always up to date

The law changes, but Nolo is on top of it! We offer several ways to make sure you and your Nolo products are up to date:

1. **Nolo's Legal Updater**
   We'll send you an email whenever a new edition of this book is published! Sign up at **www.nolo.com/legalupdater**.

2. **Updates @ Nolo.com**
   Check **www.nolo.com/update** to find recent changes in the law that affect the current edition of your book.

3. **Nolo Customer Service**
   To make sure that this edition of the book is the most recent one, call us at **800-728-3555** and ask one of our friendly customer service representatives. Or find out at **www.nolo.com**.

NOLO

please note

We believe accurate, plain-English legal information should help you solve many of your own legal problems. But this text is not a substitute for personalized advice from a knowledgeable lawyer. If you want the help of a trained professional—and we'll always point out situations in which we think that's a good idea—consult an attorney licensed to practice in your state.

NOLO

9th edition

The Copyright Handbook

How to Protect & Use Written Works

By Attorney Stephen Fishman

NOLO

NINTH EDITION	AUGUST 2006
EDITOR	RICH STIM
BOOK DESIGN	TERRI HEARSH
PROOFREADING	ROBERT WELLS
CD-ROM PREPARATION	ANDRÉ ZIVKOVICH & DOUG VARN
INDEX	MEDEA MINNICH
COVER PHOTOGRAPHY	TONYA PERME (www.tonyaperme.com)
PRINTING	CONSOLIDATED PRINTERS, INC.

Fishman, Stephen.
Copyright handbook: how to protect & use written works/by Stephen Fishman. -- 9th ed.
p. cm.
ISBN 1-4133-0533-4 (alk. paper)
1. Copyright--United States--Popular works. I. Title

KF2995.F53 2006
346.7304'82--dc22

2006043773

Quantity sales: For information on bulk purchases or corporate premium sales, please contact the Special Sales Department. For academic sales or textbook adoptions, ask for Academic Sales. 800-955-4775, Nolo, 950 Parker Street, Berkeley, CA 94710.

Acknowledgments

Many thanks to:

Jake Warner for giving me the opportunity to write a book on such an interesting subject and for his editorial contributions.

Richard Stim and Steve Elias, whose ideas and superb editing made this a much better book.

Kent Dunlap, Assistant General Counsel, U.S. Copyright Office, and Lisa Goldoftas for reviewing the chapter on copyright registration.

Attorney Katherine Hardy for reviewing portions of the manuscript.

Dedication

This book is dedicated to my mother, Helen F. Poellot.

About the Author

Stephen Fishman is a San Francisco-based attorney who has been writing about the law for over 20 years. He received his law degree from the University of Southern California in 1979. After time in government and private practice, he became a full-time legal writer in 1983. His Nolo publications include:

- *Consultant & Independent Contractor Agreements*
- *Deduct It! Lower Your Small Business Taxes*
- *Every Landlord's Tax Deduction Guide*
- *Home Business Tax Deductions: Keep What You Earn*
- *How to Safely & Legally Hire Independent Contractors*
- *Nondisclosure Agreements: Protect Your Trade Secrets & More*
- *The Public Domain: How to Find Copyright-Free Writings, Music, Art & More*
- *Tax Deductions for Professionals*
- *Web & Software Development: A Legal Guide*
- *What Every Inventor Needs to Know About Business & Taxes*
- *Working for Yourself: Law & Taxes for Independent Contractors, Freelancers & Consultants*
- *Working With Independent Contractors*

Table of Contents

5 Correcting or Changing Copyright Notice or Registration

6 What Copyright Protects

7 Adaptations and Compilations

8 Initial Copyright Ownership

12 Copyright Infringement: What It Is, What to Do About It, How to Avoid It

13 International Copyright Protection

14 Copyright in the Online World, Electronic Publishing, and Multimedia

B How to Use the CD-ROM

Index

CHAPTER

1 How to Use This Book

Here's a book about copyright for written works. It is for the entire universe of people who deal with the written word.

> **Who This Book Is For**
>
> Novelists, short story writers, poets, playwrights, screenwriters, biographers, historians, authors of how-to books, writers of scientific and technical works and other works of nonfiction, published and unpublished authors, journalists, freelance writers, persons employed by others to create written works, persons who employ others to create written works, editors who work for magazines and book publishers, established publishers, self-publishers, librarians, teachers, and literary agents.

How This Book Is Organized

This book has two parts:

- Part I (Chapters 2–4) consists of a short overview of copyright law (Chapter 2, Copyright Basics), and a "how-to" guide on copyright notice and registration with the Copyright Office.
- Part II (Chapters 5–16) serves as your copyright resource; it discusses the most important aspects of copyright law in detail. If you are unable to find the answers to your questions in Part II, the final chapter (Chapter 17, Help Beyond This Book) tells you how to do further research on your own and, if necessary, find a copyright attorney.

Which Parts of This Book You Should Read

Not everyone will want to read the whole book. Which parts you do want to read will of course depend on why you bought the book.

Most of you bought the book for one of these three reasons:

- You want to know how to satisfy the procedural requirements to obtain maximum copyright protection for a written work.
- You have a specific copyright question or problem.
- You want a general education about copyright law.

Assuming you fall into one of these three categories, here is how you can make best use of this book.

Readers Who Want to Know How to Satisfy the Procedural Requirements for Maximum Copyright Protection

If you just want to know how to place a valid copyright notice on your work (that's the © followed by a date and name you usually see on published works), read Chapter 3, Copyright Notice. Placing a valid copyright notice on your work will make it easier to enforce your copyright.

If you want to register your work with the Copyright Office, refer to Chapter 4, Copyright Registration, for a step-by-step explanation. You'll find all the registration forms you need on the CD-ROM at the end of the book. You will obtain important benefits by registering your work after it is published.

Readers Who Have a Specific Copyright Question

If you have a specific question or problem, start with the table of contents at the front of the book. For example, suppose you want to know whether you need permission to use a quotation from Abraham Lincoln that you found in a recent Civil War history. By scanning the table of contents you would discover Chapter 11, Using Other Authors' Words—probably the place to start.

If you didn't find what you were looking for in the table of contents, you could use the index at the back of the book and search under such terms as "quotations" and "public domain."

People Who Want to Learn All About Copyright

If you simply want to learn more about copyright, read Chapter 2, Copyright Basics, and then read as much of Chapters 5 through 16 as you wish. You can skip Chapters 3 and 4, since these chapters are intended for people who want to take specific steps to obtain maximum copyright protection for a written work.

What This Book Is Not About

This book only covers copyright for written works. This means it is not about:

- copyright protection for music, artwork, photography, or audiovisual works; for a detailed discussion of legal protection for music, see *Music Law: How to Run Your Band's Business*, by Richard Stim (Nolo).
- publishing contracts—although we discuss the copyright aspects of publishing contracts, this is not a book about how to negotiate or draft contracts
- protecting inventions—see *Patent It Yourself,* by David Pressman (Nolo), if you want to know about this
- protecting computer software—see *Web & Software Development: A Legal Guide,* both by Stephen Fishman (Nolo), if you want to know about this
- protecting titles, logos, or slogans—these items may be protected under the federal and state trademark laws, which have nothing to do with copyright; see *Trademark: Legal Care for Your Business & Product Name*, by Stephen Elias (Nolo).
- protecting ideas—copyright only protects words, not ideas. Ideas can be protected as trade secrets, which involves committing anyone who learns of the ideas to secrecy and maintaining security procedures to prevent the ideas from leaking out.

Icons Used Throughout the Book

Throughout the text, we have included the following icons to help organize the material.

Refers you to related information in another book or publication.

Let's you know when you can skip information that may not be relevant to your situation.

This indicates that the information is a useful copyright tip.

This caution icon warns you of potential problems.

Indicates when a form is included on the accompanying CD-ROM.

Refers you to related information in another place in the book.

■

CHAPTER

2 Copyright Basics

This chapter is an introduction to some basic copyright concepts and vocabulary. It is designed to pave the way for more detailed discussions in later chapters. We therefore urge you not to use this material to reach a final conclusion about any particular issue. Only after reading one or more of the later chapters will you be in a position to make a judgment about a particular question or course of action.

Why Have a Copyright Law?

The Founding Fathers recognized that everyone would benefit if creative people were encouraged to create new intellectual and artistic works. When the United States Constitution was written in 1787, the framers took care to include a copyright clause (Article I, Section 8) stating that "The Congress shall have Power ... To promote the Progress of Science and useful Arts, by securing for limited times to Authors ... the exclusive Right to their ... writings."

The primary purpose of copyright, then, is not to enrich authors; rather, it is to promote the progress of science and the useful arts—that is, human knowledge. To pursue this goal, copyright encourages authors in their creative efforts by giving them a mini-monopoly over their works—termed a copyright. But this monopoly is limited when it appears to conflict with the overriding public interest in encouraging creation of new intellectual and artistic works generally.

What Is Copyright?

Copyright is a legal device that provides the creator of a work of art or literature, or a work that conveys information or ideas, the right to control how the work is used. The Copyright Act of 1976—the federal law providing for copyright protection—grants authors a bundle of intangible, exclusive rights over their work. These rights include:

- reproduction right—the right to make copies of a protected work
- distribution right—the right to sell or otherwise distribute copies to the public
- right to create adaptations (or derivative works)—the right to prepare new works based on the protected work, and
- performance and display rights—the right to perform a protected work such as a stage play or display a work in public.

An author's copyright rights may be exercised only by the author—or by a person or entity to whom the author has transferred all or part of her rights. If someone wrongfully uses the material covered by the copyright, the copyright owner can sue and obtain compensation for any losses suffered.

In this sense, a copyright is a type of property—it belongs to its owner (usually the author), and the courts can be asked to intervene if anyone uses it without permission. And, like other forms of property, a copyright may be sold by its owner or otherwise exploited for her economic benefit.

How Is a Copyright Created and Protected?

A copyright automatically comes into existence the moment an author fixes her words in some tangible form—for instance, the moment a book or article is typed, handwritten, or dictated. No further action need be taken. However, it is wise to place a valid copyright notice on all published works and to register these works in the U.S. Copyright Office shortly after publication.

What Constitutes Publication

Knowing whether a work has been published or not can be important, because many important copyright rules differ for published and unpublished works. A work is published for copyright purposes when copies are sold, rented, lent, given away, or otherwise distributed to the public by the copyright owner or by others acting with the owner's permission—for example, a publisher. It is not necessary to sell thousands of copies of a work for it to be considered published. So long as copies of a work are made available to the public, the work is "published" for copyright purposes even if no copies are actually sold or otherwise distributed.

Notice

In the past, all published works had to contain a copyright notice (the © symbol followed by the publication date and copyright owner's name) to be protected by copyright. This is no longer true. Use of copyright notices is now optional. Even so, it is always a good idea to include a copyright notice on all published works so that potential copiers will be informed of the underlying claim to copyright ownership.

Registration

Prompt registration in the U.S. Copyright Office makes your copyright a matter of public record and provides a number of important advantages if it is ever necessary to go to court to enforce it. To register a work you must fill out a registration form and deposit copies of your work with the Copyright Office.

What Copyright Protects

Copyright protects an author's words if and to the extent they are original—that is, not copied from other authors' works. Since the main goal of copyright is to encourage creation of new intellectual and artistic works, it follows that copyright protection extends only to material authors write themselves.

There is also no reason to protect works whose creation is a purely mechanical or clerical act. Protecting works such as phone books or certain blank forms would not help develop the arts and sciences. An author must employ a minimal amount of creativity in creating the work. This does not mean that to be protectible a work has to be a great work of art, but a minimal amount of thought or judgment must have been involved in its creation.

A work need not be entirely new to be protectible. Copyright protects new material an author adds to a previously existing work. For example, copyright protects derivative works. A derivative work is a work that is created by adapting or transforming previously written material into a new work of authorship. Examples include a screenplay or stage play based on a novel, an English translation of a work written in a foreign language, and condensed versions of articles (such as those found in *Reader's Digest*). Copyright can also protect "compilations." These are works in which preexisting materials are selected, coordinated, and arranged so that a new work of authorship is created—for example, anthologies or catalogues.

Limitations on Copyright Protection

We've seen that the purpose of copyright is to encourage intellectual and artistic creation. Paradoxically, giving authors too much copyright protection could inhibit rather than enhance creative growth. To avoid this, some important limitations on copyright protection have been developed.

Ideas and Facts Are Not Protected

Copyright only protects the words with which a writer expressed facts and ideas. Copyright does not protect the facts or ideas themselves; facts and ideas are free for anyone to use. To give an author a monopoly over the facts and ideas contained in his work would hinder intellectual and artistic progress, not encourage it. For example, imagine how scientific progress would have suffered if Charles Darwin could have prevented anyone else from writing about evolution after he published *The Origin of Species*.

Because copyright only extends its protection to words rather than the underlying facts and ideas, works in which the particular words used by the author are important and distinctive—such as poems, novels, and plays—enjoy the most copyright protection. Works that readers buy primarily for the ideas and facts they contain, not their language, receive less protection. This includes most types of factual works, such as histories, biographies, how-to books, news stories, and so forth.

Fair Use

To foster the advancement of the arts and sciences, there must be a free flow of information and ideas. If no one could quote from a protected work without the author's permission (which could be withheld or given only upon payment of a permission fee), the free flow of ideas would be stopped dead. To avoid this, a special fair use exception to authors' copyright rights was created. An author is free to copy from a protected work for purposes such as criticism, news reporting, teaching, or research so long as the value of the copyrighted work is not diminished.

Works in the Public Domain

Any work that is not protected by copyright is said to be in the public domain. This includes works in which the copyright was lost, works in which the copyright expired, and works authored or owned by the federal government. Public domain means what it says—such works belong to the public as a whole. Anyone is free to use them any way she wishes without asking anyone's permission. And no one can ever obtain copyright protection for public domain material, no matter how she transforms it. Everything published in the United States before 1923 is now in the public domain, freely available to us all.

Copyright Ownership and Transfer of Ownership

The copyright in a protectible work is initially owned by the work's author or authors. But a person need not actually create the work to be its "author" for copyright purposes. A protectible work written by an employee as part of her job is initially owned by the employer—that is, the employer is considered to be the work's author. Such works are called works made for hire. Works created by nonemployees who sign work-for-hire agreements may also be works made for hire.

Like any other property, a copyright can be bought and sold. This is the way authors other than self-publishers profit from their work. Typically, authors sell their work to publishers for a fee or royalty. However, transfers of copyright ownership are unique in one respect: Authors or their heirs have the right to terminate any transfer of copyright ownership 35 years after it is made.

How Long a Copyright Lasts

Few things in this world last as long as copyright protection. Indeed, an author's work is likely to be long forgotten before her copyright in it expires. The copyright in works created after 1977 by individuals usually lasts for the life of the author plus an additional 70 years. The copyright in works created by employees for their employers lasts for 95 years from the date of publication, or 120 years from the date of creation, whichever occurs first.

The copyright in works created and published during 1923–1963 lasts for 95 years from the date of publication if they were timely renewed. It may be necessary to do some legwork to determine if a renewal was filed for a work. The copyright in works published during 1964–1977 lasts for 95 years regardless of whether a renewal was filed. The copyright in works created but not published before 1978 lasts at least until 70 years after the author dies.

Copyright Infringement

Copyright infringement occurs when a person other than the copyright owner exploits one or more of the copyright owner's exclusive rights without the owner's permission. This type of theft is also commonly termed copyright piracy.

The Copyright Act doesn't prevent copyright infringement from occurring, just as the laws against auto theft do not prevent cars from being stolen. However, the Copyright Act does give authors a legal remedy to use after an infringement has occurred: They may sue the infringer in federal court.

An author who wins an infringement suit can stop any further infringement, get infringing copies destroyed, obtain damages from the infringer—often the amount of any profits obtained from the infringement—and recover other monetary losses. This means in effect that an author can make a copyright pirate restore the author to the same economic position she would have been in had the infringement never occurred. And, in some cases, the copyright owner may even be able to obtain monetary penalties that may far exceed her actual losses.

Other Protections for Intellectual Property

The copyright law is not the only means available to protect products of human intellect that have some economic value. The state and federal trademark laws protect distinctive words, phrases, logos, and other symbols that are used to identify products and services in the marketplace. The federal patent law protects new inventions. State trade secret laws may protect novel and generally unknown ideas, processes, or technical designs that provide a commercial advantage in the marketplace.

Trademarks

The copyright laws do not protect names, titles, or short phrases. This is where trademark protection comes in. Under both federal and state laws a manufacturer, merchant, or group associated with a product or service can obtain protection for a word, phrase, logo, or other symbol used to distinguish that product or service from others. If a competitor uses a protected trademark, the trademark holder can obtain a court injunction and monetary damages.

> **EXAMPLE:** The word "Kleenex" is a registered trademark of the Kimberly-Clark Corporation. None of Kimberly-Clark's competitors can use this word on a box of facial tissues without Kimberly-Clark's consent. If they do, Kimberly-Clark could get a court to order them to stop and could sue for damages.

The trademark laws are often used in conjunction with the copyright law to protect advertising copy. The trademark laws protect the product or service name and any slogans used in the advertising, and the copyright laws protect any additional literal expression that the ad contains.

Patents

By filing for and obtaining a patent from the U.S. Patent and Trademark Office, an inventor is granted a monopoly on the use and commercial exploitation of her invention for a limited time. A patent may protect the functional features of a machine, process, manufactured item, method of doing business, composition of matter, ornamental design, or asexually reproduced plant. A patent also protects new uses for any such items. However, to obtain a patent, the invention must be novel and nonobvious.

> **EXAMPLE:** Mickey invents an entirely new and nonobvious type of mousetrap. He applies for a patent on his invention. If and when it's issued, no one can make, use, or sell Mickey's invention without his permission for the term of the patent (20 years from the date the patent application was filed). If they do, Mickey can sue them for patent infringement.

The basic difference between a patent and a copyright is that a patent protects ideas as expressed in an invention, whether a machine or process of some type. Copyright protects only the words an author uses to express an idea, not the idea itself.

> **EXAMPLE:** Mary has invented the widget, a device only dreamed about for decades. She obtains a patent for her invention. She manufactures and sells the widget herself. She also writes and publishes a technical manual, *The Widget Owner's Survival Guide.* The patent law prevents anyone from manufacturing and selling widgets without Mary's permission. The copyright law prevents anyone from copying the manual without Mary's permission.

Obtaining a patent can be a difficult and time-consuming process (it usually takes years). See *Patent It Yourself,* by David Pressman (Nolo), for a detailed discussion.

Trade Secrets

A trade secret is information or know-how that is not generally known in the community and that provides its owner with a competitive advantage in the marketplace. The information can be an idea, written words, a formula, a process or procedure, a technical design, a list, a marketing plan, or any other secret that gives the owner an economic advantage.

If a trade secret's owner takes reasonable steps to keep the confidential information or know-how secret, the courts of most states will protect the owner from disclosures of the secret by:

- the owner's employees
- other persons with a duty not to make such disclosures
- industrial spies, and
- competitors who wrongfully acquire the information.

That is, the trade secret's owner may be able to sue the infringer and obtain an injunction and/or damages. However, once information becomes widely known—for example, through publication—it loses its trade secret status and courts will not protect it.

EXAMPLE: Recall that Mary, in the second patent law example above, wrote a training manual for her widget invention. This manual was automatically protected by copyright. If the manual is also kept confidential (Mary only allows her employees to read it and makes them sign agreements to keep it confidential), it may also be entitled to trade secret protection. However, once Mary publishes and distributes the manual widely to the public, any trade secret protection would cease.

Since most authors want their work to be published and as widely read as possible, trade secret laws usually have little application to written works. However, trade secret protection may be important to authors of written works containing competitively advantageous information that has been kept confidential. Trade secret protection is provided only under state law, and varies from state to state.

Contract Protection for Ideas

Consider this example: Manny, a TV producer, agrees to pay Sally $10,000 for telling him an idea she has for a new TV

Some Common Copyright Misconceptions

Copyright is a fast-changing area of the law. The copyright laws were completely rewritten in 1978, and major changes were made again in 1989 and 1998. Many people who are unaware of the impact of these changes have ideas about copyright that are no longer true. For example:

- "A work must be registered with the U.S. Copyright Office to be protected by copyright."
  This hasn't been true since 1978. Copyright protection begins automatically the moment a work is set to paper or otherwise fixed in a tangible form.
- "Only works that have a copyright notice on them are protected by copyright."
  Use of copyright notices has been optional since March 1, 1989.
- "No one can use or photocopy a protected work without the owner's permission."
  This has never been true. You can photocopy or otherwise use protected works so long as the use comes within the bounds of fair use—that is, does not diminish the value of the protected work.
- "You can copyright your great ideas."
  This also has never been true. Copyright only protects the expression of an idea, not the idea itself

show. Sally tells Manny the idea, but he fails to pay. Does Sally have any recourse against Manny?

We know that copyright does not protect ideas, so Sally cannot sue Manny for copyright infringement. Her idea is not for a new invention, so she gets no help from the patent laws. And let's assume the idea is not a trade secret.

All is not lost for Sally, because some courts have held that if a person agrees to pay another person for disclosing an idea she has, the agreement constitutes an enforceable contract. This means that if the person fails to pay what he promised, the person who disclosed her idea may be able to sue and collect the promised payment. This might mean that Sally can sue Manny for breach of contract and collect the $10,000. Some courts would permit Sally the $10,000 only if her idea was novel and concrete and Manny actually used it. Others would not require this.

However, there are very few Mannys or Sallys in the real world. Rarely, if ever, will a producer, publisher, editor, or other person agree to pay an author for a mere idea. Thus, contract protection for ideas is usually more theoretical than real. The best way to protect your ideas is to disclose them only to people whose integrity can be trusted.

■

CHAPTER

3

Copyright Notice

Introduction

This chapter is about copyright notice. That's the "c" in a circle, followed by a publication date and name, usually seen on published works. The purpose of such a notice is to inform the public that a work is copyrighted, when it was published, and who owns the copyright. Before March 1, 1989, a notice was required on all published works as a condition of keeping the copyright. For works published after that date, a notice is not required. Nonetheless, it's a very good idea to provide a notice anyway on all your published works.

The use of a copyright notice is the responsibility of the copyright owner and does not require any advance permission from, or registration with, the Copyright Office.

The extent to which you need to be concerned with the material in this chapter depends upon your particular situation.

Authors of books published by established companies. As a practical matter, you don't have to worry much about the copyright notice if you're being published by an established publisher. The publisher, as a matter of course, will include copyright notices on all copies of the books they print and distribute. The author just needs to make sure that the information in the notice is correct.

Freelance writers. Freelance writers whose work appears in magazines and other periodicals are protected by the notice the publisher provides for the periodical as a whole. But some freelancers choose to include a separate notice on their work.

Self-published authors. Persons who self-publish their work must compose and format their copyright notices themselves and should carefully read this chapter, as should those who work in the publishing field.

When Copyright Notice Is Required

Copyright notice is mandatory for some works and not for others, depending upon the date of publication.

Works Published Before 1978

Until 1978, all works published in the United States had to contain a valid copyright notice to be protected by copyright. Failure to provide the notice resulted in loss of the copyright in the work—that is, the work was injected into the public domain, meaning that anyone could copy or otherwise use it without the author's permission.

Elizabeth Barrett Browning

EXAMPLE: Bernie self-published his poetry collection in 1977. He knew nothing about copyright law and failed to provide a copyright notice on the work. Shirley finds a copy of the collection in a used bookstore in 2007 and decides to include several of Bernie's poems in a compilation of modern American poetry. Since the book did not contain a copyright notice, it is considered to be in the public domain and Shirley may reproduce all or part of it without Bernie's permission.

Works Published Between January 1, 1978 and March 1, 1989

As the example above illustrates, the pre-1978 notice requirement often had draconian results—authors could lose their copyright protection just because they failed to comply with a mere technical formality. The harshness of this rule was moderated somewhat by the Copyright Act of 1976, which provided that a work without a valid notice that was published after January 1, 1978 did not enter the public domain if—within five years after the publication—the work was registered with the Copyright Office and a reasonable effort was made to add a valid notice to all copies of the work distributed after the omission was discovered. (See Chapter 4, Copyright Registration, for detailed discussion.)

Works Published After March 1, 1989

The copyright notice requirement for published works ended altogether when the United States signed the Berne Convention, an international copyright treaty. The Berne Convention is discussed in detail in Chapter 13, International Copyright Protection. All you need to know about it now is that it required the U.S. to get rid of its notice requirement, which happened on March 1, 1989. Any work printed after that date need not contain a copyright notice, even if it was originally published prior to that date.

EXAMPLE: George self-publishes a book in 1988. The work had to contain a valid copyright notice to be protected by copyright. He then reissues the book in 2007. The newly printed copies need not contain a copyright notice, but it is a good idea to provide one, anyway (see below).

Special Rules for Foreign Works

Works by foreign citizens or residents published in foreign countries without a copyright notice from January 1, 1978 through March 1, 1989 entered the public domain under the law then in effect just like any other work. However, as a result of the GATT Agreement, an international trade agreement, the U.S. copyright in these works has been automatically restored effective January 1, 1996. (See chapter 13.)

Why Provide a Copyright Notice on Published Works?

Even though a notice is not required for works printed after March 1, 1989, you should still make sure that a valid copyright notice appears on every copy of every work you publish. There are several excellent reasons for this.

Notice Makes Infringement Suits Economically Feasible

Authors and other copyright owners enforce their copyright rights by suing persons who copy their work or otherwise exercise their copyright rights without their permission. Unfortunately, copyright infringement litigation is usually very expensive (copyright attorneys usually charge at least $250 an hour). As a result, copyright infringement lawsuits may be economically feasible only if the author can obtain substantial damages (money) from the infringer.

The way to get substantial damages is to prove that the infringement was *willful*—that is, that the infringer knew that he was breaking the law but did so anyway. Courts usually award far more damages where the infringement was willful than where the infringer didn't realize what he was doing was wrong. (See Chapter 12, Copyright Infringement, for a detailed discussion of infringement suits.)

Proving willfulness can be difficult if a work lacks a valid copyright notice. The reason for this is what's known as the innocent infringement defense. If a person copies a published work that does not contain a copyright notice, the copier can claim in court that the infringement was innocent—that is, he or she didn't know the work was protected by copyright. If the judge or jury believes this, the copier may still be liable for infringement, but the damages (monetary compensation) may be drastically reduced from what they otherwise would have been. On the other hand, if there is a valid copyright notice on the work, the infringer cannot claim innocence and will be treated as a willful infringer.

EXAMPLE 1: Mary self-publishes a book without a copyright notice. Izzy copies a substantial amount of it in a book of his own. Mary sues Izzy for copyright infringement. Mary proves to the court that she suffered $25,000 in damages due to the infringement. However, Izzy, while admitting that he copied Mary's work, claims that he did not realize it was copyrighted because it lacked a copyright notice. The judge buys Izzy's story and as a result rules that Izzy need pay Mary only $5,000 in damages rather than the $25,000 required to fully compensate her.

EXAMPLE 2: Assume instead that Mary included a valid copyright notice in her book. She sues Izzy for copyright infringement. Since her book contained a valid notice, Izzy cannot argue that he did not realize the book was protected by copyright. As a result, Mary is awarded the full amount of damages required to fully compensate her: $25,000.

Copyright Notice May Deter Potential Infringers

Another important reason to place a copyright notice on all copies of your published work is that it may help deter copyright infringement. The notice lets readers know that the work is protected by copyright and may not be copied without the owner's permission. Moreover, since copyright notices appear on the vast majority of published works, a reader of a work not containing a notice might mistakenly assume that the work is not copyrighted and feel free to copy it.

Notice Protects Your Work in Countries Not Adhering to the Berne Convention

There are about half a dozen countries that do not afford copyright protection to works not containing valid copyright notices. (See Chapter 13, International Copyright Protection, for a detailed discussion.) Providing a copyright notice on your work will enable your work to be protected in these countries.

Placing a copyright notice on your published work costs nothing and may end up saving you thousands of dollars by deterring others from copying your work and enabling you to recover your full measure of damages against those who do copy it. Always, always, always place a valid copyright notice on your published work!

When to Provide Notice

A copyright notice should be included on a work when it is first published and on every subsequent published edition. A work is published for copyright purposes when it is made generally available to the public by the copyright owner or others acting with the owner's permission—a publisher, for example. It is not necessary to sell or otherwise transfer any copies of the work—publication occurs if the work is made available to the public without restriction. For example, leaving copies of a work in a public place would constitute publication, as would distributing copies on a busy street. But distributing copies to a restricted group would not constitute publication. Sending five copies of a manuscript to five publishers would not be a publication, nor would circulating copies to colleagues (a restricted group) for comment.

A copyright notice has never been required for unpublished works, and will not bar an infringer from raising the innocent infringement defense. But, under certain circumstances, it might be desirable to provide a notice on an unpublished manuscript.

Form of Notice

There are strict technical requirements as to what a copyright notice must contain. Follow these rules exactly or your notice may be found to be invalid and not accomplish its intended purpose. A valid copyright notice contains three elements:

- the copyright symbol
- the year in which the work was published
- the name of the copyright owner.

It is not required that these elements appear in any particular order in the notice, but most notices are written in the order set forth above. We'll discuss each element in turn.

Copyright Symbol

You should use the familiar © symbol—that is, the lowercase letter "c" completely surrounded by a circle. The word "Copyright" or the abbreviation "Copr." are also acceptable in the United States, but not in many foreign countries. So if your work might be distributed outside the U.S., be sure to always use the © symbol.

Adding the Word "Copyright" to Notice

Often, you'll see the word "Copyright" or the abbreviation "Copr." followed by or preceding the © symbol—for instance, "Copyright ©." Technically, this is not required—the © symbol alone is sufficient. However, it is a good idea to include the words, anyway, because they will further clarify that the work is protected by copyright.

Year of Publication

The copyright notice must also state the year the work was published. For first editions, this is easy. Put the year the work was actually published. (See "When to Provide Notice," above.)

New versions

The copyright notice for a new version of a work must contain the date that version was published. (See Chapter 7, Adaptations and Compilations, for when changes in a work make it a new version for copyright purposes.) The notice need not contain the date or dates of the prior version or versions. However, it is common practice to include such dates in the copyright notice. One reason is to let the reader know when the earlier versions were created. Another reason to do this is that it is not always easy to tell if a work qualifies as a new version under Copyright Office rules.

EXAMPLE: Sally Bowles published the first edition of her high school textbook on French in 2000. The copyright notice reads "Copyright © 2000 by Sally Bowles." The book is revised and republished as a second edition in 2005. If the second edition qualifies as a new version, the notice need only state "Copyright © 2005 by Sally Bowles." However, Sally is not sure whether the changes she made were substantial enough to make the second edition a new version. She decides to err on the side of caution and writes the notice like this: "Copyright © 2000, 2005 by Sally Bowles."

Form of date

The date is usually written in Arabic numerals—for instance, "2008." But you can also use abbreviations of Arabic numerals—for instance, "'08"; Roman numerals—for instance, "VIII"; or spelled out words instead of numerals—for instance, "Two Thousand Eight."

Copyright tip. Copyright owners sometimes state the year of publication in Roman numerals in the hope readers won't be able to decipher it and will think the work more recent than it really is. However, dates not written in Arabic numerals may not be acceptable in some foreign countries.

Copyright Owner's Name

The name of the copyright owner must also be included in the notice. Briefly, the owner is:

- the author or authors of the work
- the legal owner of a work made for hire, or
- the person or entity (partnership or corporation) to whom all the author's exclusive copyright rights have been transferred.

Honoré de Balzac

Author or authors

Unless a work is made for hire (see below), the original author or authors own all the copyright rights. Where all these rights are retained, the author's name should appear in the copyright notice.

> **EXAMPLE:** Eli Yale self-publishes a book on ivy gardening in 2008. Eli wrote the book himself and owns all the copyright rights. The copyright notice should state: "Copyright © 2008 by Eli Yale."

If there are multiple authors, they should all be listed in the copyright notice. The authors' names can appear in any order.

> **EXAMPLE:** Joe Sixpack, Louis Loser, and Benny Bigmouth write a book together about nuclear physics. All their names should appear in the copyright notice. For example: "Copyright © 2008 by Joe Sixpack, Louis Loser, and Benny Bigmouth."

Works made for hire

A work made for hire is a work made by an employee as part of her job, or a work specially ordered or commissioned under a written work-for-hire contract. (See Chapter 8, Initial Copyright Ownership.) The writer's employer or other person for whom the work was prepared is the copyright owner, and that person's (or entity's) name should appear in the copyright notice. The writer-employee's name should not be included in the notice.

> **EXAMPLE:** Archie and Marion are technical writers employed by Datavue Publications, Inc. As part of their job, they write a technical manual that Datavue publishes. Only Datavue's name should appear in the copyright notice: "Copyright © 2008 by Datavue Publications."

Transferees

If all of the copyright rights owned by the author—or by the owner of a work made for hire—are transferred to another person or entity, that name should appear in the copyright notice on all copies printed and distributed after the transfer. However, any copies printed before the transfer occurred may be distributed without updating the notice.

> **EXAMPLE:** Eli Yale self-publishes his book on ivy gardening in 2006. His name alone appears on the copyright notice. He prints 1,000 copies and, by January 2007, 500 have been sold. In February 2007, Eli transfers his entire copyright in the book to Joe Harvard, the owner of a small bookstore. Joe is

What Name Goes on the Notice Where Rights Are Transferred to Different People?

We explain in Chapter 9, Transferring Copyright Ownership, that a copyright is completely divisible—that is, the owner may transfer all or part of her exclusive copyright rights to whomever and however she wishes. For example, a copyright owner can transfer less than all of her rights and retain the others, or transfer some rights to one person or entity and all the others to other transferees. In this event, it can be confusing to determine just who the owner of copyright is for purposes of the copyright notice. The general rule is that unless the author—or owner of a work made for hire—transfers all her copyright rights to a single person or entity, the author's name should appear in the notice.

> **EXAMPLE:** Lucy has written a novel. She sells to Schultz Publishing Co. the right to publish the book in hardcover in North America. Lucy sells the paperback rights to Pequod Press. Finally, Lucy sells the right to publish her novel outside of North America to Linus Publications. Lucy's name alone should appear in the copyright notice on the hardcover, paperback, and foreign editions of her book. In contrast, if Lucy sold all her rights to Schultz, its name should appear in the notice.

The one exception to this general rule is where a collective or derivative work is created from preexisting material.

> now the copyright owner. However, Joe can distribute the 500 unsold copies without updating the copyright notice they contain, even though the notice states that Eli is the copyright owner. But if Joe prints and distributes any new copies, his name alone should appear in the copyright notice.

The most common form of transfer of rights is by a writer to her publisher. A writer can sell all or part of her copyright rights to a publisher. This is a matter for negotiation. Trade book publishing contracts typically provide the publisher with an exclusive license to exercise the rights the publisher needs (for example, the right to publish the book in all English-speaking countries). In this event, the author's name should appear in the copyright notice, not the publisher's name, because the author has retained some of her copyright rights. Another approach, commonly used in textbook publishing, is for the author to transfer all his copyright rights to his publisher. Where this occurs, the publisher's name should appear in the notice.

Form of name

Usually, the owner's full legal name is used. However, it is permissible to use an abbreviation of the owner's name; a last name alone; a trade name, nickname, fictitious name, pseudonym; initials; or some other designation, as long as the copyright owner is *generally known* by the name or other words or letters used in the notice. For example, the novelist David Cornwell could use the pseudonym John le Carré (by which he is generally known), or the International Business Machines Corporation could use the abbreviation "IBM." However, if the author is generally known only by her full name, only that name should be used in the notice.

If You Want to Remain Anonymous

The word "anonymous" should not be used in a copyright notice, because an author is obviously not generally known by that name. Likewise, it is not advisable to use a pseudonym by which you are not generally known. You can avoid revealing your name in a copyright notice, and still ensure the notice's validity, by transferring all of your copyright rights to your publisher. This way, the publisher's name may appear in the notice. Another approach would be to form a corporation, transfer your entire copyright to it, and then use the corporation's name in the notice.

If the copyright owner is a corporation, it is not necessary to include the word "Inc." in the name, even if this is part of the corporation's full legal name. Nor is it necessary for the word "by" to precede the copyright owner's name, although it is commonly used—for example, a notice can be written as "Copyright © 2008 by Joe Blow" or "Copyright © 2008 Joe Blow."

Notice on Compilations and Adaptations

Compilations and adaptations are formed all or in part from preexisting material. Nevertheless, it is usually not necessary that the copyright notice for this type of work refer to the preexisting material.

Compilations

A compilation may be a collective work—that is, a work that consists of separate and independent works assembled into a collective whole, such as encyclopedias, anthologies, and serial works like magazines, periodicals, newspapers, newsletters, and journals. A compilation may also be a work in which preexisting materials—usually data of various types—are selected, coordinated, and arranged so that a new work is created—for example, a catalogue. (See Chapter 7, Adaptations and Compilations, for detailed discussion.)

Unless a person who creates a compilation uses material in the public domain, he must either own the preexisting material used in the work or obtain the permission of those who do own it. If the creator of a compilation does not own the preexisting material, all he owns is the copyright in the compilation as a whole—that is, the copyright in the creative work involved in selecting, combining, and assembling the material into a whole work. Nevertheless, a compilation need only contain one copyright notice in the name of that copyright owner.

> **EXAMPLE:** James Henry compiles and publishes an anthology of the best American short stories of 2006. The anthology contains 12 stories. The authors of the stories gave Henry permission to publish them in the anthology but still retain all their copyright rights. The anthology need contain only one copyright notice in Henry's name: "Copyright © 2007 by James Henry." Separate copyright notices need not be provided for the 12 contributions owned by persons other than Henry.

Although an individual contribution to a compilation does not have to have its own copyright notice, a notice is permissible where the copyright in the contribution is owned by someone other than the owner of the compilation as a whole. This may help deter a potential infringer and make clear that the owner of the copyright in the compilation does not own that particular contribution.

Publication date for compilations

The copyright notice for a compilation need only list the year the compilation itself is published, not the date or dates the preexisting material was published.

> **EXAMPLE:** Josephine self-publishes an anthology of her short stories in 2005. The stories were published in various literary journals between 1999 and 2005. The notice on the anthology need only state 2005 as the publication date.

Compilations First Published Before March 1, 1989

Individual contributions to compilations first printed and distributed before March 1, 1989 are not required to bear their own copyright notices. However, it can be a good idea to provide a notice for such contributions if they have not been registered with the Copyright Office or if a transfer or license agreement was never recorded with the Copyright Office. This is because if the person named in the notice for a pre-March 1, 1989 compilation as a whole fraudulently transfers the right to copy an unnoticed contribution to a third person, the third person might not be held liable for infringement. (See discussion in Chapter 5, Correcting or Changing Copyright Notice or Registration.)

Advertisements

The rule that a single notice for a compilation as a whole covers all the material in the work does not apply to advertisements. Advertisements in serial publications such as periodicals, magazines, and newspapers must carry their own copyright notice. However, an advertisement inserted in a compilation on behalf of the copyright owner of the compilation need not contain its own notice—for example, an ad inserted in *Time* magazine by its owners urging readers to subscribe would not need its own notice.

Adaptations (Derivative Works)

An adaptation—called a derivative work in copyright jargon—is a work that is created by recasting, transforming, or adapting a previously published work into a new work of authorship. Examples include a screenplay or play based on a novel, an English translation of a work written in a foreign language, condensed versions of articles, such as those found in *Reader's Digest*, and annotations to literary works.

Unless the preexisting material used by a derivative work is in the public domain or is owned by the creator of the derivative work, the creator must obtain the copyright owner's permission to use it. (See Chapter 7, Adaptations and Compilations.)

As with compilations, the copyright notice for a derivative work need only contain the name of the owner of the copyright to the derivative work itself, not the owner of the preexisting material upon which the derivative work is based.

> **EXAMPLE:** Sally obtains Sue's permission to write a screenplay based on a novel written by Sue. Only Sally's name need appear in the copyright notice to the screenplay.

Publication date

As with collective works, the publication date in the notice for a derivative work should be the year the derivative work was published, not the year or years the preexisting material was published.

> **EXAMPLE:** Joe writes a play based on his previously published novel. The novel was published in 2006, the play in 2007. The copyright notice on the published copies of the play need only state 2007 as the publication date.

Works Containing United States Government Materials

The rule that a single general notice is sufficient for a compilation or derivative work does not always apply to publications incorporating United States government works. United States government publications are in the public domain—that is, they are not copyrighted and anyone can use them without asking the federal government's permission. However, if a work consists preponderantly of one or more works by the U.S. government, the copyright notice must affirmatively or negatively identify those portions of the work in which copyright is claimed—that is, that part of the work not consisting of U.S. government materials. This enables readers of such works to know which portions of the work are government materials in the public domain.

It's up to you to decide if your work consists preponderantly of U.S. government materials. Certainly, if more than half of your book or other work consists of federal government materials, your notice should enable readers to determine which portions of the work are copyrighted and which are in the public domain.

> **EXAMPLE:** Databest Incorporated publishes a book containing analyses of U.S. census data and including several appendixes containing U.S. Census Bureau material. The book is a collective work in which independently created contributions have been combined to form a collective whole. The appendixes amount to over half the book. The copyright notice for the work could state: "Copyright © 2007 by Databest Incorporated. No protection is claimed in works of the United States government as set forth in Appendixes 1, 2, 3, 4, 6." Alternatively, the notice could affirmatively identify those portions of the work in which copyright is claimed—that is, those portions not containing government materials, say chapters 1–10. In this event, the notice might look like this: "Copyright © 2007 by Databest Incorporated. Copyright claimed in Chapters 1 through 10."

Failure to follow this rule will result in the copyright notice being found invalid. This means that an infringer of the material in which you claim a copyright would be allowed to raise the innocent infringement defense at trial.

In addition, federal regulations require that when a contractor obtains ownership of a work created under a contract with a

U.S. government civilian agency or NASA, the copyright notice must acknowledge U.S. government sponsorship (including the contract number). The notice must be on the work when it is delivered to the government, published, or deposited for registration with the U.S. Copyright Office. (Federal Acquisition Regulation (FAR) 52.227-14; www.arnet.gov/far.) Here's a suggested format for such a notice:

COPYRIGHT STATUS: This work, authored by ____________ employees, was funded in whole or in part by ____________ under U.S. Government contract ________, and is, therefore, subject to the following license: The Government is granted for itself and others acting on its behalf a paid-up, nonexclusive, irrevocable worldwide license in this work to reproduce, prepare derivative works, distribute copies to the public, and perform publicly and display publicly, by or on behalf of the Government. All other rights are reserved by the copyright owner.

Book Dust Jackets

The copyright notice contained in a book does not serve as notice for copyrightable material on the dust jacket, even if the notice says so. This is because the dust jacket is not permanently attached to the book. If the dust jacket contains valuable material that you do not wish copied, it should bear its own copyright notice. The notice can be placed anywhere on the dust jacket. Publishers often place it on the back cover or the back inside flap.

Multimedia Works

Multimedia works, or "electronic books," combine text with visual images (both still photos and video and film clips) and sound (including music, ordinary speech, and dramatic performances). Some multimedia works consist of a printed text combined with a CD-ROM disc or other computer diskette; others are stored only on CD-ROMs or other magnetic media.

Where a work consists of a book and disc, both should contain their own copyright notice. The computer disc should have a label containing a notice. In addition, it's a good idea to include a notice on the title screen on the computer when the disc is activated, or in an "about" or credit box. Alternatively, the notice could be displayed on screen continuously when the disc is used.

Where to Place Copyright Notice

Where to place your copyright notice depends on the nature of the work. The main idea is to make it legible and readable without the aid of a magnifying glass. Remember, you want the notice to be seen by the readers so that they will know that the work is protected by copyright and who owns the copyright.

Books

If the work is a book (bound or unbound), booklet, pamphlet, or multipage folder, place the copyright notice in one of the following locations:

- the title page
- the page immediately following the title page (this is the most commonly used location for books)
- either side of the front cover
- if there is no front cover, either side of the back leaf of the copies—that is, the hinged piece of paper at the end of a book or pamphlet consisting of at least two pages
- the first or last page of the main body of the work
- if there are no more than ten pages between the front page and the first page of the main body of the work, on any page between the front page and the first page of the main body of the work, provided that the notice is reproduced prominently and is set apart from other matter on the page where it appears, or
- if there are no more than ten pages between the last page and the main body of the work, on any page between the last page of the main body of the work and the back page, provided that the notice is reproduced prominently and is set apart from other matter on the page where it appears.

Magazines and Periodicals

The copyright notice for a magazine, periodical, newsletter, journal, or other serial publication may be placed in any of the locations provided for books (above), or:

- as part of, or adjacent to, the masthead (the masthead typically contains such information as the periodical's title, information about the staff, frequency of issuance, and subscription policies)
- on the same page as the masthead, but not as part of the masthead itself, provided that the notice is reproduced prominently and set apart from the other matter appearing on the page, or
- adjacent to a prominent heading appearing at or near the front of the issue containing the periodical's title and any combination of the volume and issue number and date of the issue.

Individual Contributions to Compilations

As explained earlier, individual contributions to compilations normally do not need to contain their own copyright notices; however, it is permissible to provide one, anyway.

Contributions of one page or less

If the contribution consists of a single page or less, the optional copyright notice may be placed:

- under the title of the contribution on that page
- adjacent to the contribution, or
- on the same page if, through format and/or wording, it is clear that the notice applies only to that particular contribution.

Contributions containing more than one page

If the contribution contains more than one page, the optional copyright notice may be placed:

- under a title appearing at or near the beginning of the contribution
- on the first page of the main body of the contribution
- immediately following the end of the contribution, or
- on any of the pages where the contribution appears if it is less than 20 pages and the notice is prominent and set apart from the other matter on that page.

On same page as copyright notice for compilation

Regardless of the individual contribution's length, the copyright notice may always be placed on the same page as the copyright notice for the compilation as a whole or in a table of contents or list of acknowledgments appearing near the front or back of the compilation. However, the contribution must be listed separately by title or, if it's untitled, by a description reasonably identifying it. These locations may be the most convenient if you need to include a large number of copyright notices.

EXAMPLE 1: The *Nutne Reader*, a literary magazine, publishes an article called "Deconstructionism at a Crossroads" written by Joe Fogel, a freelance literary critic. Joe owns all the copyright rights in the article. Although the *Nutne Reader* contains its own copyright notice, at Joe's insistence it prints the following notice on the same page containing the copyright notice for the *Nutne Reader* as a whole: "'Deconstructionism at a Crossroads' Copyright © 2007 by Joe Fogel."

EXAMPLE 2: Praetorian Publishing, Inc., publishes a new translation of Caesar's *Gallic Wars*. The book also contains many new illustrations. The translation was done by Gus Augustus and the illustrations by Rene Renior. Gus and Rene have sold Praetorian only the right to publish their work in the United States and have retained their other copyright rights. The copyright notice for this compilation, combining Gus's translation with Rene's illustrations to form a collective whole, could simply state "Copyright © 2007 by Praetorian Publishing." However, if they so wish and Praetorian agrees, separate notices can also be provided for Gus's and Rene's contributions. If these notices were placed on the same page as Praetorian's notice, the copyright notice would look like this:

Copyright © 2007 by Praetorian Publishing
Translation copyright © 2007 by Gus Augustus
Ilustrations copyright © 2007 by Rene Renior

Single-Leaf Works

A single-leaf work is a work consisting of one page, whether printed on one or both sides. A book dust jacket is a good example. The copyright notice for a single-leaf work may be placed anywhere on the front or back of the work.

Other Information Near Notice

Certain other information in addition to the copyright notice itself is commonly included on the same page as the notice.

"All Rights Reserved"

The words "All rights reserved" used to be required to appear in a copyright notice to obtain copyright protection in Bolivia and Honduras. This is no longer the case. You do not need to include these words in a copyright notice. However, some publishers include them anyway out of force of habit. This does no harm.

Warning Statements

Since many people do not really understand what a copyright notice means, many publishers include various types of warning or explanatory statements on the same page as the copyright notice. The purpose is to make clear to readers that the work is copyrighted and may not be reproduced without the copyright owner's permission. It does not cost anything to place this type of statement near the copyright notice, and it may help deter copyright infringement. But remember, such statements do not take the place of a valid copyright notice as described earlier in this chapter.

Statements commonly used in books
Here are some examples of warning statements that are commonly used in books:

Except as permitted under the Copyright Act of 1976, no part of this book may be reproduced in any form or by any electronic or mechanical means, including the use of information storage and retrieval systems, without permission in writing from the copyright owner. (*Some publishers add:* Requests for permissions should be addressed in writing to [*publisher's name and address*].)

Or, more simply:

Except as permitted under the Copyright Act of 1976, this book may not be reproduced in whole or in part in any manner.

Screenplays and stage plays
Here is an example of a warning statement that may be used on a published version of a stage play or screenplay:

Caution: Professionals and amateurs are hereby warned that this material is fully protected by copyright and is subject to royalty. This play may not be used for stage production (professional or amateur), motion pictures, radio, television, public reading, or mechanical or electronic reproduction, or for any other purpose without written permission of the copyright owner. Contact [publisher's name] at [address] for information concerning licenses to dramatize this material.

Granting Permission to Use Excerpts

If you don't mind if portions of your work are copied, and want to avoid having to formally grant a license each time others want to do so, you can include a statement after the copyright notice granting permission to copy the work. This permission can be as broad or narrow as you wish. For example:

Permission is hereby granted to reprint quotations from this work up to [*number*] words in length provided that such quotations are not altered or edited in any way and provided that an appropriate credit line and copyright notice are included.

Other Material on Copyright Page

Particularly in books, certain other types of material are commonly placed on the same page as the copyright notice, even though they have nothing to do with copyright.

ISBN or ISSN number

An International Standard Book Number (ISBN) is a number preceded by the letters ISBN. An ISBN is assigned to each book by its publisher under a system administered by the R.R. Bowker Co. The number identifies the country of publication, the publisher, and the title of the book itself. It is designed to facilitate handling orders and keeping track of inventory by computer. The number has nothing to do with copyright and has no official legal status. Although not legally required, the ISBN is important for cataloguing and order fulfillment.

If you're a self-publisher, you'll need to obtain an ISBN yourself. You can apply for an ISBN online at the ISBN agency's website (www.isbn.org). You must pay a fee and you must order ISBNs in blocks of ten, 100, 1,000, or 10,000. (You can't order just one.) You can save any ISBNs you don't use for future books. The fee you pay for your ISBNs is usually a tax deductible business expense. It is the publisher's responsibility to assign numbers to each published title, enter them on computer sheets supplied by Bowker, and return the sheets to Bowker. The ISBN should be printed in nine-point type or larger on the book's copyright page. The ISBN should also appear in the lower right-hand corner of the back of the book jacket. ISBNs used to contain ten digits. However, starting in 2007, all ISBNs must have 13 digits. If you have unused ten-digit ISBNs from before 2007, you may convert them to 13-digit numbers for use in 2007 and later. For detailed information check at the ISBN agency website (www.isbn.org).

An eight-digit International Standard Serial Number (ISSN) is utilized for serial publications such as magazines, periodicals, journals, newsletters, numbered monograph series, and so on. The ISSN remains the same for each issue of a serial publication. The ISSN should be printed on the same page as the copyright notice, in the masthead area, or on the page containing instructions for ordering the publication. The ISSN program is administered by the National Serials Data Program of the Library of Congress. For more information about how to obtain an ISSN, visit the Library of Congress's ISSN website at http://lcweb.loc.gov/issn, call 202-707-6452, or email issn@loc.gov.

Library of Congress Catalog Number

The Library of Congress will preassign a Library of Congress Catalog Number (LCCN) upon request. The LCCN is the stock control number for the Library of Congress's records. The number is used by librarians for classification and ordering purposes. According to the Library of Congress, the LCCN benefits publishers because books with LCCNs are listed on a computer database that alerts librarians of forthcoming publications and enables them to select and promptly order new books.

Only U.S. publishers whose titles are likely to be widely acquired by U.S. libraries are eligible for the Cataloging in Publication (CIP) program. Book vendors, distributors, printers, production houses, and other publishing middlemen are ineligible. Self-publishers—authors and editors who pay for or subsidize publication of their own works—and publishers who specialize in publishing one or two authors are ineligible. To obtain an LCCN you must first establish a file or account with the Library of Congress. Thereafter, to obtain an LCCN you must file a CIP data sheet for each title you publish. You can obtain CIPs electronically through the Library of Congress CIP website at http://cip.loc.gov/cip. It takes about two weeks to obtain a CIP. Due to disruptions in mail service to the Library of Congress (see Chapter 4), the Library of Congress strongly encourages publishers to use its electronic system.

The LCCN should be printed on the reverse of the title page, which is usually the page where the copyright notice is placed on books. There is no charge for an LCCN, but a complimentary copy of the book must be sent to the CIP Division after it is published. This is in addition to the copies furnished to the Copyright Office as part of the registration process. (See Chapter 4, Copyright Registration.)

Copyright Notice on Unpublished Manuscripts

It has never been necessary to place a copyright notice on an unpublished manuscript, and doing so will not prevent an infringer from raising the innocent infringement defense. However, it does not seem likely that a copier could convince a judge or jury that his infringement of an unpublished manuscript was innocent if the manuscript contained a copyright notice. In addition, as with published works, placing a copyright notice on an unpublished manuscript may help to deter potential infringers.

Manuscripts sent to book and magazine publishers

Literary agents and editors advise against placing a copyright notice on a manuscript you submit to a book or magazine publisher. Publishers and editors are aware of the copyright laws and know that unpublished manuscripts are copyrighted whether or not they have a notice. Typing a notice on your manuscript makes you look like an amateur who doesn't understand the rules of the publishing game.

The one exception to this rule is where all or part of the material in the manuscript has been previously published or will be published. In this event, you should state at the bottom of the title page where the publication took place and include a notice for that publication.

> **EXAMPLE:** Nora Zorba has written a book on Greek cooking. A portion of chapter three was previously published as an article in *Culinary Magazine.* Nora should state at the bottom of the title page of her manuscript: "Portions of Chapter Three originally published in *Culinary Magazine*, December 2006. Copyright © 2006 by Culinary Publications."

Other distributions of unpublished manuscripts

It is sensible to place a copyright notice on your unpublished manuscript before sending it to persons other than publishers or editors. For example, you might want to include a notice on a manuscript that you intend to send to a colleague (or colleagues) to read. It is impossible to know just who will get their hands on your manuscript once it leaves your possession. The notice might deter a potential infringer.

Form of notice

A copyright notice for an unpublished manuscript should be in one of the following forms:

Copyright © by John Smith (This work is unpublished.)

---

or

Copyright © by John Smith (Work in Progress.)

You should not include a date in such a notice, because the date on a copyright notice denotes the date of publication.

CHAPTER

4 Copyright Registration

This chapter is about how to register your work with the Copyright Office. It covers the reasons why you should register, what types of works can be registered, and who can accomplish the registration. The chapter also explains step by step how to complete the application forms, deposit the correct material with the Copyright Office, and take the other necessary steps to complete the registration process.

What Is Copyright Registration?

Copyright registration is a legal formality by which a copyright owner makes a public record in the U.S. Copyright Office in Washington, DC, of some basic information about a copyrighted work, such as the title of the work, who wrote it and when, and who owns the copyright. When people speak of copyrighting a book or other work, they usually mean registering it with the Copyright Office.

To register, you must fill out the appropriate preprinted application form, pay an application fee, and mail the application and fee to the Copyright Office along with one or two copies of the copyrighted work.

Contrary to what many people think, it is not necessary to register to create or establish a copyright. This is because an author's copyright comes into existence *automatically* the moment an original work of authorship is written down or otherwise fixed in a tangible form. (See Chapter 2, Copyright Basics.)

Why Register?

If registration is not required, why bother? There are several excellent reasons.

Registration Is a Prerequisite to Infringement Suits

If you're an American citizen or legal resident and your work is first published in the United States (or simultaneously in the U.S. and another country) you may not file a copyright infringement suit in this country until your work has been registered with the Copyright Office. You may be thinking, "Big deal, I'll register if and when someone infringes on my work and I need to file a lawsuit." If you adopt this strategy, you may end up having to register in a hurry so you can file suit quickly. You'll have to pay an extra $685 for such expedited registration.

Compare—Works First Published Abroad

Copyright owners who are not U.S. citizens or residents and whose work is first published in most foreign countries need not register to sue for infringement in the U.S. (See Chapter 13, International Copyright Protection.) But, if they do timely register their copyrights, they will receive the important benefits discussed in the next section.

Benefits of Timely Registration

You won't need to pay the extra $685 if you register right away. Far more important, however, if you register within the time limits, you will receive a huge bonus: the right to receive special statutory damages and possibly your attorney fees if you successfully sue someone for infringing upon your work.

Normally, a copyright owner who registers her work and successfully sues an infringer is entitled to receive the amount of her losses caused by the infringement (for example, lost sales) plus any profits the infringer (and his publisher, if there is one) earned; these are called actual damages. See Chapter 12, Copyright Infringement, for detailed discussion. Unfortunately, this remedy is not as good as it sounds. Because an infringer's profits are often small, and the copyright owner's losses equally modest, actual damages are often quite small in comparison with the costs of copyright litigation (copyright lawyers typically charge between $200 and $300 per hour).

> **EXAMPLE:** Kay writes and publishes a mystery novel. Six months later, she discovers that C.C. Copycat has copied a substantial number of her words in a novel published under his own name. Copycat and his publisher earned a $10,000 profit from publishing the novel. Kay sees a knowledgeable copyright attorney. He informs her that if the case goes to trial, his attorney fees would be at least $20,000. If the only damages Kay could recover are the profits earned by Copycat and his publisher, she would lose $10,000 on the suit (assuming it goes to trial).

To give copyright owners a strong incentive to register their works and to help make copyright infringement suits economically feasible, the Copyright Act permits copyright owners who *timely* register their work and later successfully sue an infringer to be awarded statutory damages up to $150,000, plus attorney fees and court costs.

Statutory damages are special damages a copyright owner may elect to receive instead of actual damages. The amount of statutory damages awarded depends on the nature of the infringement—the more deliberate and harmful the infringement, the better the chance of obtaining a large award. (See detailed discussion in Chapter 12, Copyright Infringement.)

> **EXAMPLE:** Kay sues Copycat and his publisher and elects to receive statutory damages. The case goes to trial and Kay wins. In addition to ordering Copycat's publisher to stop selling his book, the court orders Copycat and his publisher to pay Kay $15,000 in statutory damages and to pay Kay's attorney fees and court costs—about $35,000 in all.

Importance of Timely Registration to Value of Copyright

If you fail to qualify for an award of statutory damages and attorney fees—by not timely registering your copyright—you probably can't afford a copyright infringement suit. And even if you can, the amount you will be able to collect from the infringer may not serve as a disincentive to infringement, since actual damages are hard to prove. As a practical matter, a lack of timely registration therefore makes it difficult if not impossible to enforce a copyright and, accordingly, reduces its value.

> **EXAMPLE:** Assume that Kay does not timely register her novel, and therefore cannot afford to sue Copycat and his publisher. This means she cannot prevent his copycat novel from being sold. As a result, the sales of her own novel are substantially reduced. In addition, Copycat sold a screenplay based on his novel to Repulsive Pictures. Since no producer is interested in making another whodunit movie with virtually the same plot (the plot that Copycat copied), Kay is unable to sell the screenplay rights to her novel, and its value is thus reduced.

What Is Timely Registration?

We said above that copyright owners can collect statutory damages and attorney fees if they *timely* register their work—that is, register within the time period prescribed by the Copyright Act. There are different time periods for published and unpublished works.

Published works

A published work is considered to be timely registered, entitling the copyright owner to statutory damages and attorney fees, only if it was registered:

- within *three months* of the date of the *first* publication, or
- *before* the date the copyright infringement began.

A work is published for copyright purposes when copies are made available to the public on an unrestricted basis. (See Chapter 2, Copyright Basics, for detailed discussion of what constitutes publication.)

> **EXAMPLE 1:** Assume that Kay's novel in the examples above was registered by her publisher two months after it was published. Kay is then entitled to elect to receive statutory damages and attorney fees if she sues Copycat (or anyone else) for copyright infringement.

> **EXAMPLE 2:** Assume that Kay's publisher neglected to register Kay's novel. Kay finds out about this and registers it herself nine months after publication. Copycat published his

copycat novel three months later. Kay is entitled to statutory damages and fees if she sues Copycat and his publisher, because she registered her work before Copycat copied it.

EXAMPLE 3: Assume instead that Kay's novel was never registered. After discovering Copycat's infringing novel, Kay registers her novel with the Copyright Office. If Kay sues Copycat and his publisher, she may not elect to receive statutory damages and attorney fees and costs. Reason: Kay's novel was registered neither within three months of publication nor before Copycat copied her work.

Unpublished works

The ordinary rule is that if an unpublished work is infringed upon, its author or other copyright owner is entitled to obtain statutory damages and attorney fees from the infringer only if the work was registered *before the infringement occurred.*

You cannot get around this requirement by publishing the manuscript and then registering it within three months of the publication date. The three-month rule discussed above applies only if the infringement began after first publication.

Starting in 2006, the Copyright Office instituted a new procedure that allows some unpublished works to be preregistered. The owner of a preregistered work can obtain statutory damages and attorney fees against a copyright infringer even if the work was not fully registered until after the infringement occurred. Only unpublished books, movies, music, sound recordings, computer programs, or advertising photographs may be preregistered, and only if the work is being prepared for commercial distribution.

Registration Deters Infringement

Another reason to register is that it causes the work to be indexed in the Copyright Office's records under the title and author's name. These records are open to the public and are frequently searched by persons or organizations seeking to find out whether a particular known work has been registered and, if so, who currently owns the copyright. If you have registered your work, these people may contact you and be willing to pay you a permission fee or royalty to use it. If you haven't registered, they may conclude that you're not very serious about enforcing your copyright rights. As a result, they may be inclined to use your work without asking your permission (that is, commit copyright infringement).

What Can and Should Be Registered

Any work containing material that is protected by copyright may be registered. A work need not consist entirely of protected material to be registrable. So long as a part of a work is protectible, it may be registered. The registration covers those portions of the work that are protected. (See Chapter 6, What Copyright Protects.)

Published Works

As a general rule, any published work of value should be registered within three months of publication. You can probably forget about registration, however, if your work is not worth copying (which is usually the case where the work will become outdated shortly after publication or where it is not especially new or creative), or if you aren't concerned about someone copying your work.

Unpublished Works

In deciding whether to register your unpublished work, you need to consider how many people will see it, who they are, how valuable you feel the work is, and how likely it is that someone would want to copy it.

The potential for copying exists whenever you circulate a manuscript to publishers, literary agents, personal contacts, and others. When you submit a manuscript to publishers or others, you have no control over how many people are going to read it.

However, don't be unduly paranoid about others stealing your work. The fact is that very few manuscripts are ever copied by publishers. It is usually easier and cheaper for a publisher to purchase the right to publish a manuscript than go to the trouble of copying it and risk an infringement suit.

Ideas Are Not Protected by Registration

Copyright does not protect facts or ideas, only their expression in a tangible form. (See Chapter 6, What Copyright Protects.) This means you cannot register a book or article idea. And registering a book or article proposal, outline, and/or sample chapters before submission to a publisher will not extend copyright protection to your idea.

> **EXAMPLE:** Leslie writes a detailed outline and sample chapters for a proposed book on nude skydiving. She registers the outline and chapters, and then sends them to several publishers. Larry, a freelance writer, hears about Leslie's submission from an editor acquaintance at one of these publishers and decides to write a book of his own on nude skydiving. In doing so, however, Larry does not copy anything from Leslie's outline or sample chapters (indeed, he never saw them). Leslie cannot successfully sue Larry for copyright infringement for stealing her idea for a book on nude skydiving. The fact that she registered her outline and sample chapters did not extend copyright protection to the ideas they contained.

Who Can Register?

Anyone who owns all or part of the rights that make up a work's copyright may register that work, as can that person's authorized agent (representative). This means registration may be accomplished by:

- the author or authors of a work
- anyone who has acquired one or more of the author or authors' exclusive copyright rights, or
- the authorized agent of any of the above.

Ownership of copyrights is discussed in detail in Chapter 8, Initial Copyright Ownership, and Chapter 9, Transferring Copyright Ownership. The following discussion briefly describes ownership solely for registration purposes.

Ownership by the Author(s)

Unless a work is a work made for hire (see below), the copyright initially belongs to the person or persons who created it.

Individually authored works

The copyright in a work created by a single individual is owned by that individual. An individually authored work can be registered by the author or his authorized agent (that is, someone he asks to register for him).

> **EXAMPLE:** Shelby has written a history of the Civil War. Shelby can register the book himself, or it can be registered on Shelby's behalf by his authorized agent—for example, his publisher.

Works made for hire

A work made for hire is a work created by an employee as part of her job, or a work that has been specially commissioned under a written work-for-hire agreement. For registration purposes, the author of a work made for hire is the writer's employer or other person for whom the work was prepared. It is normally the employer who registers a work made for hire, not the employee-writer.

> **EXAMPLE:** Bruno is a technical writer/translator employed by BigTech, Inc. His latest project was translating a technical manual into German. The manual is a work made for hire and should be registered by BigTech, Bruno's employer.

If you create a protectible work on a freelance basis for someone else, the question of ownership can be complex. Read Chapter 8, Initial Copyright Ownership, before completing the registration.

Joint works

If two or more persons who are not employees create a protectible work together, the work so created is called a joint work. A joint work is co-owned by its creators and can be registered by one, some, or all of the authors or by their agent.

> **EXAMPLE:** Bob, Carol, Ted, and Alice decide to write a nonfiction book entitled *The New Celibacy*. They each agree to write one-quarter of the entire work and agree that they will each own 25% of

the entire copyright. After it is written, *The New Celibacy* may be registered by any combination of Bob, Carol, Ted, and Alice or their authorized agent.

Again, for a detailed discussion of these categories, see Chapter 8, Initial Copyright Ownership.

Registration by Publishers and Other Transferees

As discussed in Chapter 2, Copyright Basics, an author's copyright is really a bundle of separate, exclusive rights. These exclusive rights include the right to make copies of an original work, the right to distribute or sell the work, the right to display the work, and the right to adapt—that is, make derivative works out of—the work. A copyright owner can sell or otherwise transfer all or part of his exclusive copyright rights. Indeed, this is usually how an author benefits economically from his work.

Transferees need to be concerned about registration because, if the work is not timely registered, they will not be entitled to obtain statutory damages and attorney fees if they successfully sue a person who infringes on the rights they purchased. (Again, registration is timely only if accomplished before an infringement occurs or within three months of publication.) Fortunately, transferees do not have to rely on authors to timely register. Anyone who obtains one or more of an author's exclusive rights is entitled to register the author's work.

Letting Your Publisher Register the Copyright

Published authors usually do not register their books themselves. Indeed, if you have signed over all of your copyright rights to your publisher, there is no reason for you to register, since you no longer have the right to commercially exploit the work. Your publisher should register the book. Even if you retain some of your rights, your publisher should accomplish the registration as an owner of an exclusive right or rights (such as the right to make copies and sell the book) or as your authorized agent.

However, you should check with your publisher one or two months after publication to make sure your book has been registered, especially if you're dealing with a very small and/or inexperienced publisher that may be lax about such matters. (Recall that to obtain statutory damages and attorney fees, your work must be registered within three months of publication or before the infringement begins.)

Of course, the situation is very different if you are self-publishing your work. In this situation, you must handle the registration yourself. This is also usually the case if you are paying a vanity press to publish your book.

> **EXAMPLE 1:** In return for a 12% royalty on each copy sold, Darlene transfers to Able Publishers all of her exclusive rights to her bowling instruction guide. Able may register the book.

> **EXAMPLE 2:** Assume instead that Darlene transfers to Able the exclusive right to sell, display, and make copies of the book, but retains her other copyright rights. As a holder of some of Darlene's exclusive rights, Able is still entitled to register the book.

If only a portion of a work's copyright is transferred, it is possible that several different persons or entities qualify to register the copyright.

> **EXAMPLE:** Bill writes a novel and grants Scrivener & Sons only the exclusive right to publish it in the United States. He also grants Repulsive Pictures the exclusive right to author and produce a screenplay based on the novel. Scrivener and Repulsive each hold one of the exclusive rights that are part of Bill's overall copyright, and Bill holds the rest. This means the novel could be registered by Bill, by Scrivener, or by Repulsive.

Although several people may be entitled to register a work, normally only one registration is allowed for each version of a published work. It makes absolutely no difference who gets the job done. The single registration protects every copyright owner.

> **EXAMPLE:** Assume that Scrivener & Sons registered Bill's novel in the example above. This means that neither Bill nor Repulsive Pictures can register it. Nor do they need to. The single registration by Scrivener covers them all—that is, they are all entitled to the benefits of registration.

Again, for a detailed discussion of the rights of copyright transferees, see Chapter 9, Transferring Copyright Ownership.

Registration as a Single Unit

A work of authorship often consists of many separate works that are combined to form a unitary whole. For example, a book will normally consist of a main text written by an author or authors. But it may also contain photographs and/or artwork supplied by the author or others. It may have a dust jacket containing artwork and/or promotional copy written by someone other than the author(s) of the text. Or, if the book is a paperback, the cover may contain artwork and copy. And it may contain an introduction or other material written by someone other than the author(s) of the main text.

The question naturally arises, "Must I register each type of authorship separately, or can I register everything together at the same time?" If your work satisfies the requirements listed below, you can register the whole work at one time. This will take less time and save on application fees. However, it could result in a smaller financial award if you sue for copyright infringement. (See "When You Register Multiple Works as a Single Unit," below.)

You can register any number of *separate* works of authorship together on one application if all of the following are true:

- They are being published for the *first* time.
- They constitute a *single unit of publication*—that is, they're sold together as a single unit with each work an integral part of the whole unit.
- The same person(s) created *all* the works in the unit, or the same person or entity has acquired ownership of *all* the copyright rights in all of the works in the unit.

Let's apply this rule to some real-life situations.

Works Containing Photographs and/or Artwork

The artwork and/or photographs a written work contains can be registered together with the text only if both of the following are true:

- They have never been published before.
- They were created by the author of the text, or the same person or entity owns the copyright to the artwork and/or photos and text.

EXAMPLE 1: Jackie is a poet and Bill a photographer. Jackie and Bill collaborate to publish a book combining Bill's photographs and Jackie's poetry. They agree to co-own the entire copyright in the work. Normally, poetry and photographs are registered separately on different application forms. However, Jackie and Bill may register the entire book at the same time for one application fee on one application form since the work is a single unit of publication and the text and photos are owned by the same persons.

EXAMPLE 2: Jim and Jean agree to produce a book on how to operate a toxic waste dump. Jim writes the text and Jean provides the pictorial illustrations for the book. Jim and Jean decide that each is the sole owner of their respective contributions. The single registration rule does not apply here. The photos and text were not created by the same persons, and they are not owned by the same persons; they were created and are owned separately by Jim and Jean. This means that Jim and Jean must each register their work separately, and each pay an application fee.

Multimedia Works

For copyright registration purposes, a multimedia work is any work which, excluding its container, combines authorship in two or more media. The authorship may include text, artwork, sculpture, cinematography, photography, sounds, music, or choreography. The media may include printed matter such as a book; audiovisual material such as videotape, slides, filmstrips; a phonorecord such as an audio tape or

When You Register Multiple Works as a Single Unit

If your work qualifies as a single unit of publication, you can register the whole thing at one time and save on registration fees. However, by doing so, you may lose the right to obtain multiple awards of statutory damages. Statutory damages are awarded by the jury or judge instead of any actual monetary losses suffered from a copyright infringement and usually range from $750 to $30,000 (but can go all the way up to $150,000 in cases of willful infringement). (See Chapter 12, Copyright Infringement.) Statutory damages sometimes far exceed the actual monetary losses from infringement. In the largest statutory damages award to date, a television production company was awarded $9 million in statutory damages against a television station owner who aired 900 television programs without permission; $10,000 in statutory damages was awarded for each program—each of which was separately registered with the Copyright Office. (*MCA Television Ltd. v. Feltner*, 89 F.3d 766 (11th Cir. 1996).)

If you register a work containing multiple works of authorship as a single unit of publication, you may be restricted to a single award of statutory damages in a copyright infringement lawsuit. If you register each type of authorship separately, you will be entitled to a separate statutory damages award for each type of infringed authorship. Here's a hypothetical example.

EXAMPLE: Mary creates and publishes a book about the Dalai Lama that contains text, photos, and drawings. Since she owns the copyright in each type of authorship, she could register it all together at one time for one $45 fee. Instead, Mary decides to register the text, photos, and drawings separately at a cost of $135 in registration fees. Mary subsequently files and wins a copyright infringement lawsuit against a website that copied the entire book without her permission. Since her actual dollar losses from the infringement were negligible, Mary asks for statutory damages. The jury awards her $15,000 ($5,000 for the infringement of the text, $5,000 for the photos, and $5,000 for the drawings). Had Mary registered the entire book together as a single unit of publication, she may have been restricted to a single statutory damages award of $5,000. By paying an extra $90 to the Copyright Office, Mary recovered an extra $10,000 in damages.

Keep in mind that most registered works are never infringed, so, one strategy you may want to consider is to register each element separately only if you believe a work is likely to be infringed. For works less likely to be copied, register all of the elements—text, photos, and artwork—as a single unit of publication.

audio disc; or any machine-readable copy such as a computer disk, tape, or chip. For example, a book combined with a filmstrip or audio tape would be a multimedia work. More important, however, written works that are combined with CD-ROM discs or other computer disks are also multimedia works, as are written works published on CD-ROMs alone along with graphics, photos, video, music, and so on.

An entire multimedia work can be registered at one time on one registration form for one registration fee provided that both of the following are true:

- The copyright claimant is the same for all elements of the work for which copyright protection is sought.
- All such elements are published at the same time as a single unit.

For a detailed discussion, see Chapter 14, Copyright in the Online World.

Artwork, Photos, and Promotional Copy on Book Dust Jackets or Covers

The artwork, photos, and/or promotional copy on a book dust jacket or cover may be registered together with the text only if both of the following are true:

- The artwork and copy have never been published before.
- The same person or entity owns the copyright to the text, cover art, and promotional copy.

Since cover art and promotional copy is normally owned by the publisher (whether created by the publisher's employees or independent contractors hired by the publisher), these items usually can be registered together with the text of the book only if the publisher acquired all the author's rights in the text.

EXAMPLE 1: Jane Milsap writes a novel and sells all her copyright rights to Acme Press. Acme employees prepare artwork and text for the cover. The text of the novel and artwork and text for the cover can be registered together on one Form TX, because Acme owns them all.

EXAMPLE 2: Bart Milsap, Jane's brother, writes a novel and grants Acme Press only the exclusive right to publish it in North America. Bart retains all his other copyright rights. Acme employees prepare artwork and text for the cover. The text of the novel and the artwork and text for the cover must be registered separately, because they are separately owned. Acme may register the artwork and cover copy together on the same form.

How to Register Artwork and Photographs

If you have to register artwork or photographs separately from the main text of a written work, you must do so on Form VA. This form is nearly identical with Form TX. A copy of the form is included on the CD-ROM at the end of this book.

Introductions, Prefaces, Bibliographies, Indexes, and Similar Items

An introduction, preface, bibliography, or index or similar material may be registered together with a work's main text only if it is being published for the first time and the person or entity that owns the copyright in the main text also owns the introduction, bibliography, index, or other item.

> **EXAMPLE 1:** Sam writes a book on the Civil War and gets the well-known Civil War expert Shelby Hand to write an introduction. Hand gives Sam's publisher the right to use the introduction only in Sam's book and retains all his other copyright rights. The introduction would have to be registered separately from the book.

> **EXAMPLE 2:** Assume instead that Acme Press, Sam's publisher, paid Hand for all his rights in the introduction and that Acme also acquired all of Sam's copyright rights in the main text. Acme could register both the text and the introduction together as a single unit. Reason: The same entity owns the copyright in both the main text and the introduction.

Different Editions With the Same Content

It is common for the same work to be published in different editions—for example, in both a hardcover and paperback edition. Where the content of the different editions is identical, only one need be registered. This would normally be the first published edition.

> **EXAMPLE 1:** Acme Publications publishes and promptly registers a hardcover edition of a book on car repair. One year later, Acme publishes the book in an identical paperback edition. The paperback need not be registered. The registration of the hardcover edition protects all the material the paperback contains.

> **EXAMPLE 2:** Assume the same facts as Example 1, except that the paperback has new cover art and copy. Acme should register the artwork and copy. But again, there is no need to reregister the text of the book.

If multiple identical editions of the same work are published simultaneously, again, only one registration need be made. In such cases, however, the applicant should deposit with the Copyright Office the edition that is the best edition. (See detailed discussion of deposits, below.)

Some Freelance Writers Must Register Separately

If you're a freelance writer and sell an article or other work to a magazine or similar publication, and the publication does not purchase copyright in the work, you must separately register it. This may not apply to you since most publications do purchase all rights (or sign work-made-for-hire agreements). However, some do not. So, examine your publishing agreement to determine what rights you're selling. If you have an oral agreement with an editor to provide an article or other work, you're not selling all your rights. (You can only transfer copyright by a signed written agreement. See Chapter 9, Transferring Copyright Ownership.) If you don't timely register such articles, you'll lose the right to obtain statutory damages and attorney fees in an infringement suit. In any event, you must register your works in order to file a copyright infringement lawsuit.

Consider Lois Morris, a freelancer who wrote a series of columns for *Allure Magazine*. She did not transfer her copyright to *Allure* and failed to separately register the columns. When she discovered two dozen columns had been reprinted in a newsletter without her permission, she sued for copyright infringement, relying on the magazine's copyright application. Her case was dismissed because she had never filed her own copyright registrations for the articles. (*Morris v. Business Concepts, Inc.*, 283 F.3d 502 (2d Cir. 2001).) Although she was entitled to later register the works and refile the lawsuit, her failure to timely file registrations resulted in a loss of potential financial damages. Therefore, to guarantee your rights, a prompt registration is recommended. Freelancers can save money by registering groups of articles at one time.

Anthologies, Newspapers, Magazines, and Other Periodicals

Anthologies, newspapers, magazines, and similar works usually contain a number of separate articles, photos, artwork, and other material. Each individual contribution must be registered by the person or entity that owns it. If the same person or entity owns all the contributions, only one registration is required. The anthology or magazine should also be registered once as a whole, usually by its publisher. Registration of newspapers, magazines, and other periodicals is discussed below.

How Many Times to Register a Single Unit of Publication

Subject to the exceptions noted below, a single unit of publication need be and can be registered only once.

Registering Unpublished Collections for a Single Application Fee

If you have a number of unpublished works, you can register them together at one time on one application form for one $45 application fee. This is so even though the works are self-contained (that is, do not constitute a single unit of publication) and would normally be registered separately. This procedure can save you a great deal of money. Four requirements must be met:

- The same person or entity must own all the copyright rights in all the unpublished works and in the collection as a whole.
- The works must be by the same author, or, if they are by different authors, at least one of the authors must have contributed to each work.
- The unpublished works must be assembled in an orderly form (one copy must be deposited with the Copyright Office).
- The collection must be given a title identifying the collection as a whole.

EXAMPLE: Joe Sixpack has written 12 unpublished short stories. He collects the stories together into a binder and calls the collection *The Unpublished Stories of Joe Sixpack*. Joe may register all 12 stories together for one $45 application fee. Note: If Joe had registered each story separately, it would have cost him $540—that is, 12 registrations times the $45 application fee. There is no limit to the number of unpublished works you can register this way. You could register your entire lifetime's worth of unpublished works for one $45 fee.

Published works

As a general rule, a published work constituting a single unit of publication can only be registered once. If the facts stated in the registration application change after the work has been registered—for instance, the work's title is changed—an application for supplemental registration should be filed with the Copyright Office to correct them. See Chapter 5, Correcting or Changing Copyright Notice or Registration.

However, there are exceptions to the general rule. If someone other than the author is identified as the copyright claimant on a registration application, the author may register the same work again in her own name as copyright claimant. A second registration may also be made if the prior registration was unauthorized or legally invalid—for instance, where registration was effected by someone other than the author, the owner of exclusive rights, or an authorized representative.

Unpublished works

A work originally registered as unpublished may be registered again after publication, even if the published and unpublished versions are identical. Even if they are identical, it is a good idea to register the published version of a previously registered unpublished work. If you ever become involved in an infringement suit, it may be very helpful to have the published version of the book on deposit with the Copyright Office. The second registration also establishes the date of publication, which may later aid you in proving that an infringer had access to your work. (See Chapter 12, Copyright Infringement.)

Registering Derivative Works and Compilations

Derivative Works

A derivative work is one created by transforming or adapting previously existing material. This includes:

- new editions of previously published works, including condensed or abridged editions or editions containing new material (new chapters, for example)
- dramatizations or fictionalizations, such as screenplays or stage plays based on novels, histories, biographies, or other works
- translations, and
- annotations, such as *Cliffs' Notes.*

These types of works are discussed in detail in Chapter 7, Adaptations and Compilations. If you're not sure whether your work is a derivative work, read that chapter before attempting to register it.

Preexisting Expression Should Have Already Been Registered

Assuming it's protectible, the preexisting expression used to create the derivative work, whether a novel, factual work, or other work, should already be registered with the Copyright Office. If not, it should be registered. The preexisting expression can be registered together with the new expression if they constitute a single unit of publication and the copyright claimant is the same. Otherwise, the preexisting expression should be registered separately by its owner.

When can a derivative work be registered?

For a derivative work to be registrable, the new expression created by the work's author must:

- be owned by the copyright claimant for the derivative work
- contain sufficient original authorship to be copyrightable as an independent work
- not be in the public domain in the United States
- be new—that is, not previously published, and
- not have been previously registered in unpublished form.

EXAMPLE: Tom writes a play based on his novel. The play is a new work based on and adapted from the novel. Tom owns the play, and it has never previously been published or registered. The play can and should be registered separately, or Tom will not be entitled to statutory damages and attorney fees if he sues someone for copying those aspects of the work not already protected by the copyright in the novel.

Registering new editions of factual works

Authors of factual works such as scientific treatises, histories, and textbooks often revise their works and publish new editions. Not all new editions can or should be registered. Look at the protected content of the various versions. If the first version you registered contains substantially the same protected content as a later version, there is no reason to register the later version; its content is protected by the initial registration. But if substantial new protectible material is added to another version, it's wise to register that version.

As a general rule, your changes are substantial enough to merit registration only if enough new expression has been added so that it is possible to tell the difference between the previous edition and the new edition. Trivial changes—such as spelling corrections—are not enough.

EXAMPLE 1: Augusta writes and publishes a college-level textbook on ancient Roman art. Two years later, she publishes a new edition of the work. The new edition is identical to the first except that Augusta corrected several spelling and punctuation errors. The Copyright Office probably will not register such a work and, indeed, there is no reason to do so since there is no new expression in the new edition that needs to be protected by registration.

EXAMPLE 2: Assume that five years later, Augusta substantially revises her book on Roman art. She adds three new chapters and makes numerous substantive changes in the other chapters. This new edition is clearly different from the original edition in a meaningful way. Augusta should register the work to protect the changes she made to her preexisting material.

As a practical matter, there is no reason to go to the trouble and expense of registration merely to protect minor changes that have no value independent from the original work. However, if you've added considerable new material to your work that has substantial value and that someone may want to copy for its own sake, registration may be prudent.

Compare—more complete version published first

If two versions of a work are published at different times, and the more complete version is published first, the less complete version may not be registered. The Copyright Office will not knowingly register a claim in a work where all of the copyrightable content has previously been published.

EXAMPLE: Schooldays Publications publishes two editions of a Spanish textbook; one version is for teachers and the other for students. The teacher's edition contains all of the text and pictorial material in the student's edition, plus additional instructions, questions, and answers. The teacher's edition was published one week before the student edition. The student edition may not be registered; all the material it contains is already protected by the registration of the teacher's edition.

Compilations

A compilation is a work created by selecting, organizing, and arranging facts or data in such a way that the resulting work as a whole constitutes an original work of authorship. Examples include anthologies, bibliographies, and catalogues of all types.

Some compilations are not considered to be sufficiently creative to merit copyright protection and may not be registered. Refer to Chapter 7, Adaptations and Compilations, for a detailed discussion of how to tell if your compilation is registrable (and ways to help make it so).

Four-Step Registration Process

To register, you must:

1. Select the appropriate registration form.
2. Fill out the registration form correctly.
3. Decide how to satisfy the Copyright Office's deposit requirements.
4. Place your application, deposit, and appropriate fee in one package and send it to the Copyright Office.

Selecting the Appropriate Registration Form

The Copyright Office has divided every conceivable type of copyrightable work into five classes and designated letter codes and has matching application forms for each class. Your copyright protection is in no way affected by which particular class your work falls in. Moreover, the Copyright Office will ordinarily go ahead and register your work even if you use the wrong application form. There's one exception: The Copyright Office will not register your work if you use a Short Form application when you should use a regular form.

Form TX: Nondramatic Literary Works

Form TX is the real workhorse in the Copyright Office's forms stable. It is used to register all types of written works (other than magazines and similar works) that are not intended to be performed before an audience. These are called nondramatic literary works (for copyright purposes, a literary work is any copyrightable work consisting of words). Form TX is used to register such works as:

- advertising copy
- articles and other individual contributions to newspapers, magazines, newsletters, or other periodicals (but

Where to Get Help

If you have difficulty understanding any aspect of the registration process, you can get help by calling the Copyright Office at 202-707-3000 between 8:30 a.m. and 5:00 p.m. Eastern time, Monday through Friday. An information specialist will be available to give you advice on selecting the proper form, filling it out, and making the required deposit. Copyright Office information specialists are very knowledgeable and helpful; however, they are not allowed to give legal advice. If you have a particularly complex problem that calls for interpretation of the copyright laws, see a copyright attorney. (See Chapter 17, Help Beyond This Book.)

Electronic Registration May Be Coming

The Copyright Office plans to replace its paper-based registration system with a paperless electronic system. This will enable copyright owners to submit a registration application and deposit over the Internet rather than sending a paper application by mail or commercial carrier. The Copyright Office hopes to implement this system during the next three or four years. You can keep posted on the progress by visiting the Copyright Office website (www.copyright.gov).

not the entire newspaper or periodical itself; see below)

- catalogues, directories, and other compilations of information
- fiction of any length
- letters and diaries
- nonfiction of any length
- poetry
- reference books, textbooks, and technical writings
- translations of works written in foreign languages, and
- written lectures, speeches, leaflets, and pamphlets.

Short Form TX

The Copyright Office has created a simplified version of Form TX called the Short Form TX. It's only one page instead of two and is easier to complete than the regular Form TX. However, the Short Form TX may only be used if all of the following are true:

- There is only one author *and* copyright owner of the work.
- The work was not made for hire—that is, was not created by an employee or freelance author under a work-for-hire agreement. (See Chapter 8, Initial Copyright Ownership.)
- The work is completely new—that is, does not contain a substantial amount of material that has been previously published or registered, or is in the public domain.

In addition, the Short Form TX must be signed by the author personally; no one can sign on his or her behalf. This means, for example, that a publisher may not sign the form on behalf of an author. This requirement likely makes the form inconvenient for most publishers to use.

Short Form TX will most likely be used by those registering unpublished works they've created themselves and self-publishers. Keep in mind, however, that the form may only be used for the first edition of a work, not a revised or updated edition.

Form PA: Plays and Screenplays

Form PA is used to register all types of published and unpublished works prepared to be performed directly before an audience, such as plays. Form PA is also used for works intended to be performed indirectly by means of a mechanical device or process. This includes screenplays, teleplays, or radio plays intended to be performed indirectly by means of a film projector, television, or radio. Form PA is also used to register song lyrics with or without accompanying music. Musical compositions are also registered on this form.

Henrik Ibsen

Form PA is also used to register multimedia works combining text with graphics, photos, videos, sounds, and so forth. See Chapter 14, Copyright in the Online World, for a detailed discussion.

Short Form PA

The Copyright Office has created a simplified version of Form PA called the Short Form PA. Its use is subject to the same restrictions as Short Form TX discussed in above.

Form SE Series: Newspapers, Magazines, and Other Periodicals

Form SE is used to register serial publications. A serial is a work that is (1) issued in successive parts, (2) logically numbered and/or dated, and (3) intended to be continued indefinitely. This includes:

- magazines and other periodicals of all types
- newspapers
- journals
- newsletters
- bulletins, and
- the minutes, journals, proceedings, or transactions of societies.

The Copyright Office has created four different registration forms for serial publications: the regular Form SE, Short Form SE, Form SE/Group, and Form G/DN. We discuss when to use what form and how to fill them out, below.

Individual Contributions to Periodicals Registered on Form TX or PA

The SE series of forms is used only to register a magazine or other serial publication as a whole. Form TX (or Form PA) must be used to register individual articles or other contributions to periodicals if the copyright is owned by someone other than the periodical.

> **EXAMPLE:** Jane has contributed a short story to the literary journal *Serendipity.* She gave the journal the right to publish her story once and has retained all other rights. Jane's story is a separate and independent work entitled to copyright protection in its own right. To register her story, she must use Form TX, the form for nondramatic literary works. But the copyright owners of *Serendipity* would use one of the SE series of forms to register the journal—a serial publication—as a whole.

Form GR/CP: Single Registration for a Group of Contributions to Serial Publications by a Single Author

Still another form, Form GR/CP, is used in conjunction with Form TX to register as a group previously published individual contributions to periodicals written by the same author.

Form VA: Visual Arts

Form VA is used to register works of visual art. These include photographs, drawings, paintings, sculpture, maps, art reproductions, jewelry designs, and architectural designs and plans. Form VA is very similar to Form TX. If you need to register photos or artwork on Form VA, refer to the discussion on Form TX, below.

Short Form VA

The Copyright Office has created a simplified version of Form VA called Short Form VA. Its use is subject to the same restrictions as Short Form TX discussed above.

Registering photographs

Authors who have photographs included in a book, article, or other written work can either register these together with the text, or register the photographs separately. (See "When You Register Multiple Works as a Single Unit," above.) You may register photographs as a group instead of registering each one separately—for example, you can use one registration for all of the photos published in a book. Photographs that are in different works—for example, in different magazine issues—can be registered together as a group for a single $45 application fee provided that all of the following are true:

- All the photographs are by the same author, who may be an individual or an employer for hire.

- All the photographs are published in the same calendar year.
- All the photographs have the same copyright claimant(s).

To register, you submit Form VA and list the titles and publication dates of each photo on Form GR/PPh/CON.

Unpublished photographs can be registered together as an unpublished collection using the procedure described above.

Choosing the Proper Form for Hybrid Works

If your work contains material falling into two or more classes—for instance, where a book contains both a written text and photographs—you need not register twice using two forms. You may use the form most appropriate to the type of authorship that predominates in the work as a whole. The following examples may help make this clear.

> **EXAMPLE 1:** Joe has written a travel guide to the Galapagos Islands. It contains 200 pages of text and 20 photographs taken by Joe. The text clearly predominates, so Joe should use Form TX (the form for nondramatic literary works) to register both the text and photos.

> **EXAMPLE 2:** Kathleen has self-published a book of her photographs and written a short caption for each photo. The photos obviously predominate in the work as a whole, so Kathleen should use Form VA (the form for pictorial works) to register the photos and captions.

You have the option of registering each type of work separately on its own form—for example, photos on Form VA and text on Form TX. This costs more, but may be advantageous if you ever sue someone for copyright infringement. (See "When You Register Multiple Works as a Single Unit," above.)

Choosing the Correct Form for Derivative Works and Compilations

If you're registering a derivative work, use the form appropriate to the derivative work itself, not the original work it was based on.

> **EXAMPLE:** Lester has written a screenplay based on his novel *Dinner With the Devil*. The novel was already registered using Form TX. The screenplay derived from the novel should be registered on Form PA (the form for plays and screenplays).

All fact compilations must be registered on Form TX. A collection of works intended to be performed before a live audience—for example, an anthology of stageplays, screenplays, or other works—would be registered on Form PA. All other collective works—for example, an anthology of short stories—should be registered on Form TX.

Where to Obtain the Forms

You can obtain the registration forms in a number of ways:

- Digital copies of the forms are on the CD-ROM at the end of this book. The forms are in Adobe Acrobat PDF format. You must have the Adobe Acrobat Reader installed on your computer to view and complete the forms. A copy of the Reader is on the CD-ROM. (See Appendix B for detailed instructions on how to use the CD-ROM.) You can complete these forms on your computer and then print them out; but before you do this, read "Printing the Forms on Your Computer," below.

- You can obtain the forms directly from the Copyright Office. Digital copies can be downloaded from the Copyright Office's website at www.copyright.gov. Hard copies can be obtained by calling the Copyright Office's Forms Hotline at 202-707-9100.

How to Complete Form TX

Form TX is for nondramatic literary works. Here's how to fill it out.

Fill Out Forms Carefully and Correctly

Type your application form or use only black ink. When filling out the form, remember that it may end up being submitted in court to help prove your infringement case. If any part of it is found inaccurate, your case could suffer—perhaps greatly. Moreover, a person who intentionally lies on a copyright registration application may be fined up to $2,500.

Printing the Forms on Your Computer

The Copyright Office is very picky about the print quality of the registration application forms you send in. This is because it produces completed registration certificates by electronically scanning the original application you submit. As a result, if you submit an application of poor print quality, you'll get a registration certificate of poor quality as well.

If you complete the digital forms on your computer, be sure to follow these instructions when you print them out:

- The forms should be printed head to head (top of page 2 is directly behind the top of page 1) using BOTH SIDES of a single sheet of paper. This means you'll have to print the first side, take the paper out of the printer, turn it over, put it back in the printer, and then print the second side. Of course, this doesn't apply to those forms that are one-sided.
- Dot matrix printer copies of the forms are not acceptable.
- Inkjet printer copies of the forms require enlarging if you use the Shrink to Fit Page option.
- To achieve the best quality copies of the application forms, it is recommended, but not required, that you use a laser printer

You will find a sample filled-out Form TX in Appendix A.

Space 1: Title Information

You must provide information about your work's title in Space 1.

Title of this work. The Copyright Office uses the title for indexing and identifying your work. If your work contains a title, fill in that wording. This should be the same title that appears on your deposit. If your work is untitled, either state "untitled" or make a title up. You need not include this made-up title on your untitled work. If you're registering a work written in a foreign language, you don't have to translate the title into English.

Titles and other identifying phrases cannot be copyrighted. This means that registration will not prevent anyone from using the title to your work, but you may have other recourse. (See Chapter 2, Copyright Basics.)

Previous or alternative titles. Provide any additional titles under which someone searching for the registration might be likely to look—for example, a foreign country where the work was originally published under a different title. However, you don't need to include any additional titles known only to you or a few readers—such as working titles.

If you're registering a new version of a work under a new title that contains substantial new material, you don't need to list the old title here.

Publication as a contribution. If the work you're registering is an individual article or other contribution to a collective work such as an anthology, newspaper, magazine, or other periodical, fill in the title of the publication after the words "Title of This Work."

> **EXAMPLE:** Kyle published an article entitled "Cave Exploration in the Andes" in *The Spelunker's Journal.* He should state: "*The Spelunker's Journal.*"

In addition, if the collective work is a serial publication such as a magazine, periodical, or newspaper, give the requested information about the issue of the serial in which the contribution appeared. The volume and issue numbers are usually found before the table of contents. The issue date is usually on the cover—for example: "June 2005" or "Winter 2005."

> **EXAMPLE:** Kyle's article was published on pages 20–30 in the June 2007 issue of *The Spelunker's Journal.* Kyle looks at the journal's masthead and sees that this issue is listed as Volume 10, Number (or issue) 6, with a June 1, 2007 publication date. Kyle would state in the first line: "*The Spelunker's Journal.*" In the second line, Kyle would indicate that the article appeared in Volume 10, Number 6, June 1, 2007, on pages 20–30.

Space 2: Author Information

Space 2 calls for information about the work's author or authors. Space 2 is divided into three identical subspaces, "a," "b," and

Copyright Office fees are subject to change. For current fees, check the Copyright Office website at *www.copyright.gov*, write the Copyright Office, or call (202) 707-3000.

Form TX
For a Nondramatic Literary Work
UNITED STATES COPYRIGHT OFFICE

REGISTRATION NUMBER

TX TXU

EFFECTIVE DATE OF REGISTRATION

Month Day Year

DO NOT WRITE ABOVE THIS LINE. IF YOU NEED MORE SPACE, USE A SEPARATE CONTINUATION SHEET.

1

TITLE OF THIS WORK ▼

PREVIOUS OR ALTERNATIVE TITLES ▼

PUBLICATION AS A CONTRIBUTION If this work was published as a contribution to a periodical, serial, or collection, give information about the collective work in which the contribution appeared. **Title of Collective Work ▼**

If published in a periodical or serial give: **Volume ▼** **Number ▼** **Issue Date ▼** **On Pages ▼**

2

a **NAME OF AUTHOR ▼** — **DATES OF BIRTH AND DEATH** Year Born ▼ Year Died ▼

Was this contribution to the work a "work made for hire"? ☐ Yes ☐ No

AUTHOR'S NATIONALITY OR DOMICILE Name of Country — OR { Citizen of ▶ ____ / Domiciled in ▶ ____ }

WAS THIS AUTHOR'S CONTRIBUTION TO THE WORK Anonymous? ☐ Yes ☐ No Pseudonymous? ☐ Yes ☐ No — If the answer to either of these questions is "Yes," see detailed instructions.

NATURE OF AUTHORSHIP Briefly describe nature of material created by this author in which copyright is claimed. ▼

b **NAME OF AUTHOR ▼** — **DATES OF BIRTH AND DEATH** Year Born ▼ Year Died ▼

Was this contribution to the work a "work made for hire"? ☐ Yes ☐ No

AUTHOR'S NATIONALITY OR DOMICILE Name of Country — OR { Citizen of ▶ ____ / Domiciled in ▶ ____ }

WAS THIS AUTHOR'S CONTRIBUTION TO THE WORK Anonymous? ☐ Yes ☐ No Pseudonymous? ☐ Yes ☐ No — If the answer to either of these questions is "Yes," see detailed instructions.

NATURE OF AUTHORSHIP Briefly describe nature of material created by this author in which copyright is claimed. ▼

c **NAME OF AUTHOR ▼** — **DATES OF BIRTH AND DEATH** Year Born ▼ Year Died ▼

Was this contribution to the work a "work made for hire"? ☐ Yes ☐ No

AUTHOR'S NATIONALITY OR DOMICILE Name of Country — OR { Citizen of ▶ ____ / Domiciled in ▶ ____ }

WAS THIS AUTHOR'S CONTRIBUTION TO THE WORK Anonymous? ☐ Yes ☐ No Pseudonymous? ☐ Yes ☐ No — If the answer to either of these questions is "Yes," see detailed instructions.

NATURE OF AUTHORSHIP Briefly describe nature of material created by this author in which copyright is claimed. ▼

NOTE

Under the law, the "author" of a "work made for hire" is generally the employer, not the employee (see instructions). For any part of this work that was "made for hire" check "Yes" in the space provided, give the employer (or other person for whom the work was prepared) as "Author" of that part, and leave the space for dates of birth and death blank.

3

a **YEAR IN WHICH CREATION OF THIS WORK WAS COMPLETED** **This information must be given in all cases.** ◀ Year

b **DATE AND NATION OF FIRST PUBLICATION OF THIS PARTICULAR WORK** **Complete this information ONLY if this work has been published.** Month ▶ ____ Day ▶ ____ Year ▶ ____ ◀ Nation

4

COPYRIGHT CLAIMANT(S) Name and address must be given even if the claimant is the same as the author given in space 2. ▼

See instructions before completing this space.

TRANSFER If the claimant(s) named here in space 4 is (are) different from the author(s) named in space 2, give a brief statement of how the claimant(s) obtained ownership of the copyright. ▼

DO NOT WRITE HERE OFFICE USE ONLY

APPLICATION RECEIVED

ONE DEPOSIT RECEIVED

TWO DEPOSITS RECEIVED

FUNDS RECEIVED

MORE ON BACK ▶ • Complete all applicable spaces (numbers 5-9) on the reverse side of this page. • See detailed instructions. • Sign the form at line 8.

DO NOT WRITE HERE

Page 1 of ____ pages

"c." Subspaces b and c are filled out only if there is more than one author.

Name of author. We discussed who the author is for registration purposes in the section "Who Can Register," above. Reread that section if you're not sure who is the author of the work being registered. If you need still more information, read Chapter 8, Initial Copyright Ownership, and Chapter 9, Transferring Copyright Ownership.

- Works *not* made for hire: Unless the work was made for hire, the person or people who created the work are the authors. Give the full name (full first, middle, and last name) of the first, or only, author. (For use of anonymous or pseudonymous names, see below.)
- Works made for hire: If the work to be registered is a work made for hire, the author for registration purposes is the employer or person or entity that commissioned the work. The full legal name of the employer or commissioning party must be provided as the name of the author instead of the name of the person who actually wrote the work.

EXAMPLE 1: Microstuff Incorporated publishes a line of computer books that are written by their in-house editorial staff. Their new title, *Computing As Therapy,* was written by Ken Grant, Microstuff's senior editor. "Microstuff Incorporated" is listed in the "Name of Author" space.

EXAMPLE 2: Jane Milsap writes a chemistry textbook and transfers to Acme Press all her copyright rights. Acme employees prepare artwork and text for the cover. Jane should be listed as author of "entire text of chemistry textbook." Acme should be listed as the author of "cover artwork and text" in Space 2b; Acme is the author because the artwork and cover copy were works made for hire prepared by its employees. (Note: Had Jane retained any of her copyright rights, the cover artwork and text and the textbook would have had to have been registered separately.)

The name of the employee who created the work made for hire may also be included if you want to make this part of the public record, but it is not required—for example: "Microstuff Incorporated, employer for hire of Ken Grant."

Harriet Beecher Stowe

Don't guess about the full legal name of a corporation, partnership, or other entity. Find out the organization's full legal name and use it—for example, do not state "ABC, Inc." when the full legal name is "Acme Book Company, Incorporated." The full legal name may be found on the entity's organizing document, such as articles of incorporation, a partnership agreement, or a registration certificate filed with the appropriate state official (often the "Secretary of State").

Anonymous or pseudonymous authors. An author's contribution to a work is anonymous if the author is not identified on the copies of the work. A contribution is pseudonymous if the author is identified under a fictitious name (pen name).

If the work is anonymous, you may:

- leave the name of author line blank (or state "N/A")
- state "anonymous" on the line, or
- reveal the author's identity.

If the work is pseudonymous, you may leave the line blank; give the pseudonym and identify it as such—for instance, "Mike Danger, pseudonym"—or reveal the author's name, making it clear which is the real name and which is the pseudonym—for example, "Harold Lipshitz, whose pseudonym is Mike Danger."

Of course, if the author's identity is revealed on the application, it will be a simple matter for others to discover it, because the application becomes a public document available for inspection at the Copyright Office.

Duration of Anonymous or Pseudonymous Works

If the author of a pseudonymous or anonymous work is not identified in the Copyright Office's records, the copyright in the work lasts for a maximum of 95 years from the date of publication, or 120 years from the date of creation, whichever is less. The copyright in works by individuals in which the author is identified lasts for the life of the author plus 70 years. This could be longer than 95 years from publication; it all depends on how long the author lives. (See discussion in Chapter 10, Copyright Duration.)

If the author absolutely does not want her name revealed to anyone, the best option may be to leave the name of author line blank, state "anonymous," or list the pseudonym without the real name. The author or her heirs can later let the Copyright Office know the author's true identity if this would extend the copyright term.

Dates of birth and death. If the author is a human being, his or her year of birth may be provided here, but this is not required (the birth year is used for identification purposes). However, if the author has died, the year of death *must* be listed unless the author was anonymous or pseudonymous. This date will determine when the copyright expires. Leave this space blank if the author is a corporation, partnership, or other organization. Corporations, partnerships, and other business entities do not "die" for copyright purposes, even if they dissolve.

Was this contribution to the work a "work made for hire"? Check the "Yes" box if the author is a corporation, partnership, or other organization. Otherwise, check the "No" box.

Author's nationality or domicile. This information must always be provided, even if the author is a business, is anonymous, or used a pseudonym. An author's citizenship (nationality) and domicile could be different. An author's domicile generally is the country where she maintains her principal residence and where she intends to remain indefinitely. An author is a citizen of the country in which she was born or later moved to and became a citizen of by complying with its naturalization requirements.

> **EXAMPLE:** Evelyn is a Canadian citizen, but she has permanent resident status and has lived year-round in Boston since 1980 and intends to remain there for the indefinite future. She is domiciled in the United States. She can state "Canada" in the citizenship blank or "U.S.A." in the domicile blank.

A legal resident of the U.S. is treated the same as a citizen for copyright purposes. If you have difficulty determining whether you are domiciled in the U.S., consult an attorney. Noncitizens usually are entitled to copyright protection in the United States. (See Chapter 13, International Copyright Protection.)

Regardless of the state or states in which it is organized and does business, the citizenship of a domestic corporation, partnership, or other organization should be given as "U.S.A."

Was this author's contribution to the work anonymous or pseudonymous? Check "Yes" box if the author is anonymous or used a pseudonym (pen name). Check the "No" box if the author is identified by her correct name. Don't check either box if the work was made for hire.

Nature of authorship. You must give a brief general description of the nature of the author's contribution to the work. Consider your words carefully, because the Copyright Office relies on the description to determine if the work can be registered. Be sure that the description matches the work deposited with your application. The Copyright Office will probably send you a letter asking you to correct and resubmit your application if the "Nature of Authorship" statement(s) describes material not included in the deposit.

Entirely new works. One of the following phrases will probably adequately describe the authorship in an entirely new work. Pick the phrase that best describes the author's contribution to the particular work (or compose a better one of your own):

- "entire text" or "entire work," if the author wrote the entire work being registered
- "entire text and illustrations" (where these are being registered as a single unit)
- "coauthor of entire text," if there were joint authors

- "nondramatic literary work"
- "book"
- "periodical"
- "novel"
- "poetry"
- "magazine article."

Do not list the work's title or describe the idea or concept embodied in the work (for example, "a book about skydiving"). Ideas and titles are not copyrightable. (See Chapter 6, What Copyright Protects.) The Copyright Office will correspond with you if your application describes your work in such terms.

Adaptations, new editions, and other derivative works. If you're registering a derivative work, describe the protectible material contributed to the work by the author. Examples of acceptable descriptions include:

- "editorial revisions," if the new material consists of editorial changes
- "editorial revisions plus additional new material" (or "Chapter 10 completely new"), if the author made editorial changes and added new material
- "editorial revisions, annotations, and other modifications"
- "Chapters 11–17," if entirely new chapters are added
- "revisions throughout, Act III completely new," if a play is revised and new material added
- "translation into English"
- "sound recording of published novel"
- "screenplay"
- "dramatization for the stage," if a play dramatizes another work such as a novel
- "dramatization for television."

A statement such as "entire work" or "derivative work" ordinarily is not acceptable for such works. Moreover, do not describe unprotectable material added to the changed version, such as material in the public domain or copyrighted material written by others that the author obtained permission to use or used without permission under the fair use doctrine. (See Chapter 11, Using Other Authors' Words.)

Compilations. If you're registering a compilation, describe both the material that has been compiled and the compilation itself. Include the terms "compilation," "selection," or "arrangement." For example:

- "Compilation and English translation," if the author translated a work into English.
- "Compilation of articles by Leroy Brown."
- "Anthology of previously published short stories."
- "Compilation of numerical data."

If the Copyright Office might question whether your compilation was the product of minimal creativity, submit a letter along with your application explaining how the compilation was created. Your letter should convince the copyright examiner that minimal creativity was employed in the selection and/or arrangement of the facts, data, or other items in your compilation. (See Chapter 7, Adaptations and Compilations.)

Information for additional authors. If there are two or three authors, go back now and fill in boxes 2b and 2c for each of them, using the above discussion as a guide. Space 2 only has enough subspaces for three authors. If the work you're registering has more than three authors, provide the required information for all the additional authors on a Copyright Office "Continuation Sheet" and clip (do not tape or staple) it to your application. There is a special continuation sheet to use with Form TX called Form TX/CON. A copy can be found on the CD-ROM at the end of this book. You can obtain additional copies from the Copyright Office.

Space 3: Relevant Dates in Which Creation of This Work Was Completed

Fill in the year in which the work you're registering first became fixed in its final form, disregarding minor editorial changes. This year has nothing to do with publication, which may occur long after creation. Deciding what constitutes the year of creation may prove difficult if the work was created over a long period of time. Give the year in which the author completed the particular version of the work for which registration is now being sought, even if other versions exist or if further changes or additions are planned.

> **EXAMPLE:** Martin finished writing an experimental novel in 2006. He couldn't find a publisher. He thoroughly rewrote the work in 2007 to make it more commercial, but still couldn't find a publisher. He finally self-published the original version of the novel in 2008. When he registers the book, the creation date will be 2006. This is because the particular version of the novel being registered was written in 2006.

Date and nation of first publication of this particular work. Leave this blank if an unpublished work is being registered. Publication occurs for copyright purposes when a work is made widely available to the public. (See Chapter 2, Copyright Basics.) Give the month, day, year, and country where publication first occurred. Give only one date. If you're not sure of the exact publication date, state your best guess and make clear it is approximate—for example, "November 15, 2005 (approx.)."

Space 4: Information About Copyright Claimants

Provide the name and address of the copyright claimant(s), which must be either:

- persons or organizations that have, on or before the date the application is filed, obtained ownership of *all* the exclusive United States copyright rights that initially belonged to the author
- the author or authors of the work (including the owner of a work made for hire, if applicable), or
- the name of a person or organization that the author or owner of all U.S. copyright rights has authorized by contract to act as the claimant for copyright registration (there is no legal requirement that such contract be in writing, but it's not a bad idea). (37 CFR § 202.3(a)(3) (1984).)

We discuss in Chapter 2, Copyright Basics, the fact that under the copyright laws an author automatically holds several different exclusive rights in the work she creates—that is, the right to reproduce the work, to distribute it, to perform or publicly display it, and to prepare derivative works based upon it. The author is entitled to transfer one or more—or any portion—of these rights in any way she pleases. But, if another person or organization acquires all these exclusive rights in a work, that person or organization is considered the copyright claimant for registration purposes, and the author is no longer the claimant.

> **EXAMPLE:** Joe, an experienced mountaineer, self-publishes a pamphlet on advanced rock climbing techniques. The Colorado Rock Climbing Club purchases Joe's entire copyright in the pamphlet and republishes it. Joe never registered the pamphlet, so the club does so. The club should be listed as the copyright claimant, not Joe.

Frequently, no one owns all the exclusive rights in the work. This may occur where an author transfers fewer than all her exclusive rights to a publisher, or where a person or entity that acquired all the author's rights transfers some, but not all, of the rights to a third party. In this event, the author must be listed as the copyright claimant, even if someone else owns most of the exclusive copyright rights.

> **EXAMPLE 1:** Assume that Joe transferred to the Rock Climbing Club only the right to publish a new edition of the pamphlet for their members and other Colorado residents. Joe retained all of his other exclusive rights. Joe is the copyright claimant.

> **EXAMPLE 2:** Assume again that the Colorado Rock Climbing Club acquired all of Joe's exclusive rights in his pamphlet. Before the pamphlet is registered, the club transfers to the Southern California Climber's Federation the right to publish and distribute the pamphlet in California. No one now owns all the exclusive rights in the pamphlet—not Joe (who owns no rights), not the club, and not the federation. When the club registers the pamphlet, Joe must be listed as the copyright claimant, because he is the author and the exclusive rights are not concentrated in one pair of hands.

In the case of a work made for hire, the author is the creator's employer, or person or entity that commissioned the work under a written work-for-hire agreement. This means the copyright claimant is either (1) the employer or commissioning party, or (2) the person or entity to whom the employer or commissioning party has transferred all of its exclusive rights in the work.

> **EXAMPLE 1:** Assume that Joe was an employee of the Colorado Rock Climbing Club and wrote the pamphlet as part of his job. The club is the copyright owner of this work made for

hire, and the club should be listed as the copyright claimant.

EXAMPLE 2: Assume that the club dissolved not long after Joe finished writing the pamphlet. Kate purchased all the club's exclusive rights in the pamphlet. When Kate registers the work, she should list herself as the copyright claimant.

A copyright claimant must be listed even for anonymous or pseudonymous works. You can provide the claimant's real name alone, the real name and the pseudonym, or the pseudonym alone if the claimant is generally known by it, or the author can authorize another person to act as the claimant (this way, the author's real name will not appear on the form).

When the name listed for the claimant is different from the name of the author given in Space 2, but the two names identify one person, explain the relationship between the two names.

EXAMPLE: John Smith is the author of the work he is registering, but all of the copyright rights have been transferred to his corporation, Smith Publishing Company, Inc., of which Smith is the sole owner. Smith should not just state Smith Publishing Company, Inc. Rather, he needs to explain the relationship between himself and his company-claimant—for example, "Smith Publishing Company, Inc., solely owned by John Smith."

Transfer. If the copyright claimant named just above is not the author or authors named in Space 2, give a brief general description of how ownership of the copyright was obtained. However, do not attach the transfer documents to the application.

This statement must show the copyright examiner that *all* the author's United States copyright rights have been transferred by a *written agreement* or by operation of law. Examples of acceptable transfer statements include: "By written contract," "Transfer of all rights by author," "By will," "By inheritance," "Assignment," or "By gift agreement."

Examples of *unacceptable* statements include:

- words indicating that possibly less than all the author's United States copyright rights have been transferred to the claimant—for example: "By license," "By permission," or "Transfer of right of first publication"
- statements suggesting that the person named as the claimant simply owns a copy of the work being registered, not the author's copyright rights—for example: "Author gave me this copy," "Found in attic trunk," "Author asked me to keep it for him"
- statements indicating that the named claimant has a special relationship to the author, but that do not show an actual transfer of ownership—for

example: "Claimant is author's publisher," "Claimant is author's agent," or "Author is president of claimant corporation."

Again, see Chapter 9, Transferring Copyright Ownership, for a detailed discussion of copyright transfers.

Note that the transfer space is used only to inform the Copyright Office about transfers that occurred before registration. All such transfers must be made in writing. (See Chapter 9, Transferring Copyright Ownership.) If a copyright is transferred after registration, there is no need to reregister. However, although not required, it is a good idea to record (send) a copy of the transfer document to the Copyright Office. Again, see Chapter 9.

If the author or owner of all rights has authorized another person or organization to act as the claimant, this should be indicated by including language like the following: "Pursuant to the contractual right from [author *or* owner of all U.S. copyright rights] to claim legal title to the copyright in an application for copyright registration."

If there's not enough space to list all the claimants on Form TX, you can list additional claimants on the reverse side of Form TX/CON.

Space 5: Previous Registration

If all the material in the work you're registering has never been registered before, check the "No" box and skip the rest of the questions.

If all or part of the work has been previously registered, check the "Yes" box. Then, you need to check the appropriate box:

- Check the first box only if you are now registering a work you previously registered when it was unpublished.
- Check the second box only if someone other than the author was listed as the copyright claimant in Space 4 in the prior registration, and the author is now registering the work in her own name—for example, where an anonymous or pseudonymous author listed an authorized agent in Space 4, above, and now wishes to reregister in her own name.
- Check the third box only if the previously registered work has been changed, and you are registering the changed version or new edition to protect the additions or revisions.

Then provide the registration number and year of previous registration in the blanks indicated. The registration number can be found stamped on the certificate of registration. It is usually a multidigit number preceded by the two-letter prefix of the application form used—for example, TX 012345. The Office places a small "u" following the prefix if the registered work is unpublished—for example, TXu 567890.

If you're not registering a derivative work or compilation, skip to Space 8, below.

Space 6: Description of Derivative Works or Compilations

Space 6 is completed only for derivative works or compilations. It should be completed only if the derivative work or compilation contains material that was:

- previously published
- previously registered, or
- in the public domain.

If the preexisting material in your derivative work or compilation was not published, registered, or in the public domain, put "N/A" in Space 6. Technically, a work based on or adapted from preexisting unpublished expression that was never registered is a derivative work. However, for reasons of administrative convenience, the Copyright Office does not require unpublished, unregistered material to be described in Space 6.

> **EXAMPLE:** Leila writes a screenplay based on her unpublished, unregistered novel. The screenplay is a derivative work, but Leila need not complete Space 6 on Form PA when she registers the screenplay.

Preexisting material (6a). For a derivative work, identify the preexisting material that has been revised, recast, transformed, or adapted—for instance, "Previously published first edition of textbook on ancient Greek history," "Public Domain French version of *Madame Bovary*," "Previously registered unpublished manuscript."

Leave Space 6a blank if you're registering a compilation.

Material added to this work (6b). For a derivative work, describe in Space 6b the new protectible material you are registering. Often, you can simply repeat what you stated in the "Nature of Authorship" line in Space 2 (above). If the application contains more than one nature of authorship statement because there was more than one author, you'll need to combine these descriptions. Be sure you describe all the new authorship.

> **EXAMPLE:** Otto and Eva have revised their published textbook. The description of Otto's authorship in space 2 states "Revised Chapters 1–8." The description of Eva's authorship states "Added new Chapter 9." They should state in space 6b, "Revised Chapters 1–8, new Chapter 9."

However, don't describe the new material in such a manner that the copyright examiner might question whether enough new material has been added to make the work registrable. For example, it's probably not wise merely to state "editorial revisions," because it is not clear from this description whether the revisions are substantial. Rather, describe the revisions—for example, "Revised foreword, typographical errors deleted, new chapter heading, and new compilation of four maps."

Space 6b must be completed for all compilations. You can simply repeat in space 6b what you stated in the "Nature of Authorship" line in space 2.

Space 7: Deposit Account and Correspondence

Deposit Account. If you have 12 or more transactions per year with the Copyright Office, you may establish a money deposit

EXAMINED BY

FORM TX

CHECKED BY

☐ CORRESPONDENCE Yes

FOR COPYRIGHT OFFICE USE ONLY

DO NOT WRITE ABOVE THIS LINE. IF YOU NEED MORE SPACE, USE A SEPARATE CONTINUATION SHEET.

5

PREVIOUS REGISTRATION Has registration for this work, or for an earlier version of this work, already been made in the Copyright Office?

☐ **Yes** ☐ **No** If your answer is "Yes," why is another registration being sought? (Check appropriate box.) ▼

a. ☐ This is the first published edition of a work previously registered in unpublished form.

b. ☐ This is the first application submitted by this author as copyright claimant.

c. ☐ This is a changed version of the work, as shown by space 6 on this application.

If your answer is "Yes," give: **Previous Registration Number** ▶ **Year of Registration** ▶

6

See instructions before completing this space.

DERIVATIVE WORK OR COMPILATION

a **Preexisting Material** Identify any preexisting work or works that this work is based on or incorporates. ▼

b **Material Added to This Work** Give a brief, general statement of the material that has been added to this work and in which copyright is claimed. ▼

7

a **DEPOSIT ACCOUNT** If the registration fee is to be charged to a Deposit Account established in the Copyright Office, give name and number of Account.
Name ▼ **Account Number** ▼

b **CORRESPONDENCE** Give name and address to which correspondence about this application should be sent. Name/Address/Apt/City/State/ZIP ▼

Area code and daytime telephone number ▶ Fax number ▶

Email ▶

8

CERTIFICATION* I, the undersigned, hereby certify that I am the

Check only one ▶
- ☐ author
- ☐ other copyright claimant
- ☐ owner of exclusive right(s)
- ☐ authorized agent of ______________________

Name of author or other copyright claimant, or owner of exclusive right(s) ▲

of the work identified in this application and that the statements made by me in this application are correct to the best of my knowledge.

Typed or printed name and date ▼ If this application gives a date of publication in space 3, do not sign and submit it before that date.

Date ▶

Handwritten signature (X) ▼

X ____

9

Certificate will be mailed in window envelope to this address:

Name ▼
Number/Street/Apt ▼
City/State/ZIP ▼

YOU MUST:
- Complete all necessary spaces
- Sign your application in space 8

SEND ALL 3 ELEMENTS IN THE SAME PACKAGE:
1. Application form
2. Nonrefundable filing fee in check or money order payable to *Register of Copyrights*
3. Deposit material

MAIL TO:
Library of Congress
Copyright Office - TX
101 Independence Avenue, S.E.
Washington, D.C. 20559-6222

Fees are subject to change. For current fees, check the Copyright Office website at www.copyright.gov, write the Copyright Office, or call (202) 707-3000.

*17 U.S.C. § 506(e): Any person who knowingly makes a false representation of a material fact in the application for copyright registration provided for by section 409, or in any written statement filed in connection with the application, shall be fined not more than $2,500.

Rev: July 2003—xxx Web Rev: July 2003 ♻ Printed on recycled paper

U.S. Government Printing Office: 2000-461-113/20,021

account to which you make advance money deposits, and charge your copyright fees against the account instead of sending a separate check each time. You must deposit at least $250 to open an account. For an application, obtain "Circular R5" from the Copyright Office. If you have a deposit account and wish to charge the registration fee to the account, state the account name and number.

Correspondence. Provide the name, address, area code and telephone number, email, and fax number (if any) of the person the Copyright Office should contact if it has questions about your application.

If the registration is being made by a corporation or other entity, list the name of the person in the organization who should be contacted. The Copyright Office makes calls between 8:00 a.m. and 5:00 p.m. Eastern time, so give the number or numbers where the contact person can be reached at these times.

Space 8: Certification

Check the appropriate box indicating your capacity as the person registering the work:

- Check the "author" box if you are the person (or one of several people) named in Space 2 (if there are several authors, only one need sign).
- Check the "other copyright claimant" box if you are not named in Space 2 as the author but have acquired all the author's rights.
- Check the "owner of exclusive right(s)" box if you only own one or more—but not all—of the exclusive rights making up the entire copyright.
- Check the "authorized agent of" box if you are not signing for yourself as an individual, but as the authorized representative of the author, another person who is the copyright claimant, or the owner of one or more—but not all—exclusive rights. Then state the name of the person or organization on whose behalf you're signing on the dotted line following the box.

Check the "authorized agent" box if you, as an individual, are signing on behalf of a corporation, partnership, or other organization that is the author, copyright claimant, or holder of exclusive rights.

After checking the appropriate box, type or print your name and date in the appropriate blanks, then sign your name on the line following "handwritten signature."

If you are registering a published work, the Copyright Office will not accept your application if the date listed in the certification space is earlier than the date of publication shown in Space 3.

Space 9: Return Mailing Address

Fill in your name and the return mailing address for your copyright registration certificate in the last box on the form.

If you're registering a group of previously published articles or other individual contributions to periodicals, turn to the section dealing with Form GR/CP, below.

How to Complete Form PA

Form PA is for works that are intended to be performed in public, such as plays and screenplays. Form PA is virtually identical to Form TX, so we'll refer to the instructions for Form TX above, where applicable.

Form PA is also used to register multimedia works combining text with graphics, photos, videos, sounds, and so forth. See Chapter 14, Copyright in the Online World, for a detailed discussion on how to complete Form PA when registering such works.

You will find a sample filled-out Form PA in Appendix A.

Space 1: Title and Date of Publication

Title of this work. Follow the instructions in "How to Complete Form TX," above.

Previous or alternative titles. Follow the instructions in "How to Complete Form TX, above".

Nature of this work. Give a brief description of the general nature of the work. For example: "screenplay," "television play," "drama," "musical play," "song lyrics."

Space 2: Author Information

Follow the instructions in "How to Complete Form TX," above. Space 2 only has enough subspaces for three authors. If the work you're registering has more than three authors, provide the required information for all the additional authors on a Copyright Office "Continuation Sheet"—Form ___ /CON—and clip (do not tape or staple) it to your application. A copy of Form ___/CON can be found on the CD-ROM at the end of this book. You can obtain additional copies from the Copyright Office.

Nature of authorship. Examples of acceptable nature of authorship descriptions include:

- "entire text" or "entire work" if the author wrote the entire work being registered
- "coauthor of entire text" if there is more than one author
- "words" if the author has written song lyrics
- "revisions throughout, Act III completely new" if a play is revised and new material added.

Space 3: Relevant Dates

Follow the instructions in "How to Complete Form TX," above.

Space 4: Copyright Claimant(s)

Follow the instructions in "How to Complete Form TX," above. If there's not enough space to list all the claimants on Form PA, you can list additional claimants on the reverse side of Form PA/CON.

Space 5: Previous Registration

Follow the instructions in "How to Complete Form TX," above.

Copyright Office fees are subject to change. For current fees, check the Copyright Office website at *www.copyright.gov*, write the Copyright Office, or call (202) 707-3000.

FORM PA

For a Work of the Performing Arts
UNITED STATES COPYRIGHT OFFICE

REGISTRATION NUMBER

PA PAU

EFFECTIVE DATE OF REGISTRATION

Month Day Year

DO NOT WRITE ABOVE THIS LINE. IF YOU NEED MORE SPACE, USE A SEPARATE CONTINUATION SHEET.

1

TITLE OF THIS WORK ▼

PREVIOUS OR ALTERNATIVE TITLES ▼

NATURE OF THIS WORK ▼ See instructions

2

a **NAME OF AUTHOR ▼**

DATES OF BIRTH AND DEATH Year Born ▼ Year Died ▼

Was this contribution to the work a "work made for hire"? ☐ Yes ☐ No

AUTHOR'S NATIONALITY OR DOMICILE Name of Country
OR { Citizen of ______ / Domiciled in ______

WAS THIS AUTHOR'S CONTRIBUTION TO THE WORK
Anonymous? ☐ Yes ☐ No
Pseudonymous? ☐ Yes ☐ No
If the answer to either of these questions is "Yes," see detailed instructions.

NATURE OF AUTHORSHIP Briefly describe nature of material created by this author in which copyright is claimed. ▼

NOTE

Under the law, the "author" of a "work made for hire" is generally the employer, not the employee (see instructions). For any part of this work that was "made for hire" check "Yes" in the space provided, give the employer (or other person for whom the work was prepared) as "Author" of that part, and leave the space for dates of birth and death blank.

b **NAME OF AUTHOR ▼**

DATES OF BIRTH AND DEATH Year Born ▼ Year Died ▼

Was this contribution to the work a "work made for hire"? ☐ Yes ☐ No

AUTHOR'S NATIONALITY OR DOMICILE Name of Country
OR { Citizen of ______ / Domiciled in ______

WAS THIS AUTHOR'S CONTRIBUTION TO THE WORK
Anonymous? ☐ Yes ☐ No
Pseudonymous? ☐ Yes ☐ No
If the answer to either of these questions is "Yes," see detailed instructions.

NATURE OF AUTHORSHIP Briefly describe nature of material created by this author in which copyright is claimed. ▼

c **NAME OF AUTHOR ▼**

DATES OF BIRTH AND DEATH Year Born ▼ Year Died ▼

Was this contribution to the work a "work made for hire"? ☐ Yes ☐ No

AUTHOR'S NATIONALITY OR DOMICILE Name of Country
OR { Citizen of ______ / Domiciled in ______

WAS THIS AUTHOR'S CONTRIBUTION TO THE WORK
Anonymous? ☐ Yes ☐ No
Pseudonymous? ☐ Yes ☐ No
If the answer to either of these questions is "Yes," see detailed instructions.

NATURE OF AUTHORSHIP Briefly describe nature of material created by this author in which copyright is claimed. ▼

3

a **YEAR IN WHICH CREATION OF THIS WORK WAS COMPLETED** **This information must be given in all cases.** Year

b **DATE AND NATION OF FIRST PUBLICATION OF THIS PARTICULAR WORK** **Complete this information ONLY if this work has been published.** Month ______ Day ______ Year ______ Nation

4

COPYRIGHT CLAIMANT(S) Name and address must be given even if the claimant is the same as the author given in space 2. ▼

See instructions before completing this space.

TRANSFER If the claimant(s) named here in space 4 is (are) different from the author(s) named in space 2, give a brief statement of how the claimant(s) obtained ownership of the copyright. ▼

DO NOT WRITE HERE OFFICE USE ONLY

APPLICATION RECEIVED

ONE DEPOSIT RECEIVED

TWO DEPOSITS RECEIVED

FUNDS RECEIVED

MORE ON BACK ▶
- Complete all applicable spaces (numbers 5-9) on the reverse side of this page.
- See detailed instructions.
- Sign the form at line 8.

DO NOT WRITE HERE

Page 1 of ______ pages

EXAMINED BY — FORM PA

CHECKED BY

☐ CORRESPONDENCE Yes

FOR COPYRIGHT OFFICE USE ONLY

DO NOT WRITE ABOVE THIS LINE. IF YOU NEED MORE SPACE, USE A SEPARATE CONTINUATION SHEET.

5

PREVIOUS REGISTRATION Has registration for this work, or for an earlier version of this work, already been made in the Copyright Office?

☐ **Yes** ☐ **No** If your answer is "Yes," why is another registration being sought? (Check appropriate box.) ▼ If your answer is No, do **not** check box A, B, or C.

a. ☐ This is the first published edition of a work previously registered in unpublished form.

b. ☐ This is the first application submitted by this author as copyright claimant.

c. ☐ This is a changed version of the work, as shown by space 6 on this application.

If your answer is "Yes," give: **Previous Registration Number ▼** **Year of Registration ▼**

6

DERIVATIVE WORK OR COMPILATION Complete both space 6a and 6b for a derivative work; complete only 6b for a compilation.

a **Preexisting Material** Identify any preexisting work or works that this work is based on or incorporates. ▼

See instructions before completing this space.

b **Material Added to This Work** Give a brief, general statement of the material that has been added to this work and in which copyright is claimed. ▼

7

a **DEPOSIT ACCOUNT** If the registration fee is to be charged to a Deposit Account established in the Copyright Office, give name and number of Account.

Name ▼ **Account Number ▼**

b **CORRESPONDENCE** Give name and address to which correspondence about this application should be sent. Name / Address / Apt / City / State / ZIP ▼

Area code and daytime telephone number ( ) Fax number ( )

Email

8

CERTIFICATION* I, the undersigned, hereby certify that I am the

Check only one ▶

☐ author

☐ other copyright claimant

☐ owner of exclusive right(s)

☐ authorized agent of ____________________

Name of author or other copyright claimant, or owner of exclusive right(s) ▲

of the work identified in this application and that the statements made by me in this application are correct to the best of my knowledge.

Typed or printed name and date ▼ If this application gives a date of publication in space 3, do not sign and submit it before that date.

Date ____________

Handwritten signature (X) ▼

☞ *x* ____________________

9

Certificate will be mailed in window envelope to this address:

Name ▼
Number/Street/Apt ▼
City/State/ZIP ▼

YOU MUST:
- Complete all necessary spaces
- Sign your application in space 8

SEND ALL 3 ELEMENTS IN THE SAME PACKAGE:
1. Application form
2. Nonrefundable filing fee in check or money order payable to *Register of Copyrights*
3. Deposit material

MAIL TO:
Library of Congress
Copyright Office
101 Independence Avenue, S.E.
Washington, D.C. 20559-6000

Fees are subject to change. For current fees, check the Copyright Office website at www.copyright.gov, write the Copyright Office, or call (202) 707-3000.

*17 U.S.C. § 506(e): Any person who knowingly makes a false representation of a material fact in the application for copyright registration provided for by section 409, or in any written statement filed in connection with the application, shall be fined not more than $2,500.

Rev: June 2002—20,000 Web Rev: June 2002 ♻ Printed on recycled paper U.S. Government Printing Office: 2000-461-113/20,021

Space 6: Description of Derivative Work or Compilation

Skip this item unless you are registering a derivative work or compilation. If you are, follow the instructions in "How to Complete Form TX," above.

Space 7: Deposit Account

Follow the instructions for Space 7 in "How to Complete Form TX," above.

Space 8: Certification

Follow the instructions for Space 10 in "How to Complete Form TX," above.

Space 9: Return Mailing Address

Fill in your name and the return mailing address for your copyright registration certificate in the last box on the form.

If you're registering a group of previously published individual contributions to periodicals, turn to the section about Form GR/CP.

Registering Newspapers, Magazines, Newsletters, and Other Periodicals: Form SE, Short Form SE, Form SE/Group, Form G/DN

Introduction

Newspapers, magazines, and other periodicals such as newsletters and journals are normally "collective works" in which a number of individual contributions such as articles, stories, cartoons, and photographs are assembled into a collective whole. Magazines and similar publications are also called serials. Both the magazine as a whole and the individual contributions are entitled to full copyright protection.

A magazine or other periodical issue is registered as a whole on one of the SE series of forms, usually by the person(s) or organization that owns the publication and/or supervises its creation. When a magazine or other periodical issue is registered as a whole, the registration protects:

- the revising, editing, compiling, and similar efforts that went into putting the issue into final form
- any individual contributions (articles and so on) prepared by the publication's employees or by nonemployees who signed work-for-hire agreements, and
- any individual contributions by freelancers to which the publication has purchased all rights.

If a periodical issue contains any independently authored contributions to which all of the rights have not been acquired by the publication, those contributions are not protected when the issue is registered as a whole. To protect their work, individual contributors who retain some of their rights must register separately.

EXAMPLE: The *Jogger's Journal* is a monthly magazine owned and published by Ededas, Inc. The July issue contains 12 articles: two articles were written by the journal's editorial staff; two were written by freelance writers who signed work-for-hire agreements; four were written by freelancers who assigned to the journal all their rights; and three were written by freelancers who assigned to the journal only the right to publish their articles for the first time in North America. When the July issue is registered, all the material in it will be protected except for the three articles to which the journal did not acquire all rights.

Four registration forms

There are four different registration forms for serial publications: Form SE, Short Form SE, Form SE/Group, and Form G/DN. Which form to use depends on the nature of the magazine or other serial work you're registering. Form SE can be used to register any serial publication, but, in practice, you'll want to use it only if you cannot use the other forms, because the filing fee is lower when you use those forms.

Form SE/Group: Group Registration of Serials

The Copyright Office now permits multiple issues of the same magazine to be registered together as a group for one application fee. For example, the same monthly magazine may now be registered three issues at a time on Form SE/Group. This way, registration need only be accomplished four times a year instead of 12. Unfortunately, there are some restrictions on which periodicals may be registered together on Form SE/Group.

Periodical must be a work made for hire

The magazine or other periodical must be a work made for hire. This means that the persons who create the periodical as a whole—that is, do the editing, compiling, and similar work necessary to put the issue in its final form—must be employees of the owner of the publication or have been commissioned to do the work under a written contract. (See Chapter 8, Initial Copyright Ownership, for a detailed discussion of works made for hire.) Most periodicals and other serial publications are works made for hire for which the owner of the publication has hired or commissioned others to compile and edit.

EXAMPLE: *Newspeak Magazine* is a weekly news magazine that is compiled and edited entirely by the publisher's editorial staff. *Newspeak* is a work made for hire, and the weekly issues may be registered together on Form SE/Group.

However, a periodical that is independently owned and created by the same individual(s) who own it—that is, not created by employees or commissioned workers—is not a work made for hire. Such a publication may not be registered on Form SE/Group. Each issue must be separately registered on Form SE (see below).

EXAMPLE: Dr. Brown, an eminent urologist, owns, publishes, writes, and edits a monthly newsletter for urologists called *Urine Analysis*. The newsletter is not a work made for hire. This means that Dr. Brown must register each newsletter issue separately on Form SE.

Group registration unavailable for periodicals published more than once a week or less than four times a year

You may register together two or more issues of the same periodical on Form SE/Group so long as they are published:

- no more frequently than once a week
- at least four times a year, and
- all issues being registered together were published within a 90-day period during the same calendar year.

EXAMPLE 1: Thirteen issues of *Newspeak Magazine* are published every 90 days. Instead of registering each issue separately on Form SE, up to 13 consecutive issues can be registered at the same time on Form SE/Group, so long as all the issues were published during the same calendar year—for example, the December 2006 and January and February 2007 issues could not be registered together, but the January, February, and March 2007 issues could be.

EXAMPLE 2: *The Nutne Reader* is a literary magazine that is published irregularly. In 2007, one issue was published in January, another in March, another in July, and another in December. The January and March issues may be registered together on Form SE/Group, since they were published within 90 days of each other. But the July and December issues must be registered separately.

Collective work authorship must be essentially all new

Form SE/Group may be used only if the collective work authorship—that is, the editing, compiling, revising, and other work involved in creating each issue as a whole—of all the issues being registered together is essentially all new in terms of when the work was done. It's not exactly clear how recently created a periodical issue must be to qualify as essentially all new, but as an outside time limit, each issue must have been created no more than one year prior to its publication.

The author and copyright claimant must be the same for all issues

The author of a magazine or other periodical issue is the person(s) or organization responsible for the creation of the issue as a whole, whether it employs an editorial staff or freelance editors or uses volunteers. The author is normally the person(s) or organization that owns the publication.

To use Form SE/Group, the author of all the periodical issues being registered as a group and the copyright claimant in the issues must be the same. As discussed above, the author of a publication is also the copyright claimant unless the author transfers all of its copyright rights to a third party. This means the author-publisher of a periodical issue would normally be the copyright claimant as well. However, if the author-publisher transferred its copyright rights to one or more of the periodical issues to a third party, those issues could not be registered on Form SE/Group.

EXAMPLE 1: *The Toxic Waste Tipster* is a monthly trade journal owned and published by a corporation called Toxic Waste Interment and Transport, Inc. (TWIT). TWIT oversees the creation of each issue through its editorial staff. TWIT is the author and copyright claimant for each issue.

EXAMPLE 2: Assume that TWIT sells the *Tipster* to the Polluters' Trade Association (PTA), effective July 2007. As of July 1, TWIT has already overseen production of all the monthly issues through September 2007. The July, August, and September issues may not be registered together on Form SE/Group because, while TWIT is the author of each, the PTA owns all the copyright rights in these issues and is the copyright claimant.

Two complimentary subscriptions must be given to the Library of Congress

Two complimentary subscriptions for the periodical must be entered for the Library of Congress. This is in addition to the normal deposit that must be submitted with your application. These subscriptions must continue for as long as you wish to use the group registration procedure.

The subscriptions must be sent *separately* to:

Group Periodicals Registration
Library of Congress
Washington, DC 20540

The *first time* a magazine or other serial is submitted for group registration, a letter confirming that two complimentary subscriptions have been given to the library must be filed at the address listed above.

The letter should identify the publisher, title(s), and volume and issue numbers that begin the complimentary subscriptions.

EXAMPLE: The publisher of *Newspeak Magazine* decides to register three months of issues together as a group. *Newspeak* gives the Library of Congress two free subscriptions to the magazine and sends the following letter to the Copyright Office General Counsel (this letter need only be sent once).

Joseph Pulitzer

Letter to Copyright Office

May 1, 20xx

Group Periodicals Registration
Library of Congress
Washington, DC 20540

Gentlemen:

The serial publication *Newspeak Magazine* has recently been submitted for group registration for the first time. This is to confirm that we have given the Library of Congress two complimentary subscriptions to *Newspeak Magazine*, commencing with Volume 52, Number 23. *Newspeak Magazine* is published by Big Brother, Inc.

Winston Smith
Newspeak Magazine
Winston Smith, Publisher

How to complete Form SE/Group

Filling out Form SE/Group is very simple.

Space 1: Title and Date of Publication

Title. Fill in the publication's complete title followed by:

- the International Standard Serial Number (ISSN) if available (see Chapter 3, Copyright Notice, for detailed discussion of ISSNs), and
- each issue's volume, number, and issue date appearing on the copies, followed by the month, day, and year of publication.

List the issues in order of publication.

No previous registration under identical title. If you have never registered the identical title before, check the box at the left.

Space 2: Author and Copyright Claimant

Name and address of the author/copyright claimant in these collective works made for hire. Give the fullest form of the author/claimant's name and mailing address. If there are joint authors and claimants, provide the names and addresses of each of them. (See Chapter 8, Initial Copyright Ownership, for discussion of joint authorship.)

For non-U.S. works. If the issues were not published in the U.S., you must list the country of which the author is a citizen or where she resides, or state the country in which the serial was published.

Certification. The application must be signed by the copyright claimant or its duly authorized agent. Type or print this person's name after the signature.

Person to contact for correspondence about this claim. In the spaces provided, indicate the name and daytime telephone number (including area code) of the person whom the Copyright Office should contact concerning the application. Also give such person's address if it is different from the address for mailing of the certificate (below).

Deposit account. If the filing fee is to be charged against a deposit account, give the name and number of the account in the space indicated. Otherwise, leave the space blank and forward the fee with your application.

Mail certificate to. Provide the complete address where your registration certificate should be sent. (The certificate is merely a stamped copy of your Form SE/Group.)

Application fee

If you don't have a deposit account with the Copyright Office, submit a check for the application fee payable to the Register of Copyrights with your application. The fee is $25 for *each* periodical issue being registered together on Form SE/Group.

Form G/DN for Newspapers

An entire calendar month's worth of daily newspaper issues can be registered at one time on Form G/DN for a single $55 fee.

What works qualify as daily newspapers

Any daily serial publication mainly designed to be a primary source of written information on current events (local, national, or international) qualifies as a daily newspaper so long as it contains a broad range of news on all subjects and activities and is not limited to any specific subject matter. Publications such as newsletters on particular subjects and daily racing forms do not qualify as daily newspapers.

Requirements for using Form G/DN

As is the case when using Form SE/Group, Form G/DN may be used only if the newspaper is an essentially all-new collective work made for hire. Virtually all daily newspapers should be able to satisfy this requirement since they are essentially all new every day and are created by employee-reporters and editors.

In addition, the author and copyright claimant must be the same person or organization. Again, this should pose no problem, because the author and claimant will normally be the owner(s) of the newspaper.

An entire month's issues must be registered

To use Form G/DN, an entire calendar month of daily newspaper issues must be registered; no more and no less. This means you'll have to register 12 times a year.

Microfilm deposit required

In one important respect, using Form G/DN is unique. Instead of the normal deposit of an actual copy of the work being registered, the newspaper issues must be deposited in the form of a positive, 35mm silver-halide microfilm.

If the newspaper is published in multiple editions, the last (final) edition of all the issues must be deposited. However, it is permissible (but not required) to also register and deposit earlier editions of the newspaper published the same day in a given metropolitan area. But national or regional newspaper editions distributed beyond a given metropolitan area must be registered and deposited separately.

Time limit for registration

Form G/DN must be filed with the Copyright Office within three months after the publication date of the last newspaper issue included in the group.

Registration fee

There is a $70 registration fee when Form G/DN is used.

Filling out Form G/DN

Form G/DN is the simplest of all registration forms. Here's how to fill it out.

Space 1: Title

Identify the work being registered in Space 1 by giving the title of the newspaper, the month and year printed on the copies, the number of issues in the group, the city and state, the edition, and, if known, the ISSN number.

Space 2: Author and Copyright Claimant

Give in Space 2 the fullest form of the author and claimant's name (this will usually be the owner of the newspaper). If there are multiple owners, give all their names.

Space 3: Date of Publication

List in Space 3 the exact full date on which the first and last newspaper issues being registered were published.

Certification; correspondence; deposit account. The copyright claimant or her authorized agent must sign in the certification space, and an address and phone number of the person to be contacted about the registered issues must be provided. If the claimant has a deposit account with the Copyright Office and wants the registration fee charged to it, the "Deposit Account" space must be filled in; otherwise, leave it blank.

Form G/DN for Newsletters

Form G/DN may also be used for group registration of newsletters. For registration purposes, a daily newsletter is serial published and distributed by mail or electronic media (for example, online, via fax, or on a CD-ROM). Publication must occur at least two days per week, and the newsletter must contain news or information of interest chiefly to a special group—for example, trade and professional associations, corporations, schools, colleges, and churches. Daily newsletters are customarily available by subscription and are not sold on newsstands.

The requirements are the same as those for newspapers covered in the preceding section, except for the following differences:

At least two issues must be registered

To use Form G/DN for a newsletter, you must register at least two issues that were published within one calendar month in the same year. The application must be filed within three months of the last publication date of the newsletter issues included in the group.

Deposit requirements

One complete copy of each newsletter issue included in the group must accompany the Form G/DN. If the newsletter is published only online, one complete printout of each issue or a computer disk or CD-ROM containing all the issues and a printout of the first and last issues included in the group must be sent. However, microfilm copies and complimentary subscriptions are required only if requested by the Copyright Office Acquisitions Division.

Short Form SE

A periodical issue that otherwise qualifies for group registration but cannot be registered on Form SE/Group because it is published too frequently or not frequently enough (such as a magazine published every four months) may be registered on Short Form SE instead *if* both of the following are true:

- The author, whether a human being or corporation or other entity, is a U.S. citizen or resides in the U.S.
- The issue was first published in the U.S.

The advantage to using Short Form SE rather than the regular Form SE is that Short Form SE is easier to fill out.

Short Form SE is nearly identical to Form SE/Group. It is filled out in the same manner as Form SE/Group (above) except that only one issue is listed in Space 1 and the date of publication of the issue being registered must be provided in Space 3. If the issue was created in a different calendar year from the year of publication, the year of creation must also be given in Space 3.

Form SE

Periodical issues that do not qualify for group registration on Form SE/Group or Form G/DN, or for individual registration on Short Form SE, must be registered individually on Form SE. This could occur, for example, where a periodical is not a work for hire.

Form SE is almost identical to Form TX discussed in "How to Complete Form TX," above. The differences in Form SE are discussed below.

You will find a sample filled-out Form SE in Appendix A.

Space 1: Title

Title of this serial. Fill in the publication's complete title. Then, in the spaces provided, give the volume and issue number, the date on the issue you are submitting with the application, and the frequency of publication of the serial—for instance, "ten times a year," "quarterly," "monthly," "bimonthly," or "weekly." You'll usually find this information in or near the publication's masthead.

Previous or alternative titles. Refer to Form TX, discussed in "How to Complete Form TX," above.

Space 2: Author Information

Follow the instructions in "How to Complete Form TX," above, with these clarifications.

Name of author. Provide the full name of the issue's author. The author is the person or organization that controls and supervises the issue's creation. (See "How to Complete Form TX," above.) This will normally be the person or organization that owns the publication. The title of a periodical itself usually should not be listed as author, because that title is usually not the owner's full legal name.

Copyright Office fees are subject to change. For current fees, check the Copyright Office website at *www.copyright.gov*, write the Copyright Office, or call (202) 707-3000.

FORM SE

For a Serial
UNITED STATES COPYRIGHT OFFICE

REGISTRATION NUMBER

U

EFFECTIVE DATE OF REGISTRATION

Month Day Year

DO NOT WRITE ABOVE THIS LINE. IF YOU NEED MORE SPACE, USE A SEPARATE CONTINUATION SHEET.

1

TITLE OF THIS SERIAL ▼

Volume ▼ **Number ▼** **Date on Copies ▼** **Frequency of Publication ▼**

PREVIOUS OR ALTERNATIVE TITLES ▼

2

a **NAME OF AUTHOR ▼**

DATES OF BIRTH AND DEATH Year Born ▼ Year Died ▼

Was this contribution to the work a "work made for hire"? ☐ Yes ☐ No

AUTHOR'S NATIONALITY OR DOMICILE Name of Country
OR { Citizen of ▶ ______ / Domiciled in ▶ ______

WAS THIS AUTHOR'S CONTRIBUTION TO THE WORK
Anonymous? ☐ Yes ☐ No
Pseudonymous? ☐ Yes ☐ No
If the answer to either of these questions is "Yes," see detailed instructions.

NATURE OF AUTHORSHIP Briefly describe nature of material created by this author in which copyright is claimed. ▼
☐ **Collective Work** Other:

b **NAME OF AUTHOR ▼**

DATES OF BIRTH AND DEATH Year Born ▼ Year Died ▼

Was this contribution to the work a "work made for hire"? ☐ Yes ☐ No

AUTHOR'S NATIONALITY OR DOMICILE Name of Country
OR { Citizen of ▶ ______ / Domiciled in ▶ ______

WAS THIS AUTHOR'S CONTRIBUTION TO THE WORK
Anonymous? ☐ Yes ☐ No
Pseudonymous? ☐ Yes ☐ No
If the answer to either of these questions is "Yes," see detailed instructions.

NATURE OF AUTHORSHIP Briefly describe nature of material created by this author in which copyright is claimed. ▼
☐ **Collective Work** Other:

c **NAME OF AUTHOR ▼**

DATES OF BIRTH AND DEATH Year Born ▼ Year Died ▼

Was this contribution to the work a "work made for hire"? ☐ Yes ☐ No

AUTHOR'S NATIONALITY OR DOMICILE Name of Country
OR { Citizen of ▶ ______ / Domiciled in ▶ ______

WAS THIS AUTHOR'S CONTRIBUTION TO THE WORK
Anonymous? ☐ Yes ☐ No
Pseudonymous? ☐ Yes ☐ No
If the answer to either of these questions is "Yes," see detailed instructions.

NATURE OF AUTHORSHIP Briefly describe nature of material created by this author in which copyright is claimed. ▼
☐ **Collective Work** Other:

NOTE

Under the law, the "author" of a "work made for hire" is generally the employer, not the employee (see instructions). For any part of this work that was "made for hire" check "Yes" in the space provided, give the employer (or other person for whom the work was prepared) as "Author" of that part, and leave the space for dates of birth and death blank.

3

a **YEAR IN WHICH CREATION OF THIS ISSUE WAS COMPLETED** This information must be given in all cases. ◀ Year

b **DATE AND NATION OF FIRST PUBLICATION OF THIS PARTICULAR ISSUE** Complete this information ONLY if this work has been published. Month ▶ ______ Day ▶ ______ Year ▶ ______ ◀ Nation

4

See instructions before completing this space.

COPYRIGHT CLAIMANT(S) Name and address must be given even if the claimant is the same as the author given in space 2. ▼

TRANSFER If the claimant(s) named here in space 4 is (are) different from the author(s) named in space 2, give a brief statement of how the claimant(s) obtained ownership of the copyright. ▼

DO NOT WRITE HERE OFFICE USE ONLY

APPLICATION RECEIVED

ONE DEPOSIT RECEIVED

TWO DEPOSITS RECEIVED

REMITTANCE NUMBER AND DATE

MORE ON BACK ▶ • Complete all applicable spaces (numbers 5-11) on the reverse side of this page. • See detailed instructions. • Sign the form at line 10.

DO NOT WRITE HERE

Page 1 of ______ pages

EXAMINED BY

FORM SE

CHECKED BY

☐ CORRESPONDENCE Yes

FOR COPYRIGHT OFFICE USE ONLY

DO NOT WRITE ABOVE THIS LINE. IF YOU NEED MORE SPACE, USE A SEPARATE CONTINUATION SHEET.

5

PREVIOUS REGISTRATION Has registration for this work, or for an earlier version of this work, already been made in the Copyright Office?

☐ **Yes** ☐ **No** If your answer is "Yes," why is another registration being sought? (Check appropriate box.) ▼

a. ☐ This is the first published edition of a work previously registered in unpublished form.

b. ☐ This is the first application submitted by this author as copyright claimant.

c. ☐ This is a changed version of the work, as shown by space 6 on this application.

If your answer is "Yes," give: **Previous Registration Number ▼** **Year of Registration ▼**

6

See instructions before completing this space.

DERIVATIVE WORK OR COMPILATION Complete both space 6a and 6b for a derivative work; complete only 6b for a compilation.

a **Preexisting Material** Identify any preexisting work or works that this work is based on or incorporates. ▼

b **Material Added to This Work** Give a brief, general statement of the material that has been added to this work and in which copyright is claimed. ▼

7

a **DEPOSIT ACCOUNT** If the registration fee is to be charged to a Deposit Account established in the Copyright Office, give name and number of Account.

Name ▼ **Account Number ▼**

b **CORRESPONDENCE** Give name and address to which correspondence about this application should be sent. Name/Address/Apt/City/State/ZIP ▼

Area code and daytime telephone number ▶ Fax number ▶

Email ▶

8

CERTIFICATION* I, the undersigned, hereby certify that I am the

Check only one ▶

☐ author
☐ other copyright claimant
☐ owner of exclusive right(s)
☐ authorized agent of ______
Name of author or other copyright claimant, or owner of exclusive right(s) ▲

of the work identified in this application and that the statements made by me in this application are correct to the best of my knowledge.

Typed or printed name and date ▼ If this application gives a date of publication in space 3, do not sign and submit it before that date.

Date ▶

Handwritten signature (X) ▼

X ______________________________

9

Certificate will be mailed in window envelope to this address:

Name ▼

Number/Street/Apt ▼

City/State/ZIP ▼

YOU MUST:
- Complete all necessary spaces
- Sign your application in space 8

SEND ALL 3 ELEMENTS IN THE SAME PACKAGE:

1. Application form
2. Nonrefundable filing fee in check or money order payable to *Register of Copyrights*
3. Deposit material

MAIL TO:
Library of Congress
Copyright Office
101 Independence Avenue, S.E.
Washington, D.C. 20559-6000

Fees are subject to change. For current fees, check the Copyright Office website at www.copyright.gov, write the Copyright Office, or call (202) 707-3000.

*17 U.S.C. § 506(e): Any person who knowingly makes a false representation of a material fact in the application for copyright registration provided for by section 409, or in any written statement filed in connection with the application, shall be fined not more than $2,500.

Rev: June 2002—20,000 Web Rev: June 2002 ♻ Printed on recycled paper

U.S. Government Printing Office: 2000-461-113/20,021

> **EXAMPLE:** *The Spelunker's Journal* is owned by the Spelunker's Society of America, a nonprofit corporation. An editor employed by the society commissions freelance writers to contribute individual articles to the journal, which the editor compiles and edits for each issue. The society is the journal's author. The society's full legal name ("Spelunker's Society of America, Incorporated") should be listed as author.

Was this contribution to the work a "work made for hire"? Read the discussion of when a periodical issue is a work made for hire in the section about registering newspapers, above, and check the appropriate box.

Nature of authorship. If the serial issue is a work made for hire, it is a collective work. A collective work is a work in which individual contributions which would be copyrightable in themselves are assembled into a collective whole by an organization and its employees. If this is the case, check this box; there is no need to describe the nature of the authorship involved in creating the issue.

However, if the serial issue was independently created by an individual or individuals, you must describe the nature of the authorship.

> **EXAMPLE:** Kay owns, publishes, writes, and edits a newsletter on environmental law. The newsletter is not a "collective work," because Kay writes the entire content herself. Kay should not check the "collective work" box. Instead, she must describe her authorship of the newsletter. She could simply state "entire text."

If the work you're registering has more than three authors, provide the required information for all the additional authors on a Copyright Office "Continuation Sheet"—Form ___/CON—and clip it (do not tape or staple it) to your application. A copy of Form ___/CON can be found on the CD-ROM at the end of this book. You can obtain additional copies from the Copyright Office.

Space 3: Relevant Dates

Follow the instructions on how to fill out Space 3 of Form TX in "How to Complete Form TX," above.

Space 4: Copyright Claimant(s)

Follow the instructions on how to fill out Space 4 of Form TX in "How to Complete Form TX," above.

Space 5: Previous Registration

Follow the instructions on how to fill out Space 5 of Form TX in "How to Complete Form TX," above.

Space 6: Description of Derivative Work or Compilation

Leave Space 6 blank if the issue contains entirely new material appearing for the first time, such as a new issue of a periodical with all new articles. Complete Space 6 only if the issue being registered contains a substantial amount of material that was:

- previously published—for example, the *Nutne Reader* is a monthly magazine that republishes articles that previously appeared in small literary journals

- previously registered—for example, the *Nutne Reader* publishes an issue containing unpublished articles that had previously been registered, or
- in the public domain—for example, to celebrate its anniversary, the *Pacific Monthly* publishes a special issue containing, in addition to the normal articles, a facsimile of its first issue, published in 1851. The 1851 issue is in the public domain.

Derivative works and compilations are discussed in detail in Chapter 7, Adaptations and Compilations. Review that chapter if you're not sure whether the periodical is a derivative work, compilation, or both.

Preexisting material (6a). If the serial is a derivative work, briefly describe in space 6a the preexisting material that has been recast, transformed, or adapted in the issue being registered—for instance, "2006 published article by Julie Blake." Don't complete this space for compilations—for instance, a magazine consisting of unaltered, previously published articles.

Material added to this work (6b). For derivative works, briefly describe in Space 6b all of the new material contained in the serial issue—for example, "Editorial revisions," "Translation," "Additional material." If the periodical issue is a compilation, describe both the compilation itself and the material that has been compiled—for example, "Compilation of previously published journal articles."

Some serials are both derivative works and compilations. For example, an issue of the *Nutne Reader* described above consisting of previously published articles would be both a compilation and a derivative work if *Nutne*'s editors made substantial editorial revisions—for instance, condensed the articles. In this event the publisher might state "Compilation of previously published articles and editorial revisions" when registering that issue of the journal.

Spaces 7–9

Follow the instructions for filling out these same spaces for Form TX, above.

Application Fee. A $45 application fee must be submitted with Form SE.

Registering a Group of Contributions to Periodicals: Form GR/CP

As discussed above, authors who retain some of the rights in their contributions to periodicals need to register them to obtain the benefits of registration for their work. This is so regardless of whether the publisher of the periodical registers the periodical issue as a whole on one of the SE series of forms.

> **EXAMPLE:** Arnie, a freelance writer, sells an article to *Newspeak Magazine.* He grants the magazine only the right to publish the article the first time in North America, and retains his other copyright

rights. When the publisher of *Newspeak* registers the issue containing Arnie's article, the article will not be covered by the serial registration. Arnie must register the article himself for it to be fully protected.

You can register each article you write individually on Form TX. However, at $45 per registration, individually registering a substantial number of articles or other periodical contributions each year can be very expensive.

Fortunately, a writer may register all of the articles he or she writes in any 12-month period as a group on one application for one $45 application fee.

Who Qualifies for Group Registration

A single copyright registration for a group of works can be made only if all of the following are true:

- All of the works are by the same author who is an individual—that is, not a work made for hire—or all the works are by the same coauthors.
- All of the works were first published as individual contributions to periodicals (including newspapers, magazines, newsletters, and journals) within any single 12-month period (not necessarily a calendar year).
- All of the works have the same copyright claimant.

EXAMPLE 1: Jean published 12 short stories in various literary journals from July 2006 to July 2007. She retained the copyright for all the stories. Each story contained a copyright notice listing "Jean Davis" as the copyright owner. Jean may register all 12 stories as a group at one time.

EXAMPLE 2: Assume that a copyright notice appeared on only eight of Jean's short stories. She could register those eight stories as a group, but not the four stories that did not have a copyright notice. For those remaining stories, Jean would have to use four Forms TX.

How to Apply for Group Registration

To apply for group registration you must complete two forms: the appropriate basic application form (Form TX or Form PA), and Form GR/CP. However, you will only be required to pay a single registration fee.

Filling out Form TX or Form PA

You'll be using Form TX unless you're registering a group of previously published plays, screenplays, song lyrics, or other dramatic works.

Space 1: (Title of this work)

State "See Form GR/CP, attached." Leave the rest of Space 1 blank.

Space 3

Give the year of creation of the last contribution you completed. Leave blank the date and nation of first publication.

You will find sample filled-out forms in Appendix A.

ADJUNCT APPLICATION
for Copyright Registration for a Group of Contributions to Periodicals

- Use this adjunct form only if you are making a single registration for a group of contributions to periodicals, and you are also filing a basic application on Form TX, Form PA, or Form VA. Follow the instructions, attached.
- Number each line in Part B consecutively. Use additional Forms GR/CP if you need more space.
- Submit this adjunct form with the basic application form. Clip (do not tape or staple) and fold all sheets together before submitting them.
- **Copyright Office fees are subject to change. For current fees, please check the Copyright Office website at www.copyright.gov or call (202) 707-3000 for current fee information.**

Form GR/CP
For Restored Works
UNITED STATES COPYRIGHT OFFICE

REGISTRATION NUMBER

TX PA VA

EFFECTIVE DATE OF REGISTRATION

Month Day Year

FORM GR/CP RECEIVED

Page ____ of ____ pages

DO NOT WRITE ABOVE THIS LINE. FOR COPYRIGHT OFFICE USE ONLY

A Identification of Application

IDENTIFICATION OF BASIC APPLICATION:
• This application for copyright registration for a group of contributions to periodicals is submitted as an adjunct to an application filed on: (Check which)

☐ Form TX ☐ Form PA ☐ Form VA

IDENTIFICATION OF AUTHOR AND CLAIMANT: (Give the name of the author and the name of the copyright claimant in all of the contributions listed in Part B of this form. The names should be the same as the names given in spaces 2 and 4 of the basic application.)

Name of Author ____________________

Name of Copyright Claimant ____________________

B Registration for Group of Contributions

COPYRIGHT REGISTRATION FOR A GROUP OF CONTRIBUTIONS TO PERIODICALS: (To make a single registration for a group of works by the same individual author, all first published as contributions to periodicals within a 12-month period (see instructions), give full information about each contribution. If more space is needed, use additional Forms GR/CP.)

☐ Title of Contribution ____________________
Title of Periodical ____________ Vol.___ No.____ Issue Date ______ Pages ______
Date of First Publication ____________ (Month) (Day) (Year) Nation of First Publication ____________ (Country)

☐ Title of Contribution ____________________
Title of Periodical ____________ Vol.___ No.____ Issue Date ______ Pages ______
Date of First Publication ____________ (Month) (Day) (Year) Nation of First Publication ____________ (Country)

☐ Title of Contribution ____________________
Title of Periodical ____________ Vol.___ No.____ Issue Date ______ Pages ______
Date of First Publication ____________ (Month) (Day) (Year) Nation of First Publication ____________ (Country)

☐ Title of Contribution ____________________
Title of Periodical ____________ Vol.___ No.____ Issue Date ______ Pages ______
Date of First Publication ____________ (Month) (Day) (Year) Nation of First Publication ____________ (Country)

☐ Title of Contribution ____________________
Title of Periodical ____________ Vol.___ No.____ Issue Date ______ Pages ______
Date of First Publication ____________ (Month) (Day) (Year) Nation of First Publication ____________ (Country)

☐ Title of Contribution ____________________
Title of Periodical ____________ Vol.___ No.____ Issue Date ______ Pages ______
Date of First Publication ____________ (Month) (Day) (Year) Nation of First Publication ____________ (Country)

☐ Title of Contribution ____________________
Title of Periodical ____________ Vol.___ No.____ Issue Date ______ Pages ______
Date of First Publication ____________ (Month) (Day) (Year) Nation of First Publication ____________ (Country)

How to complete Form GR/CP

Form GR/CP gives the Copyright Office some basic information about each individual article or other contribution being registered.

Part A

Identification of basic application. Check the box showing which basic application form you are using, either Form TX or Form PA.

Identification of author and claimant. Give the name of the author and the copyright claimant of all the contributions you're registering. These names should be the same as the names given in Spaces 2 and 4 of your basic application and must be the same for all the contributions being registered.

Part B

The Copyright Office prefers that you list the contributions in the order of their publication, giving the earliest first. You should also number each space consecutively in the box provided. Form GR/CP has space for 19 contributions. If you need to register more than that number, use an additional Form GR/CP.

For each article or other contribution being registered, provide the following.

Title of contribution. If the article contained a title or identifying phrase, use it. Otherwise, make up a title that identifies the particular contribution and distinguishes it from the other contributions you're registering.

Title of periodical and identifying information. Fill in the complete name of the periodical in which the article was first published. Give the volume and issue number (if any) and the issue date. Also, list the pages in the periodical issue on which the articles appeared.

Date and nation of first publication. Fill in the date and country in which the periodical issue that the article or other contribution appeared in was first published.

Effect of Group Registration

All of your articles or other contributions are protected by registration on the date the Copyright Office receives your application. If any of the registered articles are copied after that date, you are entitled to all the benefits of timely copyright registration (that is, statutory damages and attorney fees). However, if any of the contributions were copied before the registration date, you will not be entitled to statutory damages and attorney fees unless the registration was made within three months after the first publication of the contribution. This is not nearly as confusing as it sounds. Consider these examples.

> **EXAMPLE 1:** Percy used the group registration procedure to register ten of his published articles. The Copyright Office received Percy's application on March 15, 2006. One of Percy's articles was copied by Bob after March 15. If Percy sues Bob, he will be entitled to statutory damages and attorney fees.

EXAMPLE 2: Assume instead that Bob copied two of Percy's articles before Percy filed his group registration application on March 15. Article A was published on January 15; Article B was published in November of the preceding year. Percy is entitled to statutory damages and attorney fees for the infringement of Article A, but not for Article B. Reason: Article A was registered within three months after publication, but Article B was not.

Example 2 illustrates the one drawback of group registration: If you wait more than three months after an article is published so that you can register it together with other articles for one fee, you will lose the benefits of timely registration of that article for any infringe ment occurring before the Copyright Office receives your application. If you feel that an article or other periodical contribution is extremely valuable, make sure that it is registered within three months of publication, even if you have to register it by itself. If you publish a large number of articles every year, you should make a group registration every three months.

Satisfying Copyright Office Deposit Requirements

You must submit (deposit) one or two copies of the work being registered with your application. The Copyright Office reviews your deposit to make sure that the work is copyrightable and is accurately described on your application form. Your registration only covers the material that you deposit with the Copyright Office—except where a special deposit of less than the entire work is made, such as for a multivolume encyclopedia or automated database.

Unpublished Works

If you're registering an unpublished work, your application must be accompanied by *one complete copy* of the work—that is, the copy must contain all the material you wish to register.

Published Works

Subject to the important exceptions discussed, below, *two* complete copies of a published work must be deposited. This sounds quite simple, but there are some additional rules and limitations that we also discuss below.

Works published in two or more editions

Sometimes the same work is published simultaneously in two or more editions—for instance, in a hardcover and paperback edition, or a trade edition and a more expensively printed and bound collector's edition. Where this occurs, you must deposit the best edition of the work. The best edition is the work of the highest quality, in terms of printing and binding—for example, you would deposit a hardcover edition rather than the paperback version of a work. If there are two hardcover versions, you would deposit the edition that is the best bound, largest in size, or printed on the best paper. It's up to you to decide which edition is the best.

EXAMPLE 1: Acme Publishing Co. simultaneously publishes a novel in both paperback and hardback editions. Both editions are identical in content. The hardback is the best edition that should be deposited when the novel is registered.

EXAMPLE 2: Philip self-publishes a treatise on Byzantine art. Half the copies were printed on ordinary paper and half on archival quality paper. Philip should deposit a copy of his treatise printed on the archival quality paper; it is the "best edition."

The Copyright Office publishes a circular describing in detail all the criteria used to determine what constitutes the best edition of a work. If you're in the publishing business, you may find it useful. You may download Circular R7b from the Copyright Office website at www.copyright.gov or obtain it by calling or writing the Copyright Office.

You only need to deposit the "best edition" of the work in existence at the time you register. This means if a better edition is published after you have already registered, you do not need to deposit it with the Copyright Office.

EXAMPLE: Rachel photocopies and distributes 500 copies of a collection of her poetry. She deposits two complete copies when she registers the work. To her surprise, all 500 copies are sold within a year. She decides to self-publish another edition, but this time she has the book professionally typeset and printed by offset lithography. Although the second edition of the work is of much better print quality than the first, Rachel need not deposit it with the Copyright Office since it did not exist when she registered the work.

Make sure, however, that each of the editions has substantially the same content. If the second edition contains enough new material to be considered a new version, it must be registered separately to protect the new material.

Periodical issues

How many copies of a periodical issue need to be deposited depends on which registration form is used:

- Form SE/Group: deposit one copy of *each issue*
- Short Form SE: deposit one copy of the individual periodical
- Form SE: deposit *two copies* of the periodical issue
- Form G/DN: deposit one calendar month of daily newspaper issues on positive 35mm silver-halide microfilm, or one copy of each newsletter issue registered in a group.

Registering individual contributions to periodicals and other collective works

If you are registering an individual contribution to a collective work such as a magazine or newspaper article or a contribution to an anthology, you must register one complete copy of the best edition of the entire collective work—that is, the entire magazine or anthology. Luckily, there is an exception for newspapers: Instead of depositing the entire newspaper, you only need to deposit the section of the paper in which your article appeared. (Imagine depositing a copy of the entire Sunday *New York Times*!)

This rule also applies to registration of a group of individual periodical contributions using Form GR/CP—for instance, if you are registering 12 articles that appeared in 12 different journals, you must deposit one complete copy of *each* journal.

When only one copy need be deposited

The Copyright Office permits the deposit of one, rather than two, copies of the following types of published works:

- multimedia works; see Chapter 14, Copyright in the Online World, for a detailed discussion
- works first published outside the United States (only one copy of the first foreign edition need be deposited; it need not be the best edition)
- advertising materials (you only need to send one copy of the page in which an advertisement appeared in a periodical, not the entire periodical issue)
- lectures, sermons, speeches, and addresses published separately (that is, not as part of a collection), and
- tests and test answers published separately from each other.

Depositing Identifying Material Instead of Copies

Depositing two complete copies of some works could prove burdensome both for the applicant and the Copyright Office. For example, you would not wish to mail, and the Copyright Office would not want to store, a 30-volume encyclopedia. Indeed, the Copyright Office will not accept any item that exceeds 96 inches in any dimension.

If your work exceeds 96 inches, you'll have to deposit identifying material rather than the entire work. For example, instead of depositing every volume of an encyclopedia that takes up ten feet of shelf space, you might be able to submit photos of every volume. To prepare identifying material, first call the Copyright Office at 202-707-3000, describe your work, and find out what type of identifying material is acceptable.

Library of Congress Deposit Requirements

The Library of Congress has its own deposit requirements for published works, which are separate from those of the Copyright Office. However, the library's deposit requirements are deemed satisfied when a work is registered and a deposit made with the Copyright Office. In other words, you don't have to worry about the Library of Congress if you register your work with the Copyright Office. The one exception to this rule is deposits for machine-readable works such as automated databases. The library may demand deposit of the machine-readable copies distributed after registration has been made.

If you don't register your published work with the Copyright Office, you are supposed to deposit two copies with the Library of Congress. If you don't, the library is entitled to demand that you do so, and you are subject to monetary penalties if you do not comply. However, in practice this rarely happens. Contrary to popular belief, the Library of Congress does not collect copies of everything published in the United States.

Sending Your Application to the Copyright Office

By now you have completed your application form and have your deposit ready to go. Make a photocopy of your application form and retain it in your records along with an exact copy of your deposit.

Copyright registration fees change from time to time. So, before sending in your registration application, check to see if the registration fees have been raised. You can do this by checking the Copyright Office website at www.copyright.gov, checking the update section of the Nolo website, or calling the Copyright Office at 202-707-3000.

Application Fee

You must submit a check or money order for the application fee payable to the Register of Copyrights. The fee is nonrefundable; it will not be returned if your application is rejected. Clip your check or money order to the application. To review, currently the fees are:

Form TX	$45
Short Form TX	$45
Form PA	$45
Short Form PA	$45
Form SE	$45
Form GR/CP	$45
Short Form SE	$45
Form SE/Group	$25 per issue being registered, $45 minimum
Form G/DN	$70

When to Send Your Application

If you're registering a published work, make sure that your application is not received by the Copyright Office until after the publication date listed in Space 3 of your application. Reason: A published work cannot be registered prior to the date of publication.

Send a Single Package to the Copyright Office

All you need to do now is put your application, deposit, and check or money order for the appropriate application fee in a *single package* and send them to:

Register of Copyrights
Library of Congress
Copyright Office
101 Independence Avenue, SE
Washington, DC 20559-6000

Be absolutely sure to send the application, deposit, and fee together in one package. If you don't, all the packages you sent will be returned by the Copyright Office. (But if you send a deposit of a published work separately, the Copyright Office will turn it over to the Library of Congress rather than return it to you, so you'll get the application and fee back, but not the deposit.)

You can send your registration application by postal mail (USPS), by a commercial carrier (FedEx, UPS, DHL, and so on), or by having it hand delivered. If you send an email request from its website (http://copyright.gov/help), the Copyright Office will confirm whether it has received your application. Using USPS Express Mail or a commercial carrier can also provide tracking and delivery confirmation. You can also obtain delivery confirmation by using regular USPS mail delivery confirmation or signature confirmation services. For more information, check the USPS website (www.usps.gov).

Your Registration Is Effective When the Application Is Received

Your registration is effective on the date the Copyright Office receives all three elements: application, deposit, and application fee in proper form. This is so regardless of how long it takes the Copyright Office to process the application and send you your certificate of registration. This means you don't need to worry about not being able to obtain statutory damages or attorney fees from anyone who copies your work while your application is being processed. (Remember, you can obtain such fees and damages only if the work was registered before the infringement occurred or within three months of publication.)

EXAMPLE: Helen's cookbook is published on January 1. She sends her registration package to the Copyright Office on January 31. All the items in her package are in proper form—that is, the application form is filled out correctly and the package contains the correct deposit and $45 application fee. The Copyright Office receives her registration package on February 5. Helen receives her certificate of registration on June 15. She later discovers that Jeremy copied her work in January. If Helen sues Jeremy for copyright infringement, she will be entitled to obtain attorney fees and statutory damages. Reason: Her application was effective on the date it was received by the Copyright Office, February 5, which was within three months of publication.

Expedited Registration

A work must be registered before a copyright infringement suit may be filed. You'll need to have a copy of your registration certificate to show the court. If you need to bring an infringement suit right away but haven't registered yet, you may request that your application be given special handling by the Copyright Office. Special handling applications are processed in five to ten days, rather than the normal three to six months or more.

Special handling is available only if needed for copyright litigation, to meet a contractual or publishing deadline, or for some other urgent need. Special handling is not available for group registration of magazines or other periodicals on Form SE/Group—that is, you must register a periodical issue individually on Form SE to obtain special handling.

You must pay an additional $685 fee for special handling. You may complete the optional form reproduced on the CD-ROM at the back of this book, or send a letter along with your application containing the same information: why there is an urgent need for special handling; if special handling is needed for litigation; whether the case has been filed already or is pending; who the parties to the litigation are or will be; in what court the action has been or will be filed; and certification that your statements are true.

Send the special handling form or letter, your application and deposit, and a check or money order payable to the Register of Copyrights for $730 (the $45 application fee, plus the $685 special handling fee) all in one package to:

Screening Delay Before Applications Received

Due to the anthrax scare in late 2001, all mail sent to the Copyright Office is screened before delivery at a special facility in Washington, DC. This screening process causes a three-to-five-day delay before the Copyright Office receives your application. Mail sent by commercial carriers such as FedEx and UPS is screened as well as postal mail. This means, for example, that if you send an application by FedEx overnight delivery, the Copyright Office won't receive it overnight—the screening facility will. Since your registration isn't effective until it is received by the Copyright Office, the screening process adds a few days to the lag time before your application becomes effective.

The Copyright Office advises that to avoid damage to your deposit from Copyright Office security measures, you should package the following items in boxes rather than envelopes:

- electronic media such as audiocassettes, videocassettes, CDs, and DVDs
- microform
- photographs, and
- slick advertisements, color photocopies, and other print items that are rubber- and vegetable-based.

Special Handling
Copyright Receiving & Processing
P.O. Box 71380
Washington, DC 20024-1380

Do not send mail to this address by FedEx or any other private carrier. You may use overnight or priority USPS mail options.

The best way to request special handling for an application that has already been sent to the Copyright Office is to submit another application and deposit material identical to the ones originally submitted. In addition to the special handling request form, you must include a statement verifying that the application and deposit copies are identical to the original ones. This will allow the expedited request to go forward immediately.

Write the words "Special Handling" on the outside of the envelope. But don't put the words "Copyright Office" on the envelope.

Preregistration of Unpublished Works

In today's digital era it is common for copies of some works-in-progress to be pirated and published on the Internet and elsewhere before the work has been completed and the authorized publication or distribution has occurred. This is most common with unauthorized prereleases of movies, music, and software; but it can happen to books as well. In one case, for example, portions of former President Gerald Ford's unpublished memoirs were lifted from his publisher and published without permission in *The Nation* magazine. (*Harper & Row v. Nation Enterprises*, 471 U.S. 539 (1985).)

The Problem: Infringement Lawsuits Involving Unpublished Works

Prepublication copyright infringement has always posed a problem for copyright owners. As discussed at the start of this chapter, the statutory damages and attorney fees obtained against an infringer when a work is timely registered may often make an infringement suit worthwhile. However, the copyright law provided that such damages and fees were available for an infringed unpublished work *only* if the work was registered before the infringement occurred.

It is possible to register an unpublished work, but this poses problems. For one thing, a copy of the uncompleted work must be provided to the Copyright Office where it becomes available for inspection by the public. Many authors, publishers, and other creators don't want the public—especially the competition—to have access to what they are working on. Also, the registration only covers the work as it existed when registered. Subsequent changes would not be covered by the registration—they would have to be registered in their own right. Thus, to really be protected, a creator might have to register an unpublished work many times as it evolves and changes over time. Obviously, this is a costly and time-consuming proposition.

The Solution: Online Preregistration Without a Deposit

Starting in 2006, copyright law offered a solution to the problem outlined above. A procedure called "preregistration" was created. Creators of the works that are prone to infringement before release may preregister their work by filling out an online application at the Copyright Office website. A copy of the unpublished work need not be provided.

The copyright owner of an unpublished work that has been preregistered may file a copyright infringement suit without having to register the work with the Copyright Office. This allows a lawsuit to be filed quickly and may help the owner obtain court action to prevent distribution of the work.

Even more important, the copyright owner may obtain statutory damages and attorney fees in a successful infringement suit against anyone who pirated the unfinished work *after the preregistration was made* provided that the work is fully registered with the Copyright Office during the *earlier* of the following times:

- three months after the first publication of the work, or
- one month after the copyright owner learned of the infringement.

EXAMPLE: Copyright pirates obtain a copy of a draft version of Dan Brown's sequel to *The DaVinci Code* and release it on the Internet before the final version is published. Brown's publisher preregistered the book before the draft was stolen. As a result, the publisher can immediately file a copyright infringement suit against the copyright pirates. The publisher registers the unpublished work three weeks later. If the lawsuit proves successful, the publisher and Brown can obtain an award of their attorney fees and statutory damages.

If the copyright owner fails to meet the deadline for full registration, a court must dismiss any lawsuit brought by the owner for copyright infringement that occurred before or within the first two months after first publication. In this event, the copyright owner would have to register the work and file a new infringement suit. The late-registering owner may not obtain attorney fees and statutory damages if the suit is successful. However, this rule does not apply to infringement lawsuits for infringements occurring more than two months after first publication.

Washington Irving

Note that *preregistration is not a substitute for registration,* nor does it provide all the benefits of registration—for example, it doesn't create a legal presumption that the work is protected by a valid copyright. Its purpose is simply to advise the Copyright Office prior to the publication of a work that the work is being prepared for commercial distribution and thereby preserve your right to obtain statutory damages and attorney fees in an infringement suit. You must follow through with a full registration of the work shortly after publication or infringement of the work. The fact that a work has been preregistered does not mean that the Copyright Office necessarily will register the work when an application for registration is submitted. Also, you may register an unpublished work without preregistering it.

Is Preregistration for You?

For the vast majority of works, preregistration is a waste of money. Few works, especially written works, are infringed upon before they are published or otherwise distributed. This type of thing usually occurs with popular movies and songs. However, you may benefit by preregistering your work if you think it's likely someone may infringe your unfinished work before it is released.

How to Preregister

Preregistration is a quick, though expensive, process. The whole thing is done online through the Copyright Office website with no paper involved.

What can be preregistered?

You can preregister your work *only if*:

- it is unpublished
- its creation has begun
- it is being prepared for commercial distribution, and
- it is one of the following: a motion picture, musical work, sound recording, computer program, book, or advertising photograph.

Written works other than books may not be preregistered—for example, a screenplay not intended to be published in book form. The intended commercial distribution of the work can be in either physical or digital format—for example, e-books or CDs to be sold online.

You can't preregister ideas for new works. You must have begun to actually write the work involved, though it does not have to be finished.

Online application

You preregister by completing an online application at the Copyright Office website (www.copyright.gov). You must provide the following information:

- the work's title (a working title may be used)
- the names of the author and copyright claimant
- the date the actual writing of the book began and the date you anticipate completing it, and
- a description of the work—for example, whether it is a novel or biography, the nature of the subject matter, whether it is a later edition or

revision of a previous work, and any other details which may help identify the work in published book form.

You need not provide the Copyright Office with a copy of your unpublished work or make any other deposit. The nonrefundable filing fee for preregistration is $100.

If you fill out the application correctly, the Copyright Office will email you a notification of preregistration which will include a preregistration number and date. This is the only notice you will receive that preregistration has been made. The Copyright Office does not issue a paper certificate of preregistration.

Your preregistration is a public record. Everything you say in your preregistration application becomes a public record of the Copyright Office that can be read by others. So you might not want to say too much about your work-in-progress. Moreover, if you want to have a website using the book's title as a domain name, you may want to obtain the name before you preregister the book. Otherwise, a "cybersquatter" could learn about your title from your preregistration and register the domain name before you.

Dealing With the Copyright Office

The Copyright Office has an enormous workload (they handle over 700,000 applications per year), so it can take four

What Is Publication?

Publication" occurs for copyright purposes when the copyright owner, or someone acting with the copyright owner's authority, distributes one or more copies of the work to the general public or offers the work for distribution, public display, or public performance. Copies do not need to be sold for publication to occur—they can be leased, rented, loaned, or even given away, so long as the work has been made available to the general public.

Publication does *not* occur when:

- copies of the work are made but not distributed
- the text of the work is performed publicly (for example, a speech is presented), or
- the text of the work is displayed (for example, in a slide presentation or on television).

A "limited publication" is also not considered a publication. A limited publication occurs if copies are distributed only to:

- a selected group of people
- for a limited purpose, and
- without the right of further reproduction, distribution, or sale.

For example, it is not a publication when an author sends copies of a manuscript to several publishers seeking publication.

months (or longer) for your application to be processed. Be patient and remember that the registration is effective on the date it is received (assuming the forms were filled out properly), not the date you actually receive your registration certificate.

The Copyright Office will eventually respond to your application in one of three ways:

- If your application is acceptable, the Copyright Office will send you a registration certificate, which is merely a copy of your application with the official Copyright Office seal, registration date, and number stamped on it. Be sure to retain it for your records.
- If your application contained errors or omissions the Copyright Office believes are correctable, a copyright examiner may phone you for further information. Or he may return the application and/or deposit with a letter explaining what corrections to make.
- If the Copyright Office determines that your work cannot be registered, it will send you a letter explaining why. Neither your deposit nor fee will be returned.

If You Don't Hear From the Copyright Office

If you haven't heard anything from the Copyright Office three to six months after your application should have been received, write them and find out what went wrong (they may have lost the application, it may have never been received, or they may be very far behind in their work). In your letter identify yourself and the copyright owner, give the date of your application and the form you used, describe the work briefly, and provide the name of the author. If the Copyright Office cashed your check, you'll know that they did receive the application. Include a copy of the cancelled check with your letter. It will contain a number that will help the Copyright Office trace your application.

You'll have to pay the Copyright Office a fee to find out about the status of your application sooner than 16 weeks after the Copyright Office received it. Call the Copyright Office at 202-707-3000 to ask about this.

Extent of Copyright Examiner's Review of Your Application

The copyright examiner will examine your deposit to see whether it constitutes copyrightable subject matter and review your application to determine whether the other legal and formal requirements for registration have been met.

The rule of doubt

As a matter of policy, the Copyright Office will usually register a work even if it has a reasonable doubt as to whether the work is copyrightable or the other requirements have been met. This is called the rule of doubt. The Copyright Office takes the view that determining a copyright's validity in such cases is a task for the courts. For example, the office would ordinarily register a new edition of a previously registered work under the rule of doubt, even though it had a reasonable doubt whether the edition contained enough new expression to be registrable. When registration is made under the rule of doubt, the Copyright Office will ordinarily send the applicant a letter cautioning that the claim may not be valid and stating the reason.

Clearly unregistrable material

The Copyright Office will refuse to register a work that is without doubt unprotectable. For example, the Copyright Office would not register a title, since titles are not copyrightable, nor would a work clearly in the public domain be registered (for instance, the King James version of the Bible) unless the applicant added protectable material to it.

Presence of errors or omissions

The Copyright Office will not issue a certificate if the application contains errors or omissions or is internally inconsistent or ambiguous. Here are some of the more common errors:

- failure to sign the application
- failure to pay the application fee
- failure to provide the required number of deposit copies
- failure to adequately describe nature of authorship
- deposit does not match description of nature of authorship
- nature of authorship is described by a title or identifying phrase
- failure to provide publication date
- the work-made-for-hire box is checked, but the employer is not listed as the copyright claimant
- failure to state how ownership was transferred where copyright claimant is not the same as the author
- failure to identify adequately the material added to a new version or derivative work (Space 6b)
- date application is signed is prior to publication date in application.

The Copyright Office will ordinarily call you or send a letter asking you to fix technical errors such as these. Reread our discussion about how to complete the application forms to help you make your corrections. Send your corrected application and/or new deposit back to the Copyright Office in one package.

Be sure you respond within 120 days to any correspondence from the Copyright Office concerning your application. Otherwise, your file will be closed, your fee will not be returned to you, and you'll have to reapply by sending in a new application, deposit, and fee.

Review of Copyright Office's Refusal to Register Application

If you think the copyright examiner has wrongfully refused to register your work, you may submit a written objection to the refusal and request that the Copyright Office reconsider its action. The appeal letter should be addressed to Chief, Receiving and Processing Division, Copyright Office, P.O. Box 71380, Washington, DC 20024-1380. The first request for reconsideration must be received in the Copyright Office within 120 days of the date of the office's first refusal to register, and the envelope containing the request should be clearly marked: FIRST APPEAL. A $250 fee is charged to process an appeal.

If the claim is refused after reconsideration, the head of the appropriate Examining Division section will send you written notice of the reasons for the refusal. After this, you may again request reconsideration in writing. This second appeal must be received in the Copyright Office within 120 days of the date of the office's refusal of the first appeal, and be directed to the Board of Appeals at the following address: Copyright GC/I&R, P.O. Box 70400, Southwest Station, Washington, DC 20024.

The second appeal is handled by the Copyright Office Board of Appeals, which consists of the Register of Copyrights, the general counsel, and the chief of the Examining Division. The chair of the Board of Appeals will send you a letter setting out the reasons for acceptance or denial of your claim. The Appeals Board's decision constitutes the Copyright Office's final action. You may then bring a legal action to have a court review the Copyright Office's decision. In addition, you can bring a copyright infringement action notwithstanding the Copyright Office's refusal to register your work. You'll need to see a lawyer about this. (See Chapter 17, Help Beyond This Book.)

Full-Term Retention of Deposits and Other Ways to Preserve Deposits

Whether or not your application is accepted, your deposit becomes the property of the U.S. government and will never be returned to you. The Library of Congress may add the deposit to its own collection. If the Library chooses not to do so (which is usually the case), and your application is accepted, the Copyright Office will retain the deposit in its own storage facilities for five years. Due to a lack of storage space, the Copyright Office normally destroys all deposits of published works after five years. However, the Copyright Office may not destroy a deposit of an unpublished work without first making a copy of it.

Full-Term Retention of Deposits

People sued for copyright infringement have been known to attempt to turn the tables on their accusers and claim that the accusers actually copied from them or others. Such accusations are easily disproved if the work you claim was infringed upon was deposited with the Copyright Office before the infringing work or other work the infringer claims you copied was written and/or published. In this event, you just need to submit to the court a certified copy of the deposit you made with the Copyright Office.

The Copyright Office will provide certified copies of deposits of registered works that are involved in litigation. But, of course, such copies can only be made if the Copyright

Office still has the deposit. So you might be in for trouble if the infringement litigation takes place more than five years after the work was registered and the deposit has been destroyed by the Copyright Office.

If you want to protect against this possibility, you may request full-term retention of your deposit. Full-term retention means that the Copyright Office will retain one copy of your deposit for 95 years from the date of publication. You must request full-term retention in writing and pay a $425 fee. Only the person who made the deposit, the copyright owner, or an authorized representative may make the request. You can make this request when you register the work or any time thereafter. There is no form for this purpose. Send a letter to the Chief, Information and Reference Division, Copyright Office, Library of Congress, Washington, DC 20559, stating that you desire full-term retention of your deposit. Identify the deposit by title, author, and registration number. If you request full-term retention of your deposit when you make your initial registration, you must send the Copyright Office an additional copy of the deposit—that is, three copies of published works and two copies of unpublished works.

There is no reason to go to the trouble and expense of having the Copyright Office retain your deposit for 95 years unless the work is very valuable and you think there is a good possibility you could end up in copyright litigation more than five years after you register it—that is, after the Copyright Office would normally destroy your deposit. Keep in mind, however, that most infringements occur relatively soon after publication. Since you can make your request for full-term retention at any time, wait until four or four-and-one-half years after registration before making this decision. Things may look very different by then.

Mailing Deposit to Yourself

As an alternative to paying the Copyright Office for full-term retention, you can mail copies of your deposit to yourself (preferably by certified mail). This way, if you later become involved in infringement litigation, you can present the package in court to help prove that your work existed in a certain form as of the date of the mailing. You must not unseal or otherwise tamper with the envelope. However, this method is not foolproof, because a judge or jury might not believe that you did not tamper with the envelope (this actually happened in one case).

Depositing Screenplays With the Writers Guild of America

For screenplays and similar works, registration and deposit with the Writers Guild of America is actually better than full-term retention by the Copyright Office. The Writers Guild is the scriptwriters' union. It represents writers primarily for the purpose of collective bargaining in the motion picture, television, and radio industries. The Guild establishes guidelines regarding payment for scripts and stories and giving screen credit to authors. The Guild does not obtain employment for writers or accept or handle material for submission to production companies. Scripts, treatments, and so on must be submitted directly to production companies or through an agent.

To help writers establish the completion date and identity of works written for the entertainment industry, the Writers Guild registers scripts deposited by writers and keeps them on file. If a dispute arises as to the authorship of the material, the Guild deposit constitutes proof that the material existed in a certain form as of the date of the deposit. You need not be a member of the Writers Guild to deposit a script with the guild (indeed, you can't join until you have sold a script or story idea or performed other writing assignments).

Depositing a copy of your script with the Writers Guild is not a substitute for registration with the Copyright Office. However, the deposit will help you prove that you wrote the material deposited and when you wrote it if an authorship dispute later arises (such disputes are common in Hollywood). Moreover, many producers will not even read a script unless it has been registered with the Writers Guild.

What can be deposited

The Writers Guild will register scripts, treatments, synopses, outlines, or written ideas specifically intended for radio, television and theatrical motion pictures, video cassettes/discs, and interactive media. It also registers

A Tale of Two Writers Guild Branches

The Writers Guild is divided into two branches: Writers Guild West located in Los Angeles and Writers Guild East headquartered in New York City. Technically, the Guild West covers the area west of the Mississippi River and the Guild East covers the area east of the Mississippi. However, regardless of where you live, you may deposit your work with either branch. Since most of the film and television industries are located in Los Angeles, it's advisable to register a screenplay, teleplay, or other work designed for film or television with the Writers Guild West. This will be more convenient if you sue in Los Angeles for copyright infringement and need to have someone from the Guild testify about your deposit. (Such lawsuits must be filed where the alleged infringer resides—that is, they would likely have to be filed in Los Angeles, anyway.)

However, if your work is most likely to be produced in New York or elsewhere east of the Mississippi—for example, a stage play bound for Broadway—you may wish to deposit it with the Writers Guild East. The procedure is the same as that described here, except the fee is $22 for non-Guild members and the deposit is retained for ten years instead of five. For detailed information, visit the Writers Guild East website at www.wgae.org or call 212-767-7800.

stageplays, novels, and other books, short stories, poems, commercials, lyrics, and drawings. However, the Guild does not register or protect titles. (See Chapter 6 for information about legal protection for titles.)

Each property must be registered separately. However, three episodes, skits, or sketches for an existing television series may be deposited as a single registration.

Deposit procedure

You can deposit your work electronically over the Internet, by mail, or in person.

To use the electronic deposit procedure, you must have a digital copy of your work—for example, a Microsoft Word or Final Draft format file. To register, simply go to the Writers Guild website at www.wga.org, fill out the online registration form, provide your credit card number to pay the fee, and upload your work to the Guild. The registration fee is $20 for non-Guild members and $10 for members.

To register by mail or in person, submit one 8½ x 11-inch unbound loose-leaf copy of your work along with the registration fee. Note the specific field of writing and the proper writing credits on the title page. You must also include a cover letter providing the author's full name, Social Security number, return address, and phone number. Alternatively, the Guild has a form title page sheet on its website you can download, print out, and then fill out.

Send your deposit to: Writers Guild of America, West, Inc., Registration Department, 7000 W. 3rd St., Los Angeles, CA 90048; phone 323-782-4500; www.wga.org.

After your deposit is received, it is dated and assigned a registration number. (By the way, scriptwriting experts consider it amateurish to put this number on your script when you submit it to agents, producers, or actors.)

Duration of deposit

The Guild retains the deposit for five years. You may renew the registration for an additional five years at the conclusion of the term.

Correcting Errors After Registration Is Completed

After registration is completed, you may later wish to correct, update, or augment your registration. This is accomplished by filing an application for supplemental registration with the Copyright Office. Supplemental registration is discussed in detail in Chapter 5, Correcting or Changing Copyright Notice or Registration.

■

CHAPTER

5

Correcting or Changing Copyright Notice or Registration

Chapters 3 and 4 covered copyright notice requirements and registration with the Copyright Office, respectively. This chapter shows you how to cope with errors, omissions, or factual changes affecting your notice or registration.

Part I: Dealing With Errors or Omissions in Copyright Notice

Publishing a work without a valid copyright notice may make it more difficult to win an infringement suit or even result in loss of copyright protection; it all depends on when the publication occurred.

Works Published After March 1, 1989

As discussed in Chapter 3, a copyright notice is not required on any copies of a work published on or after March 1, 1989. This is so regardless of whether other copies of the same work were previously published before that date. (In this chapter, we'll refer to such copies as "Berne era" copies.) However, if a valid notice is not provided, an infringer may be able to claim innocence and escape paying you substantial damages. For this reason, if you discover that a copyright notice was omitted from your published work, make sure that one is included on all new copies that are printed. You may also wish to add notices to those copies that have already been distributed.

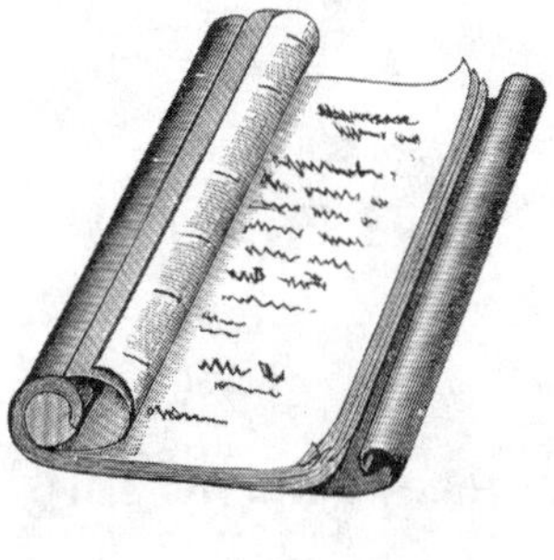

Chapter 3 noted that a valid copyright notice contains three elements: (1) the copyright symbol, (2) the publication date, and (3) the copyright owner's name. Since Berne era works need not have a copyright notice, errors or partial omissions in these elements will not affect the copyright's validity. But if the notice itself is deficient in one or more of these elements, a judge might allow an infringer to claim innocence. (See discussion in Chapter 3, Copyright Notice.) For this reason, it is advisable for the copyright owner to make sure that errors in the notice are corrected in any subsequent printings of the work. Later in this chapter we provide a detailed discussion of the types of errors that invalidate a copyright notice.

Copies Published Between January 1, 1978 and February 28, 1989

The consequences of omission of, or errors in, the copyright notice in copies of works published between January 1, 1978 and February 28, 1989, (we'll refer to these as "decennial" copies), are much more serious than those for Berne era copies.

Decennial copies must contain a valid copyright notice to be protected by copyright. However, the copyright owner will not lose her exclusive rights if any one of the following exceptions applies.

Exception #1: Only Small Number of Copies Distributed

Copyright protection will not be lost if the notice was omitted from no more than a "relatively small" number of copies distributed to the public. The "relatively small" criterion is deliberately vague, and left for the courts to decide on a case-by-case basis. Omission of notice from 1% or fewer of the published copies will probably satisfy the criteria. Omission of notice from more than 1% may or may not be too much, depending on the circumstances.

It is not legally necessary to cure the omission of copyright notices from a small number of copies. However, it is advisable to make sure that the errors in the notice are corrected in any subsequent printings or other uses of the work.

Exception #2: Corrective Measures Taken to Cure Omission Within Five Years of Publication

Even if more than a small number of copies lacked a valid copyright notice, the copyright was not invalidated if, within five years after publication, the copyright owner registered the work with the Copyright Office and made a reasonable effort to add a valid notice to all copies of the work distributed after the omission was discovered.

EXAMPLE: Sam self-published a volume of poetry in 1987. However, Sam didn't know anything about copyright, so he failed to register the book with the Copyright Office or include a copyright notice. In 1988, he found out about his error and decided to correct it in order to "rescue" his copyright. He registered the book with the Copyright Office and made a reasonable effort to add a notice to all copies of the book distributed

Henry David Thoreau

after he found out about his error. By doing so, he saved his copyright in the book from entering the public domain.

Unfortunately, by the time you're reading this book it is too late for any copyright owner to rescue her copyright by doing what Sam did in the example above. This is because such corrective efforts had to be made within five years after the work was published prior to March 1, 1989. Thus, a work published on February 28, 1989 without notice entered the public domain unless corrective action was taken by February 28, 1994, or unless another exception saving it from the public domain applies. Works published before February 28, 1989 entered the public domain earlier.

Exception #3: Omission of Notice Violates Written Agreement

Copyright protection will not be lost if the copyright owner licensed or otherwise authorized another party—for instance, a publisher—to handle her work and had a written agreement with this party requiring them to place a notice on the material when it was published, and the other party failed to do so.

Although copyright protection is not lost under these circumstances, the copyright owner cannot collect any damages from innocent infringers—that is, people who infringed the owner's copyright without knowing it due to the lack of notice. However, the copyright owner is entitled to sue the party who failed to provide the notice for any damages caused by the lack of notice. To prevent infringement from occurring in the future, the copyright owner should see to it that the errors in the notice are corrected in any subsequent printings or other uses of the work.

EXAMPLE: In 1987, Mavis signed a contract with Hackneyed Publications to publish her book. The contract contained a clause requiring Hackneyed to include a proper copyright notice on the book when it was published. Somehow, the notice was left off of over 90% of the copies Hackneyed published in 1988. Marty copied several chapters from the book in the good faith belief that it was not copyrighted due to the lack of a copyright notice. Mavis's copyright is not invalidated due to the omission, but she won't be able to collect damages from Marty. Mavis should get her publisher to add a notice to all new copies of her book and attempt to provide proper notice to those who have purchased copies lacking notice. Mavis should also consider suing Hackneyed for the damages she otherwise could have gotten from Marty.

Exception #4: Works Published Outside the U.S.

Works published outside the United States between January 1, 1978 and March 1, 1989, had to have a copyright notice, just as works published in the U.S. did. Foreign works lacking such notice entered the public domain in the U.S. unless one of the three exceptions discussed above applied. However, as a result of the GATT Agreement, an international trade agreement, the U.S. copyright in most of these works has been automatically restored effective January 1, 1996. (See Chapter 13, International Copyright Protection.)

Works Published Before 1978

All works published in the United States before January 1, 1978 had to have a valid copyright notice. If they lacked a valid notice, such works entered the public domain unless one of the following exceptions applied.

The copyright owner of any pre-1978 work saved from the public domain because one of these exceptions applies should place a valid copyright notice on the work if it is reprinted. This is not mandatory but will provide the important benefits discussed in Chapter 3.

Notice Omitted by Licensees

Works licensed to anyone before 1978 do not enter the public domain for lack of notice simply because the licensee (the publisher or other company or person) fails to include a valid copyright notice in the work.

This is because several courts have held that when such a license is entered into, the licensee impliedly agrees (that is, agrees without explicitly saying so) that it will take whatever steps necessary to protect the copyright rights retained by the copyright owner/licenser. This, of course, includes placing a valid copyright notice on all published versions of the work so that it will not enter the public domain for lack of such notice. If a licensee fails to live up to this implied promise, the courts have held that the unnoticed publication has been made without the copyright owner's authority and therefore doesn't place the work into the public domain. (*Fantastic Fakes v. Pickwick International*, 661 F.2d 479 (5th Cir. 1981).)

Notice Omitted by Accident or Mistake

There is another much more limited exception to the rule that works published before 1978 without a valid copyright notice are in the public domain. This is where the copyright owner failed to provide notice on a *particular copy or copies* by accident or mistake. Accident or mistake meant that there was an accident in the printing process or similar mechanical error—for example, lack of notice was excused where the printing matrix on which a copyright notice appeared was damaged. (*Strauss v. Penn Printing & Publishing Co.*, 220 F. 977 (E.D. Pa. 1915).) Negligence or ignorance of the notice requirement did not qualify.

This exception has rarely been successfully invoked. But even if it does apply, it only works against a person who copied the work involved after he or she actually knew it was still protected by copyright. It may not be invoked against a person who was innocently misled by the omission of the notice into believing the work was in the public domain.

Works Published Outside the U.S.

Courts have held that works published outside the U.S. before 1978 without a copyright notice did not enter the public domain in the U.S. (*Twin Books Corp. v. Walt Disney Co.*, 83 F.3d 1162 (9th Cir. 1996).) But, if such a foreign work was later published in the U.S. before 1978, it did have to comply with U.S. notice requirements. Failure to do so injected the work into the public domain unless one of the exceptions discussed above applied. However, the copyright in most such public domain works was automatically restored effective January 1, 1996 as a result of the GATT agreement, an international trade agreement discussed in detail in Chapter 13.

Types of Errors or Omissions That Invalidate a Copyright Notice

Obviously, if the work contains no copyright notice at all, the requirement for a notice has not been satisfied. However, some published works contain some, but not all, of the required elements for a valid notice. If the omissions or errors in the notice are serious enough, the notice will not be legally valid. A copy with an invalid notice is treated just the same as if it has no notice at all.

A valid copyright notice contains three elements: (1) the copyright symbol or the word "copyright," (2) the publication date, and (3) the copyright owner's name. These elements don't have to appear in any particular order (although they are usually in the order listed here).

In the past, courts were very strict about enforcing complex rules concerning the format and placement of copyright notices. Today, however, they tend to be much more lenient. A notice must contain a truly serious error or omission for the copyright to be invalidated.

The following errors or omissions will render a notice invalid.

Lack of or Error in Copyright Symbol

A copyright notice must contain either the copyright symbol "©," or the words "Copyright" or "Copr." Absence of all of these renders the notice invalid. Use of the word "Copyrighted," though technically incorrect, is also acceptable.

Sometimes the copyright symbol is not in the proper form—for example, where the letter "c" is not completely surrounded by a circle. A letter c surrounded by parenthesis, a hexagon, or some other geometric form is likely acceptable. But use of the letter c alone would likely render the notice invalid.

Error in Publication Year

The notice must also contain the date the work was published. The date can be in either Arabic or Roman numerals. A notice without a date is invalid. In addition, a copyright notice with a publication date more than one year in the future, that is, more than one year after the actual date of publication, is treated as if it had no notice at all. This is so even if only a small number of copies were distributed with the defective notice.

EXAMPLE: Isaac's book was first published in 1987, but the copyright notice lists 1989 as the publication date. The notice is invalid.

On the other hand, where the publication date is for any year *prior* to the actual publication date, the notice's validity is not affected. However, the year stated in the notice becomes the official legal publication date for copyright duration purposes.

EXAMPLE: Abraham's book was first published in 1948, but the copyright notice lists 1946 as the publication date. The notice is valid, but 1946 is now considered the date of publication for purposes of computing the duration of Abraham's copyright.

Lack of or Errors in Name

The name of the copyright owner must also be included in the notice or it will be deemed invalid. Major errors in the name, in a copyright notice—using the wrong name for example—will invalidate the notice. Minor spelling or other errors in a name, in a notice do not affect the copyright's validity. For example: Misspelling John Smith's name as "John Smythe" in a copyright notice would not affect the copyright's validity. Nor is it necessary to use the owner's full legal name. Use of a surname alone or a surname with first initial is sufficient.

Part II: Dealing With Errors or Changes Affecting Copyright Registration: Supplemental Registration

As discussed in Chapter 4, the same published work normally can only be registered once with the Copyright Office. However, a second supplemental registration may be necessary to augment your original basic registration if you later discover that you forgot something important, if you supplied the Copyright Office with the wrong information, or if important facts have changed. A special form, Form CA, is used for this purpose. Part II of this chapter shows you when a supplemental registration is appropriate and how to accomplish it.

Why a Supplemental Registration Should Be Filed (When Appropriate)

If you ever become involved in copyright litigation, your registration certificate (which is simply a copy of your basic registration application form stamped and returned to you by the Copyright Office) will be submitted into evidence to prove the existence of your copyright. It could prove embarrassing, and possibly harmful to your case, if the certificate is found to contain substantial errors, is unclear, or is ambiguous, or if important facts have changed since you registered. For this reason, you should file a supplemental registration to correct significant errors in your certificate or to reflect important factual changes.

Also, remember that your registration is a public record. By keeping your registration accurate and up-to-date, you will make it easier for those searching the Copyright Office records to discover your work and locate you. This may result in new marketing opportunities and/or help to prevent an infringement.

Corrections

A supplemental registration should be filed to correct *significant* errors that occurred at the time the basic registration was made, and that were overlooked by the Copyright Office. This includes:

- identifying someone incorrectly as the author or copyright claimant of the work
- registering an unpublished work as published, or
- inaccurately stating the extent of the copyright claim.

Errors in these important facts could cast doubt upon the validity and/or duration of your copyright and will needlessly confuse and complicate copyright litigation. They will also confuse anyone searching the Copyright Office records. Correct them as soon as you discover them.

Supplemental Registration Not Needed to Correct Obvious Errors the Copyright Office Should Have Caught

It is not necessary to file a formal supplemental registration to correct obvious errors the Copyright Office should have caught when it reviewed your application. This includes, for example, the omission of necessary information, such as the author and/or claimant's name, and obvious mistakes like listing an impossible publication date—for instance, 1003. If, when you receive your registration certificate, you discover that such errors have been overlooked by the copyright examiner, simply notify the Copyright Office and the mistake will be corrected with no need for a supplemental registration and additional fee.

Amplifications and Changes

For the same reasons discussed above, file a supplemental registration to:

- reflect important changes in facts that have occurred since the basic registration was made
- provide additional significant information that could have been provided in the original application but was not, or
- clarify or explain information in the basic registration.

If you have changed your address

File a supplemental registration to change the address listed on your certificate. It is not legally necessary for you to keep your address current in the Copyright Office's records. However, by doing so you will make it easy for people who want to use your work to locate you and arrange for permission and compensation. The harder you are to locate, the more likely it is that your copyright will be infringed.

If an author or copyright claimant was omitted

All the authors and copyright claimants must be listed in the registration. (See Chapter 4, Copyright Registration.) This means a supplemental registration should be filed if an author or copyright claimant's name was omitted.

> **EXAMPLE:** Jack and Jill coauthored a children's book. Jill completed the registration form, but later discovered that she had forgotten to list Jack as a coauthor. A supplemental registration should be filed to add Jack's name.

Change in claimant's name

A supplemental registration should be made where the name of the copyright claimant has changed for reasons other than a transfer of ownership.

Change in title of the registered work

File a supplemental registration if you changed the title of the registered work without changing its content. However, if the content of the work is changed, a new registration will have to be made (see below).

Nature of authorship needs clarification

In some cases, it is a good idea to file a supplemental registration to correct or amplify the nature of authorship statement in the original registration.

> **EXAMPLE:** Karen wrote and published a book on beekeeping in 2006. Karen never registered the book. In 2007, Karen revised and added several new chapters to her book. Karen registered this new edition with the Copyright Office. She stated "revision and chapters 9–12 added" in the nature of authorship section of her registration application. She did not complete Space 6 of the form, calling for information regarding derivative works. This registration would only protect the new material Karen added to her book; it would not protect the preexisting material that Karen never previously registered or described in her application. Karen should file a supplemental registration to change the claim to "entire text"; she should also describe the preexisting material and new material added to this derivative work as called for in Space 6 of Form TX. (See Chapter 4, Copyright Registration.) This will ensure that all the work she did will be protected by the registration.

When Supplemental Registration Is Not Appropriate

Some types of errors should not be corrected by supplemental registration. And supplemental registration may not be used to reflect some types of factual changes.

Changes in Copyright Ownership

Supplemental registration cannot be used to notify the Copyright Office of post-registration changes in ownership of a copyright, whether by license, inheritance, or other form of transfer. A special recordation procedure is used for this. (See discussion in Chapter 9, Transferring Copyright Ownership.)

Errors or Changes in Content of Registered Work

A supplemental registration cannot be filed to reflect corrections in the content of a registered work or other changes in that work. Where such changes are so substantial as to make the new work a new version, it must be registered separately and a new deposit made. If the content changes are minor, there is no need to file a new registration, since the original registration will provide adequate protection. See the detailed discussion in Chapter 4, Copyright Registration, about when a new registration must be made to protect new material.

Errors in Copyright Notice

There is no need to file a supplemental registration where you discover and correct errors in the copyright notice as discussed in Part I of this chapter.

Supplemental Registration Procedure

Filing a supplemental registration is a straightforward procedure.

When to File

You may file a supplemental registration any time during the existence of the copyright for a work that was published or registered after January 1, 1978. However, there is a time limit for works published or registered before that date. See a copyright attorney before filing a supplemental registration for a pre-1978 published work.

Who Can File

After the original basic registration has been completed, a supplemental registration may be filed by:

- any author or other copyright claimant in the work
- the owner of any exclusive right in the work (see Chapter 4, Copyright Registration), or
- the authorized agent of any of the above.

Completing the Application Form

Use the Copyright Office's official Form CA to file a supplemental registration. The form contains seven parts, lettered A through G.

Part A: Basic instructions

Part A asks for five items of information regarding your original basic registration. This information must be the same as that which already appears on your basic registration, even if the purpose of filing Form CA is to change one of these items. Refer to your certificate of registration for this information.

Title of work. Give the title as it appears in the basic registration, including any previous or alternative titles if they appear.

Registration number. This is a six- or seven-digit number preceded by a two-letter prefix—for example, TX 1234567. It should be stamped on the upper right-hand corner of your certificate of registration (the copy of your application mailed back to you by the Copyright Office).

Registration date. Give the year when the basic registration was completed.

Name of author(s) and copyright claimant(s). Give the names of all the authors and copyright claimants exactly as they appear in the basic registration.

Part B: Correction

Part B should be completed only if information in the basic registration was incorrect at the time the basic registration was made. Leave Part B blank and complete Part C instead if you want to add, update, or clarify information rather than rectify an error. Part B asks for four items of information.

Location and nature of incorrect information. Give the line number and heading or description of the space in the basic registration where the error occurred—for example, "Line 2a … Name of Author."

Incorrect information as it appears in the basic registration. Transcribe the erroneous statement in the basic registration exactly as it appears there.

Corrected information. Give the information as it should have appeared.

Explanation of correction. If you wish, add an explanation of the error or correction.

Part C: Amplification

Part C should be completed if you are filing Form CA to amplify the information in your basic registration.

Location and nature of information to be amplified. Where indicated, give the line number and heading or description of the space in the basic registration form where the information to be amplified appears.

Amplified information. Provide a statement of the added, updated, or explanatory information as clearly and succinctly as possible—for example, "change nature of authorship statement from editorial revisions to entire text."

Explanation of amplification. If you wish, add an explanation of the amplification.

Part D: Continuation

Part D is a blank space that should be used if you do not have enough space in Part B or C.

Part E: Deposit account and mailing instructions

If you maintain a deposit account with the Copyright Office, identify it in Part E. Otherwise, you will need to send a nonrefundable $100 filing fee with your form. The space headed "Correspondence" should contain the name and address of the person to be consulted by the Copyright Office if there are any problems.

Part F: Certification

The person making the supplemental registration must sign the application in Part F and check the appropriate box indicating her capacity—that is, author, other copyright claimant, owner of exclusive rights, or authorized agent.

Part G: Address for return of certificate

The address to which the Copyright Office should mail your supplemental registration certificate must be listed in Part G. Make sure the address is legible, since the certificate will be returned in a window envelope.

Filing Form CA

Send the CA form to the Copyright Office along with the $115 registration fee. Make your check or money order payable to the Register of Copyrights. No deposit is necessary for a supplemental registration. Send the form and payment to:

Register of Copyrights
Library of Congress
Washington, DC 20559

Effect of Supplemental Registration

If your application was completed correctly, the Copyright Office will assign you a new registration number and issue a certificate of supplementary registration under that number. The certificate is simply a copy of your Form CA with the new registration number, date, and certification stamped on it. Be sure to keep it in your records.

The information in a supplementary registration augments, but does not supersede, that contained in the original basic registration. The basic registration is not expunged or cancelled. However, if the person who filed the supplementary registration was the copyright claimant for the original registration (or his heir or transferee), the Copyright Office will place a note referring to the supplementary registration on its records of the basic registration. This way, anyone needing information regarding the registration will know there is a supplemental registration on file if an inquiry is made regarding the work.

■

CHAPTER

6

What Copyright Protects

We said in Chapter 2, Copyright Basics, that the copyright laws give authors and other copyright owners the exclusive right to reproduce, distribute, prepare derivative works based upon, display, and perform their work. This chapter explains that these rights extend only to a work's protected expression. It is vital to clearly understand what parts of a work constitute protected expression—and therefore belong exclusively to the author or other copyright owner—and what parts are not protected at all. Those aspects of a work that are not considered protected expression are in the public domain, free for all to use.

Only works containing protected expression may be registered with the Copyright Office in the manner described in Chapter 4, Copyright Registration. When copyright owners sell or otherwise transfer their copyright ownership rights as described in Chapter 9, Transferring Copyright Ownership, what they are selling is the right to use their protected expression. And, as described in Chapter 12, Copyright Infringement, copyright owners have valid claims for copyright infringement against persons who use their work without permission only if it is protected expression that has been used.

What Copyright Protects: Tangible, Original Expression

Described at its most fundamental level, the creation of a book, article, or other written work consists of selecting, from all the words in the English (or some other) language, a particular sequence of words and/or other symbols that communicate what the author wants to convey to her readers.

Subject to some important limitations we'll discuss below, copyright protects an author's particular choice of words from unauthorized use by others. But copyright protection does not end with the words an author uses. It also extends to an author's selection and arrangement of her material—that is, her choices as to what her work should contain and her arrangement of those items.

An author's particular choice of words and selection and arrangement of material is called her expression. This is all that copyright protects.

However, not all expression is protected by copyright. An author's expression is protected only if, and to the extent, it satisfies the following three fundamental requirements.

Requirement #1: Fixation

The most basic requirement that a person's expression must meet to qualify for copyright protection is that it must be fixed in a "tangible medium of expression." The Copyright Act is not picky about how you "fix" your expression; any medium from which your expression can be read back or heard, either directly or with the aid of a machine, will suffice. In other words, your expression will be protected if you handwrite it on a piece of paper, type it on a typewriter, save it on a computer disk, dictate it into a tape recorder, act it out in front of a video camera, or use any other means to preserve it.

Copyright protection begins the instant you fix your expression. There is no waiting period, and it is not necessary to register with the Copyright Office (but, as discussed in Chapter 4, Copyright Registration, very important benefits are obtained by doing so). Copyright protects both drafts and completed works, and both published and unpublished works.

The Copyright Act does not protect oral expressions that go unrecorded, since they aren't fixed. Likewise, copyright does not protect expression that exists in your mind but that you have not set to paper or otherwise preserved. For example, if ancient Greece had had a copyright law the same as ours, Homer's *Iliad* (which, according to tradition, Homer composed and recited in public, but never wrote down or otherwise recorded) would not have been protected by the federal Copyright Act. However, such unfixed works may be protected by state copyright laws, also known as common law copyright.

California has a law that broadly recognizes rights in unfixed original works of authorship. (Cal. Civil Code § 980.) Other states don't have such laws (though several outlaw unauthorized commercial recording of live performances). Courts in some of these states have given common law copyright protection to unfixed expressions, but the extent of such protection is far from clear. Several state courts have been reluctant to extend such protection very far. For example, a New York state court refused to give state law protection to a conversation the author Ernest Hemingway had with his biographer, A.E. Hotchner, which Hotchner reproduced years later after Hemingway's death in the book *Papa Hemingway.* The court held that for an oral statement to be protected by state law, the speaker would have to "mark off the utterance in question from the ordinary stream of speech" and indicate that he or she wished to exercise his or her control over its publication. (*Hemingway v. Random House*, 296 N.Y.S.2d 771 (N.Y. 1969).)

This means that a person who wants to protect what is said during a conversation would have to say something like, "I reserve all my copyright rights in what I'm about to say." Obviously, people rarely do this during ordinary conversation.

On the other hand, courts may be more willing to give common law copyright protection to words spoken other than in ordinary conversation—for example, to unrecorded lectures and speeches. For example, one court held that a professor's lectures were protected by common law copyright. (*Williams v. Weisser*, 273 Cal. App.2d 726 (1969).) There are distinct, identifiable boundaries to a speech or lecture—that is, a clear beginning and end—so it is easier for both the public and the courts to understand what is and is not protected.

Still other courts have refused to protect unfixed words at all. For example, a court in New York refused to grant common law copyright protection to the words spoken at a "scared straight" program in which inmates serving life sentences confronted juveniles who had begun experiencing difficulties with the law. (*Rowe v. Golden West Television Prod.*, 184 N.Y.S. 264 (1982).)

Requirement #2: Originality

A work consisting of expression that is written down or otherwise fixed in a tangible form is protected by copyright only if, and to the extent, it is original. But this does not mean that a written work must be novel—that is, new to the world—to be protected. For copyright purposes, a work is original if it—or at least a part of it—owes its origin to the author. A work's quality, ingenuity, aesthetic merit, or uniqueness is not considered. In short, the Copyright Act does not distinguish between the Great American Novel and a six-year-old's letter to her Aunt Sally; both are entitled to copyright protection to the extent they were not copied by the author—whether consciously or unconsciously—from other works. So long as a work was independently created by its author, it is protected even if other similar works already exist.

> **EXAMPLE:** Tom and Tim are identical twins who do everything together. While on a Caribbean cruise, they enjoy a spectacular sunset and are so impressed, they decide to go back to their adjoining staterooms and each write a poem about it. Not surprisingly, the poems turn out to be almost identical—after all, the twins think virtually alike. However, since they were independently created, both poems are entitled to copyright protection despite the similarities.

Derivative Works and Compilations

It is not necessary that an entire work be independently created by its author for it to be protectable. Copyright protects works created by adapting, transforming, or combining previously existing material in new ways. These types of works are called derivative works or compilations, and are discussed in Chapter 7, Adaptations and Compilations. The main point to remember about derivative works and compilations here is that they aren't protected by copyright if they infringe upon a copyright in the original works.

Requirement #3: Minimal Creativity

Finally, a minimal amount of creativity over and above the independent creation requirement is necessary for copyright protection. Works completely lacking in creativity are denied copyright protection even if they have been independently created. However, the amount of creativity required is very slight. A work need not be novel, unique, ingenious, or even any good to be sufficiently creative. All that's required is that the work be the product of a very minimal creative spark. The vast majority of written works—including catalogue copy, toy instructions, and third-rate poetry—make the grade.

But there are some types of works that are usually deemed to contain no creativity at all. For example, a mere listing of ingredients or contents, such as in a recipe, is considered to be completely lacking in creativity and is not protectable (but explanatory material or other original expression in a recipe or other list is protectable). Telephone directory white pages are also deemed to lack even minimal creativity. Other listings of data may also completely lack creativity; see the detailed discussion in Chapter 7, Adaptations and Compilations. The Copyright Office will not register such works.

Examples of Works Containing Protected Expression

Let's now put these three requirements—fixation, originality, and minimal creativity—together by looking at a list containing examples of the types of works that commonly contain protected expression:

- advertising copy
- blank forms that convey information
- catalogues, directories, price lists, and other compilations of information
- fiction of any length and quality
- instructions
- interviews, lectures, speeches, jokes, and so on that are fixed in a tangible medium of expression
- leaflets and pamphlets
- letters and diaries, whether or not they have any artistic merit or general interest
- magazines, newspapers, newsletters, periodicals, journals, and other serial publications
- nonfiction of any length and quality
- plays
- poetry
- reference books and technical writings
- screenplays
- song lyrics, whether or not combined with music
- textbooks.

Copyright Protection for Music, Movies, Sound Recordings, Computer Software, and Pictorial, Graphic, and Other Types of Work

This book focuses on copyright protection for works consisting wholly or primarily of words. However, copyright protects more than just words. Provided that the three fundamental requirements—fixation, originality, and minimal creativity—are met, copyright protects all types of expression, including music; pictorial, graphic, and sculptural works; motion pictures and other audiovisual works; sound recordings; pantomimes and choreographic works; and architectural works (architectural drawings and blueprints and the design of actual buildings). If you're interested in copyright protection for these types of works, refer to Chapter 17, Help Beyond This Book.

Computer software programs and computer databases are also entitled to copyright protection. For detailed coverage of this topic, see *Web & Software Development: A Legal Guide*, by Stephen Fishman (Nolo).

What Copyright Does Not Protect: The Boundaries of the Public Domain

Towns and cities of the 18th and 19th centuries often had a common: a centrally located unfenced area of grassland that was free for all to use. Authors also have a common: It's called the public domain. The public domain contains everything that is not protected by copyright and is therefore free for all to use without permission.

Without the public domain, it would be virtually impossible for anyone to write anything without committing copyright infringement. This is because new expression is not created from thin air; all authors draw on what has been written before. As one copyright expert has noted, "Transformation is the essence of the authorship process. An author transforms her memories, experiences, inspirations, and influences into a new work. That work inevitably echoes expressive elements of prior works." (Litman, "The Public Domain," 39 *Emory Law Journal* 965 (1990).) Without the public domain, these echoes could not exist.

For a detailed discussion of all aspects of the public domain, including how to find public domain works, see *The Public Domain: How to Find & Use Copyright-Free Writings, Music, Art & More*, by Stephen Fishman (Nolo).

Ideas and Copyright

Copyright only protects an author's tangible expression of her ideas, not the ideas themselves. Ideas, procedures, processes, systems, methods of operation, concepts, principles, and discoveries are all in the public domain, free for all to use. In effect, they're owned by everybody. (17 USC § 102(b).)

There is a good reason for this: If authors were allowed to obtain a monopoly over their ideas, the copyright laws would end up discouraging new authorship and the progress of knowledge—the two goals copyright is intended to foster.

However, although ideas are not protectable in themselves, an author's particular *selection and arrangement* of ideas may constitute protected expression. For example, an author's selection and arrangement of traits (ideas) that make up a literary character may be protected.

The Unclear Demarcation Between Ideas and Expression

It's easy to say that copyright does not protect ideas, only expression, but how do you tell the difference between an unprotected idea and its protected expression? These are very fuzzy concepts and, in fact, no one has ever been able to fix an exact boundary between ideas and expression; probably nobody ever can. But after you read the following material, you should gain a better understanding of this dichotomy.

Patent Laws Protect Ideas for Inventions

Ideas embodied in novel and nonobvious inventions can be protected under U.S. and foreign patent laws. For a detailed discussion, see *Patent It Yourself*, by David Pressman (Nolo).

Facts and Copyright

Copyright does not protect facts—whether scientific, historical, biographical, or news of the day. If the first person to write about a fact had a monopoly over it, the spread of knowledge would be greatly impeded. Another reason why copyright law does not protect facts is that an author does not independently create facts; at most, she may discover a previously unknown fact. Census-takers, for example, do not create the population figures that emerge from a census; in a sense, they copy these figures from the world around them. The Copyright Act does not protect discoveries. (17 USC § 102(b).)

So, the facts contained in works such as news stories, histories, biographies, and scientific treatises are not protectable. Subject to the important limitation of the merger doctrine discussed below, all that is protected is the author's original expression of the facts contained in such works.

Legal Protection for "Hot News"

Although facts are not protected by copyright, state unfair competition laws might protect them in certain narrowly defined situations. For example, a court has held that "hot news" is protected under such laws if the following are true:

- A person or company generates highly time-sensitive factual information at some cost or expense.
- Another person's or entity's use of the information constitutes free-riding on the fact-gatherer's costly efforts to collect the information.
- The use of the information is in direct competition with a product or service offered by the fact-gatherer.
- Other people free-riding on the fact-gatherer's efforts would threaten its ability to stay in business.

For example, it would likely be unlawful for a newspaper to copy news stories contained in a competing newspaper and print them as its own. But a company that used pagers to transmit to subscribers real-time NBA game scores and other information tabulated from television and radio broadcasts of basketball games did not commit misappropriation, because there was no free-riding involved. The company collected the scores itself; it didn't steal them from the NBA. (*National Basketball Assoc. v. Motorola, Inc.*, (105 F.3d 84 (2d Cir. 1996).)

The Merger Doctrine—When Ideas, Facts, and Their Expression Merge

Sometimes there is just one way, or only a few ways, to adequately express a particular idea or fact. If the first person to write about such an idea or fact could copyright his expression, he would effectively have a monopoly over that idea or fact itself—that is, no one else could write about it without his permission. The copyright law does not permit this, since it would discourage authorship of new works and thereby retard the progress of knowledge. In these cases, the idea or fact and its particular expression are deemed to merge and the expression—the author's words—is either treated as if it were in the public domain or given very limited copyright protection.

The merger doctrine applies mainly to factual works such as histories, biographies, and scientific treatises, rather than to works of fancy such as novels, plays, and poems. This is because the ideas and facts in factual works can often be expressed only in one particular way or only in a few ways, while the ideas contained in novels and similar works can usually be expressed in a wide variety of ways.

For example, assume you wish to write an unadorned factual account of Paul Revere's famous midnight ride during the Revolutionary War. You research Revere's life and create a work containing, in part, the following sequence of words:

On April 18, 1775, the Boston minutemen learned that the British intended to march on Concord with a detachment of 700 men. Paul Revere arranged for a signal to be flashed from the steeple of the Old North Church in Boston. Two lanterns would mean that the British were coming by water, and one, by land.

The particular selection and arrangement of words in the above paragraph appears to satisfy the three requirements for copyright protection: fixation, originality, and minimal creativity. Does this mean that if anyone used these three sentences without your permission they would be liable for copyright infringement? Because of the merger doctrine, the answer is probably not. This is because if anyone else wrote a brief factual account of Paul Revere's ride, it would necessarily have to contain sentences looking very much like those in your paragraph. This would be so even though the author had never read your account—there are just not many different ways to express the facts described in your paragraph. For example, how many different words can an author use to explain that one lantern meant that the British were coming by land and two by sea? The facts pretty much dictate the form of expression here.

As a result, if your paragraph were protected by copyright, nobody else could ever write a factual account of Paul Revere's ride without your permission. This the copyright law cannot permit, since it would effectively give you a monopoly over the facts concerning Paul Revere's ride. To prevent this, the facts of Paul Revere's ride and the words you used to express them would be deemed to merge. Some courts would hold that your paragraph was in the public domain, and could be copied verbatim (or used in any other way) without your permission. Other courts would not go quite this far; they would give your paragraph limited protection by holding that your paragraph was protected from unauthorized verbatim copying, but nothing else. (See *Landsberg v. Scrabble Crossword Game Player, Inc.*, 736 F.2d 485 (9th Cir. 1984); *Morrissey v. Procter & Gamble Co.*, 379 F.2d 675 (1st Cir. 1967).)

In contrast, the merger doctrine would not be applied to a work of fancy—for example, a poem—about Paul Revere's ride. Consider this:

> *Listen, my children, and you shall hear*
> *Of the midnight ride of Paul Revere,*
> *On the eighteenth of April, in Seventy-five.*
> *Hardly a man is now alive*
> *Who remembers that famous day and year.*
> *He said to his friend, "If the British march*
> *By land or sea from the town tonight,*
> *Hold a lantern aloft in the belfry arch*
> *Of the North Church tower as a signal light,*
> *One, if by land, and two, if by sea.*

These stanzas were written by Henry Wadsworth Longfellow over 100 years ago and are thus in the public domain because the copyright has expired—see Chapter 10, Copyright Duration. But let's pretend for purposes of our example that they were written just the other day.

This verse conveys almost exactly the same factual information as your paragraph above, yet the facts and expression would not be deemed to merge. Why? Because the author's words are embellished and highly distinctive. The sequence of words has not been dictated solely by the facts. Indeed, it is the unique word sequence itself, not the facts, that is the work's main attraction. No one needs to copy this particular word sequence in order to convey the same facts or to write another work of fancy about Paul Revere's ride. A person who copied even the first two lines would probably be found to have infringed on the copyright in the poem.

Nonfiction writers should not get the idea that they need to start writing in poetic meter to obtain copyright protection. But the more distinctive their words, the more protection they will receive. An elegantly written biography of Paul Revere will receive more protection than an unadorned factual account. Similarly, Loren Eiseley, Stephen Jay Gould, and Lewis Thomas have all written books about science whose language transcends the way their subjects are normally handled. The prose in their books receives far more protection than that of a run-of-the-mill scientific treatise. The moral is that the more effort you take to make your writing transcend the mundane and purely functional, the more copyright protection your work will receive.

Words, Names, Titles, Slogans, and Other Short Phrases

Individual words are always in the public domain, even if they are invented by a particular person. Names (whether of individuals, products, or business organizations or groups), titles, slogans, and other short phrases (for example, "I'd walk a mile for a Camel" and "No Smoking") are not protected by copyright law even if they are highly creative, novel, or distinctive, and will not be registered by the Copyright Office. (37 CFR § 202.1(a).) However, these items—especially slogans—may be protectable under the trademark laws. (See Chapter 2, Copyright Basics.)

Titles may be protectable under state law

Although titles are not protected by the Copyright Act, they may be protected under state and federal unfair competition laws (that is, laws that prohibit unfair competitive business practices). Under these laws, an author may protect a title from unauthorized use if the following are true:

- The title is strongly identified in the public's mind with the author's work.
- The author proves that the public will be confused if the title is used in another work.

This prevents a person from passing off or palming off a work on the public—that is, publishing a work with the same or similar title as a previously published, well-known work in the hope that people will buy it because they confuse it with the well-known work.

> **EXAMPLE:** A successful play called *The Gold Diggers* was made into a film entitled *Gold Diggers of Broadway*. The film's producers sued the producer of a subsequent film called *Gold Diggers of Paris* for passing off. The court held that it was unlawful for *Gold Diggers of Paris* to be marketed under that title, at least without a conspicuous disclaimer that the picture was not based on the play or the earlier picture. The court found that the title "Gold Diggers" was strongly identified in the public's mind with a series of films based on the original play. Moreover, use of the words "Gold Diggers" in the title of the defendants' film was unfair and misleading, because they would represent to the public that the film was produced by Warner Bros. Pictures and based on the play. (*Warner Bros. Pictures, Inc. v. Majestic Pictures Corp.*, 70 F.2d 310 (2d Cir. 1934).)

Titles may be protectable as trademarks

The title of a single book or other written work cannot be protected as a trademark. However, trademark protection may be available for:

- Titles for a series of books—for example, the title for a series of fishing guide books called *Fishing Hot Spots* was protectable as a trademark. (*Fishing Hot Spots, Inc. v. Simon & Schuster*, 720 F.Supp. 746 (E.D. Wis. 1989).)
- Titles of newspapers, magazines, and other periodicals—for example, the magazine called *Atlantic Monthly*. (*Atlantic Monthly Co. v. Frederick Ungar Publishing Co.*, 197 F.Supp. 524 (S.D. N.Y. 1961).)

However, if the title describes the contents of the work—which is probably the case with most titles—it must have "secondary meaning" to be eligible for trademark protection. This means that the title must become distinctive in the minds of the public over time through long, widespread use or intensive advertising. For example, the title *Aviation Magazine* was found to be descriptive of the magazine's contents and had to acquire secondary meaning to be protectable as a trademark; the court decided it lacked such meaning. (*McGraw-Hill Pub. Co. v. American Aviation Assoc., Inc.*, 117 F.2d 293 (D.C. 1940).) But the title *Photo Play Magazine*—although descriptive—was found to have attained secondary meaning and was entitled to protection. (*Photoplay Pub. Co. v. La Verne Pub. Co.*, 269 F.2d 730 (3d Cir. 1921).)

For a detailed discussion of trademarks, refer to *Trademark: Legal Care for Your Business & Product Name*, by Stephen Elias (Nolo).

Quotations

The author of a news story, biography, history, oral history, or similar work may not claim copyright ownership of statements made by others and quoted verbatim in the work. Reason: A verbatim quotation of what someone else says is not original.

> **EXAMPLE:** The author of a book about motion pictures included, in a section on John Wayne, quotations from third-person interviews and excerpts from two letters never previously published that were unearthed through the author's research. Subsequently, *Newsweek* magazine published an obituary of Wayne that used quotations from the interviews and letters contained in the author's book. The author sued *Newsweek* for copyright infringement and lost. The court held that the author held no copyright in the quotations because they were not original—that is, the author didn't say them, other people did. (*Suid v. Newsweek Magazine*, 503 F.Supp. 146 (D. D.C. 1980).)

However, this doesn't mean the quotations are always in the public domain. If the quote is written down or otherwise recorded with the speaker's authorization, it is protected by federal copyright law. The copyright is owned by the speaker. Typically, the person who writes down or records the speaker's words will have the speaker's permission to use the quotes. Such permission may be expressed or implied by the fact that the speaker consented to an interview.

In addition, a conversation reconstructed by an author from memory, rather than quoted verbatim from written notes or a recording, may be protectable by the author (not the person who made the original remarks) if some originality was involved in reconstructing the conversation. (*Harris v. Miller*, 50 U.S.P.Q. 306 (S.D. N.Y. 1941).) Moreover, the selection and arrangement of all the quotations in a book of quotations may be a protectable compilation, although the individual quotations are not protected. (*Quinto v. Legal Times of Washington*, 506 F.Supp. 554 (D. D.C. 1981).) One or more of the individual quotations in such a book could be copied without the compiler's permission, but verbatim copying of the entire book would infringe on the compiler's copyright.

But there are many instances where quotations *are* in the public domain. For example:

- A quotation by a federal government employee spoken as part of his duties is in the public domain. This includes official speeches by the president and Congresspeople.
- Quotations that are written down and published enter the public domain when the copyright in the published work expires. (See Chapter 10, Copyright Duration.)
- Quotations that are simply short phrases may also be in the public domain.
- Quotations from public domain sources—for example, from a book whose copyright has expired or never existed, such as a Shakespeare play or the King James version of the Bible—are in the public domain. Republishing them in a new work does not revive their copyright.

In addition, for a quotation to be copyrightable, it must be written down or recorded *with the speaker's authorization.* A quotation recorded without the speaker's authorization is not protected by copyright. Good examples are the many phone conversations Linda Tripp had with Monica Lewinsky that Tripp secretly recorded without Lewinsky's permission. Monica's portion of these conversations are not protected by the federal Copyright Act. Unless they can be protected under state law, they are in the public domain.

Blank Forms

Blank forms designed solely to record information are in the public domain. The Copyright Office will not register such items. (37 CFR § 202.1(c).) According to the Copyright Office, this includes such items as time cards, graph paper, account books, bank checks, scorecards, address books, diaries, report forms, and order forms.

However, forms that themselves convey information are protected and may be registered. The problem with this distinction is determining when a form does and does not convey protectable information. Even a true blank form—that is, a form consisting primarily of blank space to be filled in—can convey information. The columns or headings on a blank form may be interlaced with highly informative verbiage. Moreover, the configuration of columns, headings, and lines may itself convey information.

The courts have been inconsistent in interpreting the blank form rule and its information conveyance exception. Copyright protection has been denied to such items as a form prepared for television repairmen which contained spaces for lists of repairs and their costs (*M.M. Business Forms Corp. v. Uarco, Inc.*, 472 F.2d 1137 (6th Cir. 1973)); a time log chart which graphed hours in the business day on the vertical axis, and the day's project and activities on the horizontal axis (*Januz Marketing Communications, Inc. v. Doubleday & Co.*, 569 F.Supp. 76 (S.D. N.Y. 1982)); and a medical "superbill" form containing spaces for patient information and lists of procedures and diagnoses to be performed by doctors (*Bibbero Systems v. Colwell Systems, Inc.*, 893 F.2d 1104 (9th Cir. 1990)).

In contrast, other courts have extended copyright protection to a form used to record medical laboratory tests (*Norton Printing Co. v. Augustana Hosp.*, 155 U.S.P.Q. 133 (N.D. Ill. 1967)); record-keeping forms with instructions (*Edwin K. Williams & Co. v. Edwin K. Williams & Co.-East*, 542 F.2d 1053 (9th Cir. 1976)); and an answer sheet for a standard multiple-choice examination, designed to be graded by an optical scanning machine (*Harcourt, Brace & World, Inc. v. Graphic Controls Corp.*, 329 F.Supp. 517 (S.D. N.Y. 1971)).

The general rule appears to be that the more word sequences (as opposed to simple headings) a form contains, the more likely it is to be protectable. Forms that contain substantial textual material—for example, insurance policies, contracts, and other legal forms—are probably protectable. However, where there are only a few ways to express the facts and ideas contained in such forms, the merger doctrine comes into play to severely limit protection. For example, one court held that insurance bond forms and indemnity agreements were protectable, but because the forms contained standard language that would have to be included in any form designed to accomplish the same purpose, only verbatim copying of the forms' exact wording would constitute infringement. (*Continental Casualty Co. v. Beardsley*, 253 F.2d 702 (2d Cir. 1958).)

Compilations of Forms

To make things even more complicated, works consisting of forms designed solely for recording information may nevertheless be protectable as compilations if originality has been employed in selecting which items of information are to be recorded, and in the arrangement of such items. In this event, copyright protection extends only to the compiler's selection and/or arrangement of all the forms as a group. In one case, for example, a court held that the blank forms contained in an organizer (including calendars, telephone and address pages, and sections for recording daily activities) were not copyrightable. But the organizer as a whole was a protected compilation. However, the defendant was not liable for copyright infringement because it only copied a part of the organizer, not the whole thing. (*Harper House, Inc. v. Thomas Nelson, Inc.*, 889 F.2d 197, (9th Cir. 1989).) See Chapter 7, Adaptations and Compilations, for a discussion of compilations.

If you have produced any type of form that you want protected by copyright, by all means register it with the Copyright Office. If the Copyright Office refuses to register the form, insist that they do so under their rule of doubt. (See discussion in Chapter 4, Copyright Registration.) If anyone copies the form, you will be able to sue them for copyright infringement. But be aware that a judge might decide that your form was not entitled to copyright protection after all.

Government Works

Government edicts such as judicial opinions, legislation, public ordinances, administrative rulings, and similar official legal documents are all in the public domain. This rule applies to all levels of government—local, state, and federal—and even includes foreign government edicts.

Other types of works created by United States government officers and employees as part of their jobs are also in the public domain. This includes, for example, everything published by the United States Printing Office, IRS, Copyright Office, and Patent and Trademark Office, and all the president's official speeches. But this rule does not apply to works by state and local government employees; those works may be protected by copyright. For example, a state tax pamphlet or booklet on air pollution or water conservation published by a city or county may be protected.

Works by Federal Grantees

Works created for the federal government by independent contractors—that is, persons who are neither U.S. government officers nor employees—can be protected by copyright. However, the government may require these persons to sign work-made-for-hire agreements as a condition of receiving federal money. In this event, the U.S. government, not the individual who actually wrote the work, would be considered the author of the work; this would mean that the work would be in the public domain. See Chapter 8, Initial Copyright Ownership, for detailed discussion of work-made-for-hire agreements.

Works in Which Copyright Protection Has Expired or Was Never Obtained

The public domain also includes works whose copyright has expired and some works published without a copyright notice.

Works whose copyright has expired

Copyright protection does not last forever. When a work's copyright protection expires it enters the public domain and is freely available to anyone. All works published in the United States before 1923 are in the public domain. So are many works published during 1923–1963 for which the copyright owner failed to renew the copyright. See the detailed discussion of copyright duration and renewal in Chapter 10, Copyright Duration.

Works published without a copyright notice
Works published before March 1, 1989 without a valid copyright notice may also be in the public domain. However, you can never assume that a pre-1989 work that lacks a valid notice is in the public domain. This is because there are several exceptions to the notice requirement that may have saved the work from entering the public domain. These are discussed in detail in Chapter 5. Because of these exceptions it can be very difficult—sometimes impossible—to determine whether a pre-1989 work that lacks a notice is in the public domain.

Distinguishing Between Protected Expression and Material in the Public Domain: Putting It All Together

Now let's review the information we have just covered by looking at examples of protectable and public domain elements in works of fancy and factual works. Works of fancy include novels, short stories, plays, screenplays, and poems. A factual work is a work of nonfiction, such as a biography, history, news story, how-to book, or scientific treatise.

A Work of Fancy

Sue writes a novel about police work set in the South Bronx. Narrated by a rookie cop named Walker, the novel begins on her first day at the 41st Precinct station house, where she is shocked by its squalor. The book unfolds as a chronicle of police work and daily life in a violent neighborhood. Several chapters focus on specific topics, such as attacks on police officers. Throughout the book, Walker expresses compassion for those she considers the victims of the South Bronx, hopelessness regarding the prospects for basic improvement there, and a sense that the officers of the 41st Precinct will continue to fight a rear-guard action against lawlessness with very limited success. The book ends with her transfer to another precinct.

Unprotectable aspects of a work of fancy
We'll first examine those aspects of Sue's novel that are not protectable under the copyright law.

The idea to create a novel about police officers in the South Bronx. The underlying idea to create a certain type of work is always in the public domain. Thus, the fact that other authors have written many novels about police officers (including some set in the Bronx) does not preclude Sue (or anyone else) from writing another one.

The work's theme. The theme of Sue's novel—the hopelessness of the situation in the South Bronx and, by extension, all urban America—is in the public domain. Another novelist is free to express the same theme in her own words. A theme is an unprotectable idea, not a protectable expression.

The work's setting. A fictional work's setting—that is, the time and place in which the story occurs—is not protected by copyright. Anyone can write a story set in the 41st Precinct of the Bronx. But the particular words Sue used to describe this setting are protectable. For example, Sue described one vacant lot as "filled with the refuse of stunted lives; a dead place, with no colors and no smells ... not even the garbage smelled." This sequence of words is protected.

The work's basic plot. A fictional work's plot—that is, the sequence of events by which Sue or any other author expresses her theme or idea—is a selection and arrangement of ideas. We know that ideas themselves are not protected, but an author's selection and arrangement of ideas does constitute protected expression to the extent that it's original—that is, independently created. Thus, Sue's plot constitutes protectable expression only to the extent it was independently created by her.

Plots are rarely protectable, because there are very few independently created plots. One literary critic has noted that "authors spin their plots from a relatively small number of 'basic situations,' changing characters, reversing roles, giving modern twists to classic themes." (*The Thirty-Six Dramatic Situations*, by George Polti (The Writer, Inc.).) For example, the plot of the film *The Dirty Dozen* is basically a World War II updating of *Jason and the Argonauts;* and authors have recycled the time-tested plot of boy gets girl, boy loses girl, boy gets girl back over and over again throughout the centuries. Naturally, these basic plots are all in the public domain; otherwise, it would be very difficult, if not impossible, for anyone to create a "new" work of fancy.

Independently created variations or twists on basic plots would constitute protected expression. But there aren't very many new plot twists, either. For example, can you think of any variations on the boy meets girl scenario that haven't been done before?

The plot of Sue's novel may be described as follows: Idealistic young person joins urban police force, is assigned to inner city, sees horrors of life there, and ends up disillusioned. It's hard to see anything original in this. There are doubtless hundreds of other police stories with similar plots.

The work's scenes and situations. There are certain sequences of events, scenes, situations, or details that necessarily follow from a fictional work's given theme or setting. The French call these *scènes à faire* (that which must follow a certain situation). Sue's novel includes scenes involving drunks, prostitutes, stripped cars, rats, and a car chase. Any novel about police work in the South Bronx, West Oakland, East Los Angeles, or any other major city would likely include such elements. Such predictable—or stock—story elements are all unprotectable ideas.

However, to the extent they are original, the particular words an author uses to describe or narrate a *scène à faire* are protected, even though the idea for the scene is not. Thus, although any author can write a police novel that includes a scene involving a high-speed car chase, he could not copy the words Sue used to describe the car chase in her novel.

The work's stock characters. Similarly, there are many standard character types that have developed in fiction over time—for example, the eccentric little old lady; the tall, silent, strong cowboy; the two-fisted, hard-drinking private detective; the street-wise, fast-talking urban hustler. Since they are not original creations, these character types are not protectable; they are part of the stock of ideas that all fiction writers may draw upon. For example, one of the characters in Sue's novel is police Sergeant Jim McCarthy, a hard-drinking fourth-generation Irish cop who's seen it all. Such a sketchily drawn stock character, commonly found in police stories, would not be protected. Any author of a police thriller is free to use such a character.

Never use a well-known character—either by name or detailed description—from a copyrighted work without first consulting a copyright attorney or disguising the character to such an extent that it is not recognizable. Even if the character doesn't seem sufficiently distinctive to you to merit protection, its creator and publisher may feel quite differently and sue you for copyright infringement.

Protection for Distinctive Character

Some courts have held that distinctively "delineated" original characters are protectable. What this appears to mean is that no one can copy the particular original combination and selection of qualities—such as personality traits, physical attributes, and mode of dress—that make the character distinctive. An author's selection and combination of such distinctive qualities (ideas) is deemed to constitute protectable expression.

Unfortunately, there are no uniform standards for judging when a character is, or is not, sufficiently distinctive to be protectable. Copyright protection has been extended to such disparate characters as Tarzan, Amos & Andy, Hopalong Cassidy, and E.T., and denied to Sam Spade and the Lone Ranger. Is Sam Spade any less distinctive than Hopalong Cassidy? The only general rule is that "the less developed the characters, the less they can be copyrighted." (*Nichols v. Universal Pictures Corp.*, 45 F.2d 119 (2d Cir. 1930).) In addition, the owners of some well-known characters have sought to protect them under state and federal trademark laws. For example, Lois Lane, the Teenage Mutant Ninja Turtles, and Spiderman have all been federally registered as trademarks or service marks. State unfair competition and misappropriation laws have also been used to try to protect characters. For more information on trademarks, see *Trademark: Legal Care for Your Business & Product Name*, by Stephen Elias (Nolo).

The work's facts. Sue's novel is extremely well researched. She describes what police officers do and how they do it in great detail, and realistically catalogues the conditions of life in the South Bronx. Indeed, her novel is a better source of factual information on the South Bronx than many guidebooks or sociological studies. Of course, facts are not protectable, so all of the factual information contained in Sue's novel is in the public domain.

The work's writing style and individual words and phrases. Sue's novel is written in a highly unusual stream-of-consciousness style. She also invented new slang words and phrases for her characters to use. Neither Sue's style nor her new words and phrases are protectable. The original and creative word sequences in Sue's novel are protected by copyright, but a writing style itself is in the public domain, no matter how original it is. So are the individual words and short phrases a work contains, even if the author invented them. For example, the new words and phrases in George Orwell's *1984*—"newspeak," "I love big brother"—entered the public domain (and enriched our language) the moment Orwell published them.

The work's literary devices. Finally, literary devices such as the story within a story, flashbacks, the epistolary novel, prosodic forms, and rhetorical devices such as alliteration are all unprotectable ideas.

Protected expression in a work of fancy

You may be wondering just what *is* protected by copyright law in a work of fancy. All that is protected is the author's original expression. This includes, of course, the particular sequence of words Sue has chosen to tell her story. But her protected expression does not end there. To create her novel, Sue had to select, arrange, and combine all the unprotected elements listed above—theme, setting, plot, characters, scenes, and situations—into an integrated whole. To the extent it is original (independently created), this selection and combination also constitutes protected expression. For lack of better terms, courts sometimes call this a work's "total concept and feel" or its "overall pattern" or "fundamental essence."

A Factual Work

Commodore Hornblower spends 12 years researching the sinking of *RMS Titanic.* He scours archives in Britain and America and interviews the remaining survivors. He then writes and publishes a 500-page book describing the *Titanic*'s voyage in minute detail. The book contains many previously unknown facts; for example, that the ship's captain actually survived the sinking and lived out his life as a circus performer under an assumed name. The book ends with a startling new interpretation of the facts: The *Titanic* struck the fatal iceberg because it was sailing too fast, and it was sailing too fast because there was an out-of-control fire in one of its coal bunkers—it was desperately trying to reach port before the fire destroyed the ship.

Unprotectable elements of factual works

The following aspects of Hornblower's book are in the public domain.

Research. The facts that an author discovers in the course of research are in the public domain, free to all. This is so even if an author spends considerable effort conducting the research. Copyright does not protect the fruits of creative research, no matter how grueling or time-consuming the research may have been. Copyright only protects fixed, original, and minimally creative expression. Thus, copyright does not protect the previously unknown facts about the *Titanic*'s voyage that the commodore discovered, even though it took him 12 years to discover them. Anyone is free to use these facts—for example, that the captain actually survived the sinking—in any way she wishes. But see the discussion of plagiarism in Chapter 12, Copyright Infringement.

Quotations from public domain materials. Hornblower included in his book numerous quotations from newspaper reports about the sinking. These reports, first published before 1923, are in the public domain. Their inclusion in Hornblower's book does not revive their copyright protection. Anyone can use these quotations in a work of their own. They don't have to go back to the original sources.

Author's interpretation of facts. An author's interpretation of facts is itself a fact (or a purported fact) that is deduced from other facts. Interpretations are therefore also in the public domain. Thus, the commodore's theory as to what caused the *Titanic* to hit the iceberg (the need to reach port quickly due to the coal bunker fire) is no more protectable than the fact that the *Titanic* hit an iceberg.

Book design. The commodore's publisher spared no expense on his book. It is filled with photos and beautifully designed. Is the book's "look" protected by copyright? No. Book designs—that is, a book's physical and visual attributes—are considered to be unprotectable ideas. This includes the choice of typeface style and size, leading (space between lines of type), arrangement of type on pages and placement, and spacing and juxtaposition of text and illustrations. (46 CFR § 30651 (1981).)

Protected expression in factual works

We now turn to those aspects of a factual work that are protected by copyright.

Literal expression of facts. An author's literal expression of facts is, theoretically, entitled to protection so long as it is original. Thus, anyone who copied the commodore's words verbatim or closely paraphrased a substantial portion of the language in his book would infringe on his copyright. However, because there are often only a few ways to express the facts contained in factual works, the protection they receive may be greatly limited through application of the merger doctrine. In addition, selected passages of Hornblower's book probably could be quoted under the fair use privilege. (See discussion in Chapter 11, Using Other Authors' Words.)

Fictional elements in factual works. Hornblower was not only a dogged researcher, but had a vivid imagination as well. He included in his book certain scenes and dialogue among the *Titanic's* passengers and crew that seemed to him likely to have occurred but were still completely fictional. Fictional expressions in otherwise factual works are entitled to full copyright protection. However, if an author represents his work to be completely factual, he may not bring a copyright infringement suit against someone who, relying on such representations, copies a portion of it thinking it was unprotectable fact when it was really protectable fiction. (*Houts v. Universal City Studios*, 603 F.Supp. 26 (C.D. Cal. 1984).)

Selection or arrangement of facts. In writing his book, the commodore had to select which facts to write about and arrange them in a certain order. Is this selection and arrangement protected expression? If the commodore simply arranged the facts of the *Titanic's* voyage and sinking in chronological order, probably not. A historical chronology is itself a fact that is in the public domain.

But what if the commodore organized the facts contained in his book in an original nonchronological way; shouldn't that original arrangement be protected? Some courts say yes, others disagree. (Compare *Pacific & Southern Co. v. Duncan*, 744 F.2d 1490 (11th Cir. 1984) ("editorial judgment" makes a new presentation of facts an "original work of authorship") with *Hoehling v. Universal City Studios, Inc.*, 618 F.2d 972 (2d Cir. 1980) ("there cannot be any such thing as copyright in the order of presentation of the facts, nor, indeed in their selection").)

The DaVinci Code and the Public Domain

In 2003, Dan Brown published *The DaVinci Code,* based on a startling idea: Jesus Christ and Mary Magdalene married and had a child whose descendants are alive today. The book became the subject of a lawsuit that resulted in one of the most celebrated copyright infringement trials in history. The British authors of the 1982 nonfiction book *The Holy Blood and the Holy Grail* sued Brown's publisher in Great Britain, claiming that Brown had gotten the idea, and much else, for his novel from their book.

Brown admitted that he had relied on the book for his research, and even mentioned it in his novel. Nevertheless, the judge, applying British copyright law nearly identical to American, held that Brown had not committed copyright infringement. Brown had used many of the ideas, facts, theories, and conjectures in *The Holy Blood and the Holy Grail* to write his book, but these were not copyrightable. The architecture, structure, or way in which these facts and ideas were presented could be protected, but Brown had not appropriated the architecture of the 1982 book. Rather, he "put together these generalized facts and ideas in to a well received thriller." (*Michael Baigent and Richard Leigh v. The Random House Group Limited,* [2006] EWHC 719 (Ch).)

CHAPTER

7 Adaptations and Compilations

When 'Omer smote 'is bloomin' lyre,
He'd 'eard men sing by land an' sea;
An' what he thought 'e might require,
'E went an' took—the same as me!
—Rudyard Kipling
Barrack Room Ballads

The old saying "there's nothing new under the sun" may be the truest of all platitudes. If Kipling was right, not even the earliest authors created their works out of whole cloth. Since authorship began, authors have been borrowing and adapting what others created before them. This chapter is about works that are created by using previously existing material. It covers derivative works—works created by transforming or adapting preexisting expression—and compilations—works created by selecting and arranging preexisting material in new ways.

Derivative Works

If you take a molten lump of copper and add tin to it you'll end up with something new: bronze. A similar process of transformation can be used to create new works of authorship; that is, an author can take expression that already exists, add new expression to it, and end up with something new—that is, a new and different work of authorship. Such works are called derivative works.

> **EXAMPLE:** Sheila writes a screenplay based upon a novel. In doing so, she takes the novel's expression (words) and adds her own expression to it—she organizes the material into cinematic scenes, adds dialogue and camera directions, and deletes prose descriptions and other material that can't be filmed. The result is a new work of authorship that can be separately protected by copyright: a screenplay that is clearly different from the novel, yet clearly based upon, or derived from it.

Of course, all works are derivative to some extent. As Kipling declared, all authors "take" from each other. Authorship is more often than not a process of translation and recombination of previously existing ideas, facts, and other elements. Rarely, if ever, does an author create a work that is entirely new. For example, writers of fiction often draw bits and pieces of their characters and plots from other fictional works they have read. The same is true of writers of factual works. For example, it's likely that any new book on the impact of the electronic media on society would be derived to some extent from Marshall McLuhan's *The Medium Is the Message* (1967).

However, a work is derivative for copyright purposes only if its author has taken a *substantial* amount of a previously existing work's *expression*. As discussed in detail in Chapter 6, What Copyright Protects, copyright only protects an author's expression: the words she uses and the selection and arrangement of her material, if original. Thus, a new book on the impact of the media on society would be derivative of *The Medium Is the Message* for copyright purposes only if its author copied or paraphrased substantial portions of the words McLuhan used to express his ideas.

The ideas and facts themselves are not protectable and are therefore free for anyone to use. Likewise, this year's novel about boy meets girl is not derivative of last year's novel on the same theme unless its author copied substantial portions of its expression.

How much is substantial? Enough so that the average intended reader of the work would conclude that it had been adapted from or based upon the previously existing expression.

> **EXAMPLE 1:** Edna writes a poem about her cat. She includes one line from a poem in T.S. Eliot's cat poetry collection, *Old Possum's Book of Practical Cats.* She probably has not used enough of Eliot's expression for her poem to be considered a derivative work of *Old Possum's Book of Practical Cats.*

> **EXAMPLE 2:** Andrew Lloyd Webber and Trevor Nunn write a musical entitled *Cats.* The musical is based entirely on the poems in *Old Possum's Book of Practical Cats.* Here and there a word or two is altered to make the verses fit the music better, but the show is nothing more than Eliot's poems set to music. *Cats* is a derivative work of *Old Possum's Book of Practical Cats.*

Types of Derivative Works

There are many different types of derivative works. Let's look at those of most interest to writers in terms of the type of expression the author takes from a previously existing work and the expression she adds to it to create a new, derivative work.

Editorial revisions and elaborations

Preexisting expression taken. The entire text of any preexisting work.

New expression added. Editorial revisions and/or other new material.

> **EXAMPLE:** Dr. Blood writes a new edition of his ten-year-old textbook on heart surgery. He adds several new chapters on new surgical techniques and revises the other chapters in light of recent developments. The new edition is a derivative work based on, but designed to take the place of, the earlier edition.

Fictionalizations

Preexisting expression taken. A substantial portion of the protected expression contained in a factual work (biography, history, and so on).

New expression added. Editing, reorganization, new dialogue, descriptions, and other new material needed to transform the preexisting nonfiction work into a novel, play, screenplay, or other work of fiction.

> **EXAMPLE:** Art takes the nonfiction work *The Diary of Anne Frank* and transforms it into a stage play. To do so,

he deletes prose descriptions, adds new dialogue, organizes the work into scenes and acts, and adds new scenes and incidents that weren't in the diary. But he also retains as much of Anne Frank's expression—her words—as possible. The play is a derivative work based on the nonfiction diary.

Dramatizations

Preexisting expression taken. All or a substantial part of the expression in a fictional work not meant to be performed in public—that is, a short story, novel, or poem.

New expression added. Editing, reorganization, new dialogue and other new material needed to transform the work into a work that can be performed in public—for instance, a stage play or screenplay.

Translations into a new medium

Preexisting expression taken. All or a substantial portion of the protected expression of a work in one medium—for instance, a published book.

New expression added. Transfer of the work's protected expression into a new medium.

> **EXAMPLE:** Kitty Kelly makes a sound recording of selected highlights from her unauthorized biography of Nancy Reagan. The recording is a derivative work based on the written biography.

Translations into a new language

Preexisting expression taken. All the expression contained in a preexisting work.

New expression added. Translation of the work's expression into a new version in another language.

> **EXAMPLE:** Miguel translates Stephen King's latest bestseller into Spanish. To do so, he takes King's expression (the words contained in the novel) and replaces them with Spanish words. The resulting translation is a derivative work based on the original English-language novel.

Abridgements and condensations of fiction or nonfiction works

Preexisting expression taken. A substantial portion of work's protectable expression.

New expression added. Editing and other revisions that transform the work into a new, shorter version.

> **EXAMPLE:** *Reader's Digest* condensed books are derivative works based on the unabridged editions of the works that are condensed.

Annotations

Preexisting expression taken. All or a substantial portion of a work's protected expression.

New expression added. Notes and/or other materials that clarify the meaning of the preexisting text.

EXAMPLE: The annotated version of Lewis Carroll's *Alice in Wonderland* is a derivative work prepared from the original version of *Alice.*

When You Need Permission to Create a Derivative Work

One of the five exclusive copyright rights that automatically come into existence the moment an original work of authorship is written down or otherwise fixed in a tangible form is the exclusive right to prepare and distribute derivative works based on the work's protected expression. This means you cannot create and publish a derivative work by using someone else's protected expression without obtaining their permission. If you do, you violate that person's copyright and would be subject to a copyright infringement suit.

EXAMPLE: Rhonda writes a critically acclaimed novel. Rex writes a screenplay based on Rhonda's novel without obtaining her permission to do so. Rex sells the screenplay to a Hollywood studio. Rhonda has a valid claim against Rex for infringing on her right to create derivative works from her novel.

Such permission usually takes the legal form of an exclusive license to prepare a particular derivative work—for example, a screenplay—from the preexisting material. (See Chapter 9, Transferring Copyright Ownership.)

What Happens If You Fail to Get Permission

If you create a derivative work without obtaining permission from the owner of the copyright in the preexisting work, your original contributions will ordinarily enter the public domain. For example, if you translate a Spanish novel into English without permission, you will lose any claim to copyright protection in the original elements you added in your translation—that is, your choice of English language words to convey the meaning of the Spanish original. Anyone would be free to copy your translation without obtaining your permission, but they would have to obtain permission from the owner of the original Spanish work (but the owner of the Spanish novel would need no permission at all to copy your translation).

If you intend to create a derivative work from preexisting expression that is still under copyright, be sure to get the copyright owner's permission to use the work before you go to the time and trouble of adapting it into a new work.

When You Don't Need Permission to Create a Derivative Work

In some instances, it is not necessary to seek anyone's permission to create a derivative work, and the only legal issue the author must deal with is registering the derivative work with the Copyright Office. Registration of derivative works is discussed in Chapter 4, Copyright Registration.

Author owns right to prepare derivative works from preexisting expression

An author doesn't have to get anyone's permission to create a derivative work if she owns the entire copyright in the preexisting protected expression or the right to prepare derivative works based upon it. Authors start out owning all the copyright rights in their works, including all derivative rights, but they often transfer them to publishers, film producers, and others. An author cannot create a derivative work from her own work if she has transferred her derivative rights to others. (See Chapter 9, Transferring Copyright Ownership.)

> **EXAMPLE:** Livia writes a novel and sells the exclusive right to prepare a screenplay based upon it to Repulsive Pictures. Livia cannot write a screenplay based upon her novel without Repulsive's permission.

Preexisting material in the public domain

You don't need permission to create a derivative work based on expression that is in the public domain. Public domain material belongs to the world, and anyone is free to use it in any way she wishes. (See Chapter 6, What Copyright Protects, for a detailed discussion of the public domain.) A work may be in the public domain because it was never copyrighted or the copyright expired. The expression in such works may be used in any way without permission.

> **EXAMPLE:** You can write a screenplay based on Dickens's *Great Expectations* without obtaining anyone's permission, since the novel's copyright expired long ago.

Facts and ideas are always in the public domain. For this reason, an author need not obtain permission to use the facts or ideas contained in an otherwise protected preexisting work.

> **EXAMPLE:** Shirley, a three-year-old girl, falls into a well in Texas and is rescued one week later, miraculously still alive. The entire story was reported live on CNN and extensively covered by other news media as well. Shirley's parents write a book about the episode entitled *All's Well That Ends Well.* The book contains extensive quotations from Shirley describing her experiences (primarily in baby talk). The WOLF TV Network hires Bart to write a TV movie about the event. Bart bases the teleplay on the facts contained in newspaper accounts and the CNN coverage. He also uses some of the facts contained in *All's Well That Ends Well;* but he neither quotes nor paraphrases any of the material in the book. The teleplay is not a derivative work of *All's Well That Ends Well,* and WOLF need not obtain the permission of Shirley's parents to broadcast its TV movie.

Fair Use of Protected Expression

Even if a derivative work author uses someone else's protected expression, permission may not be required if the use constitutes a fair use. Pursuant to the fair use privilege, an author may take a *limited* amount of the protected expression in preexisting works without the copyright owner's permission. Whether or not a use is fair is determined according to the facts and circumstances of the particular case. Courts consider the purpose of the use (whether for educational or commercial purposes, for example), the nature of the preexisting expression, the amount of preexisting expression taken, and whether the use reduces the value of the copyright owner's rights in the preexisting expression. A parody of a well-known work might be one example of a derivative work that can be created without obtaining permission from the owner of the preexisting expression pursuant to the fair use privilege. Fair use is discussed in detail in Chapter 11, Using Other Authors' Words.

Derivative Work Doesn't Affect Existing Copyright Protection

The copyright status of preexisting expression used in a derivative work is unaffected by the derivative work. If the preexisting expression was in the public domain, it remains so and anyone else is free to use it. If the preexisting expression was protected by copyright, that copyright continues just as if the derivative work never existed.

EXAMPLE 1: Jillian wants to write a screenplay based upon a novel published in 1917. She pays the owner of the copyright in the novel to grant her the exclusive right to prepare derivative works based upon it. She writes the screenplay. She now owns the copyright to all the material she added to the preexisting material in order to adapt it into a screenplay. Her copyright in this material will last for the rest of her life plus an additional 70 years. However, the copyright in the novel itself is not extended or otherwise affected by Jillian's screenplay. The novel's copyright expired on Dec. 31, 1992.

EXAMPLE 2: Dr. Huxley writes an updated new edition of Charles Darwin's *The Origin of Species*. The publication of the new edition does not in any way revive the copyright in *The Origin of Species*, which expired long ago. Anyone else is free to write their own updated version of Darwin's great work, or otherwise use the material in the book.

Registering Derivative Works

A derivative work can and should be registered with the Copyright Office. This way, if anyone infringes upon the new material that has been added to the preexisting material, the derivative work author will be able to obtain statutory damages and attorney fees in an infringement suit. (See Chapter 4, Copyright Registration.)

Compilations

A compilation is a work created by selecting, organizing, and arranging previously existing material in such a way that the resulting work as a whole constitutes an original work of authorship. Compilations differ from derivative works because the author of a compilation makes no changes in the preexisting material and need not add any new material of her own. Moreover, protectable compilations can be created solely from material that is in the public domain.

Fact Compilations (Databases)

A protectable fact compilation is created by selecting and arranging facts or other items that are in the public domain. (See Chapter 6, What Copyright Protects, for a detailed discussion of what is and is not in the public domain.)

> **EXAMPLE 1:** Andrea, a baseball card dealer, compiles a catalogue listing the 500 cards in existence she deems to be the most desirable for collectors in their order of importance. Andrea sells copies of the catalogue to collectors across the country. Andrea's catalogue is a protectable compilation consisting of 500 unprotectable facts—the names of 500 baseball cards.

> **EXAMPLE 2:** Mark, an efficiency expert, takes a number of blank forms, such as a datebook and address book, and other materials in the public domain, such as a calendar, and arranges them all into a new "executive organizer." Mark's organizer is a protectable compilation consisting of unprotectable forms and calendars.

In addition to baseball card lists and executive organizers, fact compilations may include, but are not limited to, such works as automated databases (discussed in detail in Chapter 14, Copyright in the Online World), bibliographies, directories, price lists, and catalogues of all types.

> **Electronic Databases**
>
> Today, many extensive fact compilations are available only in electronic form. They may be accessed via online services like Nexis and Dialogue, or are available on computer disks. Electronic databases are discussed in detail in Chapter 14, Copyright in the Online World.

Collective Works

A compilation may also be created by selecting and arranging into a single whole work preexisting materials that are separate and independent works entitled to copyright protection in their own right. Such compilations are called collective works.

> **EXAMPLE:** Elliot compiles an anthology of the 25 best American short stories published during the 1980s. Each story is a separate and independent work that was protected by copyright the moment it was created. However, Elliot has created a new protectable collective work by selecting and arranging the stories into a collective whole—that is, a collection of the best short stories of the 1980s.

Other examples of collective works include newspapers, magazines, and other periodicals in which separately protectable articles are combined into a collective whole, and encyclopedias consisting of independently protectable articles on various topics.

Fact Compilation Combined With Collective Work

It is possible to create a compilation that includes both unprotectable facts and other items that are individually protectable.

> **EXAMPLE:** An anthology of selected articles by various historians on ancient Sparta that also contains a bibliography listing every article written on Sparta in the 20th century.

Extent of Copyright Protection for Compilations

You may be wondering why a compilation should be protected by copyright. The author of a compilation has not written anything new. For example, how can Andrea's baseball card catalogue in the example above constitute a protectable original work of authorship? Where is the originality—that is, independent creation plus minimal creativity? Andrea simply compiled a list of the names of baseball cards; none of the names on her list is individually protectable.

What makes Andrea's list protectable is the creativity and judgment she had to employ in deciding which of the thousands of baseball cards in existence belonged on her list of the 500 most desirable cards, and in deciding in what order the names should appear on the list. Similarly, Elliot in the example above used creativity and judgment in selecting which of the thousands of short stories published during the 1980s belonged in his anthology of the 25 best short stories of that decade, and in deciding on the arrangement (that is, order) of the stories. It is this selection and arrangement of the material making up a compilation that constitutes protected expression.

The copyright in a protectable fact compilation or collective work extends only to this protected expression—that is, only to the compiler's selection and arrangement of the preexisting material, not to the preexisting material itself. This is sometimes referred to as a thin copyright.

> **EXAMPLE:** The copyright in Elliot's short story anthology extends only to Elliot's selection and arrangement of the stories in his anthology, not to the stories themselves. This means that anyone could reprint the stories contained in the collection (with the copyright owners' permission) without violating Elliot's compilation copyright. But another person could not, without Elliot's permission, publish a book of the best short stories of the 1980s using the same stories in Elliot's book, printed in the same order.

Raw facts in fact compilations not protected by copyright

Since the copyright in a fact compilation extends only to the compiler's selection and arrangement of the facts, the raw facts or data themselves are not protected by copyright. The Supreme Court has stated that the raw facts may be copied at will and that a compiler is even free to use the facts contained in another's compilation to aid in preparing a competing compilation (*Feist Publications, Inc. v. Rural Telephone Service Co.,* 111 S.Ct. 1282 (1991)); but, as discussed above, the competing work may not feature the same selection and arrangement as the earlier compilation.

> **EXAMPLE:** Every month, the editors of *Harper's* magazine compile the *Harper's Index,* a listing of about 40 separate facts or statistics arranged in such a way as to comment ironically on the state of the world. Here's a sample from the May 1991 *Harper's Index:*
>
> *Death rate for American personnel stationed in the Persian Gulf, per 100,000: 69*
>
> *Death rate for men between the ages of 20 and 30 living in the United States, per 100,000: 104*
>
> *Harper's* copyright in these fact compilations extends only to the selection and arrangement of the facts, not to the facts themselves. This means that another magazine could use the individual facts contained in the *Harper's Index,* but it could not copy the arrangement of all the facts created by the *Harper's* editors. Thus, another magazine could use the statistics about death rates in the Persian Gulf War and men living in the U.S., but it could not copy the arrangement of all 40 of the statistics contained in the May 1991 *Harper's Index.*

It may seem unfair that the facts contained in a compilation gathered at great trouble and expense may be used by others without compensating the original compiler. However, recall that the purpose of copyright is to advance the progress of knowledge, not to reward authors. If the first person to compile a group of raw facts had a monopoly over them, such progress would be greatly impeded.

> **Opinions Are Not Facts**
>
> Raw facts cannot be protected by copyright. However, some things you might think are unprotectable facts really aren't. At least that's what two federal appellate courts have held. These cases involved copying of databases containing price data. In one case, someone copied the price quotations in coin dealer newsletters. In the other, the prices for used cars—listed in a used car price guide called the *Red Book*—were copied. In both cases, the courts held that the individual price quotations were copyrighted because they were entirely subjective—they were simply estimates given by the publishers of the guides. They represented the publishers' opinions of what the coins and used cars were worth, not what someone actually paid for them. The courts held that sufficient creativity was required to devise these estimates for them to be protected by copyright. (*CCC Info. Servs., Inc. v. Maclean Hunter Mkt. Reports*, 44 F.3d 61 (2d Cir. 1994); *CDN Inc. v. Kenneth A. Kapes*, 197 F.3d 1256 (9th Cir. 1999).)

The minimal creativity requirement

A work must be the product of a minimal amount of creativity to be protected by copyright. This requirement applies to fact compilations as well as all other works. The data contained in a factual compilation need not be presented in an innovative or surprising way, but the selection and/or arrangement cannot be so mechanical or routine as to require no creativity whatsoever. If no creativity was employed in selecting or arranging the data, the compilation will not receive copyright protection.

In a landmark decision on fact compilations, the Supreme Court held that the selection and arrangement of white pages in a typical telephone directory fails to satisfy the creativity requirement and is therefore not protected by copyright. (*Feist Publications, Inc. v. Rural Telephone Service Co.*, 111 S.Ct. 1282 (1991).) There are doubtless many other types of compilations that are unprotectable for the same reason.

For example, the names, phone numbers, and addresses contained in a Yellow Pages phone directory organized into an alphabetical list of business classifications have been found to completely lack creativity and therefore not to qualify for copyright protection. (*Bellsouth Advertising & Publishing Corp. v. Donnelley Information Publishing, Inc.*, 999 F.2d 1436 (11th Cir. 1993).)

How can you tell if your compilation makes the grade?

The *selection* of the data in a compilation will satisfy the minimal creativity test if the compiler has:

- chosen less than all of the data in a given body of relevant material, regardless of whether it is taken from one or more sources, or

- taken all of the data from several different sources and combined them to form a new work.

For example, there is no selectivity required to compile a list of *all* the people who have telephones in a given geographical area—that is, the compiler of a telephone directory need not employ any judgment in deciding who belongs in the directory.

A compiler's *arrangement* or coordination of the data in a compilation will satisfy the creativity requirement as long as the data is ordered into lists or categories that go beyond the mere mechanical grouping of data. Alphabetical, chronological, or sequential listings of data are purely mechanical and do not satisfy the minimal creativity requirement. This is why the alphabetical arrangement of names in a telephone directory is not minimally creative.

Representatives of the Copyright Office have indicated that in their view the following types of compilations will usually fail to satisfy the minimal creativity requirement.

Street address directories, alumni directories, membership lists, mailing lists, and subscriber lists. Where the names and addresses in these types of compilations are arranged in alphabetical or numerical order, and no selectivity was required in determining which names and addresses should be included, they would seem to contain no more creativity than telephone book white pages. Examples: an alphabetical list of all the Harvard alumni, all the members of the ACLU, or all the subscribers to *Time* magazine; a mailing list in numerical order according to zip code of all persons who have contributed more than $1,000 to the Republican Party.

Parts lists. An alphabetical or numerical list of *all* the parts in a given inventory clearly fails the creativity test: If the list is exhaustive, no selectivity is required to compile it; if it is arranged in alphabetical or numerical order, no creativity is required to arrange it.

Genealogies. A genealogy (that is, a table or diagram recording a person's or family's ancestry) consisting merely of transcriptions of public records, such as census or courthouse records, or transcriptions made from headstones in a few local cemeteries, are also deemed by the Copyright Office to lack minimal creativity. On the other hand, the creativity requirement may be satisfied where the creator of a genealogy compilation uses judgment in selecting material from a number of different sources.

The Copyright Office will not register these items unless the applicant convinces the copyright examiner that a minimal amount of creativity was required to select and/or arrange the information they contain.

De Minimis Compilations

De minimis is Latin for trifling or insignificant. A *de minimis* compilation is one that contains only a few items. Even if a *de minimis* compilation meets the minimal creativity requirement, the Copyright Office will refuse to register it. The Copyright Office considers a compilation of only three items to be clearly *de minimis*.

Making Your Compilation Protectable

There are ways you can help make your compilation satisfy the minimal creativity requirement. If you must compile a list of all of anything, don't simply arrange your data in alphabetical, numerical, or chronological order. For example, if you were compiling a bibliography of every book ever written about the Civil War, you shouldn't simply list every title alphabetically. Instead, you should employ some selectivity by breaking down your bibliography into categories—for instance, books about the causes of the war, Civil War generals, the naval war, and so on. The more judgment you use in arranging your data, the more protectable your compilation

Copyright Office Regulation

The Copyright Office has issued a regulation providing that works "consisting entirely of information that is common property containing no original authorship, such as ... standard calendars, height and weight charts ... schedules of sporting events and lists or tables taken from public documents or other common sources" are not protectable and may not be registered. (37 CFR § 202.1(d) (1984).) This is certainly true if no creativity is involved in creating such works. But, of course, a table, list, or schedule would be a protectable fact compilation if the selection and arrangement of the information it contained was minimally creative.

Noah Webster

Collective works

Collective works must also meet the minimal creativity and originality requirements. If little or no selectivity and judgment is required to create a collective work, it may not be protectable. For example, an anthology consisting of ten stories in chronological order by the same author who wrote only those ten stories in her entire life would probably not be protectable, because compiling such an anthology would require no selectivity or judgment.

Compilations containing protected expression receive greater protection

An author may add protected expression to a fact compilation or collective work. If original, such expression is protected by copyright just like any other original work of authorship. As a result, if protected expression is included throughout a compilation, it will be much more difficult and risky for users to copy the entire compilation or large chunks of it. Reason: By doing so, they would be copying not only unprotectable facts but the protected expression in the compilation as well.

> **EXAMPLE:** Robert compiles a bibliography containing the titles, authors, and publishers of every book published in the United States on the Civil War (about 50,000 in all). The bibliography is simply in alphabetical order, so it probably lacks sufficient creativity to be protectable. However, Robert also includes an introduction and annotates some of the selections with explanatory notes. Both the introduction and notes constitute protected expression. Thus, if someone copied the entire bibliography they would be copying protected expression, and therefore commit copyright infringement. Of course, anyone could still copy the individual bibliographic entries so long as they left the protected expression alone.

Other protections for compilations

Given the limitations on copyright protection for compilations, and the fact that some compilations may not qualify for any protection at all, the owners of valuable compilations may wish to find means other than copyright to protect their work. One means might be contract restrictions similar to those employed by the owners of automated databases. For example, books containing fact compilations might be leased to users on terms similar to database licenses. The lease would provide that the user may not copy the compilation without the owner's consent. However, there are many unresolved questions about the enforceability of such contracts. For further information, you should see a qualified copyright attorney.

Preexisting Material in Collective Works Must Be Used Lawfully

Recall that a collective work is a compilation in which the preexisting material consists of separate and independent works that are individually protectable. If such preexisting material is in fact under copyright, it cannot be published as part of a compilation without permission from the owner of the right to reproduce the work (presumably, such permission would have to be paid for). A compilation author who publishes such preexisting material without permission infringes on the owner's copyright and invites a copyright infringement suit.

EXAMPLE: Assume that Elliot (the compiler of the anthology of the 25 best short stories of the 1980s) obtained permission to republish 24 of the stories, but failed to get permission to publish a story written and owned by Tom. Tom is entitled to sue Elliot (and his publisher) for infringing on his exclusive right to reproduce his story.

Permission may take the form of a nonexclusive license to use the material in the collective work, an exclusive license, or even an assignment of all rights in the material. See Chapter 9, Transferring Copyright Ownership.

Use of public domain material

No permission is necessary if the preexisting material is in the public domain. As discussed in Chapter 6, What Copyright Protects, public domain material is not protected by copyright; anyone can use it however she wishes.

EXAMPLE: Assume that Elliot compiled an anthology of the best short stories of the 1880s (rather than the 1980s). He does not have to obtain permission to use the stories he selected. The copyright in all short stories written in the 1880s expired long ago, and they are all in the public domain.

Use of material created by compiler

A collective work may be created from preexisting material that the collective work author created himself. For example, Elliot could create an anthology of his own best short stories. Of course, in this event the author would not need to obtain permission to use the material (assuming he still owns the copyright).

Copyright in Preexisting Material Unaffected by Inclusion in Collective Work

The copyright status of the preexisting material used to create a collective work is unaffected by the collective work's existence. Thus, if the preexisting material was in the public domain, it remains in the public domain. If the preexisting material was protected by copyright, such protection continues without regard to the collective work—that is, the duration of copyright protection for the preexisting material remains the same, and is unaffected by a transfer of the compiler's rights in her compilation.

EXAMPLE 1: Assume again that Elliot compiles an anthology of the best short stories of the 1880s. All the stories in his anthology remain in the public domain. The fact that they were republished in Elliot's anthology does not revive the copyright in the stories.

EXAMPLE 2: Assume instead that Elliot compiles an anthology of the best short stories of the 1980s. All of the stories in the anthology are protected by copyright, so Elliot had to obtain the copyright owners' permission to include the stories in his anthology. The duration of the copyrights in the stories is not affected by the fact that Elliot republished them in his anthology years after they were created. Unless Elliot purchased all or part of the copyrights in the stories, he acquired no ownership rights in them by virtue of their inclusion in his anthology.

Registering Compilations

Fact compilations and collective works can and should be registered. This way, if someone copies the compiler's selection and arrangement, the compiler will be able to obtain statutory damages and attorney fees in an infringement suit. (See Chapter 4, Copyright Registration.)

■

CHAPTER

8 Initial Copyright Ownership

A work that satisfies the three criteria for copyright protection discussed in Chapter 6 (fixation, originality, and minimal creativity) is protected automatically upon creation. At that same moment, the author (or authors) of the work becomes the initial owner(s) of the copyright in the work. This chapter is about determining who these authors—and initial owners—are.

It is important to understand who the authors/initial owners are for these reasons:

- Their rights may differ, depending on the nature of their authorship.
- Correct identification of the authors/ initial owners is required to make a valid copyright registration.
- The nature of the authorship affects how long the copyright lasts.

There are several basic ways to author a work and thereby become its initial owner:

- An individual may independently author the work.
- An employer may pay an employee to author the work, in which case the employer is an author under the work-made-for-hire rule.
- A person or business entity may specially commission an independent contractor to author the work under a written work-made-for-hire contract, in which case the commissioning party becomes the author.
- Two or more individuals or entities may collaborate to become joint authors.

We discuss each of these types of authorship (and initial ownership) in turn.

Independent Authorship by an Individual

The individual author of a work is the initial owner of its copyright when the work-made-for-hire doctrine doesn't apply and when there is no joint authorship. The individual may exercise any of her copyright rights herself. For example, she may reproduce and sell her work herself, or authorize others to do so—that is, license a publisher. She may also transfer her ownership in whole or in part to others. (See Chapter 9, Transferring Copyright Ownership.) An individual copyright owner can do whatever she wants with her copyright in the United States; she is accountable to no one.

Impact of Community Property Laws on Copyright Ownership

In states that have community property laws, property that is acquired while people are married is usually considered to belong to both spouses equally. This means that individual authors who reside in Arizona, California, Idaho, Louisiana, Nevada, New Mexico, Texas, Washington, and Wisconsin may be required to share ownership of their copyrights with their spouses. (See discussion in Chapter 9, Transferring Copyright Ownership.)

Who Owns Copyright in Unpublished Letters

Writers and historians may be especially interested in who owns the copyright in unpublished letters. Unless written by an employee as part of her job, the copyright in a letter usually is owned by the person who wrote it. The recipient of the letter owns only the physical letter itself—that is, the paper and ink with which it was written. This means the recipient may not reproduce or publish the letter without the writer's permission. The recipient of a letter may, however, show it to others, deposit it in a library, sell it, or even destroy it. But a purchaser would acquire only the physical letter, not the copyright in the letter—that is, a purchaser could not publish or otherwise exploit the writer's copyright rights without permission.

Works Made for Hire

Not all works are initially owned by the person or persons who actually create them. If you create a protectable work on someone else's behalf, that person (or entity) may be considered the work's author and thereby initially own the copyright in the work, not you. These types of works are called works made for hire.

The owner of a work made for hire is considered to be the author of the work whether the owner is a human being or a business entity such as a corporation or partnership. As the author, the owner is entitled to register the work, exercise its copyright rights in the work such as publishing the work or adapting it to a different medium, permit others to exercise these rights, or sell all or part of its rights. The actual creator of a work made for hire has no copyright rights in the work; he may not sell it, publish it, prepare a derivative work from it, or even read it in public. All he receives is whatever compensation the hiring party gives him, whether a salary or other payment.

> **EXAMPLE:** Real estate magnate Donald Frump orders Manny, a longtime employee who serves as Donald's publicist and ghostwriter, to write his autobiography. The resulting book, entitled *The Art of the Steal,* is a worldwide bestseller. It is also a work made for hire. Donald earns $1 million in royalties and sells the film rights for another $1 million. Manny asks Donald for a 10% share of these monies, reasoning that he is entitled to them since he actually wrote the autobiography. Donald refuses, but tells Manny he'll give him a $50 a week raise. Manny can take the raise or leave it, but he is not legally entitled to any royalties from the autobiography. As far as the Copyright Act is concerned, Donald is the book's author.

Obviously, it is vitally important for all writers to understand what is and what is not a work made for hire.

Some History About Works Made for Hire

Before the Copyright Act took effect in 1978, no distinction was made between works created by employees as part of their job and commissioned works; both were automatically considered to be works made for hire unless the parties expressly agreed otherwise. No written work-for-hire agreement was ever necessary. When the 1976 Copyright Act was being drafted, organizations representing writers and other creative people strongly urged that works made for hire be limited to those created by actual employees, and that commissioned works created by nonemployees not be considered works for hire. This way, the author of a commissioned work would be the initial owner of all the rights in the work and would give to the commissioning party only those rights he expressly agreed to give up in a transfer agreement. Publishers, film producers, and others strongly opposed this. A compromise was reached that was a partial victory for writers. Under the Copyright Act, commissioned works would be works made for hire only if their creators agreed in writing; and work-for-hire status was restricted to nine categories of commissioned works listed below. Works prepared by employees continued to be works for hire just as they were before.

There Are Two Different Types of Works Made for Hire

There are probably only two reasons why you or anybody else would go to the trouble of creating a protectable work for another person or entity: (1) you are that person's employee and creating the work is part of your job, or (2) a person or entity that is not your employer—a magazine, for instance—asks you to create the work for payment or some other remuneration (the Copyright Act calls this specially requesting or commissioning a work).

As a result, there are two different types of works made for hire:

- works prepared by employees within the scope of their employment, and
- certain works prepared by nonemployees that are specially ordered or commissioned where the parties both agree in writing that the work shall be considered a work made for hire.

Let's examine each type of work made for hire.

Works Created by Employees as Part of Their Job

A natural consequence of the employer-employee relationship is that the employer owns whatever it pays an employee to create. It's assumed that an employee agrees to this when she takes a job. For example, Ford Motor Co. doesn't have to tell persons it hires to work on its assembly lines that they won't own the cars they make or have them sign contracts to this effect. Similarly, an employer doesn't have to tell an employee that it will own copyrightable works she creates on the employer's behalf—the employee is supposed to know this without being told. For this reason, no written work-for-hire contract is required in the employer-employee context.

> **EXAMPLE:** "Scoop" Jackson is hired to be a salaried reporter for the *Yakima Daily News,* which is owned by a privately held corporation. He is required to write one news story every day. These stories will be works made for hire to which the *Daily News* will own the copyright. The *Daily News* does not have to tell Scoop this and need not draw up a work-for-hire agreement for him to sign.

The example above is obvious, but the work-made-for-hire rule is not limited to works written by in-house editorial staffs. The rule extends to anything written by any employee within the scope of his employment, including reports, memoranda, letters, and in-house newsletters.

One problem in applying the work-made-for-hire rule in the employer-employee context is determining:

- just who is an employee, and
- when a work is written within the scope of employment.

Who is an employee?

The U.S. Supreme Court has held that a person is an employee for copyright purposes if the person on whose behalf the work is done has the *right to control* the manner and means by which the work is created. It makes no difference what the parties call themselves or how they characterize their relationship. If the person on whose behalf the work is done has the requisite right of control, the person hired is an employee and any protectable work he creates within the scope of his employment is a work made for hire. It also makes no difference whether the control is actually exercised, so long as the *right* to exercise it is present. (*CCNV v. Reid,* 109 S.Ct. 2166 (1989).)

If a legal dispute results as to whether the creator of a protectable work was an employee, the courts are supposed to examine a variety of factors to determine if the requisite degree of control was present in the relationship. Many of these criteria are quite broad, and there are no concrete guidelines as to how they should be applied. As a practical matter, this means that judges have great discretion in deciding who is and who isn't an employee for copyright purposes.

Two factors are of prime importance:

- whether the hiring firm pays the worker's Social Security taxes, and
- whether the hiring firm provides employee benefits.

The court held that a part-time computer programmer employed by a swimming pool retailer was not the company's employee for copyright purposes and the programmer was therefore entitled to ownership of a program he wrote for the company. The court stated that the company's failure to provide the programmer with health, unemployment, or life insurance benefits, or to withhold Social Security, federal, or state taxes from his pay, was a "*virtual admission*" that the programmer was an independent contractor. The court stressed that the company could not treat the programmer as an independent contractor for tax purposes and then turn around and claim he was an employee for copyright ownership purposes—he had to be treated the same way for both purposes. (*Aymes v. Bonelli*, 980 F.2d. 857 (2d Cir. 1992).)

In no other case has a court determined that a worker was an employee for copyright purposes where the hiring firm treated him as an independent contractor for tax purposes. *The moral is this:* If you don't pay a worker's Social Security taxes or provide him with benefits, you should assume he is an independent contractor for copyright ownership purposes.

Given the track record in the courts, you can probably safely assume that a formal salaried employee for whom you pay Social Security taxes and employee benefits would be considered an employee for copyright purposes. However, the rules are ambiguous and given to highly subjective interpretation. When anything short of a formal, salaried employment relationship is involved, there is always a risk it will not be deemed an employment relationship for copyright purposes. This could happen even though you treat such a worker as an employee for tax purposes.

Factors Considered in Determining Employee Status

Here is a list of some of the factors judges are supposed to consider in determining if a person is an employee for copyright purposes. This is not an exclusive list, and no single factor is determinative:

- the skill required to do the work
- the source of tools and materials used to create the work
- the duration of the relationship
- whether the person who pays for the work has the right to assign additional projects to the creative party
- who determines when and how long the creative party works
- the method of payment
- who decides what assistants will be hired, and who pays them
- whether the work is in the ordinary line of business of the person who pays for the work
- whether the creative party is in business for herself
- whether the creative party receives employee benefits from the person who pays for the work
- the tax treatment of the creative party.

A person who pays someone else to create a protectable work should not rely on the work-made-for-hire rule outside the context of a formal salaried arrangement. Instead, the person should have the creator transfer to him those rights that he needs. A written agreement must be signed by both parties to accomplish this.

When a work is created within the scope of employment

Not everything an employee writes belongs to his employer. An employee's writings and other copyrightable works are works made for hire only if they are created within the scope of employment. An employee's work is created within the scope of employment only if it:

- is the kind of work the employee is paid to perform
- occurs substantially within work hours at the work place, and
- is performed, at least in part, to serve the employer. (*Miller v. CP Chemicals, Inc.*, 808 F.Supp. 1238 (D. S.C. 1992) (quoting *Restatement of Agency*).)

Hans Christian Anderson

Unless an employer and employee agree otherwise, anything an employee writes outside the scope of employment is not a work made for hire. This is so even if the work arises out of the employee's activities on the employer's behalf.

> **EXAMPLE:** Recall our intrepid reporter Scoop Jackson in the example above. Assume that Scoop writes a series of articles for the *Yakima Daily News* exposing unsafe practices in the meatpacking industry. Of course, these articles are works for hire the copyright to which is owned by Scoop's newspaper. Scoop also writes a novel on his own time about a reporter who exposes the meatpacking industry. Although the novel is based on Scoop's experiences as an employee-reporter, it is not a work for hire because it was not created within the scope of his employment—that is, his job duties as a reporter did not include writing fiction.

Works created by an employee outside the scope of employment are automatically owned by the employee. Thus, it is not legally necessary to sign an agreement to this effect. However, an agreement stating that a particular work is not created within the scope of employment can be a very good idea where arguments might later develop about what the scope of employment entails. For this reason, Scoop had his employer sign the following document before he began work on the novel.

Letter to the *Yakima Daily News*

> March 1, 20xx
>
> Bill Hearst, Publisher
> *Yakima Daily News*
> 1000 Main St.
> Yakima, WA 90002
>
> Dear Bill:
>
> This letter is to confirm the understanding we've reached regarding ownership of my novel, tentatively titled *You Are What You Eat.*
>
> You acknowledge that my novel will be written on my own time and shall not be written within the scope of my employment with the *Yakima Daily News.*
>
> It is expressly agreed that I shall be the owner of all rights in the novel, including the copyright. Furthermore, the *Yakima Daily News* will sign all papers necessary for me to perfect my ownership of the entire copyright in the work.
>
> If this agreement meets with your approval, please sign below to make this a binding contract between us. Please sign both copies and return one to me. The other signed copy is for your records.
>
> Sincerely,
> *Scoop Jackson*
> Scoop Jackson
>
> I agree with the above understanding and represent that I have authority to make this agreement and to sign this letter on behalf of the *Yakima Daily News.*
>
> ______________________________
> Bill Hearst
>
> Date: March 2, 20xx

An employer and employee are free to agree that the employee will own all or part of the copyright in works she creates *within* the scope of employment. Such an agreement amounts to a transfer of copyright ownership from the employer to the employee. The employer is still considered the author of the work made for hire. To be effective, the agreement must be in writing and signed by *both* parties.

The agreement can be entered into either before or after the employee creates the work. See Chapter 9, Transferring Copyright Ownership, for a detailed discussion of transfer agreements.

EXAMPLE: Assume that Scoop Jackson in the example above wants to write a nonfiction book based on his articles about the meatpacking industry. Of course, these articles were works made for hire and Scoop's employer, the *Yakima Daily News*, is considered their author for copyright purposes. For this reason, only the *Daily News* has the right to create derivative works based upon them. Scoop gets the *Daily News* to agree to let him create a book from the articles. Scoop and the *News* must both sign a transfer agreement. It might look like the sample below.

Sample Transfer Agreement

For value received, the *Yakima Daily News* hereby assigns to Scoop Jackson the exclusive right to prepare derivative works based on the series of five articles entitled "Do You Know What You're Eating?," Parts 1–5, published in the *Yakima Daily News* during April 20xx.

Yakima Daily News, by

____

Date: ________________________

Approved and Accepted:

____

Scoop Jackson

Date: ________________________

Are scholarly writings works made for hire? Works created by professors and other scholars employed by universities, colleges, and other academic institutions pose a special problem. Prior to the adoption of the current Copyright Act in 1976, virtually all courts had held that the copyrights in lecture notes, articles, and books written by professors were owned by the professors themselves, not by the universities or colleges that employed them. However, it's unclear whether this special teacher exception to the work-for-hire rules is in effect under current copyright law. It's wise, therefore, not to rely on this exception.

So, if we assume there is no teacher exception, are faculty works made for hire? They are if (1) faculty members are employees for copyright ownership purposes and (2) the materials involved were created within the scope of employment. Unfortunately, there are no court cases to guide us.

To determine whether or not faculty members are employees, the agency law factors set forth in "Factors Considered in Determining Employee Status," above, must be applied to decide whether the requisite degree of control is present. Even if we apply these facts, there is still no clear answer. For example, faculty members typically receive employee benefits and are treated as employees for Social Security tax benefits. These are strong factors showing employee status.

On the other hand, colleges and universities typically do not exercise sufficient control over what professors write for such writings to constitute works made for hire. Although academic institutions may "require" scholars to create scholarly works or risk not being awarded tenure and other benefits ("publish or perish"), they usually do not dictate what should be written or supervise the writing process itself. The principle of academic freedom is supposed to prevent universities from controlling the ideas expressed in scholarly writings. However, no court has yet decided this question.

Even if we assume that faculty members are employees, it's not clear whether everything they create falls within the scope of employment. Applying the factors set forth above, it would seem that research publications would be within the scope of employment but textbooks would not. Faculty members are not paid by the university to write textbooks, while they are paid to produce research publications such as scholarly articles and books (again, "publish or perish").

However, as a practical matter, the question of whether faculty works are made for hire may be academic (no pun intended). There are two reasons for this. First, and probably most important, academic works usually have little or no economic value, and colleges and universities have no economic incentive to claim copyright ownership in such works. There are few examples of universities stripping faculty members of their copyright ownership.

Second, most colleges and universities now have written copyright ownership policies. Typically, these policies permit faculty members to retain ownership of works created by their own independent effort—these include, for example, journal articles, research bulletins, monographs, books, plays, poems, and works of art. However, many universities claim sole or joint ownership of works prepared with substantial use of university materials or facilities, administrative materials such as faculty memos and reports, or materials prepared as part of specially sponsored projects. Some universities claim copyright ownership of computer software. You can find links to many such policies at the CopyOwn website maintained by the University of Maryland (www.inform.umd.edu/CompRes/NEThics/copyown).

Where a university policy permits a faculty member to retain copyright ownership of his or her work—which is usually the case—the question of whether the work is a work made for hire does not arise. But, if a university does claim ownership on the basis of a copyright policy, it must be determined if the policy is legally enforceable. It *is* enforceable if the policy is contained in an employment contract signed by the faculty member. However, quite often there is no formal signed employment contract between the university and faculty member. In this event, a university might claim that copyright ownership is transferred to it by virtue of institutional policies set forth in faculty handbooks or bylaws. Whether such claims would be upheld by the courts is unclear.

The bottom line is that any faculty member should carefully investigate his or her university's copyright policies—preferably before taking the job.

Specially Ordered or Commissioned Works

We've seen above that in the employer-employee context no work-for-hire agreement is necessary, and any type of protectable work may be a work made for hire. In contrast, where a person or entity asks a writer who is not an employee to prepare a protectable work, that work may be a work for hire only if (1) both parties sign a work-for-hire agreement, *and* (2) the work is one of the types of work set out in "Nine Types of Works That May Be Considered Works Made for Hire by Nonemployees," below.

Nine Types of Works That May Be Considered Works Made for Hire by Nonemployees

- A contribution to a collective work such as a magazine or newspaper article or anthology (see Chapter 7, Adaptations and Compilations)
- a part of a motion picture or other audiovisual work such as a screenplay
- a translation
- supplementary works such as forewords, afterwords, supplemental pictorial illustrations, maps, charts, editorial notes, bibliographies, appendixes, and indexes
- a compilation (see Chapter 7)
- an instructional text
- a test
- answer material for a test
- an atlas.

Works that don't fall within one of these nine categories constitute works made for hire only if created by an employee within the scope of employment.

Special Rules for California

California law provides that a person who commissions a work made for hire is considered to be the employer of the creator of the work for purposes of the workers' compensation, unemployment insurance, and unemployment disability insurance laws. (Cal. Labor Code § 3351.5(c); Cal. Unemployment Insurance Code §§ 621, 686.) No one is entirely sure what impact this has on persons or entities who commission works made for hire. Neither the California courts nor state agencies have addressed the question. However, it may mean that the commissioning party has to obtain workers' compensation coverage for the creative party and might be liable for any injuries she sustains in the course of her work. It might also mean that special penalties could be assessed against a commissioning party who willfully fails to pay the creative party any monies due her after she is discharged or resigns.

These potential requirements and liabilities are one reason why it might be desirable for those commissioning work in California not to enter into a work-made-for-hire agreement, and instead have the creator assign the desired copyright rights to the commissioning party in advance.

Express work-for-hire contract required

A specially commissioned work constitutes a work made for hire only if the commissioning party and the creative party both sign a written contract providing that the work shall be considered a work made for hire before the work is created. The written agreement is absolutely crucial.

EXAMPLE: Steve hires Sara to write an introduction for his book. Both Sara and Steve sign a contract stating that the introduction will be a work made for hire. When Sara completes the introduction, Steve will be considered its author for copyright purposes.

Freelance contributions to magazines and other collective works

The term freelance writer usually connotes a self-employed person who contributes articles to newspapers, magazines, and similar publications. Although you may not naturally think of freelance articles as works made for hire, they are if the freelancer and the publication that buys the work both sign a work-for-hire agreement.

EXAMPLE: The editor of *The Egoist Magazine* asks Gloria, a freelance writer, if she would be interested in writing an article for the magazine on nightlife in Palm Beach. Gloria says yes. The editor then sends Gloria a letter agreement to sign setting forth such terms as Gloria's compensation and the deadline for the article and its length, and stating that the article shall be a work made for hire. If Gloria signs the agreement, her article will be a work made for hire—that is, the magazine will be the author and initial owner—instead of her.

Copyright tip for publishers and editors. Although the Copyright Act gives the publishers of magazines, periodicals, and other collective works the right to use work-made-for-hire agreements with freelance writers, this doesn't mean that they should exercise this right. Many successful freelancers simply refuse to sign work-for-hire agreements or will demand substantial extra compensation to do so. Generally, it's wiser—and more supportive of the arts—simply to have the author assign the rights that the magazine really needs, and let her retain the others.

But, if you insist on using a work-for-hire agreement, be sure to:

- get a full-blown work-made-for-hire agreement signed before the creative person starts work on the project—don't rely on informal go-aheads or engagement letters
- include an assignment to you of the creative person's copyright rights in the agreement—this way, if the finished work is for some reason determined not to be a work for hire, you'll still own all the copyright rights by virtue of the assignment.

Copyright Tip for Writers

If you sign a work-for-hire agreement, you are not considered the author of the work even though you created it. This means the commissioning party does not have to give you credit for your work. If you want credit, be sure to include in the agreement a provision requiring the commissioning party to give it to you. It should specify the size, type, and placement of your credit.

Screenplays

Screenplays are among the types of work that are considered to be made for hire if specially commissioned pursuant to a work-made-for-hire agreement. Such agreements are commonly used in the film industry. However, the Writers Guild of America (the screenwriters' union) has entered into collective bargaining agreements with the entertainment industry providing that its members are entitled to retain certain copyright rights in their made-for-hire screenplays. The Writers Guild should be consulted about this.

Supplemental works

An author or publisher who hires an independent contractor (that is, a non-employee) to compile an index or bibliography, put together an appendix, take some photographs, or create a few illustrations, maps, or charts to supplement the text would naturally assume that she will own the copyright in the work she pays for. By now you should know that this will be true only if both parties sign a work-made-for-hire agreement or the independent contractor signs an agreement assigning her rights in the work to the author or publisher. If they do neither, the contractor will own the copyright in the work he creates. However, the commissioning party will probably be entitled to use the work.

Unsolicited manuscripts are not specially commissioned works

A work is specially ordered or commissioned only if it is created at the commissioning party's request. By definition, an unsolicited manuscript is not requested and thus cannot be considered a specially ordered or commissioned work. This fact cannot be altered by contract.

> **EXAMPLE:** Archie, a beginning freelance writer, writes an article about a trip he took to Pago Pago and sends it "over the transom" to *World Travel Magazine*. The magazine accepts the article for publication and sends Archie a contract saying that the work will be a work made for hire. Although Archie's article comes within one of the nine categories of specially ordered works (it is a contribution to a collective work), it is not a work made for hire because it was not written at the magazine's request. However, if Archie signs the contract, it might be considered a transfer of his copyright in the article to the magazine.

Work-Made-for-Hire Agreements

As mentioned above, a work created by an independent contractor—that is, a person who is not an employee—can be a work for hire only if a written work-for-hire agreement is signed by both parties. The law is unclear as to whether the work-for-hire agreement must be signed before the work is started or can be signed afterwards. One court says it must always be signed beforehand. (*Schiller & Schmidt, Inc. v. Nordisco Corp.*, 969 F.2d 410 (7th Cir. 1992).) But another court ruled that the parties need only verbally agree before the work is begun that it will be a work for hire and a written agreement may be signed after the work is started or completed. (*Playboy Enters. v. Dumas,* 53 F.3d 549 (2d Cir. 1995).) Even so, it is always advisable to have a signed work-for-hire agreement in hand before work is begun, since it might be difficult or impossible to prove you had a verbal agreement with the author that the work would be a work for hire.

Authors Should Be Wary of Work-for-Hire Endorsements on Checks

Authors should be sure to carefully examine any checks they receive from magazines, newspapers, publishers, or other sources for whom they have performed freelance work on other than a work-for-hire basis. Some unscrupulous publishers add language to their checks or purchase orders stating that the work performed was a work-made-for-hire. Although the legal validity of such a provision on a check is highly questionable, it is not prudent to sign and cash such a check as issued. Instead, either cross out the offending language before cashing the check or return it to the publisher and demand a new check without the work-made-for-hire language. The latter course will result in a delay in your payment, but will help make clear to the publisher that your work is not a work made for hire.

Work-for-hire letter agreement

You don't need to use a long contract for a work-for-hire agreement; a short letter or memo can do the job. A letter agreement has two advantages: It's easy to draft and is much less intimidating to a creative person than a long contract. You should make two copies of the agreement, sign both, and send them to the creative party to sign. The creative party should keep one signed copy and return the other to you.

A Work-for-Hire Letter Agreement is included on the forms CD-ROM.

EXAMPLE: Nastassia writes a nonfiction book and asks Bill, a librarian, to compile an index for it. An index is a supplementary work, one of the nine categories of specially commissioned works. This means the index will be a work for hire if Nastassia and Bill both sign a work-for-hire agreement before Bill starts work. Nastassia could have Bill sign a letter agreement worded like the one shown below.

Standard work-for-hire contract

Some people or companies that hire independent contractors to create works for hire prefer to use longer agreements in the form of a standard contract. Such agreements typically address a number of issues that have nothing to do with copyright. You may wish to use such an agreement for a particularly

Sample Agreement

April 1, 20xx

Bill Brown
2600 State St.
Chicago, IL 6000

Dear Bill:

This letter is to confirm that I have specially ordered or commissioned you to prepare the following work: A two-level alphabetical index of at least 50 double-spaced typewritten 8.5" by 11" pages for the book entitled *The History of Sex*. The work will be delivered on computer disk in Word Perfect format.

This specially ordered or commissioned work shall be completed no later than May 1, 20xx.

You agree that this specially ordered or commissioned work is a "work made for hire," and that I, as the person for whom the work is prepared, shall own all right, title, and interest in and to the work, including the entire copyright in the work.

You further agree that to the extent the work is not a "work made for hire," you will assign to me ownership of all right, title, and interest in and to the work, including ownership of the entire copyright in the work.

You also agree to execute all papers necessary for me to perfect my ownership of the entire copyright in the work.

You represent and warrant that the work you create or prepare will be original, will not infringe upon the rights of any third party, and will not have been previously assigned, licensed, or otherwise encumbered.

As compensation for your services, I will pay you $2,000 upon satisfactory completion of the work.

Sample Agreement (continued)

If this agreement meets with your approval, please sign below to make this a binding contract between us. Please sign both copies and return one to me. The other signed copy is for your records.

Sincerely,

____

Nastassia Kinsey

I agree with the above understanding.

____

Bill Brown

Date: ________________________________

Taxpayer ID#: ____________________________

complex or expensive project, since it can provide you added protection.

The work-for-hire agreement form included in this book covers the following issues not addressed in the short letter agreement discussed above:

- **Writer's independent contractor status.** The agreement includes a lengthy provision designed to show that the writer is an independent contractor, not the hiring firm's employee. (See Clause 6.) This can be very helpful if the hiring firm is audited by the IRS or state agency and the writer's employment status is questioned.

  The key to doing this is to make clear that the writer, not the hiring firm, has the right to control how the work will be performed. You will need to emphasize the factors the IRS and other agencies consider in determining whether a client controls how the work is done. Of course, a mere recitation without adherence to these understandings won't fool the IRS. Think of this clause as a reminder to you and the writer about how to conduct your business relationship. For a detailed discussion of all the legal issues involved in hiring independent contractors, see *Working With Independent Contractors*, by Stephen Fishman (Nolo).
- **Confidentiality.** If, during the course of his or her work, the writer may have access to your valuable trade secrets—for example, business plans, methods and techniques not known by your competitors, or customer lists—it is reasonable for you to include a nondisclosure provision in the agreement. (See Clause 8.) Such a provision means that the writer may not disclose your trade secrets to others without your permission.
- **No partnership.** It's wise to make clear that you and the writer are separate legal entities, not partners or co-venturers. If the writer is viewed as your partner, you'll be liable for his or her debts and he or she will have the power to make contracts that obligate you to others without your consent. (See Clause 13.)
- **Exclusive agreement.** Business contracts normally contain a provision stating that the written agreement is the complete and exclusive agreement between those involved. This is to help make it clear to a court or arbitrator that the parties intended the contract to be their final agreement. A clause such as this helps avoid claims that promises not contained in the written contract were made and broken. (See Clause 11.)
- **Choice of law.** It's a good idea for your agreement to provide which state's law will govern if you have a dispute with the client. This is particularly helpful if you and the writer are in different states. There is some advantage to having the law of your own state govern, since your local attorney will likely be more familiar with that law. (See Clause 12.)

- **Assignment and delegation.** As a general rule, either party may assign its rights and delegate its obligations under a contract unless it's expressly prohibited. This means, for example, that the writer could hire someone else to do the work called for in the agreement. If you want to prevent a writer from delegating his or her duties under a work-for-hire agreement, you should include a clause prohibiting it without the hiring firm's consent. (See Clause 14.)
- **Arbitration.** One important function a contract can perform is to provide a means for resolving disputes. As you probably know, court litigation can be very expensive. To avoid this cost, alternative forms of dispute resolution have been developed that don't involve going to court. These include mediation and arbitration.

The work-for-hire contract contains a provision requiring the parties to take advantage of these alternate forms of dispute resolution. (See Clause 15.) You're first required to submit the dispute to mediation. You agree on a neutral third person to serve as mediator and try to help you settle your dispute. The mediator has no power to impose a decision, only to try to help you arrive at one.

If mediation doesn't work, you must submit the dispute to binding arbitration. Arbitration is usually like an informal court trial without a jury, but involves arbitrators instead of judges and is usually much faster and cheaper than courts. You may be represented by a lawyer, but it's not required.

You should indicate in the mediation/arbitration clause where the mediation or arbitration would occur. You'll usually want it in the city or county where you live or work. If you and the writer live or work a long distance apart, you'll have to agree on a location.

The text of this Work-for-Hire Agreement is contained on the CD-ROM.

EXAMPLE: AcmeSoft, Inc., a large software developer, hires Barton Finkle, a freelance translator, to translate the manual for its AcmeWrite program into French. A translation is one of the nine categories of specially commissioned works, so the translation can be a work made for hire if both parties sign a work-for-hire agreement. AcmeSoft drafts the work-for-hire contract for Barton to sign shown below.

Agreements with employees

As discussed above, protectable works created by employees within the scope of their employment automatically become works made for hire. The employee's consent is not required and an express work-for-hire agreement is not necessary. Indeed, the employer need not even inform the employee that it will own the copyright in her creations.

However, costly disputes can develop concerning whether a work is created within the scope of employment. For example, if

Work-Made-for-Hire Agreement

This Agreement is made between AcmeSoft, Inc. (Client), with a principal place of business at 122 Harr Drive, Portland, Oregon, and Barton Finkle (Writer), with a principal place of business at 1900 Leafy Lane, Ashland, Oregon.

1. **Services to Be Performed**

   Writer agrees to perform the following services: Translation into French of the AcmeSoft user manual for the program AcmeWrite 1.0.

2. **Deadline**

   Writer's work must be completed by June 15, 20___.

3. **Payment**

   In consideration for the services to be performed by Writer, Client agrees to pay Writer as follows: $10,000.

4. **Terms of Payment**

   Writer shall be paid $1,000 upon signing this Agreement and the rest of the sum described above when the Writer completes services and submits an invoice.

5. **Expenses**

   Writer shall be responsible for all expenses incurred while performing services under this Agreement.

6. **Independent Contractor Status**

   Writer is an independent contractor, not Client's employee. Writer's employees or contract personnel are not Client's employees. Writer and Client agree to the following rights consistent with an independent contractor relationship:

   - Writer has the right to perform services for others during the term of this Agreement.
   - Writer has the sole right to control and direct the means, manner, and method by which the services required by this Agreement will be performed.
   - Writer has the right to perform the services required by this Agreement at any place, location, or time.

- Client will not withhold FICA (Social Security and Medicare taxes) from Writer's payments or make FICA payments on Writer's behalf, make state or federal unemployment compensation contributions on Writer's behalf, or withhold state or federal income tax from Writer's payments.
- Writer is ineligible to participate in any employee pension, health, vacation pay, sick pay, or other fringe benefit plan of Client.
- Client shall make no state or federal unemployment compensation payments on behalf of Writer, and Writer will not be entitled to these benefits in connection with work performed under this Agreement.

7. **Intellectual Property Ownership**

To the extent that the work performed by Writer under this Agreement (Writer's Work) includes any work of Authorship entitled to protection under the copyright laws, the parties agree to the following provisions:

- Writer's Work has been specially ordered and commissioned by Client as a contribution to a collective work, a supplementary work, or other category of work eligible to be treated as a work made for hire under the United States Copyright Act.
- Writer's Work shall be deemed a commissioned work and a work made for hire to the greatest extent permitted by law.
- Client shall be the sole author of Writer's Work and any work embodying the Writer's Work according to the United States Copyright Act.
- To the extent that Writer's Work is not properly characterized as a work made for hire, Writer grants to Client all right, title, and interest in Writer's Work, including all copyright rights, in perpetuity and throughout the world.
- Writer shall help prepare any papers Client considers necessary to secure any copyrights, patents, trademarks, or intellectual property rights at no charge to Client. However, Client shall reimburse Writer for reasonable out-of-pocket expenses incurred.

8. **Confidentiality**

Writer will not disclose or use, either during or after the term of this Agreement, any proprietary or confidential information of Client without Client's prior written permission except to the extent necessary to perform services on Client's behalf.

Proprietary or confidential information includes:

- the written, printed, graphic, or electronically recorded materials furnished by Client for Writer to use
- business plans, customer lists, operating procedures, trade secrets, design formulas, know-how and processes, computer programs and inventories, discoveries, and improvements of any kind, and
- information belonging to customers and suppliers of Client about whom Writer gained knowledge as a result of Writer's services to Client.

Writer shall not be restricted in using any material which is publicly available, already in Writer's possession or known to Writer without restriction, or which is rightfully obtained by Writer from sources other than Client.

Upon termination of Writer's services to Client, or at Client's request, Writer shall deliver to Client all materials in Writer's possession relating to Client's business.

9. Terminating the Agreement

With reasonable cause, either Client or Writer may terminate this Agreement, effective immediately upon giving written notice.

10. Writer's Representations and Warranties

Writer represents and warrants that:

- Writer is free to enter into this agreement
- Writer will not violate the right of privacy or publicity or infringe upon any copyright or other proprietary right of any other person or entity.

11. Exclusive Agreement

This is the entire Agreement between Writer and Client.

12. Applicable Law

This Agreement will be governed by the laws of the state of Oregon.

13. No Partnership

This Agreement does not create a partnership relationship. Writer does not have authority to enter into contracts on Client's behalf.

14. Assignment

Writer may not assign or subcontract any rights or obligations under this Agreement without Client's prior written approval.

15. Dispute Resolution

If a dispute arises under this Agreement, the parties agree to first try to resolve the dispute with the help of a mutually agreed-upon mediator in the following location: Portland, Oregon. Any costs and fees other than attorney fees associated with the mediation shall be shared equally by the parties.

If it proves impossible to arrive at a mutually satisfactory solution through mediation, the parties agree to submit the dispute to binding arbitration in the following location: Portland, Oregon, under the rules of the American Arbitration Association. Judgment upon the award rendered by the arbitrator may be entered in any court with jurisdiction to do so.

Client:

Name of Client: AcmeSoft, Inc.

By: ______________________________
Minnie Marx

Title: Vice-President

Date: April 1, 20____

Writer:

____

Barton Finkle

Taxpayer ID Number: 123-45-6789

Date: April 1, 20____

an employee creates a work partly at home outside working hours, he or she might claim it is not a work for hire because the work was done outside the scope of employment.

For this reason, it is a very good idea to have a written agreement describing the employee's job duties so it will be clear whether a work is created within the scope of employment. It's also wise to include in the agreement a provision assigning (transferring) to you the copyright rights in any job-related works that for some reason do not constitute works made for hire.

What Happens When a Work Does Not Satisfy the Work-Made-for-Hire Requirement?

What happens if someone hires another to create a work with the belief that it will constitute a work made for hire, but it turns out that the work-for-hire requirements were not satisfied? It won't be the end of the world, but the person laying out the money might be in for an unpleasant surprise.

The creator of the work owns the copyright

First of all, since the work is not a work for hire, its creator (or creators) is the author and initial owner of all the copyright rights.

> **EXAMPLE 1:** Mark pays Sally, a freelance photographer, to take some photographs of toxic waste dumps to supplement his treatise on toxic waste management. Sally is not Mark's employee, and Sally and Mark did not sign a work-for-hire agreement. As a result, Sally owns the copyright in the photos. This means that Sally may sell them to others, reproduce them, create derivative works from them, or otherwise exercise her copyright rights in the photos.

> **EXAMPLE 2:** Marlon, a well-known actor, pays Tom $50,000 to ghostwrite his autobiography. Tom's work could constitute a work made for hire only if Tom was Marlon's employee and the work was created within the scope of employment. Assume that Marlon does not exercise sufficient control over Tom for him to be considered Marlon's employee. Who owns the copyright in Tom's work? Tom does! Tom is entitled to sell the autobiography to others, serialize it in magazines, sell it to movie producers, and so on.

Hirer has nonexclusive license to use work

At the very least, a person who pays an author to create a protectable work has a nonexclusive license to use it as intended. This seems only fair, considering that the hiring party paid for the work. A person with a nonexclusive license in a work may use the work, but may not prevent others from using it as well. Nonexclusive licenses may be implied from the circumstances; no express agreement is required. (See detailed discussion of nonexclusive licenses in Chapter 9, Transferring Copyright Ownership.)

EXAMPLE 1: Since Mark, from the above example, paid Sally to take the toxic waste photos for inclusion in his book, he would have a nonexclusive license to use them in the book. But this would not prevent Sally from allowing others to use the photographs in other publications.

EXAMPLE 2: Likewise, since Marlon paid Tom to write his autobiography, Marlon would have the right to publish it. But, again, this would only be a nonexclusive license. Tom could sell the autobiography to others.

Transfer of rights under a work-made-for-hire contract

What happens if the creator of a protectable work signed a work-for-hire contract, but the requirements for work-made-for-hire status were not satisfied? This could occur where a work-for-hire contract was signed by a nonemployee, but the work created did not fall within one of the nine categories of specially commissioned works. In this event, a court *might* interpret the contract as a transfer by the creator of his rights in the work to the hiring party.

EXAMPLE: Assume that Marlon in the example above had Tom sign a contract stating that the autobiography would be a work made for hire. Unfortunately for Marlon, the authorship of entire autobiographies does not come within one of the nine categories of specially commissioned works. This means that regardless of what Marlon's contract said, the work is not a work made for hire and Tom is the author and initial owner of the copyright.

Possible Court Help for a Failed Contract

It is possible that a court would interpret the work-made-for-hire contract as a transfer by Tom to Marlon of all his copyright rights in his work. Tom would still be the initial owner and author, but Marlon would still end up owning all the copyright rights in the work—that is, he would have the exclusive right to publish it, create derivative works based upon it, and so on. But it's also possible that a judge would rule the contract unenforceable and simply award Marlon a nonexclusive license.

Joint work created

If the hiring party and creative party worked together on the writing project, the work might constitute a joint work, with both parties being considered authors and initial copyright owners.

EXAMPLE: Assume that Marlon in the examples above worked with Tom in writing the autobiography, contributing not only ideas, but also writing portions of the book. Is Tom still the sole owner of the copyright in the autobiography? Probably not. The autobiography would probably constitute a joint work and would be jointly owned by Tom and Marlon.

Assignment of Rights as Alternative to Reliance on Work-Made-for-Hire Rule

Hopefully, it is clear by now that relying on the work-made-for-hire rule can be a risky proposition for the hiring party. Unless the hiring party is dealing with a conventional employee or commissioning one of the nine specially commissioned works discussed in "Specially Ordered or Commissioned Works," above, under an express work-for-hire contract, he can never be absolutely sure who will end up owning the copyright in the work he pays for.

The solution to this problem is to have the creator of the work transfer all or part of her rights—whatever they are—to the hiring party. As discussed above, this may mean that the creator will still be considered the author and initial owner, but the result will be that the hiring party will end up owning the copyright.

EXAMPLE 1: Assume that Marlon, in the examples above, had Tom sign an agreement assigning to him all his rights in the autobiography. Marlon would become the owner of the copyright in the autobiography by virtue of the assignment agreement.

EXAMPLE 2: Similarly, had Mark, in the examples above, had his photographer Sally assign all her rights in the toxic waste photos to him, Mark would have owned the copyright in the photos.

An assignment must be put into effect through a written transfer agreement signed by both parties. The agreement may be signed before or after the work is created. See Chapter 9, Transferring Copyright Ownership, for discussion of a simple bare-bones assignment agreement and a sample form.

You can also modify the work-for-hire agreements by deleting the work-made-for-hire language and instead including a provision like the following: "*You hereby assign to me ownership of all right, title, and interest in and to the Work, including ownership of the entire copyright in the Work. You also agree to execute all papers necessary for me to perfect my ownership of the entire copyright in the work.*"

EXAMPLE: Mark has hired Sally to take several photographs of toxic waste dumps for his book. He has her sign the following assignment letter agreement.

Jack London

Sample Assignment Letter Agreement

April 1, 20xx

Sally James
200 Beacon Hill
Boston, MA 10000

Dear Sally:

This letter is to confirm that you agree to prepare the following Work: 25 black and white photographs of the toxic waste dumps on the attached list.

The Work shall be completed no later than May 1, 20xx.

You hereby assign to me ownership of all right, title, and interest in and to the Work, including ownership of the entire copyright in the Work. You also agree to execute all papers necessary for me to perfect my ownership of the entire copyright in the work.

You represent and warrant that the work you create or prepare will be original, will not infringe upon the rights of any third party, and will not have been previously assigned, licensed, or otherwise encumbered.

As compensation for your services, I will pay you $2,000 upon satisfactory completion of the work.

If this agreement meets with your approval, please sign below to make this a binding contract between us. Please sign both copies and return one to me. The other signed copy is for your records.

Sincerely,

Mark Anthony
Mark Anthony

I agree with the above understanding.

____
Sally James
Date: April 2, 20xx
Taxpayer ID#: 123-45-6789

Assignments Can Be Terminated After 35 Years

One possible disadvantage of using an assignment of rights as opposed to a work-made-for-hire agreement is that an assignment can be terminated by the author or her heirs 35 to 40 years after it is made. (See Chapter 10, Copyright Duration, for a detailed discussion.) However, in most cases, this disadvantage is meaningless because very few works have a useful economic life of 35 years.

In addition, a work obtained by an assignment from an individual will have a different copyright term than a work made for hire. Works made for hire are protected for 95 years from the date of publication or 120 years from the date of creation, whichever comes first. Works by individuals are protected for the life of the person plus 70 years. (See Chapter 10, Copyright Duration, for a detailed discussion on how long copyright protection lasts.) Few works have a useful economic life of 70 years, let alone 95 years, so this difference is usually meaningless.

Jointly Authored Works

Things can get even more complicated when two or more individuals create a work that is not a work made for hire. Such a work is normally jointly owned by its creators—that is, each contributing author shares in the ownership of the entire work. A joint author's life is not quite as simple as that of an individual copyright owner. There may be restrictions on what each joint author can do with his or her ownership share, and joint authors must account to each other for any profits they receive from commercial exploitation of the joint work.

When Is a Work Jointly Authored?

A work is jointly authored automatically upon its creation if (1) two or more authors contributed material to the work, and (2) each of the authors prepared his or her contribution with the *intention* that it would be combined with the contributions of the other authors as part of a single unitary work. We'll refer to such works as joint works.

> **EXAMPLE:** Peter and Christianne agree to write a biography of Saddam Hussein together. Peter writes the chapters covering the first half of Saddam's life, and Christianne writes the remainder. They combine their work to form a single biography of Saddam's entire life. The biography is a joint work by Peter and Christianne.

Authors' intent is controlling factor

The key to determining whether a work is a joint work is the authors' intent *at the time the work is created.* If the authors intended that their writing be absorbed or combined with other contributions into an integrated unit, the work that results is a joint work. It is not necessary that the authors work together or work at the same time. Indeed, it is not even necessary that they know each other when they create their respective contributions.

> **EXAMPLE:** Paul writes a children's story with the intention that it be combined with a number of illustrations to be created by Jean. Unfortunately, Jean dies before she can create the illustrations. Five years later, Paul meets Mary, a successful artist. Mary reads Paul's story and tells him that she would like to create the illustrations for it. Paul agrees. Mary creates the illustrations. Mary and Paul combine Paul's story and Mary's illustrations into a single integrated work—a children's book. The book is a joint work, co-owned by Mary and Paul. This is so even though Paul had never met Mary when he wrote his story and the story was written years before Mary drew her illustrations. All that matters is that when Paul and Mary created their respective contributions they intended that they be combined with other work to form an integrated whole.

How much material must a person contribute to be a joint author?
The respective contributions made to a joint work by its authors need not be equal in terms of quantity or quality. But, to be considered a joint author, a person must contribute more than a minimal amount of work to the finished product. For example, a person who proofreads and makes spelling corrections to a book written by another is not a joint author of that book.

May a joint author only contribute ideas?
Most courts require that a person's contribution consist of protectable expression—that is, actual written work—for her to be considered a joint author. A person who contributes ideas or other unprotectable items is not entitled to an ownership interest in the work's copyright unless the parties expressly agree to it, preferably in writing. (See Chapter 6, What Copyright Protects.)

> **EXAMPLE:** Abe and Zsa Zsa agree to collaborate on a screenplay. Abe conceives a detailed and complex plot for the screenplay, but does no writing himself. Instead, he tells Zsa Zsa the plot and Zsa Zsa uses Abe's ideas to actually write the screenplay. Most courts would hold Zsa Zsa the sole owner of the copyright in the screenplay unless she and Abe had agreed otherwise.

It is always a good idea for collaborators to have a written agreement setting forth their respective interests in the work to be written. This way, if one contributor is found not to be a joint owner of the work because he did not contribute protectable expression to it, he would still be entitled (as a matter of contract law) to the ownership interest stated in the collaboration agreement.

Joint authors need not be human beings

A joint author doesn't have to be a human being. A corporation, partnership, or other business entity can also be a joint author.

> **EXAMPLE:** Sunnydale Farms, Incorporated, a large corporation that manufactures and sells gardening implements and seeds, agrees to coauthor a book on urban gardens with Ralph, a famous expert on roses. Ralph writes the chapters on growing flowers, while Sunnydale employees write the chapters on growing vegetables. The chapters written by Sunnydale's employees are works made for hire for which Sunnydale is considered the author. The resulting book is a joint work. The joint authors are Ralph and Sunnydale.

William Gilbert

Joint Works Compared With Derivative and Collective Works

What happens if the intent to combine contributions into an integrated whole arises after the contributions were created? In this event, the resulting work is not a joint work. Rather, it is either a collective work or a derivative work. It will be a collective work if the respective contributions of the authors were independently created and later simply combined into a collective whole without changing them. It will be a derivative work if the respective authors' contributions are recast, transformed, or adapted to create a new work.

> **EXAMPLE 1:** Assume that Paul in the example above wrote his children's story without any intent that it be combined with illustrations. Acme Publications purchases Paul's entire copyright in the story and decides to publish it with illustrations created by Jean. The resulting work is a collective work—that is, a work in which separately protectable works are combined into a collective whole without making any internal changes to the material. (See Chapter 7, Adaptations and Compilations, for a detailed discussion of collective works.)

> **EXAMPLE 2:** Art writes and publishes a scientific treatise on quantum theory. Several years later, Art and his colleague Marie decide to produce an updated and expanded version of the work.

This revised version of the treatise will not be a joint work, because when Art wrote his original treatise he did not intend to combine it with any other work. Rather, the revised treatise is a derivative work—that is, a work created by transforming the original treatise into a new, revised treatise. (See Chapter 7, Adaptations and Compilations, for a detailed discussion of derivative works.)

Why It Is Important to Know the Difference Between Joint Works and Derivative or Collective Works

Knowing the difference between a joint work and a derivative or collective work is important for these reasons:

- The copyright in a derivative work extends only to the material added to the preexisting material by the derivative work's authors.
- Contributors to a collective work own the copyright only in the material they contributed to the work.
- The authors of a joint work each share ownership in the entire work.

Joint Authors' Collaboration Agreement

A written collaboration agreement is not legally required to create a joint work; an oral agreement is sufficient. However, as Samuel Goldwyn supposedly once said, "An oral agreement isn't worth the paper it's printed on." It is vital that collaborators draft and sign a written agreement spelling out their rights and responsibilities. This avoids innumerable headaches later on.

An example of a completed collaboration agreement is provided below. A form agreement you can use is provided on the CD-ROM at the end of this book. The following discussion focuses on the key provisions in a collaboration agreement, many of which contain blanks you must fill in.

Collaborator's contributions

The single most important part of a collaboration agreement is the description of who will perform what work. Think carefully about this before you begin work. Some collaborators write everything together; others work independently and then review and revise each other's first drafts. By far the best practice is to write a detailed outline or synopsis of the work and indicate on it who will write each section. The outline should be attached to the collaboration agreement.

We agree to the division of labor set forth in the ☐ outline ☐ schedule attached to and made part of this agreement. [*check applicable box*]

OR

We agree to the following division of labor: *[describe who will do what]*

Collaboration Agreement

This Collaboration Agreement is made between Nastassia Kinsey whose address is 123 Grub St., Santa Longo, CA; Jack Handy whose address is 1000 Main St., Santa Longo, CA; and Bartleby Crum whose address is 77 Sunset Blvd., Los Angeles, CA.

1. Description of Work

We agree to collaborate to create the following Work: A book-length work with the working title "The History of Sex." The Work will describe how sex evolved from the first primitive life forms to the present day.

2. Collaborators' Contributions

We agree to the division of labor set forth in the outline attached to and made part of this agreement.

3. Completion Date

We shall complete our contributions by April 1, 20____, or by the date specified in a publishing contract we enter into. If we fail to do so, we may mutually agree in writing to extend the time for completion.

If we fail to agree to an extension, we shall enter into a written agreement as to which of us may complete the Work and on what terms, including what authorship credit and compensation, if any, shall be paid to the collaborator who does not participate in completing the Work. If we are unable to agree, we shall submit our dispute to mediation and/or arbitration as described below.

4. Quitting the Collaboration

If any of us wishes to quit the collaboration before the Work is finally completed and accepted by a publisher, we shall enter into a written agreement setting forth the rights of the withdrawing collaborator, including what authorship credit and compensation, if any, shall be paid to the withdrawing collaborator. If we are unable to agree, we shall submit our dispute to mediation and/or arbitration as described below.

5. Ownership

We intend that the completed Work shall be a joint work. We shall each be equal co-owners in the copyright in the Work.

Completion date

Collaborators need to decide on a realistic deadline for completion of the work. They also need to agree on what will happen if the deadline is not met—can it be extended? The following provision allows the collaborators to agree on a new deadline. If they can't agree to a new deadline, they must then decide if any of the collaborators may complete the work and on what terms. If they can't agree on anything, they have to submit the dispute to mediation and arbitration.

We shall complete our contributions by ______________ [*date*] or by the date specified in a publishing contract we enter into. If we fail to do so, we may mutually agree in writing to extend the time for completion.

If we fail to agree to an extension, we shall enter into a written agreement as to which of us may complete the Work and on what terms, including what authorship credit and compensation, if any, shall be paid to the collaborator who does not participate in completing the Work. If we are unable to agree, we shall submit our dispute to mediation and/or arbitration as described below.

Quitting the collaboration

If one collaborator wants to quit the collaboration, the agreement should provide whether the remaining collaborator(s) can complete the work and, if so, what compensation must be paid to the withdrawing collaborator. The following provision simply leaves it to the collaborators to decide how to proceed if one collaborator wants to quit. If they can't agree, they must submit the dispute to mediation/arbitration.

If any of us wishes to quit the collaboration before the Work is finally completed and accepted by a publisher, we shall enter into a written agreement setting forth the rights of the withdrawing collaborator, including what authorship credit and compensation, if any, shall be paid to the withdrawing collaborator. If we are unable to agree, we shall submit our dispute to mediation and/or arbitration as described below.

Ownership

Ownership in the completed work can be divided in any way the collaborators wish. This is so regardless of the quantity or quality of their contributions. Typically, each collaborator is given an equal ownership share—for example, two collaborators would each share an undivided one-half interest in the work; three collaborators would each own a one-third interest; and so forth. The sample agreement in this book provides for equal ownership. Materials a collaborator collects to create the work—for example, tapes or photos—are also jointly owned unless the collaborator paid for them himself or herself.

We intend that the completed Work shall be a joint work. We shall each be equal co-owners in the copyright in the Work. Materials any of us collect to prepare the Work shall belong to the collaborator who obtains them if acquired at his or her own expense. Otherwise, all materials shall be jointly owned and may be disposed of only upon all the collaborators' written agreement.

However, your ownership interests don't have to be equal. For example, if there were two collaborators, one could be given a greater ownership interest than the other. How to divide your copyright in the work is entirely up to you.

Authorship credit

How the collaborators' names appear on their completed work is often an important issue. They can be in alphabetical order or any other way. Make sure that whatever you decide is set forth in your agreement to avoid future disputes.

The Work shall contain the following credit line: [*list authors in the order their names will appear on Work*].

Payments

As with copyright ownership, the income derived from the work can be distributed among the collaborators in any way they desire. This agreement provides two options: an equal distribution or some other arrangement.

All money accruing from the exploitation of our Work shall be divided equally among us. All contracts we enter into for exploitation of the Work shall provide for equal royalty payments and statements from the payor to each collaborator.

OR

All money accruing from the exploitation of the Work shall be divided as follows: ______________________ [*describe*].

Expenses

There are two ways to deal with expenses incurred by the collaborators in creating the work: They can be shared equally, or each collaborator can be required to pay his or her own expenses. You need to decide which approach to take in your agreement by choosing one of the two provisions below.

All expenses incurred in creating the Work shall be shared equally unless we agree otherwise in writing in advance.

OR

Each of us shall pay our own expenses unless we agree otherwise in writing in advance.

Death or disability

It may seem macabre to think about, but you need to consider what will happen if one or more collaborators die or become disabled before the work is completed. Can the survivors complete the work? If so, what compensation, if any, should be paid to the disabled collaborator or the deceased collaborator's heirs? The following provision gives the surviving collaborators the right to complete the work themselves or hire someone else to help them do so. After the work is published, the deceased collaborator's estate or disabled collaborator must be paid a pro rata share of the income received from the work. This share is based on the amount of the deceased or disabled collaborator's written contribution to the completed work after deducting expenses incurred by the remaining collaborators in completing the work.

If any of us dies or becomes disabled before completion of his or her portion of the Work, the remaining collaborator(s) may complete that portion of the Work or hire someone else to do so. The deceased collaborator's estate or disabled collaborator shall be paid a pro rata share of all income received from the Work based on the amount of the deceased or disabled collaborator's written contribution to the completed Work after deducting expenses incurred in completing the Work, including any salaries, fees, or royalties paid to another to complete the Work. The remaining collaborator(s) shall have sole authority to enter into contracts or licenses for the Work.

Decision making

Unless they agree otherwise, joint authors have the right to grant third parties permission to exploit the work on a nonexclusive basis without the other authors' consent. This can lead to chaos if different authors grant nonexclusive licenses of the same rights to different people. It's best that the agreement require that all business decisions be made jointly and that all the collaborators must sign all agreements for publication or other exploitation of the work.

All editorial, business, and other decisions affecting the Work shall be made jointly by all of us and no agreement shall be valid without all our signatures.

Noncompetition

Collaboration agreements often include noncompetition provisions barring the collaborators from authoring competing works. However, you need to think carefully about including such a provision

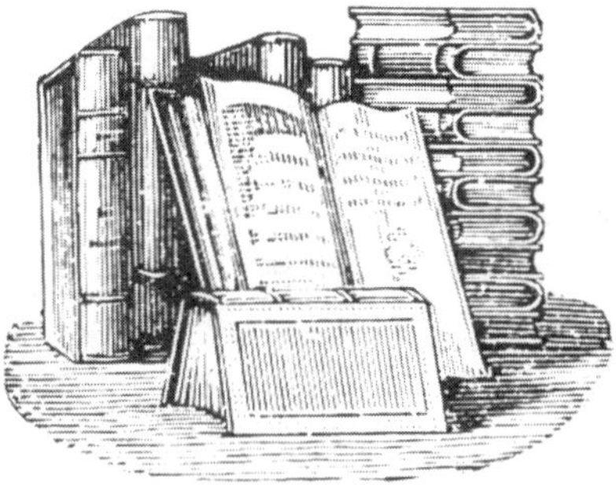

Materials any of us collect to prepare the Work shall belong to the collaborator who obtains them if acquired at his or her expense. Otherwise, all materials shall be jointly owned and may be disposed of only upon all the collaborators' written agreement.

6. Authorship Credit

The Work shall contain the following credit line: Nastassia Kinsey, Jack Handy, and Bartleby Crum.

7. Payments

All money accruing from the exploitation of our Work shall be divided equally among us. All contracts we enter into for exploitation of the Work shall provide for equal royalty payments and statements from the payor to each collaborator.

8. Expenses

All expenses incurred in creating the Work shall be shared equally unless we agree otherwise in writing in advance.

9. Death or Disability

If any of us dies or becomes disabled before completion of his or her portion of the Work, the remaining collaborator(s) may complete that portion of the Work or hire someone else to do so. The deceased collaborator's estate or disabled collaborator shall be paid a pro rata share of all income received from the Work based on the amount of the deceased or disabled collaborator's written contribution to the completed Work after deducting expenses incurred in completing the Work, including any salaries, fees, or royalties paid to another to complete the Work. The remaining collaborator(s) shall have sole authority to enter into contracts or licenses for the Work.

10. Term of Agreement

This Agreement begins on the date signed by all parties and shall continue for the duration of the copyright in the Work.

11. Decision Making

All editorial, business, and other decisions affecting the Work shall be made jointly by all of us and no agreement shall be valid without all our signatures.

Collaboration Agreement, Page 2

at all, and, if so, how broad it should be. Such a provision could make it difficult or impossible for you or your other collaborators to earn a living. If you want such a provision, it's usually best to limit its duration. You may also want to place other limitations on the restriction—for example, permitting collaborators to write magazine articles on the same topic as the work.

For a period of _____ years after completion of the Work, none of us shall participate in the preparation of any other work that directly competes with and would significantly diminish the sales of the Work.

[*OPTIONAL*]

This noncompetition agreement does not apply in the following circumstances: *[describe]* ______________________.

Warranties and indemnities

Virtually all book publishing contracts contain a warranty and indemnity clause in which the authors promise the publisher that their work does not infringe on anybody else's copyright or other rights. If it does, the authors are required to indemnify—that is, reimburse—the publisher for the costs involved in defending a lawsuit. This means that if one of your fellow collaborators violates a third person's rights, you could end up liable for the damages. The following provision protects you from this by requiring each collaborator to indemnify the other if he or she commits such a violation.

We represent and warrant to each other all of the following:

- Each of us is free to enter into this agreement.
- Our contributions to the Work are original or all necessary permissions and releases have been obtained and paid for.
- None of our contributions to the Work libel, violate the right of privacy or publicity, or infringe upon any copyright or other proprietary right of any other person or entity.

We each agree to indemnify the other(s) for any loss, liability, or expense resulting from the actual breach of these warranties.

Assignment and delegation

The following provision prevents the collaborators from assigning their contract rights or delegating their duties without the other collaborators' written permission. This means, for example, that a collaborator cannot get someone else to do his or her work without the other collaborators' consent.

None of us may assign his or her rights or delegate his or her duties under this agreement without the other collaborators' written consent. However, any collaborator may assign the right to receive royalties or other income from the Work by giving written notice to the other collaborator(s).

---

12. No Partnership

We are collaborators in this single Work. This agreement does not create a partnership relationship.

13. Exclusive Agreement

This is our entire agreement. Any other agreements previously entered into by us are superseded by it.

14. Noncompetition

For a period of two years after completion of the Work, none of us shall participate in the preparation of any other work that directly competes with and would significantly diminish the sales of the Work.

15. Derivative Works

We agree that none of us will incorporate material based on or derived from the Work in any subsequent work without the written consent of the other collaborators.

16. Warranties and Indemnities

We represent and warrant to each other all of the following:

- Each of us is free to enter into this agreement.
- Our contributions to the Work are original or all necessary permissions and releases have been obtained and paid for.
- None of our contributions to the Work libel, violate the right of privacy or publicity, or infringe upon any copyright or other proprietary right of any other person or entity.

We each agree to indemnify the others for any loss, liability, or expense resulting from the actual breach of these warranties.

17. Successors

This agreement shall benefit and bind our heirs, successors, assigns, and personal representatives.

Collaboration Agreement, Page 3

Dispute resolution

One of the most important functions of a collaboration agreement is to provide a means for resolving disputes. As you probably know, court litigation can be very expensive. To avoid this cost, alternative forms of dispute resolution have been developed that don't involve going to court. These include mediation and arbitration.

The following provision requires the collaborators to take advantage of these alternate forms of dispute resolution. You're first required to submit the dispute to mediation. You agree on a neutral third person to serve as mediator and try to help you settle your dispute. The mediator has no power to impose a decision, only to try to help you arrive at one.

If mediation doesn't work, you must submit the dispute to binding arbitration. Arbitration is usually like an informal court trial without a jury, but involves arbitrators instead of judges and is usually much faster and cheaper than courts. You may be represented by a lawyer, but it's not required. You should indicate in the following clause where the mediation or arbitration would occur. You'll usually want it in the city or county where you live. If the collaborators live a long distance apart, they'll have to agree on a location.

If a dispute arises under this agreement, we agree to first try to resolve it with the help of a mutually agreed-upon mediator in the following location [*list city or county where mediation will occur*]. Any costs and fees other than attorney fees associated with the mediation will be shared equally by each of us.

If it proves impossible to arrive at a mutually satisfactory solution through mediation, we agree to submit the dispute to binding arbitration at the following location [*list city or county where arbitration will occur*] under the rules of the American Arbitration Association. Judgment upon the award rendered by the arbitration may be entered in any court with jurisdiction to do so.

The text of this Collaboration Agreement is on the forms CD-ROM.

Joint Authors' Rights and Duties in the Absence of a Collaboration Agreement

The drafters of the Copyright Act realized that not all joint authors would be prudent enough to enter into a written (or even oral) collaboration agreement setting forth their ownership interests, rights, and duties. To avoid chaos, they made sure that the act contained provisions governing the most important aspects of the legal relationship between joint authors who fail to agree among themselves how their relationship should operate. You might think of these provisions as similar to a computer program's default settings that control the

18. Assignment and Delegation

None of us may assign his or her rights or delegate his or her duties under this agreement without the other collaborators' written consent. However, any collaborator may assign the right to receive royalties or other income from the Work by giving written notice to the other collaborators.

19. Applicable Law

This agreement will be governed by the laws of the state of California.

20. Dispute Resolution

If a dispute arises under this agreement, we agree to first try to resolve it with the help of a mutually agreed-upon mediator in the following location: Santa Longo, CA. Any costs and fees other than attorney fees associated with the mediation will be shared equally by each of us.

If it proves impossible to arrive at a mutually satisfactory solution through mediation, we agree to submit the dispute to binding arbitration at the following location: Santa Longo, CA, under the rules of the American Arbitration Association. Judgment upon the award rendered by the arbitration may be entered in any court with jurisdiction to do so.

21. Attorney Fees

If any legal action is necessary to enforce this agreement, the prevailing party shall be entitled to reasonable attorney fees, costs, and expenses in addition to any other relief to which he or she may be entitled.

Signatures:

______________________________ ______________
Nastassia Kinsey Date

______________________________ ______________
Jack Handy Date

______________________________ ______________
Bartleby Crum Date

Collaboration Agreement, Page 4

program when the user fails to make his own settings.

Ownership interests

Unless they agree otherwise, joint authors each have an undivided interest in the entire work. This is basically the same as joint ownership of a house or other real estate. When a husband and wife jointly own their home, they normally each own a 50% interest in the entire house—that is, they each have an undivided one-half interest. Similarly, joint authors share ownership of all five exclusive rights that make up the joint work's copyright.

Right to exploit copyright

Unless they agree otherwise, each joint author has the right to exercise any or all of the five copyright rights inherent in the joint work—that is, any of the authors may reproduce and distribute the work or prepare derivative works based upon it (or display or perform it). Each author may do so without the other joint authors' consent.

Right to license joint work

Unless they agree otherwise, each joint author may grant third parties permission to exploit the work—on a nonexclusive basis—without the other owners' consent. This means that different authors may grant nonexclusive licenses of the same right to different persons!

> **EXAMPLE:** Manny, Moe, and Jack are joint authors of a novel. Manny gives Publisher A the nonexclusive right to publish the book in North America. Moe gives the same right to Publisher B, and Jack to Publisher C. The result, perfectly legal, is that three publishers have the right to publish the book at the same time.

To avoid the kind of results illustrated in the above example, anyone who purchases an exclusive right in a joint work should require signatures by all the authors. (See Chapter 9, Transferring Copyright Ownership, for a detailed discussion of copyright transfers.)

Right to transfer ownership

Finally, unless they agree otherwise, each author of a joint work may transfer her entire ownership interest to another person without the other joint authors' consent. Such person then co-owns the work with the remaining authors. But a joint author can only transfer her particular interest, not that of any other author.

> **EXAMPLE:** Sue, Deborah, and Martin are joint authors of a college textbook. Sue decides to transfer her ownership interest to her son, Sam. Since Sue, Deborah, and Martin have not agreed among themselves to restrict their transfer rights in any way, Sue may transfer her interest to Sam without Deborah's or Martin's consent (but Sue could not transfer Deborah's or Martin's ownership interests to Sam without their consent). When the transfer is

completed, Sam will have all the rights Sue had as a joint author.

Duty to account for profits

Along with these rights, each joint author has the duty to account to the other joint owners for any profits received from his use or license of the joint work. All the joint authors are entitled to share in these profits. Unless they agree otherwise, the profits must be divided among the authors according to their proportionate interests in the joint work. (Note, however, that such profits do not include what one author gets for selling his or her share of the copyright.)

> **EXAMPLE:** Bill and Lee are joint authors of a novel. Bill writes a screenplay based on the novel and sells it for $10,000. Lee is entitled to one-half of the $10,000.

It may not seem fair that a joint author who goes to the time and trouble of exploiting the copyright in the joint work by publishing it or creating derivative works based upon it is required to share his profits equally with the other joint authors who did nothing. This is still another reason why it's wise to enter into a collaboration agreement.

What happens when joint authors die?

Absent a joint tenancy agreement, a deceased joint author's heirs would acquire her share in the joint work. The other joint authors do not acquire a deceased owner's share (unless, of course, the deceased owner willed it to them, or the author died without a will and another joint author was related to her and inherited her interest under the general inheritance laws).

■

CHAPTER

9 Transferring Copyright Ownership

In Chapter 8, Initial Copyright Ownership, we discuss the rights that accompany copyright ownership. Here is a brief recap. An author automatically becomes the owner of a complete set of exclusive rights in any protected expression he or she creates. These include the right to:

- reproduce the protected expression
- distribute copies of the work to the public by sale, rental, lease, or otherwise
- prepare derivative works using the protected expression (that is, adapt new works from the expression), and
- perform and display the work publicly.

These rights are exclusive because only the owner of one or more particular rights that together make up copyright ownership may exercise it or permit others to do so. For example, only the owner of the right to distribute a book may sell it to the public or permit others—a publisher, for instance—to do so.

With the important exception of self-publishers who reproduce and distribute their work themselves, authors normally profit from their copyrights by selling their rights to publishers or others to exploit. And, except where they publish works that are in the public domain (such as works originally published before 1923), publishers must acquire the right to reproduce and sell a work from its author or other copyright owner.

The Terminology of Transfers

Several different terms can be used to describe a transfer of copyright ownership rights. Many of these terms are used interchangeably and have no settled legal meaning, but here is how we'll use them in this book:

- Assignment means a transfer of all the exclusive rights that make up a copyright.
- Exclusive license means a transfer on an exclusive basis, of one or more, but less than all, of a copyright owner's exclusive rights.
- Nonexclusive license means giving someone the right to exercise one or more of a copyright owner's rights on a nonexclusive basis. Since this does not prevent the copyright owner from giving others permission to exercise the same right or rights at the same time, it is not a transfer of copyright ownership.

Again, please remember that these definitions are only for the purposes of this discussion. In the real world it makes no difference if a transfer is called an assignment, a license, a contract, or a grant of rights or is given no label. The effect of an agreement to transfer copyright ownership rights is determined according to the language it contains, not its label.

How Copyright Ownership Rights Are Transferred to Others

A transfer of copyright ownership rights must be in writing and signed by the person who owns the rights being transferred to be valid. There are two basic types of copyright transfers: exclusive licenses and assignments. Although these terms are often used interchangeably, there are some differences.

Exclusive Licenses

The term exclusive license is usually used when a copyright owner transfers one or more of her rights but retains at least some of them.

> **EXAMPLE:** Jane writes an article on economics and grants *The Economist's Journal* the exclusive right to publish it for the first time in the United States and Canada. Jane has granted the *Journal* an exclusive license. Only the *Journal* may publish the article for the first time in the U.S. and Canada. The *Journal* owns this right. But Jane retains the right to republish her article after it appears in the *Journal* and to include it in a book. She also retains the right to create derivative works from it (for example, to expand it into a book-length work), as well as other rights that weren't specifically transferred in the license.

A copyright owner's exclusive rights are almost infinitely divisible. That is, they can be divided and subdivided and licensed to others in just about any way imaginable. In the publishing business, the most common divisions are by language, type of media (hardcover and softcover books, magazines, film, video, audiotapes, computers, and so on), time, or geography.

> **EXAMPLE 1:** Jennifer writes a high school math textbook and sells Scrivener & Sons an exclusive license to distribute it in the United States only. She then grants MacKenzie Press an exclusive license to sell the book in Canada, and Trans-European Publishing Co. the right to sell it in all EC (common market) countries.

> **EXAMPLE 2:** Leo writes a biography and grants Scrivener & Sons the exclusive right to sell it in the United States in hardcover. He grants all English language rights outside the U.S. to the British publisher MacCauley & Unwin, and sells the U.S. paperback rights to Acme Press.

> **EXAMPLE 3:** Martha writes a detective novel. She grants Hardboiled Publications, Inc., the exclusive right to sell the book in the U.S. and Canada. She then gives Repulsive Pictures the exclusive right to create and distribute a film based on her work, ABC the right to use it for a television series, and Tapes Unlimited, Inc., the right to adapt it into an audiotape.

Can Copyrights Be Transferred by Email?

Can you transfer all or part of a copyright through email? That answer is unclear. Remember, the copyright law says a transfer must be in writing signed by the copyright owner to be valid. An email would not effect a valid transfer unless the electronic signature it contained was deemed to satisfy the signing requirement. The only court that has ever considered this question held that emails were not sufficient to transfer ownership. (*Ballas v. Tedesco*, 41 F.Supp.2d 531 (D. N.J. 1999).) Since that time, however, Congress enacted a law called the Electronic Signatures in Global and National Commerce Act (ESIGN for short) providing that electronic signatures are legally valid. (15 USC § 7001(a).) It remains unclear, though, how this new law applies to copyright transfers. For this reason, you should always obtain the actual signature of the owner of the copyrights you wish to obtain.

Exclusive Licensee's Rights

The holder of an exclusive license becomes the owner of the transferred right(s). As such, unless the exclusive license provides otherwise, she is entitled to sue anyone who infringes on that right while she owns it and is entitled to transfer her license to others. She may also record the exclusive license with the Copyright Office; this provides many valuable benefits.

Assignments

If an owner of all the exclusive rights in a copyright transfers the entire bundle of rights that make up his copyright simultaneously to a single person or entity, the transaction is usually called an assignment or, sometimes, an all rights transfer. An assignment must be in writing to be valid.

> **EXAMPLE:** Otto assigns Acme Romances the entire copyright in his romance novel *Love's Lost Languor*. This means that Acme, and only Acme, may publish the work or permit others to do so, or exercise any other part of the bundle of rights that make up the copyright in the work (such as authorizing someone to adapt the book into a screenplay). Otto has relinquished these rights. For all practical purposes, Acme now owns the copyright instead of Otto.

Nonexclusive Licenses Do Not Transfer Copyright Ownership

As mentioned earlier, a nonexclusive license gives someone the right to exercise one or more of a copyright owner's rights, but does not prevent the copyright owner from giving others permission to exercise the same right or rights at the same time. A nonexclusive license is not a transfer of ownership; it's a form of sharing. The most common type of nonexclusive license is one granting an author permission to quote from, photocopy, or otherwise use a protected work; such licenses are often called permissions. See Chapter 11, Using Other Authors' Words, for a detailed discussion and sample permission form.

> **EXAMPLE:** Tony, an avid parachutist, has written and self-published a pamphlet on advanced parachuting techniques. He gives the Fresno Parachuting Club permission to make 100 copies of the pamphlet and distribute them in the Fresno area. Tony retains the right to let others copy and distribute his pamphlet in Fresno (and anywhere else), or may do so himself. Tony has given the club a nonexclusive license to exercise some of his copyright rights in his pamphlet. The license is nonexclusive because the club cannot prevent Tony from letting others exercise the same rights he has granted to it.

As with exclusive licenses, nonexclusive licenses may be limited as to time, geography, or media or in any other way. They can be granted orally or in writing. The much better practice, however, is to use some sort of writing; this can avoid possible misunderstandings and gives the nonexclusive licensee certain priority rights. It is not necessary to have a formal contract filled with legalese to grant a nonexclusive license. A simple letter or memo is sufficient. Just make sure that you make clear the license is nonexclusive (use the term nonexclusive license) and spell out the terms and conditions of the license—that is, what rights are being licensed, to whom, and for how long.

Nonexclusive License May Be Implied From Circumstances

An express written or oral agreement is not always required to create a nonexclusive license. A nonexclusive license can be implied from the circumstances—that is, where the circumstances are such that a copyright owner must have intended to grant a nonexclusive license, it can be considered to exist without an actual agreement.

> **EXAMPLE:** When a person sends a letter to the editor of a newspaper or magazine, a nonexclusive license giving the publication the right to publish the letter in its letters to the editor section is implied; the newspaper or magazine need not seek the letter writer's formal permission to publish the letter

Sales of Copies Do Not Transfer Copyright Ownership

Ownership of a copyright and ownership of a material object in which the copyrighted work is embodied—such as a book or article—are entirely separate things. This means the sale or gift of a copy or copies of a book, article, or other protected work does not transfer the copyright owner's exclusive rights in the work. A copyright owner's exclusive rights can only be transferred by a written agreement. For example, a person who buys a copy of a book or manuscript owns that book or manuscript but acquires no copyright rights in the work.

EXAMPLE: Luther, an extremely wealthy and avid book collector, purchases the original manuscript of James Joyce's *Finnegan's Wake* from Joyce's estate. However, Luther does not obtain any copyright rights in the work. Although Luther owns the manuscript, he cannot reproduce and distribute it or exercise any other of the copyright owners' rights in the work without obtaining their permission.

First Sale Doctrine

Under what is known as the first sale doctrine, once a copyright owner sells or gives away a copy or copies of a book or other physical manifestation of his copyright, he relinquishes all control over that physical copy itself. The purchaser can resell the copy without the copyright owner's permission or, if the purchaser is a library, lend it to the public.

EXAMPLE: Morris has self-published 500 copies of a book on do-it-yourself plumbing. He sells all 500 copies of the book to Joe's Hardware Store but does not transfer any copyright rights to Joe's. Joe's is entitled to sell all 500 copies, rent them, give them away, destroy them, or do anything else it wants with them. But, of course, Joe's cannot reproduce the book or exercise any of Morris's other exclusive rights without his permission.

Copyright Transfers Do Not Affect Copyright Duration

Copyright transfers do not affect the duration of the copyright, even if the entire bundle of copyright ownership rights is transferred. See Chapter 10, Copyright Duration. However, a transfer itself may be limited as to time; that is, it doesn't have to be for the entire duration of the copyright.

> **EXAMPLE:** Margaret grants Green Thumb Publishing the exclusive right to publish her book on gardening in the United States for 20 years. The copyright in the book will last for the rest of Margaret's life plus an additional 70 years. The transfer to Green Thumb has no effect on this. When the 20 years are up, the transferred rights will revert to Margaret or her heirs and will last for the remainder of the copyright term.

Rights Retained by Author After Transfer

A copyright owner who transfers all or part of her bundle of exclusive rights still retains some important rights.

Right to Sublicense Under Exclusive Licenses

Whenever an author or other copyright owner assigns his or her entire bundle of copyright rights to another person or company, that person may reassign the copyright to someone else without the original owner's consent. However, this is not necessarily the case when an exclusive license is involved, since an exclusive license only transfers *part* of a copyright owner's rights.

One court held that a person or company that receives an exclusive license from an author or other copyright owner may not sublicense—that is, transfer to someone else—the rights it has received unless the license permits it or the copyright owner agrees. (*Gardner v. Nike, Inc.*, 279 F.3d 774 (9th Circuit 2002).)

This case has important ramifications for copyright owners and publishers and others to whom they grant exclusive licenses. Unless the license agreement gives them the right to sublicense the work, licensees may be prevented from fully exploiting the work they've licensed. For example, in the *Gardner v. Nike* case cited above, Nike granted an exclusive license to Sony Music Entertainment for a cartoon character named *MC Teach*. Sony had the exclusive right to use *MC Teach* in records, TV shows and movies, clothing, and educational materials. Sony then sublicensed to Gardner the right to use *MC Teach* on educational materials. Nike sued, claiming Sony couldn't sublicense *MC Teach* without Nike's permission. The court agreed, because the license agreement did not specifically permit such sublicensing. So, Sony was prevented from sublicensing *MC Teach* to Gardner unless Nike agreed. Nike was free to withhold such agreement or to demand increased license fees to permit the sublicensing.

Here are some other scenarios where this case could wreak havoc on licensees' plans:

- A publisher obtains an exclusive license to publish a book in North America. The author retains all other rights. The publishing agreement does not specifically allow the publisher to sublicense its rights in the book.

The publisher couldn't sign a license permitting another publisher to produce a Spanish language edition for sale in North America or sell North American book club rights without the author's permission.

- An author obtains an exclusive license to use several photographs in his book. He signs a license with the photographer that says he may use the photos in all editions of the book, but says nothing about whether he can sublicense the photos. When a magazine contacts him to publish an excerpt from the book, the author can't authorize use of the photos in the book unless he obtains the photographer's permission.
- A website buys a series of articles from a freelance writer. It signs an exclusive license giving it the exclusive right to use the articles on the Internet. Since the license says nothing about sublicensing, the website cannot license the articles for non-Internet uses—for example, for publication in print magazines or newspapers.

One way to avoid these issues is to include language in an exclusive license agreement permitting sublicensing. Here's an example:

[*name of person or entity receiving license*] may sublicense the rights granted in this agreement.

Alternatively, the person seeking rights can acquire copyright ownership and avoid using exclusive licenses. This can be done through an assignment or, in some cases, use of a work-made-for-hire agreement. (See Chapter 8, Initial Copyright Ownership.) This is something more and more publishers, newspapers, magazines, and others are doing.

If you would like a middle ground—where you have some say in sublicensing but you won't interfere in most sublicense agreements—you can soften the effect with a clause in which you withhold consent for sublicenses only if you have a valid business reason. What's a valid reason? Perhaps the company to which your licensee wants to grant an assignment has a reputation for not paying royalties, or maybe it is in poor financial shape. You cannot, however, withhold consent for an arbitrary reason, such as someone from the company once treated you rudely. Here's an example:

[*name of person or entity receiving license*] may not sublicense the rights granted in this agreement without the prior written consent of Licensor. Such consent shall not be unreasonably withheld.

Many exclusive license agreements contain standard "boilerplate" language stating that the agreement applies to the licensee's "successors and assigns." Whether this constitutes permission to sublicense is unclear and should not be relied upon.

The *Nike* case is only binding in the Ninth Judicial Circuit of the U.S. This includes the states of Alaska, Arizona, California, Hawaii, Idaho, Montana, Nevada, Oregon, and Washington. Courts in other parts of the country are not required to follow it, and it's possible they may not. However, you shouldn't rely on this. Whenever you sign an exclusive license, consider the subject of sublicensing.

If you're an author or other copyright owner who grants someone an exclusive license to use your work, you should decide whether to give the licensee the right to sublicense the work. This negotiation may depend on your bargaining power, but you have the legal right to refuse to grant such authority or to demand payment for sublicensing rights.

If your agreement is silent on sublicensing, and the licensee or sublicensee is located in one of the states covered by the decision (Alaska, Arizona, California, Hawaii, Idaho, Montana, Nevada, Oregon, or Washington), the licensee has no legal right to sublicense your work without your consent. If you discover that a licensee has done so, you may do what Nike did and sue for copyright infringement. Usually, however, a lawsuit won't be necessary—the licensee and/or sublicensee will probably agree to pay you for the right to sublicense. If the licensee doesn't live in one of the states directly covered by the decision, your legal situation is more problematic, since it's not clear whether courts in these other states will follow the *Nike* ruling.

Nonexclusive Licensees Have No Sublicensing Rights

Those who obtain nonexclusive licenses from copyright owners have no rights to sublicense their rights without the copyright owner's permission. Unlike the *Nike* ruling involving exclusive licenses, above, this rule is settled law throughout the U.S.

Statutory Termination of Transfers After 35 Years

A potentially important right retained by authors and their families is the statutory right to terminate transfers of copyright ownership made after December 31, 1977. This includes the original grant of rights an author gives to her publisher. These statutory termination rights can never be waived or contracted away.

What rights can be terminated?

Any transfer of copyright rights made by a living author after December 31, 1977 may be terminated. This is so whether the transfer is an assignment of the entire bundle of copyright rights or an exclusive or nonexclusive license of only certain rights. A transfer of a copyright by will that occurs after an author dies is not subject to statutory termination.

Who can exercise the termination right?

This termination right may be exercised only by the author of a work or, if the author is dead when the time to terminate arrives, by the author's widow or widower, children (including illegitimate and adopted children), and grandchildren. If an author dies without leaving a surviving spouse or children or grandchildren, the termination right ceases to exist. Note that an author cannot leave her termination rights to others in a will. When an author dies, her termination rights automatically pass on to her surviving spouse and children and grandchildren, if any. The provisions in an author's will are irrelevant.

The owner of a work made for hire, whether an individual or a business entity such as a corporation, has no statutory termination rights.

> **EXAMPLE 1:** Sam writes a book in 2000 and signs a publishing contract transferring his entire copyright to Scrivener & Sons that same year. The transfer may later be terminated by Sam or certain family members as described below.

> **EXAMPLE 2:** Sue writes a book in 2000 and transfers her entire copyright to her boyfriend Bill by a will upon her death in 2001. This transfer may not be terminated by Sue's surviving family.

When can transfers be terminated?

A transfer of the right to publish (that is, reproduce and distribute) a work may be terminated any time during a five-year period beginning either 40 years after the date of the transfer or 35 years after the date of first publication, whichever is earlier. A transfer of any other rights (for example, the right to adapt a work into a film) can be terminated any time during a five-year period beginning 35 years after the transfer was made and ending 40 years afterwards.

> **EXAMPLE:** Kelly Stewart signs a contract with Scrivener & Sons on January 1, 1980 to write a novel, and grants Scrivener the exclusive right to publish the book in the U.S. and Canada. The novel, entitled *The Voyeur*, is not published until January 1, 1990. On January 1, 1991, Kelly sells the film rights to her novel to Repulsive Pictures. The publication rights transferred to Scrivener may be terminated by Kelly or her heirs any time between January 1, 2020 and January 1, 2025, 40 to 45 years after the publishing contract was signed. This is earlier than 35 years after the date of actual publication of the book. The film rights transfer to Repulsive may be terminated between January 1, 2025 and January 1, 2031 (35 to 40 years after the transfer was made).

What happens after a transfer is terminated?

After a transfer is terminated, the terminated rights revert back to the author if he or she is still alive. If the author is dead, the rights are shared by the author's widow or widower, children, and grandchildren. However, the owners of any derivative works prepared from the work may continue to distribute such works.

> **EXAMPLE 1:** Assume that it is the year 2020. Kelly Stewart has terminated the publication rights grant she made to Scrivener & Sons in 1980. This means that Scrivener may not publish any more copies of Kelly's novel without her permission. Kelly may now resell her novel's publication rights to Scrivener or any other publisher, or self-publish her novel if she so chooses.

> **EXAMPLE 2:** Assume that it is now the year 2025. Kelly has terminated the film rights transfer she made to Repulsive Pictures back in 1991. Kelly now owns the right to make any new films based upon her novel. However, Repulsive may continue to distribute *Front Window*, a film it produced based on Kelly's novel in 1994; it just can't make any new films from the novel without Kelly's permission.

What is the termination procedure?

A written notice of termination complying with the statutory requirements must be sent to the owners of the rights being terminated and recorded with the Copyright Office. Although the termination won't be effective until 35 or 40 years after the transfer, you can serve the notice up to ten years before that. That is:

- For transfers including publication rights, the notice of termination may be served 25 years after publication or 30 years after the transfer was signed, whichever occurs first.
- For transfers not including publication rights, the notice of termination may be served 25 years after the transfer was signed.

Thus, for example, during 2007, a notice of termination may be served to terminate a transfer not involving publication rights made during 1982.

The notice of termination may be written in the form of a letter, including all the following information:

- a statement that the termination is made under 17 USC § 203
- the name of each person whose rights are being terminated or that person's successor in title, and each address at which service of the notice is being made
- the date the transfer being terminated was made, and, if the grant covered the right of publication, the date of publication
- the title of the work and the name of the author(s) and, if possible and practicable, the original copyright registration number
- a brief statement reasonably identifying the transfer to which the notice of termination applies, and the effective date of termination, and
- if the termination is made by the author's heirs, a listing of their names and relationships to that deceased author.

The notice must be served by personal service, or by first-class mail sent to an address which, after a reasonable investigation, is found to be the last known address of the person whose rights are being terminated, or his or her heirs or successors. It is also advisable to record the notice with the Copyright Office.

Filing Documents With the Copyright Office

An author or other copyright owner retains the right to file the following documents with the Copyright Office following a transfer of copyright rights.

Supplemental registrations

Certain types of new information or changes in the information supplied in the original registration may be supplemented by the author or other copyright owner according to the procedures discussed in Chapter 5, Correcting or Changing Copyright Notice or Registration, even though the author or other copyright owner no longer owns any of the copyright rights.

Notice regarding contractual termination or revocation of transfer

A copyright owner who transfers ownership of her copyright right(s) for a set term (for example, ten years) has the right to notify the Copyright Office when the term has expired so she can expressly reclaim her ownership on the record. Similarly, revocation is desirable when a transfer is revoked because the transferee did not abide by the terms of his license (for example, failed to sell a required number of copies) or for some other reason.

An owner in this situation should send the Copyright Office a letter along the following lines and also have the letter recorded.

> January 2, 20xx
>
> Dear Examiner:
>
> My copyright registration #TX 1234657 in the textbook entitled *French for First Graders* was transferred in full to Kiddie Publications for a period of ten (10) years, commencing on January 1, 20xx. This is to notify you that the transfer has terminated and I am the sole owner of copyright #TX 1234567.
>
> Sincerely,
>
> *Jacques Paul Jones*
>
> Jacques Paul Jones

Moral Rights

In many European and other countries an author automatically retains certain additional rights in his work. These are called moral rights (or *droits morals*). Moral rights are rights an author can never transfer to a third party, because they are considered an extension of her being. Briefly, they consist of the right to proper credit or attribution whenever the work is published, to disclaim authorship of unauthorized copies, to prevent or call back distribution under certain conditions, and to object to any distortion, mutilation, or other modification of the author's work injurious to her reputation. The right to prevent colorization of black and white films is an example of a moral right. Moral rights are generally of most concern to visual artists.

The Berne Convention (an international copyright treaty) requires that signatory countries extend these rights to authors. (See discussion in Chapter 13, International Copyright Protection.) In 1991, Congress amended the Copyright Act to extend certain moral rights to visual artists (see Section 106A of the Copyright Act), but the U.S. has not granted similar rights to authors. The courts will have to decide whether moral rights must be granted to writers under American copyright law pursuant to the Berne Convention.

However, American courts have recognized certain types of rights that are analogous to moral rights, although they may not be referred to as such. For example, any author of a work published in the U.S. retains the right to have his authorship continuously recognized on works that remain true to the original. Conversely, an author retains the right to have her name taken off a work that has been substantially changed from the original. These rights do not come from the Copyright Act, but rather from the trademark laws which prohibit misrepresentation of a product's origins. In addition, one court has held that unauthorized changes in a work that are so extensive as to impair its integrity constitute copyright infringement. (See *Gilliam v. American Broadcasting Cos.,* 538 F.2d 14 (2d Cir. 1976).) (The British comedy group Monty Python obtained an injunction stopping ABC from airing Monty Python programs it had obtained a license to broadcast and had heavily edited.)

Copyright Transfers Between Freelance Writers and Magazines and Other Periodicals

Now that you have a general understanding of copyright transfer law, let's see how it applies to the relationship between authors and publishers of magazines, newspapers, and similar publications (often called serial publications). Since publishers' and writers' interests differ in these transactions, we'll examine them first from an author's and then from a publisher's or editor's point of view.

Transfers From the Writer's Point of View

Publishing jargon

Editors, literary agents, and others in the publishing business have their own jargon to describe an author's copyright rights. An author attempting to sell an article or other contribution to a magazine, newspaper, or other serial publication is likely to encounter some of the following terms.

All world rights. Transfer of all world rights or all rights means that the author assigns all of his copyright rights to the magazine or other serial publication. The publication becomes the sole copyright owner. It may publish the work anywhere in the world any number of times, syndicate it, use it in databases, create derivative works from it or permit others to do so, or do anything else it wants with it. The author may not resell the work, create derivative works from it (for example, use it as a chapter in a book), or use it in any other way without the magazine's permission—the author no longer owns the work.

Compare—Work-Made-for-Hire Agreements

Magazines and other periodicals are permitted to enter into work-made-for-hire agreements with freelance contributors. Technically, a work-made-for-hire agreement is not a transfer of rights; rather, the employer is considered to be the author of the work. But the practical result is the same as a transfer of all rights: The magazine owns all the rights in the work. The only difference is that an author who makes an all-rights assignment may terminate the assignment after 35 years and retains certain moral rights. Work-made-for-hire agreements are discussed in Chapter 8, Initial Copyright Ownership.

All world serial rights. A transfer of all world serial rights means that the publisher acquires an exclusive license to publish the contribution in newspapers, magazines, and other serial publications throughout the world any number of times for the duration of the copyright term. The author of the article or other contribution may not resell it to any other serial publication anywhere in the world. But the author retains all his other rights—for instance, he may use it as a chapter in a book or sell it for adaptation as a movie or video.

First North American serial rights. A grant of first North American serial rights means that the magazine or other serial publication has an exclusive license to publish the work for the first time in North America (the U.S. and Canada). Once the work has been published, the author may resell it, create derivative works from it, or do anything else she wants with it—she owns all the other rights in the work.

Second serial rights. A transfer of second serial rights (or reprint rights) gives a magazine, newspaper, or other serial publication a *nonexclusive* license to reprint a work once after it has already appeared in another serial publication.

One-time rights. A transfer of one-time rights (also called simultaneous rights) gives the magazine or other publication the right to publish a previously unpublished work once; but, in contrast to a grant of first serial rights (above), the author may sell the work to other publications to appear at the same time. This is a nonexclusive license, rather than an ownership transfer. Newspapers often purchase one-time rights from freelance contributors.

Which rights should you sell?

It is always in a writer's best interests to retain as many rights as possible. Let's examine the consequences of an all rights grant compared with a grant of first North American rights.

> **EXAMPLE 1:** George writes a short story about a six-year-old's experiences at Christmas. In 2003, he sells all his rights in the story to *Maudlin Magazine* for $750. The story appears in *Maudlin's* December 2003 issue. The story proves to be so popular that *Maudlin* reprints it every December thereafter. Not only that, every year it sells reprint rights to the story to several other magazines and newspapers throughout the country. George gets absolutely nothing from all these reprintings.

> **EXAMPLE 2:** Assume instead that George only sold *Maudlin Magazine* first North American serial rights to his story in 2003. After *Maudlin* printed the story in North America for the first time in December 2003, it had no further rights in the story. George, and only George, could permit *Maudlin* or other magazines and newspapers to reprint it. The income George receives from these reprintings far exceeds the $750 he got from *Maudlin* for the story's initial publication.

The Real World of Publishing Practice

Traditionally, magazines and other periodicals usually only acquired North American serial rights, second serial rights, or one-time publication rights. This meant that after the article appeared in the magazine, the author could resell it elsewhere. However, things are changing fast in magazine publishing. An increasing number of magazines seek to obtain all the writer's rights or, even worse from the writer's point of view, have the writer sign a work-made-for-hire contract under which the magazine is considered to be the work's author. To put it mildly, writer's groups are bitterly opposed to this trend and advise freelancers never to sign work-made-for-hire contracts.

You'll often find that many magazines will initially ask for all your rights, but will be willing to take less if you negotiate with them. Don't be afraid to speak up and demand to be treated fairly.

Transfers From a Magazine's Point of View

If you're the editor or publisher of a magazine, periodical, or similar publication, you need to obtain the rights you need from freelancers with the least amount of paperwork and the fewest headaches possible. Be aware that a written agreement is always necessary to purchase an exclusive right from a writer—for example, first North American serial rights.

If you want to be sure a freelancer's piece will appear first and/or only in your magazine, you must use a written agreement. In the absence of a written agreement, a publisher obtains only a nonexclusive license to publish a freelancer's piece in the magazine or other periodical. Thus, the author can sell it to other magazines (or use it in any other way).

Exclusive first publication rights are of most importance to publishers of national magazines. If you're publishing a newspaper or regional publication, it probably won't matter much if the same piece appears at the same time (or has already appeared) in another periodical in a different part of the country.

Most magazines, especially regional publications, are not interested in resale rights and adaptation rights (such as film rights or the right to include the piece in a book). These rights have value only if there is a market for them; usually, there isn't.

You should develop a transfer agreement form. This may be in the form of a letter or a more formal-looking contract. See the sources listed in "Transfer Documents," below, for sample forms. If you're considering using a work-for-hire agreement, be sure to read the discussion of work-made-for-hire in Chapter 8, Initial Copyright Ownership.

Copyright Transfers Between Writers and Book Publishers

Book publishers operate differently from magazines or newspapers.

Publishing Argot

The copyright rights in a book are normally divided into two categories: the primary publication rights and subsidiary (sub) rights.

Primary publication right

The exclusive right to publish a work in book form for the first time in the English language is sometimes called the primary right. Publishing agreements vary as to the territory to which this right extends. At a minimum, a U.S. publisher will normally want the exclusive right to publish the work in the U.S. The territory is often extended to all countries in which English is spoken; these are called all English language rights. The most expansive possible grant is all world rights—that is, the right to publish the book in all countries in all languages.

Book publishers usually obtain the exclusive right to publish a work for the full copyright term, but, in some cases, a shorter period may be involved.

Hardcover and Softcover Editions

In the past, publishers specialized in selling hardcover or softcover books. This meant that the right to publish a book in hardcover and softcover editions were sold separately, usually to different publishers. Typically, the hardcover edition would be published first and then the softcover rights sold at an auction at which any number of softcover publishers could bid. Today, however, many publishers sell both hardcover and softcover books. As a result, the old softcover auction isn't nearly as common as it used to be. Instead, an author's initial grant of publication rights to a publisher will often cover both hardcover and softcover editions of the book.

Subsidiary or sub rights

All the other copyright rights in a book are called subsidiary or sub rights. These include film, television, radio, and live-stage adaptation rights; the right to publish all or part of the work in a newspaper, magazine, or other periodical prior to or after book publication; book club publication rights; the right to publish the book in a foreign language or license others to do so; the right to create and distribute nondramatic audio recordings of the work; and the right to publish braille, large-type, and other editions for the handicapped.

Importance of Foreign Language Rights

The right to translate and sell a book in a foreign language can be very important for some books, such as popular novels, art books, and children's books. These rights are usually sold language-by-language at international book fairs (such as the Frankfurt, Germany, book fair) and by international literary agents.

Transfers From an Author's Point of View

It is usually in an author's best interest to retain as many rights as possible, unless, of course, the publisher pays so much that it makes sense to assign all rights. The more bargaining power an author has, the more rights she'll likely be able to keep. However, it can make good sense to sell subsidiary rights to a publisher in return for a share of the profits (at least 50%) if the publisher is better able to market these rights than the author or the author's agent. A large full-line publisher will often know the subsidiary rights markets well and have the contacts and experience to effectively market an author's sub rights.

Transfers From a Book Publisher's Point of View

It is in a book publisher's best interest to demand an assignment of all rights from the author in return for a royalty and a share of the profits from the sale of the subsidiary rights listed earlier. This gives the publisher the right to sell all the subsidiary rights one by one and keep part of the profits. A 50–50 split of the profits from sub rights sales is common, but other divisions are also used.

Transfer Documents

Virtually all book publishers—and many magazines as well—have standard publication agreements they ask authors to sign. Such contracts usually are written by lawyers who have the publisher's best interests in mind, not the author's. If you're an author, be aware that many of the provisions in such agreements normally are subject to negotiation. The topic of author-publisher contract negotiations is beyond the scope of this book. Excellent sources on this topic include:

- *The ASJA Handbook*, by the American Society of Journalists and Authors, Inc. (This 42-page pamphlet can be obtained directly from the ASJA, 1501 Broadway, Ste. 302, New York, NY, 10036, 212-997-0947, www.asja.org.) Contains a recommended standard letter of agreement between a freelancer and a magazine, the ASJA's code of ethics, and chapters on selling books and articles.
- *The Writer's Legal Companion*, by Bunnin and Beren (Addison-Wesley). A good discussion of book and magazine contracts with sample forms; also covers libel, slander, and invasion of privacy issues.
- *Kirsch's Handbook of Publishing Law*, by Jonathan Kirsch (Acrobat Books), contains a very thorough discussion of publishing contracts and an annotated sample form.

Sample contracts and useful advice on all aspects of publishing (including finding a good agent) can also be obtained from the following writers' groups:

- The Authors Guild, Inc., 31 E. 28th St., 10th Floor, New York, NY 10016, 212-563-5904. The Guild publishes an extensively annotated sample trade book contract available only to Guild members. There is a publication requirement for membership.
- The National Writers Union, 113 University Place, 6th Floor, New York, NY 10003, 212-254-0279, www.nwu.org. This national writers' organization has no publication requirement for membership.

Minimum provisions transfer agreement must contain

If you encounter a situation where you need to draft your own transfer agreement, there are certain basic requirements that must be satisfied. To be valid, an exclusive license or assignment must be in writing and signed by the owner of the right(s) being transferred. However, in the case of a transfer between an employer and employee, the agreement must be signed by both parties.

A transfer agreement can take many forms. It may be a formal contract, a letter signed by an author, or a signed memorandum. It makes no difference if a transfer agreement is called an assignment, a license, a contract, a grant of rights, or nothing at all. The effect of the agreement is determined according to the language it contains.

Whatever a transfer agreement is called, it is important that it be accurate and complete. Listed below are the minimum provisions a transfer agreement normally must contain to be legally binding:

- The names and addresses of the copyright owner and person or entity acquiring the copyright right(s).
- A description of what rights are being transferred in what work. If the copyright owner is transferring all his rights, the following phrase may be used: "John Smith hereby transfers [or assigns] all his right, title, and interest in the novel entitled *Greed* to Mary Jones for the full copyright term." If less than the entire bundle of copyright rights is being transferred, the agreement must clearly state which right(s) are involved.

EXAMPLE: Millie, a beginning freelance writer, writes an article on dog training. Desperate to sell her work, Millie grants *Dog's Life Magazine* all world rights. One year after the article is published, Millie contacts *Dog's Life* and asks them to reassign the rights in the article to her so she can use it in a book she's writing on dog training. The *Dog's Life* editor agrees to do so for a nominal sum and tells Millie to send her a transfer agreement to sign. Millie drafts the following copyright assignment.

Copyright Assignment

Dog's Life Magazine, Inc., for value received, grants to Millie Vanilly all right, title, and interest in the copyrightable work described as follows: the article "Dog Do's and Don'ts," published in the Nov. 30, 20xx issue of *Dog's Life Magazine* at pp. 34-39.

Dog's Life Magazine

____

Edith Editor
Editor-in-Chief, *Dog's Life Magazine*
April 1, 20xx
100 Park Avenue, New York, NY 10010

____

Millie Vanilly
March 25, 20xx
10529 Grub St., Marred Vista, CA 90000

The text of this Copyright Assignment Agreement is on the CD-ROM.

EXAMPLE: Assume that *Dog's Life Magazine* in the above example refuses to grant Millie the entire copyright in her story. Instead, it agrees to give her only a nonexclusive license to use the story in her book on dog training. This means that *Dog's Life Magazine* retains all other rights in the story and can reprint it or sell it to others. *Dog's Life's* editor drafts the copyright license on the next page for Millie to sign

Copyright License

Dog's Life Magazine, Inc., for value received, grants to Millie Vanilly an

- ☐ exclusive license
- ☐ nonexclusive license to
- ☐ reproduce
- ☐ distribute
- ☐ create derivative works from
- ☐ publicly perform
- ☐ publicly display

the following copyrightable Work: the article "Dog Do's and Don'ts," published in the Nov. 30, 20xx issue of *Dog's Life Magazine* at pp. 34-39.

Millie Vanilly may sublicense the rights granted in this agreement without *Dog's Life Magazine* written consent.

This license is made subject to the following terms and conditions: the Work may only be used as part of the book by Millie Vanilly tentatively titled "Dog Training Do's and Don'ts," however it may be exploited in any language or medium now known or later invented, including, but not limited to, print, microfilm, and electronic media and in translations in all languages.

Dog's Life Magazine

______________________________ ______________
Edith Editor Date
Editor-in-Chief, *Dog's Life Magazine*
April 1, 20xx
100 Park Avenue, New York, NY 10010

______________________________ ______________
Millie Vanilly Date
March 25, 20xx
10529 Grub St., Marred Vista, CA 90000

The text of this Copyright License Agreement is on the CD-ROM.

Copies. You should have the transferor sign three original transfer documents: one for him, one for you, and one to record with the Copyright Office.

This section describes the minimum provisions a transfer document must contain to be legally valid. Unlike the examples, most publishing contracts contain many additional provisions that have nothing to do with copyright—for instance, provisions regarding royalties, delivery of manuscript, a warranties and indemnities clause, and many others.

Marriage, Divorce, and Copyright Ownership

Like everybody else, writers and other copyright owners get married and get divorced. A copyright is an item of personal property that must be given to one spouse or the other, or somehow shared, upon divorce. Every state has a set of laws about how property acquired or created by married persons is owned and divided upon divorce. These laws vary greatly from state to state. This section highlights some basic principles. You'll need to consult an attorney to answer specific questions about how the laws of your state operate.

Copyrights as Community Property

Nine states have community property laws: Arizona, California, Idaho, Louisiana, Nevada, New Mexico, Texas, Washington, and Wisconsin (in all but name). Under these laws, unless they agree otherwise, a husband and wife automatically become *joint owners* of most types of property they acquire during their marriage. Property acquired before or after marriage is separately owned.

A court in the most populous community property state—California—has held that a copyright acquired by one spouse during marriage is community property—that is, is jointly owned by both spouses. (*Marriage of Worth,* 195 Cal.App.3d 768, 241 Cal. Rptr. 135 (1987).) This means that if you are married and reside in California (or later move there), any work you have created or will create automatically would be owned jointly by you and your spouse *unless you agree otherwise* (see below). This amounts to a transfer of copyright ownership by operation of law.

> **EXAMPLE:** Emily and Robert are married and live in California. Emily writes a novel. Unless they agree otherwise, Robert automatically acquires an undivided one-half interest in the copyright the moment the work is created.

A court in Louisiana has held that copyrights are not community property in that state. (*Rodrigue v. Rodrigue,* 50 U.S.P.Q.2d

1278 (E.D. La. 1999).) Courts in the other seven community property states have yet to consider whether copyrights are community property. No one knows whether they will follow California's lead. If you're married and reside in Arizona, Idaho, Nevada, New Mexico, Texas, Washington, or Wisconsin, the most prudent approach is to assume that the copyright in any protectible work you create during marriage is community property. However, check with a family law or copyright lawyer familiar with the laws of your state before taking any action.

The following discussion briefly highlights the effect of according copyrights community property status in California.

Right to control copyrights

Normally, *either* spouse is entitled to sell community property (which would include a copyright) without the other's consent. But the profits from such a sale would themselves be community property (that is, jointly owned). The rule is different, however, as to gifts: Neither spouse can give away community property without the other's consent. However, a special provision of California law (Civil Code § 5125(d)) provides that a spouse who operates a business has the primary management and control of that business and its assets. In most cases, a married professional writer would probably be considered to be operating a business and would therefore have primary management and control over any work he or she creates (the business's assets).

This means that a married professional writer may transfer all or part of the copyright in a work he or she creates during marriage without his or her spouse's consent and/or signature on any contract. However, the author is legally required to give his or her spouse prior written notice of such transfers (but failure to do so only results in giving the nonauthor spouse the right to demand an accounting of the profits from the transfer).

When a spouse dies

Under California law (Probate Code § 201.5), each spouse may will a one-half interest in their community property to whomever they choose; this would include, of course, their interest in any community property copyright. If a spouse dies without a will, the surviving spouse acquires all the deceased spouse's community property.

Division of copyrights at divorce

When a California couple gets divorced, they are legally entitled to arrange their own property settlement, jointly dividing their property as they wish. If, however, they can't reach an agreement and submit the dispute to the court, a judge will divide the community property equally. A judge would have many options as how to divide community property copyrights—for example, she could award all the copyrights to one spouse and give the other cash or other community property of equal value; if there were, say, ten copyrights of equal value, she could give five to one spouse and five to the other; or the judge could permit each spouse to separately administer their one-half interest in all the copyrights.

Changing marital ownership of copyrights by contract

Property acquired during marriage by California residents does not *have* to be community property. Spouses are free to agree either before or during marriage that all or part of their property will be separately owned. Such an agreement must be in writing and signed by the spouse giving up his or her community property interest; in some cases, it is desirable for the spouse giving up the interest to consult a lawyer. This is something a husband and wife must discuss and decide on their own; we're not advising you to take any particular action. For detailed discussion, see *Prenuptial Agreements: How to Write a Fair & Lasting Contract*, by Shae Irving (Nolo).

Equitable Distribution States

All states other than the nine community property states listed above (with the exception of Mississippi) employ equitable distribution principles when dividing property at divorce. Equitable distribution is a principle under which assets (including copyrights) acquired during marriage are divided equitably (fairly) at divorce. In theory, equitable means equal, or nearly so. In some equitable distribution states, however, if a spouse obtains a fault divorce, the guilty spouse may receive less than an equal share of the marital property. Check with a family law attorney in your state for details.

Recording Copyright Transfers With the Copyright Office

The Copyright Office does not make or in any way participate in transfers of copyright ownership. But the office does *record* transfer documents after they have been signed by the parties. When a transfer document is recorded, a copy is placed in the Copyright Offices files, indexed, and made available for public inspection. This is similar to what happens when a deed to a house or other real estate is recorded with a county recorder's office. Recordation of transfer documents is not mandatory, but it results in so many valuable benefits that it is almost always a good idea.

Why Record a Copyright Transfer?

Because a copyright is intangible and can be transferred simply by signing a piece of paper, it is possible for dishonest copyright owners to rip off copyright purchasers.

> **EXAMPLE:** Carol signs a contract transferring the exclusive right to publish her novel, *The Goniff*, to Scrivener & Sons. Two months later, Carol sells the same rights in the novel to Acme Press. Acme had no idea that Carol had already sold the same rights to Scrivener. Carol has sold the same property twice! As a result, if Scrivener and Acme both publish the book, they'll be competing against each other (and they'll both probably be able to sue Carol for breach of contract, fraud, and other causes of action).

The Difference Between Recordation and Registration

As described in detail in Chapter 4, copyright registration is a legal formality by which an author or other copyright owner fills out a registration application for a published or unpublished work and submits it to the Copyright Office along with one or two copies of the work. If the copyright examiner is satisfied that the work contains protected expression and the application is completed correctly, the work is registered—that is, assigned a registration number, indexed, and filed in the Copyright Office's records. The copies are retained for five years. Recordation does not involve submitting copies of a work. Recordation simply means that the Copyright Office files a document so that it is available for public inspection. As mentioned above, this can be any document relating to copyright. It can be for a work that is published, unpublished, or even not yet written. A good way to distinguish the two procedures is to remember that written works containing protected expression are registered, while contracts or other documents relating to the copyright in a work are recorded.

Recordation of transfer documents protects copyright transferees from these and other abuses by establishing the legal priorities between copyright transferees if the transferor makes overlapping or confusing grants. Recordation also establishes a public record of the contents of transfer documents. This enables prospective purchasers of copyright rights to search the Copyright Office's transfer records to make sure that the copyright seller really owns what she's selling (this is similar to the title search that a homebuyer conducts before purchasing a house). Finally, recordation of a transfer document for a registered work gives the entire world constructive notice of the transfer; constructive notice means everyone is deemed to know about the transfer, whether or not they really do.

What Can Be Recorded?

Any document pertaining to a copyright can be recorded with the Copyright Office. Of course, this includes any document transferring all or part of a copyright—whether it be an exclusive license or assignment. It also includes nonexclusive licenses, wills, powers of attorney in which authors or other copyright owners give others the power to act for them, and other contracts dealing with a copyrighted work.

You can record a document without registering the work it pertains to, but important benefits are obtained if the work is registered. You can even record a document for a work that doesn't exist because it has yet to be written—for example, a publishing contract.

Effect of Recordation on Copyright Conflicts

So what happens when an unethical (or awfully forgetful) author or publisher transfers the same copyright right(s) to different persons or entities? The rules of priority for copyright transfers may be summarized as follows:

- As between two conflicting transfers of exclusive rights to a work that has been *registered with the Copyright Office*, the first transfer is always entitled to priority over the later transfer if it was recorded first.
- But even if the second transfer is recorded first, the first transfer is still entitled to protection if it's recorded *within one month* after it is signed (two months if signed outside the U.S.).
- However, if the first transfer is recorded more than one month after it's signed (or not recorded at all), the transfer that is recorded first is entitled to protection (even if it was the second one granted). (This rule does not apply if the second transfer was a gift or bequest—that is, inherited through a will.)
- But the later transfer is entitled to protection only so long as it was made in good faith and without knowledge of the earlier transfer.

A subsequent transferee will always lose out to a prior transferee who records first because such recordation gives the later transferee (and everyone else in the world) constructive notice of the prior transfer—that is, the second transferee is deemed to know about the earlier transfer whether or not he really did. This means that the second transferee cannot claim that he recorded the later transfer without knowledge of the earlier transfer.

EXAMPLE 1: Naomi writes a novel which she registers with the Copyright Office. Naomi sells the North American publication rights to the novel to Repulsive Publications on July 1. One week later, she sells the same rights to Acme Books. Assume that Repulsive recorded its transfer agreement from Naomi on August 2. Acme records its transfer agreement on August 3. Who is entitled to publish Naomi's novel? Repulsive. The first transfer is always entitled to priority if the work has been registered and the first transfer is recorded first.

EXAMPLE 2: Assume instead that Acme records its transfer agreement from Naomi on July 10. Acme did not know about the prior transfer from Naomi to Repulsive and acted in good faith. Repulsive did not record its transfer agreement until July 30. Who has the exclusive right to publish Naomi's novel? Still Repulsive. Since Repulsive recorded its transfer agreement within 30 days of the July 1 transfer, it prevails over Acme regardless of when Acme recorded.

EXAMPLE 3: Assume the same facts as in Example 2 except that Repulsive waited until August 15 to record, while Acme recorded in good faith on July 10. Who prevails? Acme. Since Repulsive waited more than 30 days to record, the first transferee to record prevails regardless of when the transfer itself was made.

EXAMPLE 4: Assume the same facts as in Example 3, except that Acme actually knew about Naomi's prior transfer to Repulsive (Naomi told them). In this event, Repulsive would prevail regardless of when it recorded.

You wouldn't buy a house or other real estate without conducting a title search. Likewise, you shouldn't spend a substantial sum to purchase all or part of a copyright without searching the Copyright Office's records to make sure the transferor owns what he's selling. See Chapter 10, Copyright Duration, for a discussion of how to search the Copyright Office's records. Take careful note, however, that such searches are not foolproof. As discussed above, under the priority rules, a transferee who records within one month after the transfer is signed (two months if signed abroad) has priority over all subsequent transfers even if they were recorded earlier. Thus, a person who received a transfer less than one month before you (two months if the transfer document was signed outside the U.S.) will have priority over you even if she records after you, provided that she records within one month after the transfer to her.

Transfers of Unregistered Works

What happens if conflicting transfers are made of a work that has not been registered? Until the work is registered, no transferee has legal priority over any other transferee.

EXAMPLE: Fouad signs a contract with ABC Publications to write a college textbook on Middle Eastern politics, and assigns ABC exclusive worldwide publication rights in all languages. One week later he signs an agreement to write an identical book for XYZ Publications and assigns them worldwide publication rights. When Fouad finishes writing the book, who owns the publication rights, ABC or XYZ? They both do until the book is registered and a transfer document is recorded. But the first one to register and record will have priority over the other. The publisher without priority may not publish Fouad's book but can probably sue him for breach of contract, fraud, and other causes of action.

Priority When a Copyright Transfer and a Written Nonexclusive License Conflict

What happens if a copyright owner grants a nonexclusive license to exercise some of his copyright rights, but later transfers those same rights (or all his exclusive copyright rights) to B? B now owns the rights A has a nonexclusive license to use. May A continue to rely on the nonexclusive license, or must he seek a new nonexclusive license from B? Luckily for nonexclusive licensees, there is a special statute giving them priority over later conflicting transfers of ownership. As long as a nonexclusive license is (1) in writing and (2) signed by the licensor, it prevails over a conflicting transfer if either of the following is true:

- The license was taken before the conflicting transfer was signed.
- The license was taken in good faith before recordation of the transfer and without notice of it.

EXAMPLE 1: Sue obtains permission from John to quote several lengthy passages from a book John has written. John signs a written nonexclusive license. A week later, John sells all his copyright rights in the book to Acme Publications. Sue may continue to quote from John's book; she need not obtain Acme's permission to do so. Her written nonexclusive license has *priority* over John's subsequent transfer to Acme.

EXAMPLE 2: Change facts: Assume that John transferred all his copyright rights in his book to Acme. However, before Acme records the transfer agreement, John grants the nonexclusive license to Sue. John does not tell Sue about the prior transfer to Acme, and she knows nothing about it. Sue's nonexclusive license still has priority.

How to Record Transfer Documents (or Other Documents Pertaining to Copyright)

To record a document with the Copyright Office, you must complete and sign the Copyright Office "Document Cover Sheet" form and send it to the Copyright Office along with the document and recordation fee.

If the work involved hasn't already been registered with the Copyright Office, it should be at the same time the document is recorded.

Step 1: Complete the Document Cover Sheet

First, complete and sign the Document Cover Sheet. A copy of the form is included on the CD-ROM at the back of the book that you can complete on your computer and then print out. You can also download the form from the Copyright Office website at www.lcweb.loc.gov/copyright or obtain a copy directly from the Copyright Office by calling the Copyright Office's Forms Hotline at 202-707-9100.

Here's how to fill out the form.

Space 1: First party given in the document

In Space 1, you must list the name of the first party listed in the document being recorded.

Space 2: First title given in the document

List here the title of the work you're recording even if you're recording more than one work.

Document Cover Sheet

UNITED STATES COPYRIGHT OFFICE

For Recordation of Documents

Volume ______ Document ______

Volume ______ Document ______

Date of Recordation M ______ D ______ Y ______
(ASSIGNED BY THE COPYRIGHT OFFICE)

Funds Received ______

Copyright Office fees are subject to change. For current fees check the Copyright Office website at *www.copyright.gov*, write to the Copyright Office, or call (202) 707-3000.

DO NOT WRITE ABOVE THIS LINE · SEE INSTRUCTIONS ON REVERSE

To the Register of Copyrights: *Please record the accompanying original document or properly certified copy thereof.*

1 First party name given in the document ______
(IMPORTANT: *Please read instruction for this and other spaces.*)

2 First title given in the document ______

3 Total number of titles in the document ______

4 Amount of fee calculated ______

5 Fee enclosed ☐ Check ☐ Money order
☐ Fee authorized to be charged to Copyright Office Deposit Account

Deposit Account number ______

Deposit Account name ______

6 Completeness of document ☐ Document is complete by its own terms ☐ Document is not complete. Record "as is."

IMPORTANT NOTE: *A request to record a document "as is" under 37 CFR §201.4(c)(2) is an assertion that: (a) the attachment is completely unavailable for recordation; (b) the attachment is not essential to the identification of the subject matter of the document; and (c) it would be impossible or wholly impracticable to have the parties to the document sign or initial a deletion of the reference to the attachment.*

7 Certification of Photocopied Document Complete this certification if a photocopy of the original signed document is substituted for a document bearing the actual original signature.
NOTE: *This space* may not *be used for documents that require an official certification.*

I declare under penalty of perjury that the accompanying document is a true and correct copy of the original document.

Signature ______ Date ______

Duly authorized agent of ______

8 Return to: Name ______

Number/Street ______ Apt/Suite ______

City ______ State ______ Zip ______

Phone number ______ Fax number ______

Email ______

SEND TO: *Library of Congress, Copyright Office, Documents Recordation Section, LM-462, 101 Independence Avenue SE, Washington, DC 20559-6000*
INCLUDE ALL THESE TOGETHER: (1) Two copies of this form; (2) payment from a Deposit Account or by check/money order payable to *Register of Copyrights*; and (3) your document.

DOCUMENT COVER SHEET PRINT REV: 01/2005—60,000 WEB REV: 01/2005 Printed on recycled paper U.S. Government Printing Office: 2004-310-462/60,096

Space 3: Total number of title(s) in the document

List the total number of titles to be recorded. This is needed to determine the recordation fee (and will be verified by the Copyright Office).

Space 4: Amount of fee calculated

State the amount of the recordation fee. The Copyright Office charges a $95 fee to record a transfer document covering one title. For additional titles, there is an added charge of $25 for each group of up to ten titles—for example, it would cost $120 to record 11 titles, $145 to record 21 titles, and so forth.

Space 5: Fee enclosed

In Space 5, indicate the method of payment.

Space 6: Completeness of document

A document being recorded with the Copyright Office should be complete on its own terms. At a minimum, it should contain (1) the names and addresses of the copyright owner(s) and person(s) or entity acquiring the copyright right(s) and (2) a description of the rights that are being transferred. The transfer document must also be signed by the transferor. See "Transfer Documents," above, for a detailed discussion. The Copyright Office will not examine your document to see if it meets these requirements. It will be recorded whether it does or not. However, if it doesn't, it may not be legally effective. If your document meets these requirements, check the first box in Space 6. If not, and you want it recorded anyway, check the second box instructing the Copyright Office to record it as-is.

Space 7: Certification of Photocopied Document

If you are submitting a photocopy, you must sign under penalty of perjury that what you have submitted is a true copy of the original.

Space 8: Return to:

Here you list your mailing address and relevant contact information.

Step 2: Send your recordation package to the Copyright Office

You need to send all the following to the Copyright Office in one package:

- the original signed Document Cover Sheet and one copy
- the proper recordation fee in a check or money order payable to the Register of Copyrights (unless you have a deposit account), and
- the document to be recorded.

Send your package to:

Documents Unit, LM-462
Cataloging Division
Copyright Office
Library of Congress
Washington, DC 20559

Within six to eight weeks, you should receive a Certificate of Recordation from the Copyright Office showing that your transfer document (or nonexclusive license) has been recorded. The original signed transfer document (or nonexclusive license) will be returned with the certificate.

■

CHAPTER

10 Copyright Duration

Copyright protection doesn't last forever, but it lasts long enough to benefit many people besides the author, potentially including children, grandchildren, great-grandchildren, publishers, agents, and other people and businesses who may have acquired an interest in the copyright.

No matter how many times a copyright is transferred, its duration does not change. The duration is determined by who the original author was and how long he or she lives or, in some cases, by the date the work was created or first published.

When a work's copyright expires, it enters the public domain; in effect, it belongs to everybody. Anyone is free to use it without asking permission, but no one can ever own it again. However, in 1998 Congress enacted the Sonny Bono Copyright Term Extension Act, which extended all copyright terms by 20 years. As explained below, one result of this law is that no new published works will enter the public domain until the year 2019.

Samuel Langhorne Clemens

Works Created During or After 1978

The great divide in determining a copyright's duration is the date January 1, 1978. The copyright in works created on or after that date usually lasts for the life of the author(s) plus 70 years. Works created before that date have a very different duration.

Single Author Works: Life Plus 70 Years

As discussed in Chapter 2, Copyright Basics, copyright protection begins when a work is created—that is, when it is written down or otherwise fixed in a tangible form. Unless one of the exceptions discussed below applies, the copyright in a work created by a single individual author on or after January 1, 1978 lasts for the life of the author plus an additional 70 years. This means, at the very least, that the copyright in an individually authored work lasts 70 years. And the copyright in a work by a young author could easily last 100 years or more, depending of course on how long the author lives.

> **EXAMPLE 1:** Bill has a fatal heart attack just as he finishes writing his epic novel on ancient Sparta. The novel's copyright will last for 70 years after Bill's death.

> **EXAMPLE 2:** Natalie completes her own epic novel on ancient Sparta when she is 30 years old. If she ends up living to 80, the copyright in her novel will last for 120 years.

Drafts and uncompleted works

Copyright doesn't just protect finished works; it also protects drafts and uncompleted works. Each draft of a work created over a period of time by an individual author is protected for the life-plus-70-year term. A work that is never completed is entitled to the same period of protection.

Works Made for Hire

As discussed in detail in Chapter 8, Initial Copyright Ownership, a work made for hire is a work created by an employee as part of his job or a work that is specially ordered or commissioned pursuant to a written work-for-hire contract. The copyright in a work made for hire lasts for 95 years from the date of its *first publication*, or 120 years from the date of its *creation*, whichever comes first. (A work is published when it is made freely available to the public; see Chapter 2, Copyright Basics, for a definition of publish.)

This means that if there were a 30-year delay between creation and publication, the copyright would last for 120 years. For example, if a work for hire was created in 2000 but not published until 2030, the copyright would expire soonest by using the 120-year-from-creation term—that is, the copyright would expire in 2120. If the 95-years-from-publication term were applied, the copyright wouldn't expire until the year 2125. Any delay between creation and publication of less than 25 years would mean that the 95-years-from-publication term should be applied, since this would result in the shortest period of copyright protection. For example, a five-year delay would result in a 95-year-from-publication term. But, if creation and publication occur within the same calendar year, as they usually do, the copyright in a work made for hire lasts for 95 years.

Joint Author Works

As discussed in detail in Chapter 8, Initial Copyright Ownership, a joint work is a work authored by two or more persons on their own behalf (that is, not a work made for hire). The copyright in a joint work lasts for the life of the last surviving author plus 70 years.

> **EXAMPLE:** Joseph Herodotus and Mary Thucydides write a history of the Persian Gulf War. Herodotus dies soon thereafter. The copyright in the work will last for the rest of Thucydides' life plus 70 more years.

If a work is created by two or more persons who work for hire, the 95- or 120-year work-made-for-hire term discussed above, applies.

> **EXAMPLE:** Two editors employed by Acme Press and two employed by Scrivener & Sons jointly author a book on publishing for their employers. The book is a joint work, co-owned by Acme and Scrivener, but the work-made-for-hire copyright term applies.

Sometimes, a work will be jointly created both by people who work for hire and people who don't. It's not exactly clear whether the life-plus-70 or work-for-hire term should apply in these situations. The Registrar of Copyrights has suggested that the life-plus-70 term should apply if at least two of the work's creators did not work for hire. It's likely the courts will adopt this rule.

> **EXAMPLE:** Acme Press has two of its editors collaborate on a book with two freelance writers. The contributions by Acme's editors are works made for hire. The contributions by the two freelancers are not works made for hire. Since two of the authors did not work for hire, the life-plus-70 rule should apply according to the Registrar of Copyrights. That is, the copyright in the work would last for the life of the last surviving freelancer plus 70 years.

What if a work is created by one or more people who work for hire and only *one* person who does not work for hire? The Registrar of Copyrights suggests that in this situation whatever copyright term is longer —life-plus-70 or the work-for-hire term— should apply.

> **EXAMPLE:** Assume that two editors employed by Acme Press and only one freelance writer write a book together. Again, the editors' contributions are works made for hire, while the freelancer's contribution is not a work made for hire. According to the Registrar of Copyrights, the copyright in the book should last for the longer of the work-made-for-hire terms or 70 years after the freelancer dies.

Anonymous and Pseudonymous Works

Obviously, there is no identified author with an interest in the copyright of an anonymous or pseudonymous work. This makes it impractical to measure the duration of the copyright against the life of the author. This means that, as with works made for hire, there is a copyright term of 95 years from the date of first publication of an anonymous or pseudonymous work, or 120 years from the date of its creation, whichever comes first.

Changing the term to life plus 70 by making identity known to Copyright Office

If the identity of the author of an anonymous or pseudonymous work is officially made known to the Copyright Office before the 95- or 120-year term expires, the copyright term changes to the life of the author plus 70 years (the same as if the true author's name had been on the copyright to begin with). Note, however, that this won't necessarily be longer than a 95- or 120-year term; it all depends on how long the author lives after the work was published.

Any person who owns all or part of the copyright in a pseudonymous or anonymous work may notify the Copyright Office of the author's true identity. This may be done by registering the work under the author's true name or, if the work has already been registered, by filing a supplementary registration with the Copyright Office. Copyright registration is discussed in Chapter 4, supplemental registration in Chapter 5.

Alternatively, it is possible to record (file) a statement with the Copyright Office setting forth the following:

- the name of the person filing the statement
- the nature of the person's interest in the copyright
- the title of the particular work affected, and
- the copyright registration number, if known.

The Copyright Office requires payment of a $95 fee to record the statement. (See Chapter 9, Transferring Copyright Ownership, for a detailed discussion of how to record documents with the Copyright Office.)

> **EXAMPLE:** Harold Lipshitz writes a detective novel under the pseudonym "Mike Danger." The book is published the same year Harold wrote it, so the copyright will last for 95 years unless Harold notifies the Copyright Office of his true identity. Harold gets to thinking: He was only 25 when he wrote the novel and his parents both lived well into their 80s, so he figures his copyright would last much longer than 95 years under the normal life-plus-70 years term. Harold sends the Copyright Office the following notice.

Sample Letter to Copyright Office

Register of Copyrights
Library of Congress
Washington, DC 20559

RE: Copyright Registration TX01234567

Dear Register:

I am writing regarding copyright registration #TX01234567, registered on 1-1-00. This work is a novel registered under the title *And Then You Die*. It is registered under the pseudonymous authorship of "Mike Danger." This is to inform you that I, Harold Lipshitz, am the author and owner of the copyright in this work. Please record this notice. A check for $80 is enclosed for the recordation fee.

Very truly yours,
Harold Lipshitz
Harold Lipshitz

If an individual author is very ill or rather elderly and not likely to live 25 years after his work is published, the work would probably receive longer copyright protection under the 95-year term for anonymous or pseudonymous works or works made for hire than under the normal life plus 70 years copyright term. The copyright term would also probably last longer if the work was written with a younger collaborator—that is, the copyright would last for 70 years after the last collaborator died. Does this mean that elderly authors should write anonymously or under a pseudonym, or, if possible, characterize their works as works made for hire or write them with youthful collaborators? In most cases, no. Very few works have a useful economic life of more than 70 years. Thus, the life-plus-70 term is usually more than adequate.

End of Calendar Year Rule

All copyright durations run until the end of the calendar year in which they would otherwise expire. For example, the copyright in a work made for hire that was first published in 2000 would expire on December 31, 2095, regardless of what month and day during 2000 it was published. Similarly, if the individual author of a work published in 1979 died in 1980, the copyright in the work would expire on December 31, 2050, regardless of the month and day of his death.

Works Created but Not Published or Registered Before January 1, 1978

With one important exception, works created before January 1, 1978, but not published or registered with the Copyright Office, are subject to the same basic copyright duration rules as those created after January 1, 1978. That is, the copyright lasts for the life of an individual author plus 70 years, or 95 or 120 years (from publication and creation, respectively) for a work made for hire or for a pseudonymous or anonymous work.

EXAMPLE: Louisa, a well-known novelist, dies in 2000 leaving behind an unpublished manuscript written in 1977. The copyright in the manuscript will last until 2070 (70 years after Louisa's death).

Given the above rule, you'd naturally assume that all unpublished works created by authors who had been dead more than 70 years on January 1, 1978 automatically entered the public domain on that date. However, this did not occur. A special rule provided that the copyright in an unpublished work created before January 1, 1978 could not expire until January 1, 2003 no matter when the author died.

Moreover, if such a work was published between January 1, 1978 and January 1, 2003, the copyright cannot expire before December 31, 2047. This is so regardless of when the author died.

EXAMPLE: Samuel, a Revolutionary War historian, finds an unknown and unpublished diary written by George Washington in 1790. Since the diary was never published (or registered with the Copyright Office), it automatically remained under copyright until December 31, 2002, even though Washington died in 1799. Samuel had the diary published in 2002. As a result, its copyright was automatically extended until December 31, 2047. The copyright in the diary is owned by whoever inherited Washington's papers, not by Samuel.

Because of these rules, recently discovered unpublished manuscripts by Jane Austen and Mark Twain were protected by copyright in the United States (but no other country). This is so even though Austen died in 1817 and Twain in 1910. The works have since been published and will be protected through December 31, 2047.

On January 1, 2003, all unpublished works by all authors who died during 1932 or earlier entered the public domain. On January 1 of every year thereafter another year's worth of unpublished works will also enter the public domain. That is, on January 1, 2004, unpublished works by authors who died during 1933 entered the public domain; on January 1, 2005, unpublished works by authors who died during 1934 entered the public domain, and so on.

In the case of unpublished works made for hire created before 1978 (works created by employees as part of their jobs or works for which a work-made-for-hire agreement was signed), the copyright lasts 120 years from the date of creation. So, all unpublished works made for hire created

Preventing Unpublished Works From Entering the Public Domain

If you own the copyright in an unpublished work created by an author who died more than 70 years ago, it's too late to save such a work's copyright. It is in the public domain. If you own an unpublished work created by a deceased author whose 70th year after death is approaching, you must publish it no later than the end of that 70th year. For example, if you own an unpublished work by an author who died during 1940, you must publish it by December 31, 2010. If you own an unpublished work by an author who died during 1941, you must publish it by December 31, 2011, and so on. It's not difficult to publish a work for copyright purposes. You don't have to have a publisher distribute it, though this would certainly qualify as publication. You just have to make copies available to the general public—for example, handing out copies on a street corner would constitute publication.

Does simply placing a work on the Internet constitute publication for copyright purposes? It's unclear, but it might not. Here is one way to definitely publish something by using the Internet. Put up a website (or use a site you already have) with a notice offering to email a copy of the work to anyone who wants one. You can charge for the copy or offer it for free, it makes no difference for publication purposes. The offer to email copies of the work to the general public constitutes a publication for copyright purposes. However, just to be on the safe side, you may want to actually email copies to a few people—four or five is plenty; these can be friends and associates. Keep copies of the emails and the website containing the notice in a safe place.

before 1883 entered the public domain on January 1, 2003. Every year thereafter, another year's worth of works for hire enter the public domain—for example, on January 1, 2004, all unpublished works made for hire created during 1883 entered the public domain; on January 1, 2005, all unpublished works for hire created during 1884 entered the public domain; and so on. This rule also applies to unpublished pseudonymous and anonymous works.

If you're the heir or transferee of a relatively unknown author who has been dead less than 70 years, and you're afraid people might think he or she has been dead more than 70 years, you can simply send a letter to the Copyright Office stating when the author died. This will prevent anyone from presuming that the author's unpublished works are in the public domain.

Works Published or Registered Before January 1, 1978

Determining the copyright term for works created before 1978 can be a complex undertaking. Under the pre-1978 copyright law (called the Copyright Act of 1909), all eligible works enjoyed an initial copyright term of 28 years from the *date of first publication* with a proper copyright notice. Before the end of the first 28 years, they could be renewed for an additional 28-year

Determining When Authors Died

All unpublished works by authors who died during 1932 or earlier are in the public domain. If the author is well known, reference works such as encyclopedias will probably reveal when (or if) he or she died. The website www.biography.com provides this information for over 25,000 people.

However, it may be difficult to determine when a particularly obscure or unknown author died. Fortunately, the Copyright Office has had a procedure in place since 2003 which allows you to safely assume that a work is in the public domain even if it's not possible to determine when the author died. The Copyright Office is required to maintain records indicating the date of an author's death or containing information that an author was alive on a certain date. Once an unpublished work becomes 100 years old you are legally entitled to assume that the work is in the public domain if you obtain a certified report from the Copyright Office indicating that nothing in its records shows that the author has been dead for less than 70 years. If it later turns out that the author in fact died less than 70 years ago, the existence of the report is a complete defense to any claim of copyright infringement. However, there is one exception: You are required to act in good faith. If you knew all along that the author died less than 70 years ago, you are not entitled to rely on such a Copyright Office report.

term by filing a renewal registration with the Copyright Office. This second term is called the renewal term.

This sounds pretty simple, but things get more complicated. The renewal term for works published before 1978 has been extended an additional 39 years to 67 years (28 + 39 = 67), for a total of 95 years of copyright protection (28 + 67 = 95).

Under the law in effect from 1909 through 1992, the renewal term was not automatic. It could be obtained only by filing a renewal registration with the Copyright Office during the 28th year after a work's publication. As you might expect, many authors failed to timely file a renewal for their work. Indeed, only about 20% of all pre-1978 published works were ever renewed.

This meant that a vast body of work entered the public domain 28 years after publication due to failure to comply with a mere technical formality. This seemed unfair to many people and, as a result, the law was changed in 1992. The new law made copyright renewals automatic—in other words, the 67-year renewal term was obtained whether or not a renewal registration was filed. Renewal registrations were made purely optional—but the law gives copyright owners who file renewal registrations some important benefits we'll discuss below.

The 1992 automatic renewal law applies only to works published between January 1, 1964 and December 31, 1977. Works published during 1923–1963 had to be renewed during the 28th year after publication or they entered the public domain, where they will forever remain.

The following sections provide some general rules that will help you decide whether a work published prior to 1978 is still protected by copyright.

Works Published Before 1923

The copyright for any work published in the U.S. before 1923 has expired. This means that the work is now in the public domain. Anyone can use it without permission or payment, but no one can ever own it.

To determine whether a book or other work was first published before 1923, simply look at the year shown in the work's copyright notice. This should be the same year as the year of first publication.

Works Published 1923–1963

Works published 1923–1963 have already entered the public domain unless a renewal registration was timely filed with the Copyright Office by the end of the initial 28-year term. If it was, the renewal term lasts for 67 years.

> **EXAMPLE 1:** The copyright in a work that was first published in 1932, and timely renewed in 1960, lasts through the end of 2027 (95 years in all).

> **EXAMPLE 2:** The copyright in a work that was first published in 1962, but not timely renewed in 1990, expired

on December 31, 1990 (the end of the initial 28-year term). The work is now in the public domain.

Congress Freezes Public Domain for 20 Years

Under the pre-1998 copyright law, the copyright for pre-1978 published works lasted 75 years from the date of publication. This meant that all works published in 1923 were due to enter the public domain in 1999; those published in 1924 would have become public domain in 2000; those published in 1925 would have become public domain in 2001, and so on every year until all pre-1978 published works entered the public domain. However, in 1998 this process was frozen for 20 years when Congress passed the Sonny Bono Copyright Extension Act. Works published between 1923 and 1978 are now protected for 95 years from the year of publication. This means works published in 1923 won't enter the public domain until 2019, those published in 1924 won't become public domain until 2020, and so on.

The 20-year copyright extension was challenged all the way to the U.S. Supreme Court which held, in a highly publicized decision, that it was constitutional. (*Eldred v. Ashcroft*, 123 S.Ct. 1505 (2003).) Thus, the extension—and the public domain freeze—is here to stay.

How to determine whether a renewal has been timely filed

As these examples illustrate, it is impossible to know how long the copyright in a work published during 1923–1963 will last unless you know whether a renewal registration was timely filed. When a book is reprinted after renewal, the copyright notice usually provides this information. Otherwise you'll need to research the Copyright Office's records to find out if a renewal was timely filed. There are three ways to do this:

1. Have the Copyright Office search its records for you. They charge $150 an hour for this service, and most searches take one hour. Unfortunately, it takes the Copyright Office six to eight weeks to conduct a search and report back to you. You can obtain much faster service for just a few dollars more by using a private search firm as described below. The Copyright Office will conduct an expedited search that takes just five business days, but this costs a minimum of $400. Again, you can obtain faster service for less by using a private search firm.

   If you still want the Copyright Office to do your search, you should call the Reference & Bibliography Section at 202-707-6850 and ask for an estimate of how long they think your search will take. Then, fill out the Search Request Form located on the CD-ROM and send it and a check in the amount of the estimate payable to the Register of Copyrights to:

Reference & Bibliography Section, LM-451
Copyright Office
Library of Congress
Washington, DC 20559

2. Have a professional search firm conduct a search for you. There are several private search firms that conduct copyright renewal searches. They may charge a little more than the Copyright Office, but they usually report back in two to ten working days. For example, Thomson & Thomson, the best known of these firms, charges $100 for a renewal search and will report back in five business days. This is a much better deal than paying $150 to the Copyright Office and having to wait up to two months for the results.

   Following is a list of copyright search firms.

Copyright Resources
616 South Carolina Ave. SE, Suite #1
Washington, DC 20003
202-544-6235
www.copyright-resources.com
email: larhoades@copyright-resources.com

Government Liaison Services, Inc.
3030 Clarendon Blvd., Suite 209
Arlington, VA 22201
800-642-6564 or 703-524-8200
www.trademarkinfo.com

Thomson & Thomson
Copyright Research Group
500 E St. SW, Suite 970
Washington, DC 20024
800-356-8630
www.thomson-thomson.com

3. Search the Copyright Office records yourself. This is relatively easy to do for works published during 1950–1963, because the records are available online at the Copyright Office website at www.copyright.gov. But researching works published during 1923–1950 is much harder, because you must manually search through the *Copyright Office Catalog of Copyright Entries* (*CCE*). This is a monumental series of annual catalogues listing and cross-referencing every work registered and renewed by the Copyright Office. The *CCE* is available to the public at the Copyright Office, located in the James Madison Memorial Building, 101 Independence Ave. SE, Washington, DC. The office is open from 8:30 a.m. to 5:00 p.m. Monday through Friday. The *CCE* can also be found in government depository libraries throughout the country. Portions of the CCE have been copied by private parties and placed online at www.digital.library.upenn.edu/books/cce and www.kingkong.demon.co.uk/ccer/ccer.htm.

For detailed guidance on how to conduct a copyright renewal search, see *The Public Domain: How to Find & Use Copyright-Free Writings, Music, Art & More*, by Stephen Fishman (Nolo).

Copying by libraries during last 20 years of copyright term. Libraries and archives are now permitted to make copies of published works during the last 20 years of their copyright term for the purposes of preservation, scholarship, or research if such works are not commercially available. See Chapter 11, Using Other Authors' Words, for a detailed discussion.

Works Published During 1964–1977

The 67-year renewal term begins automatically for works published between January 1, 1964 and December 31, 1977.

> **EXAMPLE:** Jackie published a novel in 1965. The initial 28-year copyright term for the book expired on December 31, 1993 (28 years after the year of publication). The 67-year renewal term began automatically on January 1, 1994, whether or not Jackie filed a renewal application with the Copyright Office.

However, as discussed below, important benefits can be obtained in some cases by filing an optional renewal registration with the Copyright Office.

Special Rules for Works First Published Abroad Before 1978

There are some special rules for works that were first published outside the U.S. before 1978: They may enjoy a different term of copyright protection and the copyright renewal rules no longer apply to such works.

Copyright Term for Foreign Works

Works published in almost all foreign countries are entitled to copyright protection in the U.S. (See Chapter 13 for a detailed discussion of international copyright protection.) Such works enjoy the same term of protection as works published in the U.S., with one possible exception.

The exception is that works published in a foreign country between July 1, 1909

Copyright Duration Chart

Date and Nature of Work	Copyright Term
Published before 1923	The work is in the public domain
Published 1923–1963 and never renewed	The work is in the public domain
Published 1923–1963 and timely renewed	95 years from the date of first publication
Published between 1964 and 1977	95 years from the date of publication (renewal term automatic)
Created, but not published or registered, before 1978	Single term of 120 years from creation for unpublished works made for hire, and unpublished or pseudonymous works
Created before 1978 and published 1978–2002	Copyright will expire Jan. 1, 2048

and December 31, 1977 *without* a copyright notice do not receive the same term of U.S. copyright protection as other works published before 1978. Instead, they receive the same copyright term as unpublished works: They are protected for the life of the author plus 70 years.

Such works are treated differently than other foreign works because a court has held that such works should not be considered as having acquired protection under the U.S. copyright law in effect at the time. (*Twin Books v. Walt Disney Co.*, 83 F.3d 1162 (9th Cir. 1996).)

> **EXAMPLE:** Jules, a French citizen, wrote a novel that was published in France in 1920. It did not contain a copyright notice. Jules died in 1980. The novel is protected in the U.S. until the year 2050, 70 years after he died.

However, there are two important exceptions to this rule. First, if such an unnoticed work was subsequently published in the U.S. with or without a copyright notice before 1978, it receives the same term of U.S. copyright protection as if it were first published in the U.S. that year.

> **EXAMPLE:** Jim, a German citizen, wrote a play that was published without a copyright notice in Germany in 1960 and subsequently published in the U.S. in 1970. The U.S. copyright in the work lasts for 95 years from 1970, or until 2065.

If the U.S. publication took place before 1923, the work is in the public domain in the U.S. because the copyright has expired.

> **EXAMPLE:** Assume that Jules's novel in the example above was published in the U.S. in 1922. The U.S. copyright in the novel expired in 1997 (75 years after the U.S. publication).

In addition, if the work was republished in a foreign country with a valid copyright notice before 1978, it receives the same term of U.S. copyright protection as if it were first published in the U.S. that year. If the republication took place before 1923, the work's copyright has expired.

> **EXAMPLE:** Felix published a children's book in Germany in 1922 without a copyright notice. The book was republished in Germany in 1930, this time with a valid copyright notice. The book is protected in the U.S. for 95 years from the 1930 publication with notice, or until 2025.

Renewal Not Required for Foreign Works

As a result of the GATT Agreement, an international agreement concerning foreign trade, copyright protection for some foreign works published in the U.S. before 1964 that entered the public domain because no renewal registration was filed has been restored. In other words, these works are no longer in the public domain. Instead, these works receive the same term of copyright protection they would have had if a renewal had been timely filed.

These special rules apply only to works:

- created by authors who were citizens or residents of a country that is a member of one of the major international copyright treaties such as the Berne Copyright Convention, is a member of the World Trade Organization, or has a copyright treaty with the U.S.—which includes almost all the countries of the world (see Chapter 13)
- that, if published, were first published in such a foreign country, but not published in the U.S. within 30 days following the foreign publication, and
- whose copyright protection has not expired under the copyright laws of the foreign country.

EXAMPLE: In 1950, Thames Press, a British publisher, publishes in Great Britain a novel by the English writer John Jones. Thames failed to file a renewal registration for the book in 1978, and, as a result, it entered the public domain in the U.S. on January 1, 1979. However, the U.S. copyright in the book was automatically restored by the GATT Agreement, effective January 1, 1996. This is because the work was written by a British subject and first published in Great Britain, a Berne member, and the British copyright on the book had not expired as of 1996 (British copyrights last for the life of the author plus 70 years). The book receives the same term of copyright protection in the U.S. it would have had had a renewal been timely filed—95 years from the date of publication. The novel will be protected by copyright in the U.S. until December 31, 2045.

Copyright restoration for all foreign works meeting the requirements occurred automatically on January 1, 1996. However, copyright owners of such works can't sue those who used their works without permission before 1996 because they thought they were in the public domain. The copyright owners can only bring infringement actions against those who use their works after January 1, 1996. People who used the works before that date, and continue to use them afterwards, must be given special notice before they can be sued. (See Chapter 13, International Copyright, for a detailed discussion of the impact of the GATT Agreement on U.S. copyright protection for foreign works.)

Duration of Copyright in Adaptations (Derivative Works)

As discussed in detail in Chapter 7, Adaptations and Compilations, a derivative work is a work that transforms or adapts previously existing material into a new work of authorship. A good example is a screenplay based on a novel. The copyright in a derivative work published before 1978 lasts for 95 years from publication if timely renewed, 28 years if not. The copyright in a derivative work created on or after January 1, 1978 lasts for the life of the author plus 70 years, unless it's a work for hire or a pseudonymous or anonymous work as discussed above. The creation of a derivative work has no effect on the duration of the copyright in the preexisting material it incorporates.

> **EXAMPLE:** Barbara writes a screenplay in 2000 based on a novel published by Art in 1980. The copyright in the novel will expire 70 years after Art dies. The copyright in the screenplay will expire 70 years after Barbara dies.

It is quite common for the copyright in the preexisting material to expire long before the copyright in a derivative work based upon it. In this event, others can use the preexisting material to create their own derivative works, or for any other purpose, without asking permission from the owner of the derivative work or anyone else. But others cannot use the material added to the preexisting work by the creator of the derivative work.

> **EXAMPLE:** Leslie purchases the right to create a play based from a novel published by Burt in 1932. She publishes the play in 2000. The copyright in the novel was timely renewed in 1960. Thus, copyright protection for the novel will last until 2027, while the copyright in Leslie's play will last for the rest of her life plus 70 years. After 2027, anyone may write their own play based upon Burt's novel, since it is in the public domain. But, in doing so, they could not copy from Leslie's play without her permission.

Termination of Transfers of Renewal Term Rights in Pre-1978 Works

As discussed above, works first published or registered before 1978 originally had an initial 28-year copyright term and a second 28-year renewal term. However, the renewal term has been extended twice: First, it was extended an additional 19 years to 47 years in 1978; it was then extended by an additional 20 years to 67 years in 1998. This means the owner(s) of the renewal term ownership rights in a pre-1978 work would enjoy 67 years of copyright protection provided the work was timely renewed.

A pre-1978 work's initial and renewal terms are considered to be completely separate. An author may transfer all or part of her copyright ownership rights during her work's renewal term. Such a transfer may be made any time before a work's renewal term actually begins. Indeed, before 1978, authors typically transferred their renewal term rights to their publishers and/or others when they first sold their work. This meant that in most cases publishers and other transferees, not authors or their families, would be entitled to the additional 39 years of copyright protection created by extending the renewal term to 67 years.

The whole purpose of having a renewal term was to give authors and their families a second chance to market their work. Thus, it did not seem fair that publishers should benefit from the extra 39 years added to the renewal term. To prevent this, a special provision of the Copyright Act gives authors or their heirs the right to get those extra 39 years of copyright ownership back by terminating pre-1978 transfers of renewal term rights.

> **EXAMPLE:** Art published a novel in 1952. His publishing contract contained a provision by which he transferred to his publisher his publication rights in the novel for the renewal term. Art's publisher timely filed a renewal application with the Copyright Office in 1980. The renewal term will last for 67 years, until 2047. However, Art or his surviving family can terminate the renewal rights transfer Art made to his publisher in 1952 and get back the publication rights in the novel for the last 39 years of the renewal term—that is, from 2008 until 2047.

The copyright law now gives authors or their heirs two separate chances to get back ownership of their works for all or part of the extra 39 years of copyright protection.

Works Published Less Than 61 Years Ago

A transfer of renewal rights may be terminated at any time during the five-year period beginning 56 years from the date that the work was first published. For example, a renewal rights grant for a work published in 1950 may be terminated any time between January 1, 2006 and December 31, 2011. You should think of this period as a five-year window of opportunity during which you can get back the last 39 years of copyright ownership.

Works Published More Than 61 Years Ago

What if the time period for terminating renewal rights transfers as set forth above has expired and the author or his or her heirs failed to exercise their termination rights? All is not lost. In this event, the author or his or her heirs or executor can terminate the renewal rights transfer for the last 20 years of the 95-year copyright term. To do so, they must act any time during 75 to 80 years after the work was first published. This is a second window of opportunity to get back copyright ownership.

> **EXAMPLE:** Agnes published a novel in 1930. The publishing contract contained a provision transferring her renewal term rights to her publisher. In 1958, the publisher timely renewed the copyright in the novel and owned the renewal term copyright. Agnes could have terminated the renewal term transfer by acting during 1986–1991, but she failed to do so. However, Agnes or her heirs or executor can still terminate the transfer as to the last 20 years of the novel's 95-year copyright. To do so, they must act sometime during 2005–2010—that

is, 75–80 years after the novel was first published.

What to Do

A termination of a pre-1978 transfer of renewal term rights may be accomplished by the author, or by the author's widow or widower, children, or grandchildren. If none of these are living, the termination may be accomplished by the executor or administrator of the author's estate or by the author's personal representative or trustee.

If you are the author of a pre-1978 work that still has value more than 50 years after publication, or the widow, widower, child, or grandchild of such an author, you and/or other family members should consult a copyright attorney some time during the 56th year after publication. She'll be able to determine if a terminable transfer of renewal term copyright ownership rights was made and, if so, help you take the necessary procedural steps to terminate it.

If more than 61 years have elapsed since the work was first published and the renewal rights transfer was never terminated, then calendar a new date—75 years after the work's publication—and see an attorney then.

■

CHAPTER

11 Using Other Authors' Words

To quote is not necessarily stealing. Quotation can be vital to the fulfillment of the public-enriching goals of copyright law.

—Judge Pierre N. Leval

Introduction

This chapter is about using other authors' words. Sooner or later, almost all of us feel the need to quote, closely paraphrase, photocopy, or otherwise use what others have written. Here are some examples:

- Nancy, a book reviewer, quotes several passages from a novel in the context of a published book review.
- Phil, a historian and biographer, quotes from several unpublished letters and diaries written by his subject.
- Regina, a freelance writer, closely paraphrases two paragraphs from the *Encyclopædia Britannica* in an article she's writing.
- Sylvia, a poet, quotes a line from a poem by T.S. Eliot in one of her own poems.
- Kay, a librarian, makes a photocopy of the library's only remaining copy of Stephen King's latest bestseller.
- Arnold, a high school teacher, makes 30 copies of a newspaper article to distribute to his class.

Some of these uses are lawful without obtaining the permission of the owner of the copyrighted material; others would constitute copyright infringement absent the copyright owner's consent. The purpose of this chapter is to enable you to know when permission is and is not required.

Three-Step Analysis to Determine If Permission Is Required

To determine whether you need to obtain permission to use any given item, you need to answer the following three questions. If the answer to all three is yes, you need permission; otherwise, you don't.

Are you taking an author's expression?

You only need permission to use an author's expression—that is, the particular sequence of words an author writes down or otherwise fixes in a tangible form to express her ideas, explain facts, and so on. Ideas and facts themselves are in the public domain, freely available for all to use. This idea-expression dichotomy is discussed in detail in Chapter 6, What Copyright Protects. Review that chapter to determine whether what you want to use is expression. If you're sure it isn't, you don't need permission to use it. If there's any doubt in your mind, however, assume that it is expression and go on to the next question. (Of course, photocopying another author's work always constitutes a taking of that person's expression.)

Is the author's expression protected by copyright?

Not all expression is protected by copyright. Much is in the public domain and may be used freely without seeking anyone's permission. All expression contained in works for which copyright protection has expired is in the public domain. This includes any work published in the U.S. before 1923 and works published during 1923–1963 which have not been timely renewed. Review the discussion of copyright duration and renewal in Chapter 10, Copyright Duration.

In addition, certain types of expression are not entitled to copyright protection at all; this includes, for example, works by U.S. government employees, titles and short phrases, and certain blank forms. (See Chapter 6, What Copyright Protects, for a detailed discussion.)

If the expression is protected by copyright, go on to the next question.

Does your intended use of the protected expression go beyond the bounds of fair use?

You do not need permission to use other authors' protected expression if your use constitutes a fair use. However, permission is required where the intended use of the expression goes beyond the bounds of fair use. The fair use privilege is discussed in detail below. If, after reading that discussion, you decide that your intended use of expression protected by copyright is not a fair use, you must seek permission to use it. The mechanics of seeking permission are discussed in Chapter 16.

Introduction to the Fair Use Privilege

As we discussed in Chapter 1, the purpose of the copyright laws is to advance the progress of knowledge by giving authors an economic incentive to create new works. Authors and their heirs are automatically granted the exclusive right to reproduce, adapt, perform, and display their works for at least 70 (and usually more) years; they are, in effect, granted a monopoly over the use of their work.

However, there are situations where strict enforcement of an author's monopoly would hinder, rather than promote, the growth of knowledge. An obvious example is that of a researcher or scholar whose own work depends on the ability to refer to and quote from prior scholars' work. No author could create a new work if she were first required to repeat the research of every author who had gone before her.

Of course, scholars and researchers could be required to bargain with each copyright owner for permission to quote from or refer to prior works. But this would likely prove so onerous that many scholars would hunt for another line of work, and the progress of knowledge would be greatly impeded.

To avoid these types of results, the fair use privilege was created. Pursuant to the fair use rule, an author is permitted to make *limited* use of a prior author's work without asking permission. All authors and other copyright owners are deemed to give their automatic consent to the fair use of their work by others. The fair use privilege is perhaps the most significant limitation on a copyright owner's exclusive rights.

Codification of Fair Use Privilege

The fair use privilege was originally created by judges in the 19th century. It was subsequently made a part of the Copyright Act when it was enacted in 1976. Section 107 of the act provides that:

> The fair use of a copyrighted work ... for purposes such as criticism, comment, news reporting, teaching, ... scholarship, or research, is not an infringement of copyright. In determining whether the use made of a work in any particular case is a fair use the factors to be considered ... include:
>
> 1. the purpose and character of the use, including whether such use is of a commercial nature or is for nonprofit educational purposes;
> 2. the nature of the copyrighted work;
> 3. the amount and substantiality of the portion used in relation to the copyrighted work as a whole; and
> 4. the effect of the use upon the potential market for, or value of, the copyrighted work.

When Is a Use a Fair Use?

Determining whether the fair use privilege applies in any given situation is not an exact scientific process. Rather, it requires a delicate balancing of all the factors discussed below. Probably the only useful rule for fair use is this variant of the golden rule: *"Take not from others to such an extent and in such a manner that you would be resentful if they so took from you."* (McDonald, "Non-infringing Uses," 9 *Bull. Copyright Society* 466 (1962).)

The following four factors must be considered to determine whether an intended use of an item constitutes a fair use:

- the purpose and character of the use
- the nature of the copyrighted work
- the amount and substantiality of the portion used, and
- the effect of the use upon the market for the copyrighted work.

Not all these factors are equally important in every case, but all are considered by the courts in deciding whether a use is fair. You should consider them all in making your own fair use analysis.

⚠ If you're not sure whether an intended use is a fair use, seek legal advice or get permission.

Stephen Crane

Can Fair Use Apply Where Permission Is Denied?

If you ask a copyright owner for permission to use her work and she refuses, can you then use it without permission on the grounds of fair use? The Supreme Court has said yes: "If the use is otherwise fair, no permission need be sought or granted. Thus, being denied permission to use a work does not weigh against a finding of fair use." (*Campbell v. Acuff-Rose Music, Inc.*, 114 S.Ct. 1164 (1994).)

This means that even though you're certain that your intended use is fair, you can go ahead and seek permission for the use from the copyright owner because you want to avoid the possibility of expensive litigation. If the copyright owner proves to be unreasonable and withholds permission, you can then go ahead and use the material on the basis of fair use. But, of course, the copyright owner could still sue you. If the use really was fair, you would win the suit even though you had unsuccessfully sought permission.

The Purpose and Character of the Use

First, the purpose and character of your intended use must be considered in determining whether it is a fair use. The test here is to see whether the subsequent work merely serves as a substitute for the original or "instead adds something new, with a further purpose or different character, altering the first with new expression, meaning, or message." (*Campbell v. Acuff-Rose Music, Inc.*; see "Can Fair Use Apply Where Permission Is Denied?" above.) The Supreme Court calls such a new work transformative.

This is a very significant factor. The more transformative a work, the less important are the other fair use factors, such as commercialism, that may weigh against a finding of fair use. Why should this be? It is because the goal of copyright to promote human knowledge is furthered by the creation of transformative works. "Such works thus lie at the heart of the fair use doctrine's guarantee of a breathing space within the confines of copyright." (*Campbell v. Acuff-Rose Music, Inc.*)

Following are very typical examples of transformative uses where preexisting expression is used to help create new and different works. These types of uses are most likely to be fair uses:

- **criticism and comment**—for example, quoting or excerpting a work in a review or criticism for purposes of illustration or comment
- **news reporting**—for example, summarizing an address or article, with quotations, in a news report
- **research and scholarship**—for example, quoting a passage in a scholarly, scientific, or technical work for illustration or clarification of the author's observations.

Although not really transformative, photocopying by teachers for classroom use may also be a fair use, since teaching also furthers the knowledge-enriching goals of the copyright laws.

Note that the uses listed above, with the possible exception of news reporting, are primarily for nonprofit educational purposes. Although some money may be earned from writing a review or scholarly work, financial gain is not usually the primary motivation—disseminating information or otherwise advancing human knowledge is.

If permission were required for these socially helpful uses (presumably for a fee), it is likely that few or no reviews or scholarly works would be written; neither the authors nor publishers of works that earn such modest sums could afford to pay for the necessary permissions. (Newspapers probably could afford to pay for permissions, but requiring them to do so in all cases would inevitably impede the free flow of information, and might also violate the free press guarantees of the First Amendment of the Constitution.)

In contrast, an author and/or publisher of a work written primarily for commercial gain usually can afford to pay for permission to use others' protected expression. It also seems inherently fair to require him to do so. In the words of one court, fair use "distinguishes between a true scholar and a chiseler who infringes a work for personal profit." (*Wainwright Securities, Inc. v. Wall Street Transcript Corp.,* 448 F.2d 91 (2d Cir. 1977).)

For these reasons, the fact that a work is published primarily for private commercial gain weighs against a finding of fair use. For example, using the line, "You don't need a weatherman to know which way the wind blows" (from Bob Dylan's song) in a poem published in a small literary journal would probably be a fair use; but using the same line in an advertisement for raincoats probably would not be.

However, the fact that a writer's primary motive is commercial does not always mean he can't exercise the fair use privilege. If the other fair use factors are in the writer's favor, the use may be considered a fair use. This is particularly likely where the use benefits the public by furthering the fundamental purpose of the copyright laws: the advancement of human knowledge.

> **EXAMPLE:** The authors of an unauthorized popular biography of Howard Hughes quoted from two *Look* magazine articles about Hughes. All three fair use rules were satisfied. Only a small number of words were quoted, and the authors had provided proper attribution for the quotes. In addition, the copyright owner of the articles (who turned out to be Hughes himself) had no intention of using the articles in a book, so the use was not a competitive use. A court held that the quotations qualified as a fair use. Although the biography had been published primarily to earn a profit, it also benefited the public. The court stated that "while the Hughes biography may not be a profound work, it may well provide a valuable source of material for future biographers (if any) of Hughes or for

historians or social scientists." (*Rosemont Enters. v. Random House, Inc.*, 336 F.2d 303 (2d Cir. 1966).)

It is even possible for an advertisement to constitute a fair use of protected expression if it serves the public interest as well as the advertiser's commercial interests. For example, a vacuum cleaner manufacturer was permitted to quote from an ad from a report in *Consumer Reports* comparing various vacuum cleaners (and concluding that the manufacturer's model was the best) because the ad significantly increased the number of people exposed to the Consumers Union's evaluations. The ad served the public interest by disseminating helpful consumer information. (*Consumers Union v. General Signal Corp.*, 724 F.2d 1044 (2d Cir. 1983).) The same rationale probably applies to the widespread practice of quoting from favorable reviews in advertisements for books, films, plays, and so on. However, as a general rule, you should always seek permission to quote protected material in an ad.

The Nature of the Prior Work

As we discussed in Chapter 6, What Copyright Protects, to preserve the free flow of information, less copyright protection is given to factual works (scholarly, technical, scientific works, and so on) than to works of fancy (novels, poems, plays, and so on). This is particularly true where there are only a few ways to express the facts or ideas in a factual work, and the idea or fact and its expression are deemed to merge. (See Chapter 6, What Copyright Protects.) Thus, authors have more leeway in using material from factual works than from fanciful ones, especially where it's necessary to use extensive quotations to ensure the accuracy of the factual information conveyed.

Use of unpublished materials

The extent to which unpublished materials such as letters and diaries may be quoted without permission has been one of the most controversial copyright issues in recent years.

> **EXAMPLE:** Anthony, a well-known Civil War historian, finds a letter written in 1865 by a previously unknown Civil War veteran in the attic of an old house in Georgia. The unpublished letter would remain under copyright at least until the end of 2002. (See Chapter 10 for a detailed discussion of copyright duration of unpublished works.) May Anthony quote from the letter in a book he's writing on the Civil War without obtaining permission from the letter's copyright owners (presumably, the veteran's descendants and heirs)? The answer is maybe, maybe not.

When it comes to fair use, unpublished works are inherently different from published works. Publishing an author's expression before she has authorized it infringes upon the author's right to decide when and whether her work will be made public. Obviously, this factor is not present with published works, and the Supreme Court has held that the fact that a work is unpublished weighs heavily against a finding of fair use. (*Harper & Row v. Nation Enterprises,* 471 U.S. 539 (1985).)

This in itself was not surprising. However, in a pair of highly controversial decisions, federal courts in New York, where most major publishers are located, went much farther than the Supreme Court and indicated that the unauthorized use of unpublished materials can *never* be a fair use. In the first case, (*Salinger v. Random House, Inc.*, 811 F.2d 90 (1987)), a well-known literary biographer was prohibited from quoting or closely paraphrasing in a biography of J.D. Salinger from 44 unpublished letters written by Salinger which the biographer had discovered in university research libraries. In the other case (*New Era Publications v. Henry Holt,*

Attribution Does Not Make a Use Fair, but Should Always Be Provided

Some people have the mistaken idea that they can use any amount of material so long as they give the author credit, whether in a footnote or by mentioning the title of the book after a quotation. This is simply not true. Providing credit for a quotation will not in and of itself make the use of the quote a fair use. For example, if you quote an entire chapter from another author's book without permission, your use wouldn't be considered fair even if you give that author credit.

On the other hand, it is always a good idea to provide attribution for quoted or paraphrased material. There are two reasons for this.

First, the copyright law makes it illegal to remove "copyright management information" if you know it will induce or facilitate copyright infringement. Copyright management information incudes a work's title, the author's name, and the copyright notice. It appears that copyright management information may be removed where a work is copied on the grounds of fair use, but it's a good idea to include such information anyway—this prevents even the possibility of being sued for removing such information. (For a detailed discussion of liability for removing copyright management information, see Chapter 12, Copyright Infringement.)

Second, it is likely that a judge or jury would look with disfavor on an author who attempts to pass off the words of others as his own and then has the nerve to cry "Fair use!" when he's sued for copyright infringement. They might be inclined not only to find that the use is not a fair use, but to impose particularly heavy damages in an infringement suit. If you quote someone else's work, always give that person credit. Quoting with attribution is a very good hedge against getting sued, or losing big if you are sued.

873 F.2d 576 (1989)), the court held that, but for a legal technicality, it would have been impermissible for an author to quote without permission from L. Ron Hubbard's unpublished writings in a highly critical Hubbard biography.

These decisions had a definite chilling effect on publishers—that is, books that quoted letters were rewritten to omit the quotations. And suits against other biographers were filed.

As you might expect, publishers, authors' groups, biographers, historians, and others in the literary community were highly critical of these two decisions, arguing that they enabled the heirs of well-known figures to control how scholars and others can use their unpublished writings, effectively creating a class of widow or widower censors.

After a two-year fight, the fair use provision in the Copyright Act was amended in 1992 to make clear that the fact that a work is unpublished does not act as an absolute bar to a finding of fair use. Section 107 of the Copyright Act now states: "The fact that a work is unpublished shall not itself bar a finding of fair use if such finding is made upon consideration of all … [four] fair use factors."

This amendment to the Copyright Act was intended to return the law to where it was before the controversial New York federal court decisions discussed above. The fact that a work is unpublished weighs against fair use, but it is a hurdle that can be overcome in some cases. An important case decided before the amendment became law illustrates how the law works today. In this case a biographer's unauthorized use of a modest amount of material from unpublished letters and journals by the author Richard Wright was found to be a fair use. The court held that, although the unpublished status of the material weighed against fair use, the other three fair use factors all were in the biographer's favor. (*Wright v. Warner Books, Inc.*, 953 F.2d 731 (2d Cir. 1991).)

In deciding whether your unauthorized use of unpublished material could be a fair use, focus first and foremost on the impact of your use on the value of the material. J.D. Salinger's literary agent testified at trial that Salinger could earn as much as $500,000 if he published his letters. Thus, if a biographer were permitted to publish portions of his most interesting letters first, it could have cost Salinger substantial royalties. This could not be a fair use. But you might be able to use unpublished material if it would not cost the copyright owner anything. For example, quoting a few lines from a letter written by an unknown and long-dead Civil War veteran might constitute a fair use where the letter itself has little or no intrinsic value to the veteran's heirs.

Fair use of out-of-print works

The drafters of the Copyright Act and the Supreme Court have suggested that a user may have more justification for reproducing a work without permission if it is out of print and unavailable for purchase through normal channels. (*Harper & Row v. Nation Enterprises,* 471 U.S. 539 (1985).) Thus, most courts give users more leeway when they quote from or photocopy out-of-print works. But this does not mean that any amount of material from out-of-print works may be used without permission.

The Amount and Substantiality of the Portion Used

The more material you take, the more likely it is that your work will serve as a substitute for the original and adversely affect the value of the copyright owner's work, making it less likely that the use can be a fair use. However, contrary to what many people believe, there is no absolute word limit for fair use. For example, it is not always okay to take one paragraph or less than 200 words. Copying 12 words from a 14-word haiku poem wouldn't be fair use. Nor would copying 200 words from a work of 300 words likely qualify as a fair use. However, copying 2,000 words from a work of 500,000 words might be fair. It all depends on the circumstances—for example, it may be permissible to quote extensively from one scientific work to ensure the accuracy of another scientific work.

The *quality* of the material you want to use must be considered as well as the quantity. The more important it is to the original work, the less likely is your use a fair use. For example, in one famous case, *The Nation* magazine obtained a copy of Gerald Ford's memoirs prior to their publication. The magazine published an article about the memoirs in which only 300 words from Ford's 200,000-word manuscript were quoted verbatim. The Supreme Court held that this was not a fair use because the material quoted, dealing with the Nixon pardon, was the "heart of the book ... the most interesting and moving parts of the entire manuscript." (*Harper & Row Publishers, Inc. v. Nation Enterprises,* 471 U.S. 539 (1985).)

An author of a work consisting primarily of a prior work—particularly the heart of the work, with little added or changed—will likely not be successful in invoking the fair use privilege.

As a general rule, never quote more than a few successive paragraphs from a book or article, quote one or two lines from a poem, or take more than one graphic such as a chart, diagram, or illustration. Also, be aware that although there is no legally established word limit for fair use, many publishers act as if there were one and require their authors to obtain permission to quote more then a specified number of words (ranging from 100 to 1,000 words). You should always ask your publisher about such requirements and seek to obtain any necessary permissions as soon as possible. See Chapter 16 for more information.

The Effect of the Use on the Market for, Or Value of, The Prior Work

The fourth fair use factor is the effect of the use upon the potential market for, or value, of the copyrighted work. You must consider not only the harm caused by your act of copying, but whether similar copying by others would have a substantial adverse impact on the potential market for the original work.

Since fair use is an affirmative defense to copyright infringement, it is up to the defendant—the copier—in an infringement case to show there is no harm to the potential market for the original work. This can be difficult. The more transformative the subsequent work—the more it differs from the original and is aimed at a different market—the less likely will it be deemed to adversely affect the potential market for the original.

But if you want to use an author's protected expression in a work of your own that is similar to the prior work and aimed at the same market, your intended use will probably be deemed to adversely affect the potential market for the prior work. This weighs against a finding of fair use.

James Matthew Barrie

EXAMPLE 1: Nick, a golf pro, writes a book on how to play golf. Not a good putter himself, he copies the chapter on putting from a how-to golf book written by Lee Trevino (one of the greatest putters in golf history). Since Nick intends for his book to compete with and hopefully supplant Trevino's, this use would likely not be a fair use, particularly given the large amount of copying. In effect, Nick is trying to use Trevino's protected expression to eat into the sales of Trevino's own book.

EXAMPLE 2: Ophelia, a historian, writes a study of women's roles in Elizabethan England. Working under extreme deadline pressure, somehow she unconsciously quotes or closely paraphrases many important passages in a groundbreaking study of the topic written by Horatio ten years before. Ophelia intends for her book to compete with and hopefully supplant Horatio's prior work. Ophelia's use of Horatio's material is likely not a fair use.

EXAMPLE 3: Suzy writes a guide to Social Security aimed at retirees. She borrows several charts and graphs from a prior work on the same subject aimed at the same market. This copying is likely not a fair use.

Effect of use on the market for derivative works must be considered

Since the effect of the use on the potential market for the prior work must be considered, the effect on the market for derivative works based on the original must also be analyzed. As discussed in detail in Chapter 7, Adaptations and Compilations, a derivative work is one that is based upon or recast from a prior work. One good example of a derivative work is a play or screenplay based on a novel. A finding that a work has a negative impact on the market for derivatives of an original work weighs against fair use.

> **EXAMPLE:** William writes a play about a love affair between two middle-aged people in a midwestern town. Both the plot and dialogue are borrowed liberally from the best-selling novel *The Bridges of Madison County.* William's copying from the novel is likely not a fair use. Even though the play will likely not affect sales of the novel itself, it probably would have a negative impact on the market for a play based on the novel, whether by the novelist himself or someone he gave permission to write such a play. In other words, William's play would negatively impact the market for derivative works based on *The Bridges of Madison County.*

Fair Use and the Photocopy Machine

The photocopy machine probably represents the greatest threat to copyright owners in history. With current advances in technology, it is now cheaper in many cases to photocopy an entire book than to purchase it from the publisher. Indeed, it is now possible to copy a work electronically and transfer it from one computer to hundreds of others with the push of a button.

Photocopying for Personal Use

The extent to which an individual may make photocopies of protected works for personal use is not entirely clear. Individual photocopying of one copy of an article from a magazine or periodical or small portion of a book for personal use—that is, not as part of a business activity—probably constitutes a fair use. Making one copy of a book or other work you already own for personal use also probably constitutes a fair use.

Making multiple copies of anything, or copying entire books or other works you get from libraries or friends to avoid having to buy them, probably isn't a fair use. However, there is no practical way for copyright owners to enforce their copyright rights against individual photocopiers. There are no copyright police stationed at photocopy shops.

Photocopying for Commercial Use

Photocopying for commercial purposes or to promote business activities is less likely to be a fair use than copying for personal use, particularly if multiple copies of a work are made. Publishers and other copyright owners are actively attempting to enforce their rights against commercial users. For example a group of seven major publishers obtained a $510,000 judgment against one duplicating business for copying excerpts from books without permission, compiling them into "course packets," and selling them to college students. (*Basic Books, Inc. v. Kinko's Graphics Corp.*, 758 F.Supp. 1522 (S.D. N.Y. 1991).)

What about photocopying scientific and technical journal articles and similar materials for research purposes? In the past, courts often held that this was a fair use, even where the research was done for a profit motive. One important reason for this judicial approach was that it was very difficult—and sometimes impossible—to obtain permissions from publishers of obscure, arcane journals. However, in a far-reaching decision, a federal appeals court in New York has held that this type of copying is not a fair use. The case involved systematic photocopying of technical and scientific journal articles by researchers employed by Texaco. Like many companies, Texaco obtained subscriptions for one or two copies of various expensive technical journals and then circulated them among its employee-researchers. The employees then photocopied entire articles to save for research purposes. In effect, the Texaco researchers were creating their own private libraries of journal articles.

The court held that simply because the copying was done for research did not make it a fair use. This type of wholesale archival copying was not a fair use because it was not transformative or productive—that is, Texaco's employees were just making exact copies of articles, not creating anything new. The photocopies merely served the same purpose as the original journals. The copying was done to save Texaco money on subscriptions and licensing fees. Although Texaco's copying aided research, there was no reason why it should not have to pay to make such copies.

This type of photocopying may have been customary and permissible in the past because it was difficult or impossible to obtain permission to photocopy many technical and scientific journals. But the court noted that this was no longer true, because publishers of such journals have created the Copyright Clearance Center (CCC) to serve as a central clearinghouse to license such photocopying. (See Chapter 16.) The court said that Texaco should either obtain licenses from the CCC or similar organization or buy more subscriptions for its researchers. (*American Geophysical Union v. Texaco, Inc.*, 37 F.2d 881 (2d Cir. 1994).)

Copyright tip for journal users. It's now clear that the wholesale unauthorized photocopying of journal articles that many research-oriented companies have done in the past is copyright infringement. Several publishers of journals and newsletters have won substantial judgments from large companies that have copied their works without permission. If you need to have multiple copies of journal articles, do what the court said Texaco should do: buy more subscriptions or obtain permission to make copies. If the journal publisher belongs to the Copyright Clearance Center, obtaining permission is easy.

However, there might be ways to avoid having to make multiple copies of articles and thus avoid the permissions problem. For example, it might be sufficient to create abstracts of important articles rather than copying them in their entirety. Creating an abstract or summary of an article is a fair use. You can also have employees photocopy and circulate the table of contents of journals. Employees could then check out journals from a central library as needed.

Copyright tip for journal publishers. Make it as easy as possible for those who want to photocopy or otherwise use your publication to obtain permission. Either join the Copyright Clearance Center or maintain an efficient permission department of your own.

A publisher's main problem is discovering who is doing unauthorized copying. Here is a strategy that really worked: The publisher of the *Product Safety Letter*, a journal about product liability lawsuits distributed to law firms, placed an ad in each issue offering a $2,000 reward to persons providing conclusive evidence of unauthorized photocopying of the journal. Soon, someone at a large Washington, DC, law firm notified the publisher that numerous unauthorized copies of the journal were being made for firm employees. The publisher demanded that the firm halt the copying and ultimately sued it for copyright infringement. The case was settled for an undisclosed amount, and the firm stopped making the unauthorized copies.

Photocopying by Teachers

Photocopying by teachers for scholarly or classroom use is generally favored as a fair use because it is done for nonprofit educational purposes. However, if taken to extremes, such copying would destroy the market for educational materials. In an effort to strike a balance between the needs of teachers and publishers and authors, a set of guidelines for teacher photocopying was agreed upon by representatives of author-publisher and educational organizations and unofficially endorsed by the congressional committee that drafted the Copyright Act.

Technically, the guidelines do not have the force of law, but it is highly unlikely that any court would hold that copying by a teacher within the guidelines did not constitute a fair use.

The guidelines establish *minimum* fair use standards for teachers. It is possible that teacher photocopying that exceeds the guidelines could be considered a fair use as well.

The guidelines may be summarized as follows.

Single copies

A teacher may make *one copy* of the following items for purposes of scholarly research, or use in teaching or preparing to teach a class:

- a chapter from a book (but not an entire book)
- an article from a periodical or newspaper

- a short story, short essay, or short poem, whether or not from a collective work such as an anthology, and
- a chart, graph, diagram, drawing, cartoon, or picture from a book, periodical, or newspaper.

Multiple copies for classroom use

A teacher may also make multiple copies of the items listed above (not to exceed more than one copy per pupil in the course) provided that the following are true:

- The amount of material copied is sufficiently brief.
- The copying is done spontaneously.
- The cumulative effect test is met.
- Each copy includes a notice of copyright.

Brevity

There are strict numerical limits as to how many words may be copied, but these limits may be stretched so that copies don't end with an unfinished line of a poem or an unfinished prose paragraph.

Poetry. Multiple copies may be made of a completed poem of 250 words or less that is printed on not more than two pages; up to 250 words may be copied from longer poems.

Prose. Multiple copies may be made of a complete article, story, or essay of less than 2,500 words; excerpts up to 1,000 words or 10% of the work, whichever is less, may be copied from longer works (but 500 words may be copied from works that are between 2,500 and 4,999 words long).

Illustrations. Multiple copies for classroom use may be made of one chart, graph, diagram, drawing, cartoon, or picture contained in a book or periodical issue.

Special works. The guidelines also include a category called "special works." No one is exactly sure what a special work is. However, it appears that special works include works of poetry or prose of less than 2,500 words intended for children that combine language with illustrations. Such special works may not be copied in their entirety. Only an excerpt of up to two published pages and containing not more than 10% of the words in the text may be reproduced.

Spontaneity

The idea to make the copies must come from the teacher herself, not from school administrators, the board of education, or any other higher authority. Moreover, the idea to make the copies and their actual classroom use must be so close together in time that it would be unreasonable to expect a timely reply to a request for permission from the publisher or copyright owner.

It usually takes at least a month or two for a publisher to respond to a permission request. Thus, the spontaneity requirement will probably be met where the copies are used in class less than a month after they are made. But, of course, this rule wouldn't apply if the material is included in a curriculum prepared prior to the start of the school term.

Cumulative effect of copying

The copying must not have an undue cumulative effect on the market for the copyrighted work. This test is met so long as the following are true:

- The copying is for only one course in the school where the copies are made.
- Not more than one short poem, article, story, or essay or two excerpts from longer works are copied from the same author, nor more than three from the same anthology or other collective work or periodical volume during one class term.
- There are no more than nine instances of such multiple copying for one course during one class term.

The limitations on the number of articles that can be copied does not apply to copying from newspapers, current news periodicals, and current news sections of other periodicals.

Copyright notice

A copyright notice must be included on all copies made. This can easily be accomplished by copying the page in the work where the copyright notice appears. If this is not done, the notice must be added to the copies. It should be in the exact same form as on the original work.

Photocopy charges

Finally, the teacher's students may not be charged more than the actual cost of making the photocopies.

Prohibited copying

Even if all the requirements listed above are satisfied, multiple copies may not be made to substitute for the purchase of books, publisher's reprints, or periodicals; to create anthologies or compilations; or to substitute for or replace "consumable" works such as workbooks, exercises, standardized tests, test booklets, and answer sheets.

In addition, the same teacher may not copy the same item from term to term. Thus, for example, it was not a fair use for a teacher to use the same photocopied materials for three successive school terms. (*Marcus v. Crowley,* 695 F.2d 1171 (9th Cir. 1983).)

Copying by Libraries and Archives

Fair use analysis becomes difficult when copying by libraries and archives is involved. Such institutions play a vital role in preserving and disseminating knowledge. Yet if they were permitted to engage in unfettered copying, the market for all written works would be reduced and authors' economic incentives to create new works would be diminished.

Congress has determined that certain types of unauthorized copying by libraries and archives must be permitted whether or not it would constitute a fair use under the standards discussed above.

There are two separate exemptions available for libraries and archives: The first exemption gives libraries and archives the right to make up to three physical or digital copies of any work for certain purposes. The second exemption allows copies to be made only of those works that have entered the 75th year of their copyright term.

Copying for Archival or Replacement Purposes or at User's Request

Books or other written works are often lost or become worn out. Replacing them may be difficult where the work is out of print. In this event, can a library make a new copy itself without obtaining permission from the copyright owner? Library users often ask librarians to photocopy articles from a periodicals. Can a library legally make the copy? The answer to both questions may be yes if the following special exemption applies.

Which libraries and archives may benefit from special exemption?

The exemption applies to all nonprofit libraries and archives—for example, municipal libraries, university and school libraries, government archives. However, a library or archive need not be nonprofit to qualify. A library or archive owned by a profit-making enterprise or proprietary institution may qualify for the exemption so long as the copying itself is not commercially motivated. This means that a profit may not be earned from the copies themselves—for instance, they could not be sold for a profit—but the information contained in the copies may be used to help a company make a profit-making product. For example, the exemption might be claimed by research and development departments of chemical, pharmaceutical, automobile, and oil companies; the library of a private hospital; and law and medical partnership libraries.

However, if the library or archive is not open to the general public, it must be open at least to persons doing research in the specialized field covered by the library collection who are not affiliated with the library or its owner. This requirement eliminates many libraries and archives owned by private companies that are open only to employees.

When does the exemption apply?

The special exemption may be claimed only if all of the following are true:

- The library or archive owns the work as part of its collection.
- No more than three physical or digital copies of the work are made at one time.
- No charge is made for the copying beyond the costs of making the copy.
- The copies contain the same copyright notice that the work itself contains; if the work contains no notice, a legend must be included in the copies stating that the work may be protected by copyright.

So long as these requirements are met, it is permissible for a library or archive to make an authorized photocopy of a work under the following four circumstances.

Archival reproductions of unpublished works. Up to three copies of any unpublished work may be made for purposes of preservation or security, or for deposit for research use in another library or archive. The work may be photocopied or otherwise physically reproduced, or digital copies may be made. However, if the work is digitally copied, the digital copies may not be made available to the public outside the library or archive premises. This means the digital copies could only be read on computers at the library or archive. They may not be placed on a network that people outside the library may access or the Internet. But first, the library or archives must make a reasonable effort to purchase an unused replacement at a fair price. This will always require contacting commonly known trade sources in the U.S. and, in the normal situation, the publisher or other copyright owner (if the owner can be located at the address listed in the copyright registration) or an authorized reproducing service as well.

Replacement of lost, damaged, or obsolete copies. A library or archive may also make up to three physical or digital copies of a published work that is lost, stolen, damaged, deteriorating, or stored in an obsolete format. A format is considered obsolete when the device necessary to read the work is no longer manufactured or is no longer reasonably available in the commercial marketplace. As with unpublished works, if digital copies are made, they may not be made available to the public outside the library or archive premises.

Library user requests for articles and short excerpts. A library or archive may make one copy (it doesn't have to be a facsimile) of an article from a periodical or a small part of any other work at the request of a library user or at the request of another library on behalf of a library user, provided that the following are true:

- The copy becomes the property of the library user.
- The library has no reason to believe the copy will be used for purposes other than private study, scholarship, and research.
- The library displays a copyright notice at the place where reproduction requests are accepted. (For the form of this notice and other regulations regarding it, see 37 CFR § 201.4 (1988).)

Library user requests for entire works. A library or archive may also make a copy (it doesn't have to be a facsimile) of an entire book or periodical at a library user's request (or at the request of another library on behalf of a library user) if the library determines after reasonable investigation that a copy cannot be obtained at a reasonable price, either because the work is out of print or for some other reason. The same type of investigation must be conducted as for replacement of lost or damaged copies (above). In addition, the same good faith and posting requirements must be met as for reproduction of articles and short excerpts (above).

No multiple copies

The library and archive exemption extends only to isolated and unrelated reproductions of a single copy. It does not authorize related or concerted reproduction of multiple copies of the same material, whether at the same time or over a period of time. This is so whether the copies are intended for one individual or a group. For example, if a college professor instructs her class to read an article from a copyrighted journal, the school library would not be permitted to reproduce copies of the article for the class.

No systematic copying

Systematic copying is also prohibited. This means that a library or archive may not make copies available to other libraries or groups of users through interlibrary networks and similar arrangements in such large quantities so as to enable them to substitute the copies for subscriptions or reprints that they would otherwise have purchased themselves. The National Commission on New Technological Uses for Copyrighted Works (CONTU) has developed the following guidelines as to how much copying is permissible:

- Within any calendar year, one library or archive may obtain from another library or archive not more than five copies of any factual article or articles from a single periodical published less than five years previously. The five-copy limitation applies even if each copy is of a different article or from a different issue. All that matters is that all the articles came from the same periodical and were published not more than five years before the copies are made.
- A library or archive may not obtain from another library or archive more than five copies of material other than factual periodical articles from any given work within any calendar year.
- If the requesting library or archive has on order or in its collection the item that it wants copied, but does not have the item in its possession at the time and cannot reasonably repossess it at the time, the copy made at its request will not count toward the maximum number of permissible copies.
- A library or archive may not satisfy another library's or archive's request for copies unless the request is accompanied by a representation that the request conforms with these guidelines.
- Every library or archive must keep on file each request for copies it made to other libraries or archives.

Photocopying beyond the scope of the exemption

Unauthorized copying that is not covered by, or goes beyond the limits of, the special exemption is permissible only if it is a fair use under the more flexible fair use factors discussed above.

Photocopying by library patrons

Many libraries refuse to make copies for patrons. Instead, they simply install coin-operated machines for patrons to use them selves. A library or archive is not liable for unsupervised use of photocopy machines on its premises provided that a proper warning notice is displayed. For the form of this notice and other regulations regarding it, see 37 CFR § 201.4 (1988).

Copying Works Over 75 Years Old

In 1998, the Sonny Bono Copyright Term Extension Act extended the copyright term for works published before 1978 from

75 to 95 years. The Act also included a new exemption for libraries and archives. Under this exemption, a library, archive, or nonprofit educational institution functioning as a library or archive may reproduce, display, or perform in physical or digital form for purposes of preservation, scholarship, or research a copy of a work that has entered the last 20 years of the 95-year copyright term. However, three requirements must first be met. Following a reasonable investigation, the library or archive must have determined all of the following:

- The work is not subject to normal commercial exploitation—that is, cannot be purchased from the publisher or booksellers.
- A copy of the work cannot be obtained at a reasonable price.
- The copyright owner of the work has not filed a notice with the Copyright Office that either of the first two conditions cannot be met (see below).

The exemption does not apply to unpublished works and may only be claimed by libraries or archives themselves, not by people who use them.

Few works are covered by exemption

Since the exemption only applies to works that have entered their 76th year of copyright protection, few works are currently covered. In 2006, only works published between 1923–1930 were covered; in 2007, only works published 1923–1931 were covered, and so on.

The majority of works first published in the U.S. before 1963 are in the public domain because their copyrights were never renewed. Such works may be copied freely for any purpose. Therefore, libraries and archives should first check to see if an old work they want to copy has been renewed before bothering to investigate whether this exemption applies. Note, however, that most works first published outside the U.S. before 1963 didn't have to be renewed. (See Chapter 10 for detailed discussion.)

Notice to libraries and archives

Copyright owners who own works in their last 20 years of copyright protection are allowed to file a notice with the Copyright Office stating that the work is subject to normal commercial exploitation or that a copy can be obtained at a reasonable price. If such a notice is filed, a library or archive may not utilize the exemption discussed here.

The Copyright Office has created a form for this purpose called Form NLA. A copy is included on the CD-ROM. You can also download a digital copy from the Copyright Office's website at www.lcweb.loc.gov/copyright. However, the Copyright Office will not send you a hard copy of the form. Form NLA may be filed any time during a work's last 20 years of copyright protection. The notice must be accompanied by a $50 fee for the first work covered, and an additional $20 for each additional work covered by the notice. Include a check payable to the Register of Copyrights. The notice and fee should be sent to:

NLA
Library of Congress
Copyright Office
101 Independence Ave., SE
Washington, DC 20559-6000

The Copyright Office says that the notice must be filed more than once during the last 20 years of the work's copyright life. However, it has yet to decide how often.

The notice must be signed under penalty of perjury. This means that if you claim in the notice that the work you own is subject to normal commercial exploitation or can be obtained at a reasonable price, it must be true. Don't lie in order to prevent libraries from making free copies of your work.

The Copyright Office will place the information contained in all the notices it receives in its online database called the COHD file. This may be searched online through the Copyright Office website at www.copyright.gov. Before relying on this exemption, a library or archive should search this database to see if a notice has been filed covering the work or works the library wants to copy.

Other Fair Uses

Fair use is not limited just to quotations and photocopying. Discussed below are some other types of uses that may be fair uses.

Parody

A parody is a work of fancy that ridicules another, usually well-known, work by imitating it in a comic way. Peruse the humor section of your local bookstore and you'll find many examples, such as parody versions of well-known magazines like *Cosmopolitan* (called *Catmopolitan*). Someone has even published a parody of the SAT exam called the "NSAT" (No-Sweat Aptitude Test) and a book of parody sequels to famous literary works, including titles such as *A Clockwork Tomato, 2000: A Space Iliad*, and *Satanic Reverses*.

To parody a work, it is usually necessary to use some of the original work's expression, so that readers will be able to recognize what's being parodied. However, it is rarely possible to get permission to parody or satirize someone else's work. Thus, parodies can exist only because of the fair use doctrine. Recognizing this, lower courts have historically held that parody and satire deserve substantial freedom, both as entertainment and as a form of social and literary criticism.

In a much-anticipated decision involving a parody of the song "Pretty Woman" by the rap group 2 Live Crew, the Supreme Court has strongly reaffirmed the view that a parody, like other comment and criticism, may be a fair use. Indeed, the court held that even a commercially distributed parody of a well-known song can constitute a fair use. To determine whether any parody is a fair use, all four fair use factors discussed above, must be weighed.

The Supreme Court, in *Campbell v. Acuff-Rose Music, Inc.*, 114. S.Ct. 1164 (1994), gave specific guidance on how the fair use factors should be evaluated in a parody case.

Parody: *Gone With the Wind?*

When is a work a parody and when is it not? Cases involving Dr. Seuss and the book *Gone With the Wind* show just how difficult it can be to know for sure. One thing is certain, though: If a court decides a work isn't a parody, the fair use defense will fail.

In the Dr. Seuss case, two authors wrote a book called *The Cat NOT in the Hat! A Parody by Dr. Juice*. The book told the story of the O.J. Simpson trial through poems and sketches similar to those in the famous *The Cat in the Hat* children's stories by Dr. Seuss. The work was narrated by Dr. Juice, a character based on Dr. Seuss, and contained a character called "The Cat NOT in the Hat." The story begins in Brentwood:

A happy town
Inside L.A.
Where rich folks play
The day away
But under the moon
The 12th of June
Two victims flail
Assault! Assault!
Somebody will go to jail!
Who will it be?
Oh my! Oh me!

The owners of the copyrights in Dr. Seuss sued for copyright infringement. The authors claimed that their work was a fair use of the Dr. Seuss stories because it was a parody. They argued that by applying Dr. Seuss's style to adult subject matter their work commented on the "naiveté of the original" Dr. Seuss stories as well as on society's fixation on the O.J. Simpson trial.

The court disagreed. It said that a parody was a "literary or artistic work that imitates the characteristic style of an author or a work for comic effect or ridicule." *The Cat NOT in the Hat!* didn't qualify because the authors' poems and illustrations merely retold the Simpson tale. Although they broadly mimicked Dr. Seuss's characteristic style, they did not hold it up to ridicule or otherwise make it an object of the parody. The court opined that the authors used the Seuss characters and style merely to get attention or avoid the drudgery of working up something fresh. It upheld an injunction that barred Penguin Books from distributing 12,000 books it had printed at an expense of $35,000. (*Dr. Seuss Enterprises v. Penguin Books USA, Inc.*, 109 F.3d 1394 (9th Cir. 1997).)

Four years later, the exactly opposite result was reached by another court in a case involving the legendary Civil War novel *Gone With the Wind*. The book, called *The Wind Done Gone*, chronicles the diary of a woman named Cynara, the illegitimate daughter of a plantation owner, and Mammy, a slave who cares for the owner's children. Without obtaining permission from the copyright owner of *Gone With the Wind*, the author of *The Wind Done Gone* copied the prior book's characters, famous scenes and other elements from the plot, and dialogue and

Parody: *Gone With the Wind?* (continued)

descriptions. The Margaret Mitchell estate sued both the publisher and author for copyright infringement.

The court held that *The Wind Done Gone* was protected by the fair use privilege, and thus the Mitchell estate could not obtain a court order halting its publication. The court concluded that *The Wind Done Gone* was a parody. The court held that a work is parody "if its aim is to comment upon or criticize a prior work by appropriating elements of the original in creating a new artistic, as opposed to scholarly or journalistic, work." *The Wind Done Gone* satisfied this test because it was a specific criticism of and rejoinder to the depiction of slavery and the relationships between blacks and whites in *Gone With the Wind*. (*Suntrust Bank v. Houghton Mifflin Co.*, 268 F.2d 1257 (11th Cir. 2001).)

The difference between these cases seems to be that the court didn't like The *Cat NOT in the Hat*, while it did like *The Wind Done Gone*. The *Cat* court said that authors' claim that their work commented on the naiveté of the Dr. Seuss stories was "pure shtick" and "completely unconvincing." In contrast, the *Wind* court said the book was "a critical statement that seeks to rebut and destroy the perspective, judgments, and mythology of GWTW." Subjective decisions like these show why it can be so hard to predict if a parody is a fair use or not.

Purpose and character of the use

The Supreme Court stated that the heart of any parodist's claim of fair use is that an author's preexisting work needed to be copied in order to create a new work that, at least in part, comments on or criticizes the prior author's work. However, a self-proclaimed parodist who copies a prior work merely to get attention or to avoid the drudgery in working up something fresh has a weak claim to fair use.

Does it matter that a parody might be seen to be in bad taste? The Supreme Court said no. All that matters is that the work can reasonably be perceived to contain a parodic element—in other words, it comments on or criticizes the original work in some way. Whether a parody is in good or bad taste does not matter to fair use.

The fact that a parody was commercially motivated weighs against a finding of fair use, but is not determinative by itself.

The nature of the copyrighted work

Expressive works of fancy like novels and plays are generally given greater copyright protection than more utilitarian factual works like newspaper accounts or scientific works. However, the Supreme Court stated that since parodies almost always copy publicly known expressive works, this fair use factor is not helpful "in separating the fair use sheep from the infringing goats."

The amount and substantiality of the portion used

To be effective, a parody must take enough material from the prior work to be able to conjure it up in the reader's or hearer's mind. To make sure the intended audience will understand the parody, the parodist usually has to copy at least some of the most distinctive or memorable features of the original work. Once enough has been taken from the original work to assure identification, how much more is reasonable to take will depend on the extent to which the work's overriding purpose and character is to parody the original. However, a parody composed primarily of an original work with little new material added is not likely to be considered a fair use.

Effect of the use on the market for the prior work

A finding that a parody has a detrimental effect on the market for, or value of, the original work weighs against fair use. However, the Supreme Court stated that a parody generally does not affect the market for the original work because a parody and the original usually serve different market functions. A parody is particularly unlikely

Market Effect on Derivative Works Must Be Considered

The effect of a parody on the market for derivative works based on the original must also be considered. As discussed in Chapter 7, Adaptations and Compilations, a derivative work is a work based on or recast from an original, such as a play or screenplay based upon a novel. The right to license derivative works is one of a copyright owner's most important rights. A parody may itself be a derivative work of the original it parodies. But the effect of a parody on the market for other parodies of the original need not be considered. This is because in the real world copyright owners hardly ever license parodies of their work. In other words, it is only necessary to consider the effect of a parody on the potential market for derivative works other than other parodies of the original. Again, where the copying is slight, the market effect on derivative works is also slight.

> **EXAMPLE:** William writes a one-act play that parodies the best-selling novel *The Bridges of Madison County.* In deciding whether the play is a fair use, a court must consider the effect the play has on the potential market for other plays based on the novel. But the court need not consider whether the play affects the market for other parodies of the novel, since the novel's author is unlikely to license parodies of his work.

to affect the market for the original where the copying is slight in relation to the parody as a whole.

But what if a parody is so scathing or critical of the original work that it harms the market for it? Does this weigh against fair use? The Supreme Court answered this question with a resounding no. Biting criticism is not copyright infringement, even if it effectively destroys a work both artistically and commercially.

Applying these fair use factors is a highly subjective exercise. One judge's fair use might be another's infringement. A parody will probably be deemed a fair use so long as:

- The parody has neither the intent nor the effect of fulfilling the demand for the original.
- The parodist does not take more of the original work than is necessary to accomplish the parody's purpose (the more recognizable the original work, the less needs to be taken to parody it).
- The original work is at least in part an object of the parody (otherwise there would be no need to use it).

Calligraphy

A single copy reproduction of a copyrighted work by a calligrapher for a single client is a fair use. Likewise, a single reproduction of excerpts from a work by a student calligrapher or teacher in a learning situation would be a fair use of the copyrighted work.

Copying for the Blind

The making of a single braille copy or tape recording of a copyrighted work by an individual as a free service for blind persons would probably be considered a fair use. But making multiple copies or tapes for commercial purposes would not be.

■

CHAPTER

12

Copyright Infringement: What It Is, What to Do About It, How to Avoid It

Previous chapters have discussed the steps an author or other copyright owner must take to give her work maximum protection under the copyright laws. Now we explore how these protections are enforced. This subject is referred to as copyright infringement.

When a copyright dispute arises, there are often several self-help steps a copyright owner can take. These generally amount to telling the infringer to stop the infringing activity and/or pay for the infringement. When push comes to shove, however, there is only one remedy with teeth in it. This is to ask a federal court to order the infringing activity halted and to award a judgment for damages. Because this type of litigation is procedurally complex, an attorney skilled in copyright litigation is required.

This chapter is not intended as a substitute for a good copyright attorney. Rather, its aim is to:

- help you recognize when copyright infringement has occurred
- suggest some steps an author or other copyright owner can take on her own to deal effectively with infringement without resorting to lawyers and the courts
- tell you what to expect in the event of a court action
- help you estimate what damages and other types of court relief are potentially available to you in an infringement suit
- introduce some ways to defend against infringement charges, and
- tell you how to protect yourself from infringement claims.

What Is Copyright Infringement?

In Chapter 2, Copyright Basics, we described a copyright as a bundle of five exclusive rights. These include the right to reproduce, distribute, prepare derivative works based upon, perform, and display a protected work. Subject to important exceptions discussed below, these rights cannot be exercised by anybody but the copyright owner unless the owner's permission is obtained. If copyright rights are exercised without the owner's permission, the copyright is said to be infringed.

Infringement of written works usually involves the unauthorized exercise of a copyright owner's exclusive rights to reproduce the work and prepare derivative works based on it. In plain English, this means the unauthorized *copying* of the work. This chapter focuses on infringement due to copying. However, be aware that performing a play, publishing an unauthorized copy, or reciting a written work in public also constitutes copyright infringement—unless the copyright owner's permission is obtained.

There are many ways to copy a written work. An infringer may copy another's work by means of a photocopy machine or other mechanical device, or he may do it the old-fashioned way: by transcribing verbatim or paraphrasing protected material into a work of his own. The latter type of copying need not even be done consciously to constitute infringement. A person who unconsciously copies from memory a work he's read may be a copyright infringer, but the penalties imposed on such a person would usually be less than those for a person who consciously and willfully copied another's work.

The difference between plagiarism and copyright infringement

Many people believe that plagiarism and copyright infringement are the same thing. Not so: A plagiarist is a person who poses as the *originator* of words he did not write, ideas he did not conceive, and/or facts he did not discover. For purposes of plagiarism, the material stolen need not be protected by copyright. In contrast, a copyright infringer is a person who makes unauthorized use of material protected by copyright. Absent protection, there can be no infringement. Moreover, infringement can occur even though the infringer gives proper credit to the author of the protected expression. Of course, some infringers also take credit for the work they copy; they are both plagiarists and infringers.

> **EXAMPLE 1:** Louis, a professor of French, translates a novel by the obscure 19th century French novelist Jean Valjean and publishes it under his own name. The novel is in the public domain, thus Louis has not committed copyright infringement. He is, however, a plagiarist, because he has posed as the originator of the novel.

> **EXAMPLE 2:** The publisher Scrivener & Sons publishes a paperback version of Stephen King's latest bestseller without his permission. Scrivener has infringed on King's copyright by publishing his book without permission, but it has not committed plagiarism because it has not posed as the author of the book.

> **EXAMPLE 3:** Dr. Jekyl, a biophysicist at a leading university, copies a paper written by one of his colleagues and publishes it under his own name in a scientific journal. Since the colleague's paper was protected by copyright, Dr. Jekyl is both a plagiarist and copyright infringer.

A plagiarist cannot be sued for copyright infringement if all he takes are unprotected ideas or facts, or words that are in the public domain. There is no legal requirement to provide attribution when public domain works are copied and placed into new works. (*Dastar Corp. v. 20th Century Fox Film Corp.*, 123 S.Ct. 2041 (2003).) But, publishing contracts usually contain a provision, called a warranties and indemnities clause, by which the author promises that the work he submits to the publisher is not in the public domain. So a plagiarist could be sued by his publisher for breach of contract or possibly fraud. And, aside from the possible legal consequences, being accused of plagiarism is usually not good for one's career. College professors and journalists have been fired because of plagiarism.

How to Avoid Plagiarism Charge

To avoid charges of plagiarism, authors of scholarly works (histories, biographies, legal and scientific treatises, and so on) must always give proper credit to the sources of their ideas and facts, as well as any words they borrow. Authors of less serious works, how-to books for example, should always attribute quotations, but may not always need to give credit for ideas and facts they borrow (authors of such works should discuss this with their publishers). It is neither customary nor necessary for authors of works of fancy, such as novels and plays, to credit the sources of their inspiration, whether other works of fancy, newspaper accounts, or histories. But they should, of course, give proper attribution for direct quotations.

How to Know Whether You Have a Valid Infringement Claim

If you come away with nothing else from this chapter, remember this: *The fact that another person's work is similar to your own does not necessarily mean that he has committed copyright infringement.* Infringement occurs only if all three requirements discussed below are present:

- ownership of a work protected by a valid copyright
- actual copying of the work by the alleged infringer (remember, this chapter focuses on infringement by copying; infringement of other exclusive copyright rights is also possible), and
- improper use of the work's protected expression by the alleged infringer.

We discuss each element below. Where it's clear you have a valid infringement claim, it may be possible to settle the matter without the aid of an attorney as discussed below. However, if you're not sure whether you have a valid claim, get professional help. How to find a competent copyright lawyer is discussed in Chapter 17, Help Beyond This Book.

A Work Protected by Copyright

The question of infringement does not even arise unless the work allegedly infringed is protected by copyright. This means that the work must meet the three prerequisites for copyright protection discussed in detail in Chapter 6, What Copyright Protects; that is, the work must be:

- **fixed in a tangible medium of expression.** You cannot sue anyone for copying words you have spoken but never written down or otherwise fixed in a tangible form.
- **independently created.** The material allegedly infringed upon must have been independently created. You cannot sue someone for copying words that were copied from others.
- **minimally creative.** The work you believe has been infringed upon must

have been the product of a minimal amount of creativity. You probably will not be able to successfully sue someone for copying a recipe, an alphabetically organized directory, or similar items.

Timely registration creates presumption of validity

So long as your work is registered within five years of the date of first publication, it is presumed to be protected by a valid copyright and the person(s) named in the registration certificate is presumed to be the copyright owner. This is one of the greatest benefits of copyright registration. It means that you do not have to go to the time and trouble of proving that your work is original (which can be very hard to prove) or that you actually wrote it. Rather, it's up to the alleged infringer to try to prove that the work was not original or that your copyright is invalid for some other reason.

Actual Copying by the Alleged Infringer

Second, it must be clear that the alleged infringer actually copied your work. In some cases, there may be witnesses who saw the alleged infringer copy (the infringer may have had a collaborator), or the infringer may even admit it. However, an up-front admission of copying is unusual. More typically, copyright infringement—like adultery—usually happens behind closed doors, and the participants rarely admit their involvement. For this reason, copying is usually established not through direct evidence such as witnesses or admissions, but by showing two things:

- access by the infringer, and
- that the works, or parts of them, are substantially similar.

If these are proven, copying is *inferred*, because there is no other reasonable explanation for the similarities.

Access

To prove access, you must show that the alleged infringer had access to your work—that is, the opportunity to view it. The fact that your work has been made generally available to the public through publication is sufficient to establish access. In the case of unpublished works, however, access must be shown in different ways. One way would be to show that the alleged infringer had contact with a third person—for instance, an editor—who had a copy of your manuscript in her possession. But in the absence of such contacts, you're going to have a hard time convincing anyone that the alleged infringer had access to your unpublished work.

Substantial similarity

Here, you must prove that your work and the work by the alleged infringer are so similar that copying must have occurred. Assuming the alleged infringer had access to your work, you must compare the similarities between your work and his to see if copying may reasonably be inferred. But keep in mind that similarity does not always mean that copying has occurred.

We would all like to think that no one else has ever had the same thoughts or feelings or dreams as we have had. But, in sad fact, this is simply not the case. We are not unique. As usual, Oscar Wilde said it best: "The brotherhood of man is not a mere poet's dream: it is a most depressing and humiliating reality." As a result, it's not only common that two or more people will have the same ideas at the same time and express them in similar ways, it's often inevitable.

To rule out the operation of factors that may give rise to similarity without copying—such as those listed in "Similarity Is Not Always Due to Copying," below—your work and the alleged infringer's must be so similar that these factors are not a rational explanation. Courts call this level of similarity "substantial similarity."

You don't need to engage in a hypercritical textual analysis to determine whether substantial similarity exists. Simply compare both works from all angles and ask yourself whether the average reader would conclude that the author of the later-created work copied from the first.

Of course you should look for similarities in wording, but other similarities may also help establish copying. In the case of a work of fancy, such as a novel or play, compare such aspects of the works as their themes, plots, characters, settings, moods, paces, and writing styles. For a factual work, such as a history or biography, similarities in the facts, structure, and organization of the works may help indicate copying.

Similarity Is Not Always Due to Copying

The late copyright attorney Alexander Lindey, in his classic study *Plagiarism and Originality* (Harper 1952), identified the following 14 causes, other than copying, why two works may be similar:

- the use, in both, of the same or similar theme
- the fact that commonplace themes carry commonplace accessories
- the use, in both works, of stereotypes or stock characters
- the fact that both employ the same well-weathered plot
- the limited number of plots generally
- the presence, in both, of hackneyed ingredients, episodes, devices, symbols, and language
- the fact that both authors have drawn on the world's cultural heritage, or have cast their works in the same tradition
- the imperatives of orthodoxy and convention
- the impact of influence and imitation
- the process of evolution
- the dictates of vogue or fashion
- the fact that both authors have stolen from the same predecessor
- the fact that both have made legitimate use of the same news item, historical event, or other source material, and
- the intervention of coincidence.

Publishers of certain types of works, particularly directories and other fact compilations, sometimes deliberately insert minor errors in their work to help prove copying. If the alleged infringer's work contains the same errors, copying must have occurred.

Improper Use of Protected Expression

The fact that the alleged infringer in all likelihood copied from your work will get you through the courthouse door but is not enough to establish infringement. The final and most important element of infringement is that the alleged infringer has copied your work's *protected expression.* As discussed in detail in Chapter 6, What Copyright Protects, a work's protected expression consists of the author's independently created word sequences and the selection and arrangement of her material. Everything else, including the ideas and facts the work expresses, is in the public domain, free for all to use.

There are four levels or degrees of copying of protected expression that can constitute copyright infringement:

- verbatim copying of *all* of a work's protected expression
- verbatim copying of *part* of a work's expression

Making Lists of Similarities

It may be helpful to draw up a list of similarities you discover between your work and another work you think might be infringing. You can then show the list to a copyright lawyer, who might even have it admitted into evidence if a lawsuit results. Here's a small portion of such a list prepared by the producers of the film *Star Wars*, who successfully claimed that their work had been copied by the creators of the television movie *Battlestar Galactica*:

- The central conflict of each story is a war between the galaxy's democratic and totalitarian forces.
- In *Star Wars*, the young hero's father had been a leader of the democratic forces, and the present leader of the democratic forces is a father figure to the young hero. In *Battlestar*, the young hero's father is a leader of the democratic forces.
- An entire planet, central to the existence of the democratic forces, is destroyed in both stories.
- The heroine in both stories is imprisoned by the totalitarian forces.
- A friendly robot, who aids the democratic forces, is severely injured (*Star Wars*) or destroyed (*Battlestar*) by the totalitarian forces.
- There is a scene in a cantina (*Star Wars*) or casino (*Battlestar*), in which musical entertainment is offered by bizarre, nonhuman creatures.

- paraphrasing a work's protected expression, and
- copying a work's total concept and feel or fundamental essence.

What Judges and Juries Actually Do in Infringement Cases

Judges and juries normally do not engage in a hypercritical line-by-line analysis of the works in question to determine if a defendant's paraphrasing or copying of a prior work's total concept and feel constitutes infringement. Rather, they simply ask themselves whether the average intended reader of the works would regard them as substantially similar. This is not a scientific process. It's based mostly on a judge or jury's gut impressions and sense of fairness. If the judge or jury thinks that the alleged infringer has done something wrong, they will usually find him guilty of copyright infringement.

Verbatim copying of an entire work

The most obvious type of copyright infringement occurs when an entire book, story, or article is copied verbatim (or nearly so) without the copyright owner's permission. No one can doubt that infringement has occurred when virtually every word in the alleged infringer's work is the same as yours. Indeed, when there is this much copying, many courts dispense with the need to show access; instead they presume it.

> **EXAMPLE 1:** Sally writes a short story and gives *The New Zorker* magazine permission to publish it once. Three months later, she discovers that *The Plagiarist's Review* has republished her story without asking her permission (she had retained all her other copyright rights in the story). The *Review* has clearly infringed upon Sally's copyright in her story.

> **EXAMPLE 2:** Lou publishes a monthly newsletter on trends in the publishing world. He discovers that one of his subscribers, publisher Simon and Shyster, has been making dozens of unauthorized copies of his newsletter and circulating them to its employees. This is also verbatim copying and infringes Lou's copyright.

Fortunately, most people realize that they can't get away with copying other people's work verbatim and publishing it without permission. As a result, the type of copying in Example 1 is fairly rare, probably accounting for no more than 5% of all infringement cases. Unauthorized photocopying, however, is undoubtedly very common, but very hard to discover.

Partial verbatim copying

Far more common than verbatim copying of an entire work, especially where such factual works as biographies, histories, and how-to books are involved, is verbatim (or near verbatim) copying of only a portion of a work's protected expression, whether a few lines, paragraphs, pages, or chapters. This kind of copying constitutes copyright infringement only if a substantial amount of protected expression is taken.

How much is substantial? There is no definite answer. Verbatim copying of 300 or 400 words would usually be considered substantial enough to constitute infringement. However, it is possible for less copying to be infringement if the material taken is of great value and/or highly original. For example, infringement was found where the defendant copied 12 sentences from Martin Luther King's "I Have a Dream" speech in an advertising pamphlet for funeral accessories. (*Martin Luther King, Jr., Center for Social Change, Inc. v. American Heritage Products,* 508 F.Supp. 854 (N.D. Ga. 1981).)

Paraphrasing

In the infringement context, paraphrasing means making alterations in an author's words instead of copying them verbatim. Whether done consciously, to make it appear copying has not occurred, or unconsciously, paraphrasing constitutes copyright infringement if there is a substantial amount of it. If this were not so, an infringer could get away with infringement simply by making minor changes in an original work's wording.

However, this type of close paraphrasing must be contrasted with changing an author's protected expression to such an extent that there are no recognizable similarities in the prior and subsequent works' expression. In the words of one court, "copying so disguised as to be unrecognizable is not copying." (*See v. Durang,* 711 F.2d 141 (9th Cir. 1983).)

In some cases, it can be can be very difficult to tell whether a work's protected expression has been paraphrased or an alleged infringer has merely taken the ideas and facts in the work and put them in her own words, which because of the merger doctrine (Chapter 6, What Copyright Protects), coincidence, and others factors, happen to be similar to the prior work's. It can be difficult to predict in such cases whether a judge or jury would conclude that infringement has occurred. (See "Paraphrasing Self-Test," below.)

Copying a work's total concept and feel

The final type of copying that can constitute infringement, and the most difficult to detect and prove, is unauthorized copying of a work's total concept and feel. This type of copying is often claimed to be present in infringement cases involving such works of fancy as novels, plays, and poems. This is one term courts use to describe a work's fundamental essence or overall pattern. It consists of the *totality* of all the elements an author selects and combines to form a single work of authorship. Total concept and feel includes a novelist's selection and combination of her themes, setting, stock characters, scenes, situations, literary devices, writing style, and plot. This type of infringement protects an author's selection and combination of individual elements which

Paraphrasing Self-Test

Compare the following passages taken from actual published works and decide for yourself whether the author of the second passage infringed upon the protected expression in the first passage. We also tell you what the courts decided.

Passage in first created work	Passage in subsequent work	How the courts ruled
Surprisingly, the newborn is a remarkably capable organism from the moment he begins to breathe. He can see, hear, smell, and he is sensitive to pain, touch, and change in position. The only sense modality which may not be functioning immediately at birth is taste, but even this sense develops rather quickly.	From his first breath, the child is remarkably well-equipped for life. He can see, hear, smell, touch and feel pain. All his senses, except taste, are operating immediately, and even taste develops rapidly.	Infringement. The court was probably swayed by the fact that there were over 400 examples of this type of paraphrasing from the prior work. (*Meredith Corp. v. Harper & Row, Publishers*, 378 F.Supp. 686 (S.D. N.Y. 1974).)
And second, he says that likely to aid comparisons this year was the surprisingly limited extent to which Fiber Division's losses shrank last year.	The second development likely to aid comparisons this year was the surprisingly limited extent to which the Fiber Division's losses shrank last year.	Infringement. This was just one of dozens of passages in financial reports that were closely paraphrased in a financial newspaper. (*Wainwright Sec. v. Wall Street Transcript Corp.*, 558 F.2d 91 (2d Cir. 1977).)
Ohm's Law is a very important law which you must learn. R = E/I where R = resistance in ohms E = pressure in volts I = current in ampheres.	Ohm early in the 19th century discovered that the ratio of the pressure to the current in a given circuit is constant. This is the fundamental law of the flow of electrical currents. R = E/I where R = resistance in ohms E = pressure in volts I = current in ampheres.	Infringement. The court was probably swayed by the fact that there were over 400 examples of this type of paraphrasing from the prior work. (*Meredith Corp. v. Harper & Row, Publishers*, 378 F.Supp. 686 (S.D. N.Y. 1974).)

Paraphrasing Self-Test (continued)		
Passage in first created work	**Passage in subsequent work**	**How the courts ruled**
He looks to me like a guy who makes his wife keep a scrapbook for him.	[Salinger] had fingered [Wilkie] as the sort of fellow who makes his wife keep an album of press clippings.	Infringement. The author of an unauthorized biography of J.D. Salinger paraphrased these lines from an unpublished letter by Salinger. The court characterized the biographer's passage as a close paraphrase of highly original expression. (*Salinger v. Random House,* 811 F.2d 90 (2d Cir. 1987).)
Ellen, Julia, and Rachel will be here on Tuesday; they'll stay for two days. Don't know what will happen when they get here. I'm hoping for peace and quiet.	Early in 1960, Wright wrote to Margrit de Sabloniere that Ellen, Julia, and Rachel would be arriving for a two or three day visit. Wright said that he did not know what would happen when they arrived but that he was hoping for peace and quiet.	No Infringement. The author of an unauthorized biography of Richard Wright paraphrased these lines from an unpublished letter by Wright. The court held there was no infringement because the paraphrasing constituted "straightforward factual reportage" of the "most basic and banal factual matter," not Wright's protected expression. (*Wright v. Warner Books, Inc.,* 748 F.Supp. 105 (S.D. N.Y. 1990).)

Paraphrasing Self-Test (continued)		
Passage in first created work	**Passage in subsequent work**	**How the courts ruled**
[A]s the Lord commanded he lifted up the rod and smote the waters of the river and all the waters that were in the river were turned to blood. And the fish that were in the river died; and the river stank; and the Egyptians could not drink the waters of the river; and there was blood throughout all the land of Egypt.	In accordance with the directive previously received from higher authority, he caused the implement to come into contact with the aquifer, whereupon a polluting effect was perceived. The consequent toxification reduced the conditions necessary for the sustenance of aquatic vertebrates below the level of continued viability. Olfactory discomfort standards were substantially exceeded, and potability declined. Social, economic, and political disorientation were experienced to an unprecedented degree.	No Infringement. Okay, we cheated. This is a made-up example that no court has or ever could rule on. The first passage is from Exodus in the King James Version of the Old Testament, which is in the public domain. However, even if the passage was protected by copyright, it's not likely that anyone would conclude that the second passage infringed upon it. Although we would never advise anyone to write this badly, the second passage (taken from Wydick, "Plain English for Lawyers," 66 *Calif. Law Review* 737 (1978)) is a good example of an author's taking the facts in a prior work and putting them into his own words.

are not separately protected by copyright. (See Chapter 6, What Copyright Protects.)

Remember: A work's overall pattern or fundamental essence must be copied for there to be infringement. If only a few of a work's unprotectable elements themselves are similar—for instance, stock characters, situations, or plots—there is no infringement. Most authors who bring total concept and feel suits lose their cases for this reason.

> **EXAMPLE:** Reyher published a children's story derived from an old folk tale about a child who becomes separated from her mother. To strangers, the child describes her mother as the most beautiful woman in the world. When she is finally reunited with her mother, the mother turns out to be homely in appearance. A story with an almost identical plot was subsequently published in a children's magazine. There was no verbatim copying or paraphrasing. Reyher sued the magazine for copyright infringement, claiming that her story's total concept and feel had been copied. Reyher lost. The court held that although the two stories had the same plots and similar situations, they differed in almost every other way, including the setting, theme, characterization, and mood. Thus the two works' total feel was not the same. (*Reyher v. Children's Television Workshop,* 433 F.2d 87 (2d Cir. 1976).)

Remember too that a work's fundamental essence or total concept or feel must be *original*—that is, independently created—to be protected. The less originality involved in selecting and combining a work's constituent elements, the less copyright protection it will receive. For example, works of fancy that are written according to tried-and-true formulas—for example, gothic romances, westerns, police shoot-'em-ups, and buddy movies—are accorded less protection than highly original works of art containing uncommon themes, characters, or plots.

When Copying Protected Expression Is Excused

In some cases, authors are allowed to copy other authors' protected expression without permission. This may occur through operation of the merger doctrine (legalese for situations where there are only a few ways to express an idea or fact) or where the copying constitutes a fair use of the protected expression.

Unavoidable Copying: The Merger Doctrine

Sometimes an author has no alternative but to copy or paraphrase another author's words. This occurs where there is just one way, or only a few ways, to adequately express a particular idea or fact. In these cases, the idea or fact and the way it's expressed are deemed to merge and the expression—the first author's words—is given very limited copyright protection or no protection at all. The merger doctrine applies mainly to factual works such as histories, biographies, and scientific treatises rather than to works of fancy such as novels, plays, and poems. This is because by their very nature, facts provide their own limitation of how they can be described, while the ideas present in fictional works can almost always be written in new and different ways.

As a result of the merger doctrine, in some cases verbatim copying or close paraphrasing of even a substantial number of words from a factual work may not constitute infringement. See Chapter 6, What Copyright Protects.

Fair Copying: The Fair Use Privilege

Copying of protected expression will also be excused where it constitutes a fair use of the material. The fair use privilege applies primarily in situations where an author quotes or otherwise uses a limited amount of protected expression for scholarly, educational, or other nonprofit purposes. See Chapter 11, Using Other Authors' Words.

Self-Help Remedies for Copyright Infringement

Assuming you have a valid infringement claim, you may be able to obtain a satisfactory resolution of an infringement claim on your own. Depending on the circumstances, simply sending the alleged infringer and his publisher(s) (who are also liable for any infringement; see below) a cease and desist letter may do the trick.

This sort of letter serves several functions simultaneously:

- It lets the infringer know that you believe he is infringing on your copyright.
- It establishes a date for your discovery of the infringement. This is important for purposes of the statute of limitations on copyright infringement lawsuits discussed below.
- It tells the infringer you intend to stop him.
- It gives the alleged infringer a chance to explain his conduct and perhaps offer a satisfactory compromise before you spend a lot of money initiating a lawsuit. Even if you're sure you're right, it doesn't hurt to listen to the other person's story. In addition, by giving the infringer a chance to respond, you may find out a lot about how he plans to defend a court action if you choose to bring one.

If the claimed infringement involves the Internet, a copyright owner can send a special type of cease and desist letter to an Internet Service Provider (ISP) demanding that the infringing material be removed from the Internet or access to it disabled. (See Chapter 14, Copyright in the Online World.)

Contents of a Cease and Desist Letter

A cease and desist letter should normally include:

- your name, business address and telephone number, or, if you want

to protect your privacy, some way to contact you, such as a P.O. box
- the name of your work, date of first publication, and copyright registration number if the work was registered
- the nature of the activity you believe to be an infringement of your copyright
- a demand that the infringer cease and desist from the activity and pay you for any damages you've sustained, or simply pay your damages if the infringement is not still going on, and
- a request for a response within a stated time period.

Your letter can threaten legal action, but you're probably wiser not to at this stage. The specter of imminent legal action is likely to make the other person paranoid, defensive, and unwilling to cooperate. It may also send him straight to a lawyer.

When you draft your letter, remember that you may end up wanting to use it in court. Accordingly, avoid being nasty, cute, tentative, or overly dramatic.

Cease and desist letters should be sent by certified mail, return receipt requested. If the infringer refuses to accept your letter, arrange to have it delivered personally by someone who isn't involved in the dispute and who'll be available to testify that the letter was delivered. You may have to hire a process server to deliver the letter if you don't know anyone who can do it for you.

EXAMPLE 1: Sally, a freelance writer, discovers that *The Plagiarist's Review* has reprinted without her permission an article she wrote and published several years ago and to which she retains all the copyright rights. Sally sends the magazine's editor the following letter.

January 1, 20xx

Editor in Chief
The Plagiarist's Review
100 Copycat Lane
New York, NY 10000

Dear Sir:

I recently became aware that your magazine published in its November 20xx issue an article entitled "Old Ideas In New Bottles." I originally wrote this article in January 1989 and it was first published in June 1989 in *The Patawamee Magazine*.

I own all of the rights in this article. Since I never authorized you to reprint the article in your publication, it follows that you infringed upon my copyright by doing so.

This letter is to demand that you immediately cease and desist from selling any copies of *The Plagiarist's Review* containing the infringing article. In addition, I demand to be reasonably compensated for the use of my article in the copies that have already been sold.

Please respond to this letter by January 15, 20xx.

Very truly yours,

Sally Bowles

Sally Bowles

Compromise Settlement Letter for Example 2

February 28, 20xx

President
Copycat Press
100 Grub Street
Boston, MA 10001

Dear Sir:

I recently discovered that three chapters, totalling 130 pages, from my Ph.D. dissertation, entitled *The French Chamber of Deputies, 1932–1940,* have been copied nearly verbatim in your recently published title *French History Made Easy* by Professor S.T. Coleridge. Enclosed is a copy of the chapters in question along with a copy of the dissertation's title page; note the copyright notice in my name. The dissertation was registered with the Copyright Office on July 15, 20xx; the registration number is TX123456.

I do not know Professor Coleridge, have never been contacted by him, and never gave him or anyone else permission to use any material from my dissertation, to which I own all the copyright rights.

This letter is to demand that you immediately cease and desist from selling any copies of *French History Made Easy* containing the material from my dissertation. In addition, I demand that I be compensated for the use of my dissertation in the copies that have already been sold.

Please respond to this letter by March 15, 20xx.

Very truly yours,

James C. McCarthy
James C. McCarthy

cc: Professor S.T. Coleridge
Department of Humanities, Esoterica College
Marred Vista, CA 90000

EXAMPLE 2: James obtained his Ph.D. in French history four years ago. His Ph.D. dissertation, entitled *The French Chamber of Deputies, 1932–1940*, was microfilmed and made available to researchers in various research libraries around the country. James timely registered the dissertation with the Copyright Office. He discovers that three chapters of his dissertation have, without his permission, been copied almost verbatim in a new textbook on French history "written" by Professor Coleridge and published by Copycat Press. James sends the letter shown on the previous page to Copycat Press and a copy to Professor Coleridge.

Jules Verne

Responses to Cease and Desist Letters

What happens after the alleged infringer receives your letter typically depends on the nature of the infringer and the infringing conduct. Hopefully, it will be possible for you to work out a reasonable solution, such as making the infringement legal through a license under which you're paid an agreed-upon fee for the use of your work (see Chapter 9, Transferring Copyright Ownership) and getting the infringer to stop future infringements. The fee, of course, is subject to negotiation. It should include a penalty for the inconvenience the infringer caused you—probably at least 50% more than you would have charged had the infringer asked you for permission to use your work in the first place.

Any compromise settlement should be in writing and signed by all the parties.

EXAMPLE 1: Sally Bowles in the example above agreed to grant *The Plagiarist's Review* a retroactive nonexclusive license to publish her article. In return, the *Review* promised to print a correction in a future issue stating that she was the author of the article; it also promised to publish and pay for two new articles by Sally in upcoming issues. Sally felt that was better than just getting a one-time payment for the unauthorized use of her old article.

She sends the compromise settlement letter shown below.

Compromise Settlement Letter for Example 1

Felix Franklin
Editor-in-Chief
The Plagiarist's Review
123 Copycat Lane
New York, NY 10000

Dear Mr. Franklin:

This letter embodies the terms of our settlement of the outstanding dispute arising from publication of the article "Old Ideas In New Bottles" in the November 20xx issue of *The Plagiarist's Review:*

1. Sally Bowles hereby retroactively grants *The Plagiarist's Review* a nonexclusive license to reprint her article "Old Ideas In New Bottles" in its November 20xx issue.

2. *The Plagiarist's Review* promises to print a prominently placed correction in its March 20xx issue, in words approved by Sally Bowles, informing its readers that Sally Bowles was the author of the article "Old Ideas In New Bottles" that ran in the November 20xx issue and that her name had been left off the article in error.

3. *The Plagiarist's Review* also promises to publish the following articles by Sally Bowles at its customary fee no later than December 20xx;
   - an approximately 2,000-word article tentatively entitled "What to Do If You're Accused of Plagiarism," and
   - an article of approximately 1,500 words on the subject of marketing freelance writing.

Sally Bowles
______________________________ ______________
Sally Bowles Date

______________________________ ______________
Felix Franklin, Editor-in-Chief Date
The Plagiarist's Review

EXAMPLE 2: Since James, the author of the dissertation *The French Chamber of Deputies, 1932–1940* in Example 2, above, had timely registered his dissertation with the Copyright Office, he might be entitled to substantial statutory damages if the case went to court. Accordingly, Copycat Press agreed to pay James $3,000 to settle the matter (this was 50% more than James would have charged had Copycat asked him for permission to use his work in the first place). In return, James agreed to release Copycat Press from liability for infringing on his work. James was not able to reach a settlement with Professor Coleridge, who denied copying from James's dissertation. James decided to pocket the money and forget pursuing his case against Coleridge.

James sent Copycat Press the agreement shown on the next page.

Overview of Copyright Infringement Lawsuits

If you can't satisfactorily resolve the matter yourself (perhaps with a short consultation with a copyright lawyer), you have two alternatives: forget about it or hire a lawyer and bring an infringement suit in federal court. The following is an overview of the nuts and bolts of a copyright infringement suit. It is intended to give you a general idea of what you can expect from copyright litigation, not as a substitute for further research or a consultation with an experienced copyright attorney. See Chapter 17, Help Beyond This Book, for a guide to further research and ways to find a copyright attorney.

Who Can Sue

A person or entity who files an infringement suit is called the plaintiff. The plaintiff must be someone who owns the copyright rights at issue, or who is entitled to receive royalties from them. This will typically be the author or the publisher to whom the author has sold some or all of her rights.

EXAMPLE: Bill writes a biography of Saddam Hussein and sells his reproduction and distribution rights to Scrivener & Sons. Leslie copies a substantial portion of Bill's book in her own published biography of Saddam. Both Bill and Scrivener are entitled to sue Leslie for copyright infringement of the exclusive rights to reproduce and distribute the work.

Deciding who does and doesn't own derivative rights in a work in the context of a copyright infringement action is often complex. For example, an author may transfer film rights to one person or entity, television rights to another, and foreign language translation rights to still others. And, unless prohibited in the original transfer of rights, they may be further transferred and divided—for example, the entity that buys the TV rights may transfer Japanese TV rights to someone else. Often,

Compromise Settlement Agreement for Example 2

Lisa Bagatelle
President
Copycat Press
100 Grub Street
Boston, MA 10001

Dear Ms. Bagatelle:

This letter embodies the terms of our settlement of the outstanding dispute arising from Copycat Press's publication of the book *French History Made Easy* by Professor S.T. Coleridge:

1. Copycat Press will pay James McCarthy the sum of $3,000 as compensation for the unauthorized use of material from his Ph.D. dissertation entitled *The French Chamber of Deputies, 1932–1940.*
2. Copycat Press promises not to use any of James McCarthy's work, including material from his Ph.D. dissertation, in the future without his authorization. This includes reprintings and new editions of *French History Made Easy* and other works.
3. James McCarthy agrees that this completely settles the matter in dispute between James McCarthy and Copycat Press, and releases Copycat Press from any further liability for publication of material from *The French Chamber of Deputies, 1932–1940,* by Copycat Press.

James McCarthy
James McCarthy — Date

Lisa Bagatelle, President — Date
Copycat Press

an author who transfers all or part of his derivative rights retains the right to receive part of the total fee (often a royalty) from their exploitation.

> **EXAMPLE:** Bill sells the film rights to his Hussein biography to Repulsive Pictures in return for $100,000 and a 5% share of the profits from the film. Acme Productions releases an unauthorized film based on Bill's biography. Both Bill and Repulsive may sue Acme. However, because it would get most of the recovery from a suit against Acme, Repulsive would likely carry the ball in this situation—that is, its attorneys would do most of the work and Bill would simply join along as a plaintiff.

Liability for Removing Copyright Management Information

In 1998, Congress created a new legal basis for suing copyright infringers. The Digital Millennium Copyright Act (DMCA, discussed in detail in Chapter 14) makes it illegal to remove "copyright management information" from copyrighted works and gives copyright owners the right to sue for damages people who do so. This is in addition to any rights they may already have to sue such people for copying their works.

The main intent behind the new law was to prevent infringers from removing copyright notices and other ownership information from material placed in the online world. However, the law applies both to online and other digital works and to old-fashioned paper and ink works such as books and magazines.

As a result of this law, for the first time ever U.S. authors and other copyright owners have an ironclad right of attribution—that is, the right to be identified as the owner of their works.

What is copyright management information?

Copyright management information includes:

- the title and other information identifying the work
- a work's copyright notice
- the author's name and any other identifying information about the author
- the copyright owner's name and any other identifying information about the owner
- any terms and conditions for use of the work, and
- identifying numbers or symbols on the work referring to any of the above information or Internet links to such information.

What can't you do with copyright management information?

It is now illegal to do any of the following if you know or have reasonable grounds to know that it will induce, facilitate, or conceal a copyright infringement:

- intentionally remove or alter any copyright information
- distribute, import for distribution, or publicly perform a work whose copyright management information has been removed or altered without

permission from the copyright owner or legal authority

- provide false copyright management information, or
- distribute or import for distribution a work containing false copyright management information.

For example, it is illegal to remove the copyright notice from a work and then copy and place it online without the copyright owner's permission. Similarly, it's illegal to remove the copyright notice and title page from a magazine article and make 50 copies to distribute to coworkers.

Penalties for violations

Any person injured by a violation of the law may sue the violator for damages and seek to obtain a court injunction ordering the violator to stop distributing the work from which the copyright management information was removed, altered, or falsified. Such a suit may be brought in addition to any suit for copyright infringement the person may have against the violator.

EXAMPLE 1: John is the author and copyright owner of an article about online business strategies that was published on a national magazine's website. He discovers that the article has been copied and placed on another website without his or his publisher's permission. John's name, the title of the article, the publisher's name, and the copyright notice were removed from the materials before they were placed online. John can sue the national magazine (the owners of the website) for copyright infringement because the magazine illegally copied and distributed his article. He can also sue the magazine for removing the copyright management information from his work: his name, book title, copyright notice, and publisher's name. He can obtain damages for both violations: copyright infringement and illegal removal of copyright management information. Ordinarily, both legal claims would be joined in a single lawsuit brought by John against the national magazine.

EXAMPLE 2: Sue is the author and copyright owner of a magazine article. She sends the article to a magazine. Without Sue's permission the magazine copies the bulk of the article and publishes it under the name of one of its in-house contributors. Sue can sue the magazine for copyright infringement and illegal removal of copyright management information—removing her name from her article.

If the suit is successful, the injured person may obtain from the court an award of its actual monetary damages or may instead ask for statutory damages. Such statutory damages range from a minimum of $2,500 to a maximum of $25,000 per violation. It's up to the court to decide how much to award within these limits. If the defendant is a repeat offender—has violated the law two or more times within three years—the court may increase the damage award up to three times. The court may also award the injured person attorney fees and court costs.

However, the court may reduce the damages or not award any damages at all if the offender convinces the judge that he or she was not aware and had no reason to believe that his or her acts constituted a violation. In addition, the court may not award damages against a nonprofit library, archive, or educational institution if the court finds that it was not aware and had no reason to believe that its acts constituted a violation.

A person or company that willfully violates the law for commercial advantage or private financial gain may be criminally prosecuted by the U.S. Justice Department. Penalties are steep: A first-time offender can be fined up to $500,000 and imprisoned up to five years. But nonprofit libraries, archives, and educational institutions are not subject to criminal prosecution.

Exceptions for fair use and public domain works

There are some situations where it is permissible to remove copyright management information without the copyright owner's permission.

First, the law provides that such an action is permissible if permitted by law. One case where the law may permit removing copyright management information is when material is copied on the grounds of fair use. The fair use privilege permits people to copy portions of copyrighted works without obtaining permission from the copyright owner under certain circumstances. (See Chapter 11 for a detailed discussion of fair use.) In some cases it may not be possible or convenient to include copyright management information when a work is copied on the grounds of fair use—for example, when creating a parody of a copyrighted work. In this event, its removal would likely not be considered a legal violation.

Although the law doesn't explicitly say so, it doesn't apply to works that have entered the public domain. Such works may be freely copied and altered in any way. Since no one owns a public domain work, no harm is done by removing copyright management information.

Finally, law enforcement, intelligence, and other government agencies are permitted to alter or remove copyright management information in order to carry out lawful investigative, protective, information security, or intelligence activities.

Criminal Prosecutions for Infringement

Willful copyright infringement for financial gain has long been a federal crime, punishable by imprisonment, fines, or both. However, as a practical matter this didn't mean much, because the federal authorities rarely bothered to prosecute copyright infringers. They just didn't view copyright infringement as a high-priority crime justifying allocation of limited law enforcement resources. This has changed, at least with regard to infringement of computer software—an activity software publishers claim costs them billions of dollars every year. The U.S. Justice Department and FBI have been actively going after software pirates, particularly those who use the Internet.

In the best-known case of its kind, the U.S. Attorney attempted to prosecute an MIT student who set up a computer bulletin board to dispense copyrighted software for free. The case was ultimately dismissed because the infringer didn't earn any money from his actions. (*United States v. LaMacchia*, 871 F.Supp. 535 (D. Mass. 1994).)

In response to this defeat, Congress has amended the copyright law to permit criminal prosecutions of those who commit copyright infringement, even if they don't do so for financial gain. Although the law, called the No Electronic Theft Act, was specifically intended to deal with software piracy on the Internet, it is so broadly written it could apply to other types of infringement as well.

Two different types of copyright infringement can now result in criminal liability. Let's examine both in turn.

Willful infringement not for financial gain

First, it is now a federal crime to willfully reproduce or distribute by electronic or any other means one or more copyrighted works with a total retail value of $1,000 or more within any 180-day period. This is so even though the infringer earns no money or other financial gain from the infringement.

There is a sliding scale of penalties that can be imposed against people convicted of violating this law:

- If the copyrighted works involved have a total retail value of more than $1,000 but less than $2,500, a violator can be imprisoned for up to one year and/or fined up to $100,000.
- If the offense consists of the reproduction or distribution of ten or more copies of one or more copyrighted works with a total retail value of $2,500 or more, the violator can be imprisoned for up to three years and fined up to $250,000. Jail time can be increased to six years in the case of a second offense.

This provision was specifically designed to apply to people who use the Internet or electronic bulletin boards to copy and distribute pirated software, but who don't charge users for the copies or otherwise financially benefit from the infringement.

However, this law is so broadly written it could apply to others as well, even those who don't use the Internet. Theoretically, anyone who makes an unauthorized copy of any work or works worth more than $1,000 could be subject to criminal prosecution by the federal government. For example, a group of computer scientists has expressed the concern that scientists and educators who share their articles and research with students and colleagues via the Internet could be subject to criminal prosecution. Others have expressed the fear that the law could abrogate the fair use rule that permits unauthorized copying under certain circumstances. (See Chapter 11).

These fears seem exaggerated. It's hard to believe the U.S. Justice Department would criminally prosecute a scientist or educator who shares an article with colleagues. Moreover, the requirement that the infringement be willful to be criminally liable provides some protection. Courts disagree about what "willful" means in this context, but most say that it means an intentional violation of a known legal duty. (*United States v. Moran*, 757 F.Supp. 1046, (D. Neb. 1991).) It would seem that a person who makes a copy of a work in the good-faith belief that the copying constitutes a fair use is not committing a willful copyright infringement and therefore should not be convicted under this law.

Willful infringement for financial gain

The criminal penalties are greater if a person willfully commits copyright infringement for financial gain. "Financial gain" includes receipt, or expectation of receipt, of anything of value, including the receipt of other copyrighted works.

If fewer than ten unauthorized copies are made, or the copied works have a retail value of less than $2,500, violators can be imprisoned up to one year and/or fined up to $100,000.

If the offense consists of reproducing or distributing during any 180-day period, at least ten copies of one or more copyrighted works, with a retail value of more than $2,500, violators can be jailed for up to five years and/or fined up to $250,000. Jail time can be increased to ten years in the case of a second or subsequent offense.

Who Is Liable for Infringement?

Although a primary goal may be simply to stop a publisher from selling any more copies of an infringing work, you are also entitled to collect damages from those liable for the infringement. As discussed in Chapter 4, Copyright Registration, if you timely registered your work, you may elect to receive special statutory damages and attorney fees, which is an important right when your actual damages are very small or difficult to prove.

Who may be liable for such damages and fees? Quite simply, *everybody* who participates in or contributes to copyright infringement. This may include not only the author of the infringing work, but its initial publisher and other publishers who reprint it, the publisher's printer, and even the bookstores that sell the work. Such persons or entities are liable regardless of whether they actually know that the work they published, printed, or sell infringes on another person's copyright. Moreover, corporate officers and employees—such as editors employed by publishing companies—actively involved in the infringement may be held *personally liable* along with their employers. Any person who is sued for copyright infringement is called the defendant.

How Much Time You Have to Sue: Statute of Limitations

There are strict time limits on when copyright infringement suits may be filed. If you fail to file in time, the infringer may be able to have your suit dismissed, even though you have a strong case. In cases where you have not discovered the infringement fairly promptly after it has occurred, statute of limitations questions can be tricky. It's wise to see a knowledgeable copyright lawyer about the proper application of the limitations period to your particular case.

The general rule is that an infringement suit must be filed within three years after the date the copyright owner should reasonably have discovered the infringing act occurred. In some cases, it can reasonably take a copyright owner a long time to discover that the infringement took place, especially where the infringer attempted to conceal the act of infringement. For this reason, if more than three years have passed since the infringing work was first published, don't jump to the conclusion that your suit is barred by the statute of limitations.

> **EXAMPLE:** In 2002, several professors at Esoterica College have Pinko's Copyshop photocopy portions of Bill's biography for inclusion in class materials for courses on Middle Eastern history. Bill doesn't discover this until 2007. If a court views the five-year delay as reasonable, Bill will be able to bring an infringement suit against Pinko's.

Multiple Infringements or Just One?

A factor complicating the three-year period has to do with situations in which repeated acts of infringement occur over a long period of time—for example, where a book containing infringing material is sold over a period of years. Is each sale of the book a separate infringing act, or are all the sales together one infringing act? Courts disagree with each other on this question.

> **EXAMPLE:** Acme Press begins to sell a book containing infringing material in January 1995. Carl, the copyright owner, finds out about the infringement that same year but doesn't do anything about it. However, Acme continues to sell the book through January 2001, when Carl finally decides to file suit. Some courts would permit Carl to obtain damages only for the losses he incurred due to the sales that occurred within three years before he filed suit; others would permit him to recover damages from January 1995. These courts would view all the sales of the infringing works as part of one "continuing wrong." (See *Taylor v. Meirick*, 712 F.2d 1112 (7th Cir. 1983); *Gaste v. Kaiserman*, 669 F.Supp. 583 (S.D. N.Y. 1987).

What You Can Get If You Win: Remedies for Copyright Infringement

Once you've proven the elements of infringement, the next step is to establish what remedies you're entitled to. The potential remedies include:

- **Injunctive relief.** This typically consists of a court order requiring the infringer to stop publishing the infringing work and destroy all remaining copies.
- **Actual damages and infringer's profits.** The plaintiff is entitled to be compensated for the value of lost sales (often difficult to prove) and for other losses resulting directly from the infringement. The plaintiff is also entitled to collect the amount of the defendant's profits from the infringement over and above the amount the plaintiff is awarded for her lost profits.
- **Statutory damages.** If the plaintiff's work was timely registered and she so chooses, she is entitled to receive special statutory damages provided in the copyright law (statute) instead of actual damages and other economic damages.
- **Attorney fees.** A copyright owner can also get attorney fees. Again, timely registration is required.

We'll examine each remedy in turn. Again, this isn't a complete description of the legal procedures involved but is designed to give you an overview of the available remedies.

Injunctive Relief

An injunction is a court order telling someone to stop doing something. In a copyright infringement action, the order usually is simply for the defendant to stop the infringing activity. This is commonly a quick, effective remedy because, in many cases, it is possible to get positive action from the court long before the actual trial is held to decide who wins.

Indeed, it is possible to get a temporary restraining order (TRO) almost immediately without notifying the defendant or holding a formal court hearing. A TRO may last ten days at most. A hearing must then be held on whether the judge should issue a preliminary injunction. A preliminary injunction operates between the time it is issued and the final judgment in the case. This interim court order is available when it appears likely to a federal judge, on the basis of written documentation and a relatively brief hearing at which the lawyers for each side present their view of the dispute, that (1) the plaintiff will most likely win the suit when the trial is held, and (2) the plaintiff will suffer irreparable injury if the preliminary injunction isn't granted. Ordinarily, irreparable injury is presumed to exist where someone infringes upon a copyright owner's exclusive rights. (*Apple Computer, Inc. v. Franklin Computer Corp.*, 714 F.2d 1240 (3d Cir. 1983).)

If the judge grants the injunction, the plaintiff must post a bond in an amount determined by the judge. If the injunction is later found to have been wrongfully granted, the defendant can collect from the bond the damages and costs he incurred due to the injunction.

Once a preliminary injunction is granted, it remains in effect pending a further determination of whether infringement occurred at the formal trial. In theory, a trial will probably be held one or two years later. In fact, the parties often fashion a settlement based on the results of the preliminary injunction hearing.

> **EXAMPLE:** In 1990, Nolo sued another publisher for publishing and distributing a book infringing on Nolo's title, *Dog Law,* by Mary Randolph. Nolo and Randolph were able to obtain a preliminary injunction from a federal judge barring the publisher from distributing any more copies of its book. A settlement was reached soon thereafter. The whole process took just three months from the date suit was filed.

If a settlement is not reached and a full-scale trial occurs, the same issues as those raised in the preliminary injunction hearing will be litigated in more detail. If the plaintiff again prevails, the preliminary injunction will be converted into a permanent one, either including the same terms and orders or different ones, depending on what the plaintiff proves at trial. If the plaintiff loses, the preliminary injunction (if one was granted) will be dissolved and the defendant can go back to doing what it was doing before, plus be compensated for the consequences of the lawsuit out of the bond.

Damages

If you win a copyright infringement suit, you usually have the right to collect money (called damages) from the infringer. As mentioned, if your work was timely registered with the Copyright Office, you will be entitled to choose between collecting actual damages and special statutory damages.

Actual damages and infringer's profits

Actual damages are the lost profits and/or other losses sustained as a result of the copyright infringement. In other words, actual damages are the amount of money that the plaintiff would have made but for the infringement. This may include compensation for injury to the plaintiff's reputation due to the infringement and for lost business opportunities (often difficult to prove)—for example, a lost opportunity to sign a publishing contract to write a sequel to a novel because an infringing novel hurt its sales. To obtain actual damages, the plaintiff must prove in court that the alleged losses actually occurred. Business records and witnesses (often including the plaintiff herself) must be presented to substantiate the plaintiff's actual losses.

As stated above, the plaintiff is also entitled to recover the amount of the defendant's profits from the infringement to the extent they exceed the plaintiff's recovery for her lost profits.

> **EXAMPLE:** The plaintiff is awarded $10,000 for lost sales due to the defendant's infringement. The defendant

earned $15,000 in profits from the infringement. The plaintiff is entitled to $5,000 of the defendant's profits.

To establish the defendant's profits, the plaintiff is required only to prove the infringer's gross revenue from the infringing work. The defendant's business records would usually be presented for this purpose. The defendant must then prove what its actual net profit from the infringement was—that is, the defendant must produce records or witnesses to show the amount of expenses deductible from the infringing work's gross revenues (such as printing and distribution costs) and the amount of profit, if any, attributable to the noninfringing material in the defendant's work (often difficult to prove).

Statutory damages

Statutory damages are set by the copyright law and require no proof of how much the loss was in monetary terms. However, as discussed in Chapter 4, Copyright Registration, statutory damages are only available if the work was timely registered—that is, before the infringement began or within three months of publication. Statutory damages are awarded at the discretion of the judge or jury and don't depend on having to prove a loss in any specific amount due to the infringement. Statutory damages fall within the following range:

- Absent a finding that the infringer acted either willfully or innocently, between $750 and $30,000 for all the infringements by a single infringer of a single work, no matter how many infringing acts there were. If multiple separate and independent works were infringed, statutory damages may be awarded for each work.
- If the court finds that the infringer acted *willfully*—that is, knew he had no legal right to the material he wanted, but took it anyway—it may increase the amount of statutory damages up to $150,000.
- But if the court finds that the infringer acted *innocently*—that is, he used the copyrighted material sincerely believing he had the right to do so—the judge has discretion to award as little as $200. However, if the work to which the infringer had access contained a valid copyright notice, the infringer may not claim to have acted innocently. As discussed in Chapter 3, Copyright Notice, this is why it is always a good idea to include a valid copyright notice on your work (even though a notice is not legally required for works published after March 1, 1989).

Because the actual damages (the owner's lost profits and other provable losses) caused by an infringement are often small, statutory damages may far exceed actual damages where the infringer acted willfully. A plaintiff who is eligible for both actual and statutory damages may choose which kind she wants to receive at any time, up to and during the trial. Your decision will depend on the facts of your particular case and should, of course, be made in conjunction with your attorney.

Destroying the Infringing Works

Another civil remedy for copyright infringement consists of an impound and destroy order from the court. This tells the sheriff or marshal to go to the infringer's place of business (or wherever the infringing material is located) and impound any infringing works. This can happen at any time after the suit has been filed. If the plaintiff wins, the court may order the sheriff to destroy the infringing material.

Attorney Fees and Costs

If your suit is successful and you timely registered your copyright, the court may also order the defendant to pay your attorney fees and other costs of going to court, such as filing fees. However, this is not required. It's up to the judge to decide whether to make such an award and how much it should be (the amount must be reasonable). The criteria some courts use to decide whether to award attorney fees include whether the defendant acted in bad faith or unreasonably or was otherwise blameworthy. Many courts will be especially likely to award fees to a plaintiff whose actions helped to advance the copyright law or defend or establish important legal principles.

The cost of bringing an infringement suit can be very high, easily tens of thousands of dollars. If for no other reason than to have the opportunity of recovering your attorney fees should you have to bring an infringement suit, you should always timely register your work with the Copyright Office.

If the plaintiff loses his suit, the court has discretion to award the defendant all or part of his attorney fees. In the past, many courts would award such fees to a defendant only if they found that the plaintiff's suit was frivolous or brought in bad faith. But these courts would not require this in making fees awards to plaintiffs. In 1994, the Supreme Court held that this approach was incorrect and that attorney fees must be awarded to plaintiffs and defendants in an evenhanded manner. In other words, the same criteria must be applied to both plaintiffs and defendants. (*Fogerty v. Fantasy, Inc.*, 114 S.Ct. 1023 (1994).)

What to Do If You're Accused of Infringement

What should you do if you're accused of copyright infringement? First, see how serious the claim is. If it's minor—for example, an author validly claims that you have quoted a bit too much of his work, used an illustration, or reprinted an article without permission—the matter can usually be settled very quickly for a few hundred dollars, certainly less than $1,000. This kind of thing happens all the time in publishing. There is no need to see a lawyer (who'll probably charge you at least $150 per hour) to deal with this type of minor annoyance. Have the author sign a letter releasing you from liability in return for your payment.

On the other hand, if you receive a letter from an author or author's attorney alleging a substantial claim—for example, that a book you're publishing to great success is an unauthorized derivative work and its sale should be halted immediately—it's probably time to find a copyright lawyer. If, even worse, you are served with a complaint (a document initiating a lawsuit), you must act quickly, because you may have as little as 20 days to file an answer (response) in the appropriate court. If you don't respond in time, a judgment can be entered against you. Finding a lawyer is discussed in Chapter 17, Help Beyond This Book.

However, even if the case is serious, don't despair. The fact is, many infringement suits are won by the defendant, because either the plaintiff did not have a valid claim to begin with or the defendant had a good defense. This section is not a substitute for a consultation with an experienced attorney; rather, it is designed to give you an idea of some of the things you need to discuss when you see an attorney.

Defenses to Copyright Infringement

Even if there are substantial similarities between the plaintiff's work and your work, you will not necessarily be found guilty of infringement. The similarities may simply be the result of coincidence; in this event there is no liability. But even direct copying from the plaintiff's work may be excused if it constitutes a fair use or there is another valid defense.

Possible defenses to an infringement action include many general legal defenses that often involve where, when, and how the lawsuit was brought, who was sued, and so on. We obviously can't cover all of this here. This section is limited to outlining the major defenses that are specific to copyright infringement actions. Again, if you find yourself defending a serious copyright infringement action, retain a qualified attorney!

Fair use

Authors are allowed to copy other authors' protected expression if the copying constitutes a fair use of the material. Fair use is a complete defense to infringement. See Chapter 11, Using Other Authors' Words.

The independent creation defense

As discussed in Chapter 6, What Copyright Protects, copyright protection does not prevent others from independently developing works based on the same idea or explicating the same facts. If you can convince the judge or jury that you created your work independently, not by copying from the plaintiff, you will not be held liable for infringement. In effect, you would try to prove that any similarities between your work and the plaintiff's are purely coincidental. Such coincidences are not at all uncommon.

The one sure way to show independent creation is for you to prove that your work was created before the plaintiff's. If your work was registered before the plaintiff's, this will be easy to prove.

> **EXAMPLE:** Marilyn claims that Jack turned her novel into a screenplay without her permission and sues him for infringement. Jack had deposited a copy of the allegedly infringing screenplay with the Copyright Office one year before Marilyn published her novel. Jack can prove independent creation simply by submitting a certified copy of his deposit into evidence.

In the case of unregistered works, you would have to present other evidence showing when the work was created, such as witnesses who saw you write it or dated notes and drafts.

What if the plaintiff's and your works were created at about the same time, or you can't prove when you created your work? In this event, it is very difficult, if not impossible, to prove independent creation. This is because the alleged copying need not be done consciously for the plaintiff to win. Unconscious copying also constitutes infringement (although the damages imposed may be smaller than for conscious, willful copying). Your quandary, then, is how to prove you didn't unconsciously copy from the plaintiff's work. About the best you can do in this situation is show that you created similar works in the past without copying and that you had no need to copy from the plaintiff's work. The judge or jury just might believe you.

Never assert independent creation or any other defense if it's not true. If your defense is based on lies, you'll most likely lose anyway and possibly anger the judge and/or jury. As a result, you could end up being far more severely punished than you otherwise might have been and possibly prosecuted for perjury, a felony.

Statute of limitations

A plaintiff can't wait forever to file an infringement suit. The statute of limitations is three years from the time the infringement should reasonably have been discovered (but applying this rule can be extremely tricky). If the plaintiff waited too long, the defendant may be able to have the case dismissed.

Material copied was in the public domain

If the material you allegedly copied is in the public domain, it can be used by anyone for any purpose. As discussed in detail in Chapter 6, the public domain includes:

- the ideas and facts contained in protected works
- the ideas, facts, and expression contained in works that don't qualify for copyright protection because they do not constitute original, fixed, minimally creative works of authorship
- works that might otherwise qualify for protection but are denied it, such as works by government employees, certain blank forms, titles, and short phrases, and
- works for which copyright protection has expired.

Remember, however, that so long as the plaintiff's work was registered within five years after creation, it is presumed to be protected by copyright. This means that you will bear the burden of proving the work was really not protected.

The use was authorized

In some cases, the alleged infringer isn't an infringer, but a legal transferee. For example:

- The infringer might legitimately claim to have received a license to use the plaintiff's work, and the work the plaintiff claims to infringe on his copyright falls within that license. Example: Author "A" orally tells author "B" he can copy his work, then later claims never to have granted the permission.
- Conflicting or confusing licenses or sublicenses are granted and the defendant claims to be the rightful owner of the right(s) in question.
- A transferee wasn't restricted in making further transfers and transferred the copyright to individuals unknown to the original owner.

Several examples of lawful transfers are presented in Chapter 9, Transferring Copyright Ownership. If any of these transferees were sued they would have a good defense—that is, that their use was lawful.

Public Domain Status of Foreign Work

Certain foreign works that you may have thought were in the public domain because of failure to comply with U.S. copyright formalities, such as using a copyright notice or filing a copyright renewal, are no longer in the public domain. Copyright in many of these works was automatically restored on January 1, 1996 as a result of U.S. adherence to the GATT Agreement. However, you may have special rights if you used such foreign material before 1996. (See Chapter 13, International Copyright Protection.)

Other defenses

Some of the other possible defenses to copyright infringement include such things as:

- The notion that if the plaintiff is guilty of some serious wrongdoing himself—for example, falsifying evidence—he cannot complain about your alleged wrongs.
- The notion that the plaintiff waited so long to file suit that it would be unfair to find the defendant guilty of infringement. "It is inequitable for the owner of a copyright, with full notice of an intended infringement, to stand inactive while the proposed infringer spends large sums of money on its exploitation, and to intervene

only when his speculation has proved a success. Delay under such circumstances allows the owner to speculate without risk with the other's money; he cannot possibly lose, and he may win." (*Hass v. Leo Feist, Inc.*, 234 Fed. 105 (S.D. N.Y. 1916).)

- The idea that the copyright owner knew of your acts and expressly or impliedly consented to them.

Deciding Whether to Settle or Fight

If a substantial claim is involved, the decision whether to settle the case or fight it out in court should be made only after consulting an attorney who is familiar with the facts of your particular case. However, in making this decision you need to carefully weigh the following factors:

- the likelihood the plaintiff will prevail
- how much the plaintiff is likely to collect if he does win
- the costs of contesting the case, not only in terms of money, but time, embarrassment, and adverse publicity, and
- how much the plaintiff is willing to settle for.

If the plaintiff clearly does not have a valid claim, you may be able to have his suit dismissed very quickly by filing what's called a summary judgment motion. Under this procedure the judge examines the plaintiff's claims and decides whether there is any possibility he could prevail if a trial were held. If not, the judge will dismiss the case. Of course, you must pay a lawyer to file a summary judgment motion, but, if successful, it will cost far less than taking the case to trial. Moreover, the court may be willing to award you all or part of your attorney fees. This is especially likely if the plaintiff's suit was clearly frivolous.

On the other hand, if the plaintiff does have a valid claim, paying an attorney to fight a losing battle will only compound your problems. Valid claims should be settled whenever possible. If the plaintiff was able to obtain a preliminary injunction from a federal judge, he probably has a valid claim.

How to Protect Yourself From Copyright Infringement Claims

The only way you can absolutely prevent others from accusing you of copyright infringement is never to write and publish anything. However, there are some less drastic steps you can take to help protect yourself from infringement claims:

- First and foremost, always get permission to use other authors' protected expression unless your intended use clearly constitutes a fair use. (See Chapter 11, Using Other Authors' Words.) If you're not sure whether or not you need permission, consult a copyright attorney.
- Date and keep your notes and drafts; these may help you to prove that your work was created independently from the plaintiff's.
- Promptly register your finished work with the Copyright Office; registration

conclusively establishes the date of creation of the material you deposited with your application. If you're extremely worried about being sued for infringement, it may even be worthwhile to register your unfinished drafts.

- If you're an editor for a magazine or publishing company, always promptly return manuscripts you reject; nothing arouses a writer's suspicions more than having a publisher keep a rejected manuscript and then later publish a similar work by another writer. If you already have another writer working on the same or similar idea, let the author of the rejected material know about it.
- Film and television producers and others in the entertainment industry who receive unsolicited submissions should either (1) have an established policy of returning unsolicited manuscripts unopened, or (2) refuse to read them unless the author signs a release absolving the reader from liability for infringement.

■

CHAPTER

13 International Copyright Protection

There is no single body of international copyright law. Each country has its own copyright law that applies within its own borders. However, through a series of international treaties, almost all nations have agreed to give each other's citizens the same copyright protection they afford to their own citizens. If you take the correct procedural steps, your copyright will be protected in virtually every country in the world.

We'll first examine copyright protection outside the United States for works by American citizens or permanent residents, and then turn to copyright protection within the U.S. for foreign citizens or nationals.

International Protection for U.S. Citizens and Nationals

The protection afforded to written works by the U.S. copyright laws ends at the United States borders. The extent of the protection given to work by Americans outside the U.S. is governed by international treaties. The United States and most other major industrialized countries have signed a series of international treaties, the most important of which is the Berne Convention. International copyright protection for works by U.S. citizens and permanent residents largely depends on the rights granted by these international treaties.

The Berne Convention

The world's first major international copyright convention was held in Berne, Switzerland, in 1886. The resulting agreement was called the Berne Convention for the Protection of Literary and Artistic Works, or the Berne Convention for short. The Berne Convention is the most important international copyright treaty, with the highest standards of protection. Most major industrialized countries belong to the Berne Convention. These countries include the United States (as of March 1, 1989), most of Western Europe, Japan, Canada, Mexico, and Australia.

In a nutshell, Berne member countries agree that literary, artistic, and scientific works, including all types of writing, are protected in the following ways.

Principle of national treatment

Every country that has signed the Berne Convention must give citizens or permanent residents of other Berne countries at least the same copyright protection that it affords its own nationals; this is known as national treatment. As a U.S. citizen or permanent resident, any protectable work you create or publish after March 1, 1989 (the date the U.S. joined the Berne Convention), is entitled to national treatment in every country that has signed the Berne Convention.

> **EXAMPLE:** Carl, an American citizen and resident, publishes a biography of Czar Ivan the Terrible in 2003. One year later, while browsing in a London bookstore he discovers a condensed version of his book published under another author's name by a British publisher. Since the U.S. and United

Kingdom have both signed the Berne Convention, if Carl sues the British publisher and author for copyright infringement in the British courts, he will be entitled to the same treatment as any British subject who brought this suit.

No formalities

No formalities, such as notice and registration, may be required for basic copyright protection. However, some countries offer greater copyright protection if a copyright is registered or carries a particular type of notice. For example, in Japan and Canada, registration provides a means of making your work a public record and may thus be helpful in case of an infringement action. Other countries have certain procedural requirements that must be followed before foreign works may be distributed within their borders, such as customs rules, censorship requirements, or other regulations. Compliance with these types of formalities should be taken care of by a foreign agent hired by the author's publisher or the author or author's agent.

Minimal protections required

Every Berne country is required to offer a minimum standard of copyright protection in their own country to works first published or created by nationals of other Berne countries. This protection must include:

- Copyright duration of at least the author's life plus 50 years.
- The granting of moral rights to the author. Moral rights are rights an author can never transfer to a third party because they are considered an extension of her being. Briefly, they consist of the right to claim authorship, to disclaim authorship of copies, to prevent or call back distribution under certain conditions, and to object to any distortion, mutilation, or other modifications of the author's work injurious to her reputation. The right to prevent colorization of black and white films is an example of a moral right. Moral rights are generally of most concern to visual artists.
- Some provision allowing for fair dealing or free use of copyrighted works. This includes material used in quotations for educational purposes, for reporting current events, and so forth. (In the United States, this is

Lev Tolstoi

called fair use, and it is discussed in detail in Chapter 11, Using Other Authors' Words.)

Copyright term for U.S. works in Berne countries

Under the Berne Convention, copyright protection must be granted for at least the life of the author plus 50 years. However, member countries can provide longer copyright terms if they wish. For example, most Western European countries now have a copyright term of life plus 70 years, the same as in the U.S.

> **Application of Berne Convention to Works Created Before March 1, 1989**
>
> As mentioned earlier, the United States was a latecomer to the Berne Convention; it did not join until March 1, 1989. The Berne Convention does not apply to a work first published in the U.S. before that date unless the work was also published in a Berne country at the same time (that is, within 30 days of each other). This is called simultaneous publication. Before 1989, American publishers commonly had their books published simultaneously in the U.S. and Canada and/or Great Britain (both Berne countries) so that they could receive the protection of the Berne Convention. This fact was usually indicated on the same page as the work's copyright notice.

The Universal Copyright Convention

The second most important international copyright treaty is the Universal Copyright Convention (U.C.C.). The United States joined the U.C.C. on September 16, 1955; it applies to all works created or originally published in the U.S. after that date. Where a country has signed both the U.C.C. and Berne Conventions, the Berne Convention has priority over the U.C.C. Since most major countries have now signed the Berne Convention, the U.C.C. is not nearly as important as it used to be. Indeed, it's close to becoming obsolete. The U.C.C. is relevant to works by American nationals only (1) in countries that have signed the U.C.C. but not the Berne Convention, GATT Agreement, or WIPO copyright treaty (see below), and (2) to works first published in the U.S. before March 1, 1989 that were not simultaneously published in a Berne country.

The U.C.C. is very similar to the Berne Convention, with the exception that it allows member countries to require some formalities. It requires member countries to afford foreign authors and other copyright owners national treatment. The U.C.C. also requires that each signatory country provide adequate and effective protection of the rights of foreign authors and other foreign copyright owners of literary, scientific, and artistic work, including writings and dramatic works. In addition, each country must both:

- Offer copyright protection for at least the life of the author plus 25 years.

- Offer the author exclusive rights to translate and reproduce her work, with the exception that if a work is not translated into the language of a U.C.C. country within seven years of the work's original publication (three years if the country is a developing country), the government of that country has the right to make a translation in that country's language. But the government has to pay the author a fair fee for the translation under a compulsory licensing system.

The U.C.C. does not require member countries to dispense with formalities as a prerequisite to copyright protection. But an author or copyright owner of a work first published in one U.C.C. country can avoid complying with another U.C.C. country's formalities (registration, deposit, payment of fees, and so on) simply by placing the following copyright notice on all published copies of the work: [*Date of first publication*] © [*Your name*]. Compliance with the U.S. requirements for a valid copyright notice discussed in Chapter 3, Copyright Notice, also constitutes compliance with the U.C.C. notice requirement. This is one very good reason to always affix a valid copyright notice to your published work.

GATT

In late 1994, the U.S. signed the General Agreement on Tariffs and Trade, GATT for short. GATT is a massive international treaty signed by 117 countries dealing with almost all aspects of international trade. For our purposes, what is most important about GATT is that it includes a special agreement on intellectual property called Trade Related Aspects of Intellectual Property Rights (TRIPS for short). TRIPS requires each member country to agree, at a minimum, to enact national copyright laws giving effect to the substantive provisions of the Berne Convention discussed above. However, moral rights, which are generally not recognized in the U.S., were expressly left out of TRIPS. This means that the U.S. cannot be subject to GATT dispute settlement procedures over the scope of moral rights.

TRIPS requires all GATT member countries to provide meaningful penalties for copyright infringement. These must include injunctive relief (including preliminary injunctions that can be obtained to stop infringing activities before trial) and adequate monetary damages. In addition, member countries must adopt procedures for excluding infringing goods at their borders upon application by U.S. or other copyright owners to their customs services.

GATT also includes mechanisms for settlement of country-to-country disputes regarding implementation of these requirements through the World Trade Organization, an international agency based in Geneva and similar to the World Bank. Special GATT remedies (for example, withdrawal of tariff concessions) may be imposed for violation of GATT rules.

The GATT TRIPS agreement did not take effect immediately in every country, particularly in developing countries. Most of GATT took effect in 1995 or 1996 in developed countries. However, developing countries and countries in transition from centrally planned to market economies (primarily countries that were part of the former Soviet Union or Warsaw Pact members) were given four additional years to comply with TRIPS, meaning they did not have to comply until the year 2000. What are termed "least developed countries" need not comply until 2006.

The WIPO Treaty

The U.S. has signed yet another international copyright treaty. This one was sponsored by the World Intellectual Property Organization (WIPO), a United Nations agency based in Geneva, Switzerland. The treaty is called the WIPO Copyright Treaty (WCT).

The Berne Convention was last revised in 1979, and neither it nor the U.C.C. specifically provided for copyright protection for digital works or computer software. The WCT was drafted in 1996 to help fill this gap. It was signed by the U.S. in 1996 and has been signed by most other major industrial nations.

The WCT requires member countries to enact copyright laws giving effect to the substantive provisions of the Berne Convention. But perhaps the most important aspect of the WCT is that it requires member countries to give copyright protection to works in digital form. This means, for example, that unauthorized copying of material placed on a website can constitute copyright infringement. The WCT also requires member countries to provide effective legal remedies against anyone who removes or alters rights management information from digital works—that is, electronically stored information about who owns the copyright in the work. The U.S. copyright law was amended in 1998 to comply with these requirements. (See the detailed discussion of the Digital Millennium Copyright Act in Chapter 14.)

Protections in Countries Not Covered by Conventions

There are some countries that have not signed any of the copyright treaties discussed above and that are not a party to trade agreements such as GATT. Some of these countries, for example, Taiwan, have entered into a bilateral (country-to-country) copyright treaty with the United States. Under these treaties, works by U.S. citizens are afforded copyright protection in the country involved.

In addition, many countries give foreign authors and their works copyright protection if the foreign author's country of origin provides similar treatment. This means it is possible for your work to be protected in a country that has not signed any of the multinational conventions or entered into a bilateral copyright treaty with the U.S.

However, some countries have no copyright relations with the U.S. and provide no protection for U.S. authors' works. These countries include Afghanistan, Ethiopia, Iran, Iraq, Nepal, San Marino, and Yemen.

Members of Berne Convention, U.C.C., GATT, and WCT									
Country	Berne Convention	U.C.C.	GATT	WCT	Country	Berne Convention	U.C.C.	GATT	WCT
Albania	■		■	■	Cameroon	■	■	■	
Algeria	■	■			Canada	■	■	■	
Andorra		■			Cape Verde	■			
Angola			■		Central African Republic	■		■	
Antigua and Barbuda	■		■		Chad	■		■	
Argentina	■	■	■	■	Chile	■	■	■	■
Armenia	■			■	China	■	■	■	
Australia	■	■	■		Colombia	■	■	■	■
Austria	■	■	■	■	Congo	■		■	
Azerbaijan	■	■		■	Costa Rica	■	■	■	■
Bahamas	■	■		■	Côte d'Ivoire	■		■	
Bahrain	■		■		Croatia	■	■	■	■
Bangladesh	■	■	■		Cuba	■	■	■	
Barbados	■	■	■		Cyprus	■	■	■	■
Belarus				■	Czech Republic	■	■	■	■
Belgium	■	■	■	■	Democratic Rep. of the Congo	■		■	
Belize	■	■	■		Denmark	■	■	■	■
Benin (Dahomey)	■		■	■	Djibouti	■		■	
Bhutan	■				Dominica	■		■	
Bolivia	■	■	■	■	Dominican Republic	■	■	■	■
Bosnia & Herzegovina	■				Ecuador	■	■	■	■
Botswana	■		■	■	Egypt	■		■	
Brazil	■	■	■		El Salvador	■	■	■	■
Brunei			■		Estonia	■		■	■
Bulgaria	■	■	■	■	Fiji	■	■	■	
Burkina Faso	■		■	■	Finland		■	■	
Burundi			■		France				
Cambodia		■	■		Gabon				

Members of Berne Convention, U.C.C., GATT, and WCT (continued)

Country	Berne Convention	U.C.C.	GATT	WCT
Gambia	■	■	■	■
Georgia	■	■	■	■
Germany	■		■	■
Ghana	■		■	
Greece	■		■	■
Guatemala	■	■	■	■
Guinea	■	■	■	■
Guinea-Bissau	■	■	■	
Guyana	■	■	■	■
Haiti	■	■	■	■
Honduras	■		■	■
Hong Kong, China	■		■	
Hungary	■	■	■	
Iceland	■		■	■
India			■	
Indonesia	■	■	■	■
Ireland	■	■	■	
Israel	■	■	■	
Italy	■		■	■
Jamaica	■		■	■
Japan	■	■	■	■
Jordan	■		■	■
Kazakhstan	■	■		■
Kenya	■	■	■	
Korea (North)	■			
Korea (South)	■	■	■	
Kuwait			■	
Kyrgyzstan	■		■	■
Laos		■		
Latvia	■		■	■
Lebanon	■	■		
Lesotho	■		■	
Liberia	■	■		
Libya	■			
Liechtenstein	■	■	■	
Lithuania	■		■	■
Luxembourg	■	■	■	
Macedonia	■	■	■	■
Madagascar	■		■	
Malawi	■	■	■	
Malaysia	■		■	
Maldives			■	
Mali	■		■	■
Malta	■	■	■	
Mauritania	■		■	
Mauritius	■	■	■	
Mexico	■	■	■	■
Micronesia	■			
Moldova	■	■		■
Monaco	■	■		■
Mongolia	■		■	
Morocco	■	■	■	
Mozambique			■	
Myanmar			■	
Namibia	■		■	
Nepal	■			

Members of Berne Convention, U.C.C., GATT, and WCT (continued)

Country	Berne Convention	U.C.C.	GATT	WCT
Netherlands	■	■	■	
New Zealand	■	■	■	
Nicaragua	■	■	■	■
Niger	■	■	■	
Nigeria	■	■	■	
Norway	■	■	■	
Oman	■		■	■
Pakistan	■	■	■	
Panama	■	■	■	■
Papua New Guinea			■	
Paraguay	■	■	■	■
Peru	■	■	■	■
Philippines	■		■	■
Poland	■	■	■	■
Portugal	■	■	■	
Qatar	■		■	
Romania	■		■	■
Russia	■	■		
Rwanda	■	■	■	
Saint Lucia	■		■	■
Saudi Arabia		■	■	
Senegal	■	■	■	■
Serbia and Montenegro				■
Sierra Leone			■	
Singapore	■		■	■
Slovakia	■	■	■	■
Slovenia	■	■	■	■
South Africa	■		■	
Spain	■	■	■	
Sri Lanka	■	■	■	
Sudan	■			
Suriname	■		■	
Swaziland			■	
Sweden	■	■	■	
Switzerland	■	■	■	
Taiwan			■	
Thailand	■		■	
Togo	■		■	■
Tonga	■		■	
Trinidad and Tobago	■	■	■	
Tunisia	■	■	■	
Turkey	■		■	
Uganda			■	
Ukraine	■	■		■
United Arab Emirates			■	
United Kingdom	■	■	■	
United States	■	■	■	■
Uruguay	■	■	■	
Vatican City	■	■		
Venezuela	■	■	■	
Vietnam	■			
Yugoslavia	■	■		
Zambia	■	■	■	
Zimbabwe	■		■	

Bringing Infringement Suits in Foreign Countries

If your work is infringed upon by a person or entity in a foreign country, the first thing to do is consult with an experienced American copyright attorney. Even if the infringement occurred in another country, you may be able to sue the infringer in the United States. In this event, an American court would apply the copyright law of the foreign country, not American law. If you have to file suit abroad, you'll need to hire a copyright attorney in the foreign country involved to represent you. Your American copyright attorney should be able to refer you to an experienced copyright lawyer in the country involved.

George Bernard Shaw

Before you go to the expense of filing suit, however, be sure to have your attorney explain to you what remedies (for instance, monetary damages, injunctions) you will be entitled to if the suit is successful. Remember, you'll only be entitled to the same treatment that a citizen of the country involved would receive.

Although the U.S. has been urging other nations to take copyright infringement more seriously than they have in the past, some (particularly developing) countries still do not impose meaningful penalties on infringers. This means it may not be economically worthwhile to bring infringement suits against infringers in some countries.

Protection in the U.S. for Non-U.S. Citizens

We now examine copyright protection in the United States from the point of view of non-U.S. citizens.

Foreign Works Entitled to U.S. Copyright Protection

The following works by non-U.S. citizens or permanent residents are entitled to full U.S. copyright protection.

Works first published in the U.S.

Any work first published in the U.S. is entitled to full copyright protection in the U.S., no matter what country the author is a citizen of or lives in.

EXAMPLE: Kim, a citizen and resident of South Korea, first publishes a book of poetry in the U.S. His book is entitled to full U.S. copyright protection.

Works first published in treaty countries

A work is also entitled to full copyright protection in the U.S. if it is first published in a country that has signed any of the following international copyright treaties:

- the Berne Convention
- the Universal Copyright Convention
- the GATT Agreement
- the WIPO Copyright Treaty, or
- a bilateral (country-to-country) copyright treaty with the U.S. (these countries include Taiwan and Vietnam).

Almost every country in the world has signed one or more of these treaties, including every major industrialized country. The chart above shows which country has signed which treaty. We'll refer to these countries as "treaty countries." As a result, almost all works published in foreign countries are entitled to full U.S. copyright protection.

EXAMPLE 1: Pierre, a French citizen and resident, publishes a book in France. Since France signed the Berne Convention, the work is entitled to full U.S. copyright protection.

EXAMPLE 2: Pierre, a French citizen, first publishes his work in Vietnam. The work is entitled to U.S. copyright protection because Vietnam is a treaty country.

Unpublished works

All *unpublished* works are fully protected under U.S. copyright law, no matter what country they were created in.

EXAMPLE: Maria, an Argentinian citizen and resident, creates an unpublished opera. The work is entitled to full U.S. copyright protection.

Foreign Works Not Entitled to U.S. Copyright Protection

A handful of countries have not signed any of the international copyright treaties. These are:

Afghanistan	Iraq
Ethiopia	San Marino
Iran	Yemen

A work published in any of these countries by a citizen or resident of any of these countries is not entitled to U.S. copyright protection—that is, it is in the public domain.

EXAMPLE 1: Omar, an Iraqi citizen and resident, publishes a book in Iraq. Since Iraq is one of the few countries that has signed none of the copyright treaties, Omar's work is not protected by U.S. copyright.

However, application of the rules described in the previous section, shows that a work by a citizen or permanent resident of one of these outcast countries is protected under U.S. copyright law if it is:

- *first* published in the U.S., or

- *first* published in a treaty country, or
- is unpublished.

EXAMPLE 2: Assume that Omar's book in Example 1 above was first published in the U.S. Even though Omar is an Iraqi citizen and resident, his book is entitled to full U.S. copyright protection.

EXAMPLE 3: Assume instead that Omar's book was first published in France. It is entitled to full U.S. copyright protection because it was first published in a treaty country.

EXAMPLE 4: Jaleh, an Iranian citizen, has created an unpublished screenplay. The screenplay is entitled to full U.S. copyright protection—it's protected for the rest of her life plus 70 years. This is so even though the U.S. has no copyright relations with Iran.

For copyright protection purposes, a work is first published in the U.S. or a treaty country if it was published in such a country either before or within 30 days after it was published in a nontreaty country.

EXAMPLE 5: Achmed, a citizen and resident of Nepal, published in Nepal a book on mountain climbing. Two weeks later, the book was also published in India. For copyright purposes, Achmed's book was first published in a treaty country (India) and is entitled to full U.S. copyright protection.

The copyright status of the following countries is unclear—in other words, no one is sure what protection, if any, works published in these countries are entitled to in the United States:

Kiribati	Somalia
Nauru	Syria
Paulau	Vanuatu
São Tomé and Principe	Yemen
Seychelles	

Compliance With U.S. Copyright Formalities

It is not necessary for a non-U.S. citizen to place a valid copyright notice on his published work or register it with the U.S. Copyright Office to obtain copyright protection in the U.S. Indeed, unlike the case with U.S. citizens, a non-U.S. citizen need not register a work first published abroad before filing suit in the U.S. for copyright infringement. However, as discussed in Chapter 3, Copyright Notice, and Chapter 4, Copyright Registration, extremely important advantages are gained under U.S. copyright law if a published work contains a valid copyright notice and a published or unpublished work is registered with the Copyright Office. Therefore, notice and registration are strongly advised for all foreign authors.

Restoration of Copyrights Under GATT Agreement

The GATT TRIPS Agreement required that U.S. copyright law be rewritten to restore

U.S. copyright protection for certain foreign works that:

- were published in the U.S., and
- entered the public domain in the U.S. because certain copyright formalities were not complied with.

The U.S. copyright law has in fact been rewritten to implement this provision, and works meeting the law's requirements have had their copyright restored. In other words, these works are no longer in the public domain.

The intent of the law is to put the U.S. in compliance with the Berne Convention, which never required formalities like a copyright notice or renewal to obtain copyright protection. Foreign authors who failed to comply with these unique U.S. copyright formalities are now forgiven and granted a full term of U.S. copyright protection. Unfortunately, U.S. citizens don't receive this same treatment—copyright in their public domain works has not been restored.

This is a major change in U.S. copyright law that affects not only the authors and copyright owners of the affected works, but also U.S. citizens who thought the works were in the public domain and used them without seeking permission.

Which works lost U.S. copyright protection

Works created by citizens or residents of countries other than the United States entered the public domain in the U.S. if any of the following were true:

- They were published in a foreign country between January 1, 1978 and March 1, 1989 without a valid copyright notice or were published in the U.S. any time before March 1, 1989 without a valid notice.
- They were published in the U.S. or a foreign country before January 1, 1964, but the copyright was never renewed by filing a renewal application with the U.S. Copyright Office during the 28th year after publication. (See Chapter 10, Copyright Duration.)
- They were published in the U.S. before January 1, 1978 but were not registered with the U.S. Copyright Office within six months after the Register of Copyrights notified the copyright owner that registration and deposit must be made.

It's impossible to say how many works were ever published in the U.S. before 1989 without a valid copyright notice. It's likely most works that were deemed valuable at the time did have a notice. However, notices were often left off works that were viewed as not very valuable or of only temporary interest—postcards, for example.

It's likely that by far the largest category of restored foreign works are those published before 1964 for which no renewal notice was filed during the 28th year after publication. The Copyright Office estimates that only about 15% of pre-1964 published works were ever renewed. The 15% that were renewed probably includes a large proportion of those pre-1964 works with continuing economic value. However, mistakes were frequently made and many noteworthy works were never renewed.

Copyright is also restored in works that received no copyright protection in the

U.S. because they were first published in countries with which the U.S. had no copyright relations at the time of publication. You may be surprised to know that as recently as 1973 the U.S. had no copyright relations with the Soviet Union. Works published before 1973 in the Soviet Union were in the public domain in the United States. Copyright in such works has now been restored provided they are still under protection in Russia or the other nations that made up the now defunct Soviet Union. Probably most significant among these works are those by Soviet composers such as Prokofiev and Shostakovitch.

Which works have had copyright restored

U.S. copyright is restored only in those works:

- that had at least one author who was a citizen or resident of a country other than the U.S. that is a member of the Berne Copyright Convention or World Trade Organization (a GATT member), has signed the WIPO Copyright Treaty, or has a copyright treaty with the U.S.—which includes almost all the countries of the world (see chart above)
- that, if published, was first published in one of the countries described above (not necessarily the same country as the author's), but not published in the U.S. within 30 days following the foreign publication, and
- whose copyright protection has not expired under the copyright laws of the foreign country.

The last requirement above is one that a number of foreign works may not satisfy. In almost all foreign countries, copyrights for most types of works last for the life of the author plus 50 years, or the life of the author plus 70 years (Western Europe uses the life-plus-70-year term). If the author of the foreign work died long enough ago, the work may not have qualified for copyright restoration in the U.S.

> **EXAMPLE:** Ken published a book with a copyright notice in Canada in 1940. The book was never renewed and so entered the public domain on January 1, 1969. Ken died in 1942, so the book entered the public domain in Canada on January 1, 1993 (copyrights last for the life of the author plus 50 years in Canada). Because the book was in the public domain in Canada on January 1, 1996, it didn't qualify for copyright restoration. It remains in the public domain in the U.S.

You need to know the copyright term of the foreign author's country and when the author died to know if the work was in the public domain in its home country on January 1, 1996, the date the automatic copyright restoration for foreign works took effect.

Copyright restored automatically

Copyright restoration for all foreign works meeting the above requirements occurred automatically on the date the copyright parts of the GATT Agreement became effective: January 1, 1996. These works receive the same term of copyright protection in the

U.S. they would have had had they never entered the public domain.

> **EXAMPLE:** In 1950, Thames Press, a British publisher, published in Great Britain a novel called *Sticky Wicket,* by the English writer John Jones. Thames failed to file a renewal registration for the book in 1978, and as a result it entered the public domain in the U.S. on January 1, 1979. However, the U.S. copyright in the book was automatically restored by the GATT Agreement, effective January 1, 1996. This is because the work was written by a British subject and was first published in Great Britain (a Berne member), and the British copyright on the book had not expired as of 1995 (British copyrights last for the life of the author plus 70 years). The book receives the same term of copyright protection in the U.S. it would have had had a renewal been timely filed—95 years from the date of publication. The novel will be protected by copyright in the U.S. until December 31, 2045.

Who owns restored works

The U.S. copyright in a restored work is initially owned by the author as defined by the law of the country of origin, not U.S. law. If the author died before GATT's effective date, ownership is determined under the inheritance laws of the author's country. Disputes concerning initial ownership of restored foreign copyrights are to be determined by U.S. federal courts applying the law of the country of origin.

If the author at any time assigned, licensed, or otherwise transferred all or part of his or her copyright rights, the transfer is supposed to be given effect according to the terms of the agreement. Disputes concerning copyright transfers must be resolved in U.S. state courts applying U.S. law.

Copyright infringement of restored works

No one can use a restored work for the *first* time after GATT's effective date without obtaining the copyright owner's permission, unless the use is a fair use. (See Chapter 11.) "Use" means exercising any of the copyright owner's exclusive rights to copy, initially distribute, create derivative works from, or publicly display or perform the work. The owner of a restored work can bring a copyright infringement action against anyone who unlawfully uses the work after GATT's effective date, just as for any other work. (See Chapter 12.)

Things are more complicated, however, if businesses or people used a restored work without permission before GATT's effective date because they thought it was in the public domain and continued to use the work in the same way after that date. Such people are called reliance parties. They can't be sued for copyright infringement until 12 months after the copyright owner of the restored work files a Notice of Intent to Enforce Copyright with the reliance party personally or has filed an NIE with the Copyright Office before 1998.

During this 12-month period, the reliance party may sell off previously manufactured stock, publicly perform or display the work, or authorize others to do so. A reliance party cannot make new copies of the restored work during this period or use it differently than it was used before GATT's effective date unless permission is obtained from the work's copyright owner. After the 12 months are up, the reliance party must stop using the restored work unless a licensing agreement is reached with the copyright owner for continued use of the work.

If a licensing agreement is not reached and the reliance party continues to use the restored work, the copyright owner can sue for copyright infringement for any unauthorized uses occurring *after* the 12-month period expires. But a copyright owner cannot sue a reliance party for any unauthorized uses that occurred *before* the 12-month notice period ended, provided the party used the work the same way before GATT's effective date.

> **EXAMPLE:** A cookbook by the Canadian chef Jean Valjean is published in Canada in 1960. The publisher failed to renew the copyright by filing a renewal registration with the Copyright Office during the 28th year after publication. As a result, the work entered the public domain in the U.S. on January 1, 1989. In 1993, Remainder Press republished the book in the U.S. without obtaining permission from the former copyright owners. This was perfectly legal at the time because the book was in the public domain. However, the copyright in the book was automatically restored on January 1, 1996. Nevertheless, Remainder Press continues to publish the book, just as it had before 1995. Jean Valjean, the author, sent the publisher a Notice of Intent to Enforce Copyright with Remainder on May 1, 2006. Because it published Valjean's book before and after GATT was enacted, Remainder qualifies as a reliance party. Remainder Press has until May 1, 2007 to sell off its remaining stock of the book, but cannot produce any more copies without Valjean's permission. After May 1, 2007, Remainder cannot copy, distribute, or otherwise use the book without obtaining Valjean's permission. If it does, Valjean may sue for copyright infringement for the unauthorized uses that occurred after May 1, 2007.

Special Rights for Owners of Some Pre-1995 Derivative Works

A derivative work is one based on or derived from an original work. (See Chapter 7.) Special rules apply to some derivative works based on restored works. But they only apply where the authors of the derivative work were foreign citizens or residents, or the work was first published abroad, *and* the work was later published or otherwise exploited in the U.S. without permission from the copyright owners of the original restored work. There are likely very few works that qualify. (See 17 U.S.C. § 104A(d)(3).)

Sending Notice of Intent to Enforce Copyright to reliance parties

As discussed above, the owner of a restored work has no rights against a reliance party unless a Notice of Intent to Enforce Copyright (NIE) is sent. Before 1998, the owner of a restored copyright could file an NIE with the U.S. Copyright Office or send it directly to the reliance party. As of today, however, the NIE must be sent directly to the reliance party. The Copyright Office no longer accepts NIEs. NIEs can be sent to reliance parties until the end of the U.S. copyright term for the restored work. After that date, the U.S. copyright expires and the work reenters the public domain.

NIEs must:

- be signed by the owner or the owner's agent (if signed by an agent, the agency relationship must have been set forth in writing and signed by the owner before sending the notice)
- identify the restored work and the work in which the restored work is used, if any
- include an English translation of the title and any other alternative titles known to the owner

What to Do If You're a Reliance Party

If you're a reliance party—that is, you used a restored work without permission before 1995 because you thought it was in the public domain—here's what you should do:

- First, check the Copyright Office's records to see if the owner of the work you used has filed an NIE with the Copyright Office. The Copyright Office has posted a list of all filed NIEs on its website at www.copyright.gov. You can also search for them by using the Copyright Office's online database, which is accessed from the same website.
- If an NIE has been filed, stop using the work. You'll be liable for any unauthorized uses of the work that occurred 12 months after the NIE was filed. You may wish to seek out the copyright owners of the restored work and obtain their permission to use it again.
- If no NIE has been filed with the Copyright Office, you may elect to continue to use the restored work. You won't be liable for such use until one year after the copyright owner sends you an NIE directly. Alternatively, you may stop using the work or obtain permission from the copyright owner to continue using it.

The copyright owners have until the end of the copyright term of the restored work to file the notice. After that date, the U.S. copyright expires and the work reenters the public domain.

- identify the use or uses of the restored work by the reliance party to which the owner objects—for example, unauthorized publication and distribution of the work, and
- provide an address and telephone number at which the reliance party may contact the owner.

There is no Copyright Office form for such a notice. You can simply draft a letter containing the required information.

Registering restored works with U.S. Copyright Office

It is not necessary to register a foreign work to bring a copyright infringement action in the U.S. However, registration is allowed, and doing so results in the important benefits of being able to obtain statutory damages and attorney fees in a successful infringement suit. (See Chapter 4.)

The Copyright Office created two new registration forms and a continuation page specifically designed for GATT registrations. They are:

- Form GATT, used to register individual restored works and restored works published under a single series title, and
- Form GATT/CON, a page providing additional space that may be used with either of the GATT application forms.

The forms are included on the CD-ROM or may be downloaded from the Copyright Office website at www.copyright.gov or obtained by calling the Copyright Office forms hotline at 202-707-9100.

One copy of each restored work must be submitted along with the registration application. This is called a copyright deposit. Normally, the deposit must be the first published version of a work. (See Chapter 4, Copyright Registration.) However, because some applicants may have difficulty submitting a deposit of an older work as first published, the Copyright Office permits a deposit of other than the first published edition of the work, if absolutely necessary. This can be either a reprint of the original work, a photocopy of the first edition, or a revised version including substantial copyright from the restored work with a statement of the percentage of the restored work appearing in the revision. No deposit need be made for works previously registered with the Copyright Office.

The filing fee for registering a single work or group of works published under a single series title is $45.

Miguel de Cervantes

All GATT/URAA applications for registration should be sent to:

Library of Congress, Copyright Office
Publications Section, LM 455
101 Independence Ave., SE
Washington, DC 20559-6000.

The application, fee, and deposit should be sent in a single package.

Copyright Protection in Canada

Canada's copyright law is similar, though not identical, to that of the United States. Canada is a member of all the major copyright conventions discussed above. Thus, U.S. citizens enjoy the same copyright protection in Canada as do Canadian citizens, and vice versa.

Works Protected by Copyright

The requirements for copyright protection in Canada are essentially the same as in the U.S. Protection begins automatically the moment you create an original work of authorship. Canadian law protects:

- all types of written works, such as books, pamphlets, poems, and other works consisting of text, including computer programs
- dramatic works such as films, videos, plays, and screenplays
- musical compositions
- paintings, sculpture, drawings, graphics, and other artwork
- photographs, films, and videos
- architectural works, and
- all types of recordings.

As in the U.S., copyright protection does not extend to ideas or facts, only to the way they are expressed by a particular author. Nor does copyright protect individual words, titles, short phrases, slogans, or blank forms.

Canadian Government Works Protected by Copyright

Unlike in the U.S., where works of the federal government are generally in the public domain, Canadian government works are generally protected by what is called Crown Copyright. However, an exception is made for making copies of Canadian federal laws and decisions of federally constituted Canadian courts and administrative tribunals, provided the copier ensures the accuracy of the materials reproduced and the reproduction is not represented as an official version.

Permission to reproduce other Canadian government documents can be obtained from:

Crown Copyright Officer
Canadian Government Publishing
Public Works and Government Services Canada
Ottawa ON K1A 0S9
Tel.: 613-996-6886
Fax: 613-998-1450
E-mail: copyright.droitdauteur@pwgsc.gc.ca.

Scope of Copyright Rights

The rights of a copyright owner in Canada are virtually the same as in the U.S. The owner has the exclusive right to:

- reproduce all or a substantial part of the protected work
- publish the work
- perform the work in public—for example, to perform a play in public or display in public an artistic work created after June 7, 1988
- adapt the work—for example, to convert a novel into a screenplay, translate a work into another language, or record a book on tape.

As in the U.S., the copyright owner may transfer or license any of these rights to others.

Under Canadian law, all authors also have certain "moral rights" which are stronger than in the U.S. No one is allowed to distort, mutilate, or otherwise modify an author's work in a way that is prejudicial to his or her honor or reputation. In addition, the author's name must be included on the work.

Moral rights belong only to the creator of a work—they cannot be sold or transferred to anyone else. However, authors may waive their moral rights when they sell their work. Moral rights exist for the same length of time as copyright and pass to an author's heirs, even if they do not inherit ownership of the copyright itself.

Copyright Duration

Copyrights in Canada usually last for the life of the author plus 50 years. Copyrights expire at the end of the calendar year.

The Canadian copyright in unpublished works depends on the year the works were created:

- The regular life-plus-50-year term applies to unpublished works created after July 25, 1997.
- If the author of work unpublished as of July 25, 1997 died during 1927 to 1997, the copyright lasts until December 31, 2047.
- If the author of work unpublished as of July 25, 1997 died before 1927, the work is in the Canadian public domain.

Copyright Ownership

Copyright ownership rules are very similar to those in the U.S. Any work of authorship created by an employee within the course of employment is automatically owned by the employer unless there is an agreement to the contrary.

Works created by independent contractors—that is, nonemployees—are owned by the contractor, not the hiring firm, unless there is an express or implied agreement transferring ownership to the hiring firm. For example, a work contributed by a freelance writer to a magazine is owned by the writer unless there is an agreement to the contrary.

Limited Fair Use Rights

One major difference between the U.S. and Canada is in the area of fair use. Canada has no "fair use" as such. Instead, it has what is called "fair dealing." Fair dealing is much more limited than fair use in the U.S. It allows people such as critics, reviewers, and researchers to quote from other authors' works without obtaining permission, but only for purposes of private study, research, or criticism. In the case of a published review, criticism, or newspaper summary, the user is required to give the source and the author's name, if known.

Recent amendments to the Canadian copyright laws establish a major new right to copy on the part of libraries, archives, and nonprofit educational institutions. Under these new amendments, nonprofit libraries, archives, and museums are permitted to:

- make copies of published or unpublished works that are not commercially available in a medium and of a quality that meets their users' needs in order to maintain or manage their permanent collections
- reproduce an entire article in a newspaper or magazine if the edition is at least 12 months old at the time of copying, and provided the copy is used for private study or for research purposes, and
- make a single copy of an article from a scientific, technical, or scholarly periodical at any time.

In addition, nonprofit educational institutions will be permitted to reproduce copyrighted materials for the purpose of instruction, tests, or examinations.

Copyright Notice

No copyright notice is required for works published in Canada and no legal benefits are obtained from having one. However, it's still advisable to include a notice on any work that might be distributed outside Canada, especially if it will be seen or used in the U.S.

Copyright Registration

Copyright registration is completely optional. Unlike in the U.S., it is not necessary to register to file a copyright infringement suit in Canada. The benefits of registration are much more limited than in the U.S. A person who registers a work in Canada receives a registration certificate from the Canadian Copyright Office. The certificate serves as evidence that your work is protected by copyright and that you—the person registered—are the owner. This means that in the event of a legal dispute, you do not have to prove ownership; the burden is on your opponent to disprove it. This will prove modestly beneficial if you ever sue someone for copyright infringement in Canada. It may be particularly helpful if you need to obtain a quick court injunction against a copyright pirate to stop an infringing activity.

How to register

Each separate work must be separately registered. There is no group registration of a number of works as in the U.S. The registration process is very easy. You merely fill out an extremely simple application and send it to the Canadian Copyright Office with the required fee. Unlike in the U.S., you are *not* required to deposit a copy of your work.

You can register online by filling out an electronic application form and paying the fee by credit card. Or, you can download the application and mail it in. For detailed guidance, visit the Canadian Intellectual Property Office website at http://strategis.gc.ca/sc_mrksv/cipo/cp/cp_main-e.html.

You may also obtain a copy of the application form by contacting the Canadian Copyright Office at:

Canadian Intellectual Property Office (CIPO)
Industry Canada
50 Victoria Street
Place du Portage
Hull, Quebec
K1A 0C9
819-997-1936
email: cipo.contact@ic.gc.cq

The form asks for the following information:

- **Copyright owner.** The copyright owner is the person or people who created the work, the employer of the author, or any person who obtained ownership through a transfer of copyright. Provide the owner's full legal name.
- **Nature of work.** All works are divided into categories. Works consisting of text are called literary works. This includes books, poems, song lyrics, and computer programs. Screenplays and stageplays are in the dramatic works category.
- **Title.** Provide the specific title of the complete work.
- **Author.** You need to provide the name of the person or persons who actually created the work. If the work was created by an employee or independent contractor, that person's name should be listed. The name of a corporation or other business entity is not acceptable except for photographs.
- **Publication.** If the work has been published, check the box and provide the date and place of publication. Publication occurs when copies are made available to the public. If the work is unpublished, check the appropriate box. If you register the copyright of an unpublished work, you do not have to register again after publication.
- **Signature.** The application must be signed by the copyright owner, his or her agent, or, in the case of a corporation, a director, secretary, or other principal officer of the corporation. If an agent is signing, the phrase "agent for applicant" should be inserted beneath the signature line.

Registration fee

The fee for registration is $50 in Canadian dollars if the application is submitted online; $65 if it is not. Registration is valid for as long as the copyright for the work exists. Once you register your copyright, you do not have to pay any additional fees to maintain or renew it.

Deposit With National Library

The publisher of any book published in Canada must deposit two copies with the National Library of Canada in Ottawa within one week of publication. If the book's retail value is over $50 in Canadian dollars, only one copy need be deposited. Failure to comply with the deposit requirement will not affect your copyright, but the Library may fine you.

For additional information, contact:

Legal Deposit
National Library of Canada
395 Wellington Street
Ottawa, Ontario
K1A 0N4
819-997-9565
www.nlc-bnc.ca

Additional Information

The Canadian Copyright Office has produced a very useful brochure on Canadian copyright law called *Guide to Copyright*. You can obtain a free copy from the CIPO at the address or phone number listed above. You may also download a copy from the Copyright Office website at http://strategis.gc.ca/sc_mrksv/cipo/cp/cp_main-e.html.

Copies of the Canadian Copyright Act and Rules can be found on the Canadian Intellectual Property Office website at http://strategis.gc.ca/sc_mrksv/cipo/cp/cp_main-e.html. They may also be found in many libraries. You can also buy a copy of the Act and Rules in any bookstore selling Canadian federal government publications, or order it from:

Canada Communication Group
Publishing Division
Ottawa, Ontario
K1A 0S9
819-956-4800
Fax: 819-994-1498
http://canada.justice.gc.ca

There is an excellent one-volume guide to Canadian copyright law called *Canadian Copyright Law*, by Lesley Ellen Harris. It's published by McGraw-Hill Ryerson.

Readers in the U.S. may find it easier to read about Canadian copyright law in a two-volume treatise called *International Copyright Law and Protection*, by David Nimmer and Paul Geller. It's published by Matthew Bender and available in many U.S. law libraries.

Information about all forms of intellectual property in Canada may be found on the website maintained by the Canadian Intellectual Property Office at http://cipo.gc.ca.

Marketing Your Work in Foreign Countries

If you are sharing ownership of foreign rights with your publisher, the publisher usually markets them through foreign agents with which it has established relationships and at international book fairs (the Frankfurt, Germany, book fair is the most important). If you have retained all your foreign rights and have an agent, she'll market your foreign rights through foreign subagents. If you've retained your rights and don't have an agent, you need to retain one. You can use an American agent who has contacts with foreign subagents, or directly contact agents in the particular countries in which you wish to sell your rights. The latter course will save you money since you'll only have to pay a commission to the foreign agent, not to an American agent as well. The publication *International Literary Marketplace* lists British and other foreign agents.

■

CHAPTER

14 Copyright in the Online World, Electronic Publishing, and Multimedia

The advent of the personal computer has given rise to a new medium—the online world—which has created unique problems regarding established copyright laws and principles.

The "online world," also known as cyberspace or the information superhighway, consists of millions of individual computers interconnected with each other, typically by phone lines. An individual computer user can connect with a computer hundreds or thousands of miles away and instantly send and receive immense amounts of data. A collection of interconnected computers is often called a network.

By using computer technology, any written work can be transformed into digital form—a series of ones and zeros that can be read and understood by computers. These digital copies can be stored in computers and instantaneously transmitted to other computers over networks to be read and used by people. Far more written works are available in digital form online in electronic databases than in all the libraries of the world. Widespread confusion exists as to whether and how much copyright protects written and other works in the online world or whether it can protect them at all.

Self-proclaimed experts assert that the "digital revolution" is the greatest change in human history since the invention of the printing press. This remains to be seen. But there is no denying the importance of computer technology to authors, publishers, and readers. This chapter explores how copyright applies in the brave new digital world.

What's Available Online

The online world is complex and ever-growing. At the moment, it consists of the following main areas or services.

The Internet

The Internet is a vast collection of large and small interconnected computer networks extending around the world. These networks are operated primarily by government agencies and educational institutions. The Internet as a whole is not owned or controlled by anybody, although several nonprofit organizations perform such housekeeping functions as assigning site names (known as domain names). Anyone with a computer and modem can access the Internet by obtaining an account with an Internet access provider or by using someone else's account such as a school or library. Anyone with an account can make material available on the Internet, and everybody who has an account can access this material.

The World Wide Web

The World Wide Web is the most well-known and rapidly growing part of the Internet. Technically, it consists of all the computers and their contents that can be accessed using the HyperText Transport Protocol (HTTP). The term "World Wide Web" is often used interchangeably with Internet because so much of the Internet is commonly accessed in this way.

The World Wide Web also includes the contents of all these computers, consisting of pages of text, graphics, sounds, and video that are linked to other pages or to other Internet resources. Multiple Web pages linked together at the same Internet address are called a website. The main or default page of a website is called a home page. Most Web pages contain hypertext links. These are like postal addresses. By clicking on a link, a Web user can access a particular file anywhere on the World Wide Web.

Commercial Online Services

Some of the best known parts of the online worlds are commercial online services such as America Online. These services are owned and run by private companies. To access these systems, a person must become a subscriber and pay a fee. These systems typically offer electronic mail services, online "chats" with other users, vast collections of electronic databases, and Internet access.

Private Internets

Many organizations such as private companies and public and private universities operate their own private "in-house" computer networks. These are used for email, document transfer, database storage, and access. These private internets are often called "intranets." These intranets are not open to the public. Only members of the organization that runs them are allowed access.

What Online Materials Qualify for Copyright

Copyright protects all types of works of authorship, including all kinds of written works, photos, artwork, videos, films, and sound recordings. A digital version of a work of authorship is entitled to copyright protection if the requirements discussed below are satisfied. The fact that a work in its digital form can only be read by computers—because it consists only of ones and zeros—does not affect copyright protection. Computer "language" is protectable under copyright just like recorded human words and speech.

Under the copyright laws, the moment a work of authorship is created it is automatically protected by copyright if, and to the extent, it is:

- original—that is, not copied from others
- fixed in a tangible medium of expression, and
- minimally creative. (See Chapter 6 for detailed discussion.)

All three requirements are easily met in the online world.

Originality and Creativity

The originality and creativity requirements pose no special problems at all. A work is sufficiently original if it was independently created—that is, not copied from other works.

The amount of creativity required is very slight. It's sufficient that a work be the product of a very minimal creative spark. It doesn't have to be novel, unique, ingenious, or even any good to be sufficiently creative. But still, some works of expression lack even this minimal level of creativity. One good example of "expression" that was denied copyright protection was telephone directory white pages. (See Chapter 6 for detailed discussion.)

Fixed in a Tangible Medium of Expression

A work that is original and minimally creative must also be fixed in a tangible medium of expression to be protected by copyright—for example, written down on paper or recorded on film or tape. Words that are thought or spoken but never recorded in some tangible medium are not protected.

There are many ways to "fix" an expression in the online world once it's reduced to digital form. For example, it can be fixed on a computer hard disk, floppy disk, or CD-ROM. These are tangible permanent physical media similar to phonograph records.

Rights Enjoyed by Copyright Owners Online

Under the general copyright laws, the owner of a work of authorship entitled to copyright protection automatically acquires a bundle of exclusive copyright rights. "Exclusive" means no one may exercise these rights without the copyright owner's permission. Anyone who does will be liable to the owner for copyright infringement. These exclusive rights are the:

- reproduction right—that is, the right to make copies of a protected work
- distribution right—that is, the right to initially sell or otherwise distribute copies to the public
- right to create adaptations (or "derivative works")—that is, the right to prepare new works based on the protected work, and
- performance and display rights—that is, the right to perform or display a work in public.

These exclusive copyright rights exist in the online world the same way they do in the physical world. Just as copyright protects words printed in books available to anyone with access to a bookstore or library, it also protects words which are input into computer systems and made available to people with computers and modems. It's important to remember, however, that although a copyright owner's rights are exclusive, they are subject to some important exceptions, most notably the fair use privilege.

Let's now take a closer look at what these copyright rights are and how they apply in the online world.

Reproduction Right

The reproduction right is the right to make copies of a work. This is the most fundamental copyright right. Subject to the fair use privilege, a copyright owner has the exclusive right to make copies of his or her work online. The exclusive reproduction right extends not only to text, but to graphics, pictures, and sounds.

A copy of a work of expression is made whenever the work is digitized—that is, converted to a series of binary ones and zeros that can be read by a computer—and placed into a permanent computer storage device such as a hard disk, CD-ROM, or floppy disk.

If a person downloads (transfers) this digital copy into his or her own computer and saves it on a permanent storage medium, a second copy is made. If this person prints out a hard copy of the work on paper, a third copy is made, and if he or she then transmits digital copies to other computers over a network and such copies are permanently stored, additional copies—perhaps thousands—are made.

Unless this copying is a fair use or is done with express or implied permission, it is a violation of the copyright owner's reproduction right. Much of the copying done by individuals in the online world likely qualifies as a fair use.

Are RAM copies copies?

A digital work doesn't have to be stored on permanent physical media like a hard disk to be used. Instead, it can be stored in temporary computer memory, also known as RAM (short for Random Access Memory). RAM exists only while a computer is turned on. For example, a computer user may download (copy) a work from the Internet to the RAM in his or her computer. The downloaded copy exists for as long as the computer is on—which could be minutes, hours, weeks, or longer. The computer user can read the copy on the computer display or otherwise use the copy. But once he or she turns off the computer, the copy is lost unless it is first saved to a permanent storage medium like a hard disk.

A few courts have held that a RAM copy of a work is a copy for copyright purposes. Since a RAM copy can theoretically exist for a very long time (even years if a user keeps his computer on that long), these courts view it as being sufficiently fixed to merit copyright protection. (*Advanced Computer Services v. MAI Systems Corp.*, 845 F.Supp. 356 (E.D. Va. 1994).) However, this is still an unsettled legal question.

If a RAM copy of a work is a copy for copyright purposes, simply reading or viewing a work online could technically constitute an infringement of the copyright owner's reproduction right unless it is done with permission or the act of downloading the copy into RAM qualifies as a fair use. It seems likely that simply reading or viewing a work online is a fair use (see below). Or, at the very least, it's likely people who post their works on the Internet and online services give their implied permission for others to read them—after all, why else would they place them online?

In any event, some copyright experts believe that loading a digital copy into computer RAM is not copying as defined in the copyright law, since the "copy" only exists temporarily and is lost when the computer is shut off. Under this view, reading or browsing copyrighted works online is permissible as long as a permanent copy is not made—for example, on a hard disk, floppy disk, or hard copy printout.

Distribution Right

A copyright owner has the exclusive right to distribute copies of his or her work to the public by sale, rental, or lending. This includes making a work available to the public on the Internet or a commercial online service like America Online.

But there is a very important exception to the distribution right: Once a copy is sold or otherwise distributed, the new owner of the copy may sell or otherwise transfer that particular copy without the copyright owner's permission. This is called the first sale rule. For example, if you buy a book in a bookstore, you may sell the book (technically, a copy of the underlying work of expression covered by copyright) to a used bookstore without the copyright owner's permission. But you can't make additional copies of the book. There are two exceptions to this rule: Computer programs and sound recordings can't be rented, leased, or lent to others without the copyright owner's permission. But they may be sold or given away without permission.

The first sale rule applies to digital copies as well. For example, if you purchase a CD-ROM containing an electronic book, you can sell or otherwise dispose of the CD-ROM without permission. But you can't make additional copies of the CD-ROM.

It's unclear to what extent the first sale rule applies to digital transmissions. For example, if you download a copy of a copyrighted book from the Internet with the copyright owner's permission, can you then transmit your digital copy to another computer? Some say this is permissible so long as you delete the copy stored on your own computer. They argue that this is the legal equivalent of giving away a book, since you no longer have your copy. Others say the first sale rule should be completely outlawed in the online world because it's so easy to make and transmit digital copies. So far, neither Congress nor the courts have taken up this issue.

Right to Create Derivative Works

A copyright owner also has the exclusive right to create derivative works from the original work—that is, new works based upon or adapted from the original work. (See Chapter 7 for a detailed discussion.) A user who modifies a downloaded file by annotating, editing, translating, or otherwise significantly changing the contents of the file creates a derivative work. Such a work would be an infringing work unless it was created with the copyright owner's express or implied permission or constitutes a fair use.

There is, however, one important exception to the exclusive right to create derivative works. The lawful owner of a copy of a computer program may adapt or modify it solely for his or her personal use. (17 USC § 117.) For detailed discussion, refer to *Web & Software Development: A Legal Guide,* by Stephen Fishman (Nolo).

Public Display Rights

Copyright owners not only have the exclusive right to make copies of their works, they also have the exclusive right to publicly display them. A "display" includes showing an image on a computer terminal connected with an information storage and retrieval system.

However, the fact that the display must be in public limits the display right. A public place is a place the public is free to enter without restriction other than an admission fee or an agreement to adhere to rules of comportment. It is a place where a substantial number of people outside the usual circle of family or social acquaintances are gathered. A digital transmission of a work protected by copyright which is shown on a computer in a bar, school, conference hall, or other public place is considered a public display.

A display is also considered to be public when the public can share in it individually at home. For example, a television broadcast is a public display even though each member of the viewing audience may see the broadcast in private. Online services like America Online appear very similar to television broadcasters. A photograph shown on America Online would likely be viewed as publicly displayed even though the users of America Online are in their homes.

However, it's important to differentiate between a public display and simply making material available for copying. Placing a digitized version of a photograph in a file online that users can download and view on their computers is not a public display—it is simply making a copy available to individual members of the public. But if the same photo automatically appears on the user's computer screen when he or she logged on to an online service, it would be a public display.

Public Performance Rights

The owner of a written work such as a poem or play has the exclusive right to perform it in public—for example, to recite or act it in a public place such as a theater or to broadcast it to the public on television. What constitutes a public performance is governed by rules discussed above used to determine if a display is public.

This means, for example, that a live transmission of a rock concert, movie, or radio show over a computer network would constitute a public performance of the work. Unless permission were obtained, such a transmission would constitute copyright infringement. But simply placing a digitized copy of a rock concert video online for downloading by users would not be a public performance of the concert.

An audiovisual work is "performed" whenever images and sounds are publicly displayed in any sequence. However, a single photo, painting, or sculpture does not "perform." Thus, the public performance right does not extend to pictorial, graphic, and sculptural works. The display right is considered sufficient for such works.

Fair Use Limitation on Copyright Owners' Exclusive Rights

There is an extremely important limitation on the exclusive copyright rights described above: the fair use rule. Anybody can use a copyright owner's protected expression without permission if the use constitutes a fair use. (See Chapter 11.) Fair use applies in the online world just as it does in the physical world.

It's difficult to describe any general rules about fair use, because it is always very fact-specific. However, private individuals who copy works for their own personal use have much greater fair use rights than those who copy for commercial purposes. Although no court has so ruled, it seems likely that it is a fair use for private individuals to make temporary RAM copies of online files in order to read or browse them on their computers.

It is likely also a fair use to download online files to a single hard disk, floppy disk, or other permanent computer storage device *for personal use only*, and even to print a single hard copy of an online file for personal use.

> **EXAMPLE:** Art downloads a copy of a copyrighted article from *The New York Times* Internet site and stores it on his hard disk for future reference. This is probably a fair use.

Other uses can also be a fair use. This is most likely where they are for educational, scholarly, or journalistic purposes. For example, it may be a fair use to quote a portion of an online text file in a newspaper article, college dissertation, or book.

In addition, the more "transformative" a use is, the more likely it will be a fair use. A use is transformative where the material is used to help create a new and different work, not simply copied verbatim. Be careful, however, that you don't take so much material from the original work that your work would constitute a derivative work—that is, a work "based on or adapted from the original work." Taking so much material can rarely be a fair use.

The fair use privilege is discussed in detail in Chapter 11.

Linking, Framing, and Inlining

In some cases, linking, framing, and inlining can violate copyright and other laws and should not be done without obtaining permission.

Linking

Linking is one of the most appealing features of the Internet: The use of hypertext links allows users to instantly navigate from one website to another (or within a website) by clicking on the link.

It is not a violation of copyright to create a hyperlink, but courts have held that it is a violation of the law to create a link that contributes to unauthorized copying of a copyrighted work if the linking party *knew or had reason to know* of the unauthorized copying and encouraged it.

EXAMPLE: A website posted infringing copies of a church's copyrighted handbook at its site. The website was ordered to remove the handbook, but subsequently provided links to other sites that contained infringing copies of the handbook. These links were different from traditional hyperlinks because the website knew and encouraged the use of the links to obtain unauthorized copies. The linking activity constituted contributory copyright infringement. (*Intellectual Reserve, Inc. v. Utah Ministry, Inc.*, 75 F.Supp.2d 1290 (D. Utah 1999).)

Deep linking

A link that bypasses a website's home page and instead goes to another page within the site is often called a "deep link." Some website owners object to the use of deep links. They want all the people who use their website to go first to the home page, usually because advertising is posted there. The use of deep links can cost such a website advertising revenue. In one of the first cases of its kind, Ticketmaster sued a competitor called Tickets.com partly because it linked from its website to pages deep within Ticketmaster's site. The court held that deep linking does

Limiting Liability With Disclaimers

If a website owner is concerned about liability for links but is unable or unwilling to seek permission from the linkee, a prominently placed disclaimer may reduce the likelihood of legal problems. A disclaimer is a statement denying an endorsement or waiving liability for a potentially unauthorized activity. A disclaimer is rarely a cure-all for legal claims, but if a disclaimer is prominently displayed and clearly written, a court may take it into consideration as a factor limiting damages. In some cases, such as trademark disputes, it may help prevent any liability. For example, in a case involving a dispute between websites for two restaurants named Blue Note, one factor that helped the lesser-known restaurant avoid liability was a prominently displayed disclaimer stating that it was not affiliated with the more famous restaurant. (*Benusan Restaurant v. King*, 937 F.Supp. 295 (S.D. N.Y. 1996).) To minimize liability for any activities that occur when a visitor is taken to a linked website, a webmaster may want to include a linking disclaimer on its home page or on any pages with otherwise troublesome links.

Here is a sample linking disclaimer:

By providing links to other sites, [*name of your website*] does not guarantee, approve, or endorse the information or products available at these sites, nor does a link indicate any association with or endorsement by the linked site to [*name of your website*].

not violate the copyright laws, because no copying is involved. However, the court held that Ticketmaster might have a claim against Tickets.com on other legal grounds, such as violation of trademarks or unfair business practices. (*Ticketmaster Corp. v. Tickets.com*, 54 U.S.P.Q. 2d 1344 (C.D. Cal. 2000).)

Many copyright experts believe that deep linking is not copyright infringement—after all, the author of a novel can't prevent readers from reading the end first if they so desire, so why should a website owner have the right to determine in what order a user can access a website? Nevertheless, it's prudent to be careful before deep linking to advertising-rich commercial sites. Many such sites have linking policies posted. Some well-known websites such as Amazon.com welcome deep links. If a commercial website has no posting linking policy or says that deep links are not allowed, it's wise to ask for permission before deep linking. Otherwise, you could end up getting a "cease and desist" letter from a lawyer.

Framing

"Framing" means that website A shows visitors content from website B—but inside a frame on website A. Framing may trigger a dispute under copyright and trademark law theories because a framed site arguably alters the appearance of the content and creates the impression that its owner endorses or voluntarily chooses to associate with the framer. In a 1997 lawsuit, TotalNEWS framed news content from media outlets such as CNN, *USA Today*, and *Time*. For example, the content of a CNN Web page appeared within a frame packed with advertising and information about TotalNEWS. The lawsuit settled and TotalNEWS agreed to stop framing and to only use text-only links.

A subsequent court fight involving two dental websites also failed to fully resolve the issue. Applied Anagramic, Inc., a dental services website, framed the content of a competing site. The frames included information about Applied Anagramic as well as its trademark and links to all Web pages. A district court ruled that a website containing a link that reproduced Web pages within a "frame" may constitute an infringing derivative work. The court reasoned that the addition of the frame modified the appearance of the linked site and such modifications could, without authorization, amount to infringement. (*Futuredontics Inc. v. Applied Anagramic Inc.*, 1997 46 U.S.P.Q.2d 2005 (C.D. Cal. 1997).)

Inlining

Inlining is the process of displaying a graphic file on one website that originates at another. For example, inlining occurs if a user at website A can, without leaving website A, view a "cartoon of the day" featured on website B. Inlining makes it look like the linked-to file actually originated on website A, instead of website B.

In the first case involving inlining, an image search engine called ditto.com used inline links to reproduce full-size photographic images from a photographer's website. By clicking on the link, the user was presented with a window containing a full-sized image imported from the photographer's website, surrounded by the search engine's advertising. The court held that this inlining constituted copyright infringement—it violated the photographer's exclusive right to display his images. In contrast, the court held that the search engine's practice of creating small reproductions ("thumbnails") of the images and placing them on its own website was permitted as a fair use. The thumbnails were much smaller and of much poorer quality than the original photos and served to index the images and thereby help the public access them. (*Kelly v. Arriba Soft Corp.*, 280 F.3d 934 (9th Cir. 2002).)

How Copyright Protects Different Types of Online Works

Many different types of copyrighted works are available in the online world, including text, graphics, photos, sounds, and electronic mail. Let's see how copyright protects particular types of online works.

Text Files

Digital copies of text files stored in online databases pose no special copyright problems. They are entitled to the same copyright protection as printed copies of books stored on the bookshelves of a bookstore. It is illegal for you to go into a bookstore with a portable photocopier and make copies of the books displayed there or to recite a copyrighted book on the radio without permission from the copyright owner. Similarly, you may not copy, distribute, adapt, perform, or display a digital version of a written text without the copyright owner's permission unless your use constitutes a fair use.

As mentioned above, making a single copy of a text file solely for personal use likely constitutes a fair use. In addition, a copyright owner who uploads a text file to the Internet or online service does so in order that other people can access and read it. Arguably, the act of uploading the work grants other users an implied license to download the work solely for their personal use.

Images and Sounds

Images and sounds—photos, graphics, recordings—are fundamentally no different from text files for copyright purposes. They are protected by copyright if they are original, minimally creative, and fixed in a tangible medium of expression. Subject to

Frederic François Chopin

the fair use rule, the copyright owner has the exclusive right to copy, distribute, adapt, perform, and display such works.

It is a copyright infringement, for example, to scan a copyrighted photograph and place the image on the Internet without the copyright owner's permission. It is likewise an infringement to download a protected image and use it without permission. "Use" means copying, distributing, adapting, or publicly performing or displaying the work.

EXAMPLE 1: Starware Publishing Corp. downloaded several graphics files from a computer bulletin board service and published them on CD-ROMs. The files contained 52 copyrighted photos owned by *Playboy Magazine*. *Playboy* sued Starware for copyright infringement and was awarded $1.1 million. (*Playboy Enterprises, Inc. v. Starware Publishing Corp.*, 900 F.Supp. 433 (S.D. Fla., 1995).)

EXAMPLE 2: 140 music publishers sued CompuServe alleging that the online service had infringed the copyrights in over 550 music compositions that were uploaded and downloaded to and from CompuServe by subscribers. CompuServe agreed to pay $500,000 in damages and to work with the publishers to help them license their work to online users. (*Frank Music Corp. v. CompuServe, Inc.*, No. 93 Civ. 8153 (S.D. N.Y. 1993).)

However, simply viewing an image or listening to sounds that have been placed online by the copyright owner is not an infringement. Although no court has so ruled, it seems clear that by the act of uploading such a work the copyright owner has granted other users an implied license to download it to their own computer for personal viewing or listening.

Is Modifying Images or Sounds Infringement?

It is common practice for graphic artists and others to download images from the Internet and other online sources and then modify or adapt them using computer graphics software. The altered images are often used in magazines, books, and other published works. Similarly, it's possible to download sounds and reuse bits and pieces in new recordings.

One of the exclusive rights a copyright owner has is to create derivative works from his or her work. A derivative work is one that is based on or recast from an original. (See Chapter 7.) A derivative work is created when an existing image or sound is modified or altered to form part of a new work. Such a work would be a copyright infringement unless permission is obtained to create it or it constitutes a fair use. The only exception to this rule might be where the original image or sound is so completely altered that the original source is no longer recognizable.

Websites

Websites are protected by copyright if, and to the extent, they are original. If a site contains valuable expressive material, it should contain a copyright notice. Many websites consist largely of collections of hypertext links, similar to an address book. These may be protectable as compilations if a minimal amount of creativity was required to create them. (See Chapter 7, Adaptations and Compilations.) For example, a collection of links to the best poetry sites on the Web is likely a protectable compilation—the individual links would not be protected, but copying the entire collection would be a copyright violation. Such link collections are a new form of protectable material produced by the Internet.

However, there is no copyright protection for the format of a FAQ (Frequently Asked Questions) page on a website. The FAQ format is considered common property. (*Mist-On Systems, Inc. v. Gilley's European Tan Spa*, 303 F.Supp.2d 974 (D. Wis. 2002).)

Electronic Databases

An electronic database is a collection of facts, data, or other information assembled into an organized format suitable for use in a computer. The material contained in a database may consist of text files, graphics, images, sounds, and anything else a database creator can think of. Many electronic databases are accessible online—for example, databases of magazine and journal articles may be accessed through commercial online services like Nexus and Dialog.

The individual works contained in a database may be protected by copyright as described in this section, or they might be unprotectable. Either way, there can also be a compilation or collective work copyright in the database as a whole.

Electronic Mail

Most electronic mail is trivial and ephemeral—the people who create such messages probably care little and think less about copyright protection for their "works." However, some people—scholars and scientists, for example—use electronic mail to collaborate with colleagues, communicate new and important ideas, and exchange drafts of works in progress.

Electronic mail is protected the same way as a physical letter. To the extent that it is original—that is, not copied from someone else—it is fully protected by copyright the instant it is fixed in a physical medium such as a computer hard disk.

The author of an email message owns the copyright in the message unless it was created by an employee within the scope of employment. In this event, the employer is considered the author for copyright purposes and automatically owns the copyright in the message. (See Chapter 9.)

When you receive a physical letter from someone, you don't have the right to publish it in a newspaper or book unless such a use constitutes a fair use or the owner of the letter gives you permission. The same holds true for electronic mail: Subject to the fair use rule, it would be copyright infringement for you to forward an electronic message received from someone else without permission. Likewise, modifying an electronic message without the sender's permission would violate the sender's exclusive right to create derivative works from the message.

Of course, email is distributed and modified all the time without obtaining express permission from the copyright owners. So long as this is not done for commercial purposes it probably constitutes a fair use—for example, it's undoubtedly a fair use to quote portions of an email message for a scholarly, journalistic, or educational purpose. However, some people who send email may not be aware of this and may be upset if their messages are copied without their permission. Although it's highly unlikely anyone would bother to bring a copyright infringement suit over something as valueless as email, it's good manners to ask permission before distributing another person's email.

In some cases, however, the senders of email may be deemed to have implicitly consented in advance to permit others to distribute their email—for example, when a person sends email to a Usenet newsgroup. The only reason to send such a message is to have it posted on the newsgroup so that others may read it. It's much like sending a letter to the editor to a newspaper. In such cases, the sender would likely be deemed to have consented in advance to the posting of his or her message.

Computer Conferences

Many online systems have areas where users can post messages for all to view. Software on the host computer records the messages so that each participant can read what has been written by others and then add his or her own responses. Such collections of online messages are often called conferences, discussion forums, message bases, or newsgroups.

Computer conferencing permits online users to communicate with each other on specific topics of mutual interest. Conferences are usually organized into major topics or subjects. They can last a few hours or days, or go on for years. They can be limited to a few participants or be open to anyone with access to the host computer.

The people who post messages in a given conference may create an enormous body of writing. The copyright status of a computer conference is not entirely clear. A conference could be viewed as a collective work or compilation consisting of a bunch of separately protected works. Under this approach, the copyright in each message is owned by its author and each contributor may exercise exclusive copyright rights only over the messages he or she creates. This means that unless it constitutes a fair use, no one may copy or otherwise use an individual's message without that person's permission.

Under this compilation or collective work approach, each message is separately protected. However, someone—it's unclear who—might own a copyright in the collection as a whole. Some online services claim a collection copyright in the computer conferences on their systems. If this claim is valid, a person who copies an entire conference or a substantial portion of one would violate the copyright in the collection as a whole. However, it seems likely that to assert a collection copyright in a conference, the owner of an online service would have to actively participate in shaping the conference by controlling or editing the content. For a detailed discussion of collective works, see Chapter 7, Adaptations and Compilations.

Under another approach, a conference can be considered a joint work, which qualifies as a single work for copyright purposes. Each contributor to the conference would then be deemed to be a joint author and as such would own an undivided interest in the copyright. For instance, if there were 100 contributors of one message each, each would own a 1/100 interest in the copyright to the conference. Under generally applicable joint ownership rules, each contributor would have the right to publish the whole conference (subject to accounting to the other joint authors for their pro rata share of royalties). Each contributor would also be able to sue for infringement of any portion of the conference. See detailed discussion of joint works in Chapter 8, Initial Copyright Ownership.

Blogs

It was estimated in 2006 that 75,000 new blogs are created every day. For the uninformed, a blog (short for weblog) is a website that is much like an online journal or diary. Like any other work of authorship, a blog is protected by copyright to the extent it is original.

Blogs ordinarily present far fewer copyright issues than forums or newsgroups since they are usually authored primarily by just one person. Obviously, that person owns the copyright in the work he or she creates. However, blogs often include writings, photos, artwork, music, and other copyrighted work owned by other people. In some cases these uses might be a fair use, in other cases permission should be obtained. See Chapter 11, Using Other Authors' Words, and Chapter 16, Obtaining Copyright Permissions.

Public Domain Materials

A large and growing number of public domain materials are available on the Internet. For example, Project Gutenberg is creating digitized versions of great literary works and making them available for downloading on the Internet. This is perfectly legal. When a work enters the public domain, copyright protection ceases. The work is freely available for all to use.

A work can enter the public domain for many reasons. The most common reason is that the copyright expires. Other types of works receive no copyright protection—for example, works created by the U.S. government. (See Chapter 6.) An author—that is, the person who creates a work or the owner of a work made for hire—can also dedicate an otherwise protectable work to the public domain. This can be done by stating, "This work is dedicated to the public domain" on the work. There is no need to make a filing with the Copyright Office or any other agency to dedicate a work to the public domain. Note carefully, however, that a work is *not* dedicated to the public domain simply because it is made available online.

Never assume that a work is in the public domain merely because it lacks a copyright notice. Copyright notices are optional for published works and are not required at all for unpublished material. So the fact that a work lacks a notice essentially tells you nothing about whether the work is protected by copyright.

In addition, be aware that some publications available online contain a mix of public domain material and material that is protected by copyright. Protected material does not lose its copyright protection merely because it is mixed with public domain

Google Digitizes Public Domain Books

In 2005, the Web search company Google.com announced that it had entered into agreements with several major research libraries to digitally scan millions of books from their collections and make them available on the Internet as part of Google's book search service (http://books.google.com). Google announced that it would make freely available to Internet users full copies of books published in the United States before 1923. These works are all in the public domain because their copyrights have expired. Google will allow access to only a few pages of books published after 1923. Many of these books are in the public domain because their copyrights were never renewed, but Google apparently thinks it is not feasible to research this.

The Authors Guild filed suit against Google in late 2005, claiming that its plan to make digital copies of copyrighted books without first obtaining permission from their copyright owners constituted copyright infringement. Whatever the outcome of this lawsuit, it will have no impact on Google's efforts to make pre-1923 public domain works freely available.

Google is not the only entity with big plans to digitize books. Yahoo.com, the Internet Archive, the University of California, and others have created the Open Content Alliance (www.opencontentalliance.org). The OCA plans to digitize hundreds of thousands of books and make them freely available on the Internet. Unlike Google, the OCA will digitize public domain books only.

Given all this activity, it seems certain that virtually every available book published in the United States before 1923 will be freely available on the Internet within the next ten or 20 years.

material. Copying an entire file containing such mixed material could constitute copyright infringement of the protected material.

> **EXAMPLE:** A publisher of legal databases used a computer scanner to make digital copies of legal case reports from West Publishing Co. The legal cases themselves were in the public domain, but the copies also included editorial material prepared by West that was protected by copyright. Although the database publisher deleted the protected editorial material before permanently storing the public domain cases in its database, it was still found guilty of infringement. The court held that the temporary copies of the West editorial materials infringed West's copyrights even though they were subsequently deleted. (*West Publishing Co. v. On Point Solutions Inc.*, 1994 WL 778426 (N.D. Ga. 1994).)

Copyright Infringement Online

Copyright infringement occurs every second in the online world, particularly on the Internet, which isn't controlled or supervised by anybody. Many online users have the mistaken idea that any work available online can be freely copied, distributed, and otherwise used without permission.

The problem of unauthorized copying of copyrighted works is not new. Ever since the perfection of the photocopy machine, books, articles, and other printed works have been copied and distributed without permission from, or payment to, the copyright owners. The introduction of the fax machine has made it even easier to deliver photocopies over long distances.

However, there are important limitations on distribution of unauthorized photocopies: copy quality degrades with each generation; photocopying large amounts of work can be time-consuming, expensive, and inconvenient; and a copied document is still in the same format as the original and can be easily identified as a copyrighted work.

None of these limitations exist for digital copies. Perfect digital copies can be made easily, cheaply, and quickly over and over again. Digital copies do not degrade. It is easy to disguise the origins of a digital copy by making simple format changes that require only a few keystrokes. And digital copies are easy to distribute: A copy can be posted on the Internet and easily copied by any number of users anywhere in the country or across the world.

Indeed, unauthorized copying is so ubiquitous on the Internet that some have declared that copyright is dead. However, to paraphrase Mark Twain, the reports of copyright's death are greatly exaggerated. The fact is that the copyright laws have never prevented private individuals from making unauthorized copies. What copyright has done and will continue to do even in the online era is deter the big players from stealing others' work.

For example, because they're afraid of being sued for infringement, publishers are seeking permission from their authors to reproduce the authors' preexisting works online, and are also making sure that publishing agreements for new works address electronic rights. For the same reason, commercial online services like America Online try to prevent copyrighted material from being placed on their systems without permission and quickly remove it when they find it.

The copyright laws have even had an impact on the Internet, which is the online version of the Wild West. Copyrighted photos and other materials have been removed from the Internet when copyright owners complained. And an entire website on Elvis Presley was removed when the Presley estate complained that the site violated the estate's copyright and other intellectual property rights.

Who's Liable for an Infringement?

Anyone who directly exercises any of a copyright owner's exclusive rights without permission is guilty of copyright infringement unless there is a legal excuse, such as fair use. You'll be liable, for example, if you download a protected work from the Internet and publish it in a book or CD-ROM without permission. (See Chapter 12, Copyright Infringement.)

> **EXAMPLE:** A software publisher called Wizardware downloaded from the Internet several sample "cities" created and uploaded by players of the computer game Simcity. Wizardware published the cities on a CD-ROM. Maxis Corp., owner of Simcity, sued Wizardware for copyright infringement, claiming that it owned the artwork the players used to create the cities along with the computer code that was included in the CD-ROM. The judge ordered Wizardware to stop manufacturing and selling the CD-ROM, and impounded all existing copies, until a trial could be held. (*Maxis Inc. v. Wizardware Group, Inc.*, C95-4045WHO (N.D. Cal., 1996).)

If you're liable for infringement, a court can order you to stop the infringing activity, destroy any copies you've made, and pay the copyright owner damages. This is so whether or not you knew the work you infringed upon was protected. The fact you didn't know a work was protected may affect the damages you'll be required to pay but will not relieve you of liability for infringement.

However, you don't have to infringe on someone's work yourself to be liable. A person who induces, causes, or helps someone else commit copyright infringement may be held liable as a contributory infringer. For example, you could be liable for contributory infringement if you permit someone else to use your computer and modem to transmit unauthorized copies of a work.

What about companies that provide access to the Internet (often called Internet Service Providers or ISPs) and online services like AOL? Obviously, an ISP will be liable for infringement where it or its employees actively engage in the infringement—that is, copying, distributing, or displaying a copyright owner's works without permission.

However, a far more important question is whether ISPs are liable when they don't actively participate in the infringement and instead one of their subscribers or users commits the infringement. Surprisingly few courts have considered this question, and there are no definitive answers. However, the leading cases have held that an ISP is liable for copyright infringements committed by its subscribers only if either of the following is true:

- The ISP knew about, or should have known about, the infringing activity and induced, caused, or contributed to the infringing actions.
- The ISP had the right and ability to control the infringer's acts and received a direct financial benefit from the infringement.

EXAMPLE: Dennis Erlich, a former member of the Church of Scientology, uploaded copyrighted Church material onto the Internet using the ISP Netcom to obtain Internet access. The Church sued both Erlich and Netcom for copyright infringement. The court held that Netcom was not liable for direct copyright infringement because it did not directly participate in copying and posting the Church materials on the Internet. All Netcom did was operate as an ISP. Moreover, Netcom did not receive a direct financial benefit from the alleged infringement because it only charged Erlich a flat fee for Internet access. This meant that Netcom could be held liable for Erlich's acts only if it knew about them and induced, caused, or materially contributed to Erlich's allegedly infringing conduct. (*Religious Technology Center v. Netcom On-Line Communication Serv. Inc.*, 907 F.Supp. 1362 (N.D. Cal. 1995).)

Under normal copyright infringement rules, an ISP or other entity that provides access to the Internet will likely not be held liable for subscribers' or users' infringing conduct where the ISP only passively transmitted or stored the allegedly infringing material at the user's direction, provided that the ISP didn't know or have reason to know about the infringement or receive a direct financial benefit from it. However, an ISP may become liable where it directly participates in the infringement, directly benefits from it financially, or looks the other way when it should have reasonably suspected that a subscriber or user was committing infringement. These are the *normal* copyright rules. In 1998, Congress enacted a law giving ISPs special relief from liability from copyright infringements committed by their subscribers or users and for certain other common Internet activities. (See the detailed discussion in the following two sections.)

Internet service providers should delete any infringing material they become aware of or terminate the accounts of users who commit infringement. User agreements should also prohibit users from engaging in illegal activities, including copyright infringement, and provide that the user will indemnify (repay) the operator for claims resulting from such conduct.

Internet Service Providers' Safe Harbor for Copyright Infringement Liability

It has been difficult or impossible for copyright owners to enforce their rights against individual online infringers because (1) individual infringers can be hard to find, and (2) they often have no money to pay any damages. As a result, copyright owners have frequently sued Internet Service Providers (ISPs) instead—that is, the companies that provided access to the Internet and stored and transmitted the allegedly infringing material.

The threat of such lawsuits greatly concerned ISPs and led them to lobby hard for Congress to enact a special law exempting them from liability for online copyright infringements by their subscribers or users under certain circumstances. This law, known as the Digital Millennium Copyright Act (DMCA), took effect in late 1998. Among its many provisions are new "safe harbors" exempting ISPs from liability for monetary damages resulting from copyright infringements by their users. The safe harbors also exempt ISPs from liability for common Internet practices such as caching (see below) that could raise infringement issues.

The basic intent of the DMCA safe harbors is to codify into law the holding of the *RTC v. Netcom* case discussed in the previous

Criminal Liability for Copyright Infringement

Willful copyright infringement for financial gain has long been a federal crime, punishable by both fines and imprisonment. Until recently, however, federal prosecutors rarely prosecuted copyright infringers. They just didn't think it was important enough to warrant allocation of law enforcement resources. This attitude has changed, at least with regard to computer software piracy, an activity software publishers claim costs them billions of dollars every year.

In the best-known case of its kind, the U.S. Attorney criminally prosecuted an MIT student who set up a computer bulletin board to distribute software to subscribers for free. The case was ultimately dismissed because the student earned no money from the piracy. (*United States v. LaMacchia*, 871 F.Supp. 535 (D. Mass. 1994).) In response to this defeat, Congress amended the copyright law to permit criminal prosecutions of people who copy and distribute copyrighted works but receive no money or other financial benefit from their infringement. This law was specifically designed to apply to people who use the Internet to copy and distribute pirated software, but who don't charge users for the copies. (See Chapter 12, Copyright Infringement, for a detailed discussion.)

section: that an ISP cannot be held liable for copyright infringement where it acts as a passive automatic conduit for Internet users, but does not know about or actively participate in the alleged infringement.

However, to qualify for the safe harbor exemptions, a number of complex requirements must be complied with. (See "What ISPs Must Do Now," below.)

These safe harbor rules are lengthy and complex, but they are important … not just to ISPs, but to copyright owners as well. If you believe someone has committed copyright infringement by placing your copyrighted material online without your consent, the rules may bar you from suing the ISP the infringer used to access the Internet. This may make it effectively impossible for you to obtain damages, since the infringer himself may have no money or assets. On the other hand, the rules give you a very powerful tool to have the ISP remove the infringing material without your having to go to court.

If you're a person who uses the Internet to post or email copyrighted material, the safe harbor rules may impact you greatly as well. Your ISP may remove material you've posted because someone claims it's infringing—such removal can occur without any court hearing or other legal process, and you may have no legal remedy against the ISP.

ISPs (and this includes many libraries and educational institutions) should review these safe harbor rules carefully. Any copyright owner or Internet user who has a copyright complaint that involves an ISP or one of

What ISPs Must Do Now

The safe harbor rules are complex and lengthy. Fortunately, it isn't necessary for ISPs to understand them all in detail to qualify. Here's all an ISP must do right now to qualify later for the safe harbor exemptions:

- designate an agent to whom copyright owners may send notices of claimed infringement—this involves filling out a simple form and sending it to the Copyright Office and posting the information on your website
- adopt a policy that repeat copyright infringers will have their accounts terminated and let subscribers know about it—this likely will require updating your subscriber agreement or "terms of use"
- don't go looking for copyright infringements by your subscribers or users, but if you discover one, you must take action
- comply with "standard technical measures" once they have been defined, and
- designate someone to deal with notices of claimed infringement you receive from copyright owners—prompt action will be required.

its subscribers or users should study them as well. Also, be sure to read the section regarding the procedure for removal of infringing materials, below, which describes a simple procedure a copyright owner can use to demand that the ISP remove the infringing material and what the alleged infringer can do about it.

Who may take advantage of the safe harbors?

Only ISPs can take advantage of the DMCA safe harbors. "ISP" is defined very broadly as "a provider of online services or network access, or the operator of facilities" for such services or access. This includes virtually any provider of Internet access or online network services, such as:

- conventional ISPs—that is, companies like AT&T, Microsoft, and Earthlink that provide access to the Internet to paying members of the general public
- commercial online services like AOL
- companies that operate in-house "intranets" or have bulletin boards where customers can post comments about their products
- educational institutions, such as universities and colleges, that have their own computer networks enabling students and faculty to send email and/or access the Internet, and
- libraries that provide their patrons with Internet access.

However, the safe harbors may be used only by companies and entities that operate as a conduit to the online world. They may not be used by content providers—that is, people who create and post content on websites or other areas of the Internet. Nor can they be used where an ISP knows about or actively participates in the alleged infringement.

What activities fall within the safe harbors?

If they meet the requirements for eligibility, ISPs are not liable for monetary damages for the following four activities:

- placing information on a system or network at users' direction
- use of information location tools such as hypertext links to online directories, indexes, or search engines that direct users to infringing material
- system caching, and
- temporary storage of materials, such as Web pages or chat room discussions, in the course of transmitting, routing, or providing connections.

Most ISPs routinely perform all four of these activities. However, there are separate safe harbors for each activity. A determination that an ISP qualifies for the safe harbor for one activity does not mean it qualifies for the other three. Each activity has its own set of safe harbor eligibility rules, which are discussed below.

Threshold requirements for safe harbor eligibility

Before any safe harbor can be used, an ISP must satisfy two threshold requirements:

- First, the ISP must adopt and reasonably implement a policy of terminating the accounts of subscribers who are repeat copyright infringers.

The easiest way for an ISP to do this is to add a clause implementing this policy to its subscriber agreement. If the ISP doesn't use subscriber agreements, the clause should be added to its "terms of use" that users must agree to before being allowed to use the ISP's services. If the ISP doesn't have terms of use, it should create them. All existing subscribers and users should be notified of this termination policy.

- Second, the ISP must accommodate and not interfere with "standard technical measures." These are defined as measures that copyright owners use to identify or protect copyrighted works that have been adopted as a result of a broad consensus of copyright owners and ISPs in an open, fair, and voluntary industry process. They must be available to anyone on reasonable terms and may not impose substantial costs or burdens on ISPs.

  These standard measures do not yet exist. What such measures will turn out to be is anyone's guess. They might include use of encryption to fight copyright infringers, or such technologies as digital watermarking. It's entirely up to ISPs and the copyright industries (publishers, software developers, record companies, and other content providers and owners) to decide what these measures will be. The government will play no role in this decision. Congress expects that Internet industry standards-setting organizations, such as the Internet Engineering Task Force and the World Wide Web Consortium, will establish these standards. No time limit has been imposed on making these standards.
- In addition, to qualify for the safe harbor exemptions for information storage and linking, the ISP must designate an agent to whom copyright owners can send notice of any copyright infringement they believe is occurring on the ISP's system.

Safe harbor for information stored on ISP's system by users

This safe harbor, clearly the most important of the bunch, limits the liability of ISPs for infringing material on websites (or other information repositories) hosted on their systems. To qualify for this safe harbor, the following requirements must be met:

- The infringing material must have been placed in the ISP's system at a user's direction, not by the ISP itself (or by any of the ISP's employees or agents).
- The ISP must not have known about the infringing material *and* it must not have been aware of facts or circumstances from which it should have been apparent that the infringement was occurring.
- If the ISP had the right and ability to control infringing use of the material,

the ISP did not receive a direct financial benefit from the infringing activity—for example, the infringer paid the ISP a per-transaction fee whenever it sold the infringing material to the public.

- Upon receiving notice from the copyright owner that the material is allegedly infringing, the ISP must "expeditiously" take down or block access to the material. (See below, for a detailed discussion of the notice and takedown procedure.)

If the ISP discovers or realizes that infringement is occurring on its system, or it becomes so blatantly obvious that any reasonable person should have realized it, it must act expeditiously to remove or disable access to the infringing material. This is so even where it has not received any notice from the copyright owner of the material. An ISP is not liable for removing or disabling access to material it believed in good faith was infringing. This is so even if it is ultimately determined by a court that no infringement occurred.

However, ISPs have no duty to actively monitor or police their users to make sure no infringements are occurring. Indeed, it is now clearly in the ISPs' interests *not* to monitor their users to see if infringements are occurring. If an ISP doesn't know about an infringement, it has no duty to act to stop it and can rely on the safe harbor to insulate it from damages liability if the copyright owner complains. But if the ISP knew about the infringement and did nothing, it will not qualify for safe harbor protection.

EXAMPLE: AcmeNet is an ISP that provides Internet access to subscribers and hosts their Web pages. AcmeNet made sure it complied with all the threshold requirements for safe harbor protection: It amended its subscriber agreements to adopt a policy that repeat copyright offenders would have their subscriptions terminated and appointed an agent to whom copyright owners could send notice that infringement was occurring in their system. One of AcmeNet's subscribers posts an entire issue of *Newspeak* Magazine on his website without the copyright owner's permission. AcmeNet was not aware of the posting and received no direct financial benefit from it. *Newspeak* discovered the copying and sent a notice to AcmeNet demanding that the material be removed or blocked. AcmeNet immediately complied. As a result, the safe harbor applied and AcmeNet could not be held liable for monetary damages for the copyright infringement committed by its subscriber.

Safe harbor for linking a user to a site

This safe harbor concerns the use of links, online directories, indexes, search engines, and other information location tools that help users find things on the Internet. An ISP will not be liable for linking or otherwise referring a user to a site that contains infringing material if essentially the same requirements discussed in the preceding section apply.

Safe harbor for transitory communications

This safe harbor limits an ISP's liability for copyright infringement where it merely acts as a data conduit, automatically transmitting information from one network to another at someone else's request. It covers transmissions, routing, or providing connections for the information. It also applies to the intermediate or transient copies that are automatically made when a network operates. It applies to such ISP functions as providing email service or Internet connectivity.

Unlike the safe harbors for information stored by ISPs or system caching, an ISP need not remove or block access to the allegedly infringing materials upon receiving notice of the infringement to qualify for this safe harbor.

The following requirements must be met for an ISP to qualify for this safe harbor:

- The transmission, routing, provision of connections, or copying must have occurred as part of an automatic technical process initiated by someone other than the ISP—that is, by a user or subscriber.
- The ISP must not have been involved in selecting or modifying the material or choosing its recipients.
- Any intermediate copies must not be accessible to anyone other than the intended recipients and must not be retained by the ISP for longer than reasonably necessary.

America Online attempted to use this safe harbor to avoid copyright infringement liability for USENET postings in a case involving famed science fiction writer Harlan Ellison. Ellison discovered that a fan had scanned many of his short stories and uploaded them to the USENET newsgroup alt.binaries.e-book. (USENET is an abbreviation of "User Network," an international message board for members, called peers, whose computers connect to each other via the Internet.)

Ellison filed suit against the fan and, among others, America Online (AOL), alleging copyright infringement. He claimed that AOL was liable because the newsgroup content was temporarily stored on AOL's servers that are accessed by its many subscribers.

The court concluded that AOL qualified for safe harbor protection if it could show that it had satisfied the threshold requirements discussed above. The court found that AOL did not select, modify, initiate, or direct the uploading of the copied stories or select who would receive them. The court also held that AOL's storage of USENET messages—including the copied stories—was transitory and not for longer than necessary to transmit or route them to users (even though the messages were kept on AOL's servers for 14 days). (*Ellison v. Robertson*, 357 F.3d 1072 (9th Cir. 2004).)

Safe harbor for system caching

"System caching" is a practice commonly used by ISPs to save Internet users waiting time and reduce network traffic so that the Internet works more efficiently. ISPs temporarily store or "cache" popular materials on their own system so that users' requests for the materials can be fulfilled by transmitting the stored copy, rather than going to the trouble of retrieving the material from its original network source. Some ISPs cache entire websites.

One problem with system caching is that it can result in the delivery of outdated information to subscribers and can deprive website operators of accurate "hit" information—that is, information about the number of requests for particular material on a website. This is important to website operators, because their advertising revenue is often calculated on the basis of hits. For this reason, website operators often use technology to track the number of "hits" and may require ISPs to periodically update the material they cache.

ISPs are not liable for copyright infringement for system caching if all of the following are true:

- The cached material is not modified by the ISP.
- The ISP does not interfere with technology that returns hit information to the person who posted the material, provided the technology meets certain requirements.
- The ISP limits users' access to the material in whatever way the person who posted the material requires—for example, if the person requires users to have passwords or pay a fee to access the material at the originating site, the ISP must require this for users to access the cached material.
- The ISP complies with industry standards concerning "refreshing" or reloading the material—that is, replacing the cached copies with material from the original location; these standards have yet to be negotiated.
- The ISP promptly removes or blocks access to the cached material if it is notified that it was posted at the originating site without the copyright owner's permission and that the material has been removed, blocked, or ordered to be removed or blocked at the originating site.

What happens if an ISP qualifies for a safe harbor?

The fact that an ISP qualifies for safe harbor protection does not mean it cannot be sued. The safe harbors are limitations on legal liability: Whenever a safe harbor applies, the ISP is not liable for monetary damages for any copyright infringement arising from the covered activity.

However, the ISP may still be required to comply with certain types of court injunctions. An injunction is a court order requiring someone to do something or stop doing something. A copyright owner can obtain an injunction ordering the ISP to deny access to a particular online site or to shut down the account of a person who has committed copyright infringement.

If a safe harbor can't be used, it doesn't necessarily mean the ISP is guilty of copyright infringement and liable for damages. Rather, the ISP's liability will be determined under the normal copyright rules discussed above.

Special rules for educational institutions

Ordinarily, for legal purposes an ISP is deemed to know anything its employees know and is responsible for their actions. This means that an ISP may not be able to take advantage of a safe harbor because of the knowledge or actions of its employees. For example, an ISP will not qualify for any safe harbor where an employee knew an infringement was occurring but did nothing, or actively participated in the infringement.

However, it seemed unfair to Congress to apply this rule to faculty or graduate students working for nonprofit colleges and universities. Faculty members and graduate students have a special relationship with universities when they are engaged in teaching or research—principles of academic freedom give them far more independence than typical employees. Because of this, the DMCA includes a special provision holding that universities that serve as ISPs should not be disqualified from a safe harbor because of the knowledge or actions of their faculty or graduate students.

The following conditions must be met:

- The alleged online infringement must have occurred while the faculty member or graduate student was engaged in teaching or legitimate scholarly or scientific research.
- The alleged infringement does not involve the faculty member or graduate student posting online any course materials that were required or recommended for any course during the past three years.
- The college or university must not have received more than two notifications over the past three years that the faculty member or graduate student was infringing.
- The college or university must provide all of the users of its system or network with informational materials describing and promoting compliance with copyright law—these can be Copyright Office materials or other materials such as this book. For an excellent example of such materials, see the University of Texas's Copyright Crash Course at: www.utsystem.edu/ogc/IntellectualProperty/cprtindex.htm#top.

EXAMPLE: Excelsior University operates its own online network linking students and faculty together and giving them access to the Internet and email services. Professor Smith and one of his graduate students digitally scan several technical journals and place them on Smith's Web page, which is hosted by the university. Smith and the graduate student use the journals for a research project. The university has received no complaints that Smith or the grad student have committed infringement. Thus, the university may rely on this exemption. This means the university may qualify for the safe harbor for storage of infringing materials discussed above, even though the infringement was committed by its employees.

Designating an agent

To qualify for the safe harbors for storage and linking, an ISP must designate an agent to whom copyright owners can send notices of claimed infringement. The name, address, phone number, and email address of the agent must be sent to the Copyright Office and posted on the ISP's website.

The Copyright Office has prepared a draft form for designating an agent called "Interim Designation of Agent to Receive Notice of Claimed Infringement." You can download the form from the Copyright Office's website at www.copyright.gov. When the Copyright Office adopts final regulations concerning notices, it will likely amend this form. Alternatively, you need not use the Copyright Office's form at all. You can create your own form containing the same information.

The Interim Designation must be accompanied by a $30 fee, payable to the Register of Copyrights, and sent to:

Copyright GC/I&R
P.O. Box 70400
Southwest Station
Washington, DC 20024

If you need to amend the Interim Designation, you may use the Copyright Office's "Amended Designation [etc.]" form. You will find this form at the Copyright Office website.

The designation and any amendments will be posted at the Copyright Office's website.

Procedure for ISPs' Removal of Infringing Material

To obtain safe harbor protection for storage of or linking to infringing material, Internet Service Providers (ISPs) must comply with a notice and takedown procedure. This procedure allows a copyright owner to demand that an ISP remove infringing material from its system or block access to it.

Some fear that copyright owners may use their newfound power to stamp out legitimate uses of copyrighted material on the Internet—for example, uses that fall within the fair use privilege. (See Chapter 11.) This fear was justified by an interesting experiment: A person created websites with two ISPs and then posted on them a chapter from the book *On Liberty* by John Stuart Mill, which is in the public domain, having first been published in the 19th century. He then sent the websites complaints from a fictitious John Stuart Mill Foundation claiming that the material was copyrighted and should be removed from the Internet. One ISP removed the chapter almost immediately. However, the other asked detailed questions about the infringement claim. ("How Liberty was Lost on the Internet," by Christian Ahlert, *Spiked Online*, June 1, 2004; www.spiked-online.com.)

However, the DMCA does provide some safeguards to protect against this. An ISP subscriber or user may object to the removal or disablement of the allegedly infringing material, and the ISP must put it back unless the copyright owner goes to court.

This procedure is complex, but it's vital for ISPs, copyright owners, and people who use the Internet to understand it. It involves three separate steps:

- First, the copyright owner drafts and sends to the ISP a notice claiming that infringing material is present on its system or that there are links to infringing material.
- Second, the ISP must respond to the notice in one of two ways: either (1) remove the infringing material or disable access to it, or (2) do nothing.
- Third, if the ISP has removed or disabled access to the allegedly infringing material, the user or subscriber involved can send the ISP a counter-notice stating that the material is not infringing or has been misidentified. In this event, the ISP must put the material back or restore access to it unless the copyright owner goes to court to obtain an injunction against the alleged infringer.

Copyright owner's Notice of Claimed Infringement

If a copyright owner believes that its copyrighted material has been unlawfully stored in an ISP's system or the ISP's system contains links or other locators to a site containing infringing material, the owner can send a notice to the ISP's designated agent notifying it of the claimed infringement. Any ISP receiving such a notice will have a very strong incentive to remove or disable access to the material, since doing so will relieve it of damages liability for the alleged infringement (provided that it meets all the requirements for safe harbor protection discussed above).

Using this notice and takedown procedure is not mandatory. The copyright owner can always forgo it and go straight to court and file a copyright infringement lawsuit against the infringer and/or ISP. However, anyone who believes that his or her work has been infringed on the Internet should first try to use this procedure. Filing a Notice of Claimed Infringement is not difficult and can easily be accomplished by any copyright owner without paying a lawyer. If the Notice is successful and the ISP removes the infringing material or disables access to it, there will often be no need to file an expensive action. If the infringing material is removed by the ISP, the copyright owner will still have the right to sue the infringer for damages, but in this event, the ISP will not be liable for damages.

The copyright owner should follow these steps:

Step 1

First, make sure that copyright infringement has occurred. (See Chapter 12 for a detailed discussion of what constitutes copyright infringement.) Keep in mind that not all copying is copyright infringement—some types of copying qualify as a fair use (see Chapter 11) and some things are not protected by copyright at all, such as facts and ideas (see Chapter 6). Both the person you accuse of infringement and the ISP can sue you for damages if you knowingly misrepresent—that is, lie—that copyright infringement has taken place.

Step 2

If you're convinced infringement has occurred, you must determine what ISP is involved. Remember, ISPs are companies and institutions that provide people with Internet access and host (store) websites and other materials on the Internet. The ISP is usually not the infringer, but the conduit by which the infringer has used the Internet. In some cases it will be apparent who the ISP is—for example, if the infringing material is found anywhere on the AOL system, AOL is the ISP. However, in some cases it may not be clear which ISP the alleged infringer uses. One way to determine this is to check the domain name registration records for the website where the infringing material is found. You can do this at the following website: www.netsol.com/cgi-bin/whois/whois.

Type in the domain name in the search field and you will be given access to the registration records for the domain name. If you click on the link in the "technical information" portion of these records, you will often (but not always) find the name of the ISP for the website using that domain name.

Step 3

Next, you must determine if the ISP has designated an agent to receive notifications of claimed infringement. The ISP is supposed to post this information at its website. ISPs are also required to file with the Copyright Office an "Interim Designation of Agent" form. This form gives the agent's name and address. Digital copies of these forms are posted on the Copyright Office's website at www.copyright.gov/onlinesp.

Not all ISPs have designated agents. This may be because they're unaware of the safe harbor rules or have elected not to take advantage of them. This is perfectly legal. ISPs' compliance with the safe harbor requirements is purely voluntary.

If the ISP does not have an "Interim Designation of Agent" form on file with the Copyright Office, it cannot take advantage of the safe harbor liability limitations and the procedures discussed in this section will not apply. However, you are still entitled to complain about the alleged infringement and ask the ISP to remove the infringing material. You can also sue the ISP. The normal copyright infringement liability rules will be used to determine the ISP's liability for the infringement.

Step 4

If the ISP has designated an agent, you must draft and sign a Notice of Claimed Infringement and send it to the agent. The notice must:

- identify the copyrighted work you claim was infringed (if the infringement involves many different works at a single online site, you can include a representative list rather than listing each one)
- identify the online site where the alleged infringement has occurred and identify specifically what material on the site you claim is infringing (include copies, if possible); if a link is involved, it must be identified

- give the name and contact information for the person signing the notice
- state that the information in the notice is accurate and that the complaining party "has a good faith belief that use of the material in the manner complained of is not authorized by the copyright owner, its agent, or the law"
- state, under penalty of perjury, that the signer of the notice is authorized to act on behalf of the copyright owner of the material claimed to have been infringed, and
- be signed with either a physical or electronic signature.

The notice can be either emailed or sent by postal mail to the ISP.

A form Notice of Claimed Infringement is contained on the CD-ROM.

ISP's response to Notice of Claimed Infringement

An ISP that receives a Notice of Claimed Infringement should examine it carefully to see whether it complies with the requirements set forth in the preceding section. The Notice is deemed legally null and void if it fails to identify the infringed and infringing works or fails to give adequate contact information for the sender. In this event, the ISP need take no action and the notice will not be construed as putting the ISP on notice of any infringement.

However, if the Notice is defective in any other way, the ISP has a legal duty to contact the person who sent the notice or take other reasonable steps to find out the missing information.

If the Notice is in compliance with the rules, the ISP must decide whether to remove or disable access to the allegedly infringing material. The ISP does not have to remove or disable access to such material; but, if it does so, the safe harbor will apply. Moreover, the ISP is immune from all legal liability for removing or disabling access to the material—meaning that neither the subscriber nor user nor anyone else can sue it for doing so. This is so even if it turns out that the material complained of was not infringing.

All this would seem to mean that an ISP should always remove or disable access to material that a copyright owner claims is infringing in a Notice of Claimed Infringement. However, this may not always be the case. Obviously, an ISP's subscribers will not appreciate having their material removed or disabled. If a copyright owner's allegation that the subscriber has committed infringement is clearly questionable, an ISP may prefer to stand by its subscriber. The good will and favorable publicity that could accrue from such a stance may offset the disadvantage of not being able to use the safe harbor. The ISP industry is highly competitive, so an ISP might not want to develop a reputation for caving in too easily to people who make off-the-wall copyright infringement claims.

The law imposes no specific time limit on how quickly the ISP must act. It simply says the ISP must act "expeditiously" (quickly). If the ISP does remove or disable access to the allegedly infringing material, it must "promptly" notify the subscriber or user of the action. The ball then enters the subscriber's court.

User's Counter-Notification

An ISP's subscriber or user doesn't have to take the removal of the material lying down. If the user believes that the material is not infringing or has been mistakenly identified, it can take action to have the material put back by the ISP. To do this, the user must send the ISP a Counter-Notification. The Counter-Notification must:

- identify the allegedly infringing material and give its Internet address
- state, under penalty of perjury, that the material was removed or disabled by the ISP as a result of mistake or misidentification of the material
- state that the user consents to the legal jurisdiction of the federal district court in the judicial district where the user's address is located; or, if the user lives outside the U.S., consents to jurisdiction in any federal district court where the ISP may be sued
- state that the user agrees to accept service of legal process from the copyright owner or other person who signed the Notice of Claimed Infringement
- give the user's name and contact information for the person signing the notice, and
- be signed with either a physical or electronic signature.

The Counter-Notification can be either emailed or sent by postal mail to the ISP's designated agent.

A form Counter-Notification is contained on the CD-ROM.

Upon receipt of a Counter-Notification satisfying the above requirements, the ISP must "promptly" send the copyright owner or other person who sent the Notice of Claimed Infringement a copy of the Counter-Notification and inform such person that the ISP will replace the removed material or stop disabling access to it in ten business days (days not counting weekends or holidays).

The ISP must replace the removed material or stop disabling access to it not less than ten or more than 14 business days after it received the user's Counter-Notification, *unless* the copyright owner brings a court action as described below.

By sending a Counter-Notification, the user in effect forces the copyright owner to put up or shut up. The copyright owner will have to go to court and convince a judge that it's likely that a copyright infringement has occurred. If the copyright owner doesn't want to go to court, the ISP will have to replace the removed material or stop disabling access to it.

However, you should never send a Counter-Notification just to make the copyright owner's life more difficult or where you know that you have in fact committed copyright infringement. Remember, you must promise in the Counter-Notification under penalty of perjury that the material involved is not infringing or was misidentified. If you lie, you could be prosecuted for perjury as well as sued for copyright infringement.

On the other hand, keep in mind that one ground for claiming that your use of another person's copyrighted material is not infringing is fair use. (See Chapter 11 for a detailed discussion.)

Copyright owner's response to Counter-Notification

If the subscriber sends the ISP a Counter-Notification, you can forget about getting the infringing material removed or disabled without having to go to court. Instead, you will have to file a copyright infringement lawsuit against the subscriber in federal court and ask the court to grant you an injunction ordering the subscriber to stop the infringing activity on the ISP's system. To obtain such an injunction, you'll have to convince the court that it is likely that the subscriber has committed copyright infringement.

If you don't want the ISP to put the material back or stop disabling access to it, you'll have to act quickly. Access to the material will have to be restored by the ISP no more than 14 business days after the subscriber sent it the Counter-Notification. It is, possible, however, to obtain an injunction very quickly. (See Chapter 12, Copyright Infringement, for a detailed discussion of injunctions in copyright infringement cases.)

To file your lawsuit, you'll have to know the subscriber or user's identity. The DMCA contains a procedure allowing you to subpoena the ISP and require it to give you this information.

If you miss the 14-day deadline, but later obtain an injunction, the ISP will have to remove or disable access to the material again.

Defense against abuse of notice and takedown procedure

The ISP safe harbor rules give ISPs a strong incentive to remove from their systems any material that someone claims is infringing by filing a notice of claimed infringement as described above. Free speech proponents feared that this could give some copyright owners the power to censor or otherwise prevent legal uses of their materials—uses that would constitute a fair use. This fear came to fruition in a case involving a company called Diebold Election Systems, a leading manufacturer of electronic voting systems.

Someone leaked internal Diebold documents revealing flaws in Diebold's e-voting machines. The archive was republished on numerous websites. In an attempt to stop distribution of the embarrassing emails, Diebold sent dozens of takedown notices to ISPs of the people republishing them. Diebold claimed that the email archive was copyrighted work owned by Diebold and that the republication constituted infringement for which the ISPs would be secondarily liable. Virtually all the ISPs who received the takedown notices caved in and removed the emails. However, one, OPG, didn't. Instead, it filed suit against

Diebold using a little known provision of the DMCA (Section 512(f)) which makes it unlawful to use DMCA takedown threats when the copyright holder knows that infringement has not actually occurred. Under this provision, an ISP, publisher, or copyright owner may obtain monetary damage, costs, and attorney fees against a person who makes a knowing material misrepresentation that an item is infringing in a takedown notice.

OPG won its lawsuit. The court held that the republication of the Diebold emails was a clear fair use and Diebold knew it. The court declared that "Diebold sought to use the DMCA's safe harbor provisions—which were designed to protect ISPs, not copyright holders—as a sword to suppress publication of embarrassing content rather than as a shield to protect its intellectual property." The court ordered that Diebold pay $125,000 in damages because it had materially and knowingly misrepresented in its takedown notices that copyright infringement occurred. (*Online Policy Group v. Diebold*, 2004 WL 2203382, 72 U.S.P.Q.2d 1200 (N.D. Cal. Sept. 30, 2004).)

Diebold is the first case of its kind, and this application of Section 512(f) gives ISPs and Internet publishers badly needed ammunition to fight against blatant misuse of the DMCA notice and takedown procedure. It also makes clear that a copyright owner should be sure that he or she has a valid copyright infringement claim before using the procedure.

Use of Licenses to Prevent Infringement

A license gives someone permission to do something. For example, when your state issues you a driver's license, it gives you permission to drive a car. Copyright owners can give others permission to use their works by granting licenses. (See Chapter 9.)

Licenses are often used in the online world. For example, the owners of commercial computer databases like Nexis and Lexis limit access to users who sign license agreements and agree to pay access fees. Such agreements often attempt to regulate the way users deal with online materials. For example, they may forbid users from transferring digital copies of such material to others.

A user doesn't necessarily have to physically sign a license for it to be enforceable. Online licensing agreements are likely enforceable where access to an online service, Internet site, BBS, or database is made available only after users are given the opportunity to read the agreement. Such licenses are likely not enforceable, however, where the user is not allowed to read it before being given access to protected material.

Some copyright experts assert that license restrictions that go beyond what the copyright laws allow may be unenforceable because the federal copyright laws preempt (take precedence over) state contract laws. Under this view, for example, a license restriction that attempted to do away with a user's fair use rights would be unenforceable.

However, the most significant court case to date takes the opposite view, holding that licenses can restrict the use even of information in the public domain. Matthew Zeidenberg bought a CD-ROM containing business telephone listings from ProCD. He downloaded the listings into his computer from the CD-ROM and made them available on the Internet, attaching a search program he created himself. Zeidenberg did not commit copyright infringement, because phone listings are in the public domain. (See Chapter 7, Adaptations and Compilations.) However, he did violate the terms of a shrink-wrap license agreement that came with the CD-ROM. Such license agreements, which are commonly included inside software and CD-ROM packages, typically bar purchasers from copying, adapting, or modifying the work. The court held that the shrink-wrap license was an enforceable contract. Since Zeidenberg violated the license, he was liable to ProCD for damages. (*ProCD v. Zeidenberg,* 86 F.3d 1447 (7th Cir. 1996).)

It seems likely that, as a result of this decision, even more online publishers will likely start using online licenses to control how their materials are used instead of just relying upon copyright protection.

Technological Solutions to Infringement

If copyright ceases to be an important way for content providers to protect their works, it will likely be because highly effective technological solutions to infringement will be found. This includes the use of encryption schemes—that is, translating digital works into unreadable gibberish as the military does with secret messages. Users would be able to decrypt and read a work only after paying a fee to the copyright owner. Research is also underway on embedding digital signatures into digital copies—similar to a serial number on an automobile—that enables copyright owners to identify their works even if they're heavily altered or modified.

Copyright owners are fearful that infringers may devise means of circumventing their anti-infringement technological measures—for example, devise means of "cracking" encryption codes. The Digital Millennium Copyright Act (DMCA) enacted by Congress in late 1998 includes a complex provision designed to prevent this. Following is the briefest possible overview of this statute:

- First, it makes it illegal for anyone to make, import, or sell devices or services whose primary purpose is to circumvent technological measures used to prevent unauthorized access to or copying of a work.
- Subject to several exceptions, it makes it illegal for anyone to obtain *access* to a work by circumventing any technological measure (such as encryption) that effectively controls access to the work.

  Exempt from this prohibition are nonprofit libraries, archives, and educational institutions who wish to gain unauthorized access to works solely to make a good faith determination of whether to acquire a copy. Exemptions are also given to law enforcement, intelligence, and other government activities; bona fide encryption research; security testing; and cases where the technological measure or work it protects is capable of collecting personal identifying information about online users.

In addition, four narrow exemptions were established by a regulation enacted by the Copyright Office. These exemptions permit the following activities:

- **e-book read-aloud functions.** You can circumvent controls that prevent users from enabling an e-book's read-aloud function or from using special screen readers to render the text into Braille. This exception is intended to benefit the blind and visually impaired.
- **Blocked website lists.** You can circumvent controls to access lists of blocked websites that are used in filtering software programs (sometimes referred to as censorware). This does not include lists of Internet locations blocked by software designed to protect against damage to computers, such as firewalls and antivirus software, or software designed to prevent receipt of unwanted email, such as antispam software.
- **Programs with broken dongles.** Under certain circumstances, you can circumvent "hardware locks" (known as "dongles") that prevent access to computer programs. This exception only applies to software that actually cannot be accessed due to a damaged or malfunctioning dongle, and only when the dongle cannot be replaced or repaired.
- **Obsolete computer games.** You can circumvent controls to access programs and video games distributed in formats that have become obsolete and which require the original media or hardware as a condition of access. A format is considered obsolete if the machine or system necessary to access the program or game stored in that format is no longer manufactured or is no longer reasonably available in the commercial marketplace.

These exemptions are set to expire on October 27, 2006. (Copyright Office Regulation 201.40.) A discussion of the regulation is provided at the Copyright Office website at www.copyright.gov.

- The law does not make it illegal to circumvent technological measures designed to prevent a work from being copied. This is because unauthorized copying is legal where it constitutes a fair use. This is intended to preserve the public's fair use rights. However, many copyright experts fear that fair use rights will nonetheless be eroded because the law makes it illegal to circumvent technological measures to gain access to a work. Of course, one must first gain access to a work before it can be copied, even where the copy is a fair use. These fears seemed to be justified when programmer Dmitri Sklyarov was indicted by the U.S. government for violating the DMCA. This was the first criminal prosecution under the DMCA. Sklyarov and his company created and distributed software that could permit electronic book owners to convert the Adobe e-Book format and make use of e-books without publishers' restrictions. The government alleged the software violated the DMCA's prohibition on making or selling devices whose primary purpose is to circumvent technological protections on copyrighted material. The trial judge rejected Sklyarov's claim that the DMCA only prohibited anti-circumvention devices created to infringe on copyrights and not those created to promote fair use. The judge held that the DMCA "imposes a blanket ban on trafficking in or the marketing of any device that circumvents use restrictions." Thus, it doesn't matter if a programmer markets e-book cracking software solely to enable users to copy from e-books in a way that would constitute a fair use—for example, to allow the lawful owner of an e-book to read it on another computer, to make a back-up copy, or to print the e-book in paper form. The judge said trafficking or marketing of such software violates the DMCA no matter what it's used for. (At trial, a jury acquitted Sklyarov of all charges. (*U.S. v. ElcomSoft*, No. CR 01-20138 RMW (N.D. Cal. 2002).))

- Penalties for violations are the same as for removal of copyright management information. (See Chapter 12, Copyright Infringement.)

For a detailed understanding of this incredibly complicated statute, you'll need to read the law. A copy of the DMCA is contained on the CD-ROM.

Copyright Formalities: Notice and Registration

Copyright formalities consist of placing a copyright notice on a work and registering it with the Copyright Office.

Notice

Published works should contain a valid copyright notice to prevent an alleged infringer from being able to claim that the infringement was "innocent"—that is, he didn't know the work was copyrighted. If a court buys such an "innocent infringement" defense, any damages awarded to the copyright owner may be drastically reduced. This may make it economically unfeasible for the copyright owner to file an infringement suit. (See Chapter 3, Copyright Notice.)

It's not altogether clear whether making a copy of a work available online constitutes a publication. However, you should assume that it does. Place a copyright notice on anything you don't want copied. Copyright notices and warnings contained on status screens when a user logs on to an online service or bulletin board may not serve as valid notices for all the works contained therein. So don't rely on them. Provide your own notice. The notice should contain the copyright symbol—©, publication date, and copyright owner's name. The publication date is the date you uploaded the work. If the work being uploaded has already been published in a different medium, include that publication date as well. (See Chapter 3 for detailed discussion of copyright notices.)

Registration

In addition, if you place online a digital copy of a valuable work that has never been registered with the Copyright Office, you should immediately register the work. Registration enables you to obtain statutory damages and attorney fees if you win an infringement suit.

Since it can be hard to prove how much money you actually lost when someone copies or otherwise uses your work without permission, it may not be economically

Copyright Notices on Websites

If a website contains copyrighted materials, a copyright notice should at the very least be placed on the site's home page. However, although likely not required by law, it's not a bad idea to place a notice on every page on a website. There are no special requirements for the content of a website notice. It need only consist of the word "Copyright" and/or the © symbol followed by the copyright owner's name and publication year-date. For example: "Copyright © Jack Webby 2007."

However, if you really want to make it clear that all aspects of your site are copyrighted, you could use a notice like this: "All website design, text, graphics, selection, and arrangement thereof, and software are the copyrighted works of Jack Webby, © Copyright 2007."

Some website owners are happy to permit certain types of unauthorized copying, while prohibiting others. To make it clear to Web users what types of copying are permissible, you can include a statement like the following along with the copyright notice:

- The materials on this website may be copied online, but may not be reproduced in print or on a CD-ROM without written permission.
- The materials on this website may be copied for noncommercial personal use only.
- The materials on this website may be freely copied and distributed so long as our copyright notice and website address is included.

feasible to file an infringement suit unless you can obtain statutory damages. Such damages are awarded instead of actual damages and can range from $200 to $100,000 per infringement, depending on how serious and willful the infringement was. (See Chapter 12.)

In one case, for example, *Playboy Magazine* was awarded statutory damages of $1.1 million against a publisher who downloaded 52 *Playboy* photos from a BBS and published them on a CD-ROM. The court awarded *Playboy* $20,000 in statutory damages for each copied photo. (*Playboy Enterprises, Inc. v. Starware Publishing Corp.*, 900 F.Supp. 433 (S.D. Fla., 1995).) It's likely *Playboy* would not have been awarded nearly as much had the photos not been timely registered and damages therefore limited to *Playboy*'s actual provable monetary losses.

How to register

You register websites and other online works much the same way any other material is registered. If the work consists primarily of text, use Form TX to register. If the work consists primarily of graphics, use Form VA. See Chapter 4 for a detailed discussion about how to fill out these forms.

When you register an online work, the registration extends only to the copyrightable content received by the Copyright Office in your deposit. If you characterize the work as published, the registration only covers the material published on the date of publication given in the application. Material published before this date will not be covered by the registration. This means that where an online work is frequently revised, each revision would have to be separately registered. But this is only if the online work is characterized as published. If it's unpublished, you can register any amount of material at one time as an unpublished collection for a single application fee.

It's up to you to decide whether a website has been published or not—no one knows for sure what constitutes publication on the Internet, and the Copyright Office will not second-guess you. So, if you characterize the website as unpublished, you can register all the material you've created up to the date of registration. Theoretically, you could register a frequently revised website as little as once a year or even less so long as it's characterized as unpublished. However, it's a good idea to register at least every three months. If you sue someone for copyright infringement, this avoids any possibility that the alleged infringer could claim your registration was not timely.

In addition, if your work is an online daily newsletter, newspaper, magazine, or other serial publication, you can register several weeks' or months' worth of issues together at one time for one application fee by using the Copyright Office's group registration procedure. (See Chapter 4, Copyright Registration.)

There is also a group registration procedure for electronic databases.

Deposit requirements

Deposit requirements are different for online works than for works published in the physical world. The Copyright Office gives you two deposit options.

Option 1

Under the first deposit option, you must provide a computer disk containing the entire work clearly labeled with title and author information *and* a representative hard-copy sample of the work being registered.

If the work consists of less than five pages of text or graphics, or three minutes of music, sounds, or audiovisual material, you must deposit a copy of the entire work along with a confirmation that it is complete.

If the work is longer, you must deposit five representative pages or three representative minutes. This identifying material must include the work's title and author, and a copyright notice, if any.

Option 2

Alternatively, you may deposit a hard-copy version of the entire work. No computer disk is required in this case.

Your deposit should be in a format appropriate for the type of work being registered, for example, a hard-copy printout of text or graphics or an audiocassette of music or sounds.

Works published online and off

If a work is published both online and by distributing physical copies, you must deposit the physical copies, not the online materials. For example, if a work is published as a hardbound book and also transmitted online, two copies of the hardbound book must be deposited.

Electronic Publishing and Ownership of Electronic Rights

Electronic publishing is one of the most rapidly growing and exciting areas of publishing today. But this form of publishing raises difficult copyright questions regarding ownership of electronic rights.

What Is Electronic Publishing?

"Electronic publishing" means presenting conventional print-based media such as newspapers, magazines, books, and encyclopedias in a form that readers can use on computers. This includes publishing written works on CD-ROMs and computer disks used directly in computers, and making them available in online services like Nexus that computer users access by telephone lines.

Many written works are being created expressly for electronic publication. These written materials are often combined with graphics, photos, videos, and sounds to create new types of works called multimedia works.

What Are Electronic Rights?

As used in this chapter, "electronic rights" means the legal right to reproduce, distribute, adapt, and publicly display and perform a work in electronic form. This includes:

- placing all or a substantial part of a work in its original form on magnetic media used directly in computers such as a CD-ROM (short for Compact Disc Read-Only Memory) or other computer disk
- reproducing all or a substantial part of a work in its original form in an electronic database like Lexis
- adapting a work into a multimedia work, whether distributed on a CD-ROM, computer game cartridge, or online service, and
- publishing on demand—that is, transferring a digital copy of a work from a publisher's database to a bookstore which prints it out and sells the consumer the printed copy.

Each of these uses can be regarded as a separate electronic right and dealt with separately in a publishing agreement.

Who Controls Electronic Rights?

A small war has been going on between writers and publishers over ownership of, and compensation for, electronic rights both for already existing works and those yet to be created. Ten freelance writers in conjunction with the National Writers Union filed a copyright infringement suit in New York against the *New York Times*, *Time* Inc., Mead Data Central Corp., and others, alleging that their works were copied and distributed on computer databases and CD-ROMs without their permission and without compensation.

According to the National Writers Union, many publishers are distributing authors' works electronically even though their publishing contracts do not give them the right to do so.

In the meantime, most publishers have rewritten their publishing agreements to obtain ownership of all electronic rights for all existing and future electronic media. Others, particularly magazine publishers, have started using written agreements for the first time expressly to obtain such electronic rights. Many authors' groups refer to such agreements as "contracts from hell" because they require writers to transfer rights in yet-to-be-imagined technologies without having any idea what such rights may be worth.

Initial Ownership of Electronic Rights

Electronic rights are no different from any other copyright rights. They are initially owned by a work's author.

Self-employed individuals who create written works alone or with others (the type of people we normally think of as "authors") will initially own the electronic and all other copyright rights in their works. (See Chapter 8, Initial Copyright Ownership.)

The electronic copyright in works made for hire will be initially owned by the employer or hiring party the moment the work is created. The employer or hiring party is the "author" for copyright purposes, not the person who actually created the work. This includes:

- works created by employees within the scope of their employment, and
- specially commissioned works created by independent contractors under written work-for-hire agreements. (See Chapter 8, Initial Copyright Ownership.)

Since the employer or hiring party using a work-for-hire agreement automatically owns all electronic and other copyright rights the moment a work is created, there is no need for them to obtain any additional transfer of rights from the actual creators after the work is completed.

An increasing number of magazines, newspapers, and journals are now using work-for-hire agreements with freelance writers in order to obtain all the rights in the work, including electronic rights.

Transfer of Electronic Rights by Individual Authors

With the important exception of self-publishers who reproduce and distribute their work themselves, self-employed authors normally profit from their copyrights by selling their rights to publishers or others to exploit. In today's publishing environment, such sales will typically include the transfer of the author's electronic rights.

When an author sells a book to a publisher, the publishing contract defines which rights the publisher gets and which the author keeps, if any. (See Chapter 9.) The right to license a work for use in a multimedia program or other electronic publication is usually specifically dealt with in a modern publishing agreement.

Today, most publishers insist on acquiring all electronic rights along with the right to print the work in book form. This ensures them access to an important and rapidly growing market. However, this is a matter for negotiation, as is how much an author will be paid for such rights. Experienced authors who have agents may be able to retain some or even all electronic rights to a work. Inexperienced authors will likely have difficulty retaining any such rights.

Transfers of Electronic Rights in Freelance Articles

Many articles written by freelancers and initially published in print magazines, newspapers, and journals have been digitally copied and placed on online databases such as Nexis and Lexis, on databases on CD-ROMs, and on various websites. It has been a widespread practice for publishers to do such copying themselves or allow others to do so without obtaining permission from the freelancers or paying them anything.

This practice led several freelancers to ask whether such copying was legal. In one of the most eagerly anticipated copyright decisions in recent years, the U.S. Supreme Court has answered with an emphatic "no." If a publisher has not acquired electronic rights in writing, permission must be obtained from the author to reproduce a freelance article in an electronic database. The case reverses a highly publicized lower court ruling in 1997 that such permission is not required. (*Tasini v. The New York Times Company*, 533 U.S. 483 (2001).)

Does *Tasini* Apply to CD-ROMs?

In general, permission from the writers would not be required under *Tasini* if the republication in the new media qualified as a revision of the original collective work (magazine, newspaper, or other publication). For example, permission would not be needed if a newspaper was published both in print form and online, since the online edition would surely qualify as a revision of the original print edition.

But what about republishing articles and other materials on CD-ROMs? Are these revisions? One court has said no. The case involved the publication on 30 CD-ROMs of every issue of *National Geographic* Magazine published from 1888 to 1996 (1,200 in all). A freelance photographer sued *National Geographic*, claiming it didn't have the right to make digital copies of his photos and place them on the CD-ROM. The court agreed, holding that the CD-ROM was an entirely new work—a compilation consisting of all the back issues—not a revision of the original magazine issues.

This result puzzled many copyright experts, because the CD-ROM seemed to be very similar to the microfilm that the Supreme Court in *Tasini* indicated would be a revision because copies of intact editions were stored together. Moreover, users of the CD-ROM retrieved individual articles as part of entire magazine issues, not individually as was the case with the online databases in *Tasini*.

Doubts about this decision were confirmed when another court later held that the same CD-ROM was a revision of the *National Geographic* magazine, and articles and photographs from the magazine could be republished on the CD without permission from their original authors. (*Faulker v. National Geographic Society*, 409 F.3d 26 (2d Cir. 2005).)

Nevertheless, the Supreme Court refused to reverse the decision and, as a result, prudent publishers obtain permission to include freelance materials on CD-ROMs where they haven't acquired such rights in advance. (*Greenberg v. National Geographic Society*, 244 F.3d 1267 (11th Cir. 2001).)

The case involved a lawsuit by six freelance writers against *The New York Times*; *Time* Magazine; the company that owns the massive Nexis databases; and several other publishers. All the freelancers had articles that originally appeared in print publications reproduced in Nexis and other databases without their permission. Crucial to their case was the fact that all but one of the freelancers had never signed any license agreement with their publisher. Instead, they had oral agreements and nothing was ever said about electronic rights.

The court held that when a freelancer—that is, a nonemployee—contributes an article or other material to a collective work (for example, a newspaper, magazine, periodical, journal, anthology, or encyclopedia) but does not specifically transfer all or part of his copyright rights, the collective work may only use the article or other material in:

- the original version of the collective work—for example, a specific issue or edition of a periodical
- a revision of that specific collective work—for example, later editions of a periodical such as the final edition of a newspaper, and
- a publication of a later collective work in the same series—for example, a new edition of an encyclopedia or dictionary.

Any other use of the material requires permission from the freelancer.

The publishers argued that the freelancers' permission was not required because the act of placing the articles on electronic databases constituted a revision of the original collective works. The Supreme Court rejected this argument, reasoning that electronic databases such as Nexis and Lexis are not revisions of collective works such as *The New York Times,* because the databases store and retrieve articles individually—articles that are part of a vast database of diverse texts. They do not store intact copies of newspapers or other collective works as originally published. In contrast, the court suggested that microfilm copies of newspapers and other collective works are revisions of the collective works because copies of entire intact editions are stored together on the microfilm rolls.

The *Tasini* decision has had many far-ranging consequences, some intended and some likely not intended by the writers who brought the lawsuit.

How *Tasini* impacts freelancers

The only freelancers affected by *Tasini* are those who have written articles under oral agreements or written agreements that say nothing about electronic rights. In the 1990s, many newspapers, magazines, and other collective work publishers began to require that freelancers sign agreements that included a transfer of electronic rights or all rights. As a result of *Tasini*, this practice has now become almost universal. So *Tasini* applies primarily only to older articles and other materials—those published from 1978 through the mid-1990s.

Tasini also applies to pre-1978 articles published under an oral or written agreement that did not provide that the author retained electronic rights or all copyright rights.

In 2005, an $18 million court-approved settlement was reached in the *Tasini* class action lawsuit brought on behalf of all authors who had works published after August 14, 1997 in electronic or digital form by the publishers and databases involved without first transferring their electronic rights or granting permission. Under the settlement, the publishers agreed to pay freelancers up to $1,500 for works in which the writers had registered the copyrights. Freelancers who failed to register their copyrights receive up to $60 per article. To obtain the payments, freelancers had to file a proof of claim with the court by September 30, 2005.

Some freelancers didn't like the settlement and filed an appeal that it be set aside. The appeal was ongoing in 2006, so no money had yet been paid out to authors. If the settlement goes into effect, it will be binding between the publishers involved and all freelancers who are members of the class—except for writers who removed themselves from the class by filing a document with the court by September 2005. This means that class members who didn't exclude themselves won't be able to file their own individual lawsuits against the publishers involved. However, the settlement has no effect on infringements by publishers who are not party to the settlement. A website has been set up to provide more information on the settlement (www.copyrightclassaction.com).

How *Tasini* impacts publishers

Electronic database publishers and publishers of collective works such as newspapers and magazines reacted to the *Tasini* litigation in various ways. For example, some publishers asked freelancers who had written articles covered by *Tasini* to allow them to continue to publish them in online databases. Ordinarily, no extra payment was offered for such permission. Some freelancers agreed because they didn't want their work removed from the online world and/or were afraid of being blacklisted by the publisher.

In addition, many database publishers removed from their databases all articles that might be subject to *Tasini* in an attempt to limit their liability for damages. As a result, hundreds of thousands of articles written by freelancers before the mid-1990s have been removed from electronic databases. For example, *The New York Times* has taken this approach, except where the freelancer agrees to allow the digital copy to be retained at no charge to the *Times*.

Moreover, as mentioned above, it is now a nearly universal practice for newspapers, magazines, journals, and similar publications to demand that freelancers transfer their electronic rights. This can take one of several forms:

- The freelancer can be required to sign an assignment transferring all his copyright rights to the publisher.
- The freelancer can be required to sign a work-made-for-hire agreement—in this event, the publication, not the freelancer, is considered to be the

author of the work for copyright purposes. (See Chapter 8, Initial Copyright Ownership.)

- If less than all rights are being transferred, the freelancer can be asked to specifically transfer electronic rights—a clause transferring such rights needn't be long or complex. A clause like the following will suffice: "Author grants Publisher the right to publish the work through any media deemed appropriate by the Publisher."

More and more publishers are requiring freelancers to transfer all their rights. Of course, this includes their electronic rights. For example, *The New York Times* now requires this.

How *Tasini* impacts libraries and archives

Due to the removal of articles covered by *Tasini*, librarians and archivists now have huge gaps in the online databases to which they subscribe. Some database publishers have not told their subscribers what has been removed. Many news librarians are trying to create lists of lost or damaged collections.

How *Tasini* impacts the public

The biggest loser in the *Tasini* case may be the public. Because hundreds of thousands of articles have been removed from online databases, people who want to access them will have to try and find paper copies in libraries.

Ownership of Electronic Rights in Older Works

Today, publishing agreements typically include specific provisions regarding ownership of electronic rights. However, older agreements may have nothing on the subject, because the technology wasn't known or anticipated at the time. In this event, it can be very difficult to determine who owns the electronic rights. This happened in a case involving the famous writers William Styron, Kurt Vonnegut, and Robert B. Parker. They granted Rosetta Books the right to publish digital versions ("e-books") of several of their novels. Several of the books had previously been published by Random House. Random House had signed written contracts for the books providing that it had the exclusive right to "print, publish, and sell the work in book form." Random House claimed this meant it had the exclusive right to publish the works as e-books. Random House sued Rosetta for copyright infringement and lost. The court held that the contract language did not include e-books. The court noted that, in the publishing trade, this clause is generally understood only to grant a publisher the exclusive right to publish a hardcover trade book in English for distribution in North America. (*Random House, Inc. v. Rosetta Books LLC*, 150 F.Supp.2d 613 (S.D. N.Y. 2001).)

As this case shows, interpreting a publishing agreement can be tricky. So, unless the written agreement clearly covers electronic rights, it is wise to seek legal assistance to determine who has the right to publish the work in electronic form.

Paying Authors for Online Uses of Their Works

One difficult problem facing authors and publishers is how to pay authors for online uses of their works. One approach is to form agencies to handle electronic licensing and royalty collection for freelance magazine and newspaper articles. Such collective rights agencies have long been used to license music. At least one such collective rights organizations has already been established: the Authors Registry, set up by the Authors Guild and the American Society of Journalists and Authors.

The Authors Registry, Inc.
31 East 28th St., 10th Floor
New York, NY 10016
212-563-6920
www.authorsregistry.org

Multimedia Works

Multimedia works, or "electronic books," combine text with visual images (both still photos and video and film clips) and sound (including music, ordinary speech, and dramatic performances). Some multimedia works consist of a printed text combined with a CD-ROM disk; others are stored only on CD-ROMs or other magnetic media. Software is usually included to enable the user to search, retrieve, and manipulate the material.

Multimedia works often present some difficult copyright problems. We'll examine below the copyright issues presented in obtaining permission to use third-party content in multimedia works. We'll also provide a detailed discussion of Copyright Office registration and deposit requirements for such works.

Obtaining Permissions for Multimedia Works

Many multimedia works consist, at least in part, of preexisting materials. This poses special copyright problems. Consider this example: Scrivener & Sons, a long-established book publisher, decides to enter the electronic book market. It plans to publish a multimedia history of the Persian Gulf War on a CD-ROM. Scrivener wants the disc to contain a variety of preexisting materials about the Gulf War, including:

- text from several articles and books
- photos from books, magazines, and other sources
- video clips from many television programs
- music to be used as background to the images and text, and
- third-party application software programs to support graphics, sound, and animation.

Scrivener intends to incorporate hundreds of separate items into its multimedia package. This sounds like a fine idea for a multimedia product. However, Scrivener must overcome a substantial legal obstacle before it can publish the work: It must obtain permission to use at least some of the preexisting material. Obtaining such permission can involve tracking down many different copyright owners and negotiating licenses to use their material. This can be very time-consuming and expensive. Indeed, some publishers and software developers have discovered that some multimedia works are not economically feasible in today's marketplace because the legal and licensing costs are too high.

When copyright permissions are needed

Whether permission is needed to include any given item in a multimedia work depends first, of course, on who owns it. Review the discussion of ownership of electronic copyright above, and read the detailed discussions of copyright ownerships in Chapter 8, Initial Copyright Ownership, and Chapter 9, Transferring Copyright Ownership.

Generally, permission is not needed to use materials specially created for a multimedia work, whether by employees or third parties. The publisher will automatically own materials created by employees within the scope of their employment and will routinely obtain an assignment of copyright rights from nonemployees (or have them sign work-made-for-hire agreements). For sample employment and independent contractor agreements, refer to *Web & Software Development: A Legal Guide,* by Stephen Fishman (Nolo).

However, permission may be needed to use *preexisting* materials created by nonemployees (or by employees before they became employees). Even in this event, though, permission will not be needed if the material is (1) in the public domain, or (2) the use of the material constitutes a fair use.

We discuss the public domain in detail in Chapter 6, What Copyright Protects. Review that chapter and Chapter 10, Copyright Duration, to see if a preexisting work is in the public domain and therefore has no copyright protection.

Even if a preexisting work is protected by copyright, permission will not be needed to use it if the use constitutes a fair use. Fair use is discussed in detail in Chapter 11, Using Other Authors' Words. Although Chapter 11 focuses on the fair use of writings, the principles it describes are applicable to all types of protected works—graphics, music, photos, video, and so forth.

If a preexisting work is protected by copyright and the intended use cannot qualify as a fair use, permission must be obtained to include it in a multimedia work.

Obtaining multimedia permissions

With the notable exception of the music industry, which has had a system of rights collectives in place for many decades, obtaining permission to use copyrighted materials in a multimedia project is a difficult, time-consuming, and often chaotic process.

Obtaining multimedia permissions can be especially hard because, for a variety of reasons, many copyright owners are reluctant to grant any multimedia permissions. Many copyright owners have decided not to grant multimedia permissions for the time being because the market is so new they're unsure how much such rights are worth. Others are reluctant to permit their work to be reduced to digitized form for fear they will lose control over unauthorized copying. Still others intend to launch their own multimedia ventures and don't want to help potential competitors. Some owners will grant permission, but only for exorbitant amounts of money (there are no standard rates for such permissions).

Securing a multimedia permission, then, can require a good deal of persistence, salesmanship, and creative negotiating. A two-step process should be followed:

- First, find out who owns the rights that are needed.
- Then, negotiate and have signed a written release or multimedia license agreement.

Refer to *Web & Software Development: A Legal Guide* (Chapter 13), by Stephen Fishman (Nolo), for a detailed discussion of how to obtain permission to use text, photographs, film and video, drawings and other artwork, and music. A sample website license agreement is also included.

Copyright Registration for Multimedia Works

For all the reasons discussed in Chapter 4, Copyright Registration, multimedia works can and should be registered with the Copyright Office. It is always permissible to register each element of a multimedia work separately—manual, text, photos, video, and so on. However, it may not be necessary to do so. An entire multimedia work can be registered at one time on one registration form for one $45 fee if both of the following are true:

- The copyright claimant is the same for all elements of the work for which copyright protection is sought.
- All such elements are published at the same time as a single unit (excluding preexisting elements such as photos, music, and video which will not be covered by the registration).

An example will help make these rules clear. Assume that Scrivener & Sons in the example in the above section has finished developing its multimedia history of the Persian Gulf War. The multimedia package consists of a CD-ROM containing text, photos, video, and music, and a printed manual explaining how to use the CD-ROM. Scrivener is the copyright owner of the manual, which was written by its employees. Scrivener editors and work-for-hire freelancers also wrote some of the text on the CD-ROM. All the other material on the CD-ROM was licensed by Scrivener—that is, it obtained permission to copy and distribute it on the CD-ROM from the copyright owners. Scrivener does not own the copyright in any of these individual bits of text, photos, video, or music. However, Scrivener does own a compilation copyright in the entire CD-ROM—that is, a copyright in the selection, arrangement, and coordination of all the material on the disc, which was performed by Scrivener employees and work-for-hire freelancers. This selection, arrangement, and coordination constitutes a work of authorship if original and minimally creative. (See Chapter 7, Adaptations and Compilations.)

Scrivener may register all the elements to which it claims copyright ownership—the manual, the CD-ROM text it owns, and the compilation copyright covering all the CD-ROM material—on a single application for a single fee. Why? Because the copyright claimant for all the elements of the multimedia work for which protection is sought by Scrivener is the same—Scrivener—and all these elements are being published together as a single unit at the same time.

What about registering all the individual bits of text, music, photos, video that Scrivener licensed? That's the province of the copyright owner of each individual licensed item. Scrivener may not register such material since it is not the copyright claimant (owner).

Antonin Dvořák

Multimedia Works Include More Than Just CD-ROMs

For copyright registration purposes, a multimedia work includes more than works on CD-ROM discs. Rather, a multimedia work is any work which, excluding its container, combines authorship in two or more media. The authorship may include text, artwork, sculpture, cinematography, photography, sounds, music, or choreography. The media may include printed matter such as a book; audiovisual material such as videotape, slides, filmstrips; a phonorecord such as an audio tape or audio disk; or any machine-readable copy such as a computer disk, tape, or chip. Any work combining two or more types of authorship in two or more different types of media is a multimedia work and may be registered using the procedures discussed in this section. For example, a book combined with a filmstrip or audio tape would be a multimedia work. However, since this chapter is about electronic publishing, our focus is on registering multimedia kits consisting of CD-ROM discs and written manuals.

Which form to use

Form PA is usually used for registration of multimedia works. Form PA is used to register any multimedia work containing an audiovisual element—photos, video, film clips, and so on. A multimedia work consisting solely of text is registered on Form TX. If a multimedia work does not contain any audiovisual elements, but does contain sounds in which sound-recording authorship is claimed, Form SR is used.

Filling out Form PA

Form PA is virtually identical to Form TX (the form used to register most types of written works). We discuss how to fill out Form TX in detail in Chapter 4, Copyright Registration. Following are the significant differences when registering a multimedia work on Form TX.

Space 1: Nature of This Work

State audiovisual work in the "Nature of this Work" box in Space 1.

Space 2: Name of Author

State only the name of the author(s) for the elements of the work for which copyright is claimed in this registration. If preexisting materials have been licensed from third parties, don't mention their names in Space 2. In our example above, Scrivener & Sons would be listed as the author in Space 2. The third parties from whom Scrivener licensed the material included in the work are not the authors of the work Scrivener is applying to register, and Scrivener's copyright does not cover their work.

Space 2: Nature of Authorship

The elements of the multimedia work in which original authorship is claimed should be listed here. Scrivener & Sons in our example above could state "compilation and editing of preexisting text, photographs, video clips, film clips, and music plus new original text."

Or, more broadly, if you are entitled to claim copyright in an audiovisual work, artwork on computer screens, and the text of a computer program, all embodied on a CD-ROM, Space 2 of your application would read: "audiovisual work, artwork on computer screens, and text of computer program."

If your CD-ROM claim consists solely of an original compilation of preexisting facts and data, the authorship in Space 2 would be described as "original compilation of preexisting data." Note that this nature of authorship statement is appropriate only where the applicant claims no authorship in the preexisting data, the CD-ROM contains no computer program authorship the applicant is entitled to claim copyright in, and the work is not marketed with a print manual. In this situation, you should submit a cover letter along with your application explaining what original selection, arrangement, or ordering is present—that is, explaining what work was involved in selecting and arranging the preexisting material on the CD-ROM. Such selection and arrangement must rise to the level of original authorship to be copyrightable and therefore registerable. See detailed discussion of compilation copyrights in Chapter 7, Adaptations and Compilations.

Space 6: Derivative Work or Compilation

If a multimedia work contains preexisting material such as photos, video and film clips, preexisting text, or music, Space 6 must be completed. If the work contains all new material, Space 6 can be left blank.

Space 6a must be filled in if the multimedia work is a derivative work; it is left blank if the work is just a compilation. As discussed in detail in Chapter 7, Adaptations and Compilations, a derivative work is a work that is created by adapting and recasting preexisting material into a new work of authorship. Most multimedia works containing preexisting material are derivative works—the preexisting material is edited and combined with other preexisting materials and new material to form a new original work of authorship. It's not necessary to individually list every preexisting work included in the multimedia work; a general description is sufficient. For example, Scrivener in our example above could state "previously published text, film and video footage, graphics, and music."

Space 6b: Material Added to This Work

Space 6b calls for a description of the new material added to the preexisting material in which copyright is claimed. You can simply repeat what you stated in the "Nature of Authorship" box in Space 2 above.

Deposit requirements

The Copyright Office has imposed special deposit requirements for multimedia works. One complete copy of the best edition of a multimedia work first published in the United States must be deposited with the Copyright Office. Everything that is marketed or distributed together must be deposited, whether or not you're the copyright claimant for each element. This includes:

- the ROM disc(s),
- instructional manual(s), and
- any printed version of the work that is sold with the multimedia package (for example, where a book is sold with a CD-ROM).

Multimedia works used on computers typically contain software that enables the user to operate the CD-ROM or other storage medium and access, search, and retrieve the data and produce screen displays. The deposit must include identifying material for any such software in which copyright is claimed by the applicant. (But if the software is simply licensed from a third party, no such deposit is necessary.)

The deposit must consist of a printout of the program source code or object code. However, the entire program need not be deposited. Instead, the applicant may deposit a printout of the first and last 25 pages of the source code. Or, if the program contains trade secrets, the applicant has the option of depositing:

- the first and last 25 pages of source code with the portions containing trade secrets blacked out, or
- the first and last ten pages of source code with no blacked-out portions, or
- the first and last 25 pages of object code, together with any ten or more consecutive pages of source code with no blacked-out portions, or

- for programs consisting of fewer than 25 pages, the entire program with the trade secret portions blacked out. For further details, see the Copyright Office brochure entitled "Circular 61: Copyright Registration for Computer Programs."

The Copyright Office wishes multimedia applicants to inform it as to whether the operating software is part of the multimedia work, and where it is embodied—for example, on a CD-ROM disc or other medium.

The Copyright Office has experienced some difficulty in viewing a number of CD-ROM products that have been deposited because it doesn't have the proper equipment. When this occurs, the copyright examiner will require the applicant to make a supplemental deposit of identifying material. For example, it might require a supplemental deposit of a videotape showing the audiovisual elements in which authorship is claimed.

Electronic Databases

Perhaps the most important area of electronic publishing today is the creation and economic exploitation of electronic databases. An electronic database (or automated database in Copyright Office parlance) is a body of facts, data, or other information assembled into an organized format suitable for use in a computer. The variety of information contained on electronic databases is nearly endless and growing rapidly. Everything from government documents to stock quotes to magazine and journal articles can be accessed.

Many electronic databases are available online—the database is housed in a computer in a remote location, and end users retrieve information from the database via telephone lines or computer networks. Examples include large commercial online information services such as Lexis-Nexis-Medis and Dialog. Online services such as these are actually collections of many databases provided by a variety of publishers and other sources. The services negotiate contracts with the owners of the databases for the right to distribute them, and pay royalties based primarily on how much the database is used. Costs to use such services are usually based on a subscription fee plus usage charges for actual use of particular databases.

Thousands of electronic databases are also maintained by universities, research institutions, government agencies, and large corporations. Many of these can be accessed via the Internet—a collection of thousands of regional, state, federal, academic, and corporate computer networks operated on a nonprofit basis.

Still other electronic databases are available on CD-ROM discs or other magnetic storage media. For example, a CD-ROM database containing over two million patents issued by the United States Patent and Trademark Office has recently been published. The user purchases or licenses such databases directly from the publisher and uses them directly on her own computer, rather than accessing them via an online service or computer network. This allows the database publisher to bypass the online service and market its product directly to end users.

Below, we'll look first at the nature and extent of copyright protection for such material and then show how to register an electronic database with the Copyright Office.

When Is the Data in Electronic Databases Protected by Copyright?

For electronic databases to be constructed, the computer must be told (programmed) where the information placed in it is stored and how that information can be retrieved upon request. Accordingly, when a database is actually constructed, it consists of:

- the data, and
- the database software—that is, the unique set of instructions that defines the way the data is to be organized, stored, and retrieved.

This discussion only covers copyright protection for the data in electronic databases. To learn about protecting database software, refer to *Web & Software Development: A Legal Guide*, by Stephen Fishman (Nolo).

Databases are compilations or collective works

First, a little copyright law background: A database consisting of unprotectable facts or data—for instance, names and addresses or numerical data—is a fact compilation, that is, a work created by selecting, organizing, and arranging previously existing material in such a way that the resulting work as a whole constitutes an original work of authorship. The individual materials contained in the database may not be entitled to copyright protection, but the selection and arrangement of the entire database may be.

A database that contains individually protectable works—for example, a full-text bibliographic database containing the full text of copyrighted articles—is a collective work. A collective work is a special type of compilation. It is a work created by selecting and arranging into a single whole work preexisting materials that are separate and independent works entitled to copyright protection in their own right. As with fact compilations, there may be copyright protection for the selection and arrangement of the materials making up a collective work.

Of course, some databases contain both protectable and unprotectable material, and are therefore both fact compilations and collective works. For a detailed discussion of copyright protection for compilations and collective works, see Chapter 7, Adaptations and Compilations.

Originality and minimal creativity required for protection

As discussed in detail in Chapter 7, a compilation is entitled to copyright protection only where the selection, arrangement, and/or coordination of the material is original and minimally creative. In a seminal decision called *Feist Publications v. Rural Telephone Service Co.*, 111 S.Ct. 1282 (1991), the U.S. Supreme Court held that one type of fact compilation—telephone book white pages—was not entitled to any copyright protection at all because absolutely no creativity was required to compile alphabetical white pages listings.

Copyright Does Not Protect Hard Work

In the past, some courts held that copyright protected databases and other works that lacked originality and/or creativity if a substantial amount of work was involved in their creation. These courts might have protected a telephone directory, for example, if the authors had personally verified every entry. However, the Supreme Court outlawed this sweat of the brow theory in the *Feist* decision. It is now clear that the amount of work done to create a database or other work has absolutely no bearing on the degree of copyright protection it will receive. As discussed in detail in Chapter 6, What Copyright Protects, copyright protects only fixed, original, minimally creative expressions, not hard work

The *Feist* decision caused great concern in the database industry because many databases would appear to involve no more creativity in their compiling than telephone book white pages. Does this mean they are not entitled to copyright protection? The answer is not entirely clear. However, database publishers should take heart from the Supreme Court statement in *Feist* that only a very minimal degree of creativity is required for copyright protection and that the vast majority of compilations should make the grade.

Nevertheless, for a database to be protected by copyright (and registrable by the Copyright Office), the selection, arrangement, and/or coordination involved in its creation must rise to the level of original authorship. Databases whose creation was dictated solely by mechanical or functional considerations will likely not be protectable.

Examples of databases that likely lack copyright protection include:

- exhaustive lists or collections of all the data on a given topic—for example, an alphabetical list of all the parts contained in Ford automobiles
- databases whose selection, arrangement, and/or coordination were determined by external guidelines or rules—for example, a database containing the names and addresses of contributors to the Republican Party under 50 years of age who voted for Pat Buchanan in the 1992 presidential primaries and for Ross Perot in the general election
- databases that are so commonplace in their parameters that a great possibility exists that someone else would arrive at the same selection—for example, a database of physicians' phone numbers, names, and addresses arranged according to their medical specialties.

One of the first post-*Feist* cases dealing with electronic databases illustrates that the more "value-added" features a database publisher adds to the raw facts contained in a database, the more likely it will be copyrightable. The case involved a computerized database of state trademarks. The state trademark records were themselves in the public domain. However, the publisher added to each trademark record a code indicating the type of mark, modified the state records' description of the mark to conform to standard descriptions, divided the data into separate search fields, and added search indexes to facilitate computer searches of the records. The court held that the publisher's "selection, coordination, arrangement, enhancement, and programming of the state trademark data" satisfied the originality and creativity requirements set forth in the *Feist* decision. (*Corsearch, Inc. v. Thomson & Thomson, Guide to Computer L.* (CCH) 46,645 (S.D. N.Y. 1992).) In other words, the database qualified for copyright protection.

Extent of Copyright Protection

The copyright in a fact compilation extends only to the selection, coordination, and arrangement of the data contained in the compilation and to any new expression the database author adds—for instance, instructions on how to use the database. The raw data itself are not protected. This is sometimes called a thin copyright.

A database user may extract the individual bits of data from a fact compilation database without incurring liability for copyright infringement but may not copy the entire database, since this would involve copying the copyright owner's protected expression—that is, selection and arrangement.

> **EXAMPLE:** Applied Technologies of Wisconsin created a computer program called *Market Drive* to help Wisconsin county assessors' offices compile real estate data, such as property addresses and the names of the owners, in an electronic database. The counties used the data for tax assessment purposes. A company, WIREdata, attempted to obtain the raw data from the counties to create its own database for use by real estate brokers. A court held that Applied could not sue WIREdata for copyright infringement because the raw data WIREdata wanted was in the public domain. (*Applied Technologies of Wisconsin v. WIREdata, Inc.*, 350 F.3d 640 (7th Cir. 2003).)

Copyright protection is greater where a database is a collective work—a work consisting of materials entitled to their own copyright protection. In this event, the database owner holds a thin copyright in the selection and arrangement of the entire database, and the items contained in the database may be protected individually. For example, each article contained in a full-text bibliographic database may be protected by copyright, as well as the database as a whole.

Other Means of Protecting Databases

Given the limitations on copyright protection for electronic databases, and the fact that some databases are probably not even entitled to these protections, the database industry has been placing increasing reliance on the use of contracts to prevent unauthorized use of databases. For example, the owners of databases commonly require all users to sign subscription agreements in which the user promises not to reproduce the database without the owners' permission. The extent to which such agreements are enforceable—both in legal and practical terms—is unclear. This is a matter that must be discussed with an attorney knowledgeable about the database industry.

Registering Contents of Electronic Databases

If an electronic database is protected by copyright, it should be registered with the Copyright Office for all the reasons discussed in Chapter 4, Copyright Registration. Since most databases are frequently updated or revised, the Copyright Office has instituted a special group registration procedure whereby a database and all the updates or other revisions made within any three-month period may be registered in one application. This way, a database need only be registered a maximum of four times per year, rather than each time it is updated or revised.

Database Software Must Also Be Registered

The discussion below is only about how to register the selection and arrangement of the contents of a computer automated database. It does not cover registration of computer software designed to be used with databases to facilitate retrieval of the data. Software registration is beyond the scope of this book. For coverage of this topic see *Web & Software Development: A Legal Guide*, by Stephen Fishman (Nolo).

Databases qualifying for group registration

To qualify for group registration, all of the following conditions must be met:

- All of the updates or revisions must be fixed or published only in machine-readable copies.
- All of the updates or revisions must have been created or published within a three-month period, all within the same calendar year.
- All of the updates or revisions must be owned by the same copyright claimant.
- All of the updates or revisions must have the same general title.

- The updates or revisions must be organized in a similar way.

Completing Form TX

Form TX must be submitted for a group database registration. Here's how to fill it out.

Space 1: Title

At the "Title of this Work" line, insert the following statement: "Group registration for automated database title ______________ published/unpublished (*choose one*) updates from ________ to ________." Give the earliest and latest dates for the updates included in the group registration. Remember, this time period must be three months or less, all within the same calendar year.

Use the "Publication as a Contribution" line to give the date (day, month, year) that is represented by the marked portions of the identifying material submitted as a deposit. Also indicate the frequency with which revisions are made—for example, "daily," "weekly," "monthly."

Space 2: Author(s)

You need to give the requested information about every author who contributed any appreciable amount of protectable material to the version of the work being registered. We're talking about the compilation/collective work authorship here, not the authorship of the individual articles or other works in the database. After the words "Nature of Authorship," give a brief general statement of the nature of the particular author's contribution to the work. Examples: "updates," "revisions," "revised compilation," "revised and updated text."

Space 3: Creation and Publication

Give the year in which the author(s) completed the group of updates or revisions being registered.

If the updates or revisions have been published, you must give the date (month, day, year) and nation of publication. This should be the *last* date on which revisions were added during the three-month period covered by the application. When is a database published? This is not exactly clear. For copyright purposes, publication means distributing or offering to distribute copies of a work to the public on an unrestricted basis. It is unclear whether online availability with or without printers for the user constitutes publication. The Copyright Office leaves it up to the copyright owners to determine whether their database has been published.

Space 4: Claimants

Follow the instructions in "How to Complete Form TX" in Chapter 4, Copyright Registration, on how to complete this space.

Space 5: Previous Registration

If the database has been previously registered, check the last box and give the previous registration number and date. If more than one previous registration has been made for the database, give the number and date of any one previous registration.

Space 6: Derivative Work or Compilation
Space 6 must be completed if the updates or the database and its updates contain a substantial amount of previously published, registered, or public domain material. Leave Space 6 blank if the material contained in the database and its updates is entirely new and never before registered or published.

"Preexisting Material" (Space 6a): State "previously registered material," "previously published material," or "public domain data" for a new database that has not been previously registered or published, but that contains an appreciable amount of previously registered, published, or public domain material.

For a previously published or registered database that has not been revised or updated periodically, describe the preexisting material as "previously published database" or "previously registered database," or "database prior to (*earliest date represented in the present group of updates*)."

"Material Added to This Work" (Space 6b): Describe the updates or revisions or new database being registered for the first time and specify the frequency of these updates or revisions—for example, "weekly updates," "daily revisions," or "revised compilation updated monthly."

Spaces 7 & 8
Leave these spaces blank. They're not applicable to electronic databases.

Spaces 9, 10, 11: Fee, Correspondence, Certification, Return Address
Follow the instructions in Chapter 4, Copyright Registration, on how to complete these spaces.

Deposit requirements for group registration
You must submit the following deposit with your registration application.

Identifying material. Identifying material meeting the following requirements:

- 50 representative pages of printout (or equivalent units if reproduced in microfilm) from a single-file database, or
- 50 representative complete data records (not pages) from each updated data file in a multiple-file database.

The printout or data records must be marked to show the copyrightable revisions or updates from one representative publication date (if the database is published) or from one representative creation date (if the database is unpublished) within the three-month period covered by the registration; or, alternatively, you may deposit a copy of the actual updates or revisions made on a representative date.

Descriptive statement. In addition, you must submit a brief, typed descriptive statement providing the following information:

- the title of the database
- the name and address of the copyright claimant

- the name and content of each separate file in a multiple-file database, including its subject, the origin(s) of the data, and the approximate number of data records it contains
- information about the nature, location, and frequency of the changes within the database or within the separate data files in multiple-file databases, and
- information about the copyright notice, if one is used, as follows:
  - For a machine-readable notice, transcribe the contents of the notice and indicate the manner and frequency with which it's displayed—for example, at a user's terminal only, at sign-on, continuously on terminal display, or on printouts.
  - For a visually perceptible notice on any copies of the work (or on tape reels or containers), include a photocopy or other sample of the notice.

Nongroup registration

If your database doesn't qualify for group registration, or you do not wish to use that procedure, simply complete Form TX in the same manner as for any other compilation. You should deposit the first and last 25 pages of a single-file database. If the database consists of separate and distinct data files, deposit one copy of 50 complete data records (not pages) from each file, or the entire file, whichever is less. You must also include a descriptive statement for a multiple-file database containing the same information.

If the database is fixed in a CD-ROM, deposit one complete copy of the CD-ROM package, any instructional manual, and a printed version of the work that is fixed on the CD-ROM if such an exact print version exists. The deposit must also include any software that is included as part of the package. A printout of the first and last 25 pages of the software source code is acceptable.

■

CHAPTER

15 Copyright and Taxation

This chapter provides an overview of federal taxation for writers who create copyrighted works. It is for self-employed writers—that is, writers who create their works on their own, not as employees. It focuses on tax issues of particular interest to writers, especially deducting writing expenses and the hobby loss rule.

If you handle your taxes yourself, you'll need to obtain a more detailed book specifically on taxation. Many books are available including *Deduct It!: Lower Your Small Business Taxes*, by Stephen Fishman (Nolo), and *Home Business Tax Deductions: Keep What You Earn*, by Stephen Fishman (Nolo). The IRS also has free publications on every conceivable tax topic. IRS Publication 910, *Guide to Free Tax Services*, contains a list of these publications. Some of the most useful include:

- Publication 334, *Tax Guide for Small Business*
- Publication 505, *Tax Withholding and Estimated Tax*
- Publication 937, *Employment Taxes and Information Returns*
- Publication 533, *Self-Employment Tax*, and
- Publication 535, *Business Expenses*.

You can obtain these and all other IRS publications by calling the IRS at 800-TAX-FORM, visiting your local IRS office, or downloading them from the IRS's Internet site at www.irs.gov.

Writers' Income Tax Deductions

Charles, a freelance writer, has been working on a book on international terrorism for the last two years. In the course of his research and writing he has incurred substantial expenses. This year, these included:

- $3,000 in travel and hotel expenses for trips to the Middle East and Europe to interview subjects for the book
- $2,000 for a portable computer
- $2,000 in home office expenses
- $3,000 for payments to a research assistant.

These amounted to $10,000 in writing expenses for the year. Naturally, Charles would like to know if he can use these expenses to help reduce his tax burden—that is, he wants to know if he can deduct his expenses.

A tax deduction is an expense or the value of an item that you can subtract from your gross income (all the income you earn) to determine your taxable income—the amount you earn that is subject to taxation. The more deductions you have, the lower your taxable income and the less tax you pay.

Is Writing a Hobby or Business?

Can Charles deduct his writing expenses? The answer is, "It depends." To determine whether or how an expense can be deducted, it is first necessary to figure out how Charles's writing activities should be characterized for tax purposes. With one exception (see "Writing as an Income-Producing Activity," below) these activities will be characterized either as a hobby or a business.

Tax Savings From Deductions

Only part of any deduction will end up as an income tax savings—for example, a $5,000 tax deduction will not result in a $5,000 saving. To determine how much income tax a deduction will save you, you need to know your marginal tax bracket. This is the tax bracket in which the last dollar you earn falls and it's the rate at which any additional income you earn would be taxed. To determine how much tax a deduction will save you, multiply the amount of the deduction by your top tax bracket. For example, if your top tax bracket is 28%, you will save $28 in income taxes for every $100 you are able to claim as a deductible business expense (28% x $100 = $28).

The income tax brackets are adjusted each year for inflation. For the current brackets, see IRS Publication 505, *Tax Withholding and Estimated Tax*.

In addition, you may deduct your business expenses from your state income tax. State income tax rates vary, but they average about 6%. (Alaska, Florida, Nevada, South Dakota, Texas, Washington, and Wyoming don't have state income taxes.)

If you earn income from your business, you can also deduct most of your expenses for self-employment tax purposes. The self-employment tax rate is about 15.3% on net self-employment income up to the Social Security tax cap ($94,200 in 2006).

When you add all this together, you can see the true value of a business tax deduction. For example, if you're in the 25% federal income tax bracket, your effective self-employment rate is about 13.4% because you deduct half of these taxes from your income tax. Thus, a tax would be worth as much as 25% + 13.4% + 6% = 44.4%. So you could end up deducting about 44.4% of the cost of your business expenses from your state and federal taxes. If, for example, you buy a $1,000 computer for your business, you'll save about $444 in taxes. That's a whopping tax savings. In effect, the government is paying for almost half of your business expenses. This is why it's so important to take all the business deductions to which you're entitled.

Writing as a hobby

The worst of all possible tax worlds is for your writing activities to be deemed a hobby by the IRS. A hobby is not a business, and hobbyists may not take all the tax deductions to which businesspeople are entitled. Instead, hobbyists may only deduct their expenses from the hobby from the income they earn from it. If you have no income from the hobby, you get no deduction. And you can't carry over the deductions to use them in future years when you earn income—you lose them forever. Since many writers earn little or no income from writing, those that are deemed to be hobbyists are unable to get any tax benefits from their writing expenses.

> **EXAMPLE:** Assume that Charles's writing activities were deemed a hobby by the IRS—his $10,000 in annual expenses would only be deductible from any income he earned from his hobby. Since he earned no money from writing during the year, he can't deduct any of these expenses.

Moreover, things aren't all that great even if you have income from your hobby. Your hobby expenses are only deductible as a Miscellaneous Itemized Deduction on the IRS Schedule A that you file with your Form 1040. This means you can only deduct your hobby expenses if you itemize your deductions instead of taking the standard deduction, which requires that your total itemized deductions be greater than the standard deduction ($5,100 for single people in 2006). If you do itemize, your hobby expenses will be reduced so that they are no more than your hobby income and then further reduced by an amount equal to 2% of your adjusted gross income.

> **EXAMPLE:** Assume that Charles's writing was a hobby for tax purposes and he earned $5,000 in income from it this year, along with his $10,000 in expenses. He could deduct $5,000 of these expenses as an itemized deduction—the amount equal to his writing income. However, this $5,000 deduction would be reduced by an amount equal to 2% of Charles's adjusted gross income for the year. If Charles's AGI was $100,000, there would be a $2,000 reduction. So Charles could deduct only $3,000 of his writing expenses on his Schedule A (assuming his total itemized deductions exceed the standard deduction).

You don't need to understand all this in great detail. Just be aware that a finding by the IRS that your writing activities are a hobby will be a tax disaster. The only good thing about being a hobbyist is that you don't have to pay self-employment taxes on hobby income. Writers who are in business do have to pay such taxes.

For tax purposes, a hobby is any activity you engage in primarily for a reason other than to earn a profit—for example, to have fun, pass the time, get famous, or please your spouse (or avoid your spouse), or any other reason. Or, to put it another way, if your primary motive for writing is to earn a profit, it is not a hobby. How do you show the IRS that your motive for writing is to earn a profit? You must actually earn a profit, or at least act as if you want to earn profits. This is explained in detail below.

If you *want* writing to be a hobby, not a business, that's perfectly fine. There's no law that says a writer has to be in business. Writing is a wonderful hobby. However, you should still keep track of your writing expenses—hobbyists may deduct from their hobby income the expenses that businesspeople are allowed to deduct from all their income as described below (subject to an exception for the home office deduction). Then, if you do happen to earn income from your writing, you can deduct your expenses from it. This way, you can at least avoid paying tax on all or most of this hobby income.

Writing as a business

If being deemed a mere hobbyist is the worst thing that can happen to you tax-wise, being viewed as a businessperson is the best. Businesspeople are the pampered pets of the tax code, receiving the best possible tax treatment.

If writing qualifies as business, and, like most independent writers, you are a sole proprietor, you list all your writing business expenses and income on IRS Schedule C, Profit or Loss From Business. You deduct your writing business expenses from writing business income. You pay tax only on your net business income (gross business income minus business expenses).

EXAMPLE: Assume that Charles earned $20,000 from writing for the year, and that his $10,000 in expenses qualified as current business deductions. He would deduct his $10,000 expenses from his $20,000 writing income on his Schedule C, leaving $10,000 in net writing business income subject to taxation (both income and self-employment taxes).

If, as is the case with many writers, your writing expenses exceed your writing income, or you have no writing income at all, you will have a net loss from writing for the year. You can deduct this business loss from all the income you earn for the year, whatever the source—for example, from your salary or investment income—thereby reducing your taxable income for the year.

EXAMPLE: Assume that Charles earned no money from writing for the year, but still incurred $10,000 in annual expenses that could be currently deducted. He would have a net loss from writing of $10,000. He can deduct his $10,000 writing loss from all his income for the year, which was $50,000 in interest and investment income and salary from a part-time teaching job. So, instead of having to pay income tax on $50,000 in income, he only had to pay it on $40,000 ($50,000 – $10,000). This $10,000 deduction ends up saving Charles $3,500 in federal and state income tax for the year—$3,500 he would not have had were he not engaged in the business of writing.

Net Operating Losses

Sometimes a writer's losses are so great that they will exceed his or her total income for the year. For example, assume that Charles earned only $15,000 in total income, while incurring $20,000 in currently deductible writing expenses for the year. He would have a net loss for the year of $5,000 ($15,000 – $20,000 = –$5,000). Such a loss is called a "net operating loss," NOL for short.

Although it may not be pleasant to lose money over an entire year, having an NOL does result in important tax benefits—indeed, it's a little like having money in the bank, because it can result in a quick tax refund. You can deduct the amount of an NOL against your income for previous years and thereby reduce the tax you needed to pay for those years. This is called "carrying a loss back."

Ordinarily, you may elect to carry back the loss for two years before the NOL year (the year you incurred the loss). The loss is used to offset the taxable income for the earliest year first, and then used for the next year(s). If any of the loss is left over, it may be carried forward up to 20 years—that is, used to reduce your taxable income in future years.

> **EXAMPLE:** Assume that Charles had a $5,000 NOL in 2005. He elects to carry back the loss two years—that is, to 2003. He deducts the NOL first against his taxable income for 2003. Then, if any of the NOL is unused (that is, some of it is left after reducing his tax for 2003 to zero), he then deducts it against his 2004 income. The amount of his tax savings is refunded to him by the IRS. If some of the NOL is still left over, he can use it to reduce his taxes for the next 20 years until it's all used up.

To obtain a refund due to an NOL, you must file either IRS Form 1045 or 1045X. You can get your refund faster by using Form 1045—usually you'll get it within 90 days. However, you must file Form 1045 within one year of the end of your NOL year.

The calculations involved in determining how much you can deduct from prior years' income can be complicated. Tax preparation programs like TurboTax aren't designed to handle NOLs, so it's wise to let a tax pro help you determine your NOL.

For more information on net operating losses, refer to IRS Publication 536, *Net Operating Losses (NOLs) for Individuals, Estates, and Trusts*. You can obtain this and all other IRS publications from the IRS Internet site at www.irs.gov, by calling the IRS at 800-TAX-FORM, or by visiting your local IRS office.

Writing as an Income-Producing Activity

In some cases, writing is not really a hobby or a business. This could occur where the primary motive for writing is to earn a profit, but the writer doesn't engage in writing sufficiently regularly or continuously for it to be a business. In these cases, writing could be a for-profit income-producing activity under IRC Section 212.

An income-producing activity is one you engage in primarily to earn a profit, but that does not qualify as a business. Typical income-producing activities include such things as managing rental properties or other investments. But, writing can qualify so long as your primary motive for doing it is to earn a profit.

The tax consequences of having an income-producing activity are not as favorable as being in business, but they are still better then engaging in a hobby. You're entitled to most of the same tax deductions as a businessperson (except, unlike businesspeople, you can't deduct home office expenses, or currently deduct up to $105,000 in purchases of long-term personal property under IRC 179). Unlike where writing is deemed a hobby, your deductions are not limited to the amount you earn from writing.

However, if writing is an income-producing activity instead of a business, you won't be able to deduct your expenses for the year all at once. Instead, the IRS has ruled that you must deduct them over three years—50% the first year, and 25% the next two years. (IRS Notice 88-62.)

For example, assume that Charles from the previous examples, above, was deemed to be engaged in an income-producing activity. His $10,000 in currently deductible writing expenses would have to be deducted over three years—$5,000 the first year and $2,500 the next two years.

How to Show the IRS Writing Is a Business

It should be clear by now that writers who qualify as businesspeople get the best tax treatment. Two main factors are considered by the IRS in determining whether writing is a business:

- Your primary motive for writing must be to earn a profit.
- You must engage in writing continuously and regularly over a substantial time period.

The IRS has established two tests to measure these factors. One is a simple mechanical test that asks whether you've earned a profit in three of the last five years. The other is a more complex test based on whether you behave like a business.

Note that the IRS only applies these tests if your tax returns are audited. In other words, you may mistakenly presume that writing is a business only to learn, four or five years later, that the IRS has a different opinion. In that case, you would be disallowed any improper deductions made during those years and required to pay any miscalculated taxes and penalties. The cost can be quite expensive, and for that reason we strongly recommend that you bolster your position as a business by reviewing this chapter.

Profit test

You usually don't have to worry about the IRS labeling writing as a hobby if you earn a profit from it in any three of the last five years. If your venture passes this test, the IRS must presume it is a business. This doesn't mean the IRS can't claim your writing is a hobby, but it shifts the burden to the IRS to prove it is a hobby. In practice, the IRS usually doesn't attack ventures that pass the profit test unless it's clear the numbers have been manipulated just to pass it.

You have a profit when the taxable income from an activity is more than the deductions for it. You don't have to earn a big profit to satisfy this test, and there is no set amount or percentage of profit you need to earn.

> **EXAMPLE:** Tom began to work on a new book in 1998. He earned no income from writing during 1999–2000 and therefore had no profits from writing for those years. He published the book in 2000. Due to his royalty income from the book, he earned a profit from writing during 2000 through 2003. As of 2003, he had earned a profit during three of the last five years. Thus, in 2003, the IRS must presume writing is running a business for Tom.

Unfortunately, a great many writers can't satisfy the profit test. It may take far more than five years before you see any money at all from writing, let alone turn a profit.

IRS Form 5213

The IRS has a form called Form 5213, *Election to Postpone Determination as to Whether the Presumption Applies that an Activity is Engaged In for Profit.* If you file this form, the IRS must wait an extra year before it can determine whether you've shown a profit under the profit test. This may sound like a good deal, but it isn't. Don't file this form. Doing so only alerts the IRS that you should be audited on the hobby loss issue. For this reason, almost no one ever files a 5213

Behavior test

If, like many writers, you can't satisfy the profit test, you can still show you're running a business by passing the behavior test. However, you'll have to work hard to show that you are trying your darndest to make money from writing.

Under the behavior test, the IRS looks at the following "objective" factors to determine whether you are behaving as if you honestly believe you will earn a profit from writing.

Do you act like you're in business? If you act like you're running a business, you likely want to earn a profit. Among other things, acting like a business means you keep good books and other records and otherwise carry on your writing activities in a businesslike manner.

Do you have expertise? It would look pretty odd to the IRS if, for example, a person claimed to be writing a book on nuclear physics but had no educational background or other expertise in the field. Such a person would not seem to be serious about earning money. On the other hand, a person who had a degree in physics and/or had writing credits in the field would appear to be serious about earning a profit from writing about physics. If you lack the necessary expertise, you should acquire it through study or by consulting with experts in the field.

Do you write regularly and continuously? You can work part-time at writing and still be in business. As a general rule, the more time and effort you put into writing, the more likely it will appear you want to earn a profit.

Do you have a good track record? Having a track record of success in other businesses in the past—whether or not related to writing—helps show your present writing activities are a business.

Have you earned at least some profits? Even if you can't satisfy the profit test, earning at least occasional profits helps show you're in business.

How big are your profits? Earning only small or occasional yearly profits while you have large losses and/or a large investment in an activity tends to show a lack of a profit motive. On the other hand, earning a substantial profit one year after years of losses helps show you are in a business. After all, writers often earn little or nothing for many years in the hope of a big payday down the road when their work is published or otherwise sold.

Are you rich? The IRS figures you likely have a profit motive if you don't have a substantial income from sources other than writing. After all, you'll need to earn money from your writing to survive. On the other hand, substantial income from sources other than writing may indicate a lack of a profit motive. This factor is never determinative by itself.

Are you having too much fun? Finally, activities that are inherently fun or recreational are less likely to be engaged in for profit than those that are not fun. Writing is often viewed as a "fun" activity by the IRS—particularly where the writer does a substantial amount of pleasurable traveling. This means, for example, that a writer who claims a trip to Paris as a writing business expense because his novel is set in Paris will have a harder time showing a profit motive than an accountant or computer programmer who never leaves his cubicle.

Passing the IRS behavior test

The first three factors listed above—acting like a business, expertise, and time and effort expended—are by far the most important. Studies have shown that no taxpayer who has satisfied these factors has ever been found not to have a profit motive. If you take the following steps, you'll have a good chance of passing the test:

- **Act like a businessperson.** First and foremost, you must show that you carry on your writing activities in a businesslike manner.
- **Keep good business records.** Keeping good records of your expenses and income from writing is the single most important thing you can do to show you're in business and want to earn a profit. Without good records, you'll never have an accurate idea of how you stand financially. Lack of records shows you don't really care if you make money or not. You don't need an elaborate set of books. A simple record of your expenses and income will suffice. See *Working for Yourself*, by Stephen Fishman (Nolo), for a detailed discussion of record keeping for self-employed people.
- **Persistently try to sell your work.** Writers who are in business ordinarily try to sell their work—they don't write solely for enjoyment. Authors who fail to make systematic sales efforts will usually be found to be hobbyists. Keep a record of where you submit your work and save all acceptance and rejection letters or other letters or email you receive from publishers or editors.
- **Legally protect your writings.** Any original writing is automatically protected by copyright the moment it is written down or otherwise recorded. However, you can obtain additional legal benefits by registering your works with the U.S. Copyright Office. This is inexpensive and easy to do and helps to show you're a serious businessperson. (See Chapter 4 for a detailed discussion of copyright registration.)
- **Keep a separate checking account.** Open up a separate checking account for your writing business. This will help you keep your personal and business expenses separate—another factor that shows you're running a business.
- **Get business stationery and cards.** It may seem like a minor matter, but obtaining business stationery and business cards shows you think you are in business. Hobbyists ordinarily don't have such things. You can inexpensively create your own stationery and cards yourself using off-the-shelf software products.
- **Obtain a separate phone line for your home office.** If you have an outside office, great; this will help show you're running a business. But if, like many writers, you work at home, obtaining a separate phone line for your business reinforces the idea that you're in business.

- **Join professional organizations and associations.** Join and participate in writer's organizations and associations —for example, the National Writers Union or Authors Guild.
- **Create a business plan.** It is also helpful to draw up a business plan with forecasts of revenue and expenses. For detailed guidance on how to create a business plan, see *How to Write a Business Plan,* by Mike McKeever (Nolo).
- **Have or get expertise.** If you lack all the expertise you need to be a successful writer, develop it by attending educational seminars and similar activities and/or consulting with experts. Keep records to show your attempts to gain expertise—for example, notes documenting your attendance at a writing seminar.
- **Work steadily.** People who run a business ordinarily work continuously and regularly. They don't work one day and then do nothing for the next six months. So, you can't write one short article a year and claim that writing is a business.

  You don't have to work full time on writing to show you have a profit motive, but you should work steadily rather than sporadically. This can be an important factor in an IRS determination. Long ago, the IRS ruled that a person who writes only one book as a sideline and never revises it would not be considered to be in business. In contrast, an author who prepares new editions of a book from time to time, writes other books and materials, and lectures professionally would likely be viewed as being in business. (Rev. Rul. 55-385.)

  Keep a log showing the time you spend writing; this doesn't have to be fancy—you can just mark down the time you spend on your calendar. If you're audited, this documentation will show how hard you've been working.

Writers who failed the behavior test

Following are real-life examples of writers who failed the behavior test. They may help show you how the IRS and courts apply the test.

- **The Author Who Never Sold a Book.** Bradley, a social services caseworker, worked part time at writing for over 17 years. He set up an office in a room in his home and wrote fiction. However, he only submitted one manuscript, a novel called *The Glass Mask*, to a publisher. It was rejected, and he never attempted to get it published elsewhere. The only money he ever made from writing was $700 his mother paid him to write her biography. The IRS claimed Bradley was a hobby writer, and the court agreed. The court said his failure to make systematic efforts to sell his work showed he engaged in writing "essentially for personal pleasure," not to make a profit. (*Sherman v. Commissioner*, T.C. Memo 1989-269.)

- **The Engineer's Complaint.** Bert, an intermittently employed electrical engineer, wrote various articles in his spare time. These were not on the subject of engineering, but on such topics as his hatred of the IRS and his problems with his mother. He wrote 44 such articles over a three-year period, and managed to get five published—unfortunately, for free. Although Bert claimed to have spent substantial time writing, the tax court held that he was a hobbyist. Bert failed to keep adequate books and records and the court found that his articles didn't appear to be written with the purpose of earning money from publication. Rather, his diatribes resembled diary entries or served as a means for him to let off steam about the income tax system. (*Bert v. Commissioner.* T.C. Memo, 1989-503)

Writers who passed the behavior test

The following writers passed the behavior test, even though they earned no profit from their writing during the time in question.

- **The Struggling Playwright.** Eleanor supported herself as a Hollywood screenwriter and freelance book and article writer for 28 years. Following her marriage, she continued to write magazine articles but started devoting more of her writing time to plays, which she sent to agents and producers. She lost money from these activities for eight out of 12 years. The IRS audited her and claimed that, although she had once been a professional writer, playwriting was merely a money-losing hobby she engaged in after her marriage. Eleanor appealed to the tax court and won. The court was impressed by the businesslike manner that Eleanor managed her playwriting. She spent two to four hours a day writing in her office, which measured 20' x 20' and was located in the same building as her apartment, but on a separate floor. She kept a separate bank account in which she deposited income from her writing activities and from which she paid expenses connected with her writing. She was a long-time member of the American Society of Journalists and Authors, the Dramatists' Guild and Authors' Leagues, and the American Federation of Television and Radio Actors. This all led the court to believe that Eleanor wrote her plays to earn a profit and was therefore in business. (*Howard v. Commissioner,* T.C. Memo 1981-250.)
- **The Freelancer With Great Expectations.** Seymour, a veteran writer with many articles and screenplays to his credit, spent almost a whole year in New York researching D.W. Griffith's papers at the Museum of Modern Art. He used this research to write an article on Griffith for *Film Culture Magazine* and also signed a contract to write a book on the pioneer film director.

Seymour earned no money from the article but was to be paid a royalty for the sales of his book. The IRS objected when Seymour deducted his travel expenses for the time he spent in New York, claiming he was not in business during that time. The tax court disagreed, holding that Seymour was in business because he had a good faith expectation of earning a profit from his book once it was published. (*Stern v. United States*, 71-1 U.S. Tax Cas. (CCH) P9375.)

Types of Expenses Writers May Deduct

Virtually any writing expense you incur is deductible as long as it is:

- ordinary and necessary
- directly related to your writing business, and
- for a reasonable amount.

An expense that satisfies these requirements is deductible whether your writing activity qualifies as a business, hobby, or profit-making activity, subject to the limitations on deductions for hobbies and profit activities noted above.

Ordinary and necessary

An expense qualifies as ordinary and necessary if it is common, accepted, helpful, and appropriate for your writing business. An expense doesn't have to be indispensable to be necessary; it need only help your business in some way, even in a minor way. It's usually fairly easy to tell if an expense passes this test.

EXAMPLE 1: Bill, a freelance writer, is writing a book about ancient Athens. He hires a research assistant and pays her $15 an hour. This is clearly a deductible business expense. Hiring research assistants is a common and accepted practice among professional writers. The assistant's fee is an ordinary and necessary expense for Bill's writing business.

EXAMPLE 2: Bill, the freelance writer, visits a masseuse every week to work on his bad back. Bill claims the cost as a business expense, reasoning that avoiding back pain helps him concentrate on his writing. This is clearly not an ordinary or customary expense for a freelance writer, and the IRS would not likely allow it as a business expense.

Expense must be related to your business

An expense must be related to your writing business to be deductible. That is, you must use the item you buy for your business in some way. For example, the cost of a personal computer is a deductible business expense if you use the computer to write freelance articles.

You cannot deduct purely personal expenses as business expenses. The cost of a personal computer is not deductible if you use it just to play computer games. If you buy something for both personal and business reasons, you may deduct the business portion of the expense. For example, if you buy a cellular phone and use it half the time for business calls and half the time for personal calls, you can deduct half the cost of the phone as a business expense.

However, the IRS requires you to keep records showing when the item was used for business and when for personal reasons. One acceptable form of record would be a diary or log with the dates, times, and reason the item was used. This kind of record keeping can be burdensome and may not be worth the trouble if the item isn't very valuable.

To avoid having to keep such records, try to use items either only for business or only for personal use. For example, if you can afford it, purchase two computers and use one solely for your writing and one for playing games and other personal uses.

Ralph Waldo Emerson

Writer's Brothel Expenses Not Deductible

Vitale, a retired federal government budget analyst, decided to write a book about two men who travel cross-country to patronize a legal brothel in Nevada. To authenticate the story and develop characters for the book, he visited numerous legal brothels in Nevada by acting as a customer for prostitutes. He kept a detailed journal describing his experiences at the brothels, including the dates (and sometimes the hours) of his visits, the prostitutes he met, and the amount of cash he paid each one. He wrote and published the book, called *Searchlight, Nevada*, and later claimed a deduction of $3,480 on his tax return for cash payments to prostitutes. The tax court found that writing was a business for Vitale, although he had yet to earn a profit from it. However, it denied the deduction for prostitutes, declaring that the expenditures were "so personal in nature as to preclude their deductibility." (*Vitale v. Commissioner*, T.C. Memo 1999-131.)

Deductions must be reasonable

There is usually no limit on how much you can deduct so long as it's not more than you actually spend and the amount is reasonable. Certain areas are hot buttons for the IRS—especially entertainment, travel, and meal expenses. The IRS won't allow such expenses to the extent it considers them lavish.

Also, if the amount of your deductions is very large relative to your income, your chance of being audited goes up dramatically. One analysis of almost 1,300 tax returns found that you are at high risk for an audit if your business deductions exceed 63% of your revenues. You're relatively safe so long as your deductions are less than 52% of your revenue. If you have extremely large deductions, make sure you can document them in case you're audited.

Common deductions for writing businesses

Expenses that self-employed writers may deduct from their income tax commonly include:

- commissions paid to literary agents
- attorney and accounting fees
- permissions fees
- bank fees for a writing business bank account
- costs of renting or leasing vehicles, equipment, and other property used in your business
- depreciation of business assets
- education expenses—for example, the cost of attending writing seminars or classes
- expenses for the business use of your home (this deduction may not be taken by hobby writers)
- fees you pay to people you hire to help your writing business—for example, payments to a research assistant or the cost of hiring a publicist to help you promote a book
- health insurance for yourself and your family
- insurance for your business—for example, liability and business property insurance
- office expenses, such as office supplies
- office utilities
- postage
- professional association dues
- books you need for your writing business
- repairs and maintenance for business equipment such as a photocopier or fax machine
- retirement plan contributions
- software you buy for your writing business
- subscriptions to business-related publications
- travel, meals, and business-related entertainment.

When to deduct expenses

Some expenses can be deducted all at once; others have to be deducted over a number of years. It all depends on how long the item you purchase can reasonably be expected to last—what the IRS calls its useful life.

- **Current expenses.** The cost of anything you buy for your writing business that has a useful life of less than one year must be fully deducted in the year it is purchased. This includes, for example, rent, telephone and utility bills, photocopying costs and postage, and other ordinary business operating costs. Such items are called current expenses.

Although office supplies such as stationery, paperclips, and tape may last more than one year, you can fully deduct the cost in the year you pay for them. The IRS doesn't require you to go to the trouble of deducting such trivial expenses over several years.

- **Capital expenses:** Certain types of costs are considered to be part of your investment in your business instead of operating costs. These are called capital expenses. Subject to an important exception for up to $105,000 in personal property, you cannot deduct the full value of such expenses in the year you incur them. Instead, you must spread the cost over several years and deduct part of it each year. There are two main categories of capital expenses: (1) the cost of any asset you will use in your business that has a useful life of more than one year– for cxample, equipment, software, books, furniture, and (2) business start-up costs such as fees for doing market research or attorney and accounting fees paid to set up your writing business.

Writers Need Not Capitalize Short-Term Expenses

In the past, writers used to have it tough tax-wise because they were required to capitalize all costs they incurred while creating their works. This meant they had to deduct them over several years as sales occurred. However, the tax law was changed in 1988 to provide a special exception to these capitalization rules for writers or other creative individuals. (IRC § 263A(h).) Writers may now deduct costs, other than some capital expenses as described below, in the year incurred.

Taxation of Copyright Income

Virtually any income you earn from writing—that is, creating copyrighted written works—is subject to federal income taxation. This is so whether such income takes the form of a set fee for an article or a royalty based on sales. Virtually all freelance writers are cash-basis taxpayers. This means they must pay tax on their earnings only when they are actually received, not when promised. Thus, for example, if a publisher promises to pay you a $100,000 advance when you submit a completed manuscript, you'd have to pay tax on the advance only when it was paid to you.

Prizes and awards given to writers are also taxable income, whether cash or noncash. Scholarship and fellowship grants are excluded from taxable income only to the extent they are used for tuition and course-related fees, books, supplies, and equipment at a qualified educational institution.

Self-Employment Taxes

In addition to income taxes, you'll also have to pay Social Security and Medicare taxes on the profit you earn from your writing business. These taxes are called self-employment taxes, or SE taxes. You must pay SE taxes if your net yearly earnings from your writing business are $400 or more. When you file your annual tax return, you must include IRS Form SE, showing how much SE tax you were required to pay. However, SE taxes need only be paid by writers who are in business—not by hobby writers or those for whom writing is categorized as an income-producing activity. For more information on SE taxes, see IRS Publication 533, *Self-Employment Tax.*

Income Reporting

How do the folks at the IRS find out how much you've earned from writing? Easy ... publishers tell them. Any magazine, website, publisher, or other enterprise or person that pays you $600 or more during the year as a nonemployee writer must complete a Form 1099-MISC reporting the payments. The payer must file a copy of the 1099 with:

- the IRS
- your state tax office if your state has income tax, and
- you.

To make sure you're not underreporting your income, IRS computers check the amounts listed on your 1099s against the amount of income you report on your tax return. If the amounts don't match, you have a good chance of being flagged for an audit.

Publishers and others need not file a 1099 form if you've incorporated your business and the publisher pays your corporation, not you personally.

You should receive all your 1099s for the previous year by January 31 of the current year. Check the amount of compensation listed as paid to you in each 1099 against your own records, to make sure they are consistent. If there is a mistake, contact the payer immediately and request a corrected 1099. You don't want the IRS to think you've been paid more than you really were. You don't have to file your 1099s with your tax returns. Just keep them in your records.

Capital Gains vs. Ordinary Income

As you are probably aware, the IRS taxes your income as either capital gains or ordinary income. The top capital gains tax rate is 15%, compared with 35% for ordinary income. (Note: Capital assets held for less than one year are taxed at ordinary income rates.) This means that writers with higher incomes could pay substantially less taxes if they were allowed to treat the money they receive from the sale of a copyright as a long-term capital gain rather than as ordinary income.

Capital gains treatment is available only when you sell a capital asset—this commonly includes such things as real estate and stocks and bonds. Logically, there would seem to be no reason why a copyright shouldn't also be treated as a capital asset. Unfortunately, Congress disagrees. A special provision of the tax law bars writers from obtaining capital gains treatment on money they earn from the sale of copyrighted works they create themselves. A person who is given ownership of a copyrighted work by an author is also denied capital gains treatment. (IRC § 1221(a)(3).) However, a person who inherits a copyrighted work from a deceased author may be entitled to capital gains treatment when he or she sells the work. Consult with a tax expert if you're in this situation.

Paying Your Taxes

When you're a self-employed writer—not employed to write—no income tax is withheld from your compensation and you don't receive a W-2 form. Instead, you must pay all your income and Social Security taxes to the IRS yourself in the form of periodic payments known as estimated taxes. You must pay estimated taxes if you're a sole proprietor and expect to owe at least $1,000 in federal tax for the year on your writing business income.

EXAMPLE: Joe expects to earn a profit of $10,000 from his writing business this year. He is in the 28% tax bracket, so he will owe $2,800 in taxes. Thus, he has to pay estimated taxes during the year.

There is one exception to this rule: If you paid no taxes last year, you don't have to pay any estimated tax this year no matter how much tax you expect to owe. But this is true only if you were a U.S. citizen or resident for the year and your tax return for the previous year covered the whole 12 months.

Moreover, if, in addition to being a self-employed writer, you hold a job and have taxes withheld from your paychecks by your employer, you need not pay estimated tax if the amount withheld is at least equal to the lesser of:

- 90% of your total tax due for the current year, or
- 100% of the tax you paid the previous year (110% if you earned over $150,000).

If the amount you currently have withheld from your paychecks does not meet the above test, you may be able to avoid having to make estimated tax payments by asking your employer to take more tax out of your earnings. To do this, file a new Form W–4 with your employer. Keep in mind that if you don't have more withheld each month (and make your own quarterly estimated tax payments instead), you'll have more control over your cash flow.

Estimated tax must ordinarily be paid in four installments, with the first one due on April 15, the next June 15, then September 15, and finally January 15. However, you don't have to start making payments until you actually earn income from your writing business. If you don't receive any income by March 31, you can skip the April 15 payment. In this event, you'd ordinarily make three payments for the year, starting on June 15. If you don't receive any income by May 31, you can skip the June 15 payment as well, and so on.

See IRS Publication 505, *Tax Withholding and Estimated Tax,* for a detailed explanation of estimated taxes. You can obtain the form by calling the IRS at 800-TAX-FORM, visiting your local IRS office, or downloading it from the IRS Internet site at www.irs.gov.

■

CHAPTER

16 Obtaining Copyright Permissions

This chapter covers how to get permission to use text—whether from a book, magazine, newspaper, newsletter, website, or journal. The following sections will help you identify the company or person who owns the rights to the text (the "rights holder") and offers suggestions for how to make your permissions request. It also discusses special situations that occur when using text from interviews, speeches, or print publications. At the end of the chapter, you'll find two sample text permission agreements: a short-form agreement and a longer, more detailed agreement.

This chapter is adapted from material from *Getting Permission*, by Richard Stim (Nolo).

Who Owns the Text?

The first step to obtain permission is to make sure you're asking the correct entity for permission. The owner of the text may be the company who published it, the author of the text, or no one at all. Who owns the text depends on how the rights were negotiated between publisher and author and on law and industry traditions. With the advent of online permission services, your search for the rights owner may only require a few clicks of a mouse. If these services don't offer what you need, you will need to contact either the publisher, the author, or both.

Two major industry changes may be relevant to your search: the shift in ownership of articles from author to publisher in the 1980s and the Supreme Court's 2001 decision that freelancers must be compensated for reprints of their works in electronic databases. Also, special rules apply to certain situations, such as interviews and syndicated columns.

Before seeking out the copyright owner, confirm whether permission is necessary. No permission is required if the text you want to use is in the public domain. And, many uses of text are permitted without permission under the fair use privilege. The public domain is discussed in Chapter 6, and fair use is discussed in Chapter 11.

Shifting Ownership of Articles

Before the 1980s, the author of an article was usually the primary rights holder. At that time, periodicals traditionally only asked for first "North American serial rights": the right to publish the article once in the United States and Canada. However, in the last 25 years, magazines, journals, and other periodicals have increasingly obtained reprint, syndication, and other primary rights from authors. Therefore, where multiple publishers have published an article in the last 20 years, your starting point for permission will be the original publisher of the article. For older articles, your best bet is to start by contacting the author.

Shifting Ownership of Electronic Database Reprints

The rules for ownership of electronic rights to written works changed dramatically in 2001. The U.S. Supreme Court decided that freelance writers must be compensated when their works are placed on Internet or CD-ROM databases such as Lexis-Nexis. The Court, in the case of *The New York Times v. Tasini* (533 US 483 (2001)), found that *The New York Times* and other publishers committed copyright infringement when they resold freelance newspaper and magazine articles through electronic databases without asking permission or making additional payments to the freelancers. The ruling applies to any freelancer who sold an article without expressly transferring the electronic rights to the publisher. (For a detailed discussion of the *Tasini* case, see Chapter 14, Copyright in the Online World)

If you are seeking electronic rights to an article written by a freelancer written before 1995, chances are good that the freelancer has retained the electronic rights, and you should start by contacting the freelancer. After 1995, publishers routinely obtained electronic rights from freelance authors, and you're best off contacting the publisher first.

Start With Online Permission Services

Two Internet services, RSiCopyright (www.icopyright.com) and the Copyright Clearance Center (CCC) (www.copyright.com), have drastically simplified the process of obtaining text permissions. Start your quest for permission with one of them. By using such services, you may avoid having to search for or contact the copyright owner directly. Instead, you need only identify the book, journal, or magazine article and complete an online form. If the work is part of the service's online database, you can usually obtain permission within one or two days (sometimes immediately) and pay for the rights you need by credit card. Acting as the agent and broker for publishers and authors, these permission services allow you to pick and click your way through millions of works, including books and journal and magazine articles.

Publishers set the fees with these permission brokers—for example, a national newspaper, via CCC, charges $400 to reprint an article in a book and $600 to reprint an article in a national magazine. These prices are similar to those for permissions granted without the use of an online service—but if you wish to comparison shop, you can contact the copyright owner directly following the suggestions below.

The online procedure is often far easier than the traditional system of locating and calling a publisher, negotiating permission, and signing a written agreement. If a service does not represent a publisher—that is, the publisher's works are not designated in the database—you may still use the service to inquire about the use of works on your behalf.

Copyright Clearance Center

The CCC is considered the behemoth of text permissions, as it represents over 10,000 print publishers, including *The New York Times* and *The Wall Street Journal.* This makes their website a good place to start your permissions search. Through the CCC, you can obtain permission for:

- **republication**—reproducing text in books, journals, and newsletters
- **electronic use**—reproducing text on websites, in email, in PDF format, or on CD-ROMs, and
- **photocopying**—making multiple photocopies for distribution at events or businesses.

To use the CCC's service, visit the website and complete the free registration, and you will be directed to the "Permissions Online: Services" page. (If not, click the "Services" tab.) After you choose the type of permission, a page opens allowing you to either create an order, get a quick price, or view any existing orders. (You may become frustrated using the "quick price" feature; many rights holders don't permit price quotes. In these cases, the CCC contacts the rights holder and provides you with a quote within several days.)

If you're having trouble at any point in the CCC's process, FAQs and a useful demo on the site can help you.

RSiCopyright

RSiCopyright is the innovator of online permissions, but it has a smaller database of available works than the CCC. It offers two ways of licensing reprint rights: directly through its website or by clicking on the RSiCopyright logo (see below) if it appears at the bottom of an article on the Internet.

RSiCopyright logo

If you see and click on the RSiCopyright logo, you are asked to choose whether you want to create a link to the article, reprint the article in email or on a website, or "Do Something Else." When you make the last choice, you must then complete a form that asks for your intended use—for example, to provide reprints at trade shows—and whether your use is commercial, academic, nonprofit, or governmental. Then, like the CCC, the service makes the inquiry to the copyright owner on your behalf.

Looking for Academic Articles?

Ingenta (www.ingenta.com) acts as an online intermediary for users seeking to access articles from over 28,000 academic and professional journals. If you are seeking information, content, permission to link, or online permission for academic or professional articles, check this site.

Locate the Publisher

If you cannot obtain permission through an online permission service or if you think you will get a better rate for permission by negotiating directly with the copyright owner, you'll need to search the old-fashioned way. The first step is to locate the publisher—the company that produced and distributed the work. For example, Nolo is the publisher of the book you're reading now. In the case of a quote from a magazine or journal article, the publisher is the company that produces and distributes the magazine or journal. For example, Time-Life Inc. is the publisher of *Time* magazine.

Permissions Departments

Many publishers have permissions departments or a person who handles reprints, permissions, and clearances. Information about the permissions department is usually found on or near the copyright page of a book, or in a magazine or journal's masthead page. Online magazines and book publishers' websites generally include copyright and permissions information on the introductory Web page (the index or home page).

If the book, magazine, or journal contains no specific information about permissions, direct your inquiries to the "Permissions Department" at the publisher's main business address, usually listed in the first or last few pages of a publication.

Are You Under Contract to Write a Book?

Have you signed a contract to write an article or book? Publishing contracts usually indicate who has responsibility for obtaining permission for anything you use in your article or book, either the author (you) or the publisher. Your publishing contract may also specify the language to be used in any permission agreement you obtain. Inquire whether your publisher has its own permission form you can use.

Locating Publishers

Contact information for book publishers can be located through publications such as *Books in Print, Literary Market Place,* and *International Literary Market Place,* all published by R.R. Bowker (www.bowker.com). *Books in Print* includes information about books currently available for sale and can be searched online for a fee. *Writer's Market* (Writer's Digest Books, www.writersdigest.com) provides a list of U.S book publishers as well as publishers of magazines, journals, and greeting cards.

For information on locating periodical publishers, consult *The National Directory of Magazines* and *The Standard Periodical Directory,* both published by Oxbridge Communications (www.mediafinder.com), or review *Ulrich's International Periodicals Directory* (R.R. Bowker) or *The Directory of Small Press and Magazine Editors and Publishers,* published by Dustbooks (www.dustbooks.com). For information on academic publishers, check out *The Association of American University Presses Directory,* published by the University of Chicago Press (www.press.uchicago.edu).

When There Is More Than One Publisher

Different publishers may print the same book in different versions. For example, one book may be published first in hardcover, later published in paperback by a different publisher, and then published outside the United States in a foreign language by yet a third publisher. Articles may be printed in magazines and then reprinted in digests or books by different publishers.

In cases of multiple publishers, you must find out who controls the right to reprint the work in another publication (known as "reprint rights"). The person or company who controls a work's reprint rights is known as the "primary rights holder." Often, the first publisher is the primary rights holder. In the case of a book, this is usually the hardcover publisher. You can find the name of the hardcover publisher

Distributing Photocopies at Work May Be an Infringement

Many businesses attempt to save money by photocopying an article from a journal, periodical, or book for employees or outside clients. For example, an insurance company that subscribes to a legal newsletter might make 200 photocopies and distribute photocopied newsletters to employees and customers. Though common, such photocopying is a violation of copyright law if done without permission. (See Chapter 11, Using Other Authors' Words.)

Permission to photocopy and distribute materials can be acquired directly from the publisher or from the Copyright Clearance Center (www.copyright.com) or RSiCopyright (www.icopyright.com). The CCC provides individual-permission services (as well as "repertory" or "blanket" licensing services), including its basic Transactional Reporting Service. In some cases, a business can obtain an annual blanket license that permits unlimited photocopying from the CCC's collection of 1.75 million works. These blanket licenses are based on the type of industry and the number of employees for whom photocopies will be made. For example, law firms might pay a blanket license fee of $150 per year for each professional employee.

Certain types of photocopying for educational purposes do not require permission. However, this does not extend to the wholesale copying of articles for classroom use in coursepacks. The CCC has a special program that assists educators in obtaining permission for coursepacks.

by searching an online bookstore such as Amazon (www.amazon.com) or Barnes & Noble (www.barnesandnoble.com) using the title and/or author of the book.

If the hardcover publisher tells you that it does not have the right to reprint the work, ask if the publisher knows whom you should contact. If the publisher doesn't know, contact the author. (Contacting and negotiating with authors is discussed below.)

Also, keep in mind that the primary rights holder may only control rights in one country. If you intend to reproduce a work outside that country, you may need to seek additional permission. For example, one rights holder may have the right to publish a work in the U.S., another in Great Britain, and yet another in Canada. If the work for which you're seeking permission will be distributed in the U.S., Britain, and Canada, you will need permission from all three rights holders. The primary rights holder can often lead you to foreign rights holders. If not, information about foreign publishers can be located in the publication *International Literary Market Place.*

Contact the Author

If the publisher doesn't own the rights you need, it may be able to put you in contact with the author by forwarding your request to the author or, if the author is deceased, to the author's estate. For privacy purposes, it's unlikely that the publisher will give you the author's address or phone number.

Regional Rights Versus Foreign Language Right

The territory in which a publication is distributed and the language in which it is published involve two separate rights. In other words, reprint rights are sold language by language and territory by territory. When dealing with U.S. publishers, unless you specifically ask for reprint rights in a foreign language, you will only be given the right to reprint the work in English in the territory specified. This means, for example, that acquiring "world" rights is not the same as acquiring rights in all languages. Rather, it means you have the right to publish the work in English throughout the world.

Be specific in your requests and permission agreements and keep the fees you must pay low by asking for only the rights you need. If your work will only be published in English, don't ask for foreign language rights. For example, if your magazine is distributed primarily in the U.S. and Canada, you probably only need one-time North American rights: the right to publish the work one time in the U.S. and Canada in English. However, if you print a French language edition for Canadian readers, you would need one-time North American rights and French language rights.

You may be able to locate an author using public sources, such as the Author's Registry (www.authorsregistry.org), which maintains a directory of authors and will search for one or two names, usually free of charge. Information about over 1,000 nonfiction writers may be found through the American Society of Journalists and Authors (www.asja.org).

Also, the University of Texas (http://tyler.hrc.utexas.edu) maintains a searchable database entitled WATCH (Writers, Artists, and Their Copyright Holders). This database contains the names and addresses of copyright holders or contact persons for authors and artists whose works are housed in libraries and archives in North America and the United Kingdom. The WATCH database also contains limited information on whether an author's or artist's copyrighted work has entered the public domain.

If the rights for the text are owned by two or more authors, you will need to obtain permission from only one of them—provided that your use is nonexclusive and for U.S. or North American rights. "Nonexclusive" means that other people can use the text for the same purpose as you. If you obtain permission from one of several coauthors, your permission agreement should include a statement that the rights holder has the authority to grant the rights in the agreement. For example, include a statement like "Licensor warrants that it has the right to grant permission." (This language is included in the sample licenses at the end of this chapter.) This provision places you in a better legal position if a dispute arises over your right to use the material.

You will need permission from all of the coauthors in any of the following cases:

- You want to use the text on an exclusive basis—meaning you are the only person who can use the text for a specific purpose.
- You want to use the text on a worldwide, nonexclusive basis—because some countries require consent of all co-owners even for nonexclusive uses.
- You want to use the text for a commercial purpose, to sell a service or product—for example, you want to include a quotation from a book in an advertisement (but simply using the text in a book or article you're writing for money is not considered to be a commercial purpose).

Educational Copying and Coursepacks

Some types of photocopying for educational purposes are allowed without requiring permission. However, this does not extend to the wholesale copying of articles for classroom use in coursepacks. The Copyright Clearance Center (CCC) (www.copyright.com) has a special program that assists educators in obtaining permission to include works in coursepacks.

Special Situations

Finding rights holders for certain types of text, such as syndicated columns, speeches, interviews, and letters, may prove a little tricky. Below are suggestions for getting permission to use these types of works, as well as unpublished and out-of-print texts.

Syndicated Text

Rights for works by newspaper columnists such as Dave Barry and Ann Landers are usually controlled by national syndicates. For example, to acquire permission to reprint a "Dear Abby" column in a book with an initial printing of 5,000 copies, you would first look at the column in a daily newspaper to find the syndicate's name—Universal Press Syndicate. Then, you would contact the syndicate and request permission to reprint the column.

Interviews

If you want to use an interview from a magazine or book, contact the publisher of the book or magazine. To use a written transcript of an interview from a radio or television show, contact the network or station that originally aired the show. For interviews first published on a website, contact the owner of the site, usually indicated on the bottom of the home or index page.

If you seek permission to use a transcript of a television or radio interview, most stations have permissions departments

Orphan Works

One problem that constantly bedevils people who want to obtain permission to use copyrighted works is that the copyright owner cannot be identified or located. This is particularly common for older works with little economic value. Such works are often called "orphan works." The Copyright Office conducted a detailed study of orphan works and issued a report in 2006 recommending that legislation be passed barring owners of orphan works from obtaining monetary damages in a copyright infringement suit against those who use their works without permission provided that: (1) a good faith, reasonably diligent search was made to locate the owner of the orphan work, and (2) attribution was provided to the author and copyright owner of the work, if possible and as appropriate under the circumstances. If the orphan work was used for commercial purposes, a reasonable fee would have to be paid to the copyright owner; but, if the work was not used for any direct or indirect commercial advantage, no fee need be paid if the user stops using the work upon receiving notice from the copyright owner. It remains to be seen whether this legislation will be enacted. The Copyright Office's *Report on Orphan Works* can be obtained from the Office's website (www.copyright.gov).

that will furnish you a printed version. Sometimes you can download interview transcripts from the station's website. If you want to use the actual audio or audiovisual recording of an interview, you will need to obtain the consent of the person or company who recorded the material, often the radio or television station that initially broadcast it.

If the publisher, website owner, or television or radio station is not the rights holder and cannot lead you to the rights holder, try to locate the interviewer through one of the author resources listed earlier in this chapter.

On occasion, determining the rights holder of an interview can get messy. In some cases, such as celebrity interviews, the interview subject may have placed restrictions on the use of interview material. In other situations, the interview subject may seek to prevent republication of the interview, claiming copyright ownership of his or her responses. A publication may write to you stating the following: "We are unable to grant your request because our publication holds no rights to the reuse of this material. Quotations that appear within the text remain proprietary to the speaker."

Unfortunately, sometimes a publication will provide you the interview text even if they don't own the rights to it. If you reprint the text, the interview subject could sue you for unauthorized reproduction of his or her remarks. To deal with this possibility, when seeking permission to reprint an interview, ask if there is a written consent by the interview subject on file and, if so, ask for a copy. If there is no release, ask if the rights holder is willing to sign a written assurance that it has the authority to grant the rights you need. Such a document should state: "Licensor warrants that it has the right to grant permission." This will not shield you from liability as effectively as a signed release from the interview subject, but it does provide you with some legal protection. If the interview subject later files a lawsuit, you will have a stronger case against the licensor (the rights holder) for breach of the written assurance it gave you. If you are still worried about whether you have the right to reproduce the interview, your only option is to seek a release from the interview subject.

Letters

The writer of a letter is usually the owner of the copyright in the letter. However, there are two exceptions to this rule: Letters written by employees within the course of employment are owned by the employer, and letters written by federal employees within the course of employment are in the public domain.

Don't assume that the recipient of the letter owns the rights you need. The recipient owns only the physical letter itself. For example, the owner of a letter written by Elvis Presley could sell the physical letter itself, but only the Estate of Elvis Presley could grant rights to reproduce the text of the letter. And don't assume you can use an unpublished letter, no matter how old, without permission. Review the section below, on unpublished works, first.

Speeches

Not all speeches are protected by copyright. Copyright law only protects a speech if it is written down or recorded ("fixed") and if the writing or recording was done with the speechwriter's permission. If a speaker improvises a speech and his or her words are not written down or recorded with his or her authority, the speech has no copyright protection. Both criteria, fixation (recording) and authorization, are necessary. If the text of a speech is not fixed with the authorization of the speaker, you are free to use it without violating copyright law.

Determining whether a speech has been published

If a speech is protected by copyright, it is important to determine whether the text of the speech has been published, because works that have not been published enjoy longer periods of copyright protection. Giving a speech or lecture in public does not amount to "publication." Legally, publication only occurs when copies of the speech or lecture are distributed to the public.

This rule was fortified in a case involving Martin Luther King Jr.'s "I Have A Dream" speech. A federal court of appeals ruled that Reverend King's 1963 performance of the speech to 200,000 people (and simultaneous broadcast over radio and television) did not amount to publication of the speech. (*Estate of King v. CBS, Inc.*, 194 F.3d 1211 (11th Cir. 1999).)

The Right to Use Monica's Words

Monica Lewinsky's infamous telephone conversations with confidante Linda Tripp about President Clinton are not protected under copyright law, because they were recorded by Tripp without Lewinsky's authorization. On that basis, Lewinsky has no claim against Tripp or any of the companies who have published the conversations. It's possible that her statements may be protected under principles known as "state common law" copyright, but, as a practical matter, it's difficult to enforce such claims.

This does not mean that you can lure an interview subject into a phone interview, tape it, and use it without the subject's authorization. Some states, including California, have laws prohibiting the recording of telephone conversations without the consent of both parties. In addition, publication of such conversations may trigger claims of invasion of privacy.

Who owns the copyright?

If a speech is written down before it's given, the author usually owns the copyright (assuming the author also delivered the speech—see below for rules on ghostwriters). However, if the speech was written as part of an employment obligation—for example, a speech written by the president of General

Titles and Short Phrases May Be Protected Under Trademark Law

Titles and short phrases are not protected under copyright law. Despite their public domain status, names, titles, and short phrases may be protected under trademark laws. A trademark is any word, photograph, or symbol that is used to identify specific products or services.

Permission is not required to use a trademark in any of the following cases:

- Your use is for informational or editorial purposes–for instance, you use the trademark as part of an article or story.
- Your use is part of accurate comparative product statements.

You do need to obtain permission in these cases:

- Your use is commercial and likely to create confusion among consumers.
- Your use is commercial and reflects poorly on or "tarnishes" the trademark.
- You modify the trademark.

Take, for example, the slogan "Just Do It." Because the phrase does not qualify for copyright protection, you can use it in a song lyric, movie, or book. However, because Nike has a trademark for the phrase, you cannot use it in a manner that is likely to confuse consumers into thinking that you are associated with Nike or that tarnishes Nike's reputation.

Motors for a shareholders' meeting—the author's employer owns the speech. If the speech was written by a federal government employee as part of his employment—for example, a speech by the Secretary of the Treasury to Wall Street investors—it is in the public domain. If the speech was ghostwritten—written by someone other than the speaker—the ghostwriter owns the rights, unless the ghostwriter was the speaker's employee or transferred the rights to the speaker (or someone else) under a written agreement.

If the speech was given extemporaneously (improvised, not written down in advance) but recorded with the speaker's permission, the author/speaker usually owns the copyright in the speech itself, the same way as if it was written down (as described above). But, the recording of the speech belongs to the people who recorded it—for example, a TV station news crew or a newspaper reporter. A video, film, or sound recording of a speech is a copyrighted work in its own right, owned by the person who made the work. However, a verbatim written transcription of the speech—made, for example, by a newspaper reporter at the scene—is not separately copyrightable, since the author/speaker owns the speech (but not the recording of it).

If the speech was recorded, to use the recorded copy of the speech, you'll need to obtain permission from both the author/speaker and the recorder of the speech. The same rule holds true whenever you want to use a sound recording, film, or video of a speech, instead of the written text.

If you cannot locate the speaker, contact the organization that sponsored the event. Often you can find the full text of a speech reprinted on the Internet, so a search engine may help you locate the rights holder.

Out-of-Print Works

Just because a book or magazine is out of print does not mean that its copyright has run out. Your use, without permission, may still amount to an infringement. Therefore, if you intend to use text from an out-of-print publication, start by contacting the publisher. A good way to find the name of the publisher is through online bookstores such as Amazon and Barnes & Noble, who have extensive listings of out-of-print books and publishers.

Locating the copyright owner of out-of-print works becomes more complicated if the publisher no longer exists. Authors often own the rights to their out-of-print works because publishing contracts often return rights to the author if the publisher stops selling the book. If your search for the publisher and author lead to dead ends, you will have to perform more extensive copyright research or hire a copyright search firm to determine the current owner. (See Chapter 13 for more on copyright research.)

If you're not sure whether a book is out of print, try consulting *Books Out of Print,* published by R.R. Bowker, which contains a listing of out-of-print books dating back to 1979. *Books Out of Print* is searchable (for a hefty subscription fee) at the R.R. Bowker website (www.bowker.com). Alternatively, it may be easier to check if the book is not listed as being "in print," in which case it's probably out of print. One way to find out if a book is in print is to search online bookstores. The ISBN number (see "ISBNs and ISSNs," below) located on or near the title page may help locate the book.

Unpublished Text

As with an out-of-print work, do not assume that an unpublished work is free to use. The rules regarding copyright protection for unpublished works depend on if and when the author died and, in the event the work was ultimately published, the date of publication. (See Chapter 10 for a detailed discussion of copyright duration for unpublished works.)

ISBNs and ISSNs

ISBNs (International Standard Book Numbers) and ISSNs (International Standard Serial Numbers) identify books and magazines and are sometimes required when seeking permission. ISBNs are used for books; ISSNs are used for magazines, journals, newsletters, and other serial publications. These numbers can be found on or near the title or copyright page or near the publication's UPC bar code. Since several numbers may be printed on the bar code, look for the number preceded by either "ISSN" or "ISBN."

As you can imagine, it can be quite difficult to locate copyright owners for unpublished works, because there is no publisher to contact. Copyright Office records may help, if the unpublished work was registered. Determining ownership for unpublished works is especially difficult if the author is deceased and the author's estate or heirs are hard to track down. The WATCH database may help you track down the author of an unpublished work.

Using Text From Advertisements

Text in advertisements is usually owned by the corporate sponsor of the ad. However, in some cases it may be owned by the advertising agency or publication that prepared the ad. To locate an ad agency or corporate advertiser, try using an online search engine, a Web "Yellow Pages" directory, or *The Standard Directory of Advertising Agencies* (Reed Reference Publishing).

When You Can't Find the Rights Holder

If you've used the techniques discussed in this chapter and cannot find the person or business whose permission you need, you have a few options. You could try to delve deeper into copyright records at the Copyright Office. These records may help you determine who owns the work currently, because many copyright transfers

What Does "Publication" Mean?

"Publication" occurs for copyright purposes when the copyright owner, or someone acting with the copyright owner's authority, distributes one or more copies of the work to the general public or offers the work for distribution, public display, or public performance. Copies do not need to be sold for publication to occur—they can be leased, rented, loaned, or even given away, so long as the work has been made available to the general public.

Publication does *not* occur when:

- Copies of the work are made but not distributed.
- The text of the work is performed publicly (for example, a speech is presented).
- The text of the work is displayed (for example, in a slide presentation or on television).

A "limited publication" is also not considered a publication. A limited publication occurs if copies are distributed only to:

- a selected group of people
- for a limited purpose, and
- without the right of further reproduction, distribution, or sale.

For example, it is not a publication when an author sends copies of a manuscript to several publishers seeking publication.

are recorded with the Copyright Office. Copyright Office renewal records will reveal if the publisher has failed to renew the copyright in the work—which puts the work in the public domain if it was published between 1923 and 1964. Chapter 10 offers guidance on the three most common methods of searching Copyright Office records: hiring a search firm, paying the Copyright Office to do the search for you, or searching the Copyright Office records using the Internet.

If you still cannot locate the rights holder, it may be time to consider using the material without permission. As you might imagine, this poses risks. If the rights holder finds out about your use, you (or your publisher) may receive a letter from the rights holder or an attorney demanding that you stop using the material (known as a "cease and desist letter").

Before you use any material without permission, you should answer two questions:

- How likely is it that the rights holder will see your work?
- What is your potential legal liability if you are subject to a claim of copyright infringement?

Likelihood of Discovery

The likelihood that the author or rights holder will discover your unauthorized use depends on the extent of the distribution of your work and the popularity of the rights holder's work. For example, if you use an excerpt from an obscure writer's work in a book that sells under 2,000 copies, the odds are in your favor that the writer will not learn of your use. On the other hand, if you use a well-known quote from a famous play in an article for a major magazine that sells millions of copies, your use has a much greater chance of being discovered. The more likely it is that the rights holder will see your use of the copyrighted work, the more caution you should take in proceeding without the owner's permission.

Potential Liability

When using material without authorization, there is always a risk and potential liability—meaning responsibility under the law for which you may have to pay money damages. The amount of risk depends on several factors, described below. Generally, if you can show that you made a good-faith effort to search for the copyright owner, you will probably only have to pay the rights holder the standard fee within the trade for a similar use. However, there are exceptions to this general rule. A disgruntled copyright owner may refuse to grant permission and insist that you halt distribution of your work. Alternatively, a copyright owner may demand an exorbitant payment and drag you into court.

Consider the following risk factors when proceeding without permission:

- **The investment in the project using the copyrighted work.** The more money spent on your project, the greater the risk in the event that you must halt publication. It may not be worth risking a $100,000 project for the sake of using one unauthorized illustration.

- **The diligence of your copyright search.** The more diligently you searched, the less risk. A thorough search demonstrates that you acted in good faith and may demonstrate that it's not possible to locate the copyright owner.
- **The nature of your work and how easy it would be to remove the offending portion.** There is less risk involved if it is easy for you to remove the unauthorized material from your work. For example, a photo posted on a website can be easily removed, while one printed in a book cannot without wasting any remaining inventory and reprinting the whole thing.
- **The nature of the copyrighted portion and how easy it is to replace.** Although not as important as the other factors, your risk analysis should incorporate how hard it will be to replace the material in the event that you must remove it.

EXAMPLE: Jim publishes a newsletter for seafood restaurants and wants to use material from a cookbook entitled *Steamed Eels,* published in 1977. Jim was unable to locate the publisher; his letters to the publisher were returned with a notice that the company had moved with no forwarding address. Jim later learned from a distributor that the publisher had gone bankrupt in 1983. Jim paid the Copyright Office to perform a search, which turned up only an address for the author, who died in 1986. Jim wrote to the author's last known address, but his letter was returned as undeliverable. Jim searched on the Internet for people with the same last name as the author and posted requests for information at several cooking websites. Jim documented this search and then researched the standard fee for a similar text license. Based on this, Jim proceeded to use the material without permission, citing *Steamed Eels* and its author in his work. In the event that the copyright owner turns up, Jim is prepared to pay a reasonable fee for using the work. Jim's risk is relatively low because his search was very diligent and, given the obscurity and relatively low value of the work he's copying, the financial risk for infringement is low.

When weighing risk factors, consider the expense and aggravation of the two worst-case scenarios: litigation and halting distribution of your work.

- **Litigation.** Any "wronged" party can file a lawsuit regardless of the merits of their claim. A frivolous lawsuit can drag on for months, and the attorney fees can amount to several thousand dollars. Even worse, a lawsuit based on a nonfrivolous claim (one in which there is a reasonable basis for the claim) may proceed for years, and your attorney fees can soar into the tens of thousands of dollars.
- **Halting distribution.** If a copyright owner forces you to halt distribution,

you face losing the money spent on the printing or distribution of the work, as well as the additional expenses to reprint and redistribute it. In addition, your costs may include recovery of unsold copies from distributors, notification to purchasers, and loss of revenue from advertisers. (See Chapter 12 for a detailed discussion of copyright infringement.)

Negotiating Text Permission and Fees

Obtaining permission to use text involves a four-step process:

1. First, you must clearly and specifically identify what material you want to use and how you want to use it.
2. Next, you must send a permission request letter to the publisher or rights holder.
3. Then you and the publisher or rights holder must negotiate a permission fee, if any.
4. Finally, you must get a signed permission agreement—your permission request letter may do, or you may need to draft a separate permission agreement.

Make a Request to the Rights Holder

After you identify the material and rights you need, you should send a letter to the rights holder requesting permission to use the material. Your permission request letter should provide all of the details about the text you want to use, how you expect to use it, and the permission you seek.

There are two different types of request letters you can use:

- One type of request letter simply informs the rights holder of your needs and anticipates that you and the rights holder will later complete and sign a separate permission agreement.
- The other type of request letter serves as both a request and a simple permission agreement for your use of the material. The copyright owner reviews the request and gives you permission by signing and returning the letter. This approach is recommended for simple requests to reproduce text.

The second type of letter—that serves as both a request and an agreement—is discussed later in this chapter. This section looks at a basic permission request letter that contemplates that the parties will negotiate and sign a separate permission agreement letter.

Whichever type of request letter you use, include a copy of the text that you wish to reproduce with your letter.

Keep Your Rights Request Simple

Most text permission requests are for the right to reproduce all or part of a work. For example, say you want to reproduce text in your magazine or on your website. If that's all you need, keep your rights request short and simple.

> **EXAMPLE:** Chris wants to reprint a newspaper column on his website. The request he sends is basically as follows: "I am creating a website for the Association of Barking Dog Observers (ABDO) and would like to post the Jan. 20, 1999 Dave Barry column at our site for one month. I would like to know how much it would cost to post this column. Also, I would appreciate it if you could fax or email me a sample permission agreement."

Negotiate Permission Fees

Next you'll need to work out how much you'll have to pay for the rights you've requested. The publishing industry does not have standard rates for using text. Some magazine and newspaper publishers use fixed rates for common permission situations and can furnish you with what is known as a "rate card" listing such fees. In other instances, the owner won't be able to assess the fee until after reviewing your request. Below, we've summarized some fee information.

Using text in a book

The fees for using text in a book are commonly affected by:

- The number of copies to be printed. Pricing is often calculated at print runs of 5,000, 10,000, and 100,000 copies.
- The price of the book.
- Territorial and language rights. World rights may cost double or triple the cost of U.S. rights alone. A rights holder may charge 25% more for permission to reprint in a second language.
- Whether the use is for a nonprofit purpose.
- Placement of the text within the book. For example, a half-column quote placed at the beginning of a chapter or book may result in a higher fee.

Generally you should expect to pay anywhere from $100 to $400 for use of text in a book, depending on the size of the print run and your rights request. By way of example, one national magazine charges $100 per column of text (there are three full columns to a standard page) for use in a book with a print run over 5,000 copies, and $125 for print runs over 100,000. Sometimes, the fees may seem high. For example, a professor who sought to use four lines from a poem by Emily Dickinson was quoted a fee of $200 by a university press. (Note: Because of copyright rules regarding unpublished works, not all of Dickinson's work is in the public domain.)

Using text on your website

The fees for website uses are evolving—meaning nobody is quite sure how much to charge. The fees are affected by:

- The extent of advertising on the website.
- Whether the site is intended primarily to provide information to the public (sometimes referred to as an "editorial" purpose). The rights holder may want to know whether the purpose of the site is to provide information or sell products or services.
- Whether the organization sponsoring the site is a nonprofit.
- The number of visitors to the site per day.
- Whether the text will be used in a print publication as well as the website. For example, will you use the text in a magazine and on the magazine's website?

A national magazine may charge between $100 and $500 to allow you to post an article on a website, with higher fees being charged for popular commercial sites—for example, posting a review of a movie at a high-traffic Hollywood studio website. Many publishers limit the length of time for these permissions to one year or less.

Minimizing fees

It's possible to get fees lowered or avoid them entirely by doing any combination of the following:

- Seeking a one-time nonexclusive use, as long you are not planning to write future editions or different versions of your work.
- Narrowing your permission request. The narrower your request, the less you may have to pay. For example, don't ask for "worldwide rights, all languages" if you only need "United States rights, English."
- Acquiring multiple items from one publisher. Often, you can reduce your per-item fee by licensing more than one work from the same publisher.
- Paying up front. You may be able to lower the fee by offering to pay up front instead of waiting 30 or 60 days.

Giving Credit Where It Is Due

Your permission agreement will detail your obligation to include a written credit for the author or publisher. Make sure the credit is correct as required in your permission agreement. This is a serious subject between you and the rights holder. Unless otherwise required under your permission agreement, you can group credits together on the copyright page. For example:

"Elvis's Toothbrush" originally appeared in *Meet the Stars* © 1985, by Missy Laws. Reprinted by permission of Ross Books.

"You Can Collect Toilet Paper" originally appeared in *Antique and Collecting Magazine* © 1990, by Harriet L. Rinker. Reprinted by permission of the author.

Permission Request Letter

Dear Ms. Hitchcock:

I am writing to you about your article, "Why I Hate Surround Sound." *New Audio Magazine* informed me that you were the owner of rights in the article. I'm writing a book entitled *DDA: Death to Digital Audio*, and I'd like to use an abridged version of your article in the book. The details are as follows:

Title of Your Article (the "Selection"): "Why I Hate Surround Sound"
Author: Michelle Hitchcock
Source of Article: *New Audio Magazine*
Volume, Issue, ISSN: Vol 23, No. 6, ISSN 1099-8722
Number of Pages: 4

My intended use of the Selection is as follows:

Title (the "Work"): *DDA: Death to Digital Audio*
Publisher: Cumberland Books
Type of Publication: Book (trade paperback)
Rights Needed: 1) the right to shorten or modify the Selection (I'll send you a copy of the abridged version for your approval); and 2) the nonexclusive right to reproduce the Selection in all editions of the trade paperback book, *DDA: Death to Digital Audio*.
Estimated First Print Run: 6,000
Expected Price $12.95
Projected Published Date: January 2007

I'm seeking these rights for myself and my publisher, Cumberland Books, and for any company who might acquire my rights to the book in the future. Please review this request and let me know the terms for licensing rights as well as the required credit. Once you let me know, I can prepare a permission agreement. Thank you very much.

Sincerely,

Roberta Weston
Roberta Weston

Execute a Permission Agreement

Once the rights holder has agreed to grant permission and you've agreed on a fee, you need to complete and sign a written text permission agreement. There are two ways you can go about this:

- You can convert your permission request letter into a permission agreement (a "permission letter agreement").
- You can draft and execute a detailed permission agreement that should suffice for most text-licensing situations (a "permissions agreement").

This section provides samples of each.

> **Does the Agreement Have to Be in Writing?**
>
> Unless you have an "exclusive" agreement, (see Chapter 9, Transferring Copyright Ownership), your license or permission agreement does not have to be in writing to be valid. A nonexclusive oral permission may be enforceable as long as it qualifies as a contract under general contract law principles. However, there are limits on oral agreements. For example, in most states, an oral agreement is only valid for one year. Also, it can be very difficult to prove that an oral agreement exists, not to mention to prove its terms. Because of these limitations, do not rely on an oral licensing or permission agreement—get it in writing.

Sample permission letter agreement

This short-form agreement is similar to those used by many magazines. A variation on the permission request letter above, it is intended for authors and publishers who only want to reprint text, whether in printed form or on a website. This approach—turning the request letter into an agreement—is recommended if your request is simple and you have agreed upon the terms. For example, if you want to include several paragraphs from an essay on your website, newsletter, or book, this form should be sufficient.

> **What If the Copyright Owner Furnishes the Permission Agreement?**
>
> Many publishers' permissions departments and other copyright owners will provide their own permission agreements. Read such an agreement carefully. If it contains provisions you can't understand, ask the publisher to explain them or seek legal help.

A digital copy is included on the forms CD-ROM under the file name TXTPRMLT.

Instructions for permission letter agreement

If you use this form, you don't need a separate request letter (as discussed in the

Text Permission Letter Agreement

To ____ ("Licensor"):

I am writing to you to request permission to use the following material.

Licensor Information

Title of Text (the "Selection"): ______________________________

Author: ____

Source publication (or product from which it came): ____________________

If from a periodical, the ISSN, volume, issue, and date. If from a book, the ISBN:

____

If from the Internet, the entire URL: ______________________________

Number of pages (or actual page numbers) to be used: ____________________

If you are not the copyright holder or if worldwide rights must be obtained elsewhere, please indicate that information: __________________________

____

Licensee Publication Information

The Selection will appear in the following publication(s) (the "Work"): ________

____

Title: ____

Name of publisher or sponsor ("Licensee"): __________________________

Author(s): ____

Type of publication: ____

If print publication, estimated print run: ________________

If print publication, projected publishing date: ________________

If print publication, expected price: $________________

If website, the URL: ____

If website, estimated monthly hits: ______________________________

If website, the posting date: __________________________________

Rights needed: ____

Text Permission Letter Agreement (continued)

Fee

Licensee shall pay a fee of $ ____________ to Licensor at the following address: ____ upon publication of the Work or within 6 months of executing this agreement, whichever is earlier.

Credit

A standard credit line including your company name will appear where the Selection is used. If you have a special credit line you would prefer, indicate it below:

____

Samples

Upon publication, Licensee shall furnish ______ copies of the Work to Licensor.

Signed by Licensee: ______________________________

Name: ______________________________

Title: ______________________________

Address: ______________________________

Date: ____________________

Licensor's Approval of Request

I warrant that I am the owner of rights for the Selection and have the right to grant the permission to republish the materials as specified above. I grant to Licensee and Licensee's successors, licensees, and assigns the nonexclusive worldwide right to republish the Selection in all editions of the Work.

Permission Granted by: ______________________________

Signed by Licensor: ______________________________

Name: ______________________________

Title: ______________________________

Address: ______________________________

Date: ____________________

previous section). Complete the agreement as if you were preparing the worksheet or a request letter. Below are some additional explanations for various sections:

- At the end of the *Licensor Information* section is a section the licensor—the person from whom you are requesting permission—should fill in if he or she does not own the rights you need. If this section is filled in, the licensor cannot grant you the necessary permission, so you will need to obtain permission from whomever the licensor indicates in the blank.
- It is possible that the licensor will only want to grant rights for a specific print run or for a specific period of time. Or, the licensor may not want to grant you permission to transfer the rights to someone else. In this event, modify the grant to reflect these requests—for example, strike the language regarding "successors, licensees, and assigns."
- It's possible that you will want more rights than are granted in this letter agreement. For example, you may need rights for all foreign translations and derivative rights and you may want these rights in all media. If you want a broader grant of rights, you can use the *Licensor's Approval of Request* language below to replace the language in the agreement above. Be aware that the licensor may object to such a broad grant, causing a delay in the permissions process.

Licensor's Approval of Request.

I warrant that I am the owner of rights for the Selection and have the right to grant permission to republish the materials as specified above. I grant to Licensee and Licensee's successors, licensees, and assigns the nonexclusive worldwide right to adapt and republish the Selection in all languages, in all editions of the Work, and in all versions derived from the Work in all media now known or hereafter devised.

Make the process convenient for the copyright owner. When sending your permission letter agreement, always enclose a stamped self-addressed envelope for the licensor's convenience.

Sample permission agreement

The permission agreement below is intended for authors and publishers who are negotiating for more than basic reproduction rights—for example, assembling an anthology of short stories, assembling contributions for a CD-ROM encyclopedia, or acquiring multiple or foreign rights to reproduce a work. A digital copy is included on the forms CD-ROM under the file name TXTPRM.

- In the introductory paragraph, insert the names of the licensor (the party who owns the material) and the licensee (you or the person who is seeking permission).
- In the *Licensor Information and Licensee Publication* sections, fill in the blank spaces.

Text Permission Agreement

____("Licensor") is the owner of rights for certain textual material defined below (the "Selection"). ____ ("Licensee") wants to acquire the right to use the Selection as specified in this agreement (the "Agreement").

Licensor Information

Title of Text (the "Selection"): __________________________________

Author: ____

Source publication (or product from which it came): ____________________

If from a periodical, the ISSN, volume, issue, and date. If from a book, the ISBN: ____________________________

If from the Internet, the entire URL: ______________________________

Number of pages or actual page numbers to be used: ____________

Licensee Publication Information

The Selection will appear in the following publication(s) (the "Work"): ____

(*check if applicable and fill in blanks*)

- ☐ book—title: ____
- ☐ periodical—title: ____________________________________
- ☐ event handout—title of event: ___________________________
- ☐ website—URL: ______________________________________
- ☐ diskette—title: _____________________________________

Name of publisher or sponsor: _________________________________

Author(s): ____

Estimated date(s) of publication or posting: _________________________

Estimated number of copies to be printed or produced (if a book, the estimated first print run): _______________

If for sale, the price: $ _______________

If copies are free to attendees of a program, the cost of program: ____________

If a website, the average number of visitors per month: ____________________

Grant of Rights

Licensor grants to Licensee and Licensee's successors and assigns, the: (*select one*)

☐ nonexclusive

☐ exclusive

right to reproduce and distribute the Selection in: (*select all that apply*)

☐ the current edition of the Work.

☐ all editions of the Work.

☐ all foreign language versions of the Work.

☐ all derivative versions of the Work.

☐ all media now known or later devised.

☐ promotional materials published and distributed in conjunction with the Work.

☐ other rights ____

Territory

The rights granted under this Agreement shall be for ______________________________ ____ (the "Territory").

Fees

Licensee shall pay Licensor as follows: (*select one and fill in appropriate blanks*)

☐ **Flat Fee.** Licensee shall pay Licensor a flat fee of $__________ as full payment for all rights granted. Payment shall be made:

☐ upon execution of this Agreement

☐ upon publication

☐ **Royalties and Advance.** Licensee agrees to pay Licensor a royalty of __________ % of Net Sales. Net Sales are defined as gross sales (the gross invoice amount billed customers) less quantity discounts and returns actually credited. Licensee agrees to pay Licensor an advance against royalties of $ ____________ upon execution of this Agreement. Licensee shall pay Licensor within 30 days after the end of each quarter. Licensee shall furnish an accurate statement of sales during that quarter. Licensor shall have the right to inspect Licensee's books upon reasonable notice.

(Text Permission Agreement—Page 2)

Credit & Samples

(*check if applicable and fill in blanks*)

- ☐ **Credit.** All versions of the Work that include the Selection shall contain the following statement: ______________________________
- ☐ **Samples.** Upon publication, Licensee shall furnish ____________ copies of the Work to Licensor.

Warranty

Licensor warrants that it has the right to grant permission for the uses of the Selection as specified above and that the Selection does not infringe the rights of any third parties.

Miscellaneous

This Agreement may not be amended except in a written document signed by both parties. If a court finds any provision of this Agreement invalid or unenforceable, the remainder of this Agreement shall be interpreted so as best to effect the intent of the parties. This Agreement shall be governed by and interpreted in accordance with the laws of the State of ____________________. This Agreement expresses the complete understanding of the parties with respect to the subject matter and supersedes all prior representations and understandings.

Licensor ______________________	Licensee ______________________
By: ______________________	By: ______________________
Name: ______________________	Name: ______________________
Title: ______________________	Title: ______________________
Address: ______________________	Address: ______________________
Date: ______________________	Date: ______________________
	Tax ID # ______________________

(Text Permission Agreement—Page 3)

- In the *Grant of Rights* section, complete the grant to reflect the rights that you have negotiated.
- Complete the *Territory* section to reflect the regions in which you have acquired rights—the World, the United States, Canada, or whatever region you have agreed upon. For more help, review Chapter 9.
- In the *Fees* section, check the appropriate boxes and complete the information.
- Complete the *Credit and Samples* section per your agreement with the licensor.
- A warranty is a contractual promise made by the licensor. Some licensors do not want to make promises, particularly promises that the work does not infringe any third parties' copyright or other rights. You may have to modify the *Warranty* section or strike it entirely if the licensor objects.

■

CHAPTER

17 Help Beyond This Book

Hopefully, this book provides a good basic background on most aspects of copyright of interest to writers. Additional general information can be obtained for free from the Copyright Office. The Copyright Office publishes a series of pamphlets (called "circulars") on many copyright topics. You can download digital copies of all the circulars from the Copyright Office website at www.copyright.gov. You can also have the Copyright Office fax the circulars to you or mail you copies by calling 202-707-9100.

If you have any questions that aren't answered by this book, a two-step process is suggested. First, take a look at one or more intensive background resources. These may contain all the information you need. If not, access the primary copyright resources: the copyright statutes, regulations, and case law.

Recommended reading. Use *Legal Research: How to Find & Understand the Law*, by Stephen Elias and Susan Levinkind (Nolo), or another basic legal research guide, to help you understand legal citations, how to use a law library, and understand what you find there.

Intensive Background Resources

Following are some recommended intensive background resources on copyright law. You can find others in your law library's catalogue.

Treatises, encyclopedias, and so on. The most authoritative source on copyright law is *Nimmer on Copyright*, a ten-volume legal treatise written by the late Professor Melville B. Nimmer and updated biannually by his son David, a copyright lawyer. It is published by Matthew Bender. Most public or university law libraries have this treatise. It contains thorough discussions on virtually every legal issue concerning U.S. and international copyright law.

Each point made by the treatise is supported by exhaustive citations to the relevant legal decisions, sections of the copyright statutes, and Copyright Office regulations where appropriate. Volume 10 of *Nimmer* contains a topical index, and a detailed table of contents precedes each chapter. Volume 10 also contains a table of cases and a table of statutes. These can be used to find where *Nimmer* discusses a particular copyright decision, copyright code section, or Copyright Office regulation. By using *Nimmer* you can find citations to the primary copyright materials of interest to you. You should note, however, that *Nimmer* discusses only the *law* of copyright. You will find no how-to discussions. That's what you bought this book for.

Another treatise is *Copyright Principles, Law and Practice*, by Paul Goldstein, a law professor at Stanford University. It is published by Little, Brown and Company. It contains particularly good discussions of copyright infringement and protection of ideas under express and implied contracts and other legal theories.

For the serious copyright student, an excellent one-volume resource is *Copyright Law*, by Craig Joyce et al., published by

Matthew Bender. This is a legal casebook used to teach law students. It contains the text of virtually every important copyright court decision, the copyright law and other primary materials, excerpts from law review articles, commentary by the authors (nationally recognized authorities on copyright), and other useful materials.

An extensive discussion of copyright law is contained in *American Jurisprudence, Second Series* (Am. Jur. 2d), a national legal encyclopedia that can be found in most law libraries. The article on copyright contains a detailed table of contents, and the publication contains a subject-matter index that you can access by looking under "Copyright."

If you are interested in copyright protection in the United States for works by foreign authors, or protection in other countries for works by Americans, the best starting point for your research is *International Copyright Protection*, edited by David Nimmer and Paul Geller and published by Matthew Bender. Unfortunately, this two-volume treatise does not contain an index.

Copyright Law Reporter. For the most recent information available on copyright, consult the *Copyright Law Reporter*, a weekly loose-leaf service published by Commerce Clearing House (CCH). It contains the full text or summaries of recent copyright-related court decisions and relevant discussions of new developments in copyright law. The first volume of the set contains easy-to-follow instructions on how to use this valuable resource.

Law review articles. If you have a very unusual copyright problem that is not covered by *Nimmer* or other books on copyright law, or a problem in an area in which the law has changed very recently, the best sources of available information may be articles appearing in scholarly journals called law reviews. You can find citations to all the law review articles on a particular topic by looking under "Copyright" in the *Index to Legal Periodicals* or *Current Law Index*. A key to the abbreviations used in these indexes is located at the front of each index volume. Substantial collections of law reviews are usually found only in large public law libraries or university libraries.

Forms. If you need sample agreements or other forms, consult *Lindey on Entertainment, Publishing and the Arts*, by Alexander Lindey, published by Clark Boardman Co. The first volume of this four-volume work contains sample forms on every aspect of publishing.

Primary Source Materials on Copyright

Statutes. The primary law governing all copyrights in the United States after January 1, 1978 is the Copyright Act of 1976. The Copyright Act is located in Title 17 of the United States Code. A complete copy of the Copyright Act is on the CD-ROM at the back of this book. (See Appendix B for detailed guidance on how to use the CD-ROM.) It can also be found either in the United States Code Annotated (U.S.C.A.) or United States

Code Service, Lawyers Edition (U.S.C.S.). The act has also been reprinted in Volume 4 of *Nimmer on Copyright* and in the *Copyright Law Reporter.* To find a specific statute, consult either the index at the end of Title 17 or the index at the end of the entire code.

Regulations. The United States Copyright Office has issued regulations that implement the copyright statutes and establish the procedures which must be followed to register a work. These regulations can be found in Title 17 of the *Code of Federal Regulations* (CFR), a paperback service that is updated annually. The regulations can also be found in the supplement to Title 17 of the U.S.C.A., in Volume 4 of *Nimmer on Copyright,* and in the *Copyright Law Reporter.*

Court decisions. There are several ways to find court decisions on a particular legal issue. As mentioned above, intensive background sources such as *Nimmer on Copyright*, the *Copyright Law Reporter,* and law review articles contain many case citations. In addition, the United States Code Annotated and United States Code Service both cite and briefly summarize all the decisions relevant to each section of the Copyright Act of 1976. These are located just after each section of the act. You can also find short summaries of copyright law decisions in West Publishing Company's *Federal Practice Digest* under the term "Copyright." The digest contains a detailed table of contents and a very detailed subject-matter index at the end of the set.

Case citations. Throughout the text you'll see citations like this: *Harper & Row Publishers, Inc. v. Nation Enterprises,* 723 F.2d 195 (2d Cir. 1983). This identifies a particular legal decision and tells you where the decision may be found and read. Any case decided by a federal court of appeals is found in a series of books called the *Federal Reporter.* Older cases are contained in the first series of the *Federal Reporter,* or "F." for short. More recent cases are contained in the second series of the *Federal Reporter,* or "F.2d" for short. To locate the *Harper & Row* case, simply find a law library that has the *Federal Reporter,* Second Series (almost all do), locate volume 723, and turn to page 195.

Opinions by the federal district courts (these are the federal trial courts) are in a series called the *Federal Supplement,* or "F.Supp." For example, 501 F.Supp. 848 (S.D. N.Y. 1980).

Cases decided by the U.S. Supreme Court are found in three publications: *United States Reports* (identified as "U.S."), the *Supreme Court Reporter* (identified as "S.Ct."), and the *Supreme Court Reports, Lawyer's Edition* (identified as "L.Ed."). Supreme Court case citations often refer to all three publications; for example, *Harper & Row Publishers, Inc. v. Nation Enterprises,* 471 U.S. 539, 105 S.Ct. 2230, 91 L.Ed. 405 (1985).

If you intend to do legal research yourself, be aware that interpreting statutes and cases can be difficult without legal training and a specific background in the area being researched. Before you act on anything you find in the law library, consult with a knowledgeable attorney.

Copyright Act Citation Guide

To avoid numerous footnotes, we have not provided extensive citations to the Copyright Act in the text. Listed below are all the sections of the Copyright Act that have been discussed in this book.

Subject Matter and Scope of Copyright

Sec. 101	Legal definitions of compilation, work made for hire, derivative work, and other copyright terms; works covered by Berne Convention
Sec. 102	General definition of what is protected by copyright
Sec. 103	Extent of protection for compilations and derivative works
Sec. 104	Effect of author's national origin; impact of Berne Convention
Sec. 104A	Copyright renewal
Sec. 105	No copyright in U.S. government works
Sec. 106	Copyright owners' five exclusive rights
Sec. 107	Fair use privilege
Sec. 108	Photocopying by libraries and archives
Sec. 109	First sale rule
Sec. 110	Performances and displays not constituting infringement

Copyright Ownership and Transfer

Sec. 201	General ownership provisions
Sec. 202	Ownership of copyright distinct from ownership of material object
Sec. 203	Termination of transfers and licenses
Sec. 204	Execution of transfers
Sec. 205	Recordation of transfers

Copyright Duration

Sec. 301	Copyright Act preempts other federal and state laws
Sec. 302	Post-1977 works
Sec. 303	Works created but not published before 1978
Sec. 304	Pre-1978 works
Sec. 305	Year-end termination rule

Copyright Act Citation Guide (continued)	
Notice, Deposit, and Registration	
Sec. 401	Notice requirements in general
Sec. 403	Notice for works containing U.S. government works
Sec. 404	Notice for contributions to collective works
Sec. 405	Omission of notice
Sec. 406	Error in name or date
Sec. 407	Deposit requirements
Sec. 408–410	Copyright registration
Sec. 411	Registration as prerequisite to infringement suit
Sec. 412	Registration as prerequisite to statutory damages and attorney fees
Copyright Infringement and Remedies	
Sec. 501	What constitutes copyright infringement
Sec. 502–505	Remedies for infringement
Sec. 506	Criminal liability
Sec. 507	Statute of limitations on infringement suits

Copyright Resources on the Internet

In the last few years a wide array of material on copyright has been made available on the Internet.

The Copyright Office has its own site on the Internet, under the aegis of the Library of Congress. You can read and download to your own computer frequently requested Copyright Office circulars, announcements, and the most recent proposed and final Copyright Office regulations. You can also access original and renewal registrations from 1978 to the present.

You may access the Copyright Office website by using the following URL (Web address): www.copyright.gov.

Other copyright information is available at other sites on the Internet, including copies of the Copyright Act, court decisions involving copyright, and articles on various copyright topics. The easiest way to find out what's available is to use an Internet directory such as Yahoo. Yahoo lists thousands of Internet sites by category, including a category for copyright. The Internet address, or URL, to access the Yahoo legal directory is www.yahoo.com/Government/Law. Click on Intellectual Property and then on Copyright.

Finding a Copyright Lawyer

Copyright law is a highly specialized field, and copyright attorneys know the area better than other lawyers. If you don't know of a good copyright attorney, you may be able to find one through your publisher, your literary agent, or other writers you know. Writers groups are also an excellent source of referrals to copyright attorneys, and many can be found in the publication *Literary Market Place*.

Intellectual Property Lawyers

Copyright is part of a larger specialty known as intellectual property law, which also includes patents and trademarks. Many lawyers who advertise as intellectual property lawyers can competently handle all three types of cases. But some are primarily patent attorneys who don't put much effort into the copyright side of their practice. If you are shopping for a copyright lawyer, do your best to find someone who specializes primarily in copyrights.

In addition, attorneys in many cities throughout the country operate volunteer legal aid groups that help artists and writers resolve their legal problems. These groups usually work like this: You'll generally be asked to pay a small fee ($10 to $50) to be interviewed by a paralegal or other nonattorney volunteer. If your gross household income is below a specified level (the exact amount varies among the legal aid offices), and you have a problem that requires legal assistance, you will be referred to an attorney who will represent you free of charge (except for direct out-of-pocket expenses such as filing fees, photocopying, long-distance phone calls, and so forth). However, even if you earn too much to qualify for free legal assistance, these groups should be able to refer you to an experienced copyright attorney.

You don't have to use the legal aid group located nearest to where you live. If you don't qualify for free assistance from the group nearest you, a group in a different part of the country may have a higher income-eligibility requirement that you're able to meet. California Lawyers for the Arts has no means test at all. The only drawback to using these volunteer groups is that it usually takes about three to five weeks for a volunteer attorney to get around to helping you.

Paying an Attorney

If you don't qualify for or are unable to obtain free legal assistance, you'll quickly discover that experts don't come cheap. Most copyright attorneys charge at least $200 per hour. Unless you are wealthy and/or own a very valuable work, any copyright infringement action is likely to cost more than you can afford to pay out of your own pocket. However, if your work was timely registered and you win your suit, the judge has discretion to order the defendant to pay your attorney fees. The amount of such an award is completely up to the judge; the only restriction is that the award be reasonable. If you have a good case and the defendant can afford to pay such fees and damages, an attorney might agree to take your case on a contingency basis—that is, collect his fees from any damages or fees that the court ultimately awards if your suit is successful.

What about defendants in copyright infringement suits? If you are sued for infringement and prevail at trial, the judge can order the losing plaintiff to pay all or part of your attorney fees. In the past, many courts would award such fees to a defendant only if they found that the plaintiff's suit was frivolous or brought in bad faith. But these courts would not require this in making fee awards to plaintiffs. In 1994, the Supreme Court held that this approach was incorrect and that fees must be awarded to plaintiffs and defendants in an evenhanded manner. In other words, the same criteria must be applied to both plaintiffs and defendants. (*Fogerty v. Fantasy, Inc.*, 114 S.Ct. 1023 (1994).)

The criteria some courts use to decide whether to award attorney fees to the winning side include whether the losing party's suit was frivolous or brought in bad faith, or whether the losing party otherwise acted unreasonably. Many courts will be especially likely to award fees to a prevailing party whose actions helped to advance the copyright law or defend or establish important legal principles.

Copyright and contract information hotline. The New York Volunteer Lawyers for the Arts operates a hotline that authors and artists may call to obtain answers to questions on copyright and publishing contracts. The phone number is 212-319-ARTS; call between 9:30 a.m. and 4:30 p.m. eastern time, Monday through Friday.

At least 24 states have organizations that provide legal services and information to the arts community at a reduced rate. To find such an organization near you, check the national directory on the website of the Volunteer Lawyers for the Arts (VLA), the granddaddy of the organizations (www.vlany.org). Click "Resources" on the home page and then click "National Directory."

■

APPENDIX

A Sample Forms

Single unpublished work (a novel); single author

Copyright Office fees are subject to change. For current fees, check the Copyright Office website at *www.copyright.gov*, write the Copyright Office, or call (202) 707-3000.

Form TX
For a Nondramatic Literary Work
UNITED STATES COPYRIGHT OFFICE

REGISTRATION NUMBER

TX TXU

EFFECTIVE DATE OF REGISTRATION

Month Day Year

DO NOT WRITE ABOVE THIS LINE. IF YOU NEED MORE SPACE, USE A SEPARATE CONTINUATION SHEET.

1

TITLE OF THIS WORK ▼

A Fish Story

PREVIOUS OR ALTERNATIVE TITLES ▼

PUBLICATION AS A CONTRIBUTION If this work was published as a contribution to a periodical, serial, or collection, give information about the collective work in which the contribution appeared. Title of Collective Work ▼

If published in a periodical or serial give: Volume ▼ Number ▼ Issue Date ▼ On Pages ▼

2

a NAME OF AUTHOR ▼ Felix Founder

DATES OF BIRTH AND DEATH Year Born ▼ 1955 Year Died ▼

Was this contribution to the work a "work made for hire"? ☐ Yes ☑ No

AUTHOR'S NATIONALITY OR DOMICILE Name of Country
OR { Citizen of ▶ U.S.A. / Domiciled in ▶

WAS THIS AUTHOR'S CONTRIBUTION TO THE WORK
Anonymous? ☐ Yes ☑ No
Pseudonymous? ☐ Yes ☑ No
If the answer to either of these questions is "Yes," see detailed instructions.

NATURE OF AUTHORSHIP Briefly describe nature of material created by this author in which copyright is claimed. ▼
Entire text of unpublished novel

b NAME OF AUTHOR ▼

DATES OF BIRTH AND DEATH Year Born ▼ Year Died ▼

Was this contribution to the work a "work made for hire"? ☐ Yes ☐ No

AUTHOR'S NATIONALITY OR DOMICILE Name of Country
OR { Citizen of ▶ / Domiciled in ▶

WAS THIS AUTHOR'S CONTRIBUTION TO THE WORK
Anonymous? ☐ Yes ☐ No
Pseudonymous? ☐ Yes ☐ No
If the answer to either of these questions is "Yes," see detailed instructions.

NATURE OF AUTHORSHIP Briefly describe nature of material created by this author in which copyright is claimed. ▼

c NAME OF AUTHOR ▼

DATES OF BIRTH AND DEATH Year Born ▼ Year Died ▼

Was this contribution to the work a "work made for hire"? ☐ Yes ☐ No

AUTHOR'S NATIONALITY OR DOMICILE Name of Country
OR { Citizen of ▶ / Domiciled in ▶

WAS THIS AUTHOR'S CONTRIBUTION TO THE WORK
Anonymous? ☐ Yes ☐ No
Pseudonymous? ☐ Yes ☐ No
If the answer to either of these questions is "Yes," see detailed instructions.

NATURE OF AUTHORSHIP Briefly describe nature of material created by this author in which copyright is claimed. ▼

NOTE
Under the law, the "author" of a "work made for hire" is generally the employer, not the employee (see instructions). For any part of this work that was "made for hire" check "Yes" in the space provided, give the employer (or other person for whom the work was prepared) as "Author" of that part, and leave the space for dates of birth and death blank.

3

a YEAR IN WHICH CREATION OF THIS WORK WAS COMPLETED 2000 ◀ Year This information must be given in all cases.

b DATE AND NATION OF FIRST PUBLICATION OF THIS PARTICULAR WORK Complete this information ONLY if this work has been published. Month ▶ Day ▶ Year ▶ ◀ Nation

4

COPYRIGHT CLAIMANT(S) Name and address must be given even if the claimant is the same as the author given in space 2. ▼
Felix Founder
1000 Bonito Way
Tampa, FL 10000

See instructions before completing this space.

TRANSFER If the claimant(s) named here in space 4 is (are) different from the author(s) named in space 2, give a brief statement of how the claimant(s) obtained ownership of the copyright. ▼

DO NOT WRITE HERE OFFICE USE ONLY
APPLICATION RECEIVED
ONE DEPOSIT RECEIVED
TWO DEPOSITS RECEIVED
FUNDS RECEIVED

MORE ON BACK ▶ • Complete all applicable spaces (numbers 5-9) on the reverse side of this page. • See detailed instructions. • Sign the form at line 8.

DO NOT WRITE HERE
Page 1 of ______ pages

Single unpublished work (a novel); single author (continued)

EXAMINED BY

CHECKED BY

☐ CORRESPONDENCE Yes

FORM TX

FOR COPYRIGHT OFFICE USE ONLY

DO NOT WRITE ABOVE THIS LINE. IF YOU NEED MORE SPACE, USE A SEPARATE CONTINUATION SHEET.

5

PREVIOUS REGISTRATION Has registration for this work, or for an earlier version of this work, already been made in the Copyright Office?
☐ **Yes** ☑ **No** If your answer is "Yes," why is another registration being sought? (Check appropriate box.) ▼
a. ☐ This is the first published edition of a work previously registered in unpublished form.
b. ☐ This is the first application submitted by this author as copyright claimant.
c. ☐ This is a changed version of the work, as shown by space 6 on this application.
If your answer is "Yes," give: **Previous Registration Number** ▶ **Year of Registration** ▶

6

DERIVATIVE WORK OR COMPILATION
a **Preexisting Material** Identify any preexisting work or works that this work is based on or incorporates. ▼

See instructions before completing this space.

b **Material Added to This Work** Give a brief, general statement of the material that has been added to this work and in which copyright is claimed. ▼

7

a **DEPOSIT ACCOUNT** If the registration fee is to be charged to a Deposit Account established in the Copyright Office, give name and number of Account.
Name ▼ **Account Number** ▼

b **CORRESPONDENCE** Give name and address to which correspondence about this application should be sent. Name/Address/Apt/City/State/ZIP ▼

Felix Founder
1000 Bonito Way
Tampa, FL 10000

Area code and daytime telephone number ▶ (813) 123-4567 Fax number ▶

Email ▶ felix@fish.com

8

CERTIFICATION* I, the undersigned, hereby certify that I am the
Check only one ▶
☑ author
☐ other copyright claimant
☐ owner of exclusive right(s)
☐ authorized agent of ______
Name of author or other copyright claimant, or owner of exclusive right(s) ▲

of the work identified in this application and that the statements made by me in this application are correct to the best of my knowledge.

Typed or printed name and date ▼ If this application gives a date of publication in space 3, do not sign and submit it before that date.

Felix Founder **Date** ▶ May 1, 2000

Handwritten signature (X) ▼

X Felix Founder

9

Certificate will be mailed in window envelope to this address:

Name ▼
Felix Founder

Number/Street/Apt ▼
1000 Bonito Way

City/State/ZIP ▼
Tampa, FL 10000

YOU MUST:
• Complete all necessary spaces
• Sign your application in space 8

SEND ALL 3 ELEMENTS IN THE SAME PACKAGE:
1. Application form
2. Nonrefundable filing fee in check or money order payable to *Register of Copyrights*
3. Deposit material

MAIL TO:
Library of Congress
Copyright Office - TX
101 Independence Avenue, S.E.
Washington, D.C. 20559-6222

Fees are subject to change. For current fees, check the Copyright Office website at www.copyright.gov, write the Copyright Office, or call (202) 707-3000.

*17 U.S.C. § 506(e): Any person who knowingly makes a false representation of a material fact in the application for copyright registration provided for by section 409, or in any written statement filed in connection with the application, shall be fined not more than $2,500.

Rev: July 2003—xxx Web Rev: July 2003 Printed on recycled paper U.S. Government Printing Office: 2000-461-113/20,021

Single published work; single author; photos registered separately by photographer

Copyright Office fees are subject to change. For current fees, check the Copyright Office website at *www.copyright.gov*, write the Copyright Office, or call (202) 707-3000.

Form TX
For a Nondramatic Literary Work
UNITED STATES COPYRIGHT OFFICE

REGISTRATION NUMBER

TX TXU

EFFECTIVE DATE OF REGISTRATION

Month Day Year

DO NOT WRITE ABOVE THIS LINE. IF YOU NEED MORE SPACE, USE A SEPARATE CONTINUATION SHEET.

1

TITLE OF THIS WORK ▼
All About Everything

PREVIOUS OR ALTERNATIVE TITLES ▼

PUBLICATION AS A CONTRIBUTION If this work was published as a contribution to a periodical, serial, or collection, give information about the collective work in which the contribution appeared. **Title of Collective Work ▼**

If published in a periodical or serial give: **Volume ▼** **Number ▼** **Issue Date ▼** **On Pages ▼**

2

a **NAME OF AUTHOR ▼** Jane Doe
DATES OF BIRTH AND DEATH Year Born ▼ 1955 Year Died ▼

Was this contribution to the work a "work made for hire"? ☑ Yes ☐ No

AUTHOR'S NATIONALITY OR DOMICILE Name of Country
OR { Citizen of ▶ U.S.A. / Domiciled in ▶

WAS THIS AUTHOR'S CONTRIBUTION TO THE WORK
Anonymous? ☐ Yes ☑ No
Pseudonymous? ☐ Yes ☑ No
If the answer to either of these questions is "Yes," see detailed instructions.

NATURE OF AUTHORSHIP Briefly describe nature of material created by this author in which copyright is claimed. ▼
Entire text

NOTE

Under the law, the "author" of a "work made for hire" is generally the employer, not the employee (see instructions). For any part of this work that was "made for hire" check "Yes" in the space provided, give the employer (or other person for whom the work was prepared) as "Author" of that part, and leave the space for dates of birth and death blank.

b **NAME OF AUTHOR ▼**
DATES OF BIRTH AND DEATH Year Born ▼ Year Died ▼

Was this contribution to the work a "work made for hire"? ☐ Yes ☐ No

AUTHOR'S NATIONALITY OR DOMICILE Name of Country
OR { Citizen of ▶ / Domiciled in ▶

WAS THIS AUTHOR'S CONTRIBUTION TO THE WORK
Anonymous? ☐ Yes ☐ No
Pseudonymous? ☐ Yes ☐ No
If the answer to either of these questions is "Yes," see detailed instructions.

NATURE OF AUTHORSHIP Briefly describe nature of material created by this author in which copyright is claimed. ▼

c **NAME OF AUTHOR ▼**
DATES OF BIRTH AND DEATH Year Born ▼ Year Died ▼

Was this contribution to the work a "work made for hire"? ☐ Yes ☐ No

AUTHOR'S NATIONALITY OR DOMICILE Name of Country
OR { Citizen of ▶ / Domiciled in ▶

WAS THIS AUTHOR'S CONTRIBUTION TO THE WORK
Anonymous? ☐ Yes ☐ No
Pseudonymous? ☐ Yes ☐ No
If the answer to either of these questions is "Yes," see detailed instructions.

NATURE OF AUTHORSHIP Briefly describe nature of material created by this author in which copyright is claimed. ▼

3

a **YEAR IN WHICH CREATION OF THIS WORK WAS COMPLETED** 2000 ◀ Year
This information must be given in all cases.

b **DATE AND NATION OF FIRST PUBLICATION OF THIS PARTICULAR WORK**
Complete this information ONLY if this work has been published.
Month ▶ May Day ▶ 1 Year ▶ 2000
U.S.A. ◀ Nation

4

COPYRIGHT CLAIMANT(S) Name and address must be given even if the claimant is the same as the author given in space 2. ▼
Jane Doe
123 Any Street
Anytown, KS 30000

See instructions before completing this space.

TRANSFER If the claimant(s) named here in space 4 is (are) different from the author(s) named in space 2, give a brief statement of how the claimant(s) obtained ownership of the copyright. ▼

DO NOT WRITE HERE OFFICE USE ONLY
APPLICATION RECEIVED
ONE DEPOSIT RECEIVED
TWO DEPOSITS RECEIVED
FUNDS RECEIVED

MORE ON BACK ▶ • Complete all applicable spaces (numbers 5-9) on the reverse side of this page.
• See detailed instructions. • Sign the form at line 8.

DO NOT WRITE HERE

Page 1 of ______ pages

Single published work; single author; photos registered separately by photographer (continued)

EXAMINED BY — FORM TX

CHECKED BY

☐ CORRESPONDENCE Yes

FOR COPYRIGHT OFFICE USE ONLY

DO NOT WRITE ABOVE THIS LINE. IF YOU NEED MORE SPACE, USE A SEPARATE CONTINUATION SHEET.

5 **PREVIOUS REGISTRATION** Has registration for this work, or for an earlier version of this work, already been made in the Copyright Office?

☐ **Yes** ✓ **No** If your answer is "Yes," why is another registration being sought? (Check appropriate box.) ▼

a. ☐ This is the first published edition of a work previously registered in unpublished form.

b. ☐ This is the first application submitted by this author as copyright claimant.

c. ☐ This is a changed version of the work, as shown by space 6 on this application.

If your answer is "Yes," give: **Previous Registration Number** ▶ **Year of Registration** ▶

6 **DERIVATIVE WORK OR COMPILATION**

a **Preexisting Material** Identify any preexisting work or works that this work is based on or incorporates. ▼

See instructions before completing this space.

b **Material Added to This Work** Give a brief, general statement of the material that has been added to this work and in which copyright is claimed. ▼

7 **a** **DEPOSIT ACCOUNT** If the registration fee is to be charged to a Deposit Account established in the Copyright Office, give name and number of Account.

Name ▼ **Account Number** ▼

b **CORRESPONDENCE** Give name and address to which correspondence about this application should be sent. Name/Address/Apt/City/State/ZIP ▼

Jane Doe
123 Any St.
Anytown, KS 30000

Area code and daytime telephone number ▶ (913) 123-4567 Fax number ▶

Email ▶ jane@doe.com

8 **CERTIFICATION*** I, the undersigned, hereby certify that I am the

Check only one ▶
✓ author
☐ other copyright claimant
☐ owner of exclusive right(s)
☐ authorized agent of ______
Name of author or other copyright claimant, or owner of exclusive right(s) ▲

of the work identified in this application and that the statements made by me in this application are correct to the best of my knowledge.

Typed or printed name and date ▼ If this application gives a date of publication in space 3, do not sign and submit it before that date.

Jane Doe **Date** ▶ July 1, 2000

Handwritten signature (X) ▼

X Jane Doe

9 **Certificate will be mailed in window envelope to this address:**

Name ▼ Jane Doe

Number/Street/Apt ▼ 123 Any St.

City/State/ZIP ▼ Anytown, KS 30000

YOU MUST:
- Complete all necessary spaces
- Sign your application in space 8

SEND ALL 3 ELEMENTS IN THE SAME PACKAGE:
1. Application form
2. Nonrefundable filing fee in check or money order payable to *Register of Copyrights*
3. Deposit material

MAIL TO:
Library of Congress
Copyright Office - TX
101 Independence Avenue, S.E.
Washington, D.C. 20559-6222

Fees are subject to change. For current fees, check the Copyright Office website at www.copyright.gov, write the Copyright Office, or call (202) 707-3000.

*17 U.S.C. § 506(e): Any person who knowingly makes a false representation of a material fact in the application for copyright registration provided for by section 409, or in any written statement filed in connection with the application, shall be fined not more than $2,500.

Rev: July 2003—xxx Web Rev: July 2003 Printed on recycled paper U.S. Government Printing Office: 2000-461-113/20,021

Single published work; single author; photos registered separately by photographer (continued)

Copyright Office fees are subject to change. For current fees, check the Copyright Office website at *www.copyright.gov*, write the Copyright Office, or call (202) 707-3000.

Form VA
For a Work of the Visual Arts
UNITED STATES COPYRIGHT OFFICE

REGISTRATION NUMBER

VA VAU

EFFECTIVE DATE OF REGISTRATION

Month Day Year

DO NOT WRITE ABOVE THIS LINE. IF YOU NEED MORE SPACE, USE A SEPARATE CONTINUATION SHEET.

1

Title of This Work ▼ All About Everything

NATURE OF THIS WORK ▼ See instructions: Photographs

Previous or Alternative Titles ▼

Publication as a Contribution If this work was published as a contribution to a periodical, serial, or collection, give information about the collective work in which the contribution appeared. **Title of Collective Work ▼**

If published in a periodical or serial give: **Volume ▼** **Number ▼** **Issue Date ▼** **On Pages ▼**

2

a **NAME OF AUTHOR ▼** Mike Minolta

DATES OF BIRTH AND DEATH Year Born ▼ 1940 Year Died ▼

Was this contribution to the work a "work made for hire"? ☐ Yes ☑ No

Author's Nationality or Domicile Name of Country: OR Citizen of U.S.A. / Domiciled in

Was This Author's Contribution to the Work
Anonymous? ☐ Yes ☑ No
Pseudonymous? ☐ Yes ☑ No
If the answer to either of these questions is "Yes," see detailed instructions.

Nature of Authorship Check appropriate box(es). **See instructions**
☐ 3-Dimensional sculpture ☐ Map ☐ Technical drawing
☐ 2-Dimensional artwork ☑ Photograph ☐ Text
☐ Reproduction of work of art ☐ Jewelry design ☐ Architectural work

NOTE
Under the law, the "author" of a **"work made for hire"** is generally the employer, not the employee (see instructions). For any part of this work that was "made for hire" check "Yes" in the space provided, give the employer (or other person for whom the work was prepared) as "Author" of that part, and leave the space for dates of birth and death blank.

b **Name of Author ▼**

Dates of Birth and Death Year Born ▼ Year Died ▼

Was this contribution to the work a "work made for hire"? ☐ Yes ☐ No

Author's Nationality or Domicile Name of Country: OR Citizen of / Domiciled in

Was This Author's Contribution to the Work
Anonymous? ☐ Yes ☐ No
Pseudonymous? ☐ Yes ☐ No
If the answer to either of these questions is "Yes," see detailed instructions.

Nature of Authorship Check appropriate box(es). **See instructions**
☐ 3-Dimensional sculpture ☐ Map ☐ Technical drawing
☐ 2-Dimensional artwork ☐ Photograph ☐ Text
☐ Reproduction of work of art ☐ Jewelry design ☐ Architectural work

3

a **Year in Which Creation of This Work Was Completed** 2000 Year. **This information must be given in all cases.**

b **Date and Nation of First Publication of This Particular Work** **Complete this information ONLY if this work has been published.** Month May Day 1 Year 2000 U.S.A. Nation

4

COPYRIGHT CLAIMANT(S) Name and address must be given even if the claimant is the same as the author given in space 2. ▼
Mike Minolta
100 Grant St.
Chicago, IL 50000

See instructions before completing this space.

Transfer If the claimant(s) named here in space 4 is (are) different from the author(s) named in space 2, give a brief statement of how the claimant(s) obtained ownership of the copyright. ▼

DO NOT WRITE HERE OFFICE USE ONLY
APPLICATION RECEIVED
ONE DEPOSIT RECEIVED
TWO DEPOSITS RECEIVED
FUNDS RECEIVED

MORE ON BACK ▶ • Complete all applicable spaces (numbers 5-9) on the reverse side of this page. • See detailed instructions. • Sign the form at line 8.

DO NOT WRITE HERE

Page 1 of _____ pages

Single published work; single author; photos registered separately by photographer (continued)

EXAMINED BY — FORM VA

CHECKED BY

☐ CORRESPONDENCE Yes

FOR COPYRIGHT OFFICE USE ONLY

DO NOT WRITE ABOVE THIS LINE. IF YOU NEED MORE SPACE, USE A SEPARATE CONTINUATION SHEET.

5

PREVIOUS REGISTRATION Has registration for this work, or for an earlier version of this work, already been made in the Copyright Office?

☐ Yes ☑ No If your answer is "Yes," why is another registration being sought? (Check appropriate box.) ▼

a. ☐ This is the first published edition of a work previously registered in unpublished form.

b. ☐ This is the first application submitted by this author as copyright claimant.

c. ☐ This is a changed version of the work, as shown by space 6 on this application.

If your answer is "Yes," give: **Previous Registration Number** ▼ **Year of Registration** ▼

6

DERIVATIVE WORK OR COMPILATION Complete both space 6a and 6b for a derivative work; complete only 6b for a compilation.

a. Preexisting Material Identify any preexisting work or works that this work is based on or incorporates. ▼ **a**

See instructions before completing this space.

b. Material Added to This Work Give a brief, general statement of the material that has been added to this work and in which copyright is claimed. ▼ **b**

7

DEPOSIT ACCOUNT If the registration fee is to be charged to a Deposit Account established in the Copyright Office, give name and number of Account.

Name ▼ **Account Number** ▼ **a**

CORRESPONDENCE Give name and address to which correspondence about this application should be sent. Name/Address/Apt/City/State/ZIP ▼ **b**

Mike Minolta
100 Grant St.
Chicago, IL 50000

Area code and daytime telephone number (211) 555-1234 Fax number ( )

Email

8

CERTIFICATION* I, the undersigned, hereby certify that I am the

check only one ▶
- ☑ author
- ☐ other copyright claimant
- ☐ owner of exclusive right(s)
- ☐ authorized agent of ______ Name of author or other copyright claimant, or owner of exclusive right(s) ▲

of the work identified in this application and that the statements made by me in this application are correct to the best of my knowledge.

Typed or printed name and date ▼ If this application gives a date of publication in space 3, do not sign and submit it before that date.

Mike Minolta **Date** July 1, 2000

Handwritten signature (X) ▼

x *Mike Minolta*

9

Certificate will be mailed in window envelope to this address:

Name ▼ Mike Minolta

Number/Street/Apt ▼ 100 Grant St.

City/State/ZIP ▼ Chicago, IL 50000

YOU MUST:
- Complete all necessary spaces
- Sign your application in space 8

SEND ALL 3 ELEMENTS IN THE SAME PACKAGE:
1. Application form
2. Nonrefundable filing fee in check or money order payable to *Register of Copyrights*
3. Deposit material

MAIL TO:
Library of Congress
Copyright Office
101 Independence Avenue, S.E.
Washington, D.C. 20559-6000

Fees are subject to change. For current fees, check the Copyright Office website at www.copyright.gov, write the Copyright Office, or call (202) 707-3000.

*17 U.S.C. § 506(e): Any person who knowingly makes a false representation of a material fact in the application for copyright registration provided for by section 409, or in any written statement filed in connection with the application, shall be fined not more than $2,500.

Rev: August 2003—30,000 Web Rev: June 2002 ♻ Printed on recycled paper U.S. Government Printing Office: 2003-496-605/60,029

Single published work; five joint authors; publisher acquired all copyrights

Copyright Office fees are subject to change. For current fees, check the Copyright Office website at *www.copyright.gov*, write the Copyright Office, or call (202) 707-3000.

Form TX
For a Nondramatic Literary Work
UNITED STATES COPYRIGHT OFFICE

REGISTRATION NUMBER

TX TXU

EFFECTIVE DATE OF REGISTRATION

Month Day Year

DO NOT WRITE ABOVE THIS LINE. IF YOU NEED MORE SPACE, USE A SEPARATE CONTINUATION SHEET.

1

TITLE OF THIS WORK ▼
The History of Music

PREVIOUS OR ALTERNATIVE TITLES ▼

PUBLICATION AS A CONTRIBUTION If this work was published as a contribution to a periodical, serial, or collection, give information about the collective work in which the contribution appeared. Title of Collective Work ▼

If published in a periodical or serial give: Volume ▼ Number ▼ Issue Date ▼ On Pages ▼

2

a NAME OF AUTHOR ▼ Peter Piccolo
DATES OF BIRTH AND DEATH Year Born ▼ 1940 Year Died ▼
Was this contribution to the work a "work made for hire"? ☐ Yes ☑ No
AUTHOR'S NATIONALITY OR DOMICILE Name of Country OR { Citizen of ▶ U.S.A. Domiciled in ▶
WAS THIS AUTHOR'S CONTRIBUTION TO THE WORK Anonymous? ☐ Yes ☑ No Pseudonymous? ☐ Yes ☑ No If the answer to either of these questions is "Yes," see detailed instructions.
NATURE OF AUTHORSHIP Briefly describe nature of material created by this author in which copyright is claimed. ▼ Wrote chapters 1-4

b NAME OF AUTHOR ▼ Vicky Viola
DATES OF BIRTH AND DEATH Year Born ▼ 1950 Year Died ▼
Was this contribution to the work a "work made for hire"? ☐ Yes ☑ No
AUTHOR'S NATIONALITY OR DOMICILE Name of Country OR { Citizen of ▶ U.S.A. Domiciled in ▶
WAS THIS AUTHOR'S CONTRIBUTION TO THE WORK Anonymous? ☐ Yes ☑ No Pseudonymous? ☐ Yes ☑ No If the answer to either of these questions is "Yes," see detailed instructions.
NATURE OF AUTHORSHIP Briefly describe nature of material created by this author in which copyright is claimed. ▼ Wrote chapters 5-10

c NAME OF AUTHOR ▼ Mary Maestro
DATES OF BIRTH AND DEATH Year Born ▼ 1950 Year Died ▼
Was this contribution to the work a "work made for hire"? ☐ Yes ☑ No
AUTHOR'S NATIONALITY OR DOMICILE Name of Country OR { Citizen of ▶ U.S.A. Domiciled in ▶
WAS THIS AUTHOR'S CONTRIBUTION TO THE WORK Anonymous? ☐ Yes ☑ No Pseudonymous? ☐ Yes ☑ No If the answer to either of these questions is "Yes," see detailed instructions.
NATURE OF AUTHORSHIP Briefly describe nature of material created by this author in which copyright is claimed. ▼ Wrote chapters 11-15

NOTE
Under the law, the "author" of a "work made for hire" is generally the employer, not the employee (see instructions). For any part of this work that was "made for hire" check "Yes" in the space provided, give the employer (or other person for whom the work was prepared) as "Author" of that part, and leave the space for dates of birth and death blank.

3

a YEAR IN WHICH CREATION OF THIS WORK WAS COMPLETED 2000 ◀ Year This information must be given in all cases.

b DATE AND NATION OF FIRST PUBLICATION OF THIS PARTICULAR WORK Complete this information ONLY if this work has been published. Month ▶ April Day ▶ 15 Year ▶ 2000 U.S.A. ◀ Nation

4

COPYRIGHT CLAIMANT(S) Name and address must be given even if the claimant is the same as the author given in space 2. ▼
Scrivener & Sons Publishing Co., Inc.
12345 Park Ave.
New York, NY 10000

See instructions before completing this space.

TRANSFER If the claimant(s) named here in space 4 is (are) different from the author(s) named in space 2, give a brief statement of how the claimant(s) obtained ownership of the copyright. ▼
By written contract

DO NOT WRITE HERE OFFICE USE ONLY
APPLICATION RECEIVED
ONE DEPOSIT RECEIVED
TWO DEPOSITS RECEIVED
FUNDS RECEIVED

MORE ON BACK ▶ • Complete all applicable spaces (numbers 5-9) on the reverse side of this page. • See detailed instructions. • Sign the form at line 8.

DO NOT WRITE HERE
Page 1 of ______ pages

Single published work; five joint authors; publisher acquired all copyrights (continued)

EXAMINED BY | FORM TX

CHECKED BY

☐ CORRESPONDENCE Yes

FOR COPYRIGHT OFFICE USE ONLY

DO NOT WRITE ABOVE THIS LINE. IF YOU NEED MORE SPACE, USE A SEPARATE CONTINUATION SHEET.

5

PREVIOUS REGISTRATION Has registration for this work, or for an earlier version of this work, already been made in the Copyright Office?

☐ **Yes** ☑ **No** If your answer is "Yes," why is another registration being sought? (Check appropriate box.) ▼

a. ☐ This is the first published edition of a work previously registered in unpublished form.

b. ☐ This is the first application submitted by this author as copyright claimant.

c. ☐ This is a changed version of the work, as shown by space 6 on this application.

If your answer is "Yes," give: **Previous Registration Number ▶** **Year of Registration ▶**

6

DERIVATIVE WORK OR COMPILATION

a **Preexisting Material** Identify any preexisting work or works that this work is based on or incorporates. ▼

See instructions before completing this space.

b **Material Added to This Work** Give a brief, general statement of the material that has been added to this work and in which copyright is claimed. ▼

7

a **DEPOSIT ACCOUNT** If the registration fee is to be charged to a Deposit Account established in the Copyright Office, give name and number of Account.

Name ▼ **Account Number ▼**

b **CORRESPONDENCE** Give name and address to which correspondence about this application should be sent. Name/Address/Apt/City/State/ZIP ▼

Scrivener & Sons Publishing Co., Inc.
12345 Park Ave.
New York, NY 10000

Area code and daytime telephone number ▶ (212) 123-4567 Fax number ▶

Email ▶

8

CERTIFICATION* I, the undersigned, hereby certify that I am the

Check only one ▶
- ☐ author
- ☐ other copyright claimant
- ☐ owner of exclusive right(s)
- ☑ authorized agent of Scrivener & Sons Publishing Co.

Name of author or other copyright claimant, or owner of exclusive right(s) ▲

of the work identified in this application and that the statements made by me in this application are correct to the best of my knowledge.

Typed or printed name and date ▼ If this application gives a date of publication in space 3, do not sign and submit it before that date.

Maxwell Perkins **Date ▶** May 1, 2000

Handwritten signature (X) ▼

X Maxwell Perkins

9

Certificate will be mailed in window envelope to this address:

Name ▼
Scrivener & Sons Publishing Co., Inc.

Number/Street/Apt ▼
12345 Park Ave.

City/State/ZIP ▼
New York, NY 10000

YOU MUST:
- Complete all necessary spaces
- Sign your application in space 8

SEND ALL 3 ELEMENTS IN THE SAME PACKAGE:
1. Application form
2. Nonrefundable filing fee in check or money order payable to *Register of Copyrights*
3. Deposit material

MAIL TO:
Library of Congress
Copyright Office - TX
101 Independence Avenue, S.E.
Washington, D.C. 20559-6222

Fees are subject to change. For current fees, check the Copyright Office website at www.copyright.gov, write the Copyright Office, or call (202) 707-3000.

*17 U.S.C. § 506(e): Any person who knowingly makes a false representation of a material fact in the application for copyright registration provided for by section 409, or in any written statement filed in connection with the application, shall be fined not more than $2,500.

Rev: July 2003—xxx Web Rev: July 2003 Printed on recycled paper U.S. Government Printing Office: 2000-461-113/20,021

Single published work; five joint authors; publisher acquired all copyrights (continued)

CONTINUATION SHEET FOR APPLICATION FORMS

FORM ____ /CON
UNITED STATES COPYRIGHT OFFICE

REGISTRATION NUMBER

PA PAU SE SEG SEU SR SRU TX TXU VA VAU

EFFECTIVE DATE OF REGISTRATION

(Month) (Day) (Year)

CONTINUATION SHEET RECEIVED

Page ______ of ______ pages

- This Continuation Sheet is used in conjunction with Forms CA, PA, SE, SR, TX, and VA, **only**. Indicate which basic form you are continuing in the space in the upper right-hand corner.
- If at all possible, try to fit the information called for into the spaces provided on the basic form.
- If you do not have enough space for all the information you need to give on the basic form, use this Continuation Sheet and submit it with the basic form.
- If you submit this Continuation Sheet, clip (do not tape or staple) it to the basic form and fold the two together before submitting them.
- **Space A of this sheet is intended to identify the basic application.** **Space B is a continuation of Space 2 on the basic application. Space B is not applicable to Short Forms.** **Space C (on the reverse side of this sheet) is for the continuation of Spaces 1, 4, or 6 on the basic application or for the continuation of Space 1 on any of the three Short Forms PA, TX, or VA.**

DO NOT WRITE ABOVE THIS LINE. FOR COPYRIGHT OFFICE USE ONLY

A Identification of Application

IDENTIFICATION OF CONTINUATION SHEET: This sheet is a continuation of the application for copyright registration on the basic form submitted for the following work:

- TITLE: (Give the title as given under the heading "Title of this Work" in Space 1 of the basic form.)

The History of Music

- NAME(S) AND ADDRESS(ES) OF COPYRIGHT CLAIMANT(S): (Give the name and address of at least one copyright claimant as given in Space 4 of the basic form or Space 2 of any of the Short Forms PA, TX, or VA.)

Scrivener & Sons Publishing Co., 12345 Park Ave., New York, NY 10000

B Continuation of Space 2

d NAME OF AUTHOR ▼ Ted Timpani
DATES OF BIRTH AND DEATH Year Born ▼ 1955 Year Died ▼

Was this contribution to the work a "work made for hire"? ☐ Yes ☑ No

AUTHOR'S NATIONALITY OR DOMICILE Name of Country
OR { Citizen of ▶ U.S.A. / Domiciled in ▶ ______ }

WAS THIS AUTHOR'S CONTRIBUTION TO THE WORK
Anonymous? ☐ Yes ☑ No
Pseudonymous? ☐ Yes ☑ No
If the answer to either of these questions is "Yes," see detailed instructions.

NATURE OF AUTHORSHIP Briefly describe nature of the material created by the author in which copyright is claimed. ▼
Chapter 16

e NAME OF AUTHOR ▼ George Eastman
DATES OF BIRTH AND DEATH Year Born ▼ 1945 Year Died ▼

Was this contribution to the work a "work made for hire"? ☐ Yes ☑ No

AUTHOR'S NATIONALITY OR DOMICILE Name of Country
OR { Citizen of ▶ U.S.A. / Domiciled in ▶ ______ }

WAS THIS AUTHOR'S CONTRIBUTION TO THE WORK
Anonymous? ☐ Yes ☑ No
Pseudonymous? ☐ Yes ☑ No
If the answer to either of these questions is "Yes," see detailed instructions.

NATURE OF AUTHORSHIP Briefly describe nature of the material created by the author in which copyright is claimed. ▼
Illustrations

f NAME OF AUTHOR ▼
DATES OF BIRTH AND DEATH Year Born ▼ Year Died ▼

Was this contribution to the work a "work made for hire"? ☐ Yes ☐ No

AUTHOR'S NATIONALITY OR DOMICILE Name of Country
OR { Citizen of ▶ ______ / Domiciled in ▶ ______ }

WAS THIS AUTHOR'S CONTRIBUTION TO THE WORK
Anonymous? ☐ Yes ☐ No
Pseudonymous? ☐ Yes ☐ No
If the answer to either of these questions is "Yes," see detailed instructions.

NATURE OF AUTHORSHIP Briefly describe nature of the material created by the author in which copyright is claimed. ▼

Use the reverse side of this sheet if you need more space for continuation of Spaces 1, 4, or 6 of the basic form or for the continuation of Space 1 on any of the Short Forms PA, TX, or VA.

Single published work; five joint authors; publisher acquired all copyrights (continued)

CONTINUATION OF (Check which): ☐ Space 1 ☐ Space 4 ☐ Space 6

C
Continuation of other Spaces

Certificate will be mailed in window envelope to this address:

Name ▼

Number/Street/Apt ▼

City/State/ZIP ▼

YOU MUST:
- Complete all necessary spaces
- Sign your application

SEND ALL 3 ELEMENTS IN THE SAME PACKAGE:
1. Application form
2. Nonrefundable fee in check or money order payable to *Register of Copyrights*
3. Deposit Material

MAIL TO:
Library of Congress, Copyright Office
101 Independence Avenue, S.E.
Washington, D.C. 20559-6000

D

Fees are subject to change. For current fees, check the Copyright Office website at www.copyright.gov, write the Copyright Office, or call (202) 707-3000.

Rev: June 2002—20,000 Web Rev: June 2002 Printed on recycled paper

U.S. Government Printing Office: 2000-461-113/20,021

Single work made for hire; previously published under another title and revised; a derivative work

Copyright Office fees are subject to change. For current fees, check the Copyright Office website at *www.copyright.gov*, write the Copyright Office, or call (202) 707-3000.

Form TX
For a Nondramatic Literary Work
UNITED STATES COPYRIGHT OFFICE

REGISTRATION NUMBER

TX TXU

EFFECTIVE DATE OF REGISTRATION

Month Day Year

DO NOT WRITE ABOVE THIS LINE. IF YOU NEED MORE SPACE, USE A SEPARATE CONTINUATION SHEET.

1

TITLE OF THIS WORK ▼
What is DOS

PREVIOUS OR ALTERNATIVE TITLES ▼
HTML for Everyone

PUBLICATION AS A CONTRIBUTION If this work was published as a contribution to a periodical, serial, or collection, give information about the collective work in which the contribution appeared. **Title of Collective Work ▼**

If published in a periodical or serial give: **Volume ▼** **Number ▼** **Issue Date ▼** **On Pages ▼**

2

a **NAME OF AUTHOR ▼** Acme
DATES OF BIRTH AND DEATH Year Born ▼ Year Died ▼

Was this contribution to the work a "work made for hire"? ☐ Yes ☑ No

AUTHOR'S NATIONALITY OR DOMICILE Name of Country
OR { Citizen of ▶ U.S.A. / Domiciled in ▶ }

WAS THIS AUTHOR'S CONTRIBUTION TO THE WORK
Anonymous? ☐ Yes ☑ No
Pseudonymous? ☐ Yes ☑ No
If the answer to either of these questions is "Yes," see detailed instructions.

NATURE OF AUTHORSHIP Briefly describe nature of material created by this author in which copyright is claimed. ▼
Entire text

b **NAME OF AUTHOR ▼**
DATES OF BIRTH AND DEATH Year Born ▼ Year Died ▼

Was this contribution to the work a "work made for hire"? ☐ Yes ☐ No

AUTHOR'S NATIONALITY OR DOMICILE Name of Country
OR { Citizen of ▶ / Domiciled in ▶ }

WAS THIS AUTHOR'S CONTRIBUTION TO THE WORK
Anonymous? ☐ Yes ☐ No
Pseudonymous? ☐ Yes ☐ No
If the answer to either of these questions is "Yes," see detailed instructions.

NATURE OF AUTHORSHIP Briefly describe nature of material created by this author in which copyright is claimed. ▼

c **NAME OF AUTHOR ▼**
DATES OF BIRTH AND DEATH Year Born ▼ Year Died ▼

Was this contribution to the work a "work made for hire"? ☐ Yes ☐ No

AUTHOR'S NATIONALITY OR DOMICILE Name of Country
OR { Citizen of ▶ / Domiciled in ▶ }

WAS THIS AUTHOR'S CONTRIBUTION TO THE WORK
Anonymous? ☐ Yes ☐ No
Pseudonymous? ☐ Yes ☐ No
If the answer to either of these questions is "Yes," see detailed instructions.

NATURE OF AUTHORSHIP Briefly describe nature of material created by this author in which copyright is claimed. ▼

NOTE
Under the law, the "author" of a "work made for hire" is generally the employer, not the employee (see instructions). For any part of this work that was "made for hire" check "Yes" in the space provided, give the employer (or other person for whom the work was prepared) as "Author" of that part, and leave the space for dates of birth and death blank.

3

a **YEAR IN WHICH CREATION OF THIS WORK WAS COMPLETED** This information must be given ◀ Year in all cases.
2000

b **DATE AND NATION OF FIRST PUBLICATION OF THIS PARTICULAR WORK** Complete this information ONLY if this work has been published.
Month ▶ April Day ▶ 15 Year ▶ 2000
U.S.A. ◀ Nation

4

COPYRIGHT CLAIMANT(S) Name and address must be given even if the claimant is the same as the author given in space 2. ▼
Acme Press
1234 Computer Rd.
Silicon Valley, CA 90000

See instructions before completing this space.

TRANSFER If the claimant(s) named here in space 4 is (are) different from the author(s) named in space 2, give a brief statement of how the claimant(s) obtained ownership of the copyright. ▼

DO NOT WRITE HERE OFFICE USE ONLY
APPLICATION RECEIVED
ONE DEPOSIT RECEIVED
TWO DEPOSITS RECEIVED
FUNDS RECEIVED

MORE ON BACK ▶ • Complete all applicable spaces (numbers 5-9) on the reverse side of this page.
• See detailed instructions. • Sign the form at line 8.

DO NOT WRITE HERE
Page 1 of _____ pages

Single work made for hire; previously published under another title and revised; a derivative work (continued)

EXAMINED BY | FORM TX

CHECKED BY

☐ CORRESPONDENCE Yes

FOR COPYRIGHT OFFICE USE ONLY

DO NOT WRITE ABOVE THIS LINE. IF YOU NEED MORE SPACE, USE A SEPARATE CONTINUATION SHEET.

5

PREVIOUS REGISTRATION Has registration for this work, or for an earlier version of this work, already been made in the Copyright Office?
☑ Yes ☐ No If your answer is "Yes," why is another registration being sought? (Check appropriate box.) ▼
a. ☐ This is the first published edition of a work previously registered in unpublished form.
b. ☐ This is the first application submitted by this author as copyright claimant.
c. ☐ This is a changed version of the work, as shown by space 6 on this application.
If your answer is "Yes," give: **Previous Registration Number ▶** TX-123456 **Year of Registration ▶** 1995

6

DERIVATIVE WORK OR COMPILATION
a **Preexisting Material** Identify any preexisting work or works that this work is based on or incorporates. ▼
First edition of work, published under title "HTML for Everyone"

See instructions before completing this space.

b **Material Added to This Work** Give a brief, general statement of the material that has been added to this work and in which copyright is claimed. ▼
Revised chapters 1-8, chapter 9 entirely new

7

a **DEPOSIT ACCOUNT** If the registration fee is to be charged to a Deposit Account established in the Copyright Office, give name and number of Account.
Name ▼ **Account Number ▼**

b **CORRESPONDENCE** Give name and address to which correspondence about this application should be sent. Name/Address/Apt/City/State/ZIP ▼
Acme Press
1234 Computer Rd.
Silicon Valley, CA 90000
Area code and daytime telephone number ▶ (408)-123-4567 Fax number ▶
Email ▶

8

CERTIFICATION* I, the undersigned, hereby certify that I am the
Check only one ▶
☑ author
☐ other copyright claimant
☐ owner of exclusive right(s)
☐ authorized agent of Acme Press
Name of author or other copyright claimant, or owner of exclusive right(s) ▲
of the work identified in this application and that the statements made by me in this application are correct to the best of my knowledge.

Typed or printed name and date ▼ If this application gives a date of publication in space 3, do not sign and submit it before that date.
Susan Succubus **Date ▶** May 1, 2000

Handwritten signature (X) ▼
X Susan Succubus

9

Certificate will be mailed in window envelope to this address:

Name ▼ Acme Press
Number/Street/Apt ▼ 1234 Computer Rd.
City/State/ZIP ▼ Silicon Valley, CA 90000

YOU MUST:
- Complete all necessary spaces
- Sign your application in space 8

SEND ALL 3 ELEMENTS IN THE SAME PACKAGE:
1. Application form
2. Nonrefundable filing fee in check or money order payable to *Register of Copyrights*
3. Deposit material

MAIL TO:
Library of Congress
Copyright Office - TX
101 Independence Avenue, S.E.
Washington, D.C. 20559-6222

Fees are subject to change. For current fees, check the Copyright Office website at www.copyright.gov, write the Copyright Office, or call (202) 707-3000.

*17 U.S.C. § 506(e): Any person who knowingly makes a false representation of a material fact in the application for copyright registration provided for by section 409, or in any written statement filed in connection with the application, shall be fined not more than $2,500.

Rev: July 2003—xxx Web Rev: July 2003 Printed on recycled paper U.S. Government Printing Office: 2000-461-113/20,021

Published book; derivative work based on previously published article; joint authors: one the author of the text, the other the photographer; text and photos registered together as a single unit of publication

Copyright Office fees are subject to change. For current fees, check the Copyright Office website at *www.copyright.gov*, write the Copyright Office, or call (202) 707-3000.

Form TX
For a Nondramatic Literary Work
UNITED STATES COPYRIGHT OFFICE

REGISTRATION NUMBER

TX TXU

EFFECTIVE DATE OF REGISTRATION

Month Day Year

DO NOT WRITE ABOVE THIS LINE. IF YOU NEED MORE SPACE, USE A SEPARATE CONTINUATION SHEET.

1 TITLE OF THIS WORK ▼
The Sex Life of the Gnu

PREVIOUS OR ALTERNATIVE TITLES ▼
What the Gnu Knew

PUBLICATION AS A CONTRIBUTION If this work was published as a contribution to a periodical, serial, or collection, give information about the collective work in which the contribution appeared. Title of Collective Work ▼

If published in a periodical or serial give: Volume ▼ Number ▼ Issue Date ▼ On Pages ▼

2 **a** NAME OF AUTHOR ▼ Nastassia Kinsey
DATES OF BIRTH AND DEATH Year Born ▼ 1960 Year Died ▼

Was this contribution to the work a "work made for hire"? ☐ Yes ☑ No
AUTHOR'S NATIONALITY OR DOMICILE Name of Country
OR { Citizen of ▶ U.S.A. / Domiciled in ▶
WAS THIS AUTHOR'S CONTRIBUTION TO THE WORK Anonymous? ☐ Yes ☑ No Pseudonymous? ☐ Yes ☑ No
If the answer to either of these questions is "Yes," see detailed instructions.

NATURE OF AUTHORSHIP Briefly describe nature of material created by this author in which copyright is claimed. ▼
Entire text

b NAME OF AUTHOR ▼ George Eastman
DATES OF BIRTH AND DEATH Year Born ▼ 1950 Year Died ▼

Was this contribution to the work a "work made for hire"? ☐ Yes ☑ No
AUTHOR'S NATIONALITY OR DOMICILE Name of Country
OR { Citizen of ▶ U.S.A. / Domiciled in ▶
WAS THIS AUTHOR'S CONTRIBUTION TO THE WORK Anonymous? ☐ Yes ☑ No Pseudonymous? ☐ Yes ☑ No
If the answer to either of these questions is "Yes," see detailed instructions.

NATURE OF AUTHORSHIP Briefly describe nature of material created by this author in which copyright is claimed. ▼
Photographs

c NAME OF AUTHOR ▼
DATES OF BIRTH AND DEATH Year Born ▼ Year Died ▼

Was this contribution to the work a "work made for hire"? ☐ Yes ☐ No
AUTHOR'S NATIONALITY OR DOMICILE Name of Country
OR { Citizen of ▶ / Domiciled in ▶
WAS THIS AUTHOR'S CONTRIBUTION TO THE WORK Anonymous? ☐ Yes ☐ No Pseudonymous? ☐ Yes ☐ No
If the answer to either of these questions is "Yes," see detailed instructions.

NATURE OF AUTHORSHIP Briefly describe nature of material created by this author in which copyright is claimed. ▼

NOTE
Under the law, the "author" of a "work made for hire" is generally the employer, not the employee (see instructions). For any part of this work that was "made for hire" check "Yes" in the space provided, give the employer (or other person for whom the work was prepared) as "Author" of that part, and leave the space for dates of birth and death blank.

3 **a** YEAR IN WHICH CREATION OF THIS WORK WAS COMPLETED 2000 ◀ Year
This information must be given in all cases.

b DATE AND NATION OF FIRST PUBLICATION OF THIS PARTICULAR WORK
Complete this information ONLY if this work has been published.
Month ▶ May Day ▶ 15 Year ▶ 2000
U.S.A. ◀ Nation

4 COPYRIGHT CLAIMANT(S) Name and address must be given even if the claimant is the same as the author given in space 2. ▼
Nastassia Kinsey
100 Tenth St.
New York, NY 10000

George Eastman
123 Kodak St.
Rochester, NY 12345

See instructions before completing this space.

TRANSFER If the claimant(s) named here in space 4 is (are) different from the author(s) named in space 2, give a brief statement of how the claimant(s) obtained ownership of the copyright. ▼

DO NOT WRITE HERE OFFICE USE ONLY
APPLICATION RECEIVED
ONE DEPOSIT RECEIVED
TWO DEPOSITS RECEIVED
FUNDS RECEIVED

MORE ON BACK ▶ • Complete all applicable spaces (numbers 5-9) on the reverse side of this page.
• See detailed instructions. • Sign the form at line 8.

DO NOT WRITE HERE
Page 1 of ______ pages

Published book; derivative work based on previously published article; joint authors: one the author of the text, the other the photographer; text and photos registered together as a single unit of publication (continued)

EXAMINED BY

FORM TX

CHECKED BY

☐ CORRESPONDENCE Yes

FOR COPYRIGHT OFFICE USE ONLY

DO NOT WRITE ABOVE THIS LINE. IF YOU NEED MORE SPACE, USE A SEPARATE CONTINUATION SHEET.

5

PREVIOUS REGISTRATION Has registration for this work, or for an earlier version of this work, already been made in the Copyright Office?
☐ Yes ☑ No If your answer is "Yes," why is another registration being sought? (Check appropriate box.) ▼
a. ☐ This is the first published edition of a work previously registered in unpublished form.
b. ☐ This is the first application submitted by this author as copyright claimant.
c. ☐ This is a changed version of the work, as shown by space 6 on this application.
If your answer is "Yes," give: **Previous Registration Number** ▶ **Year of Registration** ▶

6

DERIVATIVE WORK OR COMPILATION
Preexisting Material Identify any preexisting work or works that this work is based on or incorporates. ▼ **a**

What the Gnu Knew (an article in International Geographic, vol. 60, no. 1)

See instructions before completing this space.

Material Added to This Work Give a brief, general statement of the material that has been added to this work and in which copyright is claimed. ▼ **b**

Text has been substantially revised and expanded, 50 new photographs

7

DEPOSIT ACCOUNT If the registration fee is to be charged to a Deposit Account established in the Copyright Office, give name and number of Account. **a**
Name ▼ **Account Number** ▼

CORRESPONDENCE Give name and address to which correspondence about this application should be sent. Name/Address/Apt/City/State/ZIP ▼ **b**

Nastassia Kinsey and George Eastman
100 Tenth St.
New York, NY 10000

Area code and daytime telephone number ▶ (212) 123-4567 Fax number ▶
Email ▶ kinsey@kinky.com

8

CERTIFICATION* I, the undersigned, hereby certify that I am the
Check only one ▶
☑ author
☐ other copyright claimant
☐ owner of exclusive right(s)
☐ authorized agent of ______
Name of author or other copyright claimant, or owner of exclusive right(s) ▲

of the work identified in this application and that the statements made by me in this application are correct to the best of my knowledge.

Typed or printed name and date ▼ If this application gives a date of publication in space 3, do not sign and submit it before that date.

Nastassia Kinsey **Date** ▶ June 1, 2000

Handwritten signature (X) ▼

X *Nastassia Kinsey*

9

Certificate will be mailed in window envelope to this address:

Name ▼
Nastassia Kinsey
Number/Street/Apt ▼
100 Tenth St.
City/State/ZIP ▼
New York, NY 10000

YOU MUST:
• Complete all necessary spaces
• Sign your application in space 8

SEND ALL 3 ELEMENTS IN THE SAME PACKAGE:
1. Application form
2. Nonrefundable filing fee in check or money order payable to *Register of Copyrights*
3. Deposit material

MAIL TO:
Library of Congress
Copyright Office - TX
101 Independence Avenue, S.E.
Washington, D.C. 20559-6222

Fees are subject to change. For current fees, check the Copyright Office website at www.copyright.gov, write the Copyright Office, or call (202) 707-3000.

*17 U.S.C. § 506(e): Any person who knowingly makes a false representation of a material fact in the application for copyright registration provided for by section 409, or in any written statement filed in connection with the application, shall be fined not more than $2,500.

Rev: July 2003—xxx Web Rev: July 2003 ♻ Printed on recycled paper U.S. Government Printing Office: 2000-461-113/20,021

Single published work; publisher acquired all rights in text; text and work for hire cover art and copy registered together as a single unit of publication

Copyright Office fees are subject to change. For current fees, check the Copyright Office website at *www.copyright.gov*, write the Copyright Office, or call (202) 707-3000.

Form TX
For a Nondramatic Literary Work
UNITED STATES COPYRIGHT OFFICE

REGISTRATION NUMBER

TX TXU

EFFECTIVE DATE OF REGISTRATION

Month Day Year

DO NOT WRITE ABOVE THIS LINE. IF YOU NEED MORE SPACE, USE A SEPARATE CONTINUATION SHEET.

1

TITLE OF THIS WORK ▼
The Plagiarist's Handbook

PREVIOUS OR ALTERNATIVE TITLES ▼

PUBLICATION AS A CONTRIBUTION If this work was published as a contribution to a periodical, serial, or collection, give information about the collective work in which the contribution appeared. Title of Collective Work ▼

If published in a periodical or serial give: Volume ▼ Number ▼ Issue Date ▼ On Pages ▼

2

a NAME OF AUTHOR ▼ Charles C. Copycat
DATES OF BIRTH AND DEATH Year Born ▼ 1955 Year Died ▼

Was this contribution to the work a "work made for hire"? ☐ Yes ☑ No

AUTHOR'S NATIONALITY OR DOMICILE Name of Country
OR { Citizen of ▶ U.S.A. / Domiciled in ▶

WAS THIS AUTHOR'S CONTRIBUTION TO THE WORK
Anonymous? ☐ Yes ☑ No
Pseudonymous? ☐ Yes ☑ No
If the answer to either of these questions is "Yes," see detailed instructions.

NATURE OF AUTHORSHIP Briefly describe nature of material created by this author in which copyright is claimed. ▼
Entire text

b NAME OF AUTHOR ▼ Acme Press
DATES OF BIRTH AND DEATH Year Born ▼ Year Died ▼

Was this contribution to the work a "work made for hire"? ☐ Yes ☑ No

AUTHOR'S NATIONALITY OR DOMICILE Name of Country
OR { Citizen of ▶ U.S.A. / Domiciled in ▶

WAS THIS AUTHOR'S CONTRIBUTION TO THE WORK
Anonymous? ☐ Yes ☑ No
Pseudonymous? ☐ Yes ☑ No
If the answer to either of these questions is "Yes," see detailed instructions.

NATURE OF AUTHORSHIP Briefly describe nature of material created by this author in which copyright is claimed. ▼
Cover artwork and copy

c NAME OF AUTHOR ▼
DATES OF BIRTH AND DEATH Year Born ▼ Year Died ▼

Was this contribution to the work a "work made for hire"? ☐ Yes ☐ No

AUTHOR'S NATIONALITY OR DOMICILE Name of Country
OR { Citizen of ▶ / Domiciled in ▶

WAS THIS AUTHOR'S CONTRIBUTION TO THE WORK
Anonymous? ☐ Yes ☐ No
Pseudonymous? ☐ Yes ☐ No
If the answer to either of these questions is "Yes," see detailed instructions.

NATURE OF AUTHORSHIP Briefly describe nature of material created by this author in which copyright is claimed. ▼

NOTE
Under the law, the "author" of a "work made for hire" is generally the employer, not the employee (see instructions). For any part of this work that was "made for hire" check "Yes" in the space provided, give the employer (or other person for whom the work was prepared) as "Author" of that part, and leave the space for dates of birth and death blank.

3

a YEAR IN WHICH CREATION OF THIS WORK WAS COMPLETED 2000 ◀Year
This information must be given in all cases.

b DATE AND NATION OF FIRST PUBLICATION OF THIS PARTICULAR WORK
Complete this information ONLY if this work has been published. Month ▶ May Day ▶ 15 Year ▶ 2000
U.S.A. ◀ Nation

4

COPYRIGHT CLAIMANT(S) Name and address must be given even if the claimant is the same as the author given in space 2. ▼
Acme Press
1000 Summit Drive
Phoenix, AZ 80000

See instructions before completing this space.

TRANSFER If the claimant(s) named here in space 4 is (are) different from the author(s) named in space 2, give a brief statement of how the claimant(s) obtained ownership of the copyright. ▼
Written transfer of all right, title, and interest

DO NOT WRITE HERE OFFICE USE ONLY
APPLICATION RECEIVED
ONE DEPOSIT RECEIVED
TWO DEPOSITS RECEIVED
FUNDS RECEIVED

MORE ON BACK ▶ • Complete all applicable spaces (numbers 5-9) on the reverse side of this page.
• See detailed instructions. • Sign the form at line 8.

DO NOT WRITE HERE
Page 1 of ______ pages

Single published work; publisher acquired all rights in text; text and work for hire cover art and copy registered together as a single unit of publication (continued)

EXAMINED BY

FORM TX

CHECKED BY

☐ CORRESPONDENCE Yes

FOR COPYRIGHT OFFICE USE ONLY

DO NOT WRITE ABOVE THIS LINE. IF YOU NEED MORE SPACE, USE A SEPARATE CONTINUATION SHEET.

5

PREVIOUS REGISTRATION Has registration for this work, or for an earlier version of this work, already been made in the Copyright Office?
☐ **Yes** ☑ **No** If your answer is "Yes," why is another registration being sought? (Check appropriate box.) ▼
a. ☐ This is the first published edition of a work previously registered in unpublished form.
b. ☐ This is the first application submitted by this author as copyright claimant.
c. ☐ This is a changed version of the work, as shown by space 6 on this application.
If your answer is "Yes," give: **Previous Registration Number** ▶ **Year of Registration** ▶

6

DERIVATIVE WORK OR COMPILATION
a **Preexisting Material** Identify any preexisting work or works that this work is based on or incorporates. ▼

b **Material Added to This Work** Give a brief, general statement of the material that has been added to this work and in which copyright is claimed. ▼

See instructions before completing this space.

7

a **DEPOSIT ACCOUNT** If the registration fee is to be charged to a Deposit Account established in the Copyright Office, give name and number of Account.
Name ▼ **Account Number** ▼

b **CORRESPONDENCE** Give name and address to which correspondence about this application should be sent. Name/Address/Apt/City/State/ZIP ▼
Acme Press
1000 Summit Drive
Phoenix, AZ 80000
Area code and daytime telephone number ▶ (602) 666-6666 Fax number ▶
Email ▶

8

CERTIFICATION* I, the undersigned, hereby certify that I am the
Check only one ▶
☐ author
☐ other copyright claimant
☐ owner of exclusive right(s)
☑ authorized agent of Acme Press
Name of author or other copyright claimant, or owner of exclusive right(s) ▲
of the work identified in this application and that the statements made by me in this application are correct to the best of my knowledge.

Typed or printed name and date ▼ If this application gives a date of publication in space 3, do not sign and submit it before that date.
Chandler Bartlett **Date** ▶ July 1, 2000

Handwritten signature (X) ▼
X ___*Chandler Bartlett*___

9

Certificate will be mailed in window envelope to this address:
Name ▼ Acme Press
Number/Street/Apt ▼ 1000 Summit Drive
City/State/ZIP ▼ Phoenix, AZ 80000

YOU MUST:
• Complete all necessary spaces
• Sign your application in space 8
SEND ALL 3 ELEMENTS IN THE SAME PACKAGE:
1. Application form
2. Nonrefundable filing fee in check or money order payable to *Register of Copyrights*
3. Deposit material
MAIL TO:
Library of Congress
Copyright Office - TX
101 Independence Avenue, S.E.
Washington, D.C. 20559-6222

Fees are subject to change. For current fees, check the Copyright Office website at www.copyright.gov, write the Copyright Office, or call (202) 707-3000.

*17 U.S.C. § 506(e): Any person who knowingly makes a false representation of a material fact in the application for copyright registration provided for by section 409, or in any written statement filed in connection with the application, shall be fined not more than $2,500.

Rev: July 2003—xxx Web Rev: July 2003 ♻ Printed on recycled paper U.S. Government Printing Office: 2000-461-113/20,021

Published compilation (anthology); publisher registers for the authors

Copyright Office fees are subject to change. For current fees, check the Copyright Office website at *www.copyright.gov*, write the Copyright Office, or call (202) 707-3000.

Form TX
For a Nondramatic Literary Work
UNITED STATES COPYRIGHT OFFICE

REGISTRATION NUMBER

TX TXU

EFFECTIVE DATE OF REGISTRATION

Month Day Year

DO NOT WRITE ABOVE THIS LINE. IF YOU NEED MORE SPACE, USE A SEPARATE CONTINUATION SHEET.

1

TITLE OF THIS WORK ▼

The Best Short Stories of 2000

PREVIOUS OR ALTERNATIVE TITLES ▼

PUBLICATION AS A CONTRIBUTION If this work was published as a contribution to a periodical, serial, or collection, give information about the collective work in which the contribution appeared. Title of Collective Work ▼

If published in a periodical or serial give: Volume ▼ Number ▼ Issue Date ▼ On Pages ▼

2

a NAME OF AUTHOR ▼ Alan Allenby

DATES OF BIRTH AND DEATH Year Born ▼ 1950 Year Died ▼

Was this contribution to the work a "work made for hire"? ☑ Yes ☐ No

AUTHOR'S NATIONALITY OR DOMICILE Name of Country OR { Citizen of ▶ U.S.A. / Domiciled in ▶

WAS THIS AUTHOR'S CONTRIBUTION TO THE WORK Anonymous? ☐ Yes ☑ No Pseudonymous? ☐ Yes ☑ No If the answer to either of these questions is "Yes," see detailed instructions.

NATURE OF AUTHORSHIP Briefly describe nature of material created by this author in which copyright is claimed. ▼ Anthology of previously published short stories

b NAME OF AUTHOR ▼

DATES OF BIRTH AND DEATH Year Born ▼ Year Died ▼

Was this contribution to the work a "work made for hire"? ☐ Yes ☐ No

AUTHOR'S NATIONALITY OR DOMICILE Name of Country OR { Citizen of ▶ / Domiciled in ▶

WAS THIS AUTHOR'S CONTRIBUTION TO THE WORK Anonymous? ☐ Yes ☐ No Pseudonymous? ☐ Yes ☐ No If the answer to either of these questions is "Yes," see detailed instructions.

NATURE OF AUTHORSHIP Briefly describe nature of material created by this author in which copyright is claimed. ▼

c NAME OF AUTHOR ▼

DATES OF BIRTH AND DEATH Year Born ▼ Year Died ▼

Was this contribution to the work a "work made for hire"? ☐ Yes ☐ No

AUTHOR'S NATIONALITY OR DOMICILE Name of Country OR { Citizen of ▶ / Domiciled in ▶

WAS THIS AUTHOR'S CONTRIBUTION TO THE WORK Anonymous? ☐ Yes ☐ No Pseudonymous? ☐ Yes ☐ No If the answer to either of these questions is "Yes," see detailed instructions.

NATURE OF AUTHORSHIP Briefly describe nature of material created by this author in which copyright is claimed. ▼

NOTE

Under the law, the "author" of a "work made for hire" is generally the employer, not the employee (see instructions). For any part of this work that was "made for hire" check "Yes" in the space provided, give the employer (or other person for whom the work was prepared) as "Author" of that part, and leave the space for dates of birth and death blank.

3

a YEAR IN WHICH CREATION OF THIS WORK WAS COMPLETED 2000 ◀ Year This information must be given in all cases.

b DATE AND NATION OF FIRST PUBLICATION OF THIS PARTICULAR WORK Complete this information ONLY if this work has been published. Month ▶ May Day ▶ 15 Year ▶ 2000 U.S.A. ◀ Nation

4

COPYRIGHT CLAIMANT(S) Name and address must be given even if the claimant is the same as the author given in space 2. ▼

Alan Allenby
1000 Allen Street
Allentown, PA 20000

TRANSFER If the claimant(s) named here in space 4 is (are) different from the author(s) named in space 2, give a brief statement of how the claimant(s) obtained ownership of the copyright. ▼

See instructions before completing this space.

DO NOT WRITE HERE OFFICE USE ONLY

APPLICATION RECEIVED

ONE DEPOSIT RECEIVED

TWO DEPOSITS RECEIVED

FUNDS RECEIVED

MORE ON BACK ▶ • Complete all applicable spaces (numbers 5-9) on the reverse side of this page. • See detailed instructions. • Sign the form at line 8.

DO NOT WRITE HERE

Page 1 of ____ pages

Published compilation (anthology); publisher registers for the authors (continued)

EXAMINED BY | FORM TX

CHECKED BY

☐ CORRESPONDENCE Yes

FOR COPYRIGHT OFFICE USE ONLY

DO NOT WRITE ABOVE THIS LINE. IF YOU NEED MORE SPACE, USE A SEPARATE CONTINUATION SHEET.

5

PREVIOUS REGISTRATION Has registration for this work, or for an earlier version of this work, already been made in the Copyright Office?

☐ **Yes** ☑ **No** If your answer is "Yes," why is another registration being sought? (Check appropriate box.) ▼

a. ☐ This is the first published edition of a work previously registered in unpublished form.

b. ☐ This is the first application submitted by this author as copyright claimant.

c. ☐ This is a changed version of the work, as shown by space 6 on this application.

If your answer is "Yes," give: **Previous Registration Number** ▶ **Year of Registration** ▶

6

DERIVATIVE WORK OR COMPILATION

a **Preexisting Material** Identify any preexisting work or works that this work is based on or incorporates. ▼

Anthology of previously published short works

See instructions before completing this space.

b **Material Added to This Work** Give a brief, general statement of the material that has been added to this work and in which copyright is claimed. ▼

7

a **DEPOSIT ACCOUNT** If the registration fee is to be charged to a Deposit Account established in the Copyright Office, give name and number of Account.
Name ▼ **Account Number** ▼

b **CORRESPONDENCE** Give name and address to which correspondence about this application should be sent. Name / Address / Apt / City / State / ZIP ▼

John Smith, Acme Press
10 Grub Street
Boston, MA 01234

Area code and daytime telephone number ▶ (617) 123-4567 Fax number ▶

Email ▶ john@cicine.com

8

CERTIFICATION* I, the undersigned, hereby certify that I am the

Check only one ▶
☐ author
☐ other copyright claimant
☐ owner of exclusive right(s)
☑ authorized agent of Alan Allenby
Name of author or other copyright claimant, or owner of exclusive right(s) ▲

of the work identified in this application and that the statements made by me in this application are correct to the best of my knowledge.

Typed or printed name and date ▼ If this application gives a date of publication in space 3, do not sign and submit it before that date.

John Smith **Date** ▶ April 1, 2000

Handwritten signature (X) ▼

X John Smith

9

Certificate will be mailed in window envelope to this address:

Name ▼	John Smith, c/o Acme Press
Number/Street/Apt ▼	10 Grub Street
City/State/ZIP ▼	Boston, MA 01234

YOU MUST:
• Complete all necessary spaces
• Sign your application in space 8

SEND ALL 3 ELEMENTS IN THE SAME PACKAGE:
1. Application form
2. Nonrefundable filing fee in check or money order payable to *Register of Copyrights*
3. Deposit material

MAIL TO:
Library of Congress
Copyright Office - TX
101 Independence Avenue, S.E.
Washington, D.C. 20559-6222

Fees are subject to change. For current fees, check the Copyright Office website at www.copyright.gov, write the Copyright Office, or call (202) 707-3000.

*17 U.S.C. § 506(e): Any person who knowingly makes a false representation of a material fact in the application for copyright registration provided for by section 409, or in any written statement filed in connection with the application, shall be fined not more than $2,500.

Rev: July 2003—xxx Web Rev: July 2003 Printed on recycled paper U.S. Government Printing Office: 2000-461-113/20,021

Single author; contribution to collective work

Copyright Office fees are subject to change. For current fees, check the Copyright Office website at *www.copyright.gov*, write the Copyright Office, or call (202) 707-3000.

Form TX
For a Nondramatic Literary Work
UNITED STATES COPYRIGHT OFFICE

REGISTRATION NUMBER

TX TXU

EFFECTIVE DATE OF REGISTRATION

Month Day Year

DO NOT WRITE ABOVE THIS LINE. IF YOU NEED MORE SPACE, USE A SEPARATE CONTINUATION SHEET.

1

TITLE OF THIS WORK ▼
The Red-Faced Killer

PREVIOUS OR ALTERNATIVE TITLES ▼
N/A

PUBLICATION AS A CONTRIBUTION If this work was published as a contribution to a periodical, serial, or collection, give information about the collective work in which the contribution appeared. Title of Collective Work ▼
Mysteries Unlimited

If published in a periodical or serial give: Volume ▼ Number ▼ Issue Date ▼ On Pages ▼

2

a NAME OF AUTHOR ▼ Kay Hurst
DATES OF BIRTH AND DEATH Year Born ▼ 1941 Year Died ▼

Was this contribution to the work a "work made for hire"? ☑ Yes ☐ No
AUTHOR'S NATIONALITY OR DOMICILE Name of Country
OR { Citizen of ▶ U.S.A. / Domiciled in ▶
WAS THIS AUTHOR'S CONTRIBUTION TO THE WORK
Anonymous? ☐ Yes ☑ No
Pseudonymous? ☐ Yes ☑ No
If the answer to either of these questions is "Yes," see detailed instructions.

NATURE OF AUTHORSHIP Briefly describe nature of material created by this author in which copyright is claimed. ▼
Anthology of previously published short stories

NOTE

Under the law, the "author" of a "work made for hire" is generally the employer, not the employee (see instructions). For any part of this work that was "made for hire" check "Yes" in the space provided, give the employer (or other person for whom the work was prepared) as "Author" of that part, and leave the space for dates of birth and death blank.

b NAME OF AUTHOR ▼
DATES OF BIRTH AND DEATH Year Born ▼ Year Died ▼

Was this contribution to the work a "work made for hire"? ☐ Yes ☐ No
AUTHOR'S NATIONALITY OR DOMICILE Name of Country
OR { Citizen of ▶ / Domiciled in ▶
WAS THIS AUTHOR'S CONTRIBUTION TO THE WORK
Anonymous? ☐ Yes ☐ No
Pseudonymous? ☐ Yes ☐ No
If the answer to either of these questions is "Yes," see detailed instructions.

NATURE OF AUTHORSHIP Briefly describe nature of material created by this author in which copyright is claimed. ▼

c NAME OF AUTHOR ▼
DATES OF BIRTH AND DEATH Year Born ▼ Year Died ▼

Was this contribution to the work a "work made for hire"? ☐ Yes ☐ No
AUTHOR'S NATIONALITY OR DOMICILE Name of Country
OR { Citizen of ▶ / Domiciled in ▶
WAS THIS AUTHOR'S CONTRIBUTION TO THE WORK
Anonymous? ☐ Yes ☐ No
Pseudonymous? ☐ Yes ☐ No
If the answer to either of these questions is "Yes," see detailed instructions.

NATURE OF AUTHORSHIP Briefly describe nature of material created by this author in which copyright is claimed. ▼

3

a YEAR IN WHICH CREATION OF THIS WORK WAS COMPLETED 1996 ◀ Year This information must be given in all cases.

b DATE AND NATION OF FIRST PUBLICATION OF THIS PARTICULAR WORK Complete this information ONLY if this work has been published. Month ▶ March Day ▶ 1 Year ▶ 2000
U.S.A. ◀ Nation

4

COPYRIGHT CLAIMANT(S) Name and address must be given even if the claimant is the same as the author given in space 2. ▼
Kay Hurst
2400 Great Lakes Way
Detroit, MI 48219

See instructions before completing this space.

TRANSFER If the claimant(s) named here in space 4 is (are) different from the author(s) named in space 2, give a brief statement of how the claimant(s) obtained ownership of the copyright. ▼

DO NOT WRITE HERE OFFICE USE ONLY
APPLICATION RECEIVED
ONE DEPOSIT RECEIVED
TWO DEPOSITS RECEIVED
FUNDS RECEIVED

MORE ON BACK ▶ • Complete all applicable spaces (numbers 5-9) on the reverse side of this page.
• See detailed instructions. • Sign the form at line 8.

DO NOT WRITE HERE
Page 1 of ______ pages

Single author; contribution to collective work (continued)

EXAMINED BY

FORM TX

CHECKED BY

☐ CORRESPONDENCE Yes

FOR COPYRIGHT OFFICE USE ONLY

DO NOT WRITE ABOVE THIS LINE. IF YOU NEED MORE SPACE, USE A SEPARATE CONTINUATION SHEET.

5

PREVIOUS REGISTRATION Has registration for this work, or for an earlier version of this work, already been made in the Copyright Office?
☐ **Yes** ☑ **No** If your answer is "Yes," why is another registration being sought? (Check appropriate box.) ▼
a. ☐ This is the first published edition of a work previously registered in unpublished form.
b. ☐ This is the first application submitted by this author as copyright claimant.
c. ☐ This is a changed version of the work, as shown by space 6 on this application.
If your answer is "Yes," give: **Previous Registration Number** ▶ **Year of Registration** ▶

6

DERIVATIVE WORK OR COMPILATION
a **Preexisting Material** Identify any preexisting work or works that this work is based on or incorporates. ▼

See instructions before completing this space.

b **Material Added to This Work** Give a brief, general statement of the material that has been added to this work and in which copyright is claimed. ▼

7

a **DEPOSIT ACCOUNT** If the registration fee is to be charged to a Deposit Account established in the Copyright Office, give name and number of Account.
Name ▼ **Account Number** ▼

b **CORRESPONDENCE** Give name and address to which correspondence about this application should be sent. Name/Address/Apt/City/State/ZIP ▼

Kay Hurst
2400 Great Lakes Way
Detroit, MI 48219

Area code and daytime telephone number ▶ (333) 123-4567 Fax number ▶
Email ▶

8

CERTIFICATION* I, the undersigned, hereby certify that I am the
Check only one ▶
☑ author
☐ other copyright claimant
☐ owner of exclusive right(s)
☐ authorized agent of ______
Name of author or other copyright claimant, or owner of exclusive right(s) ▲
of the work identified in this application and that the statements made by me in this application are correct to the best of my knowledge.

Typed or printed name and date ▼ If this application gives a date of publication in space 3, do not sign and submit it before that date.

Kay Hurst **Date** ▶ April 21, 2000

Handwritten signature (X) ▼

X ____ Kay Hurst ____

9

Certificate will be mailed in window envelope to this address:

Name ▼
Kay Hurst

Number/Street/Apt ▼
2400 Great Lakes Way

City/State/ZIP ▼
Detroit, MI 48219

YOU MUST:
- Complete all necessary spaces
- Sign your application in space 8

SEND ALL 3 ELEMENTS IN THE SAME PACKAGE:
1. Application form
2. Nonrefundable filing fee in check or money order payable to *Register of Copyrights*
3. Deposit material

MAIL TO:
Library of Congress
Copyright Office - TX
101 Independence Avenue, S.E.
Washington, D.C. 20559-6222

Fees are subject to change. For current fees, check the Copyright Office website at www.copyright.gov, write the Copyright Office, or call (202) 707-3000.

*17 U.S.C. § 506(e): Any person who knowingly makes a false representation of a material fact in the application for copyright registration provided for by section 409, or in any written statement filed in connection with the application, shall be fined not more than $2,500.

Rev: July 2003—xxx Web Rev: July 2003 ♻ Printed on recycled paper U.S. Government Printing Office: 2000-461-113/20,021

Group of contributions to periodicals in a 12-month period; a single author

Copyright Office fees are subject to change. For current fees, check the Copyright Office website at *www.copyright.gov*, write the Copyright Office, or call (202) 707-3000.

Form TX
For a Nondramatic Literary Work
UNITED STATES COPYRIGHT OFFICE

REGISTRATION NUMBER

TX TXU

EFFECTIVE DATE OF REGISTRATION

Month Day Year

DO NOT WRITE ABOVE THIS LINE. IF YOU NEED MORE SPACE, USE A SEPARATE CONTINUATION SHEET.

1

TITLE OF THIS WORK ▼
See Form GR/CP attached

PREVIOUS OR ALTERNATIVE TITLES ▼

PUBLICATION AS A CONTRIBUTION If this work was published as a contribution to a periodical, serial, or collection, give information about the collective work in which the contribution appeared. Title of Collective Work ▼

If published in a periodical or serial give: Volume ▼ Number ▼ Issue Date ▼ On Pages ▼

2

a NAME OF AUTHOR ▼ Kay Hurst

DATES OF BIRTH AND DEATH Year Born ▼ 1941 Year Died ▼

Was this contribution to the work a "work made for hire"? ☐ Yes ☑ No

AUTHOR'S NATIONALITY OR DOMICILE Name of Country OR { Citizen of ▶ U.S.A. Domiciled in ▶

WAS THIS AUTHOR'S CONTRIBUTION TO THE WORK Anonymous? ☐ Yes ☑ No Pseudonymous? ☐ Yes ☑ No If the answer to either of these questions is "Yes," see detailed instructions.

NATURE OF AUTHORSHIP Briefly describe nature of material created by this author in which copyright is claimed. ▼
Entire text of short stories

NOTE

Under the law, the "author" of a "work made for hire" is generally the employer, not the employee (see instructions). For any part of this work that was "made for hire" check "Yes" in the space provided, give the employer (or other person for whom the work was prepared) as "Author" of that part, and leave the space for dates of birth and death blank.

b NAME OF AUTHOR ▼

DATES OF BIRTH AND DEATH Year Born ▼ Year Died ▼

Was this contribution to the work a "work made for hire"? ☐ Yes ☐ No

AUTHOR'S NATIONALITY OR DOMICILE Name of Country OR { Citizen of ▶ Domiciled in ▶

WAS THIS AUTHOR'S CONTRIBUTION TO THE WORK Anonymous? ☐ Yes ☐ No Pseudonymous? ☐ Yes ☐ No If the answer to either of these questions is "Yes," see detailed instructions.

NATURE OF AUTHORSHIP Briefly describe nature of material created by this author in which copyright is claimed. ▼

c NAME OF AUTHOR ▼

DATES OF BIRTH AND DEATH Year Born ▼ Year Died ▼

Was this contribution to the work a "work made for hire"? ☐ Yes ☐ No

AUTHOR'S NATIONALITY OR DOMICILE Name of Country OR { Citizen of ▶ Domiciled in ▶

WAS THIS AUTHOR'S CONTRIBUTION TO THE WORK Anonymous? ☐ Yes ☐ No Pseudonymous? ☐ Yes ☐ No If the answer to either of these questions is "Yes," see detailed instructions.

NATURE OF AUTHORSHIP Briefly describe nature of material created by this author in which copyright is claimed. ▼

3

a YEAR IN WHICH CREATION OF THIS WORK WAS COMPLETED 1998 ◀ Year This information must be given in all cases.

b DATE AND NATION OF FIRST PUBLICATION OF THIS PARTICULAR WORK Complete this information ONLY if this work has been published. Month ▶ Day ▶ Year ▶ ◀ Nation

4

COPYRIGHT CLAIMANT(S) Name and address must be given even if the claimant is the same as the author given in space 2. ▼
Kay Hurst
2400 Great Lakes Way
Detroit, MI 48219

See instructions before completing this space.

TRANSFER If the claimant(s) named here in space 4 is (are) different from the author(s) named in space 2, give a brief statement of how the claimant(s) obtained ownership of the copyright. ▼

DO NOT WRITE HERE OFFICE USE ONLY
APPLICATION RECEIVED
ONE DEPOSIT RECEIVED
TWO DEPOSITS RECEIVED
FUNDS RECEIVED

MORE ON BACK ▶ • Complete all applicable spaces (numbers 5-9) on the reverse side of this page. • See detailed instructions. • Sign the form at line 8.

DO NOT WRITE HERE

Page 1 of ______ pages

Group of contributions to periodicals in a 12-month period; a single author (continued)

EXAMINED BY — FORM TX

CHECKED BY

☐ CORRESPONDENCE Yes

FOR COPYRIGHT OFFICE USE ONLY

DO NOT WRITE ABOVE THIS LINE. IF YOU NEED MORE SPACE, USE A SEPARATE CONTINUATION SHEET.

5

PREVIOUS REGISTRATION Has registration for this work, or for an earlier version of this work, already been made in the Copyright Office?
☐ **Yes** ☑ **No** If your answer is "Yes," why is another registration being sought? (Check appropriate box.) ▼
a. ☐ This is the first published edition of a work previously registered in unpublished form.
b. ☐ This is the first application submitted by this author as copyright claimant.
c. ☐ This is a changed version of the work, as shown by space 6 on this application.
If your answer is "Yes," give: **Previous Registration Number ▶** **Year of Registration ▶**

6

DERIVATIVE WORK OR COMPILATION
a **Preexisting Material** Identify any preexisting work or works that this work is based on or incorporates. ▼

b **Material Added to This Work** Give a brief, general statement of the material that has been added to this work and in which copyright is claimed. ▼

See instructions before completing this space.

7

a **DEPOSIT ACCOUNT** If the registration fee is to be charged to a Deposit Account established in the Copyright Office, give name and number of Account.
Name ▼ **Account Number ▼**

b **CORRESPONDENCE** Give name and address to which correspondence about this application should be sent. Name/Address/Apt/City/State/ZIP ▼

Kay Hurst
2400 Great Lakes Way
Detroit, MI 48219

Area code and daytime telephone number ▶ (333) 123-4567 Fax number ▶
Email ▶

8

CERTIFICATION* I, the undersigned, hereby certify that I am the
Check only one ▶
☑ author
☐ other copyright claimant
☐ owner of exclusive right(s)
☐ authorized agent of ____________
Name of author or other copyright claimant, or owner of exclusive right(s) ▲

of the work identified in this application and that the statements made by me in this application are correct to the best of my knowledge.

Typed or printed name and date ▼ If this application gives a date of publication in space 3, do not sign and submit it before that date.

Kay Hurst **Date ▶** May 1, 1998

Handwritten signature (X) ▼

X ____ Kay Hurst ____________

9

Certificate will be mailed in window envelope to this address:

Name ▼
Kay Hurst

Number/Street/Apt ▼
2400 Great Lakes Way

City/State/ZIP ▼
Detroit, MI 48219

YOU MUST:
- Complete all necessary spaces
- Sign your application in space 8

SEND ALL 3 ELEMENTS IN THE SAME PACKAGE:
1. Application form
2. Nonrefundable filing fee in check or money order payable to *Register of Copyrights*
3. Deposit material

MAIL TO:
Library of Congress
Copyright Office - TX
101 Independence Avenue, S.E.
Washington, D.C. 20559-6222

Fees are subject to change. For current fees, check the Copyright Office website at www.copyright.gov, write the Copyright Office, or call (202) 707-3000.

*17 U.S.C. § 506(e): Any person who knowingly makes a false representation of a material fact in the application for copyright registration provided for by section 409, or in any written statement filed in connection with the application, shall be fined not more than $2,500.

Rev: July 2003—xxx Web Rev: July 2003 ♻ Printed on recycled paper U.S. Government Printing Office: 2000-461-113/20,021

Group of contributions to periodicals in a 12-month period; a single author (continued)

ADJUNCT APPLICATION
for Copyright Registration for a Group of Contributions to Periodicals

- Use this adjunct form only if you are making a single registration for a group of contributions to periodicals, and you are also filing a basic application on Form TX, Form PA, or Form VA. Follow the instructions, attached.
- Number each line in Part B consecutively. Use additional Forms GR/CP if you need more space.
- Submit this adjunct form with the basic application form. Clip (do not tape or staple) and fold all sheets together before submitting them.
- Copyright Office fees are subject to change. For current fees, check the Copyright Office website at *www.copyright.gov*, write the Copyright Office, or call (202) 707-3000.

FORM GR/CP
For a Group of Contributions to Periodicals
UNITED STATES COPYRIGHT OFFICE

REGISTRATION NUMBER

TX PA VA

EFFECTIVE DATE OF REGISTRATION

Month Day Year

FORM GR/CP RECEIVED

Page _____ of _____ pages

DO NOT WRITE ABOVE THIS LINE. FOR COPYRIGHT OFFICE USE ONLY

A Identification of Application

IDENTIFICATION OF BASIC APPLICATION:
• This application for copyright registration for a group of contributions to periodicals is submitted as an adjunct to an application filed on: (Check which)

☑ Form TX ☐ Form PA ☐ Form VA

IDENTIFICATION OF AUTHOR AND CLAIMANT: (Give the name of the author and the name of the copyright claimant in all of the contributions listed in Part B of this form. The names should be the same as the names given in spaces 2 and 4 of the basic application.)

Name of Author Kay Hurst

Name of Copyright Claimant Kay Hurst

B Registration for Group of Contributions

COPYRIGHT REGISTRATION FOR A GROUP OF CONTRIBUTIONS TO PERIODICALS: (To make a single registration for a group of works by the same individual author, all first published as contributions to periodicals within a 12-month period (see instructions), give full information about each contribution. If more space is needed, use additional Forms GR/CP.)

1. Title of Contribution The Green-Nosed Killer
   Title of Periodical Mysteries Unlimited Vol. 11 No. 6 Issue Date 6/97 Pages 18-34
   Date of First Publication June (Month) 15 (Day) 2000 (Year) Nation of First Publication U.S.A. (Country)

2. Title of Contribution The Red-Nosed Killer
   Title of Periodical Mysteries Unlimited Vol. 11 No. 8 Issue Date 8/97 Pages 3-28
   Date of First Publication June (Month) 15 (Day) 2000 (Year) Nation of First Publication U.S.A. (Country)

3. Title of Contribution The Black-Nosed Killer
   Title of Periodical Mysteries Digest Vol. 81 No. 8 Issue Date 1/98 Pages 94-116
   Date of First Publication January (Month) 15 (Day) 1998 (Year) Nation of First Publication U.S.A. (Country)

4. Title of Contribution The Noseless Killer
   Title of Periodical Mysteries Magazine Vol. 28 No. 4 Issue Date 4/98 Pages 80-101
   Date of First Publication April (Month) 1 (Day) 1998 (Year) Nation of First Publication U.S.A. (Country)

☐ Title of Contribution ____
Title of Periodical ____ Vol.___ No.___ Issue Date ____ Pages ____
Date of First Publication ____ (Month) (Day) (Year) Nation of First Publication ____ (Country)

☐ Title of Contribution ____
Title of Periodical ____ Vol.___ No.___ Issue Date ____ Pages ____
Date of First Publication ____ (Month) (Day) (Year) Nation of First Publication ____ (Country)

☐ Title of Contribution ____
Title of Periodical ____ Vol.___ No.___ Issue Date ____ Pages ____
Date of First Publication ____ (Month) (Day) (Year) Nation of First Publication ____ (Country)

Group of contributions to periodicals in a 12-month period; a single author (continued)

FORM GR/CP

DO NOT WRITE ABOVE THIS LINE. FOR COPYRIGHT OFFICE USE ONLY.

B Continued

☐ Title of Contribution ______
Title of Periodical ______ Vol.___ No.___ Issue Date ___ Pages ___
Date of First Publication ______ (Month) (Day) (Year) Nation of First Publication ______ (Country)

☐ Title of Contribution ______
Title of Periodical ______ Vol.___ No.___ Issue Date ___ Pages ___
Date of First Publication ______ (Month) (Day) (Year) Nation of First Publication ______ (Country)

☐ Title of Contribution ______
Title of Periodical ______ Vol.___ No.___ Issue Date ___ Pages ___
Date of First Publication ______ (Month) (Day) (Year) Nation of First Publication ______ (Country)

☐ Title of Contribution ______
Title of Periodical ______ Vol.___ No.___ Issue Date ___ Pages ___
Date of First Publication ______ (Month) (Day) (Year) Nation of First Publication ______ (Country)

☐ Title of Contribution ______
Title of Periodical ______ Vol.___ No.___ Issue Date ___ Pages ___
Date of First Publication ______ (Month) (Day) (Year) Nation of First Publication ______ (Country)

☐ Title of Contribution ______
Title of Periodical ______ Vol.___ No.___ Issue Date ___ Pages ___
Date of First Publication ______ (Month) (Day) (Year) Nation of First Publication ______ (Country)

☐ Title of Contribution ______
Title of Periodical ______ Vol.___ No.___ Issue Date ___ Pages ___
Date of First Publication ______ (Month) (Day) (Year) Nation of First Publication ______ (Country)

☐ Title of Contribution ______
Title of Periodical ______ Vol.___ No.___ Issue Date ___ Pages ___
Date of First Publication ______ (Month) (Day) (Year) Nation of First Publication ______ (Country)

☐ Title of Contribution ______
Title of Periodical ______ Vol.___ No.___ Issue Date ___ Pages ___
Date of First Publication ______ (Month) (Day) (Year) Nation of First Publication ______ (Country)

☐ Title of Contribution ______
Title of Periodical ______ Vol.___ No.___ Issue Date ___ Pages ___
Date of First Publication ______ (Month) (Day) (Year) Nation of First Publication ______ (Country)

☐ Title of Contribution ______
Title of Periodical ______ Vol.___ No.___ Issue Date ___ Pages ___
Date of First Publication ______ (Month) (Day) (Year) Nation of First Publication ______ (Country)

☐ Title of Contribution ______
Title of Periodical ______ Vol.___ No.___ Issue Date ___ Pages ___
Date of First Publication ______ (Month) (Day) (Year) Nation of First Publication ______ (Country)

Rev: June 2002—20,000 Web Rev: June 2002 Printed on recycled paper U.S. Government Printing Office: 2000-461-113/20,021

Original screenplay by a single author

Copyright Office fees are subject to change. For current fees, check the Copyright Office website at *www.copyright.gov*, write the Copyright Office, or call (202) 707-3000.

FORM PA
For a Work of the Performing Arts
UNITED STATES COPYRIGHT OFFICE

REGISTRATION NUMBER

PA PAU

EFFECTIVE DATE OF REGISTRATION

Month Day Year

DO NOT WRITE ABOVE THIS LINE. IF YOU NEED MORE SPACE, USE A SEPARATE CONTINUATION SHEET.

1

TITLE OF THIS WORK ▼
And Then You Die

PREVIOUS OR ALTERNATIVE TITLES ▼

NATURE OF THIS WORK ▼ See instructions
Screenplay

2

a **NAME OF AUTHOR ▼** David Griffith
DATES OF BIRTH AND DEATH Year Born ▼ 1935 Year Died ▼

Was this contribution to the work a "work made for hire"? ☐ Yes ☑ No
AUTHOR'S NATIONALITY OR DOMICILE Name of Country: OR { Citizen of U.S.A. / Domiciled in
WAS THIS AUTHOR'S CONTRIBUTION TO THE WORK Anonymous? ☐ Yes ☑ No Pseudonymous? ☐ Yes ☑ No — If the answer to either of these questions is "Yes," see detailed instructions.

NATURE OF AUTHORSHIP Briefly describe nature of material created by this author in which copyright is claimed. ▼
Entire text

NOTE
Under the law, the "author" of a "work made for hire" is generally the employer, not the employee (see instructions). For any part of this work that was "made for hire" check "Yes" in the space provided, give the employer (or other person for whom the work was prepared) as "Author" of that part, and leave the space for dates of birth and death blank.

b **NAME OF AUTHOR ▼**
DATES OF BIRTH AND DEATH Year Born ▼ Year Died ▼

Was this contribution to the work a "work made for hire"? ☐ Yes ☐ No
AUTHOR'S NATIONALITY OR DOMICILE Name of Country: OR { Citizen of / Domiciled in
WAS THIS AUTHOR'S CONTRIBUTION TO THE WORK Anonymous? ☐ Yes ☐ No Pseudonymous? ☐ Yes ☐ No — If the answer to either of these questions is "Yes," see detailed instructions.

NATURE OF AUTHORSHIP Briefly describe nature of material created by this author in which copyright is claimed. ▼

c **NAME OF AUTHOR ▼**
DATES OF BIRTH AND DEATH Year Born ▼ Year Died ▼

Was this contribution to the work a "work made for hire"? ☐ Yes ☐ No
AUTHOR'S NATIONALITY OR DOMICILE Name of Country: OR { Citizen of / Domiciled in
WAS THIS AUTHOR'S CONTRIBUTION TO THE WORK Anonymous? ☐ Yes ☐ No Pseudonymous? ☐ Yes ☐ No — If the answer to either of these questions is "Yes," see detailed instructions.

NATURE OF AUTHORSHIP Briefly describe nature of material created by this author in which copyright is claimed. ▼

3

a **YEAR IN WHICH CREATION OF THIS WORK WAS COMPLETED** 2000 Year — **This information must be given in all cases.**

b **DATE AND NATION OF FIRST PUBLICATION OF THIS PARTICULAR WORK** — **Complete this information ONLY if this work has been published.** Month Day Year Nation

4

COPYRIGHT CLAIMANT(S) Name and address must be given even if the claimant is the same as the author given in space 2. ▼
David Griffith
666 Hollywood Blvd.
Hollywood, CA 90000

See instructions before completing this space.

TRANSFER If the claimant(s) named here in space 4 is (are) different from the author(s) named in space 2, give a brief statement of how the claimant(s) obtained ownership of the copyright. ▼

DO NOT WRITE HERE / OFFICE USE ONLY:
APPLICATION RECEIVED
ONE DEPOSIT RECEIVED
TWO DEPOSITS RECEIVED
FUNDS RECEIVED

MORE ON BACK ▶ • Complete all applicable spaces (numbers 5-9) on the reverse side of this page. • See detailed instructions. • Sign the form at line 8.

DO NOT WRITE HERE
Page 1 of pages

Original screenplay by a single author (continued)

EXAMINED BY — FORM PA

CHECKED BY

☐ CORRESPONDENCE Yes

FOR COPYRIGHT OFFICE USE ONLY

DO NOT WRITE ABOVE THIS LINE. IF YOU NEED MORE SPACE, USE A SEPARATE CONTINUATION SHEET.

5

PREVIOUS REGISTRATION Has registration for this work, or for an earlier version of this work, already been made in the Copyright Office?

☐ **Yes** ☑ **No** If your answer is "Yes," why is another registration being sought? (Check appropriate box.) ▼ If your answer is No, do **not** check box A, B, or C.

a. ☐ This is the first published edition of a work previously registered in unpublished form.

b. ☐ This is the first application submitted by this author as copyright claimant.

c. ☐ This is a changed version of the work, as shown by space 6 on this application.

If your answer is "Yes," give: **Previous Registration Number** ▼ **Year of Registration** ▼

6

a **DERIVATIVE WORK OR COMPILATION** Complete both space 6a and 6b for a derivative work; complete only 6b for a compilation.
Preexisting Material Identify any preexisting work or works that this work is based on or incorporates. ▼

See instructions before completing this space.

b **Material Added to This Work** Give a brief, general statement of the material that has been added to this work and in which copyright is claimed. ▼

7

a **DEPOSIT ACCOUNT** If the registration fee is to be charged to a Deposit Account established in the Copyright Office, give name and number of Account.
Name ▼ **Account Number** ▼

b **CORRESPONDENCE** Give name and address to which correspondence about this application should be sent. Name/Address/Apt/City/State/ZIP ▼

David Griffith
666 Hollywood Blvd.
Hollywood, CA 90000

Area code and daytime telephone number (213) 666-6666 Fax number ( )

Email dave@nation.com

8

CERTIFICATION* I, the undersigned, hereby certify that I am the

Check only one ▶
- ☐ author
- ☐ other copyright claimant
- ☐ owner of exclusive right(s)
- ☐ authorized agent of ______

Name of author or other copyright claimant, or owner of exclusive right(s) ▲

of the work identified in this application and that the statements made by me in this application are correct to the best of my knowledge.

Typed or printed name and date ▼ If this application gives a date of publication in space 3, do not sign and submit it before that date.

David Griffith **Date** May 1, 2000

Handwritten signature (X) ▼

x *David Griffith*

9

Certificate will be mailed in window envelope to this address:

Name ▼	David Griffith
Number/Street/Apt ▼	666 Hollywood Blvd.
City/State/ZIP ▼	Hollywood, CA 90000

YOU MUST:
- Complete all necessary spaces
- Sign your application in space 8

SEND ALL 3 ELEMENTS IN THE SAME PACKAGE:
1. Application form
2. Nonrefundable filing fee in check or money order payable to *Register of Copyrights*
3. Deposit material

MAIL TO:
Library of Congress
Copyright Office
101 Independence Avenue, S.E.
Washington, D.C. 20559-6000

Fees are subject to change. For current fees, check the Copyright Office website at www.copyright.gov, write the Copyright Office, or call (202) 707-3000.

*17 U.S.C. § 506(e): Any person who knowingly makes a false representation of a material fact in the application for copyright registration provided for by section 409, or in any written statement filed in connection with the application, shall be fined not more than $2,500.

Rev: June 2002—20,000 Web Rev: June 2002 ♲ Printed on recycled paper U.S. Government Printing Office: 2000-461-113/20,021

Unpublished song lyric; single author

Copyright Office fees are subject to change. For current fees, check the Copyright Office website at *www.copyright.gov*, write the Copyright Office, or call (202) 707-3000.

FORM PA
For a Work of the Performing Arts
UNITED STATES COPYRIGHT OFFICE

REGISTRATION NUMBER

PA PAU

EFFECTIVE DATE OF REGISTRATION

Month Day Year

DO NOT WRITE ABOVE THIS LINE. IF YOU NEED MORE SPACE, USE A SEPARATE CONTINUATION SHEET.

1

TITLE OF THIS WORK ▼
Why Did You Tell Me You Loved Me When You Really Loved My Pick-up

PREVIOUS OR ALTERNATIVE TITLES ▼
Shoo-Be-Do-Be-Doo

NATURE OF THIS WORK ▼ See instructions
Song lyric

2

a NAME OF AUTHOR ▼
Hank Hutchins, Jr.

DATES OF BIRTH AND DEATH
Year Born ▼ 1945 Year Died ▼

Was this contribution to the work a "work made for hire"? ☐ Yes ☑ No

AUTHOR'S NATIONALITY OR DOMICILE
Name of Country
OR { Citizen of U.S.A. / Domiciled in

WAS THIS AUTHOR'S CONTRIBUTION TO THE WORK
Anonymous? ☐ Yes ☑ No
Pseudonymous? ☐ Yes ☑ No
If the answer to either of these questions is "Yes," see detailed instructions.

NATURE OF AUTHORSHIP Briefly describe nature of material created by this author in which copyright is claimed. ▼
Words

b NAME OF AUTHOR ▼

DATES OF BIRTH AND DEATH
Year Born ▼ Year Died ▼

Was this contribution to the work a "work made for hire"? ☐ Yes ☐ No

AUTHOR'S NATIONALITY OR DOMICILE
Name of Country
OR { Citizen of / Domiciled in

WAS THIS AUTHOR'S CONTRIBUTION TO THE WORK
Anonymous? ☐ Yes ☐ No
Pseudonymous? ☐ Yes ☐ No
If the answer to either of these questions is "Yes," see detailed instructions.

NATURE OF AUTHORSHIP Briefly describe nature of material created by this author in which copyright is claimed. ▼

c NAME OF AUTHOR ▼

DATES OF BIRTH AND DEATH
Year Born ▼ Year Died ▼

Was this contribution to the work a "work made for hire"? ☐ Yes ☐ No

AUTHOR'S NATIONALITY OR DOMICILE
Name of Country
OR { Citizen of / Domiciled in

WAS THIS AUTHOR'S CONTRIBUTION TO THE WORK
Anonymous? ☐ Yes ☐ No
Pseudonymous? ☐ Yes ☐ No
If the answer to either of these questions is "Yes," see detailed instructions.

NATURE OF AUTHORSHIP Briefly describe nature of material created by this author in which copyright is claimed. ▼

NOTE
Under the law, the "author" of a "work made for hire" is generally the employer, not the employee (see instructions). For any part of this work that was "made for hire" check "Yes" in the space provided, give the employer (or other person for whom the work was prepared) as "Author" of that part, and leave the space for dates of birth and death blank.

3

a YEAR IN WHICH CREATION OF THIS WORK WAS COMPLETED This information must be given in all cases.
2000 Year

b DATE AND NATION OF FIRST PUBLICATION OF THIS PARTICULAR WORK
Complete this information ONLY if this work has been published.
Month Day Year
Nation

4

COPYRIGHT CLAIMANT(S) Name and address must be given even if the claimant is the same as the author given in space 2. ▼
Hank Hutchins, Jr.
1000 Country Road
Graceland, TN 20000

See instructions before completing this space.

TRANSFER If the claimant(s) named here in space 4 is (are) different from the author(s) named in space 2, give a brief statement of how the claimant(s) obtained ownership of the copyright. ▼

DO NOT WRITE HERE / OFFICE USE ONLY
APPLICATION RECEIVED
ONE DEPOSIT RECEIVED
TWO DEPOSITS RECEIVED
FUNDS RECEIVED

MORE ON BACK ▶ • Complete all applicable spaces (numbers 5-9) on the reverse side of this page.
• See detailed instructions. • Sign the form at line 8.

DO NOT WRITE HERE
Page 1 of pages

Unpublished song lyric; single author (continued)

EXAMINED BY

FORM PA

CHECKED BY

☐ CORRESPONDENCE Yes

FOR COPYRIGHT OFFICE USE ONLY

DO NOT WRITE ABOVE THIS LINE. IF YOU NEED MORE SPACE, USE A SEPARATE CONTINUATION SHEET.

5

PREVIOUS REGISTRATION Has registration for this work, or for an earlier version of this work, already been made in the Copyright Office?

☐ Yes ✓No If your answer is "Yes," why is another registration being sought? (Check appropriate box.) ▼ If your answer is No, do **not** check box A, B, or C.

a. ☐ This is the first published edition of a work previously registered in unpublished form.

b. ☐ This is the first application submitted by this author as copyright claimant.

c. ☐ This is a changed version of the work, as shown by space 6 on this application.

If your answer is "Yes," give: **Previous Registration Number ▼** **Year of Registration ▼**

6

a **DERIVATIVE WORK OR COMPILATION** Complete both space 6a and 6b for a derivative work; complete only 6b for a compilation.
Preexisting Material Identify any preexisting work or works that this work is based on or incorporates. ▼

See instructions before completing this space.

b **Material Added to This Work** Give a brief, general statement of the material that has been added to this work and in which copyright is claimed. ▼

7

a **DEPOSIT ACCOUNT** If the registration fee is to be charged to a Deposit Account established in the Copyright Office, give name and number of Account.
Name ▼ **Account Number ▼**

b **CORRESPONDENCE** Give name and address to which correspondence about this application should be sent. Name/Address/Apt/City/State/ZIP ▼

Hank Hutchins, Jr.
1000 Country Road
Graceland, TN 20000

Area code and daytime telephone number (444) 444-4444 Fax number ( )

Email hank@elvis.com

8

CERTIFICATION* I, the undersigned, hereby certify that I am the

Check only one ▶
- ✓ author
- ☐ other copyright claimant
- ☐ owner of exclusive right(s)
- ☐ authorized agent of ____________
  Name of author or other copyright claimant, or owner of exclusive right(s) ▲

of the work identified in this application and that the statements made by me in this application are correct to the best of my knowledge.

Typed or printed name and date ▼ If this application gives a date of publication in space 3, do not sign and submit it before that date.

Hank Hutchins, Jr. **Date** Sept. 1, 2000

Handwritten signature (X) ▼

x *Hank Hutchins, Jr.*

9

Certificate will be mailed in window envelope to this address:

Name ▼
Hank Hutchins, Jr.

Number/Street/Apt ▼
1000 Country Road

City/State/ZIP ▼
Graceland, TN 20000

YOU MUST:
- Complete all necessary spaces
- Sign your application in space 8

SEND ALL 3 ELEMENTS IN THE SAME PACKAGE:
1. Application form
2. Nonrefundable filing fee in check or money order payable to *Register of Copyrights*
3. Deposit material

MAIL TO:
Library of Congress
Copyright Office
101 Independence Avenue, S.E.
Washington, D.C. 20559-6000

Fees are subject to change. For current fees, check the Copyright Office website at www.copyright.gov, write the Copyright Office, or call (202) 707-3000.

*17 U.S.C. § 506(e): Any person who knowingly makes a false representation of a material fact in the application for copyright registration provided for by section 409, or in any written statement filed in connection with the application, shall be fined not more than $2,500.

Rev: June 2002—20,000 Web Rev: June 2002 ♻ Printed on recycled paper U.S. Government Printing Office: 2000-461-113/20,021

Three monthly issues of a monthly magazine registered as a group on Form SE/Group

Copyright Office fees are subject to change. For current fees, check the Copyright Office website at *www.copyright.gov*, write the Copyright Office, or call (202) 707-3000.

FORM SE/Group
UNITED STATES COPYRIGHT OFFICE

REGISTRATION NUMBER

EFFECTIVE DATE OF REGISTRATION

APPLICATION RECEIVED

ONE DEPOSIT RECEIVED

EXAMINED BY CORRESPONDENCE ☐

DO NOT WRITE ABOVE THIS LINE.

1

TITLE ▼ ISSN▼

The Toxic Waste Tipster

List in order of publication

No previous registration under **identical title** ☐

	Volume▼	Number▼	Issue date on copies▼	Month, day, and year of publication ▼
1.	VIII	1	January 2000	January 4, 2000
2.	VIII	2	February 2000	February 3, 2000
3.	VIII	3	March 2000	March 2, 2000
4.				
5.				
6.				
7.				
8.				
9.				
10.				
11.				
12.				
13.				
14.				

2

NAME AND ADDRESS OF THE AUTHOR/COPYRIGHT CLAIMANT IN THESE COLLECTIVE WORKS MADE FOR HIRE ▼

Toxic Waste Interment & Transport, Inc.
P.O. Box P-U
New York, NY 10012

FOR NON-U.S. WORKS: Author's citizenship ▼ Domicile ▼ Nation of publication ▼

CERTIFICATION*: I, the undersigned, hereby certify that I am the copyright claimant or the authorized agent of the copyright claimant of the works identified in this application, that all the conditions specified in the instructions on the back of this form are met, that I have deposited two complimentary subscription copies with the Library of Congress, and that the statements made by me in this application are correct to the best of my knowledge.

Handwritten signature (X) *John Durtt* Typed or printed name John Durtt

PERSON TO CONTACT FOR CORRESPONDENCE ABOUT THIS CLAIM

Name John Durtt Daytime telephone (212) 123-4567

Address (if other than given below)

Fax Email john@dirt.com

Certificate will be mailed in window envelope to this address:

Name▼ Toxic Waste Interment & Transport, Inc.

Number/Street/Apt ▼ P.O. Box P-U

City/State/ZIP▼ New York, NY 10012

DEPOSIT ACCOUNT

Account number

Name of account

MAIL TO:
Library of Congress
Copyright Office
101 Independence Avenue, S.E.
Washington, D.C. 20559-6000

*17 U.S.C. §506(e): Any person who knowingly makes a false representation of a material fact in the application for copyright registration provided for by section 409, or in any written statement filed in connection with the application, shall be fined not more than $2,500.

Rev: June 2002—20,000 Web Rev: June 2002 Printed on recycled paper U.S. Government Printing Office: 2000-461-113/20,021

Single magazine issue

Copyright Office fees are subject to change. For current fees, check the Copyright Office website at *www.copyright.gov*, write the Copyright Office, or call (202) 707-3000.

Short Form SE
For a Serial
UNITED STATES COPYRIGHT OFFICE

Registration Number

Effective Date of Registration

Examined By

Application Received

Correspondence ☐

Deposit Received
One | Two

Fee Received

DO NOT WRITE ABOVE THIS LINE.

1 TITLE OF THIS SERIAL AS IT APPEARS ON THE COPY

The Toxic Waste Tipster

Volume▼	Number▼	Date on copies▼	ISSN▼
VIII	12	December 2000	1234678

2 NAME AND ADDRESS OF THE AUTHOR AND COPYRIGHT CLAIMANT IN THIS COLLECTIVE WORK MADE FOR HIRE

Toxic Waste Interment & Transport, Inc.
P.O. Box P-U
New York, NY 10012

3 DATE OF PUBLICATION OF THIS PARTICULAR ISSUE

Month ▼	Day ▼	Year ▼
January	2	1998

YEARINWHICHCREATIONOF THISISSUEWASCOMPLETED (IF EARLIERTHANTHEYEAROF PUBLICATION):
Year ▶ 2000

CERTIFICATION*: I, the undersigned, hereby certify that I am the copyright claimant or the authorized agent of the copyright claimant of the work identified in this application, that all the conditions specified in the instructions on the back of this form are met, that the statements made by me in this application are correct to the best of my knowledge.

Handwritten signature (X) John Durtt

Typed or printed name of signer John Durtt

PERSON TO CONTACT FOR CORRESPONDENCE ABOUT THIS CLAIM

Name ▶ John Durtt
Address (if other than given below) ▶
Daytime phone ▶ (212) 123-4567
Fax ▶ ( )
Email ▶ john@dirt.com

DEPOSIT ACCOUNT

Account number ▶
Name of account ▶

Certificate will be mailed in window envelope to this address:

Name▼
Toxic Waste Interment & Transport, Inc.
Number/Street/Apt ▼
P.O. Box P-U
City/State/ZIP▼
New York, NY 10012

YOU MUST:
- Complete all necessary spaces
- Sign your application

SEND ALL 3 ELEMENTS IN THE SAME PACKAGE:
1. Application form
2. Nonrefundable $30 filing fee in check or money order payable to *Register of Copyrights*
3. Deposit material

MAIL TO:
Library of Congress
Copyright Office
101 Independence Avenue, S.E.
Washington, D.C. 20559-6000

Fees are subject to change. For current fees, check the Copyright Office website at www.copyright.gov, write the Copyright Office, or call (202) 707-3000.

*17 U.S.C. §506(e): Any person who knowingly makes a false representation of a material fact in the application for copyright registration provided for by section 409, or in any written statement filed in connection with the application, shall be fined not more than $2,500.

Rev: June 2002—20,000 Web Rev: June 2002 Printed on recycled paper

U.S. Government Printing Office: 2000-461-113/20,021

Single issue of a magazine published three times a year; single author; not a work made for hire

Copyright Office fees are subject to change. For current fees, check the Copyright Office website at *www.copyright.gov*, write the Copyright Office, or call (202) 707-3000.

FORM SE
For a Serial
UNITED STATES COPYRIGHT OFFICE

REGISTRATION NUMBER

U

EFFECTIVE DATE OF REGISTRATION

Month Day Year

DO NOT WRITE ABOVE THIS LINE. IF YOU NEED MORE SPACE, USE A SEPARATE CONTINUATION SHEET.

1 TITLE OF THIS SERIAL ▼
Urine Analysis: The Urologist's Journal

Volume ▼	Number ▼	Date on Copies ▼	Frequency of Publication ▼
17	2	May 2000	3 times per year

PREVIOUS OR ALTERNATIVE TITLES ▼

2 **a** NAME OF AUTHOR ▼ Dr. Lou Brown
DATES OF BIRTH AND DEATH Year Born ▼ 1935 Year Died ▼

Was this contribution to the work a "work made for hire"? ☐ Yes ☑ No
AUTHOR'S NATIONALITY OR DOMICILE Name of Country OR { Citizen of ▶ U.S.A. / Domiciled in ▶ }
WAS THIS AUTHOR'S CONTRIBUTION TO THE WORK Anonymous? ☐ Yes ☑ No Pseudonymous? ☐ Yes ☑ No If the answer to either of these questions is "Yes," see detailed instructions.

NATURE OF AUTHORSHIP Briefly describe nature of material created by this author in which copyright is claimed. ▼ ☐ Collective Work Other: Entire text

NOTE
Under the law, the "author" of a "work made for hire" is generally the employer, not the employee (see instructions). For any part of this work that was "made for hire" check "Yes" in the space provided, give the employer (or other person for whom the work was prepared) as "Author" of that part, and leave the space for dates of birth and death blank.

b NAME OF AUTHOR ▼
DATES OF BIRTH AND DEATH Year Born ▼ Year Died ▼

Was this contribution to the work a "work made for hire"? ☐ Yes ☐ No
AUTHOR'S NATIONALITY OR DOMICILE Name of Country OR { Citizen of ▶ / Domiciled in ▶ }
WAS THIS AUTHOR'S CONTRIBUTION TO THE WORK Anonymous? ☐ Yes ☐ No Pseudonymous? ☐ Yes ☐ No If the answer to either of these questions is "Yes," see detailed instructions.

NATURE OF AUTHORSHIP Briefly describe nature of material created by this author in which copyright is claimed. ▼ ☐ Collective Work Other:

c NAME OF AUTHOR ▼
DATES OF BIRTH AND DEATH Year Born ▼ Year Died ▼

Was this contribution to the work a "work made for hire"? ☐ Yes ☐ No
AUTHOR'S NATIONALITY OR DOMICILE Name of Country OR { Citizen of ▶ / Domiciled in ▶ }
WAS THIS AUTHOR'S CONTRIBUTION TO THE WORK Anonymous? ☐ Yes ☐ No Pseudonymous? ☐ Yes ☐ No If the answer to either of these questions is "Yes," see detailed instructions.

NATURE OF AUTHORSHIP Briefly describe nature of material created by this author in which copyright is claimed. ▼ ☐ Collective Work Other:

3 **a** YEAR IN WHICH CREATION OF THIS ISSUE WAS COMPLETED 2000 ◀ Year This information must be given in all cases.
b DATE AND NATION OF FIRST PUBLICATION OF THIS PARTICULAR ISSUE Complete this information ONLY if this work has been published. Month ▶ May Day ▶ 1 Year ▶ 2000
U.S.A. ◀ Nation

4 COPYRIGHT CLAIMANT(S) Name and address must be given even if the claimant is the same as the author given in space 2. ▼
Dr. Lou Brown
123 Colonic Highway
Runnymeade, VA 40000

See instructions before completing this space.

TRANSFER If the claimant(s) named here in space 4 is (are) different from the author(s) named in space 2, give a brief statement of how the claimant(s) obtained ownership of the copyright. ▼

DO NOT WRITE HERE OFFICE USE ONLY
APPLICATION RECEIVED
ONE DEPOSIT RECEIVED
TWO DEPOSITS RECEIVED
REMITTANCE NUMBER AND DATE

MORE ON BACK ▶ • Complete all applicable spaces (numbers 5-11) on the reverse side of this page. • See detailed instructions. • Sign the form at line 10.

DO NOT WRITE HERE

Page 1 of _____ pages

Single issue of a magazine published three times a year; single author; not a work made for hire (continued)

EXAMINED BY — FORM SE

CHECKED BY

☐ CORRESPONDENCE Yes

FOR COPYRIGHT OFFICE USE ONLY

DO NOT WRITE ABOVE THIS LINE. IF YOU NEED MORE SPACE, USE A SEPARATE CONTINUATION SHEET.

5

PREVIOUS REGISTRATION Has registration for this work, or for an earlier version of this work, already been made in the Copyright Office?
☐ Yes ☑ No If your answer is "Yes," why is another registration being sought? (Check appropriate box.) ▼
a. ☐ This is the first published edition of a work previously registered in unpublished form.
b. ☐ This is the first application submitted by this author as copyright claimant.
c. ☐ This is a changed version of the work, as shown by space 6 on this application.
If your answer is "Yes," give: **Previous Registration Number** ▼ **Year of Registration** ▼

6 See instructions before completing this space.

DERIVATIVE WORK OR COMPILATION Complete both space 6a and 6b for a derivative work; complete only 6b for a compilation.
a **Preexisting Material** Identify any preexisting work or works that this work is based on or incorporates. ▼

b **Material Added to This Work** Give a brief, general statement of the material that has been added to this work and in which copyright is claimed. ▼

7

DEPOSIT ACCOUNT If the registration fee is to be charged to a Deposit Account established in the Copyright Office, give name and number of Account.
a **Name** ▼ **Account Number** ▼

b **CORRESPONDENCE** Give name and address to which correspondence about this application should be sent. Name/Address/Apt/City/State/ZIP ▼

Dr. Lou Brown
123 Colonic Highway
Runnymeade, VA 40000

Area code and daytime telephone number ▶ (804) 123-4567 Fax number ▶
Email ▶

8

CERTIFICATION* I, the undersigned, hereby certify that I am the
Check only one ▶
☑ author
☐ other copyright claimant
☐ owner of exclusive right(s)
☐ authorized agent of ______
Name of author or other copyright claimant, or owner of exclusive right(s) ▲

of the work identified in this application and that the statements made by me in this application are correct to the best of my knowledge.

Typed or printed name and date ▼ If this application gives a date of publication in space 3, do not sign and submit it before that date.
Dr. Lou Brown **Date** ▶ July 1, 2000

Handwritten signature (X) ▼
X Lou Brown

9

Certificate will be mailed in window envelope to this address:

Name ▼
Dr. Lou Brown
Number/Street/Apt ▼
123 Colonic Highway
City/State/ZIP ▼
Runnymeade, VA 40000

YOU MUST:
- Complete all necessary spaces
- Sign your application in space 8

SEND ALL 3 ELEMENTS IN THE SAME PACKAGE:
1. Application form
2. Nonrefundable filing fee in check or money order payable to *Register of Copyrights*
3. Deposit material

MAIL TO:
Library of Congress
Copyright Office
101 Independence Avenue, S.E.
Washington, D.C. 20559-6000

Fees are subject to change. For current fees, check the Copyright Office website at www.copyright.gov, write the Copyright Office, or call (202) 707-3000.

*17 U.S.C. § 506(e): Any person who knowingly makes a false representation of a material fact in the application for copyright registration provided for by section 409, or in any written statement filed in connection with the application, shall be fined not more than $2,500.

Rev: June 2002—20,000 Web Rev: June 2002 Printed on recycled paper U.S. Government Printing Office: 2000-461-113/20,021

APPENDIX

B How to Use the CD-ROM

Forms discussed in this book are included on a CD-ROM in the back of the book. This CD-ROM, which can be used with Windows computers, installs files that you use with software programs that are already installed on your computer. It is *not* a stand-alone software program. Please read this appendix and the README.TXT file included on the CD-ROM for instructions on using the Forms CD.

Note to Mac users: This CD-ROM and its files should also work on Macintosh computers. Please note, however, that Nolo cannot provide technical support for non-Windows users.

How to View the README File

If you do not know how to view the file README.TXT, insert the Forms CD-ROM into your computer's CD-ROM drive and follow these instructions:

- Windows 98, 2000, Me, and XP: (1) On your PC's desktop, double click the My Computer icon; (2) double click the icon for the CD-ROM drive into which the Forms CD-ROM was inserted; (3) double click the file README.TXT.
- Macintosh: (1) On your Mac desktop, double click the icon for the CD-ROM that you inserted; (2) double click on the file README.TXT.

While the README file is open, print it out by using the Print command in the File menu.

Two different kinds of forms are contained on the CD-ROM:

- Word processing (RTF) forms that you can open, complete, print, and save with your word processing program, and
- Forms from the United States Copyright Office (PDF) that can be viewed only with Adobe Acrobat Reader 4.0 or higher (see below). Some of these forms have "fill-in" text fields and can be completed using your computer. You will not, however, be able to save the completed forms with the filled-in data. PDF forms without fill-in text fields must be printed out and filled in by hand or with a typewriter.

At the end of this appendix you will find a list of forms, their file names, and file formats.

Installing the Form Files Onto Your Computer

Before you can do anything with the files on the CD-ROM, you need to install them onto your hard disk. In accordance with U.S. copyright laws, remember that copies of the CD-ROM and its files are for your personal use only.

Insert the Forms CD and do the following:

Windows 98, 2000, Me, and XP Users

Follow the instructions that appear on the screen. (If nothing happens when you insert the Forms CD-ROM, then (1) double click the My Computer icon; (2) double click the icon for the CD-ROM drive into which the Forms CD-ROM was inserted; and (3) double click the file WELCOME.EXE.)

By default, all the files are installed to the \Copyright Forms folder in the \Program Files folder of your computer. A folder called "Copyright Forms" is added to the "Programs" folder of the Start menu.

Macintosh Users

Step 1: If the "Copyright Handbook CD" window is not open, open it by double clicking the "Copyright Handbook CD" icon.

Step 2: Select the "Copyright Forms" folder icon.

Step 3: Drag and drop the folder icon onto the icon of your hard disk.

Using the Word Processing Files to Create Documents

This section concerns the files for forms that can be opened and edited with your word processing program.

All word processing forms come in rich text format. These files have the extension ".RTF." For example, the form for the Copyright Assignment discussed in Chapter 8 is on the file Assignment.rtf. All forms, their file names, and file formats are listed at the end of this appendix.

RTF files can be read by most recent word processing programs including all versions of MS Word for Windows and Macintosh, WordPad for Windows, and recent versions of WordPerfect for Windows and Macintosh.

To use a form from the CD to create your documents you must: (1) open a file in your word processor or text editor; (2) edit the form by filling in the required information; (3) print it out; and (4) rename and save your revised file.

The following are general instructions. However, each word processor uses different commands to open, format, save, and print documents. Please read your word processor's manual for specific instructions on performing these tasks.

Do not call Nolo's technical support if you have questions on how to use your word processor.

Step 1: Opening a File

There are three ways to open the word processing files included on the CD-ROM after you have installed them onto your computer.

- Windows users can open a file by selecting its "shortcut" as follows: (1) Click the Windows "Start" button; (2) open the "Programs" folder; (3) open the "Copyright Forms" subfolder; (4) open the "RTF" subfolder; and (5) click on the shortcut to the form you want to work with.
- Both Windows and Macintosh users can open a file directly by double clicking on it. Use My Computer or Windows Explorer (Windows 98, 2000, Me, or XP) or the Finder (Macintosh) to go to the folder you installed or copied the CD-ROM's files to. Then, double click on the specific file you want to open.

- You can also open a file from within your word processor. To do this, you must first start your word processor. Then, go to the File menu and choose the Open command. This opens a dialog box where you will tell the program (1) the type of file you want to open (*.RTF); and (2) the location and name of the file (you will need to navigate through the directory tree to get to the folder on your hard disk where the CD's files have been installed). If these directions are unclear you will need to look through the manual for your word processing program—Nolo's technical support department will *not* be able to help you with the use of your word processing program.

Where Are the Files Installed?

Windows Users: RTF files are installed by default to a folder named \Copyright Forms\RTF in the \Program Files folder of your computer.

Macintosh Users: RTF files are located in the "RTF" folder within the "Copyright Forms" folder.

Step 2: Editing Your Document

Fill in the appropriate information according to the instructions and sample agreements in the book. Underlines are used to indicate where you need to enter your information, frequently followed by instructions in brackets. Be sure to delete the underlines and instructions from your edited document. You will also want to make sure that any signature lines in your completed documents appear on a page with at least some text from the document itself. If you do not know how to use your word processor to edit a document, you will need to look through the manual for your word processing program—Nolo's technical support department will *not* be able to help you with the use of your word processing program.

Editing Forms That Have Optional or Alternative Text

Some of the forms have optional or alternate text:

- With optional text, you choose whether to include or exclude the given text.
- With alternative text, you select one alternative to include and exclude the other alternatives.

When editing these forms, we suggest you do the following:

Optional text
If you *don't want* to include optional text, just delete it from your document.

If you *do want* to include optional text, just leave it in your document.

In either case, delete the italicized instructions.

Alternative text
First delete all the alternatives that you do not want to include, then delete the italicized instructions.

Step 3: Printing Out the Document

Use your word processor's or text editor's "Print" command to print out your document. If you do not know how to use your word processor to print a document, you will need to look through the manual for your word processing program—Nolo's technical support department will *not* be able to help you with the use of your word processing program.

Step 4: Saving Your Document

After filling in the form, use the "Save As" command to save and rename the file. Because all the files are "read-only," you will not be able to use the "Save" command. This is for your protection. *If you save the file without renaming it, the underlines that indicate where you need to enter your information will be lost, and you will not be able to create a new document with this file without recopying the original file from the CD-ROM.*

If you do not know how to use your word processor to save a document, you will need to look through the manual for your word processing program—Nolo's technical support department will *not* be able to help you with the use of your word processing program.

Using United States Copyright Office Forms

Electronic copies of useful forms from the United States Copyright Office are included on the CD-ROM in Adobe Acrobat PDF format. You must have the Adobe Reader installed on your computer to use these forms. Adobe Reader is available for all types of Windows and Macintosh systems. If you don't already have this software, you can download it for free at www.adobe.com.

All forms, their file names, and file formats are listed at the end of this appendix. These form files were created by the United States Copyright Office, not by Nolo.

Some of these forms have fill-in text fields. To create your document using these files, you must: (1) open a file; (2) fill in the text fields using either your mouse or the tab key on your keyboard to navigate from field to field; and (3) print it out.

Forms without fill-in text fields cannot be filled out using your computer. To create your document using these files, you must: (1) open the file; (2) print it out; and (3) complete it by hand or typewriter.

Step 1: Opening a Form

PDF files, like the word processing files, can be opened one of three ways.

- Windows users can open a file by selecting its "shortcut" as follows: (1) Click the Windows "Start" button; (2) open the "Programs" folder; (3) open the "Copyright Forms" subfolder; (4) open the "PDF" folder; and (5) click on the shortcut to the form you want to work with.
- Both Windows and Macintosh users can open a file directly by double clicking on it. Use My Computer or

Windows Explorer (Windows 98, 2000, Me, or XP) or the Finder (Macintosh) to go to the folder you created and copied the CD-ROM's files to. Then, double click on the specific file you want to open.

- You can also open a PDF file from within Adobe Reader. To do this, you must first start Reader. Then, go to the File menu and choose the Open command. This opens a dialog box where you will tell the program the location and name of the file (you will need to navigate through the directory tree to get to the folder on your hard disk where the CD's files have been installed). If these directions are unclear you will need to look through Adobe Reader's help—Nolo's technical support department will *not* be able to help you with the use of Adobe Reader.

Where Are the PDF Files Installed?

Windows Users: PDF files are installed by default to a folder named \Copyright Forms\PDF in the \Program Files folder of your computer.

Macintosh Users: PDF files are located in the "PDF" folder within the "Copyright Forms" folder.

Step 2: Filling in a Form

Use your mouse or the Tab key on your keyboard to navigate from field to field within these forms. Be sure to have all the information you will need to complete a form on hand, because you will not be able to save a copy of the filled-in form to disk. You can, however, print out a completed version.

NOTE: This step is only applicable to forms that have been created with fill-in text fields. Forms without fill-in fields must be completed by hand or typewriter after you have printed them out.

Step 3: Printing a Form

Choose Print from the Acrobat Reader File menu. This will open the Print dialog box. In the "Print Range" section of the Print dialog box, select the appropriate print range, then click OK.

List of Forms Included on the Forms CD-ROM

The following files are in rich text format (RTF):

Form	File name
Work Made for Hire Agreement	Agreement.rtf
Copyright Assignment	Assignment.rtf
Collaboration Agreement	Collaboration.rtf
Copyright License	Copyright.rtf
Counter-Notification in Response to Claim of Copyright Infringement	Counter.rtf
Work for Hire Letter Agreement	Letter.rtf
Notice of Claimed Copyright Infringement	Notice.rtf
Copyright Permission Request	Permission.rtf
Search Request Form	Search.rtf
Text Permission Agreement	TextAgreement.rtf
Text Permission Letter Agreement	TextLetter.rtf

The following files are in Adobe Acrobat PDF format (asterisks indicate forms with fill-in text fields):

Form	File name
Sonny Bono Copyright Extension Act	bono.pdf
Copyright Act	circ92.pdf
Form CA*	formca.pdf
Form CON*	formcon.pdf
Document Cover Sheet*	formdoc.pdf
Form GATT/CON*	formgatc.pdf
Form GATT*	formgatt.pdf
Form G/DN*	formgdn.pdf
Form GR/CP	formgr_cpwi.pdf
Form PA*	formpa.pdf
Short Form PA*	formpas.pdf

List of Forms Included on the Forms CD-ROM (continued)

Form	File name
Form SE*	formse.pdf
Form SE/Group*	formseg.pdf
Short Form SE*	formses.pdf
Form TX*	formtx.pdf
Short Form TX*	formtxs.pdf
Form VA*	formva.pdf
Short Form VA*	formvas.pdf
Form NLA	nla.pdf
Form NLA/CON	nlacon.pdf

Index

D

G

H

I

O

P

Remember:

Little publishers have big ears.
We really listen to you.

Take 2 Minutes & Give Us Your 2 cents

Your comments make a big difference in the development and revision of Nolo books and software. Please take a few minutes and register your Nolo product—and your comments—with us. Not only will your input make a difference, you'll receive special offers available only to registered owners of Nolo products on our newest books and software. Register now by:

PHONE 1-800-728-3555	**FAX** 1-800-645-0895	**EMAIL** cs@nolo.com	or **MAIL** us this registration card

fold here

NOLO

Registration Card

NAME ____________________ DATE ____________________

ADDRESS ____

____

CITY ____________________ STATE __________ ZIP __________

PHONE ____________________ EMAIL ____________________

WHERE DID YOU HEAR ABOUT THIS PRODUCT? ____________________

WHERE DID YOU PURCHASE THIS PRODUCT? ____________________

DID YOU CONSULT A LAWYER? (PLEASE CIRCLE ONE) YES NO NOT APPLICABLE

DID YOU FIND THIS BOOK HELPFUL? (VERY) 5 4 3 2 1 (NOT AT ALL)

COMMENTS ____

WAS IT EASY TO USE? (VERY EASY) 5 4 3 2 1 (VERY DIFFICULT)

We occasionally make our mailing list available to carefully selected companies whose products may be of interest to you.

❑ If you do not wish to receive mailings from these companies, please check this box.

❑ You can quote me in future Nolo promotional materials.

Daytime phone number ____________________.

COHA 9.0

Nolo *in the* NEWS

"Nolo helps lay people perform legal tasks without the aid—or fees—of lawyers."

—USA TODAY

Nolo books are ..."written in plain language, free of legal mumbo jumbo, and spiced with witty personal observations."

—ASSOCIATED PRESS

"Nolo publications...guide people simply through the how, when, where and why of law."

—WASHINGTON POST

"Increasingly, people who are not lawyers are performing tasks usually regarded as legal work... And consumers, using books like Nolo's, do routine legal work themselves."

—NEW YORK TIMES

"...All of [Nolo's] books are easy-to-understand, are updated regularly, provide pull-out forms...and are often quite moving in their sense of compassion for the struggles of the lay reader."

—SAN FRANCISCO CHRONICLE

fold here

Place stamp here

NOLO
950 Parker Street
Berkeley, CA 94710-9867

Attn: COHA 9.0